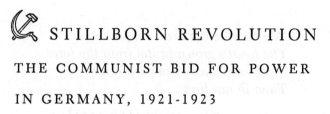

STILLBORN REVOLUTION

THE COMMUNIST BID FOR POWER

IN GERMANY, 1921-1923

We had fed the heart on fantasies,
The heart's grown brutal from the fare;
More substance in our enmities
Than in our love . . .

WILLIAM BUTLER YEATS

Stillborn Revolution

THE COMMUNIST BID FOR POWER

IN GERMANY, 1921-1923

 BY WERNER T. ANGRESS

PRINCETON, NEW JERSEY

PRINCETON UNIVERSITY PRESS

1963

To Curt Bondy,

FRIEND AND TEACHER

PREFACE

IT IS NOT EASY in our troubled times to approach the issue of Communism calmly. The fears and hostilities generated by the contemporary East-West struggle tend to intrude even into the sphere of scholarly investigation, where they disturb its traditional sense of perspective and objectivity. In this study I have made an effort not to project the emotion-ridden present into the past. The book is not meant to be either an indictment or an apologia; it merely tries, with as much detachment as possible, to reconstruct a significant phase in the history of German Communism.

The principal concern of this study is what I should like to call the *Kampfzeit* of the German Communist Party.[1] The phase properly extends from November 1918, to the end of 1923, but since the earlier Communist attempts to capture power in 1918-1919 have been variously treated by German and non-German scholars, I have focused on the subsequent period which, up to now, has not received the attention it deserves. A summary account of the preceding stages has been given in the first three chapters to acquaint the reader with the general background and some of the basic problems which bear on the topic. The remaining nine chapters are devoted to the years 1921 through 1923, with emphasis on the March uprising in 1921 and the projected October revolution in 1923.

The present rulers of East Germany have endowed the history of the German Communist Party during the Weimar era with an aura of glorification. Numerous monographs and articles extolling the party's revolutionary tradition are published every year. That these scholarly endeavors serve a special purpose is apparent from the preface of an official East German publication.

"The popularization of the German Communist Party's revolutionary tradition is designed, particularly in the present situation, to mobilize the working masses in their struggle for the peaceful reunification of Germany, on a democratic basis, and in opposition to West German militarism, vengefulness, and imperialist war preparations. At the same time, the publication of this volume serves the purpose of facilitating and improving the propaganda

---

[1] For the application of the term *Kampfzeit* in this connection I am indebted to the unpublished M.A. thesis of Mr. Thomas A. Baylis, "East Germany's Rulers: a Study in the Evolution of Totalitarian Leadership," submitted to the Department of Political Science at the University of California, Berkeley, in 1961, p. 19.

work of our party [the SED] as well as the historical study of the German labor movement in our . . . institutes of higher learning."[2]

Such a "revolutionary tradition" undoubtedly exists. The question is, why was a successful Communist revolution never accomplished in Germany, not even at a time when circumstances seemed to favor it? Until the end of 1923, the Weimar Republic resembled a storm-tossed ship adrift on turbulent waters; Germany was still suffering from the aftereffects of a lost war, of a political revolution, and of a peace treaty which the greater part of the nation resented. Furthermore, unsettled political conditions at home, and lingering hostility and suspicion on the part of the victorious Allies abroad, retarded restoration of Germany's economic stability. It was against this background that the German Communist Party entertained hopes of capturing control of the young republic. The nature of these hopes, the attempts undertaken to realize them, and the reasons why they failed are the object of this study.

A number of scholars have dealt in one way or other with the revolutionary phase of German Communism, and while the literature on this topic is discussed more thoroughly in the bibliographical essay, I want to refer here briefly to three of the best-known studies, those by Edward H. Carr, Ruth Fischer, and Ossip K. Flechtheim.[3] Of these, Carr's work proves by far the most useful and reliable, but since the author's main concern is the Soviet Union he approaches the German problem from the point of view of Bolshevik policies. Ruth Fischer's account, apart from being partisan, unreliable, and devoid of organization, hardly mentions the March uprising of 1921, and presents other vital aspects of the period in a rather haphazard fashion. Flechtheim's pioneering study on the history of the German Communist Party in the Weimar Republic, though a valuable survey, devotes but sixty-odd pages to the time span between 1918 and 1923. Moreover, the book suffers from the author's tendency to rely too uncritically upon Communist

[2] *Zur Geschichte der Kommunistischen Partei Deutschlands; eine Auswahl von Materialien und Dokumenten aus den Jahren 1914-1946*, ed. Marx-Engels-Lenin-Stalin Institut beim Zentralkomitee der SED (Berlin, 1955), p. 5.

[3] Edward Hallett Carr, *A History of Soviet Russia: The Bolshevik Revolution 1917-1923*, III (New York, 1953), and *A History of Soviet Russia: The Interregnum 1923-1924* (New York, 1954); Ruth Fischer, *Stalin and German Communism: A Study in the Origins of the State Party*, preface by Sidney B. Fay (Cambridge, Mass., 1948); Ossip K. Flechtheim, *Die Kommunistische Partei Deutschlands in der Weimarer Republik* (Offenbach, 1948).

interpretations of the time, and upon some anti-Communist accounts as well.

This is not intended to convey the impression that I have found any of these books useless. On the contrary, I have profitably drawn on all of them, and have found that even Ruth Fischer's account, when used with caution, will yield valuable information unobtainable elsewhere. But in none of them has the revolutionary phase of the German Communist Party been subjected to a detailed critical analysis, and so a number of vital questions have remained unexplored. For example, while most historians would generally agree that Communist tactics during this period split the German working-class movement irrevocably, and that this split had far-reaching consequences for the republic, both the origins of this split and its inevitability are too often simply taken for granted. Surely the Communists did not intend to alienate the majority of workers outside the ranks of the German party. If so, why should they have tried so hard to rally the masses behind their banner, or resorted to the precarious contortions of the united front policy? To answer these questions it proved essential to examine carefully the declining quality of party leadership, the increase of Bolshevik influence, the intraparty struggles, and the gradual liquidation of Rosa Luxemburg's concepts of party autonomy and democracy. This study also hopes to demonstrate through its investigation of the party's revolutionary mission—its theoretical basis, practical application, and effects—that the Communist objective of capturing power was unrealistic, and the measures taken to that end ill-starred.

The nature of this topic posed the special problem of finding reliable sources. Apart from the partisanship displayed in the majority of secondary works, the difficulties encountered in working with Communist material need hardly be mentioned. The conspiratorial sphere in which the Communists operated, and their proclivity for subordinating truth to propaganda have often made it difficult to distinguish facts from fiction. Furthermore, the destruction of valuable documents by the National Socialist regime and by bomb damage during the Second World War has depleted source material which was never abundant to begin with. Fortunately, the records which have survived indicate that during the early postwar years the debates at Communist congresses, and the tone of the party press, were more candid and less restrictive than became the norm after Stalin's rise to power. Nevertheless, the process of evaluating the extant material at times resembled detective work. Whenever conflicting evidence made a definite conclusion impossible, I have so indicated in a footnote.

The present book is a drastic and extensive revision of a dissertation submitted to the Graduate Division of the University of California, Berkeley, for the degree of Doctor of Philosophy in History. During the varying stages of research I have received advice and assistance from a number of persons and institutions. I wish to express my sincere appreciation to my colleagues at Berkeley who read the manuscript and commented on it, notably Professors Hans Rosenberg, Carl E. Schorske, and Raymond J. Sontag.

I am greatly indebted to Dr. Fritz T. Epstein, who suggested the topic to me; to Professor Carl A. Landauer, whose constructive and detailed criticism during the initial stages of research proved especially helpful in view of his personal experience with the German political scene in general, and the German labor movement in particular; and to Professor Harold J. Gordon, Jr., who read the final draft of the manuscript and whose careful, detailed, and perceptive critical suggestions have been invaluable.

I want to acknowledge gratefully the assistance I received from the University of California, Berkeley, which granted me a University Faculty Fellowship for the summer of 1958; and from the University's Institute of Social Sciences which financed, and arranged for, the typing of the manuscript.

My thanks are due to the staff of the Hoover Institution on War, Revolution, and Peace at Stanford University, Stanford, California, and to Mrs. Agnes F. Peterson in particular, for their courtesy and assistance. The wealth of otherwise unattainable material which the Hoover Institution made available to me proved invaluable.

I also wish to thank the staff of the General Library at the University of California, Berkeley, for helping me to secure books, documents, and other material I needed, a task which was not always easy, and for which the Interlibrary Borrowing Service under the direction of Mrs. Margaret D. Uridge deserves my special and warm appreciation.

I owe a special debt of gratitude to Mrs. Janet Purcell and the entire administrative staff of the History Department at the University of California, Berkeley, for their unflagging cooperation and

Preface

patience whenever I needed their assistance; to Miss Jacqueline Strain, who proofread the manuscript and helped with the editing; and to Mrs. Cornelia Pimentel for her assistance in proofreading and compiling the index.

To Princeton University Press and its editorial staff I want to express my sincere appreciation.

Finally, to Ruth Angress, who throughout the period of work on this book provided encouragement, criticism, and help, I owe much more than any formal statement can possibly convey.

The responsibility for shortcomings, errors, and views expressed is entirely my own.

Berkeley, California
September 1962

LIST OF ABBREVIATIONS

ADGB	*Allgemeiner Deutscher Gewerkschaftsbund* (General Federation of German Trade-Unions)
Afa	*Allgemeiner freier Angestelltenbund* (General Federation of Employees)
C.I.	Communist International
Comintern	Communist International
C.P.	Communist Party
DGB	*Deutscher Gewerkschaftsbund* (Federation of German [Christian] Trade-Unions)
ECCI	Executive Committee of the Communist International
EKKI	*Exekutivkomitee der Kommunistischen Internationale*
IAH	*Internationale Arbeiterhilfe* (International Workers Aid)
Inprecorr	International Press Correspondence
Inprekorr	*Internationale Presse-Korrespondenz*
KAG	*Kommunistische Arbeitsgemeinschaft* (lit., Communist Working Cooperative, actually a Communist parliamentary splinter group, headed by Paul Levi)
KAPD	*Kommunistische Arbeiterpartei Deutschlands* (German Communist Workers Party)
K.I.	*Kommunistische Internationale* (Communist International)
Komintern	*Kommunistische Internationale* (Communist International)
KPD	*Kommunistische Partei Deutschlands* (German Communist Party)
M.E.L.S.I.	Marx-Engels-Lenin-Stalin *Institut*
M-Apparat	*Militär-Apparat* (Military Group)
M-P	*Militär-Politisch* (Military-Political)
N-Apparat	*Nachrichten-Apparat* (Intelligence Group)
Narkomindel	*Narodnyi Komissariat Inostrannykh Del* (People's Commissariat of Foreign Affairs)
NEP	New Economic Policy
NSDAP	*Nationalsozialistische Deutsche Arbeiterpartei* (National Socialist German Workers Party)
OMS	*Otdel Mezhdunarodnoy Svyazi* ([Comintern's] Department for International Liaison)
Orbüro	*Organisationsbüro* (Organizational Department)

List of Abbreviations

Orgesch — *Organisation* Escherich

Polbüro — *Politisches Büro* (Political Department)

Profintern — *Krasnyi Internatsional Professional'nykh Soyuzov* (Red International of Trade-Unions)

REVKO — *Revolutionskomitee* (Revolutionary Committee)

RGI — *Rote Gewerkschaftsinternationale* (Red International of Trade-Unions, or Profintern)

RKP — *Rossiiskaya Kommunisticheskaya Partiya* (Russian Communist Party)

SED — *Sozialistische Einheitspartei Deutschlands* (German Socialist Union Party)

SPD — *Sozialdemokratische Partei Deutschlands* (German Social Democratic Party)

T-Apparat — *Terror-Apparat* (Terror Group)

USPD — *Unabhängige Sozialdemokratische Partei Deutschlands* (Independent Social Democratic Party of Germany, or Independents)

VKPD — *Vereinigte Kommunistische Partei Deutschlands* (Unified German Communist Party)

WUMBA — *Waffen-und Munitionsbeschaffungsamt* (Office for the Procurement of Arms and Ammunition)

Z-Apparat — *Zersetzungs-Apparat* (lit., Undermining Group; designed to spread sedition among the army and police forces)

CONTENTS

CONTENTS

PART ONE

BACKGROUND

CHAPTER I

BIRTH: THE PARTY AND
ITS HERITAGE

❧ THE GERMAN COMMUNIST MOVEMENT grew out of a radical opposition faction within the leadership of the German Social Democratic Party. The faction was small, a mere handful of men and women who constituted the party's extreme left wing. Its most notable representatives were Rosa Luxemburg, Karl Liebknecht, and Franz Mehring. The eventual schism between the radical Left and the party majority was preceded by a decade of intraparty controversy over policies and principles. Beginning in 1905-1906 with a heated debate over the use or misuse of the mass strike, discord within the Socialist camp grew more bitter and intense with every crisis.[1]

The underlying issue of the prolonged conflict was a difference of outlook on how a Socialist party was to proceed in creating a Socialist state. After a dynamic start in the nineteenth century, the SPD (*Sozialdemokratische Partei Deutschlands*) had lost much of its revolutionary *élan*, and by the beginning of the twentieth, largely as a result of Revisionism and growing trade-union influence, the trend of the party was toward respectability and moderation. The moderate majority, which included the party's executive, emphasized domestic reform of German and Prussian institutions, and concentrated on increasing Socialist representation in the Reichstag. Although the SPD continued to pay lip service to the principle of Socialist revolution, in practice its main concern was with the immediate question of how to achieve a higher standard of living, as well as political and social equality for the workers within the institutional framework of the state.

The radicals scoffed at what they considered the bread-and-butter orientation of the party majority. They rejected the concepts

[1] For the brief summary of the well-known events concerning the split of the German Social Democratic Party and the origins of the German Communist Party I am indebted to Carl Schorske, *German Social Democracy 1905-1917; The Development of the Great Schism* (Cambridge, Mass., 1955) and Eugen Prager, *Geschichte der U.S.P.D.* (Berlin, 1922); see also A. Joseph Berlau, *The German Social Democratic Party 1914-1921* (New York, 1941) and Arthur Rosenberg, *Entstehung und Geschichte der Weimarer Republik* (Frankfurt am Main, 1955).

of gradualism and reform, and criticized the leadership for centering its efforts and attention on domestic issues rather than on the
foreign political scene where the future world order would ultimately be decided. They put their faith in revolutionary mass action
rather than in a numerically strong, but politically impotent, Reichstag representation; and they aimed at the forceful overthrow of
that very society within the framework of which the party majority
wanted to strengthen the position of the working class by ceaseless,
but peaceful, day-by-day demands.

At the Jena Party Congress in September 1913, two crucial issues
had to be decided. Should the SPD vote for military tax increases
in the Reichstag, and should it prepare for the use of the mass strike
as a means by which to press for reform of the antiquated and class-
bound Prussian electoral system? The radicals lined up against the
military tax bill and for the general strike measure, thereby voting
on both issues in opposition to the party majority. As the debate
preceding the vote had been acrimonious, the cleavage within the
party became sharper than ever. But even more significant was the
fact that the radicals received support from a group of party functionaries who, up to the Jena Congress, had vacillated between "reformism" and "revolution." These "left centrists," led by Georg Ledebour and Hugo Haase, now threw in their lot with the radical
faction headed by Rosa Luxemburg and Karl Liebknecht. Four
years later, both groups were jointly to form the Independent Socialist Party (USPD), with the Luxemburg-Liebknecht group constituting the extreme left wing which became the nucleus of the
German Communist Party (KPD).

At the outbreak of war, the SPD presented for the last time a
unified front to the outside world. Although a heated debate in the
party caucus on whether to vote war credits had preceded the
crucial Reichstag session of August 4, 1914, party discipline prevailed once more, as left centrists and radicals reluctantly lined up
with other party delegates in making unanimous the vote in favor
of war credits.

This outward display of unity was of short duration. Under the
impact of the war and the hardships it imposed on the working class
in particular, intraparty strife re-emerged and grew sharper as the
months went by. Despite the party executive's demand for ironclad
discipline, conflicting views on what attitude the SPD should adopt

4

concerning the war accentuated the prewar divisions and rendered unity illusory. The party majority, under the leadership of Friedrich Ebert, put patriotism above Socialist ideology and adhered to the *Burgfrieden* which the emperor had proclaimed in August 1914. The left centrists took a middle position between the party majority and the left radicals. They did not oppose the war outright but rejected the official government position on war aims—a victorious peace with annexations—by refusing to vote further war credits in December 1915. Their attitude contrasted with that of the party majority, which also opposed the government's war aims but was unwilling to translate this opposition into action.

The attitude of the radicals on the extreme left wing of the party was even more uncompromising than that of the left centrists. Liebknecht had been the first Social Democratic Reichstag delegate to break party discipline when he voted against war credits in December 1914. But he, Luxemburg, and a few like-minded intellectuals in the radical camp pushed their protest further. From 1915 on the *Gruppe Internationale* (literally, "Group International"), as the radicals called themselves after a periodical they began to publish in April of that year, started to agitate openly against the "imperialist" war. Writing from prison, where she spent a substantial part of the war years for political dissent, Rosa Luxemburg expressed the ideas of her faction most succinctly in an article which has become known as the "Junius Brochure."

"Thus we are faced today . . . with this choice: either the triumph of imperialism and decline of all civilization, as in ancient Rome . . . or the victory of Socialism, that is the conscious fight of the international proletariat against imperialism and its method—war . . . . The future of civilization and mankind will depend on whether the proletariat will cast its revolutionary sword into the scales with manly resolution. . . . Millions of proletarians, speaking all tongues, are now dying on the field of dishonor, of fratricide, of self destruction, the slave song on their lips. . . . Indeed, we resemble the Jews whom Moses led through the desert. But we are not lost, and we shall be victorious, if we have not forgotten how to learn. And if today's leader of the proletariat, Social Democracy, should prove incapable of learning, then it will perish. . . ."[2]

[2] Rosa Luxemburg, "Die Krise der Sozialdemokratie (Junius-Broschüre)," *Ausgewählte Reden und Schriften*, 1 (Berlin, 1955), pp. 270-271. The brochure was

Background

Although Luxemburg, Liebknecht, and other members of the radical faction spent the better part of the war behind bars, there were always enough of them at liberty to carry on their agitation against the war and the society which they held responsible for it. Nor did imprisonment prove an insurmountable obstacle to Rosa Luxemburg whose articles, written in her cell, were smuggled out and disseminated. The articles were initially circulated on mimeographed sheets, and in the fall of 1916 appeared in print under the name of "Spartacus Letters." This title inspired the "Group International" to adopt, informally, the additional name of *Spartakusgruppe*, popularly known as "Spartacists." The official name *Spartakusbund* (Spartacus League) was not adopted until November 11, 1918, after the revolution had broken out. The *Spartakusbund* was the immediate forerunner of the German Communist Party.

It is surprising, given the divisions within the SPD, that the party stayed together as long as it did, until the spring of 1917. By then the time for a break had arrived, though it turned out to be at first a two-way rather than a three-way split. Moreover, the initiative for the break was taken by the party executive rather than by the two opposition factions. The impetus for the party leadership to purge the ranks of the SPD was, in turn, provided by the German government.

In August 1916, the generals von Hindenburg and Ludendorff were appointed to head the Supreme Command of the German armed forces. This move, under the pressure of Ludendorff, led to increased military influence on the policies of the German government. It led especially to a more rigorous enforcement of the state-of-siege law, a measure which had been in effect since 1914, and which was designed to protect the country against spies, saboteurs, and radical agitators. The law was now applied with renewed vigor, particularly against the two left-wing factions of the SPD. By continuing their agitation against the war and the governmental war aims, their orators became liable to prosecution, and frequently to prison terms. The activities of the SPD's rebellious minority proved a constant source of embarrassment to the party executive. In order to remedy the situation, the executive let it be known that party

---

written in April 1915, was smuggled out of the Berlin prison in which Luxemburg was confined, and was published in Zürich in the spring of 1916.

discipline, which had been allowed to lapse shortly after the outbreak of the war, would again be strictly enforced, and that violators would have to face the consequences. This left the two opposition factions with the choice of submitting to the dictates of the executive, or facing expulsion. Drawn closer together by the crisis they both faced, left centrists and Spartacists met in January 1917 for a conference to discuss what steps they should take to meet the challenge of the executive. Neither group wanted a break with the mother party, but opinions differed on how to remain in the SPD without submitting to the authority of its leadership. In the end, a rather conciliatory compromise solution, sponsored by the left centrists, was adopted, but the efforts expended on this conference proved entirely wasted. A few days after its participants had dispersed, the party council announced that by holding a separate conference the two factions had forfeited their right to remain within the Social Democratic Party. The decision left the expelled members no choice but to form an organization of their own. They did so early in April 1917, when both factions met at Gotha where they founded the Independent Social Democratic Party (USPD, or Independents). Although in drafting a party program the left centrists and Spartacists rarely saw eye to eye, the latter, comprising a small minority even in the new splinter party, resolved to stay with it, at least for the time being, "in order," as Liebknecht put it, "to drive them forward, to have them within reach of our whip."[3]

The split of the SPD, long since pending, had finally materialized and proved irrevocable. Despite subsequent shifts of alignment, especially on the part of the USPD—which, after a brief but eventful existence, disappeared from the political scene in 1922—the German working-class movement after April 1917 remained divided into a moderate and a radical wing. Divided it went through the revolution of November 1918; divided it remained under the Weimar Republic; divided it surrendered to Hitler in 1933. After 1918, the standard-bearer of the radical wing became the German Communist Party.

[3] *The Communist International 1919-1943, Documents,* ed. Jane Degras, I (1919-1922), issued under the auspices of the Royal Institute of International Affairs (London-New York-Toronto, 1956), p. 74. In order to avoid confusion with other works pertaining to the Communist International, the work hereafter will be cited as Degras, ed., *The Communist International 1919-1943, Documents,* I.

Background

The origins of the Communist movement in Germany are inextricably connected with the personality and ideas of Rosa Luxemburg.[4] The most gifted and most articulate of the Spartacists, she was forty-seven years old when the German Empire collapsed in November 1918, and she had already devoted over thirty years to the revolutionary movement, first in the Polish, then in the German Social Democratic Party. Born in Zamosc, a small town in Russian Poland, she was the daughter of a well-to-do Jewish businessman. When she was three years old, her father removed his family to Warsaw because he "could not stand life with Jews" in Zamosc.[5] Here the Luxemburg family embraced the cause of Polish nationalism. Rosa, though in sympathy with Polish national aspirations, soon began to go her own way, and at the age of sixteen she joined a clandestine revolutionary Socialist group in Warsaw. Because of her affiliation with this group she was forced to flee to Zürich, Switzerland, in 1889, where she attended the university, established contact with other political exiles, mostly Russians, and became an expert Marxist theorist. From Zürich she studied the Socialist movements in Germany and France, but in these early years Poland remained her chief concern. Though an exile, she became in 1894 a co-founder of the Social Democratic Party of the Kingdom of Poland and Lithuania. She was still an ardent Polish nationalist, but did not advocate independence for Poland: she believed instead that it was the primary task of the Polish revolutionary movement to overthrow the autocracy of the Russian Tsar with the aid of the Russian working class.[6]

The period of her Swiss exile, which ended in 1898 when she settled permanently in Germany, established her as a leading figure among Europe's Socialists. Even then she was a controversial person

[4] A definitive biography of Rosa Luxemburg is still wanting. The most useful one, available in English, is by Paul Frölich, *Rosa Luxemburg,* trans. Edward Fitzgerald (London, 1940). A very concise, but searching, evaluation of her political ideas has been written by Francis Ludwig Carsten, "Rosa Luxemburg, Freedom and Revolution," *Soviet Survey,* No. 33 (July–September 1960), pp. 93-99. A recent East German study by Fred Oelssner, *Rosa Luxemburg, Eine Kritische Biographische Skizze* (Berlin, 1956), is patronizingly critical while trying to salvage her propaganda value. See also Henriette Roland-Holst-van der Schalk, *Rosa Luxemburg, Ihr Leben und Wirken* (Zürich, 1937), the memorial of a friend, and Max Hochdorf, *Rosa Luxemburg, Das Leben einer Revolutionärin* (Berlin, n.d.), the journalistic account of a German liberal writer.

[5] Judd L. Teller, *Scapegoat of Revolution* (New York, 1954), p. 164.

[6] Carsten, p. 93.

8

who was either revered or hated, but could not be ignored. The key to Rosa Luxemburg's personality was her independence of mind, her sharp, honest, uncompromising intellect, and the strength of her convictions. Although she was younger than most of the other prominent Socialist leaders she never hesitated to disagree with them, at times violently and aggressively.

This is not the place to dwell on the complex arguments over theory in which she engaged with such men as Eduard Bernstein and Karl Kautsky. May it suffice to say that, following Marx, she believed firmly in the inevitable collapse of capitalism as the result of natural social laws. This belief she shared with many other Marxist theoreticians, but she differed with most of them on the inter-relationship between the "inevitable historical process" and the role of the proletariat within this process.[7] Borrowing a phrase from Marx's *The Eighteenth Brumaire of Louis Bonaparte*, she expressed her ideas on this interrelationship most succinctly in the "Junius Brochure" which she wrote during the war.

"Men do not make history of their own free will, but they do make their own history. The proletariat is dependent in its action on the given degree of maturity in social development existing at the time, but social development does not proceed independent of and apart from the proletariat, and the proletariat is as much its cause and mainspring as it is its product and consequence. The action of the proletariat is a determining factor in history. . . . The victory of the socialist proletariat will be the result of iron historical laws, and it will depend on a thousand steps in a previous, laborious and all-too-slow development. However, it will never be fulfilled unless the material conditions brought together slowly by the historical process are vitalized with the life-giving spark of conscious will-power generated in the great masses of the people."[8]

Her faith in the masses was deep and genuine, a sentiment which early in the twentieth century involved her in a debate with Lenin. In 1902, Lenin had published *What Is To Be Done?*, in which he called for a revolutionary party controlled by a small, secretly organized and centrally directed band of professional revolutionaries,

[7] Frölich, *Rosa Luxemburg*, pp. 64-66. For a fuller discussion of her Marxist views see *ibid.*, pp. 54-78, and *passim*.

[8] Luxemburg, "Die Krise der Sozialdemokratie," *Ausgewählte Reden und Schriften*, I, p. 269. I have used Frölich's translation, *op.cit.*, pp. 65-66.

who would demand and enforce iron discipline. He was convinced that only with such an organization, run by men who possessed single-mindedness of purpose, could a revolutionary movement ever be successful. Rosa Luxemburg, on the basis of her experience in the Polish and German parties, disagreed with the underlying scepticism of Lenin's point of view. She put her faith in the masses rather than in a centralized bureaucratic party machine, and in spontaneity rather than in manipulation and tight organization. When Lenin two years later reiterated his position in *One Step Forward, Two Steps Back,* and used the phrase: "Bureaucracy versus democracy is . . . the organisational principle of the revolutionary Social-Democrats as opposed to the organisational principle of the opportunist Social-Democrats,"[9] Luxemburg replied in an article published in *Die Neue Zeit.*

"The conditions of Social-Democratic activity are fundamentally different. This activity develops historically from the elementary class struggle, subject to the dialectical antithesis that the proletarian army recruits its forces only during the course of the struggle itself, and realizes the true nature of its final task only in the course of the struggle. Organization, education, and struggle are thus not mechanically separated elements nor are they separate in time . . . they are various aspects of the same process. On the one hand, and apart from the general principles of the struggle, there can be no complete and previously accepted fighting tactics drilled into members of a Social-Democratic organization by its Central Committee, and on the other hand the very process of struggle which creates the organization causes a continual fluctuation of the Social-Democratic sphere of influence. *From this it follows that the Social-Democratic form of organization cannot be based on blind obedience and on the mechanical subordination of all members to some centralized power.* . . . The ultra-centralism demanded by Lenin develops, it seems to us, not from positive creative ideas, but from a sterile, bureaucratic attitude. Its chief aim is to control the activity of the party rather than to fructify it, to limit rather than to develop it, to dragoon the movement rather than to educate it."[10] She concluded her article

[9] V. I. Lenin, *One Step Forward, Two Steps Back* (London, 1941), p. 255.
[10] Rosa Luxemburg, "Organisationsfragen der russischen Sozialdemokratie," *Die Neue Zeit,* xxii, ii, No. 41 (1903-1904), pp. 488, 492; I have used the translation in Frölich, *Rosa Luxemburg,* pp. 103-105. My italics.

with the observation: "Mistakes made by a genuinely revolutionary working-class movement are historically incomparably more fruitful and valuable than the infallibility of the best Central Committee."[11]

Although Rosa Luxemburg personally liked and respected Lenin, she never became reconciled to his views on the fundamental question of organization. Nor was it only Lenin with whom she differed on this matter. In 1906 she published a lengthy treatise on *Mass Strike, Party and Trade-Unions* in which she directed her acid criticism against another champion of strict and centralized organization, the German trade-union movement.[12] Here, too, she professed her faith in the spontaneity and the revolutionary will of the people, which she contrasted contemptuously with the mentality of the trade-union leaders who dreaded the prospect of seeing their precious organizations imperiled by revolutionary mass action. Dislike for, and contempt of, organization became virtually an obsession which haunted her until the end of her life.

A year after the outbreak of war she wrote:

"It was precisely the powerful organization, precisely the highly praised discipline of German Social Democracy, which made it possible for a handful of parliamentarians to command this organism of four million people to about-face within twenty-four hours, and to hold the very bastion which they had been organized to storm. . . . The better the education, the organization, the famous discipline . . . the more effective is the war effort of German Social Democracy."[13] In April 1917, at the Founding Congress of the Independent Social Democratic Party, a spokesman of the Spartacist faction acted entirely in accordance with the wishes of the imprisoned Rosa Luxemburg when he demanded that the local organizations within the new party should be granted the most far-reaching freedom of action, and that the main share of influence in future *Aktionen* be left to the masses.[14]

Throughout the remaining years of her life she held fast to her trust in the spontaneity of the proletariat as a whole, and her dis-

[11] Luxemburg, "Organisationsfragen . . . ," *ibid.*, No. 43 (1903-1904), p. 535.
[12] Rosa Luxemburg, "Massenstreik, Partei und Gewerkschaften," *Ausgewählte Reden und Schriften*, I, pp. 157-257, esp. pp. 218-225. See also the very cogent discussion of Schorske, pp. 54-58.
[13] Rosa Luxemburg, "Der Wiederaufbau der Internationale," *Ausgewählte Reden und Schriften*, II, p. 521.
[14] Prager, p. 145.

trust of rigid and centralized party control of the revolutionary movement. At the same time she rejected as irresponsible adventures all premature uprisings launched by a handful of eager activists. Only when a genuine revolutionary situation existed and the masses were ready to rise against the old order were the party leaders to place themselves at the head of the movement in order to provide aim and direction for the fighting proletariat.

It was quite in keeping with her convictions that even as momentous an event as the Russian Revolution did not blur her vision. To be sure, the course of that revolution which she followed from her prison cell elated her, and at the same time taxed her patience at being imprisoned. After the treaty of Brest-Litovsk she was haunted by fears that a victorious imperial Germany might still crush the new Soviet state, and she watched eagerly for any indications that the German proletariat was ready to follow the Russian lead. She smuggled urgent appeals from her cell to the workers outside, demanding that they save the Russian Revolution by taking action in Germany.[15] But despite her genuine concern she did not ignore the flaws which she discerned in the new Russia. While she generously acknowledged the initial achievements of Lenin and Trotsky, and recognized the tremendous importance of the revolution for the working classes everywhere, certain aspects of the revolutionary process in Russia disturbed her deeply. Apart from criticizing Lenin's agrarian policy and the dissolution of the constitutent assembly by the Bolsheviks, she raised her strongest objections against the use of terror and the curtailment of democracy and freedom. While conceding that democratic institutions had their shortcomings, she charged that to cure such institutions by abolishing them altogether was worse than the disease itself.[16] After a scathing indictment of the restricted electoral law devised by the Bolshevik leaders she turned her attention to civil liberties.

"Freedom for the supporters of the government alone, only for the members of one party—however numerous they may be—that is no freedom at all. Freedom is always freedom for the one who dissents, not because of a fanatical sense of 'justice,' but because

---

[15] Frölich, *Rosa Luxemburg,* pp. 261-264.

[16] Rosa Luxemburg, *Die Russische Revolution,* ed. Paul Levi (Berlin, 1922), p. 103. Paul Levi had persuaded the author not to publish the brochure at the time when it was written, and it finally appeared posthumously. See Roland-Holst, pp. 159-160.

all that is enlightening, healing, and purifying in political freedom depends on this definition and becomes ineffective if 'freedom' becomes a privilege."[17] Nowhere else in her political writings did she express her idealism, her fundamental faith in humanity more clearly than in her criticism of the achievements of her Russian friends. It was this spirit, this combination of faith and uncompromising, independent judgment which gave her a stature among the German radicals never attained by any of her successors.

It was Rosa Luxemburg's tragedy that the course of the German revolution in November 1918 played havoc with her idealism and strong sense of justice. The sectarian and utopian traits of the Spartacists, whose most prominent leader she was, were revealed during the weeks after the collapse of the German Empire. Torn between the Bolshevik example, her own convictions, and the actual events in Germany, she tried to the last to reconcile these contradictions, hoping to refashion the country in the image of her lifelong vision. In the *Rote Fahne* of November 18 she stated the objectives of the Spartacists in an article entitled "The Beginning."

"The abolition of capitalist rule and the realization of a socialist order of society—this and nothing else is the historic theme of the German Revolution. It is a tremendous task which cannot be performed overnight with a few decrees from above, but only through the conscious action of the toiling masses in city and country. . . . The path of the revolution follows clearly from its objective, its method derives from its mission: *All power into the hands of the toiling masses, into the hands of the workers' and soldiers' councils* . . . this must be the guiding principle for all measures taken by the revolutionary government."[18]

The initial course of events seemed to favor the objectives of the Spartacus League. Mass demonstrations and the formation of workers' and soldiers' councils gave the impression that Germany had reached a decisive political turning point. But the picture was deceptive. Behind the tumult and the shouting, the red flags, and the *ad hoc* revolutionary committees existed strong sentiments for a return to normal conditions. When Friedrich Ebert's Provisional Government of Social Democrats and Independents promised to restore order, most Germans were prepared to support it. For the

[17] Luxemburg, *Die Russische Revolution*, p. 109.
[18] *Die Rote Fahne*, No. 3, November 18, 1918. Italics in the original.

moment, at least, political likes and dislikes receded into the background, and a stunned and confused nation rallied unenthusiastically behind a few Socialist leaders who had become the chief source of authority.

To this general pattern the Spartacists did not conform. Together with other splinter groups which then constituted the amorphous radical left wing of the German working-class movement,[19] the Spartacists disagreed with the majority of labor on the nature and objectives of the November revolution. This majority, consisting of the SPD and most trade-unions, maintained that the mission of the revolution had been accomplished after the people had overthrown the imperial government, had eliminated the monarchy, and had paved the way for the establishment of democratic, parliamentary institutions by calling for elections to a National Constituent Assembly. Interpreting the revolution exclusively in political terms, they placed their primary emphasis on changing the political institutions of the state. Once this was accomplished and the political situation was firmly consolidated, the SPD and its supporters expected that a transformation of German society along the traditional lines of Socialist doctrine would gradually but inevitably follow, particularly if the Socialists should obtain a parliamentary majority as they confidently anticipated.[20]

In contrast to the Social Democrats, and consistent with their entire outlook, the Spartacists were not satisfied with the mere political achievements of the revolution which, in their opinion, did not go far enough. The revolution which they wanted to see, and were determined to make, would terminate only in a truly Socialist state, governed by a dictatorship of the proletarian masses. This, they maintained, could not be accomplished by parliamentary

[19] Of these, the most significant, besides the Spartacus League, was that of the *Revolutionäre Obleute* (Revolutionary Shop Stewards), a group which emerged during the war from the trade-union movement. Politically, the Revolutionary Shop Stewards were loosely connected with the USPD. Another organization, variously referred to as *Linksradikale* (Left Radicals), *Internationale Kommunisten Deutschlands* or, after their newspaper, *Gruppe Arbeiterpolitik*, was largely restricted to Bremen and had closer ties to the Russian Bolsheviks than to the German Spartacists. See Ossip K. Flechtheim, *Die KPD in der Weimarer Republik* (Offenbach a.M., 1948), pp. 12-13, and *passim*; and Walter Tormin, *Zwischen Rätediktatur und sozialer Demokratie; Die Geschichte der Rätebewegung in der deutschen Revolution 1918/19. Beiträge zur Geschichte des Parlamentarismus und der politischen Parteien*, Heft 4 (Düsseldorf, 1954), pp. 40-44, 86-89, and *passim*.

[20] Tormin, p. 69.

majority decisions or by decrees of the Provisional Government, but only by a concerted effort on the part of the masses, by strikes, demonstrations, and similar fighting tactics. The idea of a National Assembly was in their eyes a betrayal of the revolutionary cause, as it was liable to prove a back door to power for the bourgeoisie. For this reason Rosa Luxemburg, Karl Liebknecht and other Spartacist leaders threw their entire support behind the workers' and soldiers' councils, even though few of these councils shared the radical philosophy of the Spartacists.[21] For this reason the Spartacists also rejected an invitation to join the Provisional Government and instead turned against it, assailing Ebert and his colleagues in their press and through street corner orators as "traitors to the working class."

As usual, the Independent Socialists occupied a position between the SPD and the Spartacists, with the right wing of the USPD favoring the former, the left wing favoring the latter. But despite these internal divisions, the USPD as a whole sided with the SPD on the issue of National Assembly versus workers' and soldiers' councils.[22]

Officially, the Spartacists were still affiliated with the Independent Social Democratic Party. But in the weeks following the collapse of the Empire, the precarious ties which connected them with the mother organization were sorely strained when the Spartacists embarked upon a political course of their own. Rosa Luxemburg and her handful of loyal lieutenants, most of them intellectuals like herself, most of them men and women who had been in the SPD for over a decade and had joined its radical opposition faction, refused to concede that their battle was lost. Far from abandoning the struggle to carry the revolution on to what she considered its logical, and only acceptable, conclusion, Rosa Luxemburg proceeded to outline the aims of her faction in the *Rote Fahne* on December 14, 1918.

Entitled "What Does the Spartacus League Want?",[23] the principal theme of the editorial was an appeal to the German workers to continue the revolution until the final objective, the Socialist state, had been attained. "The realization of the Socialist order of society is the most tremendous task ever faced by a class and a

[21] *ibid.*, p. 70.
[22] *ibid.*, pp. 69-71.
[23] "Was will der Spartakusbund?", *Die Rote Fahne*, No. 29, December 14, 1918.

revolution." Whereas revolutions in the past had been made by small special interest groups who had exploited the masses to do their bidding, the Socialist revolution would be carried through by the toiling masses themselves. "The liberation of the working class must be the task of the working class proper." The bourgeois revolutions of the past had relied on bloodshed, terror, and political assassination. "The proletarian revolution does not require terror to reach its objective; it hates and despises murdering human beings . . . because it fights institutions, not individuals."

The key passage of the editorial expressed Rosa Luxemburg's vision of the society which, she hoped, the revolution would create: "The essence of a Socialist society consists in this, that the great toiling mass ceases to be a regimented mass, and instead lives and directs the whole political and economic life in conscious and free self-determination. . . . The proletarian masses must learn to become the thinking, free, and active guides of this process [of production] rather than remain dead machines employed by the capitalists. . . . They must acquire the sense of responsibility of active members of the commonweal, which is the sole owner of all social wealth. They must develop zeal without the employer's whip, highest productivity without capitalist drivers, discipline without a yoke, and order without regimentation. Highest idealism in the interest of the commonweal, strictest self-discipline, a true civic spirit of the masses, these constitute the moral basis of a Socialist society."[24]

She warned, however, that the proletariat still faced the unabated resistance of the old ruling class and the bourgeoisie, who would not hesitate for a moment to sow dissension among the people, and who would turn any National Assembly into a weapon against the toiling masses. To forestall this danger, the proletariat must do everything in its power to break the resistance and the remaining influence of the capitalist-imperialist exploiters.

How was this to be accomplished? Rosa Luxemburg answered this question in a program which she set forth as the demands of the Spartacus League. The first section dealt with security measures such as the disarmament of all potential "counterrevolutionaries," the creation of a workers' militia, and the trial of war criminals by a revolu-

[24] *ibid.* My translation is based in part on that of Carsten, p. 99.

tionary tribunal. The second section related to political and social measures, including the abolition of separate states and the creation of a unified German republic; it rejected elections for a National Assembly and called for the bestowal of all power on the workers' and soldiers' councils; the remaining part of this section was concerned with the regulation of hours, working conditions, food supply and health problems. The economic part of the Spartacist demands was in the third section, and may be summed up under the general heading of "total socialization" of all business enterprises and industry. The fourth section called for the immediate establishment of contact with proletarian organizations in other countries in the interest of lasting peace and international fraternization.

The program closed with a promise and a threat: "The Spartacist League is not a party which wants to come to power over the heads or by means of the toiling masses. The Spartacus League is only the most determined [*zielbewusst*] segment of the proletariat . . . [and] will never assume the power of government unless it be by the clear, unequivocal will of the vast majority of the proletarian masses throughout Germany. . . . The victory of the Spartacus League does not stand at the beginning but at the end of the revolution: it is identical with the victory of the many millions of proletarian workers. Onward, proletarians! Into battle! There is a world to be conquered, and a world against which to fight. In this last class struggle of history for the highest objective of humanity, let the enemy hear this word: thumb upon the eye, and knee upon the chest!"[25]

The final bloodcurdling phrase notwithstanding, the general tenor of the editorial expressed once again the genuine idealism, the basically humanitarian outlook of its author. But at the same time the expectations of Luxemburg and her associates, implicit in the demands they set forth, revealed the curious absence of a sense of reality and of proportion. They chose to ignore the true state of mind of the masses to whom they appealed, an attitude which was to become a chronic feature of German Communism. They failed to appreciate the fact that the German people in 1918 were convinced that the revolution had already established a new order of society, and that the people, after four years of war which had ended

[25] *Die Rote Fahne*, No. 29, December 14, 1918.

in defeat, were tired of strife and chaos. Under these circumstances the Spartacist program was utopian and the determination of the leaders to put it into practice quixotic.

But this was exactly what they set out to do, only to suffer a serious setback nearly at once. Even before they published their program on December 18, the Spartacists followed two major lines of approach. They did everything they could to keep the picture of the unfinished revolution constantly before the public eye; and they opposed elections for a National Assembly, demanding instead that all power be entrusted to the workers' and soldiers' councils.

The council movement had sprung up spontaneously at the outset of the revolution. The majority of councils was composed of moderates, including not only Social Democrats and Independent Socialists, but also middle-class representatives. The objectives of the councils were predominantly of a practical, immediate nature. While they varied locally with respect to specific objectives, their principal concerns were the maintenance of order, regulation of food supplies, and direction of the transportation system. In short, they took over the functions of local government, and in general tried to fill the administrative gap created by the collapse of the Empire. Only a minority of councils was controlled by radicals who wanted to emulate the Russian example by demanding that all political power be vested in the council system (*Räte System*). Thus, whereas the overwhelming majority of the councils considered their existence temporary, pending an eventual return to legally established political authority, the radical minority wanted the councils to become and remain this political authority. The radical viewpoint was, of course, propagated and shared by the Spartacist leaders.[26]

All hopes of the Spartacists that the radical viewpoint would ultimately capture the council movement, thereby keeping the revolutionary trend alive and going, were shattered just at the time that Luxemburg's editorial was published. The first National Congress of German Workers' and Soldiers' Councils convened in Berlin from December 16 to 20 to deliberate on whether the future

---

[26] By far the best up-to-date account of the council movement is Tormin's study. On the function and character of the councils see especially pp. 89-94. See also Eric Waldman, *The Spartacist Uprising of 1919 and the Crisis of the German Socialist Movement: A Study of the Relation of Political Theory and Party Practice* (Milwaukee, 1958), pp. 93-98.

of the nation was to be entrusted to a democracy or a dictatorship, to a National Assembly or a perpetual council system. The verdict, rendered on December 19 by a margin of 400 to 50, was in favor of democracy and elections for a National Assembly.

The decision was not surprising in view of the general desire for a return to orderly and stable conditions, and the Spartacists had done their share to strengthen this desire. In part, at least, the vote reflected a mounting revulsion among the majority of German labor against the ceaseless radicalism of the left extremists. As Oscar Cohen, sponsor of the crucial motion on the issue of National Assembly versus councils, put it: "We Social Democrats must take at last a most decisive and persistent stand against the way in which our clean, clear, good Socialist ideology is constantly being sabotaged and discredited by Bolshevist perverseness." The statement was greeted with stormy applause.[27]

This charge was essentially the result of two closely connected factors, the shrill and aggressive tone of the Spartacist press and speeches, and the effect of this violent language on the activists in the streets. All policies and slogans originated with the small group of leaders around Rosa Luxemburg and Karl Liebknecht, many of them intellectuals, all of them devoted Marxists. Among others, the group included Franz Mehring and Clara Zetkin, the oldest members of the radical wing in the Socialist movement and, of the younger generation, Leo Jogiches, August Thalheimer, Paul Levi, Wilhelm Pieck, Ernst Meyer, Hugo Eberlein, and Hermann and Käte Duncker. The more unfavorable the situation looked to these men and women, the more determined they became to keep the flickering revolutionary flame burning. The results were disappointing. The masses whom the Spartacists hoped to sway to their side remained hostile to the often unrestrained language of the *Rote Fahne*. The majority of workers were faithful Social Democrats, many of them organized trade-union members as well, and as such were accustomed to preserve discipline and to shun violence. It was different with the Spartacist rank and file. The total membership of the Spartacus League was small in 1918, with estimates ranging from several hundreds to several thousands.[28] But although numerically few in proportion to the rest of German labor, these

[27] Tormin, p. 98.
[28] Flechtheim, p. 29.

activists made up the deficiency by resorting to acts of lawlessness. They took the appeals to drive the revolution forward more literally than Luxemburg and her friends ever intended them to do. What the Spartacist leadership hoped to bring about was a proletarian *levée en masse*; what they actually accomplished was to unleash a series of disconnected, disorganized, undisciplined, and usually aimless street brawls, especially in Berlin and other large cities.

The chief factors responsible for this situation were the heterogeneous composition of the Spartacist membership and the absence of any effective organization capable of controlling the rank and file. Whereas the core of the Spartacists' supporters was composed of trained and dedicated Marxist revolutionaries, the extremist philosophy of the movement had also attracted elements holding what some scholars have termed "unrestrained utopian," "ultra-radical," and "revolutionary-romantic" views.[29] These people were often adherents of an anarcho-syndicalist rather than of a Marxist tradition and did not prove amenable to any discipline. The ranks of this lunatic fringe within the Spartacus League were swelled, during the revolutionary upheavals in November, by an assorted conglomeration of shiftless drifters and downright criminals who, under the pretext of fighting for the revolution, tried to benefit from it. It was largely this combination of lunatic fringe and *Lumpenproletariat* which engaged in looting, started unauthorized local riots, and committed other excesses, thereby giving the Spartacist League an unsavory reputation.

Such a group would have been hard to control even if an organization with the authority to do so had existed. This, however, was not the case. Luxemburg's philosophy of decentralization, democracy, and autonomy, which she had developed in reaction to the rigid discipline and hierarchical structure of the German Social Democrats and to Lenin's authoritarian concept of control by a small party elite, now proved to be a real disadvantage. At a time of acute crisis the Spartacist leaders found themselves unable to exercise any effective authority over their rank and file.[30] The price they paid was a growing isolation of their radical movement from

---

[29] See, for example, Rosenberg, *Entstehung und Geschichte*, pp. 293-294; Waldman, p. 98; Flechtheim, p. 41.
[30] Schorske, pp. 323-324.

the majority of the German working class, a trend which was to prove irreversible.

The adverse vote by the National Congress of Workers' and Soldiers' Councils was a severe blow to the Spartacist leaders and forced them to rethink their next moves. Luxemburg's first reaction to the repudiation of the council system was unconcealed anger and disappointment. Referring to the delegates at the congress as "Ebert's Mamelukes" she charged in the *Rote Fahne* that "the composition of this congress, its attitude from start to finish, bear living proof of its determined . . . partiality for the camp of Scheidemann's counterrevolution. . . . The congress . . . has crowned its work by depriving the workers' and soldiers' councils of all power and by handing it over to the Ebert clique."[31] The bitterness of her denunciation was the measure of her disappointment. For a brief span she clung to the hope that the councils themselves might repudiate the resolution of the congress. But the councils did nothing of the sort, and Luxemburg had no choice but to accept the setback.

During the Christmas season of 1918 street fighting occurred in Berlin between government forces and a contingent of mutinous sailors, the *Volksmarinedivision*. The Spartacus League played no prominent part in these clashes, largely because Luxemburg and her friends were preoccupied with a reappraisal of their policies. One of its first results was the decision to participate in the election campaign for the National Assembly, after Ebert's Provisional Government had fixed January 19 as the date when the elections were to be held. Rosa Luxemburg expounded the reasons for her reversal on this issue in the *Rote Fahne* on December 23.

"We are now in the midst of revolution, and the National Assembly is a counterrevolutionary fortress which has been erected *against* the revolutionary proletariat. It is our task to storm this fortress and tear it to the ground. We must utilize the elections and the floor of the National Assembly proper to mobilize the masses *against* the National Assembly. . . .

"Our participation in the elections is necessary, not because we want to make laws in cooperation with the bourgeoisie and its stooges, but in order to chase the bourgeoisie and its stooges from the temple, in order to storm the fortress of the counterrevolution

[31] *Die Rote Fahne*, No. 35, December 20, 1918.

and to hoist upon it the flag of the victorious proletarian revolution."[32]

The announcement that she had changed her position on the election issue came at a moment when she was also attempting to regain influence with the USPD. Ever since 1917, when the party was founded, the Spartacists had lived uneasily under what they called its "protective roof." But in practice the Spartacus League had gone its own way, and the ties which connected it to the mother party had worn thin. In December 1918 the Spartacists believed that the time had come to choose between two alternatives: either to re-establish close contact with the USPD, and especially its rank and file, or to break away from the Independents altogether. Luxemburg and most of her associates favored the first solution, because they had noticed that many members of the USPD had recently shown signs of impatience with their leaders' inclination to temporize on burning political issues. Rosa Luxemburg hoped that the Spartacists might benefit from their discontent. She accordingly approached the leaders of the USPD and urged them to call a party congress prior to the elections for the National Assembly, ostensibly to make plans for the coming campaign. The proposal was rejected on December 24.[33]

This negative reply prompted the Spartacists to make their final break with the USPD, a move which had lately been urged upon them with growing insistence by a small, independent, rival organization, the Left Radicals, also called "International Communists of Germany."[34] The Left Radicals had their center in Bremen and branches in North Germany, Saxony, and the Rhineland. Though this organization was in accord with the Spartacists on many fundamental principles, disagreement on a number of minor matters had prevented an amalgamation of the two groups in the past. One particular obstacle standing in the way of a merger was the affiliation of the Spartacus League with the USPD. It was overcome by the political mentor of the Left Radicals, Karl Radek, a man who until 1924 was to play a vital role in the German Com-

[32] *ibid.*, No. 38, December 23, 1918. Italics in the original.
[33] Frölich, *Rosa Luxemburg*, pp. 311-312; Wilhelm Pieck, *Gesammelte Reden und Schriften*, 1 (Berlin, 1959), p. 437; Willy Brandt und Richard Lowenthal, *Ernst Reuter, Ein Leben für die Freiheit* (Munich, 1957), p. 119.
[34] See above, n.19.

munist movement. Radek, who had followed Lenin to Russia in 1917, came to Germany in mid-December 1918. He attended a special conference of the Left Radicals, held in Berlin on December 24, and prevailed on this organization to pass a resolution inviting the Spartacus League to join forces and to form a German Communist Party, provided that the Spartacists left the USPD.[35]

Rosa Luxemburg was at first reluctant to take such a step. She not only disliked and distrusted Radek, the principal sponsor of the proposed merger, but she was also impressed by the warning of her close friend Leo Jogiches that the time was not yet ripe for founding a Communist Party. Eventually, however, she gave her consent, especially when she perceived that most of her other colleagues, Liebknecht included, did not share her misgivings and those of Jogiches. On December 29, 1918, a National Conference of the Spartacus League convened on the premises of the Prussian diet in Berlin and voted in favor of founding a new party. The official Founding Congress opened the following day and sat until January 1, 1919. Eighty-seven delegates from the Spartacus League and the Left Radicals represented altogether forty-seven localities. In addition, sixteen guests attended the ceremony.

The formal founding of the new organization presented no major difficulties, and after a brief debate the delegates agreed on the name *Kommunistische Partei Deutschlands (Spartakusbund)*, commonly abbreviated to KPD. Once this formality was settled, a crucial debate arose over the question whether the new party should participate in the elections for the National Assembly, or boycott them. Rosa Luxemburg had already expressed herself on December 23 in favor of participation, and had since then secured the support of the other Spartacist leaders. But as soon as the proposal reached the floor of the congress it met with opposition. Luxemburg had entrusted the presentation of the issue to one of the younger Spartacist leaders, the lawyer Dr. Paul Levi. His speech evoked a stormy reaction. The majority of the assembled delegates were revolution-

[35] Flechtheim, p. 45; Waldman, pp. 150-151, incl. n.92; Günter Benser, in "Das Verhältnis der Bremer Linksradikalen zur Spartakusgruppe," a contribution to an East German historical colloquium the proceedings of which were published by the Institut für Marxismus-Leninismus beim ZK der SED under the title *Die Gründung der Kommunistischen Partei Deutschlands* (Berlin, 1959), pp. 113-122, gives a laudatory account of the Bremen group but fails to mention Radek. For a more detailed account on Radek's role see Ch. II and *passim*.

ary zealots who were unable to comprehend why the small group of Spartacist leaders advocated participation in the elections when they also consistently rejected the National Assembly in principle. These men and women still believed that the dictatorship of workers' and soldiers' councils was just around the corner, despite the recent decisions of the National Congress of Councils, and Rosa Luxemburg admonished them in vain.

"Comrades, you make it too easy for yourselves with your radicalism. We must not . . . abandon the necessary seriousness and calm reflection. To cite the Russian example as an argument against participation in the election will not do. When the National Assembly there was dispersed, the Russian comrades had already the government of Lenin [and] Trotsky. We still have Ebert [and] Scheidemann. The Russian proletariat could look back to a long epoch of revolutionary struggles. We stand at the beginning of revolution. . . . Your activism may seem simpler and easier, [but] our tactics envision a longer road. . . . We want for this struggle [ahead] as additional support the floor of the National Assembly."[36] Her words were received with weak applause. Nor was Liebknecht any more successful when he asked the delegates whether "our past parliamentary activities in the Reichstag had been altogether valueless?" The majority of the delegates remained unconvinced and voted 62 to 23 against participation.[37]

The result of the vote confirmed the suspicions of Luxemburg and Jogiches that the founding of the party had been premature. Nor was it much consolation that the program adopted by the new party conformed essentially with the general principles which Luxemburg had published on December 16, after the spirit of these principles had been flagrantly disregarded in the vote on election participation. The decision to boycott the coming elections was in effect a repudiation of Luxemburg's fundamental concept on how a radical minority should conduct revolutionary policy. It also revealed, at least by implication, that many of the delegates were not averse to embarking on political adventures, an attitude which

---

[36] *Die Rote Fahne*, No. 45, December 31, 1918. My account of the founding of the KPD owes much to the following studies: Flechtheim, pp. 45-47; Tormin, pp. 110-113; Frölich, *Rosa Luxemburg*, pp. 312-315; Brandt and Lowenthal, pp. 119-121; Waldman, pp. 149-158; Rosenberg, pp. 320-323; see also the very selective account of events in Pieck, *Gesammelte Reden und Schriften*, I, pp. 456-461.

[37] *Die Rote Fahne*, No. 45, December 31, 1918.

in party lingo was known as "putschism." But the argument that the Spartacist leaders should have defied and, if necessary, split the new party then and there, as Lenin would have done had he been in Luxemburg's position, is unconvincing.[38] Luxemburg was not Lenin, and she did not share many of his views on how to lead a revolutionary party. It was one thing to have split the SPD, a measure which she had actively and wholeheartedly supported because the issues dividing that party had involved irreconcilable political principles. But it did not occur to her to split an organization which she had just helped to vote into existence merely because of a disagreement on tactics, or on the principle of party discipline. It was her misfortune, and that of the new party as well, that the dilemma she faced proved beyond a solution. Thus, by their acquiescence, she and the other Spartacist leaders inadvertently encouraged the already far from negligible influence of the party's most irresponsible elements.[39]

The last major issue which confronted the Founding Congress was the attitude which the KPD should assume toward the Revolutionary Shop Stewards. This radical group had sprung from the trade-union movement, specifically the Berlin metal workers, and had hardly any locals outside the capital. The group had been formed in 1914 as an anti-war movement which operated within the labor unions. When the first mass strikes occurred in the summer of 1916, the Revolutionary Shop Stewards began to make active preparations for the revolution they anticipated. In contrast to the Spartacists they did not believe in mass action as the key to revolution, but in conspiracy conducted by a small group of militants. Their political aims were vague, except for their general advocacy of a proletarian dictatorship to be established through revolutionary councils. They admired the Bolsheviks, but they did not, as a group, have contact with the Russian revolutionaries, nor did they subscribe to a revolutionary theory such as Marxism represented. They relied on recruiting their strength from within the factories, preferably among union members, and saw in the "shops" rather than in any given party the strongholds for revolutionary action.

[38] Rosenberg, p. 322. For the reaction of Luxemburg and Jogiches, see Brandt and Lowenthal, p. 120.

[39] Rosenberg, p. 322; Friedrich Stampfer, *Die vierzehn Jahre der ersten deutschen Republik*, 3rd ed. (Hamburg, 1947), p. 89.

Although they remained trade-union members and belonged nominally to the USPD, they conducted their policies independently of either.[40]

The relationship between the Revolutionary Shop Stewards and the Spartacus League had been anything but congenial prior to the revolution in Germany. A rapprochement between the two groups occurred only two months before the collapse of the Empire, and some degree of cooperation became inevitable after November 9, 1918, especially when the Spartacists realized that the Revolutionary Shop Stewards were energetic and successful champions of the council system. Despite this fact, the different philosophies, tactics, and objectives of the two groups led repeatedly to altercations.[41]

Several representatives of the Revolutionary Shop Stewards attended the Founding Congress of the German Communist Party as guests. In the course of the proceedings the Spartacist, or, as they now called themselves, Communist, leaders entered into negotiations with the Revolutionary Shop Stewards and invited them to join the new party. But whether the Shop Stewards did not like the tone of the debates at the congress, or whether they were suspicious of the direction in which the new party seemed to be headed, especially in view of the reputation for rioting which the Spartacists had won, they hedged and stated conditions. They demanded that the resolution to boycott the coming elections be revoked; that they, the Shop Stewards, be granted parity with the Communists in determining the program, tactics, and publications of the projected enlarged organization; and, finally, that the additional name of "Spartacus League" be dropped from the name of the Communist Party. These conditions proved unacceptable to the KPD, and fusion with the Revolutionary Shop Stewards was regretfully rejected.[42]

[40] Tormin, pp. 41-44.

[41] *ibid.*, pp. 42-44.

[42] *Die Rote Fahne*, No. 2, January 2, 1919; Brandt and Lowenthal, p. 120; Flechtheim, p. 46; Tormin, pp. 112-113; Waldman, pp. 156-157. According to Edward Hallett Carr, *A History of Soviet Russia: The Bolshevik Revolution 1917-1923*, III (New York, 1953), p. 106, the real obstacle to an amalgamation of KPD and Revolutionary Shop Stewards was Rosa Luxemburg, who distrusted the radicalism of the Shop Stewards. This contention is not borne out by Luxemburg's comments on this issue (*Rote Fahne*, No. 2, January 2, 1919); see also Rosenberg, pp. 322-323.

It should be added that a possible additional reason for the wariness of the Shop Stewards may have been the open hostility which the delegates displayed vis-à-vis

The Party and Its Heritage

When most of the items on the agenda had been settled, the delegates turned their attention to party organization. Hugo Eberlein, one of the younger Spartacist leaders, presented the matter to the congress. After posing the rhetorical question of whether the new party wanted to be merely an electioneering club or a political fighting organization, he settled the matter at once by outlining his concept of how a political fighting organization should operate. The informal organization of the Spartacus League, which had never enjoyed legal status, was no longer feasible. The struggles ahead demanded leadership more centralized than the Spartacus League had required. To meet this condition, Eberlein suggested that the loose and improvised leadership setup of the past be reconstituted into a formal, elective *Zentrale*. But he stressed at once that this body must not be permitted to become a dictatorial agency. Full autonomy was to be granted to the Communist locals in the various parts of the country. Nor should the *Zentrale* be given authority to exercise rigid control over local party publications. The principal duty of the *Zentrale* would be to keep an eye on the domestic scene, and to provide political and ideological guidance.[43]

In the ensuing debate, which preceded the election of the *Zentrale*, another Spartacist leader, Ernst Meyer, suggested that the *Zentrale* be supplemented by a national committee (*Reichsausschuss*) consisting of representatives from the various national districts. No action was taken at the time on Meyer's suggestion. The delegates then agreed to "elect" all members of the old Spartacist leader group into the new *Zentrale*, and to add one representative from the Left Radicals, Paul Frölich. Their tenure of office was to extend until the next party congress. Aside from Frölich, the *Zentrale* included Rosa Luxemburg, Karl Liebknecht, Leo Jogiches, August Thalheimer, Hermann and Käte Duncker, Wilhelm Pieck, Ernst Meyer, Paul Levi, Hugo Eberlein, and Paul Lange.[44]

---

the German trade-union movement. The matter was debated on the floor, and Rosa Luxemburg pointed out in the course of the deliberations that the trade-unions had acted in the past as "firm supporters of the bourgeois state and society." No formal vote on whether the new party should participate in the trade-union movement was taken, but the issue was referred to a committee for further deliberation (*Die Rote Fahne*, No. 1, January 1, 1919); see also Carr, III, p. 104.

[43] *Die Rote Fahne*, No. 2, January 2, 1919.

[44] *Die Rote Fahne*, No. 2, January 2, 1919; it is interesting to note that six out of twelve members in the first KPD *Zentrale* held a doctoral degree. See the unpubl.

Thus the KPD began its history by pouring old wine into new bottles, retaining the leaders who had founded the party, and consequently also the traditional principles of decentralization and party democracy. In the course of the following five years, as four of the most prominent Spartacist leaders were either killed or expelled from the party, these principles were to be steadily undermined, but the party's organizational setup which evolved from the Founding Congress remained by and large unchanged. To the *Zentrale*, elected at party congresses which convened at irregular intervals, fell the direction of policy and the coordination of party activities. The number of members elected to the *Zentrale* was flexible and was changed at nearly every party congress. The members of the *Zentrale*, as a body, shared all responsibility for party policy. It soon became customary, however, to recognize one member as the principal leader, even when no official mention of his position was indicated in party records. The recognition of a definite hierarchy was eventually formalized when the party created offices within the *Zentrale*, and designated a chairman, a vice-chairman, secretaries, and alternates.

The party gradually grew larger, and the basis of leadership was extended in December 1920 by the creation of a Central Committee. It was composed of delegates from each of the party's twenty-eight districts. The Central Committee met with the *Zentrale* at joint conferences whenever major policy decisions had to be made, or other weighty matters required discussion. It served in addition as a control agency over the activities of the *Zentrale*. As the delegates to this committee represented their respective geographical districts, where the views of the party members did not always coincide with those of the *Zentrale*, it was here, in the Central Committee, that opposition factions could form and exercise an often formidable influence on the party.[45]

---

diss. of Otto Wenzel, "Die Kommunistische Partei Deutschlands im Jahre 1923" (Freie Universität Berlin, 1955), p. 124, n.1.

[45] In general, the organizational process of the KPD closely followed that of the Russian Communist Party, as Bolshevik influence on the German party grew stronger. It was no coincidence that, following the Russian pattern, the term *Zentrale* was replaced by *Zentralkomitee* after Stalin's favorite German Communist, Ernst Thälmann, became party chairman in the fall of 1925. This change in terminology has frequently caused confusion. Some authors, Ruth Fischer among them, have failed to distinguish between *Zentrale*, *Zentralkomitee*, and *Zentralausschuss*, and have indiscriminately translated all three terms as "Central Committee." To

The Party and Its Heritage

At no time since the outbreak of the November revolution were the Communists as isolated as they were immediately after the founding of their new party.[46] The councils, the Revolutionary Shop Stewards, even the recently defeated *Volksmarinedivision* began to keep their distance. It was therefore an ironic twist of fate that the disastrous January uprising in Berlin, which has gone down in history as "Spartacus Putsch," was started, not by the KPD, but by the Independent Socialists and the Revolutionary Shop Stewards. As the most recent historian of this event points out, it was not "the product of a deliberate plan" formulated by any particular political faction, but rather the result of "a violent outburst of the sharp hostility which then existed between the socialist factions."[47] Briefly, the genesis of the January riots was as follows. As a result of disagreements which arose over the manner in which the provisional German government had put down the mutinous *Volksmarinedivision* in December, the members of the USPD represented in the government resigned on December 29. Their example was followed by their colleagues in the Prussian cabinet. Only Berlin's Police President Emil Eichhorn, a left-wing Independent, failed to follow the lead of his party colleagues. When the Prussian Minister of the Interior Paul Hirsch asked Eichhorn to resign from his office, Eichhorn refused. He received immediate support from his own party and from the Revolutionary Shop Stewards, who decided to call a mass demonstration in the center of the city for January 5. This plan was communicated to the KPD leaders, who decided to join the other two organizations. The mass demonstration was well attended, and its sponsors felt encouraged to exploit the favorable response of the populace toward taking more drastic steps. In the evening of January 5 delegates from the Revolutionary Shop Stewards, the USPD leadership, and the KPD (Liebknecht and Pieck) held a conference and resolved to overthrow the government. They formed a provisional revolutionary committee of which Liebknecht was one of the three directors. While the committee debated on

---

avoid such confusion in this study, *Zentrale* will be always rendered in the original, and "Central Committee" will refer exclusively to the *Zentralausschuss*.

[46] Both Tormin (pp. 112-113) and Waldman (p. 157) point out that the abortive negotiations with the Revolutionary Shop Stewards left the KPD numerically weak, and accentuated the party's isolated position.

[47] Waldman, pp. 184-185, 214.

how to proceed, and eventually issued a proclamation which declared the Ebert government "deposed," undisciplined, leaderless bands rioted in the streets, occupied the offices of leading newspapers, and engaged in skirmishes with the police.[48]

Rosa Luxemburg, Leo Jogiches, and other members of the *Zentrale* realized as early as January 6 that the entire undertaking was senseless. The revolutionary committee proved incompetent, and the riots in the streets of Berlin lacked direction and coordination and served no useful purpose. On January 8 the *Zentrale* held a meeting in the course of which the "uprising" was sharply criticized. The attending members even considered an official disavowal of Liebknecht's claim to speak for the entire Communist Party.[49] On January 9 Radek, still illegally in Berlin, urged the KPD leaders to try to terminate the riots as soon as possible. But Rosa Luxemburg and her colleagues wavered. While they disapproved of the adventure, they were also loath to abandon the fighting workers to their fate, quite apart from the fact that they knew how difficult it would prove to restrain the mobs over whom they had little, if any, control. In the end, the *Zentrale* settled for a compromise. Although they recognized the hopelessness of the situation, and knew that the overwhelming majority of the Berlin workers rejected and resented the riots, they decided to print "defensive" slogans in the *Rote Fahne* in an attempt to give the uprising the appearance of being a heroic struggle against "counterrevolutionary" attacks.[50] The dilemma which the Communists faced in these days was subsequently described by Clara Zetkin, who based some of her observations on a letter from Leo Jogiches.

"The aim of the struggle could be only a forceful defense against the blow of the counterrevolution. Thus: reinstatement of Eichhorn in his office; removal of the troops . . . ; arming of the workers, and transfer of military power to the revolutionary-political representatives of the proletarians. . . . The situation created a difficult and conflict-laden task for the young Communist Party which Rosa Luxemburg led. It could not make the objective . . . 'overthrow of

---

[48] See esp. *ibid.*, pp. 171-185; also Rosenberg, pp. 328-330.

[49] Paul Levi, *Was ist das Verbrechen? Die Märzaktion oder die Kritik daran? Rede auf der Sitzung des Zentralausschusses der V.K.P.D. am 4. Mai, 1921* (Berlin, 1921), 33-34; Frölich, *Rosa Luxemburg*, pp. 321-322.

[50] Flechtheim, p. 48.

the government' its own; it had to reject it, but at the same time it could not lose touch with the masses who had become engaged in the struggle. . . . For this purpose the Communist Party had to show its own face . . . without damaging the proletarian, revolutionary solidarity which it owed to the fighters. Thus its role in the struggle had to be simultaneously negative-critical and positive-encouraging."[51]

Such a task proved too difficult for the party, and in the end led nowhere. The KPD certainly was unable to stop governmental countermeasures. As early as January 8, the government mobilized every available military unit in order to dislodge the insurgents from those city districts still held by them. The operation was directed by Gustav Noske, himself a member of the Provisional Government. During the night of January 10 to 11 the troops, many of them led by former imperial officers, began to advance on the center of Berlin, and three days later the uprising was completely suppressed.

On January 14, 1919, Rosa Luxemburg's last editorial appeared in the *Rote Fahne* under the caption: "Order Rules in Berlin." It was a bitter, resigned, but balanced appraisal of the recent events. Only the last paragraph of the editorial reflected once again a deep-seated optimism, an irrepressible faith in the eventual triumph of *her* revolution: " 'Order Rules in Berlin.' You dull henchmen [*Schergen*]! Your 'order' is built on sand. Tomorrow the revolution will 'rise again with clattering noise,' and to your horror will proclaim to the sound of trumpets: I was, I am, I shall be!"[52]

It was the last time that she addressed herself to the public. On the following day she and Karl Liebknecht were arrested, and on their way to prison were murdered by officers and men of a Berlin cavalry regiment.

The martyr's death they shared linked them so closely in the minds of their followers that subsequent Communist tradition has usually referred to them jointly, as if they had been a couple of revolutionary Dioscuri. But they were, in fact, very dissimilar individuals whose characters, aims, and ideas differed widely. Rosa

[51] Clara Zetkin, "Um Rosa Luxemburgs Stellung zur russischen Revolution," *Ausgewählte Reden und Schriften*, ii (Berlin, 1960), pp. 445-446.
[52] Rosa Luxemburg, "Die Ordnung herrscht in Berlin," *Ausgewählte Reden und Schriften*, ii, pp. 708-714.

Luxemburg was first and foremost a Marxist theorist, but Lieb-knecht was a man of action rather than a thinker. Although he was virtually born into the Marxist revolutionary movement, he never became well versed in Marxian theory. He shared with Luxemburg the dream of a future Socialist society but had no clear idea of how it should be realized. Lacking both Luxemburg's sensibility and her sensitivity, his approach to revolution was impulsive, pragmatic, and at times downright rash. While his rousing oratory, his personal courage and the sincerity with which he stated his convictions made him one of the most effective radical agitators, his lack of critical judgment at times involved him in adventures without regard for the possible consequences. Of all the Spartacist leaders, Liebknecht was probably the greatest admirer of the Bolsheviks, whose revolution won his unqualified and enthusiastic admiration. The differences which existed between German and Russian conditions he tended to ignore.[53]

Luxemburg was aware of Liebknecht's weak points, and usually distrusted his judgment and methods even though she valued him as a person. Of the two, she possessed the more independent mind, was more discerning and more prone to reject any move that smacked of irresponsible putschism. Liebknecht's proclivity for rushing headlong into ill-conceived adventures rarely met with her approval. She also disagreed with him on Russia. Though she, too, welcomed the October Revolution and shared in his admiration for the men who led it, she was much more critical of Russian developments than he was. She strongly disapproved of certain Bolshevik measures, and she rejected the idea of blindly modeling the German revolutionary movement on its Russian counterpart. Unlike Lieb-knecht, she saw the vast difference which distinguished Russian conditions from German, and she sensed danger for her own party should it ever become dependent on Bolshevik influence. She had denounced in the past Lenin's concept of the elite, the tightly organized revolutionary party of experts, and her verdict on this

[53] Carr, *The Bolshevik Revolution*, III, pp. 104-105; Brandt and Lowenthal, p. 120; Frölich, *Rosa Luxemburg*, p. 208; but cf. Rosenberg, p. 332, who draws no distinction between the fundamental attitudes of Liebknecht and Luxemburg. The best and most recent treatment of Liebknecht's ideas, his position in the party, and his relations with Rosa Luxemburg is in Karl W. Meyer, *Karl Liebknecht: Man Without a Country*, introd. C. V. Easum (Washington, D.C., 1957), pp. 127-173, and *passim*.

matter did not change. She remained loyal to her own conviction that a revolutionary party had to be independent, had to be democratically led, and had to be rooted in the support of the masses.

These ideas were the legacy which she bequeathed to her party. But this legacy became the property of only a few intellectuals within it. The great majority of German Communists, leaders and rank and file alike, either failed to understand her meaning altogether, or misinterpreted her, sometimes intentionally, to suit their purposes of the moment.[54] That the spirit of Leninism was to triumph over her own after her death was largely due to the dynamism of the Bolshevik movement, which succeeded in bringing German Communism into its orbit, and eventually under its control. Another factor which contributed heavily to undermining the effectiveness of Rosa Luxemburg's theories was her failure to apply them consistently in practice, when the time to do so arrived toward the end of her life. For although her assassination and Liebknecht's were acts of senseless brutality, there is little doubt that the political circumstances which led to their deaths were to some extent of their own making. During the first weeks after the collapse of the Empire they had misinterpreted events in Germany and had misjudged the temper of the people. Their lifelong dream that the fall of the Empire would bring with it the victory of the proletariat died slowly, as they clung for weeks to the belief that the political tide would turn in their favor. Only after the National Congress of Councils endorsed the elections to the National Assembly, did Luxemburg realize that victory was still far off, while Liebknecht still refused to admit even temporary defeat.

Toward the end of December, when it became quite obvious that the masses were not behind the Spartacists, Luxemburg reluctantly consented to the creation of a Communist Party. The moment was ill-chosen. The Spartacists were supported by only an insignificant number of German workers; they could not depend on controlling even that number; and they lost the "protective roof" of the USPD. The Founding Congress of the KPD confirmed Luxemburg's and Jogiches' initial misgivings when the delegates disregarded the advice of the Spartacist leaders on the crucial election issue. A few days later the new party became involved in the Eichhorn affair.

[54] Paul Levi, *Unser Weg; Wider den Putschismus.* Mit Anhang: *Die Lehren eines Putschversuches* von Karl Radek (Berlin, 1921), p. 34.

Luxemburg and Liebknecht disagreed on what attitude the Communists should adopt in this crisis, and neither of them succeeded in gaining control over the undisciplined crowds in the streets. These errors, which were largely of a tactical nature, were compounded by still graver psychological errors of judgment. In the two months between the fall of the Empire and the January disturbances in Berlin, the Spartacists kept up a ceaseless and vituperative hate campaign against Ebert's Provisional Government. In view of the uneasy atmosphere created by national defeat, hunger, and general uncertainty, their radical slogans sounded more ominous than was warranted by the actual strength of their movement. The tone of the *Rote Fahne*, the oratory of Liebknecht, Pieck, and others, and the sporadic local riots and strikes, although often unconnected with the Spartacists, all contributed to a popular image of the Spartacists as bloodthirsty extremists who wanted to liquidate everyone except proletarians. Public resentment naturally enough centered on the Communist leaders, and in particular on "Red Rosa," whose editorials in the *Rote Fahne* gave the average citizen the impression that they were inciting immediate civil war. Only a few close friends knew Rosa Luxemburg's real position, and of those not all were in agreement with her. Blinded by her unbounded faith that the masses would eventually rally behind the banner of the "true" proletarian cause, she did not recognize that her fine distinction between preparing the ground for a revolution and actually starting one was easily missed by minds less subtle than her own. The government and the public understood little and cared less about the complexities of Luxemburg's ideas; they only knew that radical slogans caused bloodshed, and they wanted to silence those who issued the slogans.

The bad reputation which the KPD acquired in the January days of 1919 had a lasting effect on the party's relations with other German labor organizations. Communist violence, real or alleged, caused particularly strong resentment among the Social Democratic workers and the trade-union members. Although there were occasions in the years to come when the Communists succeeded in establishing some degree of cooperation with moderate labor groups, such harmony was always superficial and of brief duration. The German Communists never overcame the basic distrust which their actions evoked in this early period. Social Democratic sentiments

to this effect were revealingly expressed in a poem printed by
Vorwärts, the principal organ of the SPD, on January 13, 1919.
Entitled "The Morgue," its last stanza read:

> Rows of hundreds of dead are everywhere—
> Proletarians!
> Karl, Rosa, Radek and Co. don't care—
> None of them lies there, none of them lies there!
> Proletarians![55]

Two days later, however, Karl and Rosa were among the rows of
corpses.

Their deaths gave the German Communist Party a legend, and
at the same time helped to obscure the guiding principles which
Rosa Luxemburg had tried to impress upon the movement she
helped to found. Only a handful of party functionaries knew her
opposition to the meaningless uprising which claimed her as a
victim, or were aware of her misgivings concerning Liebknecht's
hapless role in the Eichhorn affair. The rank and file, then and later,
saw in her only the martyred leader whose fate they mourned; they
ignored her teachings. True, there was a party program which professed the rejection of terror and premature uprisings, but few Communists seem to have heeded the program which Luxemburg had
drafted. After January 1919 Liebknecht's activist spirit was to per-
meate German Communism for several crucial years, but it was

---

[55] "Das Leichenhaus," *Vorwärts*, No. 22, January 13, 1919. The lines read in the
original:

> Vielhundert Tote in einer Reih'—
> Proletarier!
> Karl, Rosa, Radek und Kumpanei—
> Es ist keiner dabei, es ist keiner dabei!
> Proletarier!

The same paper had expressed similar sentiments the previous day in another
poem, entitled "In der Nacht zum 7. Januar"; the second stanza read:

> Ich sah der Masse räuberische Streife
> Sie folgten Karl, dem blinden Hödur, nach.
> Sie tanzten nach des Rattenfängers Pfeife,
> Der ihnen heuchlerisch die Welt versprach.
> Sie knieten hin vor blutigen Idolen
> Bauchrutschten vor der Menschheit Spott und Hohn,
> Vor Russlands Asiaten und Mongolen,
> Vor Braunstein, Luxemburg und Sobelsohn [Radek].
> O kehret um, ihr aufgehetzten Horden!
> Ihr ruft nach Freiheit nur, um sie zu morden.
> *Vorwärts*, No. 21, January 12, 1919

fused with the image of Rosa Luxemburg as her followers wanted to remember her. Her death became a symbol for thousands of party members, though few of them ever realized that the uprising in which she and Liebknecht perished had been started in opposition to her better judgment. Thus the memory of the undaunted revolutionary leader was kept alive in Communist annals, while her humanitarian, compassionate idealism, along with her sober counsels, were gradually consigned to oblivion.[56]

Ebert's Provisional Government emerged strengthened rather than weakened from the bloody January events, and throughout the Reich freecorps under Noske's direction put down local disorders wherever they occurred. Elections for the National Assembly were held on January 19, 1919, without the participation of the KPD, and the constituent body convened in Weimar on February 6. The SPD, which had received 37.8% of the total vote, formed a coalition government with the Democratic and Center parties, a constellation which became known as the "Weimar Coalition." During the following months the republic consolidated its position by defeating a short-lived soviet republic in Bavaria,[57] concluding a

---

[56] For a brief, but cogent, discussion of Rosa Luxemburg's place in contemporary Communist tradition see Werner Conze, "Die Befestigung der KPD-Tradition durch Mehring und Rosa Luxemburg," *Historische Zeitschrift*, CLXXXVIII, No. 1 (August 1959), pp. 76-82, esp. pp. 76-78; see also Carsten, p. 99.

[57] Although Communists played a leading role in the brief but stormy episode of the Bavarian soviet republic in April 1919, the movement as such was largely autonomous. There is no evidence to show that the *Zentrale* in Berlin was in any way connected with the events in Bavaria. The Communists, then and now, have given little emphasis to this chapter of proletarian history and seem to consider it of mere peripheral interest. Thus Wilhelm Pieck in "Kurze Geschichte der Arbeiterparteien," *Jahrbuch für Politik, Wirtschaft, Arbeiterbewegung 1922-1923* (Hamburg, n.d.), pp. 639-649, does not mention it, but lists it in the appended table of events, without comment (p. 650). Only one entry, a telegram of Lenin's to the Bavarian soviet republic, is devoted to the episode in *Zur Geschichte der Kommunistischen Partei Deutschlands; Eine Auswahl von Materialien und Dokumenten aus den Jahren 1914-1946*, published and edited by the Marx-Engels-Lenin-Stalin Institut beim Zentralkomitee der SED, 2nd ed. (Berlin, 1955), p. 79. Three documents pertaining to the role played by the Bavarian branch of the KPD are included in *Dokumente und Materialien zur Geschichte der deutschen Arbeiterbewegung*, Reihe II, 1914-1945, III, Januar 1919–Mai 1919, published and edited by the Institut für Marxismus-Leninismus beim Zentralkomitee der Sozialistischen Einheitspartei Deutschlands (Berlin, 1958), pp. 379-381, although additional documents pertaining to other aspects of the Bavarian soviet republic are included.

peace treaty with the Allies, and adopting a constitution. These were steps forward, but they by no means represented the end of all difficulties for Germany. Although economic prospects were initially brightened by gradually increasing imports, which eased the critical food shortage, and by rather rapidly increasing exports, the value of the mark depreciated steadily, a trend indicative of the republic's precarious financial position.[58] The winter of 1919-1920 saw the creation of the provisional *Reichswehr,* and also military operations in the Baltic region against Bolshevik forces. It was here that the notorious freecorps grew strong and aggressive, fighting to protect the borders of a republic which they deeply despised.

For the German Communists the year 1919 proved to be grim and discouraging. Their two most capable leaders were dead, and party leadership rested for a few months in the hands of Leo Jogiches, the friend and former mentor of Rosa Luxemburg. The party itself was suspect and exposed to further repressions, in the event of any domestic disturbances in which it might become involved. Such an occasion was not long in coming. Unemployment and rising prices led in February 1919 to a series of strikes in various parts of the country, especially in central Germany. On March 3 the movement spread to Berlin, where it developed into a general strike and led to street fighting and looting, but collapsed on March 8 after military forces had been called in to restore order. Two days later Leo Jogiches was arrested and shot to death by a police officer. Although this time the *Zentrale* had appealed to the workers not to engage in futile skirmishes with the police, the disturbances in the streets were blamed on the KPD because of its reputation for trouble-making, and the authorities proceeded to curb its activities as much as possible. Under a state-of-siege law the Prussian government banned the *Rote Fahne* on March 3. The party moved the newspaper office from Berlin to Leipzig, and the *Rote Fahne* was published there from April 11 to May 9, when the Saxon government in turn forbade its publication. From that day until December 12, 1919, the party's chief organ remained banned. In addition, many Communists were arrested and held in prison for months

[58] Costantino Bresciani-Turroni, *The Economics of Inflation: A Study of Currency Depreciation in Post-War Germany,* foreword by Lionel Robbins, translated by Millicent E. Sayers (London, 1937), pp. 28-30, 51-54.

before they were brought up for trial. Throughout the year, the party remained in a semi-legal state of existence.[59]

By the summer of 1919 the first revolutionary wave in Germany, which had followed in the wake of the Armistice in 1918, reached a temporary standstill. The conclusion of the peace treaty in June, the adoption of the constitution in August, and the success of Noske's police actions in putting down disturbances throughout the country gave the new state for the first time a semblance of stability. But Noske's rigorous measures were bitterly resented by a large part of German labor, not only by the Communists. In addition, the failure of the Social Democrats to initiate the socialization of basic industries proved disappointing to many workers who had expected that such measures would surely be taken by the young republic.[60] These workers also demanded a stronger voice in the country's economic affairs, and wanted to see the elimination of influence by members of the old military and bureaucratic caste, many of whom had remained in office. Thus, despite the positive achievements to which the republic could point toward the end of the year, it had at the same time alienated part of the German working class and thereby endangered the hard-won domestic peace.[61]

The KPD, isolated and despised, remained throughout 1919 a small and ineffective platoon which wanted very much to be an army. The majority of the dissatisfied elements among labor found the USPD more congenial than the Communists, who were virtually outlaws, and who had alienated even other radical groups by their brush-fire tactics, their boycott of the elections, and their hostility to the trade-unions. To recapture lost ground, the party had to win the confidence of the masses. This was clearly recognized by the party's new leader, Paul Levi. A lawyer by profession and a Marxist

[59] *Die Rote Fahne*, No. 45, March 3, 1919; No. 47, April 11, 1919; No. 70, May 11, 1919; No. 67 [*sic*], December 12, 1919. See also Flechtheim, pp. 51-52; Rosenberg, pp. 332-334; Brandt and Lowenthal, pp. 128-129; Gustav Noske, *Von Kiel bis Kapp; Zur Geschichte der deutschen Revolution* (Berlin, 1920), pp. 76-93, and *passim; Dokumente und Materialien zur Geschichte der Deutschen Arbeiterbewegung,* III, *passim.*

[60] For an excellent summary of the socialization problem, which also includes an up-to-date bibliography, see Karl Dietrich Erdmann, *Die Zeit der Weltkriege,* vol. IV of Bruno Gebhardt, *Handbuch der Deutschen Geschichte* (Stuttgart, 1959), pp. 89-92. See also Klemens von Klemperer, *Germany's New Conservatism; Its History and Dilemma in the Twentieth Century,* foreword by Sigmund Neumann (Princeton, 1957), pp. 80-91.

[61] Rosenberg, pp. 334-335.

by conviction, Levi was 36 years old when the death of Leo Jogiches made him a logical choice for the most influential position in the party's high command.[62] Well known as a loyal disciple of Rosa Luxemburg, Levi's succession was not contested, but his position was problematic from the start. Although few questioned Levi's genuine devotion to the cause of revolutionary Socialism, his personality was not such as to win him the spontaneous support of his colleagues, or make him popular with the rank and file.[63] Although he was a fine speaker and a clever writer, his incisive logic and biting wit usually hovered above the level of a typical proletarian audience. Almost everything that he did or said had an irritating effect on at least some of those with whom he came into contact. His scepticism, his studied air of indolence and aloofness bred resentment, if not distrust. Many of his associates did not appreciate his private

[62] Franz Borkenau, *The Communist International* (London, 1938), p. 151. Officially, at least, the *Zentrale* had no formal chairman until December 1920, when the left wing of the USPD amalgamated with the KPD to form what was temporarily called the VKPD (*Vereinigte Kommunistische Partei Deutschlands*, or United Communist Party of Germany). It was then that Levi assumed the chairmanship. As there was no election to the *Zentrale* until the Second Party Congress met in October 1919, Levi's position of leadership could have come about only by informal common consent. It is not even certain that he was a member of the *Zentrale* which was elected anonymously in October 1919, though the fact that he delivered the keynote address to the congress makes it very probable that he was. He was definitely not a member of the *Zentrale* which was elected at the Third Party Congress held in February 1920 in Karlsruhe, because he was in prison. Two months later, at the Fourth Party Congress held in Berlin, Levi was elected to the *Zentrale* over his protest. He was re-elected at the Fifth Party Congress in November 1920, also held in Berlin. See Kommunistische Partei Deutschlands, *Bericht über den 2. Parteitag der Kommunistischen Partei Deutschlands (Spartakusbund) vom 20. Oktober bis 24. Oktober 1919* (Berlin, n.d.), pp. 6-26, 59-60.
—*Bericht über den 3. Parteitag der Kommunistischen Partei Deutschlands (Spartakusbund) am 25. und 26. Februar 1920* (Berlin, n.d.), p. 69.
—*Bericht über den 4. Parteitag der Kommunistischen Partei Deutschlands (Spartakusbund) am 14. und 15. April, 1920* (Berlin, n.d.), p. 78.
—*Bericht über den 5. Parteitag der Kommunistischen Partei Deutschlands (Sektion der Kommunistischen Internationale) vom 1. bis 3. November 1920 in Berlin* (Berlin, 1921), pp. 55, 192.
—*Bericht über die Verhandlungen des Vereinigungsparteitages der U.S.P.D. (Linke) und der K.P.D. (Spartakusbund). Abgehalten in Berlin vom 4. bis 7. Dezember, 1920* (Berlin, 1921), pp. 216, 270.
[63] During the Third World Congress of the Communist International in the summer of 1921, Lenin, in a talk with Clara Zetkin, had this to say about Levi: "You know how highly I value Paul Levi and his capacity. I got to know him in Switzerland and placed great hopes in him. He proved true in the times of worst persecution, was brave, clever, unselfish. I believed that he was firmly bound to the proletariat, although I was aware of a certain coolness in his attitude to the workers. Something of a 'please keep your distance.'" Quoted in Clara Zetkin, *Reminiscences of Lenin* (London, 1929), p. 31.

tastes, which inclined toward the artistic and especially literature and poetry, and they did not forgive him his habit of seeking refuge from the humdrum of party routine and political maneuvers in versatile interests and activities which were far removed from the aims of a revolutionary party.[64] But Levi was still the best man whom the KPD had to offer in the spring of 1919, and while he is said to have deplored the party's choice, he accepted his position for better or worse.[65]

The party was in poor straits when Levi assumed its leadership. Its virtually illegal status under the state-of-siege law made all political activities difficult and dangerous, doubly so because the authority which the *Zentrale* could exert over the local organizations was limited.[66] Luxemburg, Liebknecht, and Jogiches were dead, many other leaders in prison, and prospects for an improvement of the party's position were dim. Within the German labor movement the KPD was comparable to an unlicensed side show which featured "Wild Men" as its special attraction. Levi was determined to change all this. He was convinced that the Communists were themselves responsible for their uncomfortable position.[67] Twice within three months they had joined battle against overwhelming odds with incredibly small forces, only to be defeated each time. No substantial support had been forthcoming, because the party's reputation for irresponsibility and terrorism had alienated too many workers who might otherwise have sympathized with the Communist objectives. If the KPD was to survive, it had to break out of its isolation, recapture the confidence of at least the left wing of the USPD, and try to transform it from its present sectarian status into a strong mass party.[68] To this end the *Zentrale* would have to purge party

[64] This charge has been acidly expounded by Karl Radek, "Der Fall Levi," *Soll die Vereinigte Kommunistische Partei Deutschlands eine Massenpartei der revolutionären Aktion oder eine zentristische Partei des Wartens sein?*, 2nd ed. (Hamburg, n.d.), pp. 89-119, esp. p. 105. For a characterization of Levi, see also Carl von Ossietzky, "Als Gast Herr Dr. Paul Levi," *Die Weltbühne*, xxv/i, No. 23 (June 4, 1929), pp. 841-844; and Carl von Ossietzky, "Paul Levi," *ibid.*, xxvi/i, No. 8 (February 18, 1930), pp. 280-282.

[65] Levi, *Was ist das Verbrechen?*, p. 41; Wilhelm Pieck, "Party and Leader Crises in the Communist Party of Germany," *The Communist International, Organ of the Executive Committee of the Communist International*, xviii-xix, New Series (London, n.d.), p. 67.

[66] Rosenberg, p. 335; Pieck, "Kurze Geschichte der Arbeiterparteien," *op.cit.*, p. 646.

[67] Borkenau, *Communist International*, p. 152.

[68] Brandt and Lowenthal, p. 129.

membership of all extremist elements, tighten the reins of leadership, and discourage putschism. Levi resolved to make it impossible
for any faction within the KPD ever again to involve the party in
a futile adventure, particularly in an armed uprising which lacked
mass support.[69]

Levi proceeded carefully. Rather than purge the party outright of
its lunatic fringe by expulsion, he adopted a policy by which the
extremist element was driven into opposition to the *Zentrale,* a
maneuver which ultimately led to an open split. Levi's task was
facilitated by the fact that the party was divided on a number of
crucial issues, all of which centered around the problem of what
tactics to adopt. There were three major points of controversy:
National Bolshevism, the attitude to trade-unions, and participation
in the parliamentary life of the state.[70]

National Bolshevism was a peculiar phenomenon which occurred
on and off during the history of the Weimar Republic. It involved
at all stages an attempt, initiated by either the extreme political
Right or Left, to build a bridge between them and thus create a
national front of the people. The common enemies were in all cases
the bourgeois democratic republic and the Entente powers, whereas
Soviet Russia was seen even by the nationalist advocates of such a
common front as a potential German ally.[71]

The 1919 version of National Bolshevism was sponsored by two
Communist leaders from Hamburg, Dr. Heinrich Laufenberg and
Fritz Wolffheim, who advocated a Jacobin war against the Western
Allies. In such a war the German proletariat was to take the lead in
creating a red army, which would be open to nationalist freecorps
volunteers, and thus organized would strike out against the West.
The French and Belgian proletariat would be persuaded to join
their German comrades against their own capitalist exploiters, and

[69] Borkenau, *Communist International,* p. 152.

[70] Ruth Fischer, *Stalin and German Communism: A Study in the Origins of the
State Party,* preface by Sidney B. Fay (Cambridge, 1948), p. 118.

[71] The most recent study of National Bolshevism in the Weimar Republic is
Otto Ernst Schüddekopf, *Linke Leute von Rechts; Die nationalrevolutionären
Minderheiten und der Kommunismus in der Weimarer Republik* (Stuttgart, 1960).
Other accounts worth consulting are Erich Müller, *Nationalbolschewismus* (Ham-
burg, 1933); Karl O. Paetel, "Der deutsche Nationalbolschewismus 1918-1932; Ein
Bericht," *Aussenpolitik,* 3. Jahrgang, No. 4 (April 1952), pp. 229-242; Armin
Mohler, *Die Konservative Revolution in Deutschland 1918-1932; Grundriss ihrer
Weltanschauung* (Stuttgart, 1950), pp. 59-65, and *passim*; Klemperer, pp. 139-150.
For a discussion of a later stage of National Bolshevism see below, Ch. XI.

help smash the chains of the Versailles treaty. Laufenberg and Wolffheim actually attempted to translate their theories into practice, but apart from isolated local rapprochements between radical workers and freecorps units the scheme brought no results.[72] Initially even Radek, who since February 1919 had been held a prisoner in Berlin by the German government, was fascinated by some of the implications National Bolshevism offered, though he did not endorse the Laufenberg-Wolffheim movement. In the following year, Lenin himself officially branded it as a Communist heresy.[73] Throughout the better part of 1919, however, the Hamburg circle around Laufenberg and Wolffheim remained influential in party affairs, particularly since they also led the opposition against participation in trade-unions and parliament.

At the Founding Congress of the KPD, the majority of the delegates had come out against such participation. Rosa Luxemburg, who had opposed the boycott of the elections, had clearly sided with the majority on the trade-union issue. The party had carried out its resolution to abstain from voting in the elections, but had taken no steps to have its members withdraw from the trade-unions. Now, months after the Founding Congress had adjourned, both issues were revived. In August 1919 they were heatedly debated during a clandestine party meeting at Frankfurt am Main. But nothing was settled there, and further debate was deferred until October of the year when the Second Party Congress was scheduled to meet at Heidelberg. During the debates at the Second Congress the delegates split into two camps. The *Zentrale*, led by Levi, presented a number of theses which censured Communist abstention from participation in elections and trade-unions. In short, Levi demanded a reversal of the party's original position on these issues. The opposing camp, led by Laufenberg and Wolffheim, called for the withdrawal from all German trade-unions and the formation of a new, big union which presumably was to be run by the Communists.[74]

The key to Levi's political maneuver lay with the eighth of the theses which he submitted to the congress. It stated that "Members

[72] Schüddekopf, *Linke Leute von Rechts*, pp. 107-120; Paetel, p. 230.

[73] Fischer, pp. 92-93; Vladimir Ilitch Lenin, *"Left-Wing" Communism: An Infantile Disorder; An Attempt at a Popular Discussion on Marxist Strategy and Tactics* (New York, 1934), pp. 25-58, *passim*.

[74] Carr, *The Bolshevik Revolution*, III, pp. 104, 136; Flechtheim, pp. 59-60; cf. Fischer's rather colored account of the same events, pp. 118-119.

of the KPD who do not concur with these views will have to leave the party."[75] Laufenberg, speaking in the name of the opposition faction, complained that the theses, notably the eighth, were designed to force a party split. His complaint was justified. Shortly before Levi submitted the theses he had received a letter from the imprisoned Radek, who implored Levi not to make the two issues a matter of party discipline, but to rely on persuasion. Levi ignored Radek's plea and presented his theses to the congress in the original version. When the vote was taken, the *Zentrale* carried the day and the Laufenberg-Wolffheim faction announced their secession from the KPD.[76]

For the moment at least, common sense had triumphed. Levi's roughshod tactic was prompted by his belief in Luxemburg's maxim that German Communism could succeed only through mass support. Thus the extremists had to go in order to make the party more respectable. But in carrying out his plan Levi went much further than Luxemburg had been willing to go at the Founding Congress. Besides reversing the party's position on the trade-union and election issues, he did what Luxemburg had refused to do, he split the party. His decision to do so was that of a reasonable man who hoped to introduce an element of sanity into the German revolutionary movement. But reason and revolution rarely mix, and his good intentions were in the long run condemned to failure. His later critics charged him retrospectively with "opportunism," a term which in party lingo usually referred to policies of compromise and moderation,[77] and from their point of view they were undoubtedly right. Since Levi was a pessimist by nature he may have

---

[75] Quoted in Flechtheim, p. 59.

[76] *ibid.*, p. 60; Carr, *The Bolshevik Revolution*, III, p. 137.

[77] See, for instance, Kommunistische Partei Deutschlands, *Bericht über die Verhandlungen des 2. Parteitages der Kommunistischen Partei Deutschlands (Sektion der Kommunistischen Internationale), abgehalten in Jena vom 22. bis 26. August 1921* (Berlin, 1922), p. 151. After the KPD merged with the left wing of the USPD in December 1920, the party congresses were given a new numbering system. Thus the Unification Congress of December 1920 counted as the First, the congress held at Jena in August 1921 as the Second Congress. Thereafter, the party instituted a dual system of numbering whereby the following congress, held in Leipzig in January 1923, came to be called the "III. (8.) *Parteitag.*" In order to distinguish the two "second congresses" from each other, I shall henceforth cite the one above as follows: *Verhandlungen des 2. Parteitages (Jena 1921).*

For a definition of "opportunism" in the Communist meaning see *Handbuch des Weltkommunismus*, eds. Joseph M. Bochenski and Gerhart Niemeyer (Munich, 1958), pp. 136-137, 147.

sensed as early as 1919 that world revolution was still a long way off, and, although he remained a revolutionary Marxist, he endeavored to lead the party along the path of prudence. It was virtually inevitable that under these circumstances he would sooner or later come into conflict with his less restrained peers.

One immediate effect of the split was a reduction of the party's strength from approximately 107,000 to about 50,000 members. Its strongest organizations, those in northern Germany, the Rhineland, parts of Saxony, and nearly all of Berlin joined the seceding faction and founded a rival party in April 1920. The Communist Workers Party of Germany (*Kommunistische Arbeiterpartei Deutschlands*, or KAPD), as it was called, soon acquired a deserved reputation as a movement that was more akin to Anarcho-Syndicalism than to Communism. Although the KAPD remained a small party which never exerted any significant influence on German politics, it was for several years a thorn in the side of the KPD.[78]

The KPD entered the year 1920 reduced in numbers, but temporarily consolidated. The party's fortunes were to take a turn for the better toward the end of the year, but the first four months were far from promising. The Third Party Congress, which met in Karlsruhe on February 25 and 26, 1920, was prematurely dissolved by the police, and the few sessions which were held reflected an atmosphere of resignation rather than of revolution. The party was subject to constant harassment by the authorities. Paul Levi had been arrested in Bremen shortly before the congress convened, and some of his colleagues shared his fate after the police raid on the delegates in Karlsruhe.[79]

[78] Brandt and Lowenthal, p. 129; Flechtheim, p. 60; Fischer, p. 119; Borkenau, *The Communist International*, p. 153.

The history of the KAPD remains to be written, but some information is provided by the following accounts: Schüddekopf, *Linke Leute von Rechts*, pp. 108-109, and *passim*; Wilhelm Pieck, "Kurze Geschichte der Arbeiterparteien," *op.cit.*, pp. 644-645, a very biased commentary; Erich Everth, "Deutscher Kommunismus," *Die Neue Rundschau*, xxxii: 1, No. 1 (January 1921), pp. 78-80; Anonymous, "Die Roten Kämpfer: Zur Geschichte einer linken Widerstandsgruppe," *Vierteljahrshefte für Zeitgeschichte*, vii, No. 4 (October 1959), pp. 441-446. The author of this article claims (p. 441) that Levi split the party at the behest of the Bolsheviks, but gives no evidence to bear out his claim. The following account, cited in Fischer, p. 119, was not available to me: Bernhard Reichenbach, "Zur Geschichte der KAPD," *Archiv für die Geschichte des Sozialismus und der Arbeiterbewegung*, xiii, (Leipzig, 1928), pp. 117-140.

[79] KPD, *Bericht über den 3. Parteitag*, p. 90, and *passim*; Brandt and Lowenthal, p. 131; Carr, *The Bolshevik Revolution*, iii, pp. 170-171; *Die Rote Fahne*, No. 18, February 29, 1920, and No. 19, March 1, 1920.

The low ebb of Communist morale became very evident three weeks after the Third Party Congress. On March 13, 1920, Wolfgang Kapp and General Walther von Lüttwitz staged a right-wing putsch and formed a short-lived government after their forces had occupied the capital. The legitimate government fled Berlin and established itself in Stuttgart. But after four days the Kapp Putsch was defeated by a general strike, led by the trade-unions.[80] Here was a unique occasion for the Communists to join wholeheartedly in what was for once a genuine mass movement, and to show that they were really what they had always claimed to be—the vanguard of the proletariat. But the KPD leadership did not see it that way. With Levi still in prison, the *Zentrale* in Berlin decided initially to ignore Kapp, Lüttwitz, the Ehrhardt Brigade and all the rest. A leaflet which the party issued on March 13 advised against support of the general strike which the SPD and trade-unions had proclaimed, and warned the proletariat "not to lift a finger for the democratic republic."[81] On March 14, the *Rote Fahne* printed a leading article on the subject.

"The Ebert-Republic, the bourgeois democracy, can no longer be saved; it is merely an empty pretence, merely a cracked mask for the capitalist dictatorship. . . . The revolutionary proletariat remains in chains. Thousands of revolutionary leaders are in protective custody, in prison, in the penitentiary. The situation is crystal clear. The watchword is evident: All revolutionary workers must rally around the red flag of the proletarian dictatorship."[82]

But the situation was not crystal clear. Later in the day, when the Communist leaders realized that they were out of step with their own rank and file, they reversed their position and supported the general strike. But by then the party had lost every opportunity to play a leading role in what proved to be the high point of working-class solidarity in the era of the Weimar Republic.[83]

[80] The best recent account of the well-known Kapp Putsch is Robert G. L. Waite, *Vanguard of Nazism; The Free Corps Movement in Postwar Germany 1918-1923* (Cambridge, Mass., 1952), pp. 140-167. For a somewhat different viewpoint, see Harold J. Gordon, Jr., *The Reichswehr and the German Republic 1919-1926* (Princeton, 1957), pp. 90-125. The former emphasizes the role of the freecorps, the latter that of the Reichswehr.

[81] Flechtheim, p. 62; Carr, *The Bolshevik Revolution*, III, p. 172.

[82] *Die Rote Fahne*, No. 30, March 14, 1920.

[83] Flechtheim, pp. 62-63; Brandt and Lowenthal, pp. 131-134. See also Radek's criticism of the party in Exekutive der Kommunistischen Internationale, *Protokoll*

Background

Meanwhile large-scale disturbances had erupted in the Ruhr region. This movement, which was initially directed against the Kapp Putsch, very soon developed into an industrial uprising, with the avowed objective of overthrowing the republican government and establishing a proletarian dictatorship. A Red Ruhr Army was hastily formed, and the government of Friedrich Ebert, which had hardly recovered from the right-wing putsch, now had to send police and army forces against the left-wing insurgents in the Ruhr. Local Communist organizations participated in the Ruhr fighting, but formed only an insignificant contingent alongside insurgents who were either unaffiliated anarcho-syndicalist elements, or belonged to the KAPD, the USPD, and even the SPD. The Communists in the Ruhr gained no effective control over the insurgent forces, nor were they supported from the *Zentrale*. The uprising was defeated by the first week of April, along with similar radical upheavals in Chemnitz and other parts of central Germany.[84]

When the Fourth Party Congress convened in Berlin on April 14, the attitude of the KPD, during the Kapp Putsch and the subsequent uprisings in the Ruhr and in central Germany, was the key issue on the agenda. After the customary wrangles and mutual recriminations the congress passed a vote of censure against several members of the *Zentrale* who were held most responsible for the party's errors of the preceding weeks. The debates revealed that party unity was again tenuous at best, only half a year after the first major split. The factions were not yet clearly arrayed, but all indications pointed toward another polarization of forces into "right" and "left." Enough unity existed, however, to approve the party's participation in the coming Reichstag elections, and to agree on the development of intensified Communist activities in the trade-unions.[85]

---

des III. Kongresses der Kommunistischen Internationale (Moskau, 22. Juni bis 12. Juli 1921) (Hamburg, 1921), p. 457. Hereafter cited as *Protokoll des III. Kongresses der K.I.*

[84] Waite, pp. 172-182; Gordon, pp. 125-129; Werner T. Angress, "Weimar Coalition and Ruhr Insurrection, March–April 1920: A Study of Government Policy," *The Journal of Modern History*, XXIX, No. 1 (March 1957), pp. 1-20.

[85] Flechtheim, pp. 64-66; Brandt and Lowenthal, p. 135; Carr, *The Bolshevik Revolution*, III, p. 174; Pieck, "Kurze Geschichte der Arbeiterparteien," *op.cit.*, pp. 646-647; *Die Rote Fahne*, No. 53, April 18, 1920. The Fourth Party Congress was the first in over a year which met openly; the period of virtual illegality was over. See Degras, ed., *The Communist International 1919-1943, Documents*, I, p. 83.

The results of the election to the first Reichstag, held on June 6, 1920, revealed to the Communists how little of an impression they had yet made on the German labor movement. The KPD received 589,000 votes as compared to 6,104,400 for the SPD, and 5,046,800 for the USPD. Whereas the Social Democrats sent 102 delegates to the Reichstag, and the Independent Social Democrats 84, the Communists sent two, Levi and Zetkin.[86] Left to its own devices, the KPD might conceivably have remained in the doldrums indefinitely. But just when party morale had reached another nadir an outside force, the Executive Committee of the Communist International in Moscow, prepared to take a more active hand in the affairs of German Communism.[87]

[86] Germany. Statistisches Reichsamt, *Statistisches Jahrbuch für das Deutsche Reich*, XLIX (Berlin, 1930), p. 561. Although the KPD was entitled to four delegates, they were apparently represented by only two; see Germany, *Verhandlungen des Reichstags, 1. Wahlperiode 1920, Anlagen zu den stenographischen Berichten*, vol. 363 (Berlin, 1924), p. 31.

[87] Brandt and Lowenthal, p. 136.

CHAPTER II

GROWTH: THROUGH THE COMINTERN
TO MASS PARTY STATUS

ON JANUARY 24, nine days after the death of Rosa Luxemburg and Karl Liebknecht, a radiotelegram from Moscow issued an invitation to thirty-nine revolutionary working-class movements all over the world to attend the Founding Congress of the Third (Communist) International. The organization which headed the list was the KPD (Spartacus League). This was not accidental; it was the recognition by the Russian Bolsheviks that the new German party was the most important revolutionary movement outside Russia proper.

Despite this distinction, the KPD *Zentrale* received the invitation unenthusiastically. Much as the German Communists admired Lenin and his achievements, they were still strongly influenced by Rosa Luxemburg's critical attitude toward the Russian developments, and were not prepared to welcome the new International with open arms. News that an invitation to a founding congress was imminent had reached Rosa Luxemburg a few days before she was murdered.[1] The idea as such was not new to her. The founding of a Communist International constituted a logical sequel to the Bolshevik revolution, and Lenin had submitted a plan to this effect to the Central Committee of the Bolshevik party as early as April 1917.[2] Luxemburg and her colleagues in the *Zentrale* did not object in principle that a counterpart to the "opportunist" Second International be created. At the same time, the German Communist leaders were wary of an organization which the Bolsheviks could so easily dominate. Luxemburg in particular believed that if such an organization were founded before at least some strong revolutionary mass parties existed in the West, a Bolshevik-dominated International might deter the organic growth of such movements.[3] Prompted by her scepticism, and in anticipation of a formal invitation from Moscow, Luxemburg took the precaution to select a

[1] Carr, *The Bolshevik Revolution 1917-1923*, III (New York, 1953), p. 121, n. 1.
[2] Degras, ed., *The Communist International 1919-1943*, Documents, I (1919-1922, issued under the auspices of the Royal Institute of International Affairs (London-New York-Toronto, 1956), p. 1.
[3] Borkenau, *The Communist International* (London, 1938), p. 161.

delegate who was to represent the KPD whenever the prospective congress would be ready to meet. She chose Hugo Eberlein, a fellow Spartacist leader, and instructed him to vote against the creation of a new International because the KPD deemed it premature.

When the KPD *Zentrale* received the invitation, Leo Jogiches decided to carry out Rosa Luxemburg's instructions and sent Hugo Eberlein to Moscow, where the congress convened on March 2, 1919. Eberlein, faithful to his mandate, stated his party's opposition to the founding of the Third (Communist) International, but in the end was persuaded to abstain from the final vote, so as not to destroy the unanimity of the congress. Thus the Comintern, as it became commonly known, was founded without the formal approval of the most important non-Russian revolutionary movement, a peculiar irony in view of the fact that the platform of the new International, according to the invitation, was "worked out on the basis of the program of the Spartakusbund in Germany and of the Communist Party (Bolsheviks) in Russia."[4]

Although for the moment the KPD had asserted its independence vis-à-vis the Russians, the party's initial attitude remained a mere gesture. Eberlein not only signed the manifesto of the congress, but the KPD became the first Communist party outside Russia which joined the Comintern. This was the beginning of a gradual process by which German Communism became subject to Bolshevik interference, just the development which Luxemburg had anticipated and tried to prevent. Whereas Lenin had originally

[4] Degras, ed., *The Communist International, Documents*, I, p. 2. The program which the KPD adopted when the party was founded had made no mention of the Bolsheviks; see Kommunistische Partei Deutschlands, *Bericht über den Gründungsparteitag der Kommunistischen Partei Deutschlands (Spartakusbund), vom 30. Dezember 1918 bis 1. Januar 1919* (Berlin, n.d.), pp. 33-34.

The two most recent accounts of these events are Günther Nollau, *Die Internationale; Wurzeln und Erscheinungsformen des proletarischen Internationalismus* (Cologne, 1959), pp. 47-50; and Stanley W. Page, *Lenin and World Revolution* (New York, 1959), pp. 122-133. See also Carr, *The Bolshevik Revolution*, III, pp. 116-131. Originally two delegates, Eugen Leviné and Hugo Eberlein, were to attend the congress, but only Eberlein (whose pseudonym was "Max Albert") made his way across the frontier. For Eberlein's principal speeches at the congress, see Exekutive der Kommunistischen Internationale, *Der I. Kongress der Kommunistischen internationale. Protokoll der Verhandlungen in Moskau vom 2. bis zum 19. März 1919* (Hamburg, 1921), pp. 132-134, 146-147; hereafter cited as *Der I. Kongress der K.I., Protokoll.*

conceived of his prospective creation as a genuinely international organization to which he had referred as "the forerunner of the international republic of soviets,"[5] the Comintern was destined from birth to serve first and foremost the Russian state. Although world revolution was written on its banners and was expounded in the theses which the First Congress adopted, this objective remained dependent on Russian conditions and subject to Bolshevik control. The mere fact that Comintern headquarters was in Moscow, and remained there, showed that the Bolshevik leaders intended to retain full control, notwithstanding Zinoviev's vague assurances that the seat of the new organization would be transferred "as quickly as possible to another capital, for example, Paris."[6] Many a foreign delegate to the Executive Committee of the Comintern (ECCI) learned sooner or later that he was working *"pour les commissaires russes,"* a lesson which the German Communists learned too.[7]

The strength of Russian influence in the Comintern was already reflected in the composition of its first executive committee. Zinoviev became president, and Radek, although appointed *in absentia* because he was imprisoned in Berlin, became secretary of the ECCI. Angelica Balabanov was appointed as his substitute. Furthermore, the Russian delegation represented in the ECCI consisted of Lenin (as chief delegate), Trotsky, Bukharin, and Zinoviev, who thus acted in a dual capacity.[8]

The two whose influence on German Communism proved to be most immediate and fateful were Zinoviev and Radek. Grigori Evseyevich Zinoviev, originally Apfelbaum, was a peculiar choice for so important a post. An intellectual whose arrogance and predi-

---

[5] Quoted in Carr, *The Bolshevik Revolution*, III, p. 125.
[6] Quoted *ibid.*, p. 124.
[7] For the "Theses on Bourgeois Democracy and Proletarian Dictatorship Adopted by the First Comintern Congress," and for Eberlein's signature at the end of them see Degras, ed. *The Communist International, Documents*, I, pp. 7-47, esp. pp. 17-24, 38-47. On Russian influence on the Comintern see Carr, *The Bolshevik Revolution*, III, pp. 125-126, and *passim.* Also Theodore H. von Laue, "Soviet Diplomacy: G. V. Chicherin, Peoples Commissar for Foreign Affairs, 1918-1930," *The Diplomats*, eds. Gordon A. Craig and Felix Gilbert (Princeton, 1953), pp. 243-244, which gives a brief but excellent description of the relationship between the Russian Foreign Office and the Comintern.
[8] Von Laue, pp. 237-238. For Balabanov's account of the congress see Angelica Balabanoff [sic], *My Life as a Rebel* (New York and London, 1938), pp. 212-220.

lection for luxurious living were anything but proletarian,[9] he had jumped on the Bolshevik band-wagon in 1917 only at the last minute. Among the other Bolshevik leaders he had a reputation for cowardice, duplicity, and selfishness. Despite his lack of physical courage he often overrated the chances for political action, at least when the lives of others were at stake, and when matters went wrong he usually either refused to admit failure, or tried to shift the blame. According to Borkenau, Zinoviev made his way in the party by boundless submissiveness to Lenin after the revolution had succeeded.[10] Judging from an oblique reference in his political testament, Lenin must have been quite aware of Zinoviev's lack of revolutionary audacity.[11] On the other hand, Zinoviev's weaknesses were at least partly balanced by his unmatched gift for oratory, a quality which made him useful to the Bolshevik cause. Trotsky, though certainly no unbiased witness, has given Zinoviev generous credit for his ability to sway audiences, "to penetrate the heart of the demos and play upon its strings." In certain moments "he was an ideal mechanism of transmission between Lenin and the masses —sometimes between the masses and Lenin." But Trotsky's final judgment of Zinoviev is devastating.

"The agitator of the revolution lacked revolutionary character. When it was a question of conquering minds and hearts Zinoviev remained a tireless fighter, but he suddenly lost his fighting confidence when he came face to face with the necessity for action . . . then his insinuating, almost feminine voice, losing its conviction, would expose his inner weakness."[12]

Although neither Lenin nor Trotsky had any illusions as to Zinoviev's strength of character, they did not deprive the Bolshevik movement of his talents. World revolution required agitation and Zinoviev, in Lenin's words, was "an agitator and nothing but an agitator."[13] Thus Zinoviev was among the members of the committee which prepared the plans for founding the Third International, and at the congress proper Lenin appointed him president

[9] Gustav Hilger and Alfred G. Meyer, *The Incompatible Allies, A Memoir-History of German-Soviet Relations 1918-1941* (New York, 1953), pp. 117-118.

[10] Borkenau, *The Communist International*, p. 163.

[11] Isaac Deutscher, *Stalin, A Political Biography* (London-New York-Toronto, 1949), p. 249.

[12] Leon Trotsky, *The History of the Russian Revolution*, transl. Max Eastman (Ann Arbor, n.d.), II, pp. 46-47.

[13] *ibid.*, I, p. 301.

of the Executive Committee of the Third International. We do not know what was in Lenin's mind when he made head of the Comintern a man who was deemed unsuitable for a major post in the Soviet government. But whatever his reasons may have been, he entrusted to Zinoviev the organization of world revolution.[14]

Karl Radek, elected secretary of the ECCI, was one of the most fascinating and complex figures among the Bolshevik leaders. He was born in 1885 as Karl Bernardovich Sobelsohn in the Austrian part of Galicia. His early career as a radical was as colorful as it was turbid. Until 1908 he was active in the Polish Socialist movement, where he first came into conflict with his teacher, Rosa Luxemburg. That same year he went to Germany, joined the SPD, and became contributing editor to various Socialist publications. He also continued to keep his hand in the affairs of the Polish Social Democratic Party until he was expelled in 1912, allegedly for petty theft. By that time his pronounced left-wing radicalism and his acid newspaper articles had made him enemies in the German Social Democratic Party as well. And when the Polish Socialists requested the German party to expel him, the executive of the SPD availed itself of the opportunity to rid the party of a very uncomfortable troublemaker. Radek's cup of iniquity was considered full to the brim.[15]

When war broke out, Radek went to Switzerland where he joined Lenin with his coterie of exiles, and in April 1917 was among those who accompanied Lenin through Germany in the famous "sealed" train so obligingly furnished by General Ludendorff. Radek did not, however, participate in the actual events of the Russian Revolution, but stayed in Stockholm; there he made

---

[14] Franz Borkenau, *Der europäische Kommunismus; Eine Geschichte von 1917 bis zur Gegenwart* (Bern, 1952), p. 32. Equally uncomplimentary characterizations of Zinoviev can be found in *Balabanoff*, pp. 220-222; Paul Levi, *Was ist das Verbrechen?* (Berlin, 1921), p. 35; and Oscar Blum, *Russische Köpfe* (Leipzig-Vienna-Bern, 1923), pp. 109-111.

[15] *Akten betreffend den Russischen Bolschewisten Karl Radek (Sobelsohn)*, Auswärtiges Amt, Germany, file Deutschland 131, adh. 3, No. 2, microfilm, container 38, frame not numbered, National Archives, Washington, D.C. All documents in this collection will subsequently be cited as follows: Germany, Auswärtiges Amt, microfilm, container, and frame number.

This film, the frames of which are not consecutively numbered, contains the German intelligence file on Radek from December 1917 to February 1920. See also Fischer's analysis of Radek, *Stalin and German Communism* (Cambridge, Mass., 1948), pp. 201-210. According to her and according to the intelligence files, Radek adopted his *nom de guerre* after he had been charged with petty theft. Radek is derived from the Polish "Kradek," which means thief.

international contacts for the Bolsheviks, whose ranks he did not formally join until he arrived in Russia sometime after November 1917.[16]

For the next few months the versatile linguist, "who was perfectly at home in Russian, Polish and German and incorrectly fluent in three or four other languages,"[17] assisted Trotsky, then Peoples' Commissar for Foreign Affairs, in transacting whatever foreign political business there was. Radek's primary task during the winter of 1917 to 1918 consisted of spreading propaganda to the German trenches and winning converts to the Bolshevik cause among prisoners of war. Radek attended the peace negotiations between Germany and Russia at Brest-Litovsk as a "Polish member" of the all-Russian delegation and as "representative of the Social Democracy of Poland and Lithuania," the Polish Socialist Party of the left. When the train in which he and Trotsky traveled arrived at the railroad station in Brest-Litovsk, Radek grabbed a suitcase of Bolshevik propaganda pamphlets and began to distribute them to the German soldiers before the eyes of the German diplomats and officers assembled on the platform to greet the Russian plenipotentiaries. His impudence infuriated especially the German General Max Hoffmann who still saw in the Galician-born Radek an Austrian citizen.[18] When in March 1918 Georgi V. Chicherin replaced Trotsky as Commissar for Foreign Affairs, Radek was entrusted with the direction of the Central European Division of Narkomindel, the Russian Commissariat for Foreign Affairs. These early ties with Narkomindel enabled him to keep in close touch with the Russian diplomatic branch after he became associated

[16] Ruth Fischer states (p. 204) that Radek had to stay in Stockholm because the Provisional Government denied him entry into Russia as an Austrian citizen. Balabanoff mentions only that the Swiss Socialist Robert Grimm was denied entry, and states that Radek was the Bolshevik representative in Stockholm (pp. 146-147, 169, 171-172). Radek's presence in Stockholm is variously mentioned in *Akten betreffend den Russischen Bolschewisten Karl Radek (Sobelsohn)*, *op.cit.*, *passim.* See also *The Letters of Lenin*, eds. Elizabeth Hill and Doris Mudie (New York, 1937), pp. 424-426, containing instructions sent by Lenin to Radek in Stockholm on April 12, 1917; and Trotsky, *The Russian Revolution*, II, p. 97, referring to a similar correspondence. Thus Radek may have remained in Stockholm because Lenin wanted him there, and not because he was barred from entering Russia.

[17] Edward Hallett Carr, *German-Soviet Relations Between the two World Wars, 1919-1939* (Baltimore, 1951), p. 4.

[18] Isaac Deutscher, *The Prophet Armed: Trotsky, 1879-1921* (New York and London, 1954), p. 360. Carr, *The Bolshevik Revolution*, III, p. 37. Fischer, p. 204.

with the Comintern, the revolutionary arm of the Soviet state.[19] By this time, Soviet Russia had become his adopted country, and he served her faithfully for nearly two decades.

Throughout his political career Radek remained a controversial figure. Even his appearance was disturbing, and he seemed to take a certain pleasure in shocking people. A stranger who met him for the first time would see a little man with a huge head, topped by a shock of unruly, slightly receding hair, with protruding ears, and chewing on a pipe held between tobacco-stained teeth. In Moscow during the early 1920's he liked to wear a shaggy beard, which lent added prominence to his Jewish features and gave him the expression of a Talmudic scholar. But whenever he went abroad on a mission the beard came off, and Hilger relates that a clean-shaven Radek was always an indication to the personnel of the German Embassy in Moscow that he had recently been out of the country.[20] An ugly pair of spectacles, behind which his clever eyes appeared slightly veiled, completed the picture of this revolutionary intellectual.[21] For Radek was an intellectual. His three-room apartment in the Kremlin was crowded with books and other reading material, scattered all over chairs, tables, and shelves. His biting sarcasm and witticisms were notorious. Not even the sacrosanct Russian Communist Party and its Bolshevik leaders were spared by his sharp tongue. Many people disliked him profoundly,[22] but as Lenin's special confidant and a follower of Trotsky he could afford to ignore most of his antagonists, the more so since his work for the Bolshevik cause, erratic though it was at times, revealed originality, insight, and dedication. In contact with foreign diplomats, particularly the Germans, Radek could be utterly charming. The revealing frankness with which he discussed the most delicate political questions

[19] Von Laue, pp. 241-242. Carr, *The Bolshevik Revolution*, iii, p. 68. Cf. the rather muddled version in Fischer, p. 204.

[20] Hilger and Meyer, pp. 155-156.

[21] *ibid.*, pp. 71-74; Fischer, pp. 204-205; Blum, pp. 87-92; Ypsilon, *Pattern for World Revolution* (Chicago-New York, 1947), pp. 78-80, and *passim*; George Grosz, *Ein kleines Ja und ein grosses Nein; Sein Leben von ihm selbst erzählt* (Hamburg, 1955), pp. 174-175.

[22] See, for instance, Balabanoff, pp. 167, 246-248; Toni Sender, *The Autobiography of a German Rebel* (New York, 1939), p. 73. Borkenau, *The Communist International*, p. 164, calls him a cynic "too clever to be either heroic or even consistent," a judgment which may not be too far off the mark. Frölich, *Rosa Luxemburg*, trans. Edward Fitzgerald (London, 1940), p. 211, comments on Luxemburg's dislike of Radek.

bordered at times on Bismarckian bluntness and rarely failed to impress his listeners. No other Bolshevik functionary could promote simultaneously the revolutionary policies of the Comintern and the diplomatic objectives of Narkomindel as flexibly and brazenly as could Radek, who had a foot in both camps. Considering that these two agencies did not always agree on what constituted the best interests of the Soviet Union, Radek's ability to balance between them was no mean feat. One effect of his dual role was that the German diplomats who dealt with him trusted him as a rule whenever he talked diplomacy, but rightly considered him an enemy as soon as he meddled in German domestic affairs. This was the man who until the end of 1923 was Lenin's expert on German affairs.[23]

The outbreak of the German revolution in November 1918 fostered hopes among the Bolsheviks that Germany would follow the Russian example. But after the initial wave of excitement had subsided the course of German events did not follow a radical pattern. Furthermore, the German Provisional Government refused to accept a token shipment of Russian grain, and did not recall Adolf Joffe, the Soviet representative who had been expelled by the imperial government, to his post. To remedy the situation, in December the Central Executive Committee of the Russian Communist Party appointed five men who were to be sent to Germany. Ostensibly, they went to Germany because they were invited to attend the first All-German Congress of Workers' and Soldiers' Councils, scheduled to meet in Berlin on December 16, 1918. Their true mission, however, was to try to drive the German revolution further to the left. The five men, Nikolai Bukharin, Adolf Joffe, Christian Rakovsky, E. Ignatov, and Karl Radek, only got as far as Minsk where German officials turned them back by order of the

[23] Apart from Hilger and Meyer, pp. 73-74, evidence of trust placed in Radek by German diplomats was variously expressed in the correspondence between the German Foreign Office and the German Embassy in Moscow. See, for instance, "Consul General Schmidt-Rölke to German Foreign Office, December 12, 1921," Auswärtiges Amt (RAM), microfilm, container 1405, frames D 552334-552335; "Ambassador von Brockdorff-Rantzau to German Foreign Office, May 7, 1923," Auswärtiges Amt (RAM), microfilm, container 1406, frame D 552956; "Counselor of Embassy von Radowitz to Ago von Maltzan, personal, August 13, 1923," *ibid.*, frame D 553190. Cf. *Akten betreffend den Russischen Bolschewisten Karl Radek (Sobelsohn)*, *passim*, which reveal profound distrust of Radek by the German authorities at that time (1917-1920).

Ebert government. Four members of the mission resigned themselves to their ill luck, but Radek refused to be stopped. He disguised himself as an Austrian soldier returning from a Russian prisoner of war camp and, accompanied by two emissaries of the Russian Communist Party, made his way across the demarcation line and into Germany.[24]

Because of his delay Radek arrived in Berlin too late to attend the Congress of Workers' and Soldiers' Councils, which had already adjourned, but in time to participate in the Founding Congress of the German Communist Party. In his capacity as official representative of the Bolsheviks, he addressed the congress on the subject of the Russian and German revolutions. It was at this time, prior to his appearance on the platform, that he and Liebknecht engaged in hectic arguments with Luxemburg and Jogiches over whether to cut the ties with the Independent Social Democrats. As has been shown earlier, Radek's and Liebknecht's views prevailed.

Radek's first interference in the affairs of the German Communists was followed on many similar occasions during the next few years, when he was to be a frequent, although not universally welcome, guest inside the German borders. He came first and foremost because he was the official Russian expert on Central European affairs, but there was also a less obvious reason for his visits. For Radek, the Polish Jew and Bolshevik revolutionary, loved Germany and was attached to German culture by strong emotional bonds.[25] These sentiments he ingeniously combined with a sincere desire to bestow upon the object of his love the blessings of a new, Russian-style social order.

The suspicion held in official German circles that Radek had been prominently involved in the January disturbances led to his arrest on February 12, 1919, by the Berlin police.[26] The circum-

[24] Carr, *The Bolshevik Revolution*, III, pp. 94-101; Günther Rosenfeld, *Sowjetrussland und Deutschland, 1917-1922*, Schriften des Instituts für Geschichte, Reihe 1, Band 8 (Berlin, 1960), pp. 142-153; this is an East German publication. The two emissaries with whom Radek went across the border were Nicolai Rackow, alias Felix Wolf, and Ernst Reuter, subsequently a leading KPD functionary and at the end of his life Lord Mayor of West Berlin; see Brandt and Lowenthal, *Ernest Reuter* (Munich, 1957), pp. 112-113. (All three accounts differ on minor details but agree on the essentials.)

[25] Hilger and Meyer, p. 73.

[26] Evidence for Radek's implication in the January uprising proved disappointingly

stances of his sojourn in Moabit prison and, subsequently, of his confinement in private quarters, have been related many times.[27] He was held incommunicado for the first five months, but from August on a steady stream of visitors descended on his "political salon," as Radek called it. Here the prisoner, part host, part exotic curiosity, presided, conversed, and counseled. His guests represented all walks of German society: army and navy officers, statesmen, industrialists, labor leaders, newspaper editors, university professors, and officials of the SPD, the USPD, and the KPD. For Radek as well as for many of his visitors these were fruitful months. While it may be an exaggeration to say that Radek's political ideas, which he developed for the benefit of some of his listeners, "led to the Russo-German Treaty of Rapallo," they undoubtedly helped to prepare the ground for an eventual rapprochement between Germany and the Soviet Union.[28] Radek's efforts in the fall of 1919 to "sell" such a rapprochement to prominent Germans were favored by the strong public resentment against the Versailles treaty, a sentiment which was particularly prevalent among the personnel of the German Foreign Office.[29] Thus, when Radek in January 1920 finally returned to Russia, he could do so with the satisfactory feeling that he had not wasted his time in prison.

---

inconclusive for the German government, a fact which emerges from a telegram which the German Foreign Office sent on February 25, 1919, to Edgar Haniel von Haimhausen, then on a diplomatic mission to Spa. See *Akten betreffend den Russischen Bolschewisten Karl Radek.*

[27] Carr, *The Bolshevik Revolution*, iii, pp. 133-135, 312-317; the same author has translated Radek's own recollections of this period: "Radek's 'Political Salon' in Berlin 1919," *Soviet Studies*, iii, No. 4 (April 1952), pp. 411-430. See also Lionel Kochan, *Russia and the Weimar Republic* (Cambridge, 1954), pp. 17-20; Gerald Freund, *Unholy Alliance; Russian-German Relations from the Treaty of Brest-Litovsk to the Treaty of Berlin,* introduction by J. W. Wheeler-Bennett (New York, 1957), pp. 46-49; Hilger and Meyer, pp. 189-192; Fischer, pp. 205-208.

[28] The assertion concerning Rapallo is in Kochan, p. 17.

[29] Wipert von Blücher, *Deutschlands Weg nach Rapallo; Erinnerungen eines Mannes aus dem zweiten Gliede* (Wiesbaden, 1951), p. 50. Walther Rathenau, one of Radek's visitors, wrote in a letter of January 26, 1920, that he was in favor of establishing economic relations with Russia, but that the present government did not agree with him on this matter. He also mentioned that he had studied the problem of Russo-German relations for several months, and that he had discussed it with "all available authoritative (*massgebende*) persons from both sides." *Briefe,* ii (Dresden 1926), p. 220. General Hans von Seeckt, who had also established contact with the imprisoned Radek, wrote on January 31, 1920: "Since I hold an eventual political and economic agreement with Great-Russia a fixed objective of our policy, we must at least make an effort not to turn Russia into an enemy." *Seeckt, Aus seinem Leben, 1918-1936,* ed. Friedrich von Rabenau (Leipzig, 1940), p. 252.

Background

Throughout the balance of 1919, while Radek sat comfortably behind bars, the Bolshevik leaders were virtually out of touch with German developments. The Soviet state was embroiled in civil war and confronted by foreign intervention. Communications with the outside world were accordingly difficult to establish, and the Bolsheviks had to confine their activities largely to the issuing of propagandist manifestos.[30] Aside from Radek, who hardly counted under the circumstances, the only contact with the Bolsheviks which was available to the KPD was a "West European Bureau" of the Comintern, situated in Berlin. It was organized by a Bavarian Communist, who called himself "Thomas," and a Pole, M. G. Bronsky. But except for an intermittent and illegal courier service, the Bureau had no means of communication with Moscow and was mostly left to its own devices.[31] In this atmosphere of isolation the KPD was marking time and was trying to find its bearings in the gradually stabilizing German scene. Levi, steering a cautious course, was convinced that the revolution was a "long process of rise and fall, of flow and ebb," a notion which had taken hold of Radek and Bronsky as well.[32] From their vantage point inside Germany, they could see that the first revolutionary wave was in the process of subsiding. This development convinced them that the Communists would have to concentrate their efforts on winning the masses and on organizing them in preparation for the next wave which would eventually come, though not very soon. Levi's maneuvers at the Heidelberg Party Congress were in line with this interpretation of the situation, and although Radek did not then agree with Levi's policy of splitting the party, he had come to share Levi's pessimistic outlook. This was reflected in the address which was read in Radek's name at the congress.[33] Considering the cir-

[30] Three of these are reprinted in Degras, ed., *The Communist International, Documents*, I, pp. 50-58.

[31] Fischer, pp. 134-135, incl. n. 18; Nollau, pp. 114-115; Carr, *The Bolshevik Revolution*, III, pp. 132-136, 321.

[32] *Bericht über den 2. Parteitag der KPD* (Berlin, n.d.), p. 61, as quoted in Freund, p. 54. Carr, *The Bolshevik Revolution*, III, p. 133, n. 2, quotes Thomas as having said, two years later, that "the overthrow of the premature Bavarian Soviet republic also meant the collapse of the German revolution." Freund's interpretation of Levi's policies, and the statements on Luxemburg made in this connection, are misleading (p. 54).

[33] See Karl Radek, *Zur Taktik des Kommunismus: Ein Schreiben an den Oktoberparteitag der KPD* (n.p., 1919), as cited in Carr, *The Bolshevik Revolution*, III, p. 139, n. 1.

cumstances of the KPD, and the fact that Bela Kun's short-lived uprising in Hungary had collapsed late in the summer of 1919, such pessimism was justified.

When Radek returned to Moscow in January 1920, he found the Soviet government in an ambivalent state of mind. On the one hand, the Bolsheviks were as determined as ever to extend the Communist revolution westward, and believed that the chances to do so were favorable. On the other hand, the Russian rulers were not averse to establishing contact with capitalist countries, not because they shared Radek's dim views with regard to revolutionary prospects, but because they wanted to break through the isolation in which the revolution and the civil war that followed it had placed them.[34] Such contacts were conceived primarily in economic terms, with a view to the possible resumption of trade with the West, and some tentative feelers were extended to Great Britain in pursuit of this policy. The Bolshevik leaders, from Lenin downward, were cheered by the fact that the fortunes of the Soviet state had lately taken a turn for the better. In November 1919 Victor Kopp had gone to Berlin as Russian plenipotentiary for prisoner of war affairs, a piece of official business which brought Russia into direct diplomatic contact with Germany. Kopp's formal recognition was granted in February 1920.[35] Furthermore, the Allied Supreme Council had just lifted the blockade which had been imposed upon Russia in October 1919, and the civil war was virtually won.

This was the general political atmosphere which Radek encountered upon his return to Moscow. But since he had surveyed the situation from a different vantage point from that of his fellow Bolsheviks, his views on the prospects for world revolution were more pessimistic than theirs, and colored his ideas on the nature of Russia's foreign relations in the foreseeable future. In his address at Heidelberg, Radek had said: *"The problem of the foreign policy of Soviet Russia and, unless the world revolution announces itself*

[34] I am aware of the fact that in summarizing these complex developments I am laying myself open to a charge of oversimplification. In view of the fact that this chapter is still introductory in nature I had no choice but to accept this risk. For a more penetrating analysis see especially Carr, *The Bolshevik Revolution*, III, pp. 148-164, esp. pp. 150-154; Xenia Joukoff Eudin and Harold H. Fisher, in collaboration with Rosemary Brown Jones, *Soviet Russia and the West 1920-1927; A Documentary Survey* (Stanford, 1957), pp. xxxvii, 19-20.

[35] Freund, p. 51.

*more quickly than hitherto, of all other countries in which the
working class is victorious, consists in arriving at a* modus vivendi
with the capitalist states. . . . The possibility of peace between
capitalist and proletarian states is no utopia."[36] This evaluation was
in accordance with the impressions he had gained in Germany. It
was in line with his attempts to win influential Germans over to the
idea of a Russo-German rapprochement. Finally, it was in line with
his rejection of left-wing National Bolshevism of the Laufenberg-
Wolffheim brand.

Lenin did not agree with Radek's analysis, although he soon endorsed his stand on National Bolshevism and "left-wing" Communism.[37] Lenin considered the tentative feelers which the Soviet
Union extended to the West early in 1920 merely as a means of
improving the economic conditions of his war-ravaged country. A
modus vivendi, such as Radek envisaged, was at that time still far
from his mind. The objective of extending the revolution westward
at the first possible opportunity remained unaffected by the apparent international "thaw." In this respect, Lenin's fundamental
position remained consistent with the closing words of his address
at the Founding Congress of the Comintern: "Victory of the proletarian revolution throughout the world is certain. The founding of
the International Soviet Republic will come."[38] He remained convinced that it was essential to secure the victory of the Russian
revolution by carrying it abroad to western Europe and especially to
Germany—a defeated, impoverished country, bitterly hostile to the
Western victors, and with a large and politically conscious proletariat. But to what extent was this proletariat ready to support the
Communist cause, and what was the KPD doing to secure such
support? These were the principal questions which Lenin had to
face.

He proceeded to do so with his customary sense of realism. His

[36] Quoted in Carr, *The Bolshevik Revolution,* III, p. 319; the italics are Radek's.
[37] Lenin, *"Left-Wing" Communism* (New York, 1934), pp. 56-58, and *passim.*
In this book, which was written after the Kapp Putsch, Lenin attacked the Laufenberg-Wolffheim brand of National Bolshevism and in the process implied also that
he did not think much of Radek's prison conversations with prominent Germans
as far as they had entailed any projects, however vague and inconclusive, concerning
a possible collaboration between Germany and the Soviet Union against the Entente
powers; see Carr, *The Bolshevik Revolution,* III, pp. 321-322. For further discussion of *"Left-Wing" Communism,* see below.
[38] *Der I. Kongress der K. I., Protokoll,* p. 202.

optimism with regard to the over-all prospects for world revolution did not blind him to the fact that the political effectiveness of the KPD was so far extremely limited. Ever since 1918 the KPD had been regarded in Moscow as one of the most promising revolutionary movements in Europe, second only to the Bolsheviks themselves. But at the moment it did not live up to these expectations. Lenin came to the conclusion that the German party would have to expand in order to gain influence, and he lost no time in exploring ways and means by which other segments of the German proletariat could be induced to join the ranks of the KPD. His attention focused on the Independent Social Democratic Party, which at the time seemed a likely prospect for Communist overtures.[39] After the Spartacists had seceded from the USPD, that party had retained a left wing which was constantly at loggerheads with the right wing. The left wing, following the example of its counterpart in the KPD, rejected participation in parliamentary elections and the trade-unions, and after March 1919 demanded that the USPD affiliate with the Communist International. The first two issues were temporarily settled by a compromise in March 1919, at a party congress held in Berlin. The question of affiliation with the Comintern was postponed until November, when another congress was scheduled to convene at Leipzig. When that time came, the majority of delegates voted to break with the Second International, but took no decision on whether to join the Third. The delegates resolved instead to refer the matter to a future conference, where it would be discussed in conjunction with the possibility of founding a comprehensive organization that would include all revolutionary Socialist movements.[40]

On February 5, 1920, the ECCI sent a letter to the Executive of the Independent Social Democratic Party, a copy of which went to the *Zentrale* of the KPD. The letter revealed Moscow's displeasure with the compromise which the Independents had arrived at in Leipzig. It listed very methodically all the faults which the Comintern detected in the policies of the Independents and analogous parties, such as that of Jean Longuet in France and the Independent

[39] Carr, *The Bolshevik Revolution*, III, pp. 166-168, 171, 175-176.
[40] Prager, *Geschichte der U.S.P.D.* (Berlin, 1922), pp. 191-195, 202-205, 211-212; Flechtheim, *Die K.P.D. in der Weimarer Republik* (Offenbach, 1948), pp. 67-68; Degras, ed., *The Communist International, Documents*, I, pp. 74-75.

Labour Party in England; it rejected the formation of another, all-inclusive International, and invited the Independents to commence negotiations concerning the party's admittance to the Comintern. In conclusion, the ECCI suggested that the USPD should purge its leadership, and expressed the hope that the party would soon amalgamate with the KPD.[41]

This letter initiated a new phase in Comintern strategy. It consisted of a concerted effort to wean labor movements with strong left wings away from their leaders and to attract their rank and file to the Communist camp. The onslaught was principally directed against labor organizations which either were still affiliated with the Second International, or were on the verge of leaving it and had extended feelers toward the Communist International.[42] The Bolsheviks employed all the weight of the immense reputation which they then enjoyed among working people throughout the world to brand the leaders of such Socialist parties as traitors, and to urge their followers to purge their parties of these "Kautskyists."[43] The idea for this approach had been conceived by Lenin in the summer of 1919, and it was accepted, and subsequently applied, by the Comintern.[44] The German Independent Social Democrats had the dubious honor of being the first major party to become the target of Lenin's schism theory.

Bolshevik expectations that Germany was drifting rapidly toward a new threshold of revolution rose to a high pitch in March 1920 because of the Kapp Putsch and its corollary, the proletarian uprising in the Ruhr region and central Germany. On March 25 the ECCI issued another one of its manifestos which praised the Berlin workers, damned the Social Democrats, and exhorted the German proletariat to seize arms and fight.[45] A few days later Lenin addressed the Ninth Congress of the Russian Communist Party, and compared the Kapp Putsch with the Kornilov interlude during the Russian Revolution. In the process of his address he exclaimed

[41] Excerpts in Degras, ed., *The Communist International, Documents*, i, pp. 75-80.

[42] Carr, *The Bolshevik Revolution*, iii, pp. 183-184. The various parties are discussed in Ossip Pjatnizki, *Die einundzwanzig Aufnahmebedingungen der Kommunistischen Internationale* (Moscow-Leningrad, 1934), pp. 16, 32-37. See also the interpretation of Borkenau, *Der europäische Kommunismus*, pp. 35-37.

[43] See, for example, Lenin, *"Left-Wing" Communism*, pp. 15, 19, and *passim*.

[44] Carr, *The Bolshevik Revolution*, iii, p. 183.

[45] Excerpts in Degras, ed., *The Communist International, Documents*, i, pp. 83-85.

confidently that "the time is not far off when we shall march hand in hand with a German Soviet Government."[46] Although events did not bear out these hopes, Lenin undeterredly pursued his objective of strengthening the revolutionary movement in Germany.

A few weeks after the Kapp Putsch, in April 1920, Lenin wrote *"Left-Wing" Communism, An Infantile Disorder*, which served a dual purpose. One of its functions was to criticize those left-wing elements within Communist parties, and notably in the KPD, which opposed participation in trade-unions and parliaments, and held National Bolshevist views.[47] With many illustrations from the Russian Revolution Lenin drove home the point that the "Leftists" were wrong, the Bolsheviks right, and that Moscow expected erring members of Communist parties everywhere to correct their ideas accordingly. The second function of the pamphlet was to win new followers for Communism. Apart from his efforts to convince his readers that the policies he advocated were vital tactical aspects of the universal class struggle, Lenin's appeal to keep party discipline was intended to make the Communist movement more attractive to potential recruits from other parties, especially to those who were also trade-union members and had no desire to leave their unions. Closely connected with this aspect of his argument was Lenin's attempt to drive a wedge between the Socialist leaders and their followers. His criticism of the "Left" was interspersed with vilifications of what he called "opportunist leaders [Kautsky, Hilferding ... Crispien, Ledebour and others]—who have proven their inability to understand the significance of the Soviet power and the dictatorship of the proletariat."[48] These and similar references to leaders of the USPD were an unmistakable invitation to those workers who did understand the significance to break with their leaders and to join the Communists. Finally, leaving no margin for error concerning his meaning, Lenin openly encouraged the "proletarian wing" of the Independent Social Democrats to join forces with the KPD.[49] This suggestion he was to follow up a few months later by personal discussions with representatives of both parties during the Second World Congress of the Comintern.

☆ ☆ ☆

[46] Quoted in Kochan, p. 26.
[47] Lenin, *"Left-Wing" Communism*, pp. 24-42, 48-58.
[48] *ibid.*, p. 55; see also pp. 88-89, and *passim*.
[49] *ibid.*, pp. 55, 87.

Background

Before the Second World Congress of the Communist International opened in Petrograd on July 12, 1920, the Soviet Union had become involved in a war with Poland. Throughout the month of May Polish armies were advancing eastward, and in the south "White" forces under General Wrangel resumed fighting from the Crimea, thus rekindling the civil war. But in June the tide began to turn in favor of the Bolsheviks. Russian forces launched a series of successful counterattacks and reached the outskirts of Warsaw by the middle of August. It was against this background of momentary military success that the delegates to the Second World Congress of the Communist International assembled at Petrograd on July 19.[50]

Of 217 delegates from 41 countries who attended the congress, Germany was represented by no less than three different parties, the KPD, the KAPD, and the USPD.[51] The delegates of the latter two parties had come as guests; they had only consultative powers, without the right to vote on the proceedings. The KPD delegation, led by Levi, arrived in a belligerent frame of mind. During the past six months the German Communists had suffered a series of humiliations. They resented the fact that the ECCI had negotiated over their heads with the Independents and with the Communist left-wing rebel faction, which had seceded from the KPD after the Heidelberg Congress and in the spring of 1920 had founded the KAPD.[52] Furthermore, the memories of the party's bungling tactics during the Kapp Putsch still smarted, and although Lenin had by and large endorsed Levi's position in this affair, he

[50] The congress remained in Petrograd only for one day. It then moved to Moscow, where the proceedings were resumed on July 23; they were concluded on August 7, 1920.

[51] Degras, ed. *The Communist International, Documents,* I, p. 109. Of the 217 delegates only 169 had voting rights.

[52] *ibid.,* pp. 92-99, 100-101; Carr, *The Bolshevik Revolution,* III, p. 170. The KPD delegation was composed of four members beside Levi: Jakob Walcher, Ernst Meyer, Rosi Wolffstein, and one Budich. In addition, a German delegate to the Communist Youth International, Walter Löwenhain, attended the sessions, according to Margarete Buber-Neumann, *Von Potsdam nach Moskau; Stationen eines Irrweges* (Stuttgart, 1957), p. 81. The protocol of the Second World Congress lists as the only German delegate to the Communist Youth International one Leinhardt, and it is conceivable that this was Löwenhain's *nom de guerre;* see Kommunistische Internationale, *Der zweite Kongress der Kommunistischen Internationale: Protokoll der Verhandlungen vom 19. Juli in Petrograd und vom 23. Juli bis 7. August 1920 in Moskau* (Hamburg, 1921), p. 781; hereafter cited as *Der II. Kongress der K.I., Protokoll.*

had been quite critical of the KPD's behavior during the German crisis. Finally, the outcome of the Reichstag election of June 6, 1920, had been disappointing for the Communists. The KPD had received only a fraction of the labor vote, a little over a half a million, whereas the USPD had polled nearly five million, and the SPD over six million votes. But the chief grievance of the KPD delegation was the presence of two KAPD representatives at the congress. They had been invited because the Bolsheviks were still hoping that the refractory Heidelberg secessionists could be persuaded to return to the fold.[53] To make this step more palatable to the KAPD, the Bolshevik leaders had initially tried to grant the two KAPD representatives full voting rights, but they gave up this attempt when Levi announced in the name of the KPD delegation that he and his comrades would leave the congress if the KAPD representatives were thus favored.[54]

Levi's attitude was determined by his basic disagreement with the Bolsheviks on what direction the future course of the KPD should take. Lenin continued to believe that the mass of workers in western Europe were fundamentally revolutionary, and were only restrained by their "opportunist" leaders from throwing in their lot with the Communists. Once these leaders were removed from their positions of influence, the rank and file would soon support the only true revolutionary movement—Communism. Levi, the disciple of Rosa Luxemburg, and far more sceptical than she had ever been, was convinced that in Germany, at least, the process of revolutionizing large masses of workers would be a long and difficult uphill struggle. He did not share Lenin's belief that the process could be accelerated by simply discrediting a few labor leaders, although he agreed with Lenin that it would be desirable to create a Communist mass party in Germany. Both men wanted the left

[53] Degras, ed., *The Communist International, Documents*, I, pp. 93-99 (extracts from an open letter from the ECCI to the members of the German Communist Labour Party). See also Lenin, *"Left-Wing" Communism*, pp. 85-86.

[54] Kommunistische Partei Deutschlands, *Bericht über den 5. Parteitag der Kommunistischen Partei Deutschlands (Sektion der Kommunistischen Internationale) vom 1. bis 3. November 1920 in Berlin* (Berlin, 1921), pp. 27-28, 36. See also Radek, "Der Fall Levi," *Soll die Vereinigte Kommunistische Partei Deutschlands eine Massenpartei der revolutionären Aktion oder eine zentristische Partei des Wartens sein?*, 2nd ed. (Hamburg, n.d.), p. 104 (Radek supported Levi's position on this issue); Brandt and Lowenthal, p. 138; and Carr, *The Bolshevik Revolution*, III, p. 188, n. 3.

wing of the USPD to join the Comintern, preparatory to a subsequent merger with the KPD. But whereas Levi was primarily interested in facilitating this political marriage by being conciliatory to the Independents, Lenin was more concerned with devising safeguards against the possibility that a merger would bring "opportunist" elements into the Communist movement. To guard against the danger of creating a mass party in which lukewarm revolutionary sentiments might prevail, the Bolshevik leaders toyed with the idea of bringing into the projected party the same radical firebrands who had split away from the KPD at Heidelberg in October 1919. Apparently Moscow deemed comrades afflicted with "left-wing infantile disorders" less dangerous to the cause than proletarians suffering from the cancer of "reformism" or "opportunism."[55]

Since Levi did not agree with Lenin on the situation in Germany, he failed to share the latter's apprehensions concerning the Independents. On the other hand, he was determined to bar the rebellious KAPD sectarians from rejoining the KPD because he was convinced that they would hinder fusion with the left-wing Independents. In the end he won his point, and the idea of persuading the KAPD to rejoin forces with the KPD was abandoned for the time being. Levi, however, could not prevent the Comintern from accepting the KAPD a few months later as a "sympathizing party with consultative voice."[56] This honor made such a deep impression on the KAPD that its executive never bothered to apply for full membership.

The concession which Levi obtained on this particular issue remained his only victory at the Second World Congress. The Bolshevik leaders were not in a bargaining mood. The war against Poland went exceedingly well in late July and early August as the Red Army moved closer to Warsaw, and the military successes created an atmosphere of hopeful anticipation at the congress. Was it not possible, after all, that the victories of the Red Army might spark the eagerly anticipated revolutions in central and western Europe? To what extent even Lenin was affected by the buoyant

[55] For a fuller discussion see Page, pp. 158-166, and Brandt and Lowenthal, pp. 138-139. See also Fischer, p. 143.

[56] Degras, ed., *The Communist International, Documents,* I, p. 206; Pieck, "Kurze Geschichte der Arbeiterparteien," *Jahrbuch für Politik, Wirtschaft, Arbeiterbewegung 1922-1923* (Hamburg, n.d.), p. 645; Anonymous, "Die Roten Kämpfer," *Vierteljahreshefte für Zeitgeschichte,* VII, No. 4 (October 1959), p. 441.

optimism of the moment may be illustrated by an incident which occurred at the congress and involved Levi and two other German delegates. Standing before a large strategic wall map of which Zinoviev has left us a vivid description,[57] Lenin invited the three Germans to join him and began to explain the military situation. He said that according to Trotsky's estimates the Red Army would reach the eastern frontier of Germany within the next few days, and, turning to his listeners, he asked: "In your opinion, Comrades, what forms will the uprising in East Prussia take?" The three Germans stared at him in amazement. East Prussia was known as one of the most conservative German regions, and an uprising of the East Prussian peasants in support of the Red Army sounded like a poor joke to Levi and his colleagues. One of them, Ernst Meyer, gave a sceptical reply. This irritated Lenin, who now turned to Levi and asked: "And you, Comrade Levi, do you also agree that there will be no uprising?" Levi remained silent, and Lenin terminated the conversation by remarking acidly: "In any case, you ought to know that we of the Central Committee [of the Russian C.P.] hold quite a different opinion."[58]

Under the impact of the favorable news from the front, the tone of the Bolshevik delegation at the sessions of the congress was peremptory, and their attitude determined and unconciliatory.[59] Of the parties which had signified interest in joining the Comintern, only two were represented at the congress, the French Socialist Party and the German Independent Social Democratic Party.[60]

[57] Quoted in Kochan, pp. 29-30; also Carr, *The Bolshevik Revolution*, III, p. 188.

[58] Buber-Neumann, p. 81; Brandt and Lowenthal, p. 138, refer to the same episode, citing Balabanoff as their source. I have not found any reference to this incident in the English edition of Balabanoff's book.

Toward the end of the congress Levi expressed himself on the Russo-Polish war "for the record." He stressed the sympathy of the German proletariat with the Russian cause, assured the congress that the German workers would rush to the aid of the Soviet Union if the Entente should try to march through Germany—or even with Germany—to assist Poland, but said not a word about a general German uprising in support of Russia, aside from the rather hypothetical situation to which he had referred earlier. Only his closing words may have heartened his Russian listeners: "And when the Red Army will approach the German border in the course of its fight with Poland's White Army, it . . . will hear but one shout of the German proletariat, the shout: 'Long live Soviet Russia!'" A shout, then, was apparently all that Levi would concede to the Russians by way of a promise; see *Der II. Kongress der K.I., Protokoll*, pp. 673-674 (translated and delivered in the third person by Radek).

[59] For a fuller account see Carr, *The Bolshevik Revolution*, III, pp. 187-193; also Prager, p. 221.

[60] Pjatnizki, p. 13.

Their delegates, it will be recalled, had only consultative rights, but they attended the sessions and held discussions with the Russians. The Independents had sent four delegates, Wilhelm Dittmann, Arthur Crispien, Ernst Däumig, and Walter Stoecker, who were to negotiate with the ECCI on the conditions required for affiliation with the Comintern.[61] The conditions, they soon discovered, were stringent. The Bolshevik leaders made it clear from the outset that the Communist International must become "a single communist party having branches in different countries."[62] The individual sections would have to accept unconditionally the theses and directives issued by the ECCI. To make sure that only organizations willing to abide by these strictures would join, the Russians had drawn up a set of twenty-one conditions which each party applying for membership had to accept before it could become a bona fide section of the Comintern. Every one of the conditions was designed to give the ECCI the authority to control all aspects of world Communism from its centralized location—which was, and remained, Moscow. Objectives, tactics, organization, publications, even the precise terminology by which each section was to be known were spelled out in the set of conditions.[63] The demands made upon a prospective new member party may be compared to the requirements for joining a monastic order. The candidate had first to renounce all former ties and associations before he could be admitted. Of special importance were the last two conditions. They were added during the proceedings by Lenin and by an Italian delegate, Amadeo Bordiga, respectively.[64] Lenin demanded that two-thirds of the central committees and other important party agencies be composed of comrades who had publicly and unequivocally advocated that their party affiliate with the Comintern *prior* to the Second World Congress (Condition No. 20). Bordiga demanded that all party members be automatically expelled from their organizations if they rejected in principle the conditions and theses adopted by the Comintern (Condition No. 21). These two conditions made schisms within the prospective new member parties inevitable, as

[61] Prager, p. 219.
[62] *Der II. Kongress der K.I., Protokoll*, p. 111 (Carr, *The Bolshevik Revolution*, III, p. 190, erroneously cites p. 102).
[63] For details see Pjatnizki, pp. 18-32, 59-68; and *Der II. Kongress der K.I., Protokoll*, pp. 387-395.
[64] *Der II. Kongress der K.I., Protokoll*, pp. 235-236, 285.

they disqualified most of these parties' leaders from membership in the Comintern. It was precisely for this reason that they had been introduced.[65] For was it not conceivable that some of the old party leaders preferred to hold their noses and sign on the dotted line rather than see their organizations split? And could not these leaders then try to recapture lost ground within the Comintern? The commission which drew up the twenty-one conditions proved unwilling to take these chances and phrased the draft accordingly, in order to eliminate all loopholes through which undesirable "opportunists" might slip into the inner sanctum of the proletarian vanguard.

Despite the high-handed manner by which the Bolsheviks imposed the twenty-one conditions upon the congress, they were able to repulse every challenge from the floor and to establish their leadership in the Comintern unequivocally. They could do so largely because of the prestige they enjoyed as the first successful revolutionary party in the world. This prestige was increased, at the time the congress met, by the steady advance of the Red Army against Warsaw, a development which added to their determination to spread the revolutionary gospel westward and create the proletarian millennium.[66]

The confident mood of the Russians found only a dim echo among the delegates from the USPD, whose reaction to the twenty-one conditions was far from enthusiastic. All four delegates initially agreed that some of the stipulations were unacceptable, but after discussions with representatives from the ECCI and the KPD, two of them, Däumig and Stoecker, were persuaded to accept all conditions.[67] This meant that the USPD delegation was divided before

[65] Pjatnizki, p. 31; Carr, *The Bolshevik Revolution*, III, p. 195; see also pp. 199-200 for Carr's analysis of the Bolshevik "split method."

[66] Carr, *The Bolshevik Revolution*, III, pp. 197-199, 217; Borkenau, *The Communist International*, p. 187.

[67] Prager, p. 221. How thoroughly Däumig and Stoecker were converted is evident from their propagandist efforts prior to the specially scheduled party congress of the USPD at Halle (see below). Däumig wrote: "Underlying the theses and conditions which the Second Congress of the Moscow International has postulated lie the correct estimate of the world situation on the one hand, and the experience gained from the Russian struggle on the other. The point in question is not a split of the proletariat, as the opportunist leaders claim, but the rallying of revolutionary and active vanguards of the proletariat on a clear and unequivocal theoretical basis." And Stoecker: ". . . we must keep in mind that our Russian comrades have undergone a lengthy revolutionary apprenticeship." Ernst Däumig, *Für die dritte*

it had even started home, a situation which boded ill for the subsequent fate of that party.

It was only natural that Levi should take part in the struggle for the political salvation of the Independents, and in open session he criticized their party's sins as severely as did Radek and Lenin.[68] But in contrast to the Russians, Levi doubted the wisdom of the twenty-one conditions. They were, he remarked, poorly formulated, an "imperfect lawyer's job." What was really needed, according to Levi, was to show the rank and file of the USPD what was wrong with their party, and especially with their leaders. If the KPD wanted to give the masses, including the left wing of the USPD, a clear idea of what was at stake for the German proletariat, then the Communists would have to offer them lucid criticism and a precise political program. "In this sense we shall proceed with our criticism," Levi said in closing, "not for our sake, but for the sake of the masses within the U.S.P. . . ."; and he ended, with a fine touch of irony, by quoting two lines from the Swiss poet Conrad Ferdinand Meyer:

> Amor, who loves and tortures you,
> wants you cleansed, and blissful too.[69]

When the congress was over, Levi left Moscow in a somber frame of mind. The methods which the Bolsheviks had employed in their dealings with the Independents disturbed him. He also disliked the monopolistic position which the Russian delegation had assumed within the Comintern. Finally, he objected to the fact that on Zinoviev's insistence the congress had written into the statutes which it adopted that the creation of illegal organizations

---

Internationale (Berlin, 1920), pp. 6, 56-57, as quoted in Hans Martin Meyer, *Die politischen Hintergründe des Mitteldeutschen Aufstandes von 1921* (diss. Friedrich-Wilhelms-Universität zu Berlin, 1935), p. 29.

[68] *Der II. Kongress der K.I., Protokoll,* pp. 353-362, *passim;* but note his very fair, and nearly apologetic, attitude vis-à-vis Dittmann, *ibid.,* pp. 396-397.

[69] *ibid.,* pp. 361-362. The lines he quoted (p. 362) read in German:

> Amor, der dich liebt und peinigt
> will dich selig und gereinigt.

However, Levi quoted incorrectly; he should have said: "Eros, der dich sucht und peinigt . . ." ("Die gegeisselte Psyche").

According to Ruth Fischer (p. 144) Levi tried to make light of the twenty-one conditions, which he presented as a mere formality, an entrance fee that was easy to pay. If he did so, he was hiding his true opinion.

was mandatory for every Communist party.[70] Levi's general dissatisfaction heightened when he discovered after the congress was over that Radek, Zinoviev and Bukharin had tried behind his back to persuade his colleague Ernst Meyer to form a "left-wing" opposition faction within the KPD. On his journey back to Berlin, Levi complained bitterly about the distrust which he had encountered in Moscow, and at home he told his friends in the USPD what he thought of the twenty-one conditions.[71]

The Independents faced a difficult decision. As soon as the USPD delegation had returned from Moscow the party began a debate on whether or not they should affiliate with the Comintern and accept its conditions. Weeks before a special congress was scheduled to discuss the matter, the party divided into two warring factions, and the controversy became so acrimonious that a split seemed inevitable. The showdown came on October 12, 1920, when the special congress convened at Halle. The meeting hall was decked out with Soviet emblems and Communist propaganda posters, a courtesy bestowed by the local USPD organization which had been entrusted with the arrangements and which favored acceptance of the twenty-one conditions. Leaving nothing to chance, the Russians had sent their heaviest artillery, in the person of Zinoviev, to plead the case of the Comintern. Zinoviev was accompanied by Solomon A. Lozovsky, president of the recently founded Communist Trade-Union International (Profintern). The delegates sat by factions, the advocates of the twenty-one conditions on one side of the hall, their opponents on the other. The atmosphere was tense, if not hostile. The central event of the proceedings was a verbal duel between Zinoviev and Dr. Rudolf Hilferding, who spoke for the right wing of his party. Zinoviev's impassioned four-hour speech was an impressive piece of oratory, despite his halting German. Drawing generously on the Bolshevik experience, he concentrated on the theme that a revolution in the west was imminent, and chal-

[70] Levi's attitude emerged from several unsuccessful motions which he made in the course of debate. One of them was that the center of the ECCI should be removed from Moscow toward the west, preferably to Germany, another, that a plenary session of the ECCI be held every three months; *Der II. Kongress der K.I., Protokoll*, pp. 584-587.

[71] Brandt and Lowenthal, p. 139; Levi, *Was ist das Verbrechen?*, p. 41; Radek, "Der Fall Levi," *op.cit.*, p. 104. It appears from a passing remark made in his first address to the congress that Trotsky was also annoyed with Levi; see *Der II. Kongress der K.I., Protokoll*, p. 91.

lenged his listeners to join the ranks of those who would spearhead it. The audience was spellbound, but only a handful of delegates from the right wing changed sides. The balance of the forces was not essentially altered. Hilferding ridiculed Zinoviev's assertions in an exhaustive rebuttal. He denied that conditions for a revolution were ripe and lectured the chairman of the ECCI on the fallacy of applying Russian conditions and experiences to Germany. Arguments and counterarguments by various speakers continued for the next five days. The decisive vote was taken on October 16, when 236 delegates signified their acceptance of the twenty-one conditions, and 156 rejected them. The Comintern had achieved for the first time a split in a major European labor party.[72]

Had the vote which was taken at Halle been representative of the party's rank and file, the split would have boosted the membership of the KPD to the half million mark by the time the merger took place. As it was, only 300,000 out of roughly 890,000 Independents joined the German Communist Party in December 1920.[73] While

[72] Prager, pp. 222-226; Carr, *The Bolshevik Revolution*, III, pp. 217-220; Fischer, p. 145; Stampfer, *Die vierzehn Jahre der ersten deutschen Republik*, 3rd ed. (Hamburg, 1947), pp. 212-216; Sender, pp. 174-178; G. Sinowjew (Zinoviev), *Zwölf Tage in Deutschland* (Hamburg, 1921), pp. 11-56; Zinoviev claims (p. 11) in contrast to Prager (p. 224) that over thirty delegates switched sides during the proceedings.

[73] Ruth Fischer's claim (p. 146) that "the split brought the majority of the USPD to the Comintern" is a gross exaggeration. Pieck, "Kurze Geschichte der Arbeiterparteien," *op.cit.*, pp. 642-643, states that the USPD had 893,000 members as of October 1920. The figure is based on a report of that party's executive and constitutes the strength before the split. Pieck claims it to be an exaggeration. Flechtheim, p. 70, who bases himself on Ernst Drahn, *Handwörterbuch der Staatswissenschaften*, VII, 4th ed. (Jena, 1926), p. 535, gives the strength of the USPD before the split as 800,000. Everth, "Deutscher Kommunismus," *Die Neue Rundschau*, XXXII: 1, No. 1 (January 1921), p. 81, states that the right wing of the USPD remained the stronger one after the split, and names a ratio of approximately five to one. This seems too high an estimate. Borkenau, *Der europäische Kommunismus*, p. 39, claims also that only a minority of the USPD's rank and file joined the KPD.

Estimates as to the strength of the German Communist Party after unification fluctuate between 350,000 and 500,000. The lower figure is probably correct. Pieck, "Kurze Geschichte der Arbeiterparteien," *op.cit.*, p. 647, gives "approximately 380,000." Radek disputed the figure of 500,000 at the Third World Congress of the Comintern and insisted that the party had only 350,000 members; see Kommunistische Internationale, *Protokoll des III. Kongresses der Kommunistischen Internationale (Moskau, 22. Juni bis 12. Juli 1921)*, (Hamburg, 1921), p. 457; hereafter cited as *Protokoll des III. Kongresses der K.I.* Ruth Fischer, contradicting herself on what she said on p. 146, gives the strength of the KPD as 350,000 on p. 172. Paul Levi, *Unser Weg; Wider den Putschismus. Mit Anhang: Die Lehren eines Putschversuches, von Karl Radek*, 2nd ed. (Berlin, 1921), p. 3, names 500,000. Carr, *The*

there may have been many private reasons why so many Independents failed to follow the lead of the majority of delegates at Halle, two developments seem to have been most decisive. One was the change of fortunes in the Russo-Polish war, the other the creation of a Communist Trade-Union International.

By the end of August the Russian advance on Warsaw was halted, with the aid of a French military mission under General Weygand. Throughout September Polish forces drove the Red Army back, until an armistice was concluded in October. Failure of the Polish proletariat to rise in support of the Bolshevik "liberators" dealt a severe blow to Moscow's hopes that western Europe was ripe for a revolution.[74] The lesson of this defeat could hardly pass unnoticed by the German workers.

The creation of the Profintern, the Communist Trade-Union International, likewise proved detrimental to the Communist cause. The decision to create such an organization had been made at the Second World Congress.[75] And in the months that followed, Moscow actively propagated the idea.[76] The move was primarily directed against the Socialist-run International Federation of Trade-Unions, also called the Amsterdam or "Yellow" Trade-Union International. The attempt to split this older organization was only moderately successful, but it caused confusion in the ranks of European labor. Many workers found it difficult to understand why the Comintern demanded on the one hand that Communists must not refuse to work within the existing trade-unions of their respective countries, and on the other hand made every effort to split the trade-union movement on the international level. The onslaught against the Amsterdam organization elicited only a weak response from German labor, including a majority of the USPD's rank and file. The trade-unions had traditionally exercised a stronger hold on the German workers than had any political party, a fact which

Bolshevik Revolution, III, p. 223, incl. n. 4, accepts the figure of 350,000. Heinz Schürer, *Die politische Arbeiterbewegung Deutschlands in der Nachkriegszeit 1918-1923* (diss. Leipzig, 1933), p. 48, also disputes the figure of 500,000.

The membership figure of the KPD prior to unification was officially given as 78,715 as of October 1, 1920; KPD, *Bericht über den 5. Parteitag*, p. 6.

[74] Eudin and Fischer, p. 5; Carr, *The Bolshevik Revolution*, III, p. 215.

[75] *Der II. Kongress der K.I., Protokoll*, pp. 500-501, 520, and *passim*.

[76] Degras, ed., *The Communist International, Documents*, I, pp. 185-188.

had been clearly demonstrated during the Kapp Putsch.[77] The strongest, longest, and loudest disturbance during the Halle Congress was evoked by the president of the newly created Profintern, Lozovsky, when he abused the Amsterdam International Federation.[78] Although Lozovsky's blustering performance did not deprive the Comintern of a majority vote in Halle, the bulk of the active trade-union members among the left-wing Independents on the local level simply refused to abide by the decision of their delegates to join the Communist camp.[79]

The official ceremony by which the dissident Independents were admitted into the KPD was conducted at a "Unification Congress" held in Berlin from December 4 to 7, 1920. Ruth Fischer, who was one of the Communist delegates from Berlin, has left a vivid description of the setting in which the event took place: "The large meeting hall in the *Lehrervereinshaus* in Berlin's Alexanderplatz was elaborately decorated with a wealth of red cloths draped over pictures of Lenin and Trotsky, of Liebknecht and Luxemburg, of Zinoviev. Communist sergeants at arms were posted at all the doors. There was an artistic frame of classical music and revolutionary poetry. The USPD delegates, mostly workers from the bench, were disgusted by the new official pomp; they had looked forward to a sober analysis of the German situation, concrete proposals on what to do next. Paul Levi gave them instead a speech on the economic situation of the world, in which a wealth of statistics was combined with varied news of events in Asia and in the Anglo-American world, and which ended with the bombast, 'Enter, ye workers of Germany, enter [our new party], for here are thy gods.' "[80]

Levi was followed by other speakers of whom two, Ernst Däumig and Wilhelm Koenen, were "New Communists" (*Neukommunisten*), as the secessionists from the USPD were called. Four of the other most prominent speakers, Heinrich Brandler, Fritz Heckert, August Thalheimer, and Clara Zetkin were veteran Spartacists.[81]

[77] Carr, *The Bolshevik Revolution*, III, p. 218.
[78] *loc.cit.*; Prager, p. 226.
[79] Borkenau, *The Communist International*, p. 200; Evelyn Anderson, *Hammer or Anvil; The Story of the German Working-Class Movement* (London, 1945), p. 77, incl. n. 1.
[80] Fischer, p. 147. Cf. Carr, *The Bolshevik Revolution*, III, p. 223, n. 3, where he doubts that the disgust of the Independents was as strong as Miss Fischer alleges.
[81] These speeches, as was customary, covered all major aspects of party policy.

When the delegates proceeded to elect officers, Levi and Däumig became the two chairmen of the *Zentrale*, theoretically with equal rights.[82] Before the congress, the Comintern, and Radek in particular, had tried behind Levi's back to undermine his position in the party, but the attempt miscarried. Levi's reputation, especially with the newcomers, was such that no effort was made to block his election.[83] To make sure at the start of the proper revolutionary spirit, Radek drafted a "Unification Manifesto" and railroaded it through the congress without discussion. It contained one clause which might have aroused Levi's disapproval had it been submitted to debate.

"Whereas a party commanding the allegiance of ten thousands must win its supporters primarily through propaganda, a party that numbers hundreds of thousands in its organization, and is speaking for millions, must win supporters primarily by deeds, through action. The United Communist Party has sufficient strength to move into action on its own responsibility whenever events permit or require it."[84] This clause was to be used on more than one occasion by Communist activists to justify schemes of armed insurrection.

The unification with the left wing of the USPD gave the German Communists a feeling of accomplishment and triumph. The sectarian stage was past, and they liked to think of themselves as a rising power on the German political scene. If some of the party

---

Däumig elaborated on the program and aims which Levi had outlined before him. Brandler spoke on the trade-unions and factory councils, Koenen on party organization, Thalheimer on agriculture, Heckert on unemployment, and Zetkin on the women's question (Flechtheim, p. 71).

For a period over a year after the Unification Congress, the Communists called their party the "United" (*Vereinigte*) German Communist Party, abbreviated to VKPD. As this was a temporary measure of little significance, I shall refrain from confusing the reader with additional abbreviations, and shall continue to refer to the KPD.

[82] In addition, the following officers were elected: Secretaries of the *Zentrale* were Clara Zetkin, Wilhelm Koenen, Heinrich Brandler, Walter Stoecker, Wilhelm Pieck, Otto Brass, and Hermann Remmele. Alternates: Adolf Hoffmann, August Thalheimer, Kurt Geyer, Fritz Heckert, and Otto Gäbel. Of these, Däumig, Koenen, Stoecker, Brass, Hoffmann, and Geyer came from the USPD; see Kommunistische Partei Deutschlands, *Bericht über die Verhandlungen des Vereinigungsparteitages der U.S.P.D. (Linke) und der K.P.D. (Spartakusbund). Abgehalten in Berlin vom 4. bis 7. Dezember,* 1920 (Berlin, 1921), pp. 216, 270.

[83] Brandt and Lowenthal, pp. 141-142. According to Radek, Levi became chairman because the newcomers from the USPD had demanded it; see *Protokoll des III. Kongresses der K.I.,* p. 550.

[84] Quoted in Brandt and Lowenthal, p. 141.

leaders experienced occasional doubts as to whether an organization of 350,000 members was indeed a mass party, they did not parade their faintheartedness. Nor did many of them seem to have given thought to the fact that the KPD owed its present success not to its own persuasiveness, but to Moscow, and that Bolshevik influence on their party had consequently grown stronger. Fewer and fewer Communist leaders were still guided by Luxemburg's teachings, and even those few were soon to be silenced, Levi among them. Luxemburg's picture continued to adorn the meeting halls of the German Communist Party, but her spirit, her ideas were rapidly fading.

CHAPTER III

PROBLEMS OF ADJUSTMENT: THE PARTY IN THE YOUNG REPUBLIC

THE MERGER of the KPD with the left wing of the USPD took place against a background of national and international difficulties which had dogged the young republic throughout 1920. In November of that year the eminent theologian and sociologist, Ernst Troeltsch, jotted down the following observations on Germany.

"The pressure from the Entente destroys living conditions and radicalizes the hungry masses; the success of Bolshevism in Germany encourages further destructive hopes among the Entente. As a result, the strangest paradoxes arise: one part of the laboring class becomes violently nationalist, whereas segments of the bourgeoisie turn Bolshevist. Strong foes of the Entente are forced into the camp of Entente capitalism from fear of Bolshevism, while radical opponents of working class domination [are being driven] in despair toward Bolshevism."[1] Although Troeltsch's appraisal proved to be somewhat overpessimistic, it illuminates the atmosphere in which it was written.

On June 6, 1920, when the German people went to the polls to elect the first postwar Reichstag, the majority of voters repudiated the Weimar Coalition government which had guided the affairs of the republic since February 1919. The losses of the Center Party, the Democratic Party, and the Social Democratic Party became the gains of the German People's Party and the German Nationalist People's Party on the right, and of the Independent Social Democratic Party on the left. The Communists, it may be recalled, did not fare too well with their half million votes.

The outcome of the election reflected above all a general discontent with the SPD, which had the heaviest losses of the three coalition parties. Many middle-class voters laid the guilt for the proletarian uprising in central Germany and the Ruhr squarely upon the Social Democratic government of Prussia, and they also

[1] Ernst Troeltsch, *Spektator-Briefe. Aufsätze über die deutsche Revolution und die Weltpolitik* 1918/22, introd. Friedrich Meinecke, ed. Hans Baron (Tübingen, 1924), p. 162.

77

resented the fact that the names of the Socialist members of the Reich cabinet had been affixed to the appeal for a general strike during the Kapp Putsch. On the left, a sizable number of workers expressed their lack of confidence in a Socialist party which had not introduced Socialism, had not substantially improved economic conditions, and had dispatched Reichswehr and freecorps units against fellow workers.[2]

Whereas in the country as a whole both the left and right political wings were strengthened, Bavaria moved predominantly toward the right. Here the monarchist sympathizer Gustav Ritter von Kahr had established a government on March 16, 1920, and for the next three years Bavaria remained a bulwark of reaction and particularism, a center of anti-republican intrigues, and a harbor for freecorps fighters after their organizations were outlawed elsewhere in Germany by the end of May 1920.

Two days after the Reichstag elections, the cabinet of Chancellor Hermann Müller, a Social Democrat, resigned, and on June 25 a coalition government of middle-class parties was formed by a member of the Center Party, Konstantin Fehrenbach. Neither the SPD nor the National People's Party was represented in the new cabinet. The various posts were distributed among the Center Party, the Democratic Party, and the German People's Party.

The new government faced its most urgent problems in the sphere of foreign policy. Until January 10, 1920, when the Versailles treaty went into effect, Germany had restricted her reparations payments to the delivery of merchant ships and the relinquishment of assets in the countries of her former enemies. Large shipments of coal had been made as well. But after January 1920 direct money payments became due. During the first months of the year Germany held preliminary discussions with the Allies, in an attempt to determine the sum which she was expected to pay in reparations. No decision was reached, and in June the Allied Supreme Council invited a German delegation to a conference at Spa for negotiations. The talks centered around the questions of coal deliveries and

[2] For the long-range significance of the election see Arnold Brecht, *Vorspiel zum Schweigen. Das Ende der deutschen Republik* (Vienna, 1948), pp. 170-172; see also Erich Eyck, *Geschichte der Weimarer Republik*, I, pp. 220-222; Angress, "Weimar Coalition and Ruhr Insurrection. . . ," *Journal of Modern History* xxix, No. 1 (March 1957), pp. 19-20.

Germany's military disarmament, although the conference had been called for the purpose of discussing reparations in general. The Germans were in an uncomfortable position. They had to admit that they were lagging behind in their obligations to deliver coal, and pleaded strikes and floods as the reasons for the delay. The Allies, and notably France, charged that Germany was deliberately holding back, and demanded an annual delivery of thirty million tons of coal. This the German delegation rejected as impossible, and in the end the matter was temporarily settled by a compromise: for the next six months, Germany was expected to deliver twelve million tons of coal to the Allies.

Concerning disarmament, the Germans conceded that they had not yet reduced the size of their army to the 100,000 men required by the peace treaty. After lengthy and acrimonious discussions, Germany was given an additional six months to comply with the demands for demobilization of her armed forces. The Allies warned at the end of the conference that they would occupy a strip of German territory on the right bank of the Rhine if Germany failed to demobilize, or defaulted on her assigned quota of coal deliveries.

Because the Spa Conference concentrated on these two issues, little progress was made toward a solution of German reparations in general. Although the Entente powers reached an agreement among themselves on how to divide the German payments, once they were forthcoming, no understanding was reached on either the total sum or the rate of payments. In the absence of a definite solution of these matters, another conference, this time of financial experts, was scheduled to meet in Brussels in December. When the financial experts failed to reach a conclusion in Brussels, the Allied statesmen resolved to meet again in Paris, in January 1921, but this time without the presence of German representatives. The Paris meeting brought the Allies one step forward. They agreed that Germany's payments should be distributed over a period of forty-two years, and that the annual sum was to increase over a period of eleven years from two to six billion gold marks. The first payment of two billion was to become due on May 1, 1921. The German government was immediately informed of this plan, which caused deep consternation throughout the country. The Allies scheduled another conference for March 1, 1921, in London, where the proposal was to be formally submitted to Germany for her acceptance.[3]

When Germany began negotiations with the Western Allies in Spa, the Russo-Polish war posed additional problems on her eastern frontier. The Russian summer offensive against Warsaw, which was then in full swing, was received with mixed feelings in German official circles and by the public at large. The rapid advance of the Russians caused alarm in the Wilhelmstrasse, but at the same time raised the prospect of possible border revisions favorable to Germany if Poland should be defeated. Equally ambivalent was the attitude of General Hans von Seeckt, commander of the German Reichswehr. While he was fully alive to the immediate threat posed by the advance of Russia's Red Army, he welcomed the initial defeat of Poland, a tool of France. And finally, whenever Soviet Russia was mentioned while the Reichstag debated the Spa conference from July 26 to 28, the sentiments expressed by the speakers fluctuated between apprehension and admiration.[4]

Many middle-class Germans watched with trepidation the approach of Trotsky's Red Army to the East Prussian border, while others, notably young nationalists and freecorps leaders, frankly admired the Russian successes and talked about joining the Bolsheviks in their efforts to smash the Polish state.[5] Such an attitude stemmed in part from the traditional Prussian admiration for Rus-

[3] In addition to the general accounts of this phase of German foreign policy given by Stampfer, *Die vierzehn Jahre der ersten deutschen Republik*, 3rd ed. (Hamburg, 1947), Rosenberg, *Entstehung und Geschichte der Weimarer Republik* (Frankfurt a. M., 1955), Eyck, *et al.*, see especially Viscount D'Abernon, *The Diary of an Ambassador, I, Versailles to Rapallo 1920-1922* (New York, 1929), pp. 57-125, and Ludwig Zimmermann, *Deutsche Aussenpolitik in der Ära der Weimarer Republik* (Göttingen-Berlin-Frankfurt, 1958), pp. 83-92. On the reparation problem see Carl Bergmann, *Der Weg der Reparation von Versailles über den Dawesplan zum Ziel* (Frankfurt, 1926) and E. Weil-Raynal, *Les Réparations Allemandes et La France*, I-III (Paris, 1947) for the respective German and French points of view.

[4] Blücher, *Deutschlands Weg nach Rapallo* . . . (Wiesbaden, 1951), pp. 98-101; Theodor Schieder, *Die Probleme des Rapallo-Vertrags; eine Studie über die deutsch-russischen Beziehungen 1922-1926*, Arbeitsgemeinschaft für Forschung des Landes Nordrhein-Westfalen, Heft 43 (Cologne and Opladen, 1956), pp. 21-27, notably on the attitude of the Reichswehr; Rabenau, ed., *Seeckt, Aus seinem Leben 1918-1936* (Leipzig, 1940), pp. 252-253, and *passim*; Freund, *Unholy Alliance* (New York, 1957), pp. 74-77; Prager, *Geschichte der U.S.P.D.* (Berlin, 1922), pp. .220-221; Germany, *Verhandlungen des Reichstages: Stenographische Berichte*, vol. 364, pp. 251-353, *passim*. In the course of the debates Foreign Minister Dr. Walther Simons assured the house that the Soviet Republic did not intend to carry the war beyond the German-Polish border (*ibid.*, p. 265).

[5] Schüddekopf, *Linke Leute von Rechts* (Stuttgart, 1960), pp. 121-126; Zimmermann, *Deutsche Aussenpolitik*, p. 88.

sia, which at times overshadowed the Bolshevik phobia, but resentment over French support of Poland entered the picture as well. This resentment and the unconciliatory attitude which the Entente powers displayed in their negotiations with Germany suggested to a growing number of Germans a possible rapprochement with Russia as a means of redressing the unfavorable balance in the West. Hostility toward the Western Allies also accounted for the widespread pro-Russian sympathies of German labor, including its overwhelmingly non-Communist wing. Early in August the SPD, USPD, KPD, and the trade-unions issued a joint appeal to all German workers not to permit foreign troop transports bound for Poland to pass through German territory, and dock workers in German harbors refused to handle munitions destined for Poland.[6] The popular agitation which the Russo-Polish war had aroused died down only at the end of August, 1920, when the Red Army was driven back toward the Russian frontier.

During that month another crisis developed in Upper Silesia. Under the provisions of the peace treaty the Allies had gained the right to send troops through Germany to any territory where plebiscites were scheduled to be held in the near future. Upper Silesia was one such territory. During the Russo-Polish war the French used their privilege to send troop transports to that region, a move which raised suspicions in Germany that the transports were bringing reinforcements to the Poles. But the increase of French forces in Upper Silesia alone was sufficient to arouse the hostility of the local population which, during the latter part of August, staged protest strikes and engaged in skirmishes with French troops. Although order was eventually restored to the troubled region, these incidents left an atmosphere of mutual suspicion and hostility which boded ill for the plebiscites scheduled to be held in Upper Silesia during the spring of 1921.[7]

Although foreign political problems were trying, and opinion on how to deal with them divided, the multiple pressures which confronted Germany from abroad were in 1920 still less detrimental to her national unity than the disputes on domestic affairs. One of the most pressing, and politically most divisive issues concerned the

[6] Stampfer, p. 200.
[7] Carl Severing, *Mein Lebensweg*, I (Cologne, 1950), pp. 302-305.

Bavarian homeguards (*Einwohnerwehren*). They had sprung up in Bavaria and elsewhere in the spring of 1919, and were represented as auxiliary forces to help the regular police in maintaining order. Before long they attracted the suspicion of the Inter-Allied Military Control Commission, and the Commission demanded in a note of April 7, 1920, that the German government disband all homeguards, which were held to exist in violation of the disarmament clause of the peace treaty. The German government, eager to avoid further friction with the Allies, acted promptly. The day after the note was received, the Ministry of the Interior instructed all German state governments to comply with the Allied demand. The order was obeyed by Prussia, the largest German state, but evoked open and uncompromising opposition from the second largest, Bavaria. Ritter Gustav von Kahr, who had formed a right-wing government during the Kapp Putsch, was an outspoken advocate of Bavarian particularism and as such was a tireless opponent of the national government in Berlin. With Kahr at the helm, Bavaria not only refused to disband its own homeguards, but in May 1920 sponsored a nationwide organization of all homeguards which were not yet banned by the individual states. Its founder was a Bavarian Forestry Councillor (*Forstrat*), Dr. Georg Escherich, who called his creation *"Organisation Escherich."* It was soon to gain notoriety as *"Orgesch."* Escherich had coordinated the Bavarian homeguards since their formation in 1919, and Bavaria remained the center and stronghold of the entire movement.

The homeguards were discussed at Spa in conjunction with the general question of German disarmament. The Allies insisted that all paramilitary organizations be dissolved at once, and the German government relayed the order to the states. The problem caused Berlin a series of embarrassments for months: the Allies repeated their demands at regular intervals and the government passed them on, but met with stubborn resistance from Bavaria. The *Orgesch*, organized and controlled by an official of that state, remained a major controversial issue between Germany and the Entente until June 1921, when the organization finally disarmed and disbanded.[8]

---

[8] On the homeguards, often referred to as "civil guards" or "citizens' corps," and especially on the *Orgesch*, see Karl Schwend, *Bayern zwischen Monarchie und Diktatur. Beiträge zur Bayerischen Frage in der Zeit von 1918 bis 1933* (Munich, 1954), pp. 159-170; Werner Gabriel Zimmermann, *Bayern und das Reich 1918-*

Party Problems in the Young Republic

Aside from the fact that the *Orgesch* created unnecessary problems in the foreign political sphere, and accentuated the growing rift between Munich and Berlin, the existence of a right-wing middle-class homeguard with distinct anti-republican sentiments proved disturbing to German labor. It did not go unnoticed on the political left that the German government handled the homeguard question with what looked like inexhaustible patience, although it had never hesitated in the past to proceed with great promptness against any disturbances caused by workers. Labor also resented the fact that the Kapp Putsch rebels were either not punished at all, or given very mild sentences. These grievances, which the working class shared with many middle-class liberals, gave the KPD valuable propaganda material in its efforts to discredit the republic. What could be easier than to link the *Orgesch* to counterrevolutionary conspiracies condoned by the "bourgeois-capitalist" state? The Communists lost no opportunity to use this argument until the demise of the *Orgesch* rendered it ineffective. But since the republic never lacked militant right-wing organizations, the party had no trouble in finding suitable substitutes for the homeguards presided over by Forestry Councillor Escherich.

Frustrating diplomatic negotiations with the Entente in the West, tense and uneasy relations with the neighbors in the East, and political stresses and strains at home—this was Germany's harvest after two years of peace. To make matters worse, the republic faced serious economic difficulties. The unprecedented hardships of four years of war, followed by the stringent provisions of the peace treaty, made economic recovery a Herculean task. Territorial losses deprived Germany of farm lands, equipment, raw materials, and financial assets, and frequently caused dislocation of her industries.[9] The required surrender of merchant ships and rolling stock hamstrung foreign trade, as well as the transportation of goods and passengers within the country. Overshadowing these losses was the reparations problem, which posed innumerable dif-

1923; *der bayerische Föderalismus zwischen Revolution und Reaktion* (Munich, 1953), *passim*. Waite, *Vanguard of Nazism* (Cambridge, Mass., 1952), pp. 197-202; Carl Landauer, "The Bavarian Problem in the Weimar Republic, 1918-1923," Part I, *The Journal of Modern History*, XVI, No. 2 (June 1944), pp. 101-102.

[9] Bernhard Harms, "Das neue Deutschland im neuen Europa," in *Strukturwandlungen der deutschen Volkswirtschaft*, I (Berlin, 1928) pp. 21-26.

ficulties to the reconstruction of the German economy, and which had a demoralizing effect on the nation. Finally, in addition to these factors, Germany's economic recovery was severely impeded by a seemingly perpetual financial crisis which manifested itself drastically in a steady depreciation of the country's currency.

This study is not the place to dwell on the complex and controversial causes of the German postwar inflation, so it will suffice to outline its course very briefly. The depreciation of the mark began during the war, when the imperial government resorted to a large-scale issue of bank notes in order to finance the growing expenditures of the Reich. The republican government continued this practice after the collapse of the Empire while trying simultaneously, albeit with very limited success, to restore stable financial conditions by a reform of the taxation system. The currency continued to depreciate in relation to the dollar, a development which was accompanied by a steady increase of the floating debt, a growing volume of paper currency, and rising food costs. The depreciation took an alarming downward step after June 1919, probably in consequence of the psychological impact which the signing of the peace treaty had upon German business interests. The value of the mark continued to decline through February 1920, then leveled off and slightly improved until August of that year when its downward trend was resumed. This continued, except for a few brief intervals, until the exchange rate of the mark to the dollar assumed astronomic proportions in the summer and fall of 1923.[10]

Needless to say, the steady depreciation of the currency affected the morale as well as the morals of a nation still dazed by the impact of over four years of a war which had ended in defeat and political turmoil.[11] Inflation robbed the middle-income groups of their savings, destroying their confidence in the state and the political system on which it was based. The working class felt its impact most keenly through the steadily rising cost of food. In an attempt to

[10] The most authoritative work on the German inflation is still Costantino Bresciani-Turroni, *The Economics of Inflation; A Study of Currency Depreciation in Post-War Germany*, trans. Millicent E. Sayers, foreword by Lionel Robbins (London, 1937); the above summary is based on this work, pp. 25-62.

[11] For a vivid, though somewhat sensational, description of the impact the inflation had on the nation see Hans Ostwald, *Sitten-Geschichte der Inflation. Ein Kulturdokument aus den Jahren des Marktsturzes* (Berlin, 1931).

adjust wages to this trend, labor resorted to strikes which abounded during the first five postwar years. But since wage increases thus obtained were still paid in depreciating paper money, real wages continued to fall behind and, in a vicious circle, led to new wage demands, more strikes, and an acceleration in the printing of paper money.[12]

That such a combination of misfortunes proved disheartening to an observer like Ernst Troeltsch was understandable. How could he escape the impression that the country was ripe for Marx's proverbial Communist specter? In addition to the various political problems which confronted the republic at home and abroad, the defeated country presented an appearance of drabness and poverty. Its people lacked confidence in the future. The nation was bewildered by the foreign political developments which had made Germany a pawn of the victorious powers; it was demoralized by the economic situation, especially the inflation, which even to the government seemed beyond immediate remedy. In the face of adversity, national unity disintegrated to an alarming extent. The polarization of the republic into right and left political extremes, so evident in the June elections, progressed steadily during the balance of the year. The nationwide swing to the right, following the Kapp Putsch, had assumed reactionary proportions in some parts of the country, with a resulting provocative effect on labor.[13] The rapprochement and eventual fusion between the KPD and the left wing of the USPD were indicative of growing restlessness among the working class. Nor could it be ignored that large segments of German labor displayed pro-Russian sympathies during the Russo-Polish war. The majority of workers, to be sure, opposed Communism at home, and they cheered for a Russian victory largely because of their hatred for the Entente, but a genuine admiration for the "fatherland of the working class" and dissatisfaction with conditions in Germany also colored their attitude. In short, it had been a grim year. When it came to a close, its most succinct epitaph appeared

---

[12] Gerhard Kessler, "Die Lage der deutschen Arbeiterschaft seit 1914," *Strukturwandlungen der Deutschen Volkswirtschaft*, I, ed. Bernhard Harms (Berlin, 1928), pp. 445-450; see also Theodor Leipart, "Die Arbeitnehmer in Deutschland," *Zehn Jahre Deutsche Geschichte 1918-1928*, 2nd ed. (Berlin, 1928), pp. 341-342, which in contrast to Kessler's study emphasizes labor's point of view.

[13] Here again Troeltsch's analysis, pp. 125-149, is particularly cogent.

in the *Rote Fahne*: "Crises everywhere. Solutions nowhere: this is the signature of the year 1920."[14]

☆ ☆ ☆

Within two years after it was founded, the KPD had come to consider itself a mass party with a membership of approximately 350,000. The unification took place at a time when the republic, which the party eventually hoped to "bury," was in difficult straits. On the surface, therefore, the Communists had every reason to be pleased with their achievements. But despite their increase in strength, which gave them a more prominent political status, they still constituted a decided minority of German labor. If they wanted to realize their avowed objective, the seizure of power through revolution, they had first to gain the confidence and wholehearted support of the majority of workers.

This proved to be far from easy, as the party was soon to find out. The Communists could strengthen their movement only by breaking the hold which the older, established working-class organizations, notably the SPD and the trade-unions, had over their members. Even the recent split of the USPD had proved somewhat of a disappointment, in that only a fraction of its rank and file actually joined the KPD. The prospects for winning large numbers of converts from the SPD were therefore proportionally less promising. The former mother-party had the advantages of tradition, experience, and organization, all of which had a stronger appeal to the average German worker than anything the upstart KPD could offer. The typical Social Democrat was by and large disciplined and fundamentally averse to political radicalism. He tended to look with pride on the past achievements of a party to which his father, and sometimes his grandfather, had belonged. He had probably entered the SPD's youth group as a *Jungarbeiter* (young worker), and in time had become a regular party member who paid his dues, attended the party's political and social functions, read its publications, and bought its inexpensive burial insurance. In short, the SPD was as much an institution as it was a political party, and it could confidently claim and receive the loyal support of most of its adherents.

14 *Die Rote Fahne*, No. 1, January 1, 1921.

Party Problems in the Young Republic

The attitude of the KPD toward the Social Democrats was an ambiguous compound of antagonism and missionary zeal. By official Communist standards the Social Democrats were traitors to the revolutionary cause, and the hostility which the Communists showed toward the SPD was real enough. Their wartime break with the mother-party was not just a tactical move, prompted by political convenience; it was the expression of deep-felt dissent. The rise of Bolshevism in Russia and the course of the German revolution a year later combined to make this break irrevocable.

Even before the German Communists became subject to domination from Moscow they had admired, though not always uncritically, the Soviet Union and the men who created it. After their own disastrous failure to emulate the Bolshevik example, their admiration for Russia was complemented by mounting hostility toward the SPD which, in their view, had deprived the German proletariat of its victory. Their hostility grew more pronounced with every subsequent defeat. Whereas the Social Democrats had sat in the government, the Communists were ostracized. Whereas the Social Democrats sacrificed socialization in Germany to the interest of democracy, the Communists were prepared to destroy democracy in the interest of the proletarian dictatorship. Under these circumstances there could be no common meeting-ground between the two working-class parties.[15]

But there was another side to the picture. The contempt and hatred of the Communists for the SPD was accompanied by the practical consideration that without the rank and file of that "traitorous" party the Communists could not make a successful revolution in Germany. This realization gradually forced the KPD into an uncomfortable position. While the Communists condemned the tactics of the SPD as "opportunist" and "reformist," at the same time they tried to attract its members toward their own camp. The problem of how to square this political circle was to occupy the German Communists and their Bolshevik advisers for years to come.

The efforts of the KPD to extend its appeal to non-Communist

[15] This theme is more fully developed in chapter 5 of Flechtheim, *Die K.P.D. in der Weimarer Republik* (Offenbach, 1948), entitled "Zur Ideologie und Soziologie der KPD," pp. 185-223, esp. pp. 196-198. This brief discussion owes much to Flechtheim's treatment of the issue.

labor were impaired by the party's unfavorable reputation. Widespread dislike for, and distrust of, Communist tactics, created during and after the revolution, affected not only the middle class but also the majority of labor. In the days before the KPD was branded as "Moscow's mouthpiece," it was not uncommon for a non-Communist worker to feel a high regard for the Soviet Union but loathe the Communists at home. This antagonism was particularly pronounced in the SPD and the largest German trade-union federation, the *Allgemeiner Deutscher Gewerkschaftsbund* (ADGB), which had close connections with the Social Democrats. The latter always stressed their superiority to the Communists, claiming that the backbone of the SPD was formed by skilled labor, while the KPD recruited its followers largely from the unskilled, the unemployed and unemployable—in short, from the *Lumpenproletariat*.[16]

Although this charge contained an element of truth, its over-all validity was questionable. Despite its numerous shortcomings the KPD was not just a conglomeration of hoodlums, as its enemies maintained. Viewed in retrospect, the early stages of the Communist movement still convey an aura of genuine idealism, of dedication to its mission, of open, though often unbridled, dissent such as existed at the same time in the United States among the Wobblies of the Pacific Northwest. Before rigid dogmatism and bureaucratization stultified spontaneity and introduced both cynicism and crude conformity to Communism, its devotees saw revolution still as a liberating force which would improve society without enslaving it. The idealist element predominated among the leaders of the KPD, many of whom, it will be recalled, were intellectuals of middle-class origin. This, as Robert Michels has shown, was not unprecedented.[17] The history of past revolutionary movements shows numerous instances of dedicated idealists from an upper class assuming the leadership of a popular movement. Nor is it al-

[16] Seymour Martin Lipset, "Party Systems and the Representation of Social Groups," *European Journal of Sociology*, I, No. 1 (1960), pp. 10-11, reissued by the Institute of Industrial Relations, University of California, Berkeley, Reprint No. 161. Also Flechtheim, p. 215.

[17] Robert Michels, *Zur Soziologie des Parteiwesens in der Modernen Demokratie. Untersuchungen über die Oligarchischen Tendenzen des Gruppenlebens* (Leipzig, 1911), pp. 224-226.

together valid to ascribe this phenomenon merely to "guilt feelings of the privileged," as a recent German study maintains.[18]

It is, of course, nearly impossible to ascertain why each individual party leader became a Communist. Political conviction, personal circumstances, economic and social conditions—these and others could all be determining factors, though the first tended by and large to be decisive. It was so for Rosa Luxemburg, Karl Liebknecht, and the other Spartacist veterans who had virtually grown up with the vision of revolution and, in contrast to most of their Social Democratic peers, remained faithful to it. An examination of why some members of the younger generation joined the party in the immediate postwar era reveals that here also political conviction was the strongest motivation. Thus Ernst Reuter discovered Communism as a prisoner of war in Russia, during the revolution. Margarete Buber-Neumann was persuaded to join by the party's youth organization which, she believed, strove for liberty and a better future independently of the party bureaucracy. Finally, Alfred Kantorowicz, though he actually joined the party only in 1931, became a radical Marxist during the period of monetary inflation, "in unheated student quarters, and with the daily turnip soup in the *Mensa*. . . ."[19]

Political idealism was not confined to the leaders, but it was probably less pronounced among the party's rank and file. The typical party member at this lower level tended to join the KPD because he was dissatisfied with the way in which existing conditions affected his personal affairs. Since Communism promised to change these conditions, and advocated radical measures to do so, it held a special appeal for the activist and the rebel. There is no doubt that the party's revolutionary *esprit de corps* attracted on the whole a rougher and tougher breed of supporters than did the SPD, and it was inevitable that among them was also a sizable number of neurotic, shiftless, and unruly members. Even after the Heidelberg Congress, where Levi had forced many of the more undesirable *enragés* out of the party, enough of them remained, or subsequently joined, to perpetuate the party's reputation for recklessness and

[18] Margret Boveri, *Der Verrat im XX. Jahrhundert*, III, *Zwischen den Ideologien* (Hamburg, 1957), pp. 25-27.
[19] Brandt and Lowenthal, *Ernst Reuter* (Munich, 1957), pp. 79-124, *passim*; Buber-Neumann, *Von Potsdam nach Moskau* (Stuttgart, 1957), p. 64; Alfred Kantorowicz, *Deutsches Tagebuch*, I (Munich, 1959), pp. 17-18.

irresponsibility. It was also undeniable that the ratio of unemployed tended to be higher in the KPD than in the SPD. On the other hand, the assertion of the Social Democrats that the "aristocracy" of labor was in their own ranks while the riffraff joined the Communists was a gross exaggeration. The KPD enjoyed substantial support from various well-paid trades which the Social Democrats included in the labor aristocracy, among them the construction workers, miners, metal workers, pipe layers, and steel workers, both skilled and unskilled. Conversely, some of the most loyal supporters of the SPD came from predominantly unskilled or underpaid trades, such as textile workers and farm laborers.[20]

The ill repute in which the Communists were held by the mass of their fellow proletarians was no secret to Paul Levi. He realized that the now enlarged party had to find ways and means of establishing closer relations with other German labor organizations in order to break out of its uncomfortable isolation. This, as Levi well knew, was no easy project. The first obstacle he encountered was the restlessness which prevailed in the ranks of the party. The Independents had split at Halle primarily over the issue of world revolution. The 300,000 secessionists who opted for joining the KPD did so in the belief that world revolution was imminent, and that their new party would soon lead them into action.[21]

To restrain these newcomers without disillusioning them was a major task in itself, but Levi faced additional opposition from a growing and articulate left-wing faction of party functionaries. The center of this "Left Opposition" was in Berlin, where three leaders of the local Communist organization advocated support for a more dynamic policy than Levi had proposed.[22] The most prominent of them was Ernst Reuter, whose party name was "Friesland." He was chairman and first secretary of the party district Berlin-Brandenburg, and speaker of his district's delegation to the Central Committee.[23] In the winter of 1920, Reuter-Friesland obtained the

[20] Flechtheim, pp. 206-216, esp. 208. A thorough sociological study of the KPD, though badly needed, would be a nearly impossible undertaking in view of the absence of reliable data.

[21] Carr, *The Bolshevik Revolution*, III (New York, 1953), pp. 219, 222; Meyer, *Die politischen Hintergründe* . . . (diss. Friedrich-Wilhelms Universität zu Berlin, 1935), p. 38; Brandt and Lowenthal, p. 143.

[22] Carr, *The Bolshevik Revolution*, III, p. 332.

[23] Berlin-Brandenburg was District I of the German Communist Party Organization. It was represented in the Central Committee, aside from Reuter-Friesland, by

support of two junior colleagues, Ruth Fischer and Arkadi Maslow. All three were "outsiders" in the sense that none of them had gone through the ranks of the Spartacus League. Reuter-Friesland, who had been active in the SPD before the war, became a Communist while a prisoner of war in Russia, and upon his return to Germany literally drifted into the KPD at about the time it was founded.[24] Ruth Fischer, who as a student belonged to the radical wing of the Austrian Social Democratic Party, and participated in the founding of the Austrian Communist Party, came to Berlin in 1919, joined the KPD, and within a year made her mark in the party as a temperamental orator and tireless worker.[25] Maslow was the son of Russian parents who had settled in Germany before the war. Like Reuter and Fischer, he had attended a university. Although the three young intellectuals—Reuter, the oldest, was 31 at the end of 1920—were political upstarts in the eyes of their Spartacist comrades, they did not hesitate to voice their opinions on matters affecting party policy. And since they were party leaders of the vital Berlin district, their opinions began to carry weight.

Levi, however, decided to ignore the various pressures brought upon him to initiate a more forceful policy, and set out to improve the party's public relations. On January 8, 1921, the *Rote Fahne*

Paul Wegmann and Karl Winkelsässer; see KPD, *Bericht über die Verhandlungen des Vereinigungsparteitages der U.S.P.D. (Linke) und der K.P.D. (Spartakusbund). Abgehalten in Berlin vom 4. bis 7. Dezember, 1920* (Berlin, 1921), p. 270, and Brandt and Lowenthal, p. 142.

[24] Brandt and Lowenthal, pp. 120-121.

[25] Ruth Fischer, born in 1895 as Elfriede Eisler, came from a Jewish-Viennese middle-class family. Her father, Dr. Rudolf Eisler, was a distinguished writer and Secretary of the Viennese Sociological Society. As a student at the University of Vienna, where she took eight semesters of philosophy and economics, she became interested in the Austrian labor movement, joined the Social Democrats, and married a fellow Socialist, Dr. Friedländer. The marriage ended in divorce, and "Fritzi" Eisler, who had little faith in the weak Austrian Communist Party which she helped to found, went to Berlin in 1919 and joined the KPD. In Germany she decided to adopt the maiden name of her mother, Ida Fischer, and to change her first name to Ruth. In order to acquire German citizenship she went through the formality of a second marriage with the treasurer of the KPD, one Herr Golke, but continued to call herself Ruth Fischer. She died in March 1961 in Paris. See Wenzel, "Die Kommunistische Partei Deutschlands im Jahre 1923" (unpubl. diss., Freie Universität Berlin, 1955), pp. 32-33, incl. n.6; *Wer ist's?*, ed. Herrmann A. L. Degener, 9th ed. (Berlin, 1928), p. 349; cf. the very vivid, but inaccurate profile of Miss Fischer by Johannes Fischart, "Neue Politikerköpfe: Ruth Fischer," *Die Weltbühne*, xx, No. 19 (May 8, 1924), pp. 618-620, and the equally unreliable version in Georg Schwarz, *"Völker höret die Zentrale, KPD bankrott"* (Berlin, 1933), p. 75 and *passim*.

carried an Open Letter addressed to a number of German labor organizations, ranging from the respectable *Allgemeiner Deutscher Gewerkschaftsbund* to the extremist KAPD.[26] The letter, which Levi had drafted with Radek's blessing, if not Radek's assistance, was an appeal for working-class solidarity and as such foreshadowed the united front tactics of the future.[27] The Communists invited their fellow proletarians to submit to the government a joint demand for specific concessions, in the political and economic spheres, which would benefit all workers. The demands ranged from an improvement of unemployment legislation and ceilings on food prices to the dissolution of all bourgeois defense organizations, the creation of proletarian ones, an amnesty for all political prisoners, and the resumption of economic and diplomatic relations with Soviet Russia. The letter emphasized that close cooperation of all labor organizations was necessary in view of deteriorating economic conditions, and closed on the rather defiant note that the Communists would wage this struggle alone should their fellow workers decline to join them.

The response to this appeal was negative. With the exception of an insignificant Syndicalist organization, the *Freie Arbeiterunion Deutschlands*, all recipients of the Open Letter, including both Socialist parties, rejected the Communist offer.[28] The rebuff encouraged the Left Opposition to launch another round of criticism against Levi's "opportunistic" tactics, a move which undermined confidence in his leadership.[29] But to all appearances Levi remained unmoved by the vehemence of his critics and continued to solicit support from non-Communist labor.

[26] *Die Rote Fahne*, No. 11, January 8, 1921.

[27] The accounts vary on who drafted the letter. Fischer, *Stalin and German Communism* (Cambridge, Mass., 1948), p. 171, who gives the wrong publication date (January 6), states flatly that the letter was Radek's work. Flechtheim, p. 72, ascribes it to Levi alone. Carr, *The Bolshevik Revolution*, III, p. 333, speculates that it might have been drafted jointly by Radek and Levi. Borkenau, *Der europäische Kommunismus* (Bern, 1952), p. 45, holds the same opinion more positively. Brandt and Lowenthal, p. 144, name Levi as the author but add that Radek had given his consent. The East German symposium *Die Märzkämpfe 1921*, Marx-Engels-Lenin-Stalin Institut beim ZK der SED (Berlin, 1956), p. 16, hereafter cited as M.E.L.S.I., *Märzkämpfe 1921*, gives no author at all.

[28] Exekutivkomitee der Kommunistischen Internationale, "Monatsschau der Kommunistischen Internationale, Januar-Februar 1921," *Die Kommunistische Internationale*, II, No. 16 (Hamburg, 1921), p. 753; hereafter cited: EKKI, *Kommunistische Internationale*.

[29] Carr, *The Bolshevik Revolution*, III, p. 334; Brandt and Lowenthal, p. 144.

Party Problems in the Young Republic

One step in this direction was an attempt to create a party tradition, the absence of which put the Communists at a disadvantage vis-à-vis the Social Democrats. In pursuit of such a tradition the *Zentrale* proceeded to utilize the political martyrdom of Luxemburg and Liebknecht. No party meetings were held without their pictures on the wall, and no speaker failed to pay tribute to them, a device which was usually the only emotional stimulus an audience would receive from otherwise hackneyed orations.[30] This formula, of making political hay with the only Communist leaders who enjoyed a measure of popularity beyond the confines of the party, was accordingly employed on the anniversary of their death, January 15, 1921. The *Zentrale* called on all party districts to stage organized demonstrations, but the spotlight was on Berlin where the Communists marched to the graves of "Karl and Rosa" in the Friedrichsfelde cemetery.[31] Margarete Buber-Neumann, who was one of the marchers, has left us her impressions of the event.

"Marching in the rank ahead of me was Mother K. [Mrs. Buber-Neumann's aged landlady]. She shouted every few minutes with contagious enthusiasm 'long live [*Hoch*] the victory of the working class!' or 'the world revolution!' or 'the October revolution!' Those who marched in front and behind of us would respond every time with a thundering '*Hoch! Hoch! Hoch!*' Every enthusiastic '*Hoch!*' was followed by a hate-filled 'Down with the murderers of the workers!' whereupon the crowd exploded in a threefold 'Down! [*Nieder*] Down! Down!' A worker a few rows behind me carried . . . Käthe Kollwitz' picture of the murdered Liebknecht on his bier, the bloody bandage around his forehead. . . . Over and over again [the marchers] struck up the funeral march, '*Unsterbliche Opfer, ihr sanket dahin . . .*' [immortal victims, you have perished . . .], and each time I experienced a choking feeling in my throat."[32]

Besides the Open Letter and political demonstrations, Levi also carried his propaganda into the Reichstag. On February 2, 1921, during a debate on foreign policy, he delivered a lengthy speech in

[30] Everth, "Deutscher Kommunismus," *Die Neue Rundschau*, XXXII, I, No. 1 (January 1921), p. 73.

[31] EKKI, *Kommunistische Internationale*, II, No. 16, p. 753. *Schulthess' Europäischer Geschichtskalender*, Neue Folge, LXII, 1921, Erster Teil, ed. Ulrich Thürauf (Munich, 1926), p. 9, hereafter cited as *Schulthess'*, 1921, claims that the demonstrations were held on Sunday, January 16, and that participation was weak.

[32] Buber-Neumann, pp. 62-63.

which he advocated a German alliance with Soviet Russia. The war, he stated, had changed the European constellation of powers. "No longer do imperialist powers face other imperialist powers, but the oppressed nations of the entire world face the oppressors, headed by the states of the Entente." Levi suggested to the government that the only consequence of this situation for an oppressed nation like Germany was to look toward the East, for "the leader of the oppressed throughout the world . . . is Soviet Russia." Charging that the nation's leaders had accepted President Wilson's Fourteen Points and the Versailles peace treaty from fear of Bolshevik Russia, he called them "a puny generation" [*ein kleines Geschlecht*], and concluded his speech with the appeal "Proletarians, your lives . . . are at stake; help your brothers throughout the world; join the front of the oppressed!"[33]

The speech, which was greeted with open derision by the house, had an unforeseen sequel elsewhere. Two Communist functionaries of the party's Munich organization misinterpreted the meaning of Levi's oratory and thought that he had advocated a resumption of the discredited National Bolshevist line. Without checking with the *Zentrale* in Berlin, they issued an appeal which called on nationalist German youth to join forces with the proletariat and Soviet Russia. Once this was done, the peace treaty could be torn up, and the weapons which the Allies wanted Germany to surrender would instead be used against the Entente capitalists.[34]

More significant than the incident in Munich were the repercussions of Levi's speech in Berlin. Here the spokesmen for the Left Opposition were up in arms against their party chairman. Ruth Fischer charged during a meeting on February 8 that Levi had recommended a military alliance with Soviet Russia to the German bourgeoisie. During the week that followed, she and Ernst Reuter-

[33] *Reichstag, Stenographische Berichte*, vol. 347, pp. 2316-2319. Levi's advocacy of an alliance with Soviet Russia probably would not have met with Luxemburg's approval.

[34] EKKI, *Kommunistische Internationale*, II, No. 16, pp. 758, 762; Heinrich Euler, *Die Aussenpolitik der Weimarer Republik 1918-1923. Vom Waffenstillstand bis zum Ruhrkonflikt* (Aschaffenburg, 1957), p. 203. The authors responsible for the appeal were disciplined as soon as the new *Zentrale* under Brandler was formed, not before. While Levi was still chairman, the *Rote Fahne* published only a mild reproof, an attitude which was severely censured a few days later by Ernst Reuter-Friesland in the same paper; *Die Rote Fahne*, No. 61, February 6, 1921, and No. 71, February 12, 1921.

Friesland elaborated their charges against Levi's alleged public endorsement of a Russo-German military alliance in the *Rote Fahne*.[35] They drew pointed comparisons between his Reichstag speech and the National Bolshevist theories which Laufenberg and Wolffheim had advocated a few months earlier. The bitter tone of their attacks illustrated the growing schism over policy which was dividing the party. It was obvious that the Left was out to discredit Levi and, if possible, to oust him from his leading position: in their opinion Levi was a stumbling block on the party's path to revolution.[36] They disapproved of his overtures to non-Communist labor, including the Open Letter campaign, because they considered his approach "opportunist" and detrimental to the Communist objective. Their criticism of his Reichstag speech was but a variation on the same theme. Levi's advocacy of a Russo-German alliance, they argued, confused and misled the workers. They asserted that he did not really believe in the feasibility of such an alliance, and that his slogan was merely a political maneuver of very dubious propaganda value. But even if such an alliance should be realized, it would only work to the advantage of the German bourgeoisie, not the proletariat. For the power position of the German ruling class, which was now being undermined by the policies of the Entente, would be given a new lease on life by an alliance with Russia, and at the expense of the proletarian revolution at home. The aim of the KPD should be instead to show the German working class how to emulate the Russian Bolsheviks by establishing a proletarian dictatorship in Germany. Only then, after a successful revolution had been made, would an alliance with Soviet Russia be meaningful.

The attack by the Left was directed against Levi and the other members of the *Zentrale* who approved of his policy. It was not directed against Soviet Russia and its Bolshevik rulers. The party chairman stood accused of wanting to rescue the floundering German bourgeoisie by harnessing the republic to the "fatherland of the proletariat," thereby obstructing revolution in Germany. The question arises, however, whether Reuter-Friesland, seeing beyond his immediate objective of discrediting Levi, sensed the danger that

[35] Brandt and Lowenthal, pp. 146-149; *Die Rote Fahne*, No. 69, February 11, 1921; No. 71, February 12, 1921; No. 75, February 15, 1921.
[36] The intraparty debate on the prospects for revolution is treated below, Ch. IV.

the chances for a revolution in Germany might eventually be sacrificed to the interests of Soviet diplomacy. If so, the future was to bear out his presentiments.

Before the month was out, Paul Levi resigned as chairman of the *Zentrale,* very much to the satisfaction of his critics in the party. But it was not they who had prompted him to take this step. Levi's decision was taken after a conflict with representatives of the ECCI, and the issue was not the KPD but the Italian Socialist Party.

The Italian Socialists had joined the Comintern in September 1919. Two months later, they had captured one-third of the total of five million votes in the Italian parliamentary elections,[37] but despite their success at the polls, the Italian Socialists lacked cohesion and effective, unified leadership. The party was composed of three factions and was led, nominally at least, by Giacinto Serrati who headed the center faction, the "Maximalists," numerically the strongest of the three. A sizable right wing was led by Filippo Turati, who had unsuccessfully opposed his party's affiliation with the Comintern. But no attempt was made to expel the right wing, nor did Turati consider secession from the party. The left wing, which eventually became the Communist Party of Italy, was led by Amadeo Bordiga and Nicola Bombacci. During the Second World Congress of the Comintern, where only the center and left wing of the Italian Socialist Party were represented, Serrati became engaged in heated disputes with Bordiga, Bombacci, and the Bolshevik leaders.[38] In contrast to the left-wing faction of his party, he objected to those of the twenty-one conditions which required the expulsion of "opportunists" from all parties either affiliated with the Comintern, or about to affiliate.[39] Although he was otherwise in general agreement with the objectives of the Comintern, Serrati, basically a tolerant man, was reluctant to have to expel Turati's right wing merely because the ECCI demanded it. No agreement

[37] Degras, ed., *The Communist International, Documents,* I, Royal Institute of International Affairs (London-New York-Toronto, 1956), p. 70; *Jahrbuch für Politik, Wirtschaft, Arbeiterbewegung 1922-23* (Hamburg, n.d.), p. 831.

[38] For the most crucial debates see *Der Zweite Kongress der K.I., Protokoll der Verhandlungen vom 19. Juli in Petrograd und vom 23. Juli bis 7. August 1920 in Moskau* (Hamburg, 1921), pp. 250-252, 282-286, 288-293, 338-353, 654-656, and *passim.*

[39] See above, Ch. II.

on this question was reached in Moscow, and the decision was deferred until the next congress of the Italian Socialist Party, scheduled to be held in Leghorn from January 15 to 21, 1921.

The congress convened at Leghorn in an atmosphere of tension and bitterness. Widespread labor disturbances had occurred in northern Italy and parts of Sicily during the autumn months of 1920. Metal workers had occupied factories in the Milan region and had staged sitdown strikes, frequently accompanied by violence and breaches of the law. A sporadic revolutionary wave seemed about to sweep the country, but after a few weeks of disorder, which reached its climax in September, the strike movement collapsed. Its inglorious end had repercussions within the Italian Socialist Party. Charges of treason and treasonable complacency were raised by the Bordiga-Bombacci faction against Turati and Serrati and, when the Leghorn Congress opened, all remaining traces of unity had vanished. The spirit of animosity which prevailed among the delegates was further aggravated by the presence of two ECCI emissaries, the Hungarian Matyas Rakosi and the Bulgarian Christo Kabakchiev. They had instructions to demand the unequivocal acceptance of the twenty-one conditions by the Italian Socialist Party, and they executed their mission with a maximum of arrogance and tactlessness. Serrati faced a dilemma. He did not want to break with the Comintern, but he was equally unwilling to expel Turati and his followers, especially since such a move would risk losing the support of the trade-unions.[40]

In his search for an answer to this difficult choice, Serrati turned for advice to the delegate of the German Communist Party, Paul Levi. The rudeness and contempt which Rakosi and Kabakchiev had displayed in their dealings with the Italians taxed Levi's patience, and revived his lingering irritation over the high-handed manner in which the Comintern had treated the visiting delegations at the Second World Congress. When his attempts to find an

[40] For the Italian episode and the Leghorn Congress see Carl A. Landauer, *European Socialism, A History of Ideas and Movements*, I (Berkeley, n.d.), pp. 885-887; Carr, *The Bolshevik Revolution*, III, pp. 225-226, 334; Balabanoff, *My Life as a Rebel* (New York and London, 1938), pp. 285-287; EKKI, *Kommunistische Internationale*, II, No. 16, pp. 753, 755; Brandt and Lowenthal, p. 145; Borkenau, *The Communist International* (London, 1938), pp. 208-212; Meyer, pp. 42-43; and Fischer, pp. 113-116, who has the Leghorn Congress meet in April rather than in January.

acceptable middle ground between the positions of the ECCI and Serrati were sabotaged by the two emissaries, Levi's patience reached an end. He supported Serrati when the latter finally rejected the crucial twenty-first condition, on the ground that to accept it would ruin the Italian Socialist movement. While defending Serrati's decision, Levi also censured the behavior of the Comintern emissaries and condemned their obvious attempts to split the Italian Socialist Party. But a split could no longer be avoided. Serrati and Turati with their followers seceded from the Communist International, and the left-wing Bordiga-Bombacci faction left the Italian Socialist Party, reaffirmed their allegiance to the Comintern, and founded the Communist Party of Italy.[41]

Levi returned from the Leghorn conference in an irritable mood. The behavior of Rakosi and Kabakchiev had antagonized him, and though he was careful not to criticize their role at Leghorn in public, he voiced misgivings about the wisdom of the split as such in carefully couched words in the *Rote Fahne*. His comments drew a sharp reply from Radek, who devoted three editorials in the same paper to Levi's heretical views, and warned him in private that "before you will be allowed to attack us we shall draw the sword against you."[42]

Now the ring of antagonists began to close in on the party chairman. The wrath of the ECCI, which Levi had incurred by his hostile attitude to its two emissaries at Leghorn,[43] merged with the

[41] The accounts disagree on how forcefully Levi supported Serrati, though there is general consensus that Levi tried to avoid a split, and that he sympathized with Serrati's position. See Rakosi's report, in *Protokoll des III. Kongresses der K.I.* (Moskau, 22. Juni bis 12. Juli, 1921) (Hamburg, 1921), p. 329; Heckert's report, *ibid.*, pp. 242-246; Levi's own account in *Was ist das Verbrechen?* (Berlin, 1921), p. 42; Borkenau, *The Communist International*, p. 212; Brandt and Lowenthal, p. 145; Carr, *The Bolshevik Revolution*, III, p. 225; Flechtheim, p. 72. For a very biased interpretation see Wilhelm Pieck, "Der Parteikonflikt in der Vereinigten Kommunistischen Partei Deutschlands," *Die Kommunistische Internationale*, II, No. 18 (Hamburg, 1921), p. 97.

[42] Quoted in Brandt and Lowenthal, p. 145; *Die Rote Fahne*, No. 37, January 23, 1921; No. 41, January 26, 1921; No. 42, January 26, 1921 (evening ed.) and No. 43, January 27, 1921. Radek signed only with the initials "P.B.," probably with reference to his former pen name, "Parabellum."

[43] According to a confidential report from Curt Geyer, who in February 1921 was the official KPD representative to the ECCI in Moscow, and whose report was intercepted by German intelligence agents, Zinoviev and other unidentified ECCI functionaries were highly critical of the Levi-Däumig *Zentrale* prior to the resignation of Levi and his four colleagues. Geyer quoted Zinoviev to have said that the Communist International had accepted too many people into its organization; that

revolt of the Left Opposition at home. The first Levi crisis (a second one followed in April 1921) came to a head during a Central Committee meeting, held in Berlin from February 22 to 24. Initially, the proceedings seemed to go well for Levi. When the representatives of the Left Opposition introduced a motion to reverse the policy of seeking the cooperation of other German labor organizations, the majority not only defeated it but passed a vote of censure against the sponsors.[44] This was a distinct victory for Levi, but his triumph was short-lived, as became evident when the debate moved on to the recent split of the Italian Socialist Party. The Central Committee meeting was attended by one of the ECCI emissaries who had been at Leghorn, Matyas Rakosi, and his verbal duel with Levi was resumed with fresh vigor.[45] This time, however, Levi himself was the target of the aggressive little Hungarian. Rakosi took the initiative by defending the split of the Italian Socialist Party. In the course of the debate he threatened that similar measures might have to be taken against other parties, possibly even against the KPD.[46] Levi rose to the challenge by rejecting once again the Comintern's schism policy, which he considered detrimental to any party trying to win mass support, and he warned that "repeated splits will mean the end of Communism and the Communist movement for a long time to come."[47]

When the vote was taken as to whether Levi's position was right or wrong, the delegates repudiated his views 28 to 23. Levi immediately announced his resignation as chairman. He was joined by four of his colleagues in the *Zentrale*, co-chairman Ernst Däu-

---

it would be better not to admit any more, and to concentrate now on the removal of the "Serratis." Geyer explained that Zinoviev meant by "Serratis" all those who opposed the present, putschist-oriented tactics of the ECCI, especially Levi and his friends. Geyer added that the ECCI favored the activist faction around Ernst Reuter-Friesland, Paul Frölich, Ernst Meyer, etc. over the "opportunist" Levi-Däumig faction. See "State Commissioner Weismann to German Foreign Ministry, May 2, 1921," Auswärtiges Amt, Germany, microfilm, container 1405, frames D552277-D552280, National Archives, Washington, D.C.

[44] Brandt and Lowenthal, p. 149.

[45] Carr, *The Bolshevik Revolution*, III, p. 334, who apparently bases his account on Borkenau, *The Communist International*. pp. 212-213, claims that Kabakchiev was likewise present, a claim which is unsubstantiated. For Rakosi's side of the story see *Protokoll des III. Kongresses der K.I.*, pp. 330-332.

[46] Carr, *The Bolshevik Revolution*, III, pp. 335, note 1, and 389. Levi, *Unser Weg*, 2nd ed. (Berlin, 1921), pp. 46-47.

[47] Quoted in Brandt and Lowenthal, p. 150.

mig, Clara Zetkin, Otto Brass, and Adolf Hoffmann. In a joint statement which was published in the *Rote Fahne*, they justified their
resignation by declaring that they could not accept the responsibility for carrying out a party policy with which they fundamentally
disagreed.[48]

The resignation of Levi and his friends was a turning point in the
history of the KPD. Whatever their personal convictions on the
prospects of a German revolution may have been—and in Levi's
case the strength of his convictions remains subject to reasonable
doubts—the party leaders who resigned their offices in February
1921 were independent-minded individuals with a highly developed
sense of responsibility. Whether their resignations were prompted
solely by political considerations, or whether personal pique entered
in as well, remains an open question. But there is little doubt that
all of them resented the arbitrary and dictatorial methods of the
Comintern, methods in which they sensed danger for the future
of German Communism. Clara Zetkin, who had been in the labor
movement since the days of Bismarck's anti-Socialist laws, in the
spring of 1921 was still opposed to Bolshevik interference in the
affairs of the German party.[49] Levi's distrust of the Russian leaders
and their methods was even stronger, and more lasting. He had
adopted Rosa Luxemburg's scepticism toward Moscow's tutelage,
had found ample confirmation for his attitude in his repeated
personal contacts with leading Bolsheviks, and during his term as
party chairman had been guided by the maxim of his dead teacher
—that a revolutionary party in Germany could never be successful
unless it received mass support. Däumig, a former leader in the
Revolutionary Shop Steward movement which had always prided
itself upon its rugged individualism, was equally disinclined to take

[48] Kommunistische Partei Deutschlands, *Bericht über die Verhandlungen des 2.
Parteitages der Kommunistischen Partei Deutschlands (Sektion der Kommunistischen
Internationale), abgehalten in Jena vom 22. bis 26. August, 1921* (Berlin, 1922),
pp. 60-61, hereafter cited as *Bericht über die Verhandlungen des 2. Parteitages,* 1921;
Die Rote Fahne, No. 98, February 28, 1921; Radek, "Der Fall Levi," *Soll die
Vereinigte Partei Deutschlands . . . ,* 2nd ed., (Hamburg, n.d.), pp. 106-107.

[49] See Balabanoff, pp. 288-290, for an appraisal of Zetkin's personality and views.
Zetkin's conversion to the Bolshevik point of view became evident *after* the Third
World Congress of the Comintern in the summer of 1921. Compare her attitude at
the congress in *Protokoll des III. Kongresses der K.I.,* pp. 278-300, with an address
to the Italian Socialist Party which she gave on October 10, 1921: "Um Sein oder
Nichtsein der Italienischen Sozialistischen Partei," *Ausgewählte Reden und Schriften,*
II (Berlin, 1955), pp. 357-380.

orders from Zinoviev's *missi dominici*. With Hoffmann and Brass, a newcomer from the Independents, Däumig preferred to serve the party as a "common soldier" rather than as an "officer" in a *Zentrale* where the right to disagree would henceforth be limited.[50]

With the formation of the new *Zentrale*, control over the affairs of the party passed into the hands of men less independent-minded and imaginative than Levi and his four colleagues. Heinrich Brandler and Walter Stoecker shared the chairmanship.[51] Paul Frölich,

[50] For the "common soldier" and the "right to disagree" see Radek, "Der Fall Levi," *op.cit.*, pp. 107, 113-119.

[51] Heinrich Brandler was born on July 5, 1881, at Warnsdorf in Austria-Hungary. He acquired German citizenship in 1918, when he served for six weeks in the Bavarian government as *Unterstaatssekretär*. Brandler, by trade a construction worker, had a bona fide proletarian background. Before the war he had been active in the SPD and the trade-union movement. During the war he joined the Spartacus League. He became well known and respected in labor circles during the Kapp Putsch, when he occupied and held the city of Chemnitz virtually without bloodshed until after the proletarian uprising in the Ruhr and central Germany collapsed. In nearly all accounts there is general agreement as to his honesty, self-respect, and his ability as an organizer. But although he had proved himself a capable leader on the local level, as chairman of the party's Chemnitz organization, his provincial outlook, inadequate education, and political naïveté did not qualify him particularly well for the party chairmanship. But Ruth Fischer's statement (p. 180) notwithstanding, it was Brandler and not Ernst Meyer who succeeded Levi as party chairman. Brandler remained in this position until April 18, 1921, when he was arrested in connection with the party's March uprising of that year. He was tried for high treason, and sentenced to five years fortress imprisonment on June 6, 1921. But he served only four months of his sentence. In November 1921 he was released, and the party sent him to Moscow as the KPD representative to the ECCI, a position which he held until his return to Germany in August 1922. Sometime in 1921, the exact date cannot be established, the *Zentrale* was divided into an organizational and a political section, the *Orgbüro* and the *Polbüro*. Upon his return to Germany in August 1922, Brandler became secretary of the *Polbüro*. In February 1923 he was re-elected into the *Zentrale* and resumed the leadership of the party. For his activities in 1923 and beyond see below, Chs. xi and xii.

Walter Stoecker had joined the party from the USPD in December 1920. He, too, had a trade-union background. He served the party loyally throughout the period of the Weimar Republic, and was killed by the National Socialist regime sometime between 1933 and 1945.

For Brandler's background see the following: *Der Hochverratsprozess gegen Heinrich Brandler vor dem ausserordentlichen Gericht am 6. Juni, 1921 in Berlin* (Berlin, 1921), pp. 5-6; Borkenau, *The Communist International*, p. 159; Wenzel, pp. 36-37; Radek, "Der Fall Levi," *op.cit.*, p. 98; KPD, *Bericht über die Verhandlungen des 2. Parteitages*, 1921, pp. 7-8, 438; Kommunistische Partei Deutschlands, *Bericht über die Verhandlungen des III. (8.) Parteitages der Kommunistischen Partei Deutschlands (Sektion der Kommunistischen Internationale) abgehalten in Leipzig vom 28. Januar bis 1. Februar 1923* (Berlin, 1923), pp. 57-58, 441, hereafter cited as *Bericht über die Verhandlungen des III. (8.) Parteitages*. The confusing method of giving two numbers to each party convention was presumably the result of a party decision to include the conventions of the Spartacus League in the numbering system. Apparently this system was found wanting since the following congress

Background

Ernst Meyer, Paul Böttcher, and Max Sievers became secretaries, and Paul Wegmann replaced Adolf Hoffmann as alternate.[52] These new leaders undoubtedly considered themselves as much the successors to Rosa Luxemburg, and heirs to her tradition, as did Levi and his friends. But the subsequent weeks were to show that in this respect the Brandler *Zentrale* labored under a misconception. Under its new leadership the party was to ignore Luxemburg's repeated warning against a policy of putschism, was to disregard her plea for independence from outside interference, and thus was to pave the way for an increase of Bolshevik influence on German Communism in the years to come.

---

was assigned the Roman numeral ix, without a second number, thus compounding confusion.

[52] KPD, *Bericht über die Verhandlungen des 2. Parteitages, 1921,* p. 7. The Berlin Opposition, i.e., Reuter-Friesland, Fischer, and Maslow, had voted with the majority against Levi. But although their influence on the new leaders was to increase during the interim between Levi's resignation and the March uprising, they did not obtain seats on the new *Zentrale*; Brandt and Lowenthal, p. 151.

PART TWO
THE "UNAUTHORIZED" BID
FOR POWER (1921)

CHAPTER IV

THE GENESIS OF THE
MARCH UPRISING

ANY INQUIRY into the origins of that complex series of events which in Communist parlance has become known as the *März Aktion* of 1921 must take into account the KPD's rise to the status of mass party. Although its estimated importance may have been unrealistic when compared to the overwhelming labor support that was given to the two Socialist parties, the mere concept of being an organization which claimed half a million members created in party ranks a confident and optimistic mood. Veteran Spartacists and newcomers from the Independents alike expected the party to follow henceforth a more dynamic, more activist course, and watched eagerly for any indication of growing Communist influence on the German domestic scene.[1] Electoral gains in Prussia, Lippe-Detmold, Hamburg, and even an increased Communist vote in union elections of the Berlin woodworkers and railway workers were interpreted as signs of mounting party strength.[2] The buoyant spirit of the rank and file was in sharp contrast to the continued cautious policies of Levi. The result was a progressive dissatisfaction with the *Zentrale* among the party membership, a development which in the weeks following the unification congress of December 20 led to an increase of independent activities on the part of local Communist organizations. By far the most serious effect of this trend was an increase in sporadic underground work.

It had been resolved at the Second World Congress of the Communist International that all Communist parties were immediately to form "illegal organizations . . . for the purpose of carrying out

---

[1] Brandt and Lowenthal, *Ernst Reuter* (Munich, 1957), p. 143; Carr, *The Bolshevik Revolution*, III (New York, 1953), p. 332; H. M. Meyer, *Die politischen Hintergründe* . . . (diss. Friedrich-Wilhelms-Universität zu Berlin, 1935), p. 44; also the references which Radek and Koenen made in this connection at the Third World Congress, *Protokoll des III. Kongresses der K.I.* (Moskau, 22. Juni bis 12. Juli, 1921) (Hamburg, 1921), pp. 311, 659. Ruth Fischer, *Stalin and German Communism* (Cambridge, Mass., 1948), p. 171, links the disenchantment of the Independent newcomers that followed soon after the unification with the KPD to the beginnings of the New Economic Policy in Russia, although NEP was officially promulgated only in March 1921.

[2] M.E.L.S.I., *Märzkämpfe 1921* (Berlin, 1956), p. 18.

systematic underground work. . . ."[3] This was presented as a defensive measure made necessary by reactionary persecutions of Communists everywhere. Underground organizations for illegal political work had existed in Germany ever since the war years, but they had originated with the Revolutionary Shop Steward movement, not with the Spartacists. In the summer of 1918 the Shop Stewards had come under the leadership of Ernst Däumig, who was then still a member of the Independent Social Democratic Party.[4] The two organizations had an informal and noncommittal relationship. The Revolutionary Shop Stewards were the earliest advocates of a system of workers' councils, and in November 1918 were far more influential in creating them than were the Spartacists. Even before the revolution broke out they had begun to buy weapons and to form secret military detachments, referred to as *Der Apparat* (the apparatus) and directed by Däumig in close cooperation with two other Shop Steward leaders, Emil Barth and Richard Müller. *Der Apparat* formed the model for future Communist underground organizations.[5]

After the November revolution and the founding of the KPD, such Communist underground organizations sprang up haphazardly throughout Germany but remained without effective coordination and control from the *Zentrale* in Berlin. During the proletarian uprising in the Ruhr region in March and April 1920, the police discovered in several local party offices blueprints for a red army and other documents pertaining to Communist military plans.[6] Whether the organizations responsible for these materials were offshoots of the old Däumig apparatus, or whether they were the more recent creations of local KPD cells is impossible to say. But on no occasion between 1918 and 1920 was the role of Communist underground organizations of vital importance, because, lacking central direction, they were weak and ineffective.[7]

[3] *Der Zweite Kongress der K.I., Protokoll der Verhandlungen vom 19. Juli in Petrograd und vom 23. Juli bis 7. August 1920 in Moskau* (Hamburg, 1921), pp. 758-759.

[4] Tormin, *Zwischen Rätediktatur und Sozialer Demokratie* . . . , Beiträge zur Geschichte des Parlamentarismus. . . , Heft 4 (Düsseldorf, 1954), p. 42.

[5] *ibid.*, pp. 42-44; Fischer, p. 173; Erich Wollenberg, *Der Apparat. Stalins Fünfte Kolonne* (Bonn, 1952), p. 9.

[6] Angress, "Weimar Coalition and Ruhr Insurrection. . . ," *Journal of Modern History*, xxix, No. 1 (March 1957), pp. 3-5, incl. nn. 16, 22.

[7] Fischer, p. 173. For very harsh criticism of the illegal party organizations by the

Genesis of the March Uprising

Communist underground work intensified after unification with the left-wing Independents. Two principal illegal *"Apparate"* were created prior to 1921, an N-group (*Nachrichtenapparat*) for intelligence work, and an M-group (*Militärapparat*) intended to train cadres of Communist fighters. Both groups had the additional mission of maintaining liaison with Russian agents passing illegally through Germany.[8] The formation of these groups was in accordance with the directives of the Second World Congress, which the party was obligated to obey. There is no indication, however, that they functioned efficiently, or that they were effectively supervised and coordinated by the *Zentrale* while Levi was still its chairman. Moreover, basic disagreement existed between the *Zentrale* and the party's underground on what the functions of the illegal groups were to be. The latter stressed the need for storing weapons and ammunition for future use, while the *Zentrale* tried to divert the conspiratorial ambitions of the would-be underground fighters into relatively harmless channels. This was done by forming them into study groups on military theory and by using them as guards at party meetings.[9] But it was in the nature of the situation that the restraining efforts made by the leadership met with only limited success. Local Communist underground organizations frequently acted on their own initiative and, as was inevitable, incidents occurred which aroused the suspicion of the German authorities that the KPD was secretly but actively preparing for revolution.

On January 19, 1921, Prussian police raided Communist offices in Essen, Düsseldorf, Elberfeld, and Luenen, near Dortmund, arrested a number of Communist leaders, and confiscated party files.

Communists themselves see Kommunistische Partei Deutschlands, *Taktik und Organisation der revolutionären Offensive. Die Lehren der Märzaktion* (Leipzig-Berlin, 1921), pp. 128-129, and ff., *passim*; hereafter cited as *Taktik und Organisation*.

[8] Wollenberg, p. 9; Fischer, pp. 173-174; "Bericht des preussischen Staatskommissars Dr. Weismann," Auswärtiges Amt, Germany, microfilm, container 1405, frames D552166-D552168, National Archives, Washington, D.C.

Fischer mentions also the creation of Z-groups, *Zersetzungsgruppen*, designed to infiltrate hostile political and military organizations in order to undermine them and to collect information; and T-groups, *Terrorgruppen*, which were used for sabotage and the liquidation of traitors (p. 174). Buber-Neumann, *Von Potsdam nach Moskau* (Stuttgart, 1957), p. 68, also mentions these two organizations, but states that she was at the time unaware of the existence of any underground organizations. She only noticed some occasional theft of dynamite. According to Wollenberg (p. 11), the Z- and T-groups were created at a later date. Weismann's report makes no mention of them either.

[9] Fischer, pp. 173-174.

On the basis of what Dr. Robert Weismann, Prussian State Commissioner for Safeguarding Public Security, termed "partial confessions," and after an examination of the captured material, Weismann reported to his superiors that he had discovered evidence for the existence of a red army. Its headquarters, the report said, was in Berlin, and several subordinate command posts (*Kommandobehörden*) were in western and central Germany. Weismann claimed to have found proof beyond doubt that the organization was designed to overthrow, by force, government and constitution: its ultimate objective was to establish a dictatorship of the proletariat.[10]

On February 3, 1921, State Commissioner Dr. Weismann made another discovery. This one involved the Soviet Mission in Berlin, headed by Victor Kopp. It appears that staff members of this mission were engaged in a series of occupations totally unconnected with their official duty of negotiating with the Germans for the exchange and repatriation of prisoners of war.[11] A number of copied documents, which had found their way into Weismann's office, contained strong indications that the Soviet Mission was involved in smuggling arms and explosives, furthering Communist propaganda, and financing Communist underground activities in Germany and other parts of Europe.[12] Later in the month, raids on Communist party offices in Magdeburg, Stendal, and Frankfurt am Main led to the arrest of several local KPD functionaries. Dynamite, arms, and other military equipment had been found.[13]

[10] "Report of the Prussian State Commissioner, Dr. Weismann, January 20, 1921," Auswärtiges Amt, Germany, microfilm, container 1405, frames D552147-D552149, D552166-D552168.

[11] Hilger and Meyer, *The Incompatible Allies* (New York, 1953), p. 65. Connected with these negotiations were the unofficial attempts of both sides to prepare for the resumption of Russo-German commercial and diplomatic relations; *loc.cit.*, and Freund, *Unholy Alliance* (New York, 1957), p. 84.

[12] "Report of the Prussian State Commissioner Dr. Weismann, February 3, 1921," Auswärtiges Amt, Germany, microfilm, container 1405, frames D552184-D552193.

[13] H. M. Meyer, p. 62. Prussia, Landtag, *Niederschriften über die von dem Untersuchungsausschuss zur Nachprüfung der Ursachen, des Umfangs und der Wirkungen des kommunistischen Aufstandes in Mitteldeutschland im März 1921 in mündlicher Verhandlung erhobenen Beweise: Sammlung der Drucksachen des Preussischen Landtags (Anlagen zu den Sitzungsberichten)*, Drucksache Nr. 4140, 1. Wahlperiode, 1. Tagung, begonnen am 10. März, 1921, VIII (Berlin, 1923), pp. 2, 97, and *passim*; hereafter cited as *Preussischer Untersuchungsausschuss.*
For the origins, procedure, and achievements of this investigation committee see Winfried Steffani, *Die Untersuchungsausschüsse des Preussischen Landtages zur Zeit der Weimarer Republik. Ein Beitrag zur Entwicklung, Funktion und politischen Bedeutung parlamentarischer Untersuchungsausschüsse*, Kommission für Geschichte

Alarmed by these ominous discoveries, a number of German, and particularly Prussian officials became firmly convinced that the KPD was preparing for an uprising sometime in the spring.[14] Throughout the first two months of 1921, rumors of a red underground army caused particular concern in official quarters. State Commissioner Weismann maintained in his report of January 20 that the KPD was directly supporting the formation of such an army.[15] His assertion was based on documents found during raids on the party offices in the Rhineland. But either because the evidence proved too inconclusive, or because the *Zentrale* habitually (and perhaps not always untruthfully) denied all knowledge of these uncovered plots, Weismann refrained from taking statewide action against the party as a whole. He continued instead to rely on preventive measures, keeping the party's activities under constant surveillance in the expectation that sooner or later local organizations would become careless enough to lay themselves open to police raids.[16] Thus, despite their suspicions of Communist intentions, the authorities took no steps to arrest the *Zentrale*. Levi was allowed to travel abroad to attend the Leghorn conference and, understandably enough, nothing was done about the delicate problem posed by Victor Kopp's Soviet Mission.

How correct were the appraisals concerning the threat of an armed Communist insurrection that were voiced by various German officials early in 1921? Ironically enough, no specific plans for such an uprising existed prior to March of that year; and when the uprising did occur, unprepared, improvised, and absolutely un-

---

des Parlamentarismus und der politischen Parteien, xvii (Düsseldorf, 1960), pp. 138-144.

[14] Mention of this was made in an unsigned memorandum of January 27, 1921, to the German Foreign Office, though the report also emphasizes the internal difficulties which the Communist Party faced at the time, and concludes that for the moment no *Aktion* on the part of the KPD was anticipated. See "Sonderbericht über die deutsche Arbeiterbewegung No. 31. . . ," Auswärtiges Amt, Germany, microfilm, container 1405, frames D 552177-552178; see also Weismann's analysis, *ibid.*, frame D 552168; and the statement by Dr. Gottfried von Dryander during the investigation of the March action that the Federal Commissioner for Safeguarding Public Security, Dr. Peters, had warned on February 15, 1921 that a Communist uprising was imminent; *Preussischer Untersuchungsausschuss*, p. 108.

[15] "Report of the Prussian State Commissioner, Dr. Weismann, January 20, 1921," Auswärtiges Amt, Germany, microfilm, container 1405, frame D 552148.

[16] *Preussischer Untersuchungsausschuss*, pp. 1, 2. Fischer (p. 174) states that those arrested on conspiracy charges were denied open party support.

organized, no red army materialized even in central Germany, the heart of the insurgent region.[17] This is not to say that the KPD was a peaceful club. Nor does it mean that among the German Communists there were not some who seriously advocated a revolutionary offensive at the earliest possible opportunity. But dedication to the principle of revolution and actual preparation for such an event are not the same, and while the KPD never denied that revolution was its ultimate aim, no practical measures to implement it seem to have been taken by the *Zentrale*, certainly not while Levi was still its chairman.[18] The plots which the German authorities discovered during January and February were examples of the same naïve and irresponsible "putschist" attitude which since the days of Luxemburg and Liebknecht had made it so hard for the party leadership to control the radical elements, especially on the local level. Moreover, the tendency to indulge in cloak and dagger games was hard to block after the ECCI had made underground work by all Communist parties mandatory. But the government officials who sounded the alarm and predicted bloodshed in the near future can hardly be blamed for being misled by overenthusiastic Communist busybodies. Only when the insurrection finally came, at Easter, and apparently justified the most dire predictions of the German security agencies, did it become evident that the KPD had acted on impulse and faith, without benefit of either organization or preparation.

The various steps which led to the March uprising are even today a matter of controversy. Whoever wants to reconstruct the complex and involved circumstances must take into consideration that both the Communists and the various government representatives have

[17] In his deposition before the Investigation Committee of the Prussian Diet, which was commissioned to trace the origins of the Communist uprising in March 1921, Dr. Weismann denied on May 9, 1921, that a nationwide Communist underground army ever existed, thus directly contradicting the reports he had issued in January 1921. Weismann made it clear that his negative findings included the central German region as well, i.e., that part of the country where Communist strength was particularly heavy (see H. M. Meyer, p. 63). Testimony to the effect that no red army existed anywhere in Germany during 1921 were also given by the Prussian Minister of the Interior Carl Severing; the Prussian *Ministerialdirigent* Dr. Wilhelm Abegg; and the *Oberpräsident* of the Prussian province of Saxony, Otto Hörsing; *Preussischer Untersuchungsausschuss*, pp. 1, 3, 101, 118, 120.

[18] A few months later, Radek referred to the party's illegal organization as "illusions" which at best existed on paper; "whatever there was, was undisciplined." *Protokoll des III. Kongresses der K.I.*, p. 471.

tried to obscure many of the issues in their respective accounts. To this must be added that official Communist interpretation moved through several phases before the final version was adopted at the Third Congress of the Communist International in the summer of 1921. According to this version, which is still upheld today, the March uprising was the result of calculated provocation of the workers by the Prussian government. Because it contained a few grains of truth, this formula proved to be the most feasible way in which a number of very inconvenient facts could be left unexplained in official Communist annals, past and present.[19]

The key factor that made a Communist insurrection possible in the first place was the change in leadership of the *Zentrale*. Heinrich Brandler, the new chairman, was a simple and pedestrian man whose intellectual qualities were overshadowed by most of his more sophisticated colleagues, especially Ernst Meyer, Paul Frölich, and August Thalheimer. Levi had led the party without paying too much attention to views which did not coincide with his, thereby alienating large segments of the party, but Brandler went to the other extreme and too often accepted the opinions of others as his own. He had proved his mettle in the past in trade-union work, and during the proletarian uprisings that followed in the wake of the Kapp Putsch he acted as a capable though cautious commander of the armed Saxon workers. But now he had assumed a much greater responsibility, and he was to show before long how difficult it was to live up to it.

It soon became apparent that the switch in the Communist high command caused a great deal of consternation within the party.[20] Although Levi had been a controversial figure from the first to the last day that he served as chairman of the *Zentrale*, he still commanded the allegiance of many party members who saw in him the heir and disciple of Rosa Luxemburg, and who respected his ability

[19] For an early example of this thesis see O. Kilian, "The Truth about the March Action in Central Germany," *International Press Correspondence*, I, No. 12 (November 29, 1921), pp. 95-96; hereafter cited as *Inprecorr*. For a recent example, see M.E.L.S.I., *Märzkämpfe 1921*, pp. 21-26, and *passim*.

[20] *Protokoll des III. Kongresses der K.I.*, pp. 313, 353; Wilhelm Pieck, "Der Parteikonflikt in der Vereinigten Kommunistischen Partei Deutschlands," *Die Kommunistische Internationale*, II, No. 18 (Hamburg, 1921), p. 98; Levi, *Unser Weg*, 2nd ed. (Berlin, 1921), pp. 6-11, *passim*. The second edition of Levi's pamphlet, which has the same title as the first, contains a special "Introduction to the Second Edition."

even when they did not care for his personality. The fact that Zetkin, Brass, Däumig, and Hoffmann, some of them old war-horses who had won renown in the prewar SPD, had declared their solidarity with Levi created additional unrest and uncertainty in party circles. Thus the new Brandler *Zentrale* faced a difficult situation from the start. On the one hand Moscow, where Levi's cavalier attitude toward revolution had incurred strong disapproval, wanted the German party to adopt a more vigorous policy, although what exactly was expected of the KPD remained for the time being uncertain.[21] On the other hand, the resignation of the Levi faction had aggravated rather than eliminated the internal crisis of the party. How could Moscow's expectations be met when the Communist leadership was divided on the principal issue of the day, the prospects for a proletarian revolution in Germany? On this point all factions disagreed. While it was generally recognized, in a vague and hazy way, that the Communists as the vanguard of the proletariat had to win influence over the masses in order to lead them to victory, the propitiousness of the moment as well as the tactics to be applied toward this end remained constant subjects of controversy among the party hierarchy.

Up to the moment when the Levi *Zentrale* resigned, the views of the party's right wing had determined policy and set the course. While its spokesmen had admitted to the presence of "objective" factors which favored revolution, particularly rising unemployment, the threatened financial collapse of the state, and the growing misery of the masses, they had maintained that such "subjective" factors as the relative strength of the Communists vis-à-vis the state, and the absence of a genuine revolutionary spirit among German labor, offset the aspects favorable for a successful revolutionary movement.[22] The right wing, under Levi's guidance, had advocated that for the moment the only feasible slogan which the party could

---

[21] K.P.D., *Bericht über den 5. Parteitag der K.P.D. (Sektion der Kommunistischen Internationale) vom 1. bis 3. November 1920 in Berlin* (Berlin, 1921), pp. 27-28, 36; and Curt Geyer's report (see above, Ch. iii) in "Report of the Prussian State Commissioner Dr. Weismann, May 2, 1921," Auswärtiges Amt, Germany, microfilm, container 1405, frame D 552280. Here Geyer points out that in February 1921 Russian members of the ECCI expressed the desire to see a rapprochement, and possibly a fusion, between the KPD and the KAPD in order to boost the revolutionary spirit of the former. See also Zinoviev's comments at a later date in *Protokoll des III. Kongresses der K.I.*, pp. 181-182, 186.

[22] H. M. Meyer, pp. 43-45.

employ with any hope of success was that of "Alliance with Soviet Russia." Levi thought this slogan particularly opportune in view of the growing tension between Germany and the Western Allies, a theory which he elaborately defended before and after the March uprising. In April 1921 Levi wrote: "With the Paris demands [*Diktat*] the German Reich entered upon a new, acute crisis, and this acute crisis, as was self-evident, had to be utilized for an *Aktion*. . . . The former *Zentrale* accepted the slogan [Alliance with Soviet Russia] . . . unanimously. . . . At the first sign of crisis it [the KPD] marched forward with the corresponding slogan . . . [and] this slogan—'Alliance with Soviet Russia'—had to become, of course, the leitmotif of all Communist propaganda during the weeks preceding the actual crisis. . . . We were convinced that this common struggle . . . would for the first time really close the ranks of the party."[23]

Whatever Levi may have meant with his vague reference to an *Aktion* in the event of possible conflict between Germany and the West, he had certainly not visualized a putsch. This is evident from his own interpretation: "During times of crisis when the masses are in a state of political turmoil . . . the Communist party has the duty to show a positive way out of the present dangers. The slogans of the V.K.P.D. must not be humdrum, everyday slogans, but must issue directly from any given crisis. . . . Such a slogan can only be 'Alliance with Soviet Russia'. . . . It had been issued as a concrete slogan, i.e. one which could also be immediately realized *by the bourgeois government*, and at the same time could guide the proletariat in its struggle for the fulfilment of these demands."[24]

In short, the party's right wing set its hopes upon a possible conflict between Germany and the Western Allies, a conflict which might lead to a Russo-German alliance. How exactly the German Communists were to profit from such an alliance Levi never made clear. What he did make clear was his determination not to permit rash actions to anticipate events, but to wait for an international crisis, and meanwhile to prepare the proletariat for a war in which

[23] Levi, *Unser Weg*, 2nd ed., p. 6. The Paris *Diktat* mentioned by Levi referred to the decisions concerning reparation payments, disarmament, etc., reached by the interallied conference held in Paris from January 24-29, 1921. These demands were submitted to Germany for consideration.
[24] *ibid.*, p. 8; italics mine.

the Western powers would be faced by the Soviet Union and its ally—the German bourgeois republic!

It will be recalled that Levi's views had evoked vehement criticism from the Left Opposition.[25] In contrast to Levi and the majority of his colleagues in the *Zentrale*, the Berlin Left believed that a new revolutionary wave was in the offing, and that the party had to prepare its own members and as many non-Communist workers as possible for the event.[26] On February 12 the *Rote Fahne* had published an article by Reuter-Friesland in which he had clearly enunciated the position of the Left.

"We were all of the opinion, up to now, that the German bourgeoisie is not oppressed, that the German bourgeoisie enjoys life, and that it counts on the fraternal support of the Entente imperialists while oppressing the German proletariat . . . ; it is exactly for this reason that we have made it our task to fight against every nationalist slogan. Let me remind you that the Communist party neither approved of the Versailles treaty, nor opposed it, but demanded *the revolutionary solution of the world crisis. . . .*

"For the time being, the German proletariat must first solve its mission in Germany. *Hic Rhodus, hic salta!. . . .* Let the German proletariat first break the resistance of this [bourgeois] society; let the German proletariat first secure possession of all factories and [other] enterprises; then we shall see how this struggle for liberation waged by the German workers will affect the proletariat of England, France . . . of the western countries. . . . We do not want contrived [*an den Haaren herbeigezogen*] measures designed to convince either the German workers or the Executive [of the Comintern] how active we are. We want to show the German working masses the clear, unequivocal, though difficult road to the German revolution."[27]

The conflicting opinions on party strategy were still a burning issue when Levi and his friends resigned, saddling the Brandler *Zentrale* with the thankless task of choosing a proper solution. It soon became apparent that the views of the Left were gaining ground. They did so despite the fact that this faction was not repre-

[25] See above, Ch. III.
[26] *Protokoll des III. Kongresses der K.I.*, p. 532 (Heckert's report); *Taktik und Organisation*, p. 15; Brandt and Lowenthal, p. 149.
[27] *Die Rote Fahne*, No. 71, February 12, 1921; emphasis in the original.

sented in the new *Zentrale,* and that its criticism of the right wing had been voted down in the same meeting which had culminated in the resignation of the Levi group. But the spokesmen of the left wing were also in control of the party's strong and radical Berlin organization, which Reuter and two of his colleagues represented in the Central Committee. And since the *Zentrale* likewise had its headquarters in Berlin, it was constantly exposed to the influence of the Reuter-Fischer-Maslow triumvirate. After Levi and his friends were no longer in positions of authority, the Berliners had the field largely to themselves, and they made good use of their opportunity.[28]

The Left tried hard to convince the new leadership that now was the time to show the German working class the road to the German revolution. This approach had in its favor the awareness of the new *Zentrale* that Moscow and large segments of the KPD expected German Communism to adopt a more vigorous approach toward its ultimate objective. Nevertheless, the underlying preconceptions held respectively by the Berliners and the Brandler *Zentrale* were fundamentally different. While Reuter, the most prominent figure of the Left, wanted the party prepared to make use of the new revolutionary wave which he sincerely anticipated,[29] the Brandler *Zentrale* wanted to conjure up a revolutionary situation, even though few of its members shared Reuter's optimistic view of the revolutionary wave on the horizon. They were primarily concerned to demonstrate that the KPD, under new management, would no longer be a do-nothing party, but a party of action, and that it would daringly lead the lethargic German workers out of the bondage of bourgeois capitalist exploitation. With the Communist mission thus formulated in theory, the sole remaining question was how to go about it in practice. To find the answer, the new party leaders began to scan the national and international scenes in the hope that they would somehow, somewhere, find both an occasion and a justification for an *Aktion.*[30]

[28] Levi, *Unser Weg,* 2nd ed., p. 7.

[29] Brandt and Lowenthal, p. 149.

[30] How strong this line of thought was among the Communist leaders is evident from their defense of it in *Taktik und Organisation,* pp. 3, 4, 6, 13, 14, 15, 20, 21, and *passim.* This symposium, compiled by the promoters of the so-called "theory of the revolutionary offensive," was later officially disavowed by the Comintern and the KPD because it conflicted with the ultimate "interpretation" of the March action as

During the first three months of 1921 the international situation was tense. The Allied conference which was held at Paris between January 24 and 29 had yielded some definite proposals for German reparation payments, and a German delegation was invited to come to London on March 1 to negotiate on the foundation laid by the Paris conference. Public opinion in Germany was unanimously hostile to the Paris decisions, and the German plenipotentiaries were not expected to display a very conciliatory attitude in London.[31] This expectation proved to be correct, and the negotiations which began on March 1 ended in an impasse. An ultimatum to comply with Allied demands on reparations was rejected by Germany on March 7, and at 7 A.M. of the following day French troops occupied the cities of Duisburg, Düsseldorf, and Ruhrort in the Ruhr region. The situation was critical, and no rapid solution was in sight. The Allies remained firm, threatened that further sanctions might be applied, and demanded payment of twenty million gold marks by May 1. In addition, a new customs line was drawn along the Rhine, which cut off normal commercial intercourse between the Reich and its territory on the left bank of the river.

Difficulties between Germany and the Western Allies were intensified in the East by the approaching plebiscite in Upper Silesia, which was to determine where the German-Polish frontier would be drawn. Throughout 1920, and especially in August of that year, armed clashes between Poles and Germans had occurred sporadically along the disputed border region. The threat of new outbursts of violence remained constant. As the day of the plebiscite approached (March 20, 1921), tension mounted in Upper Silesia, partly because of renewed anti-German agitation in the Polish press. The situation was decidedly dangerous.[32]

One domestic problem, Bavaria, flared up with fresh bitterness early in 1921. All attempts by the German government to make

---

adopted by the Third World Congress. The contributions to the symposium show that the Communist leaders were aware of the unrevolutionary spirit which prevailed among the non-Communist German workers. This was also frankly admitted by Fritz Heckert at the Third World Congress (*Protokoll des III. Kongresses der K.I.*, p. 532). Three of the contributors to the symposium, August Thalheimer, Hermann Remmele, and Paul Frölich, were members of the Brandler *Zentrale*. So was Fritz Heckert.

[31] D'Abernon, *The Diary of an Ambassador*, I (New York, 1929), pp. 126, 132.
[32] *Frankfurter Zeitung*, No. 190, March 12, 1921.

Bavaria disband her civil guards (*Einwohnerwehren*), particularly the controversial *Orgesch*, had failed. The Bavarians justified their obstinacy with the argument that the civil guards alone stood between the security of the population and Communist anarchy.[33] On February 5, 1921, a conference of prime ministers from the individual German states (*Länder*) met in Berlin to discuss the whole sordid question once again. The Allied conference at Paris had issued a final injunction on January 29 under which the German government was instructed to enforce the disbanding of all paramilitary organizations inside the Reich by June 30, 1921. But despite the urgency of the matter, the conference of prime ministers reached no agreement. The central government insisted that the Allied demands would have to be met, and Bavaria's Minister President von Kahr refused to comply. Kahr added that Bavaria would await the outcome of the London conference before making a decision. This stand was reaffirmed on February 8 by a council of the Bavarian ministry, and reiterated by Kahr before the Bavarian diet on February 17 and March 7. At this point the German government finally lost patience. Faced with Allied sanctions in the West on account of the reparations deadlock, and threatened by possible international complications arising from the Upper Silesian plebiscite, the government was determined to stave off additional trouble with the Allies by taking a firm stand on the civil guard issue. On March 12, a draft bill was introduced in the Reichsrat, the German upper house representing the individual states, which provided for general German disarmament in accordance with articles 177 and 178 of the peace treaty. The bill went to the Reichstag on March 14, was slightly revised in committee, and finally passed into law on March 19, 1921. It was another two and a half months, however, before Bavaria finally admitted defeat and agreed to comply with the law. In the meantime, the issue continued to hang in the balance.[34]

The combination of domestic and foreign political problems which the republic faced by the end of February was indeed formidable—a fact which was not lost on the German Communists.

[33] Schwend, *Bayern zwischen Monarchie und Diktatur* (Munich, 1954), p. 163; H. M. Meyer, p. 58, n. 5.

[34] *Schulthess' Europäischer Geschichtskalender*, N. F., LXII, 1921 (Munich, 1926), pp. 52, 54-55, 57, 61-62, 79, 102-103, 105, 108-109, 192; Schwend, pp. 166-169.

But although they recognized the political potentials of the situation, they were so overwhelmed by what appeared to be a wealth of opportunities that they did not know how to deal with them. The Brandler *Zentrale* resembled a group of explorers at the edge of a vast wilderness, impatient to go, but undecided where to start and how to proceed. Thus in the absence of a clear and suitable plan the Communist leaders resorted to half-measures and improvisations. The program—if the muddle which resulted can be honored with this term—consisted merely of a formula which had served the KPD repeatedly, albeit ineffectually, in the past: strengthen the party, prepare it for action, and infuse revolutionary spirit into the German working class! But there was as yet no clear conception of what kind of action the party was to prepare, nor any clear idea as to what exactly it was to accomplish. In the absence of more substantial plans, the *Zentrale* restricted its activities for the moment to the dissemination of revolutionary propaganda to the masses, leaving the rest of its program to the future.[35] In spite of the recent fiasco of the first Open Letter (January 8, 1921), the *Zentrale*, mindful of the fact that persistence was a virtue, published another manifesto in the *Rote Fahne* on March 4. The appeal was addressed "To the German Proletariat," and began with the jeering observation that the diplomatic negotiations at London had led the German capitalists nowhere. Their surrender to the demands of the Entente powers was imminent, and the present negotiations had but one objective, to sell out German workers in order to reap benefits for German capitalists. The working class had only one alternative—the overthrow of the bourgeois government. No God was going to help the workers; they must help themselves. Then the tone became shrill.

"The German working class faces once again an hour of destiny. Your fate will not be decided in London, but in Germany and by

[35] The ineptness of the Brandler *Zentrale* prior to the March uprising was not only noted by Levi (*Unser Weg*, 2nd ed., pp. 6-11, and *passim*), but aroused comments from various speakers during the Third World Congress of the Comintern. Thus a delegate from the KAPD castigated Paul Frölich's faulty propaganda; Wilhelm Koenen, a member of the *Zentrale*, admitted to the shortcomings of the party's policies prior to the *Aktion*, but blamed them on the Levi faction; Heckert took a very similar line to Koenen's; and Radek delivered his customary vitriolic sarcasm in his assessment of the clumsy tactics employed by the Brandler *Zentrale* prior to March 17, 1921; *Protokoll des III. Kongresses der K.I.*, pp. 239, 313, 461-462, 532-533.

you. . . . The choice is yours. . . . You cannot evade this struggle. . . .
Hesitate no longer. You have nothing to lose. Be resolved to take
action. Demonstrate on Sunday [March 6], stir up all who are
dilatory. March against your oppressors! Against the dual yoke of
foreign and German exploiters! For the Communist reconstruction!
Away with all bourgeois governments! For the rule of the working
class! Alliance [*Schutz-und Trutzbündnis*] with Soviet Russia! Economic Union with Soviet Russia!"[36]

This appeal elicited a letter from Paul Levi the following day.
Directing himself to the *Zentrale*, the former party chairman called
the appeal mere irresponsible propaganda, and its slogans unconvincing except to members of the KPD. He charged that the *Zentrale* had surrendered to the Berlin Left when the new line of propaganda was adopted. Instead of expounding highly unrealistic aims
in the appeal, the *Zentrale* should have retained "Alliance with
Soviet Russia" as its only slogan, without the other nonsense which
at the moment could have no effect on most Germans. His letter
closed with the words: "I see in the general attitude a weakness of
the German *Zentrale*, the consequences of which I am as yet unable
to foresee."[37]

This letter resulted in a meeting on March 8 in Berlin between
the members of the *Zentrale* and the Communist Reichstag delegation, which included Levi and Zetkin. Levi's account of this meeting is the only available source. According to him, all but one member of the *Zentrale*, Paul Frölich, proved amenable to his criticism
of the most recent party line. Frölich defended the appeal, and
demanded that once matters came to a head the party should issue
the slogan: "Overthrow the Government and Elect Workers'
Councils."[38] Although no formal decision was taken on the matter,
Levi left the conference apparently in the belief that he had convinced all members of the *Zentrale*, except Frölich, of the clumsi-
ness and untimeliness of the party's latest approach to revolution.
He was soon to learn that he had been mistaken.

For in the first days of March, 1921, the German Communists
received an unexpected visit. From the East appeared three emis-

[36] *Die Rote Fahne*, No. 105, March 4, 1921; also quoted in Levi, *Unser Weg*,
2nd ed., pp. 7-8. This appeal does not appear in the documentary annex of the
East German M.E.L.S.I. symposium, *Die Märzkämpfe 1921*.
[37] Levi, *Unser Weg*, 2nd ed., pp. 8-9.
[38] *ibid.*, p. 10.

saries of the ECCI, the Hungarians Bela Kun and Joseph Pepper, alias Pogany, and the Pole August Guralsky, alias Kleine. The latter two, it appears, kept discreetly in the background and left the transaction of business to Kun. After a short and unhappy career as leader of the Hungarian Communist revolt in 1919, Bela Kun had found a job and a home with the Executive Committee of the Third (Communist) International, where he soon made a name for himself by his unscrupulous tactics and extreme left-wing orientation.[39] Sir Harold Nicolson, who met Kun in April 1919, has given a thumbnail sketch of the then triumphant revolutionary chief: "A little man of about 30: puffy white face and loose wet lips: shaven head: impression of red hair: shifty suspicious eyes: he has the face of a sulky and uncertain criminal."[40] And now Kun had come with his fellow travelers to Germany in order to launch the KPD on the road to revolution.[41]

[39] Brandt and Lowenthal, p. 151.

[40] Harold Nicolson, *Peacemaking 1919* (London, 1945), p. 244. For similar adverse appraisals of Kun see Balabanoff, *My Life as a Rebel* (New York and London, 1938), p. 224, and Borkenau, *The Communist International* (London, 1938), pp. 114-115.

[41] The precise circumstances of this interlude are still largely a matter of conjecture. For instance, we do not know with any degree of certainty who exactly was responsible for sending the Kun mission in the first place; what the motives were which prompted the decision; and whether Kun left Moscow with precise instructions, or simply with the authority to use his own discretion once he had appraised the situation. Until very recently the theory prevailed that Kun and his attendants were sent to Germany by the Bolshevik leaders for the express purpose of creating a revolutionary situation. The object of such a move, according to this theory, was to divert attention away from the embarrassing Kronstadt revolt which shook the Soviet Union in the first part of March. This view, with slight variations, can be found in Flechtheim, *Die K.P.D. in der Weimarer Republik* (Offenbach, 1948), p. 73; H. M. Meyer, pp. 30-37, 65-67; Heinz Schürer, *Die Politische Arbeiterbewegung Deutschlands in der Nachkriegszeit, 1918-1923* (diss. Leipzig, 1933), p. 48; Walter G. Krivitsky, *In Stalin's Secret Service: An Exposé of Russia's Secret Policies by the former Chief of the Soviet Intelligence in Western Europe* (New York-London, 1939), p. 32; and even Nollau, *Die Internationale* (Cologne, 1959), p. 62.

Recent scholarship has corrected this conventional theory. Carr, *The Bolshevik Revolution*, III, p. 335, note 2, and Brandt and Lowenthal, pp. 153-154, agree that the Kronstadt revolt as such could not have been a decisive factor as it broke out *after* the emissaries had left Russia (presumably on March 1, 1921, at the latest). Brandt and Lowenthal also refute the theory that the Russian leadership as a whole created an artificial revolution in Germany in order to render the introduction of the New Economic Policy in Russia unnecessary. The authors point out that Lenin submitted the fundamental outlines of NEP to the Politburo on February 8; that the Politburo agreed to the proposals on March 7, and formally adopted them at the Tenth Congress of the Russian Communist Party on March 15, 1921. The authors argue further that since Lenin introduced NEP in Russia when he realized that the revolutionary wave in Europe was on the decline, he would have hardly

Genesis of the March Uprising

The situation which they encountered upon their arrival proved very favorable for their plans. The leaders of the KPD, eager to prove their mettle but at a loss how to proceed, were easy prey for Kun who, in their eyes at least, represented the will of the Kremlin. Whether the party's appeal of March 4 was the handiwork of the *"Turkestaner,"* as Levi called them, is doubtful; it is certain only that no final decision was taken during the first two weeks of March. Kun used this time to convince the *Zentrale* that the KPD must exploit the unique combination of national and international crises for an action of its own. The party, Kun urged, must take the offensive even if it should have to resort to provocative measures. Once an offensive was launched, two to three million German workers

---

chosen this particular moment for endorsing a reckless, adventurous policy in Germany.

But these arguments still do not answer the question of who was responsible for encouraging the KPD to stage an armed insurrection. Brandt and Lowenthal (153) suggest that the instigators of the plan must be sought among the "little bureau" of the ECCI, which included Zinoviev, Bukharin, and Radek. Carr surmises that Kun might have had Zinoviev's blessings for urging a more active policy on the German *Zentrale*, and that Kun, on his own responsibility, may have used the Kronstadt uprising as an argument for persuading the KPD to take action (335, n. 2; 338). Since it is very likely that by March 1921 Kun himself may have been a member of the "little bureau" (he, like Radek and two others, was added to the bureau between the Second and Third World Congresses), it is conceivable that Zinoviev gave him a liberal degree of leeway; (see Degras, ed., *The Communist International, Documents*, I, Royal Institute of International Affairs [London-New York-Toronto, 1956], pp. 453-454 on Kun's membership in the "little bureau"). Ruth Fischer (pp. 174-175) writes that "the action in Germany . . . had been concocted by a caucus of the Russian party, centering around Zinoviev and Bela Kun." She claims that it was planned prior to the Kronstadt rebellion in order "to divert the Russian workers from their own troubles." A similar view is expressed in Borkenau, *The Communist International*, p. 213. Leon Trotsky, *The Third International after Lenin* (New York, 1936), p. 89, states that "the entire ultra-Left wing of the Comintern of that time advocated the line of the March 1921 days," and singles out Bukharin in particular for having expressed the "opinion that unless the proletariat in Europe was 'galvanized' . . . the Soviet power was threatened with certain destruction." It appears, then, that the plan for a German uprising in March 1921 originated in the circle to which Zinoviev, Bukharin, and Kun belonged; but who among these was the spiritual father of the project will probably never be answered.

The accounts differ on the composition of the Kun mission. Borkenau, *The Communist International*, p. 213, and Krivitsky, p. 32, mention only Kun. Carr, *The Bolshevik Revolution*, III, p. 335, Brandt and Lowenthal, p. 151, Buber-Neumann, p. 67, and Flechtheim, p. 73, mention all three men. Fischer, p. 175, mentions Kun and Guralsky, but not Pogany. Rosenberg, *Entstehung und Geschichte der Weimarer Republik* (Frankfurt am Main, 1955), p. 390, refers only to commissars of the Third International; and Levi, who criticizes the *"Turkestaner"* in both of his pamphlets, refrains tactfully from identifying them by name. See below, Ch. VI, on how the delicate subject of the Kun mission was handled during the Third World Congress of the Comintern.

would follow the lead of the Communists. Kun was generous with optimistic estimates, and his enthusiasm captured the imagination of most members of the *Zentrale*. By March 10 Kun felt sufficiently sure of his success to reveal his ideas to Clara Zetkin, who was so shocked by what she had heard that she immediately informed Paul Levi and told him that she refused to have any further conversations with Kun unless witnesses were present. On March 14 Levi himself talked to Kun and was treated to the same grandiloquent schemes which had outraged Clara Zetkin a few days earlier. One might have expected that the former party chairman would have tried his utmost to block Kun's ventures then and there, that he would have used whatever authority his opinion still carried to beat the alarm, to warn his comrades not to listen to a tempter whose ineptness had been so clearly revealed during the Hungarian revolution of 1919. But if Levi did so he has left no record of his attempts. Perhaps he refused to take Kun's revolutionary overtures seriously; perhaps he put his faith in the sanity of his former colleagues or, conscious of his political eclipse, fatalistically shrugged off any further responsibility. Whatever his reasons may have been, Levi resolved to take a vacation and, shortly after his talk with Kun, departed for Vienna, with Italy as his ultimate destination.[42]

[42] The only contemporary accounts of the events related above are in Levi's two pamphlets, *Was ist das Verbrechen?* (Berlin, 1921), pp. 8-9, and *Unser Weg*, pp. 21-22, 28. But Levi, who was still a party member when he wrote *Unser Weg*, and an "independent" Communist when he wrote *Was ist das Verbrechen?*, treated the entire Kun interlude with discretion, and carefully refrained from mentioning names. The same cautious silence on this matter prevailed at the Third World Congress which met in the summer of 1921 (see below, Ch. VI). But although neither Kun nor his companions were mentioned by name during the proceedings, several speakers alluded obliquely to their role in Germany (*Protokoll des III. Kongresses der K.I.*, pp. 263, 295, 297, 299, 305, 317, 425-426, 455). Kun himself spoke only twice; once on a point of order, and again to read a list of names (*ibid.*, pp. 47, 650). The curtain of silence has never been officially lifted by the Communist world. In May 1923, for instance, Wilhelm Pieck denied in the *Rote Fahne* that Kun had been in Germany in March 1921 (*Die Rote Fahne*, No. 102, May 8, 1923). The letter has been reprinted in the appendix of *Die Märzkämpfe 1921*, pp. 164-167. Only Clara Zetkin talked out of turn, apparently inadvertently, when she wrote her *Reminiscences of Lenin* (London, 1929). The little book was written in 1924, completed in January 1925, and published four years later. In it she relates how she and Lenin discussed the so-called "theory of the [revolutionary] offensive," which had been the ideological basis for the March uprising, and quotes Lenin as follows: "Is it a theory anyway? Not at all, it is an illusion . . . sheer romanticism. That is why it was manufactured in the 'land of poets and thinkers,' with the help of my dear Bela, who also belongs to a poetically gifted nation and feels himself obliged to be always more left than the left" (pp. 25-26).

Genesis of the March Uprising

On March 16 and 17, 1921, the *Zentrale* met with the Central Committee in Berlin for a high-level conference, to determine what strategy the KPD was to adopt in the immediate future. Brandler presided and delivered the keynote address, which began with an analysis of the political situation as he saw it. The analysis presented the assembled functionaries and the Communist newspaper editors from every German district with a number of amazing statements. In addition to a sweeping and rapid recapitulation of all existing crises at home and abroad, which ranged from the effects of the London conference and the Upper Silesian plebiscite to the counter-revolutionary plans of the *Orgesch*, Brandler outdid himself by conjuring up the acute possibility of war between the United States and Great Britain. The new party chairman, perhaps affected by Kun's optimism, stated that the chances of conflicts along Germany's borders were nine to one, and that in the event of their outbreak the influence of the KPD would extend beyond the four to five million [sic!] Communists.

"I maintain that we have in the Reich today two to three million non-Communist workers who can be influenced by our Communist organization, who will fight under our flag . . . even in an offensive action [started by the KPD]. If my view is correct, then the situation obligates us to deal with the existing tensions at home and abroad no longer passively; we must no longer exploit . . . [them] merely for agitation, but we are obligated . . . to interfere through *Aktionen* in order to change matters in our sense."[43]

See also the following on the Kun mission: Brandt and Lowenthal, pp. 151-155; Carr, *The Bolshevik Revolution*, III, pp. 335-338, *passim*; Borkenau, *The Communist International*, pp. 212-214; Krivitsky's (rather overdrawn) account, p. 32. Cf. Radek, "Der Fall Levi," *Soll die Vereinigte Kommunistische Partei Deutschlands . . .*, 2nd ed. (Hamburg, n.d.), pp. 107-119, *passim*, in which the issue is carefully avoided. Flechtheim, p. 73, is inaccurate.

[43] Levi, *Unser Weg*, pp. 22-23. Here again, Levi does not mention Brandler by name but merely refers to a "responsible speaker." But the official party report of the conference in *Bericht über die Verhandlungen des 2. Parteitages der K.P.D. (Sektion der K.I.), abgehalten in Jena vom 22. bis 26. August, 1921* (Berlin, 1922), p. 61, lists Brandler as the principal speaker. So do Radek and Malzahn in *Protokoll des III. Kongresses der K.I.*, pp. 463 and 553. Cf. Brandler's apologia, *War die Märzaktion ein Bakunisten-Putsch?* (Berlin-Leipzig, 1921), pp. 12-20, where he tries to refute Levi's charges.

It appears that Levi obtained the minutes of the conference from Frau Anna Geyer whose husband, Kurt Geyer, was an alternate (*Beisitzer*) in the *Zentrale*, and at the time the party's delegate to the ECCI in Moscow. Frau Geyer, acting in a secretarial capacity, had access to the files and, being in sympathy with the Levi

The speech was followed by a general discussion in which the members of the *Zentrale* voiced their support of Brandler's theses.[44] The most enthusiastic endorsement came from Paul Frölich, who called the projected plan of action a "complete break with the past" because the Communists, up to then always on the defensive, had finally reached the point when they would have to challenge fate by way of revolution.[45] Frölich elaborated that "we must now . . . go over to the offensive. . . . We can aggravate the existing [international] complications tremendously by calling on the masses in the Rhineland to go on strike, thereby sharpening . . . the prevailing differences between the Entente and the German government."[46] In Bavaria the party's task would be provocation of the civil guards, in order to stir up trouble in that region.[47]

Similar sentiments were voiced by Ernst Reuter-Friesland, who represented the Berlin organization in the Central Committee. He told the conference that the party must take action now, even if the Communists should find themselves fighting alone in the coming struggle.[48] But the activists were not unopposed.[49] Dissenting voices were raised, one of them by Heinrich Malzahn, a union official, member of the Reichstag, and an adherent of the Levi faction. Malzahn, unimpressed by Brandler's rhetoric which struck him as exceedingly hazy, suggested that it was inadvisable to sanction blindly any future commitment by the party for a revolutionary offensive.[50] But his objections and those raised by like-minded sceptics carried no weight. The opponents of the suggested policy of action were hesitant and irresolute in their attempts to combat the bravado of the assembled party leaders.[51] "The best lack all convictions, while the worst are full of passionate intensity," wrote

---

faction, made them available to the former party chairman upon his return from his journey abroad; See *Protokoll des III. Kongresses der K.I.*, pp. 594-595; also 581-582.

[44] *Taktik und Organisation*, p. 28.

[45] *Protokoll des III. Kongresses der K.I.*, pp. 465, 553.

[46] Levi, *Unser Weg*, p. 23.

[47] *ibid.*, pp. 23-24.

[48] *Protokoll des III. Kongresses der K.I.*, pp. 553, 574.

[49] In *Bericht über die Verhandlungen des 2. Parteitages*, 1921, p. 61, reference is made to only one dissenting vote when the decisions of the conference were adopted. During the preceding debate, however, opposition to the projected plans was voiced by more than one delegate; *Taktik und Organisation*, p. 28.

[50] *Protokoll des III. Kongresses der K.I.*, p. 553.

[51] *ibid.*, p. 575; *Taktik und Organisation*, p. 28.

William Butler Yeats in 1919, and his words well sum up the atmosphere in which the KPD leadership in March 1921 decided to embark upon revolution. Kun and his friends, though not personally in evidence during the conference, ultimately carried the day. In a series of resolutions it was decided to alert the party and to work toward a further increase of tensions wherever feasible. The party was to engage in armed struggles as soon as the combination of crisis atmosphere and Communist agitation produced an outbreak of violence anywhere. The overthrow of the existing German federal government was to be the first objective of the projected operation. "Overthrow the Government" was to serve as a fighting slogan in conjunction with the familiar demand, "Alliance with Soviet Russia." Finally, in order not to jeopardize needlessly the success of the whole scheme, the conference resolved to make every effort to postpone the *Aktion* until after Easter week, a period unsuitable for strikes since factories were closed.[52]

The decision was reached, the plans were laid, but the party's freedom of action was lost even before the conference voted to adjourn. In her last editorial, published in the *Rote Fahne* on January 13, 1919, Rosa Luxemburg had warned that "the revolution just does not operate of its own accord, on an open battlefield, and according to a plan cleverly laid by 'strategists.' Its opponents can *also* take the initiative; moreover, they usually avail themselves of

[52] *Taktik und Organisation*, p. 28; cf. the more carefully worded official account in *Bericht über die Verhandlungen des 2. Parteitages*, 1921, p. 61. Some members of the *Zentrale* hoped that beyond the overthrow of the government, which was only the first objective of the KPD, a successful revolution would enable the Communists to capture power of the state, and then to establish the dictatorship of the proletariat. This is evident from the record of the hearing which the *Zentrale* gave Levi on May 4, 1921, when he appealed his expulsion from the party; Levi, *Was ist das Verbrechen?*, pp. 14-16.

Brandt and Lowenthal, pp. 154-155, have developed another theory. They argue that the Communist leaders had no illusions about the party's prospects for capturing power of the state, though this fact did not prevent them from unleashing a bloody civil war. The authors speculate that Kun may have tried to force the Reichswehr, acting in response to the chaos created by the Communists, to establish a military dictatorship. The Reichswehr, once in control of the state, would then make an alliance with Soviet Russia against the Entente. Such speculation is farfetched and unconvincing. The authors' account exaggerates and misrepresents the closeness of the contacts which then existed between Reichswehr and Red Army. Furthermore, it is very unlikely that Kun, a Comintern agent, would have wittingly or unwittingly pursued a political course which did not coincide with the objectives of the Communist International, but rather with those of the rival Russian foreign office.

it more often than does the revolution."[53] Brandler, his colleagues, and Kun and company were soon to learn how true her observation was. While the conference was still in session, on March 17, the Communist leaders received word that the Social Democratic *Oberpräsident* (approx.: governor) of the Prussian province of Saxony, Otto Hörsing, had the day before issued a proclamation announcing his intention to dispatch police forces into the Eisleben-Mansfeld districts of the province. The proclamation stated that the purpose of this measure was the restoration of order and security in that strike-ridden industrial region.[54] The occasion for which the *Zentrale* had been waiting so eagerly had arrived, but prematurely, and from an unexpected quarter. All of a sudden the Communists were forced to face an unforeseen situation in which their opponents had taken the initiative.

Situated in the heart of Germany, the Prussian province of Saxony and the neighboring states of Thuringia and Saxony formed an economic unit which in industrial importance ranked with the Ruhr region and Upper Silesia. Prussian Saxony was the home of the Leuna Works which produced gasoline and chemicals; it was also a mining center where lignite, potash, and copper slate were dug. It rated high in steel production and had a number of processing industries.

The region was densely populated by industrial workers and had already seen labor trouble before the war. In January 1910, during a strike wave in the Mansfeld coal district, the regular army was sent in to maintain order.[55] The district of Halle, one of six regional organizations which as early as 1913 belonged to the left wing of the SPD, was expelled by that party in the fall of 1916, and in the spring of 1917 participated in the founding of the Independent Social Democratic Party.[56] After the November revolution, radicalism in

---

[53] Luxemburg, *Ausgewählte Reden und Schriften*, II (Berlin, 1955), p. 711; italics in the original.

[54] Text in *Die Rote Fahne*, No. 128, March 17, 1921.

[55] Schorske, *German Social Democracy 1905-1917* (Cambridge, Mass., 1955), p. 180; cf. Gustav Noske, *Erlebtes aus Aufstieg und Niedergang einer Demokratie* (Offenbach-Main, 1947), p. 204, where the author maintains that the Mansfeld mining region was politically untroubled and quiet until 1918.

[56] Schorske, pp. 282-283, including Table III; M.E.L.S.I., *Märzkämpfe 1921*, p. 19.

the region became endemic. The rapidly expanding lignite mining and chemical industries attracted many newcomers, especially from the western provinces, after Germany, under the terms of the peace treaty, lost the large hard coal deposits of Alsace-Lorraine and Eupen-Malmedy. The new arrivals included a good number of rootless and shiftless people, many of whom had been toughened, if not brutalized, by years of trench warfare. Apart from these local conditions, the region shared with the rest of the country the political confusion, economic dislocation, and the disillusionment and demoralization which followed in the wake of the lost war. Itinerant agitators, roving from mining town to mill town, addressed audiences of disgruntled and hungry workers who listened eagerly to anyone who offered to improve their miserable lot.[57] Immediately after the war the region became a stronghold of the USPD, but, as economic conditions deteriorated further, the Communists gained ground. In the elections to the Prussian diet on February 20, 1921, in the electoral district of Halle-Merseburg, the KPD obtained 197,113 votes as compared to 70,340 for the SPD, and 74,754 for the USPD.[58]

The Prussian government realized as early as 1919 that the province of Saxony, notably the Halle district, was a center of economic and political unrest. Wildcat strikes, clashes between workers and police, and thefts in factories and on the farm lands occurred with increasing frequency. After the Kapp Putsch, a state of siege was proclaimed in the province and was not lifted until September 1920. In the following month the Prussian Minister of the Interior Carl Severing suggested to the *Oberpräsident* of Prussian Saxony, Otto Hörsing, that a drastic reorganization of the police in the troubled region was essential if order and security were to be restored. It was also known that the population had surrendered only a small number of arms after the upheavals which had followed the Kapp Putsch, and the existence of undiscovered arms caches was a constant source of concern to the Prussian authorities.[59]

[57] Noske, *Erlebtes aus Aufstieg und Niedergang einer Demokratie*, p. 204; Stampfer, *Die vierzehn Jahre der ersten deutschen Republik*, 3rd ed. (Hamburg, 1947), p. 218.
[58] M.E.L.S.I., *Märzkämpfe 1921*, p. 20.
[59] Walter Drobnig, *Der mitteldeutsche Aufstand 1921: seine Bekämpfung durch die Polizei* (Lübeck, 1929), p. 2. This is an account by a police major who took part in suppressing the uprising.

The situation continued to deteriorate during the winter months of 1920-1921. The Prussian government received complaints from factory owners and farmers who charged that thefts were increasing. All attempts to prevent theft by means of private plant detectives, bodily searches, and stricter supervision were answered by spontaneous strikes, beating of guards, sabotage, and other terroristic acts. Conditions were particularly tense in the Leuna Works near Merseburg, and in the Eisleben copper slate works. Both industrial plants were harassed by strikes at the end of January and the beginning of February, 1921. At Leuna the issue was a demand for shorter hours, at Eisleben resistance to the presence of plant detectives. Both strikes were settled, apparently by promises on the part of management which satisfied the workers.[60]

In view of the constant stream of complaints which reached the office of the *Oberpräsident*, Hörsing called a conference at Merseburg for February 12 to which he invited the *Landräte*, mayors, and chief representatives of industry from the region. The discussions at the conference revealed a gloomy picture, and Hörsing was particularly shocked by reports that farmers had their manure carted away under cover of darkness.[61] It is uncertain whether the decision to send a police expedition into the Eisleben-Mansfeld districts was reached on that occasion or only on February 28, when Hörsing called another conference with the same participants. In any event, plans for such a measure were definitely made in February.[62] The original plan called for the occupation of Eisleben by 300 policemen, and of Hettstedt by 200. The occupation was not to commence before March 19 in order not to jeopardize the plebiscite in Upper Silesia, scheduled for March 20. Hörsing was afraid that an operation at an earlier date might harm the German cause in the plebiscite

[60] For details on the situation in Prussian Saxony prior to the March uprising see, for the government's point of view, the testimonies of Severing, Hörsing, Weismann, and lesser figures in *Preussischer Untersuchungsausschuss*, pp. 1-2, 41-42, 66, 76-100, 109, 113-115; also Drobnig, p. 3. Cf. the Communist point of view in *Taktik und Organisation*, pp. 31-32, and M.E.L.S.I., *Märzkämpfe 1921*, pp. 66-76.

[61] *Preussischer Untersuchungsausschuss*, p. 115.

[62] Hörsing stated in his testimony before the investigation committee of the Prussian Landtag that the decision for the measures outlined above was taken during the conference of February 12, 1921 (*ibid.*, p. 116). But in a document entitled "Auszug aus einem Bericht Hörsings 'Die Ursachen des Aufstandes in Mitteldeutschland' vom 4. Mai 1921 an das preussische Ministerium des Innern," reprinted in M.E.L.S.I., *Märzkämpfe 1921*, p. 168, it appears from Hörsing's presentation that a final decision was only reached on February 28, 1921.

by reducing rail transportation needed to take voters to the region, and by prompting possible sympathy strikes on the part of railway personnel.

It seems that up to this point Hörsing considered the pacification of his bailiwick as strictly his own responsibility, to be handled by local officials and local police forces. Though he kept the Prussian government abreast of developments, Hörsing was apparently not eager to have his superiors interfere in what he believed were his own affairs. There was in addition a distinct difference of opinion as to what exactly the projected police occupation was to accomplish, and against whom it was to be primarily directed. Hörsing went out of his way to emphasize the non-political nature of the disturbances, and before and after the uprisings in central Germany insisted that all his efforts were directed toward restoring the authority of the state (in this case, Hörsing's authority), which was being undermined by criminal elements and trouble makers.[63]

In contrast to Hörsing's parochial views, the Prussian State Commissioner for Safeguarding Public Security, Dr. Weismann, saw central Germany primarily as a political powder-keg which at any moment could be blown sky high by Communist conspirators. But Weismann was in a difficult position. His suspicions were largely based on intuition, a fact which he admitted after the uprising, and as he was unable to prove that left-wing radicals in Prussian Saxony were planning a revolt, he could not convince either Severing or Hörsing of the validity of his point of view.[64]

Severing's ideas on how to handle the unruly province differed from both Hörsing's and Weismann's. Severing was willing to allow the *Oberpräsident* a free hand as long as unrest remained restricted to Prussian Saxony and did not acquire political overtones. Thus he kept in touch with developments and, although he was unimpressed by Weismann's somber predictions of a putsch, he did not rule out the possibility that the Communists would sooner or later exploit

[63] For Hörsing's views see *Preussischer Untersuchungsausschuss*, pp. 118, 120; for Weismann's, *ibid.*, pp. 5-7. According to Drobnig, pp. 3-4, the occupation by the police was initially to be restricted to the Mansfeld district. The area of occupation was extended only on March 14, the day after the plot against the *Siegessäule* (see below) was discovered.

[64] *Preussischer Untersuchungsausschuss*, pp. 6-7. However, compare his earlier statement (pp. 2-3) where he supported Hörsing's and Severing's assertions that the police action was planned exclusively as a "war on crime," not as an anti-Communist crusade.

the tensions in the Mansfeld region. In such a case, Severing was determined to "clear the air" by every means at the disposal of the Prussian government.[65]

The moment when Severing decided to interfere arrived on March 13, 1921. On that day, an unsuccessful attempt was made to dynamite the *Siegessäule* (victory column), a famous and venerable landmark in the heart of Berlin. Twelve pounds of high explosives, packed in a cardboard box, were discovered by visitors to the monument on the morning of March 13. Only a defective fuse had prevented damage, and possibly casualties.

A number of East German historians, who in February 1956 conducted a colloquium on the March uprising, have once again proffered a charge, which dates back to 1921, that the attempt against the *Siegessäule* was part of a deliberate plot by the Prussian government to implicate the Communists, and that the dynamite was in fact placed by police spies.[66] Since this charge constitutes the key argument on which the Communists, then and now, have based their interpretation of the origins of the March uprising, it will be necessary to dwell briefly on the bomb plot.

When the dynamite was discovered, 50,000 marks were offered as a reward to anyone who could lead the police to the persons who had placed it. In addition, a thorough description of the bomb and its wrappings appeared in the newspapers. The description stated that six kilograms of dynamite had been placed in a cardboard box marked "Dr. Oetkers Saucenpulver," that the color of the box was brown, and that the detonation caps were marked "Anhaltische Sprengwerke." On March 21, thus after the police occupation in central Germany had begun, the Berlin police arrested eleven persons, some of whom carried membership cards of the KAPD. These men confessed that they placed the bomb. The explosion, according to the testimony of some, was intended to intimidate the popula-

---

[65] *ibid.*, pp. 95-113, esp. pp. 101-102, 107, 109; furthermore, Severing's memoirs, *Mein Lebensweg*, 1 (Cologne, 1950), pp. 321-323. Neither account is entirely convincing, however, and must be supplemented by Weismann's testimony with its barely concealed resentment at Severing's preference for Hörsing's rather than Weismann's own interpretation of the situation in Prussian Saxony; see *Preussischer Untersuchungsausschuss*, pp. 6-7.

Severing's presentation of events seems to be colored by his attempt to justify his own position which at the time was being attacked by the Right as "too lax"; *Schulthess'*, 1921, pp. 116-118.

[66] *Taktik und Organisation*, p. 62; M.E.L.S.I., *Märzkämpfe 1921*, pp. 23, 71-72.

tion, initiate a new revolutionary wave and, incidentally, mark the first anniversary of the Kapp Putsch. None of the persons arrested revealed the identity of the man who had given them their orders. None of them was a member of the KPD.[67]

There is little doubt that this project was neither conceived nor executed by any political party, but was a typical example of "individual terror" on the part of revolutionary cranks, who abounded in Germany during the postwar period. According to the account of Max Hoelz, one of the most colorful revolutionaries of this period,[68] the idea of blowing up the monument came from a freewheeling radical named Ferry, alias Hering. Ferry met Hoelz in Berlin (no date is indicated, except that Hoelz went to Berlin in December 1920), and asked for money with which to buy explosives necessary for his plot. He promised in return to manufacture bombs and hand grenades for Hoelz. The deal went through, to the satisfaction of both individuals concerned.[69]

The *Siegessäule* incident convinced Severing of the need for a large-scale, state-supported operation in central Germany. Since all indications pointed toward the plot's having originated in the prov-

[67] For coverage of the bomb plot see the following newspapers: *Vorwärts*, No. 122, March 14; No. 123, March 15; No. 136, March 22; No. 138, March 23; No. 140, March 24; Nos. 142-143, March 26; No. 148, March 30, 1921. *Frankfurter Zeitung*, No. 193, March 14; No. 197, March 15; No. 218, March 23; No. 224, March 25, 1921.

Severing stated in his testimony (*Preussischer Untersuchungsausschuss*, p. 106) that the explosives were wrapped in a copy of the *Hettstedter Zeitung*, a clue for the police to direct their search toward Prussian Saxony (see also Severing, *Mein Lebensweg*, I [Cologne, 1950], p. 322). This vital piece of evidence was never mentioned in the newspapers, although the police had taken great pains to describe other details of the bomb with minute thoroughness. Why was this bit of information withheld from the public? Here is definitely a weak link in the case for the Prussian government, unless one assumes that this particular clue was kept secret in order not to forewarn the plotters. But why, then, did the press report that the detonation caps were marked "*Anhaltische Sprengwerke*"? This clue pointed after all to the same region. However, the East German historians have not even bothered to point out this inconsistency in Severing's story but have stuck, without further ado, to the blunt charge of police provocation.

[68] On Hoelz's role in the revolutionary movement see below Ch. v.

[69] Max Hoelz, *From White Cross to Red Flag; the Autobiography of Max Hoelz, Waiter, Soldier, and Revolutionary Leader* (London-Toronto, 1930), pp. 126-129. A list of arrested plotters, given in *Vorwärts*, No. 156, April 4, 1921, contains neither a Ferry nor a Hering. But on the following day, *ibid.*, No. 157, April 5, 1921, the paper reported a confession by the defendants that the man who assigned them the mission to blow up the monument was called Ferry; and when they were shown pictures of Hoelz, they claimed that he and Ferry were identical. Neither the account of Hoelz nor the statement of the defendants sounds very convincing, and it may well be that the full truth of the matter will never be known.

ince of Saxony, Severing dispatched police agents of the criminal detachment to the region, with instructions to investigate whether dynamite had been stolen there.[70] He also ordered police reinforcements from Berlin and other places to be alerted for the projected operation, and arranged with Hörsing that another conference be called at Merseburg on March 17.[71] One day before the conference was held, Hörsing published his proclamation to the workers in the central German industrial districts. It was a lengthy appeal which began with a description of diverse lawless acts that of late had increased in number and severity. Wildcat strikes, robbery, looting, and terrorist activities by roving armed bands headed the list of offenses. The damages done to agricultural and industrial property were mentioned, and also bodily injuries inflicted on guards who had tried to prevent theft and looting. The appeal called attention to the fact that workers who had refused to go on strike had been threatened, and at times brutally beaten. Furthermore, lawfully elected factory councils had been replaced on many occasions by so-called action committees. Hörsing pointed out that his impression during a recent tour of inspection had been that these outrages were not instigated by Communists, but by "international criminals" who were posing as Communists and were using the most absurd slogans in their attempts to stir up trouble.

The appeal closed as follows:

"In the interest of labor, agriculture, industry, commerce, and trade I have given orders that strong contingents of police forces will be sent into many towns of the industrial region within the next few days. . . . The police forces will treat with equal firmness both the criminals themselves and all those who should attempt to pre-

---

[70] Severing stated in his testimony that additional dynamite was found in Berlin, following a police search on March 14, and that all clues pointed to central Germany (*Preussischer Untersuchungsausschuss*, p. 97). According to Hörsing, no theft of explosives was reported to him prior to the discovery of the plot on the *Siegessäule*, but such thefts were subsequently discovered by police investigators sent by Severing to central Germany on March 14 (LHA Magdeburg, c 20 1 b 4797, x, no pages given, as quoted in M.E.L.S.I., *Märzkämpfe 1921*, p. 72). In his testimony, Hörsing was less specific on this point (*Preussischer Untersuchungsausschuss*, p. 116). The East German publication implies that these belated reports of theft were mere fabrications on the part of the government. This charge fails to take into account the possibility that small thefts of explosives could have easily escaped notice in a mining area unless special efforts were made to keep a close check on available stock at all times.

[71] *Preussischer Untersuchungsausschuss*, pp. 97, 116.

vent the forces from carrying out their duty, offer open opposition, or try to incite the population . . . in an effort to hinder the police forces in the execution of their mission."[72]

The conference on March 17 was attended by Hörsing, Severing, Weismann, the highest administrative official of the district of Merseburg, *Regierungspräsident* von Gersdorff, and representatives of all political parties except the Communists.[73] The discussion was primarily concerned with strategy, and two days later, March 19, the police occupation began.[74]

Who, then, bore the largest share of responsibility for the ensuing disorders? The Communists put the entire blame on the Prussian government in general, and on Severing in particular, charging that the workers of central Germany were to be provoked into active opposition, so that Severing could crack down and settle accounts with the Communists.[75] But the proponents of this theory conveniently disregard a number of relevant facts. They discount, or even deny, the role played by Bela Kun and his fellow *"Turkestaner,"* who spent the first half of March trying to sell their plan for a revolution to the *Zentrale* of the KPD. They also misrepresent the tenor of the debate at the Central Committee meeting on March 16 and 17, falsify the reasons why the conference was called in the first place, and do not mention either the *Zentrale's* intention to prepare for an uprising before Hörsing's appeal became known to the delegates, or the objections that were raised against these plans by some of the functionaries present. Although the fact is mentioned that one faction at the conference favored a theory of revolutionary offensive, no attempt has been made to point out the effect of this theory on the decisions taken by the party caucus on March 17.[76] True, the uprising which the KPD originally conceived was to have taken place after the Easter holidays, and, according to the party theoreticians,

---

[72] Text reproduced in *Die Rote Fahne*, No. 128, March 17, 1921.

[73] *Schulthess'*, 1921, p. 105 gives the date of the conference as March 18, but both Severing and Hörsing testified that it was held on the day after Hörsing published his appeal, thus making it March 17. Since *Schulthess'* gives the wrong date for the plot on the *Siegessäule* (*ibid.*, p. 105) I have accepted the date given by Hörsing and Severing; *Preussischer Untersuchungsausschuss*, pp. 97-98, 116.

[74] *Preussischer Untersuchungsausschuss*, p. 98; *Schulthess'*, 1921, p. 106.

[75] M.E.L.S.I., *Märzkämpfe 1921*, pp. 21-26, 66-76, and *passim*; also Walter Ulbricht, *Zur Geschichte der deutschen Arbeiterbewegung; Aus Reden und Aufsätzen*, I (Berlin, 1953), p. 50.

[76] M.E.L.S.I., *Märzkämpfe 1921*, pp. 37-45.

was to have grown out of international complications. What happened instead was that the Prussian government unwittingly anticipated the insurrectionist intentions of the *Zentrale* by its decision to execute a police occupation of Prussian Saxony.[77] Taken unawares, the Communists, for reasons which will be discussed shortly, allowed themselves to become involved in a struggle at a time and place not of their own choosing, and under circumstances that favored the Prussian government, which had seized the initiative.

It is conceivable that the March uprising would not have occurred at all if the bomb plot against the *Siegessäule* had not prompted the Prussian government to make a show of force. Persuaded by Severing, Hörsing revised his earlier plan to deal with the disturbances in the province exclusively with his own police forces. The area of occupation, which originally was to be confined to the Eisleben-Mansfeld districts, was extended to include the Merseburg area as well, and the number of police contingents was doubled by calling on outside reinforcements.[78] These measures gave the operation from the beginning an appearance quite out of proportion to its alleged objective, the suppression of a local crime wave. The man behind these changes was Severing.[79] There is good reason to believe that after the *Siegessäule* plot Severing, and through him Hörsing, were converted to Weismann's point of view that the series of incidents discovered during the early part of 1921 were indicative of a contemplated Communist putsch. They happened to be right, but the indications on which the Prussian officials based their assumptions were largely incidental and not part of the actual plan which the KPD finally adopted on March 17.

Despite their suspicions, Severing, Hörsing, and Weismann upheld the official version that the police occupation of Prussian Saxony had no political motives, but was entirely a measure designed to stamp out crime.[80] In view of the fact that the Communists were

---

[77] See Levi's poignant observation on this issue, *Was ist das Verbrechen?*, pp. 9-11.

[78] *Preussischer Untersuchungsausschuss*, pp. 107, 116; Drobnig, pp. 5-8.

[79] *Preussischer Untersuchungsausschuss*, p. 107; Severing, *Mein Lebensweg*, I, p. 322.

[80] Behind this attitude may have been the desire to keep any possible conflict in the region from developing into a civil war. For the same reason, the Prussian government refrained from calling on the army to assist in the police operation, except for "borrowing" one battalion of artillery; *Preussischer Untersuchungsausschuss*, pp. 98-99.

the only political party not represented at the Merseburg conference of March 17, coupled with the large-scale preparations for the impending move, the argument is unconvincing. It was nevertheless maintained after the uprising had been crushed, except for a revealing remark made by Severing. He was questioned by a member of the investigation committee appointed by the Prussian diet as to whether it was true that the police forces employed in Prussian Saxony were intentionally kept below the numbers required for a quick operation lest "the thunderstorm would not have broken, leaving the atmosphere sultry." Severing denied the intention but agreed that the relative weakness of the police proved a blessing in disguise, because it brought the simmering insurrection out into the open where it could be fought.[81] In his memoirs, Severing went even further by adding that "it was not, after all, the objective of the police action merely to punish the misdeeds of a few evildoers, but to pacify the region by means of a thorough disarmament action (*Entwaffnungsaktion*)."[82] To this extent, and only to this extent, can the Communist charge of government "provocation" be considered justified. But it must also be kept in mind that the Prussian officials were leaning over backward not to challenge the KPD openly, going so far as to maintain the legal fiction of an operation against crime. Under these circumstances, the Communist leaders could easily have ignored Hörsing's appeal.[83] That they chose not to do so was to cost the life of many a comrade from the rank and file.

[81] Severing's remark appeared first in a German magazine, *Der getreue Eckart*. It was picked up by the *Berliner Tageblatt* on April 7, 1921, and was quoted by the Communists in *Taktik und Organisation*, p. 32. Severing's commentary on his remark before the investigation committee is in *Preussischer Untersuchungsausschuss*, p. 105.

[82] Severing, *Mein Lebensweg*, I, p. 323.

[83] This point was made by Levi at the meeting of the Central Committee on May 4, 1921; *Was ist das Verbrechen?*, pp. 38-39.

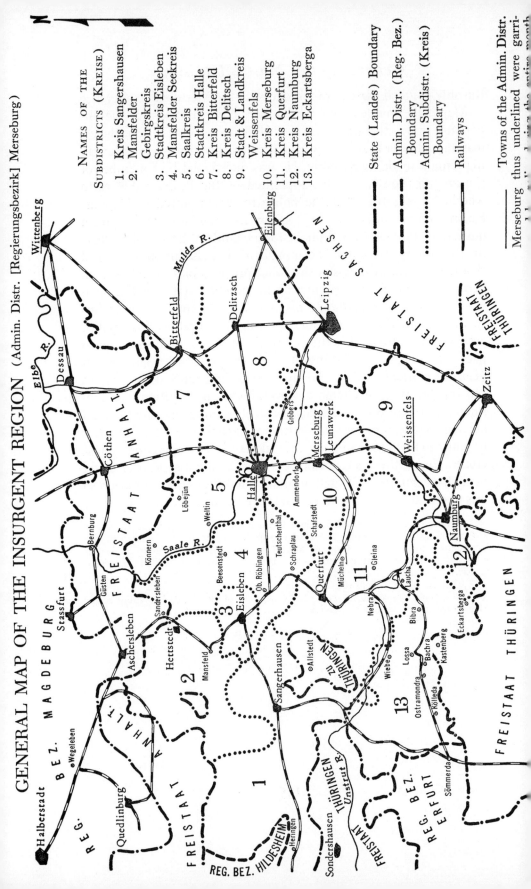

GENERAL MAP OF THE INSURGENT REGION (Admin. Distr. [Regierungsbezirk] Merseburg)

NAMES OF THE
SUBDISTRICTS (KREISE)

1. Kreis Sangershausen
2. Mansfelder
   Gebirgskreis
3. Stadtkreis Eisleben
4. Mansfelder Seekreis
5. Saalkreis
6. Stadtkreis Halle
7. Kreis Bitterfeld
8. Kreis Delitsch
9. Stadt & Landkreis
   Weissenfels
10. Kreis Merseburg
11. Kreis Querfurt
12. Kreis Naumburg
13. Kreis Eckartsberga

State (Landes) Boundary
Admin. Distr. (Reg. Bez.)
   Boundary
Admin. Subdistr. (Kreis)
   Boundary
Railways

Towns of the Admin. Distr.
thus underlined were garri-
Merseburg

CHAPTER V

THE MARCH UPRISING
AND ITS FAILURE

HÖRSING'S MOVE became known at the Central Committee meeting on the morning of March 17 and found the Communist leaders unprepared. As there were at the moment no details, apart from the text of the appeal, the assembled delegates refrained from dealing with the unexpected development except for agreeing on the advisability of postponing any direct involvement in central Germany until after Easter. The four-day holiday, from Good Friday to Easter Monday, was held to be unsuitable for strikes and related actions. The party organizations in the affected region were advised, presumably through those of their members who attended the conference in Berlin, that they should merely threaten to call a general strike once the police marched in, but were not to carry out the threat until the plants and mines were actually occupied. Before the day was over, however, this prudent attitude was abandoned by the *Zentrale* in favor of a barely disguised attempt to exploit the new situation. According to the Communist version, the initial desire to avoid a struggle in Prussian Saxony prior to Easter week was foiled by the Mansfeld miners, who reacted to Hörsing's "provocation" by precipitating a spontaneous uprising, and thereby compelled the KPD to rush to their assistance.

In the light of subsequent events this argument is not convincing. It is much more likely that, after the immediate impact of Hörsing's appeal had worn off, at least some members of the *Zentrale* experienced a change of heart by the time the conference adjourned on March 17. Once again, all signs point to the machinations of Kun with his flair for concocting ill-starred revolutions. In view of the delicacy of his mission, neither he nor his associates attended the Central Committee meeting—the presence of the Comintern agents was to be known only to a restricted circle. It stands to reason, however, that Kun was informed of the outcome of the conference as soon as it stood adjourned, and that he then gave his views on the situation. If Kun had come to Germany with the express purpose of goading the KPD into action, the news of Hörsing's intention to move police into Prussian Saxony was in perfect accordance with his plans. All he had to do was to persuade those members of the *Zentrale* who had already fallen under his influence that the projected police occupation offered an excellent opportunity for the German Communists to launch the revolution which they had just decided was in the offing anyway. He may well have pointed out that any delay would diminish the chances for a successful operation. There were nine more days until Good Friday (March 25), time enough for Hörsing's forces to get a firm foothold in the occupied region unless they were met by organized resistance. And who but the KPD could furnish the leadership for such resistance?

Whatever the circumstances which prompted the *Zentrale* to reverse its earlier decision to postpone action, the fact remains that from March 17 on the KPD sounded and acted like a party resolved upon revolution. At the same time, in order to justify the party in the eyes of the working class in general, and of the Communist rank and file in particular, great pains were taken to give the impression that German Communism was merely responding to the wishes of the treacherous bourgeoisie.[1]

---

[1] It is exceedingly difficult to establish with any degree of certainty what decisions were taken on March 17, on what basis they were taken, and who took them. The available evidence is scanty, and those accounts which exist are either vague, or contradictory, or both.

The intention to postpone action until after Easter week, as well as the instructions to the party organizations in central Germany, are related in KPD, *Taktik und Organisation der revolutionären Offensive* (Leipzig-Berlin, 1921), p. 28. Since this publication was written by proponents of the so-called "theory of the revolutionary offensive," and was subsequently banned by the KPD, there is no reason to doubt its veracity on these particular points. Furthermore Levi, in *Unser Weg* (Berlin, 1921), pp. 26-27 and *Was ist das Verbrechen?* (Berlin, 1921), pp. 12-13, takes issue with the *Zentrale* for having blamed the Mansfeld workers for the failure of the uprising because they allegedly broke discipline when they engaged in combat with the police. Radek adopted a very similar attitude at the Third World Congress. He charged that the *Zentrale* first bombarded the assembled party functionaries at the crucial Central Committee meeting with wild revolutionary theories, and then instructed those among them who represented districts from central Germany to avoid at all costs any conflict before Easter (*Protokoll des III. Kongresses der K.I.* [Moskau, 22. Juni bis 12. Juli 1921] [Hamburg, 1921], p. 463; also Heckert's statement on this issue, *ibid.*, pp. 534-535). Finally, the decision to postpone action is mentioned by Brandler, *War die März Aktion ein Bakunisten-Putsch?* (Berlin-Leipzig, 1921), pp. 16-17. The records of the KPD state only that no decisions were taken by the conference because its members lacked the necessary information upon which to base them (*Bericht über die Verhandlungen des 2. Parteitages der K.P.D.* [Sektion der K.I.] *abgehalten in Jena vom 22. bis 26. August 1921* [Berlin, 1922], p. 61). Carr, *The Bolshevik Revolution*, III (New York, 1953), pp. 335-337, leaves the question open. So does Flechtheim, *Die K.P.D. in der Weimarer Republik*

The March Uprising and Its Failure

On March 17, the Communist press, led by the *Rote Fahne*, opened a propaganda barrage so violent as to be inconsistent with the party's alleged intention to hold the line until after Easter week. Under the heading "The Counterrevolution Strikes," the early edition of the *Rote Fahne* carried a leading article urging the proletarians to abandon their previous passivity, which had merely encouraged the reactionaries. "It is not enough," the paper warned, "to

---

(Offenbach, 1948), pp. 73-74, whose account follows largely those of Borkenau, Schürer, and Rosenberg. Ruth Fischer, *Stalin and German Communism* (Cambridge, Mass., 1948), p. 175, treats the entire March uprising in a very cursory manner, and the East German symposium (M.E.L.S.I., *Märzkämpfe 1921* [Berlin, 1956], *passim*) repeats the hoary legend that the KPD acted partly in self-defense, partly in defense of the miners and workers in Prussian Saxony.

Where does this maze of inconclusive evidence leave us? It appears safe to say that the official party policy agreed upon on March 17 was indeed to postpone any *Aktion* until after Easter. Nevertheless, this plan was rendered inoperative nearly at once. Was there, perhaps, an unofficial party policy, one which was not communicated to the general body of functionaries? It appears from Brandt's and Lowenthal's biography of Ernst Reuter that this is a distinct possibility. The authors, who had access to documents and verbal statements from surviving witnesses which were not utilized by any other accounts, quote a memorandum which Ernst Reuter-Friesland wrote in conjunction with several friends in November or December 1921. The memorandum was written with reference to a series of devastating articles, published in the Social Democratic organ *Vorwärts* in November 1921. The articles presented documented charges that the Communists had artificially engineered the March uprising, and in the process had committed acts of sabotage designed to provoke both the police and the local population (this interlude is discussed below, Ch. VII.) One sentence in Reuter's memorandum reads as follows: "Even some members of the *Zentrale* were not informed about very important occurrences which, in connection with the discussion of the *Vorwärts* revelations, have now been established as being true, or as essentially true" (Brandt and Lowenthal, *Ernst Reuter* [Munich, 1957], p. 194; see also pp. 192-193, and for an even more specific indictment pp. 201-202).

The implication which can be drawn from Reuter's statement is that the *Zentrale* was composed at the time of "initiated" and "uninitiated" members, and we may assume that the first category included Brandler, Frölich, Thalheimer and Ernst Meyer as adherents of Kun. Frölich and Thalheimer, moreover, were the most outspoken proponents of the theory of the revolutionary offensive. To these must be added Hugo Eberlein. Although he was not a member of the *Zentrale*, he headed the party's military-political organization and was directly implicated in those acts of terrorism which *Vorwärts* exposed in November 1921. But he was also the first Communist functionary who, in a party meeting right after the uprising, blamed the failure of the March uprising on the "breach of discipline" allegedly committed by the proletariat in Central Germany (Levi, *Was ist das Verbrechen?*, p. 13). This would explain the origin of the fiction, perpetuated ever since, that the KPD had warned the Mansfeld miners to remain calm until after Easter, but then was compelled to intervene in their behalf when they ignored the Communist directives. Thus it would appear that, from March 17 until the end of the insurrection, Kun and his small band of initiates concealed their tactics from some of their colleagues and from the party at large, and that they accounted for all deviations from the officially adopted plans by blaming uncontrollable outside forces.

139

announce the struggle by way of demonstrations. Only the immediate fight of the proletarian masses against . . . the counterrevolution can frustrate its criminal intentions." There was but one way out of the present crisis: alliance with Soviet Russia which, however, could only be realized "over the bodies of the bourgeoisie." Excerpts from Hörsing's appeal appeared in the early edition, and the full text was printed in the evening edition of the *Rote Fahne*.[2] The Communist targets on March 18 were the *Orgesch* and the SPD. Pointing to Bavaria's refusal to disarm her civil guards, the paper commented at length on the helplessness of the unarmed workers. "The gang of majority Socialists" had agreed that, under the pretext of law, armed might in Prussian Saxony should be permitted to march against "the naked chest of the working class."

"The bourgeoisie stands in arms and refuses to surrender them . . . and the German workers have no weapons! It was not the *Entente* that disarmed them—the *Entente* cannot even disarm the *Orgesch*. The German bourgeoisie and the rabble of Social Democratic leaders have wrested the weapons out of the hands of the proletarians. . . . Now the law means nothing any more; nor does Versailles. Weapons will decide, and the counterrevolutionaries refuse to surrender theirs. . . . *Every worker will simply ignore the law [pfeift auf das Gesetz] and must seize a weapon wherever he may find one!*"[3]

This blast, drafted by Kun himself,[4] led to the confiscation of the issue by the Prussian authorities, whereupon the identical text was promptly reprinted in the *Rote Fahne* on the following day.[5] The entire approach was so clumsy that it met with the disapproval even of Ernst Reuter-Friesland, who registered a protest with the *Zentrale*.[6] Yet the same argument was put forth on March 18 in the Reichstag where the KPD deputy Däumig demanded that the proletariat be armed because the Reichswehr was counterrevolutionary and anti-proletarian.[7]

[2] *Die Rote Fahne*, Nos. 127, 128, March 17, 1921. In view of the fact that the early edition appeared while the Central Committee was still in session, the radical tone of the leading article gives rise to the suspicion that it stemmed from Kun's pen, and that he may have written it on his own responsibility. The fact that he was the author of the extremely violent editorial which appeared the following day (Brandt and Lowenthal, p. 153) lends substance to this hypothesis.

[3] *Die Rote Fahne*, No. 129, March 18, 1921; italics in the original.

[4] Brandt and Lowenthal, p. 153.

[5] *Die Rote Fahne*, No. 131, March 19, 1921.

[6] *Protokoll des III. Kongresses der K.I.*, p. 575; Brandt and Lowenthal, p. 157.

[7] *Reichstag, Stenographische Berichte*, vol. 348, pp. 3207-3210, esp. 3209.

The March Uprising and Its Failure

On March 19, the day the police occupation of Prussian Saxony went into effect, the *Rote Fahne* announced that the Central Committee had decided at its recent meeting to mobilize the party, organizationally and spiritually, for the coming struggle against a bourgeoisie which was collaborating with the *Entente* in a joint effort to exploit the workers. "The difficulties faced by the government in the Upper Silesian plebiscite and the sanctions make it essential that the proletariat develop the greatest possible activity!" All workers would have to be prepared to fight in answer to Hörsing's provocation.[8]

Although the logic of the article left much to be desired, inasmuch as collaboration between Germany and the *Entente* powers was mentioned in one breath with Allied sanctions, the general tenor was clear enough. Every stop of the propaganda organ was pulled in order to bracket events in Prussian Saxony with all the other crisis factors, real or imaginary, that loomed so large in the imagination of the party strategists. It was quite in line with this policy to devote the evening issue of the *Rote Fahne* on March 19 to the problem in Upper Silesia, where the plebiscite was scheduled to be held the next day. The paper pointed out that Polish and German counterrevolutionaries were facing each other in Upper Silesia and were ready to engage in combat. The *Orgesch* in that part of the country was spoiling for a fight because the spirit of nationalism there was strong. The Silesian plebiscite, the *Rote Fahne* informed its readers, was no local affair but concerned every proletarian. The adventure planned by the German counterrevolutionaries in these regions was to be the first battle of the *Orgesch*, to be followed by a second, the battle against the German proletariat. "Once the Polish and German counterrevolutionaries in Upper Silesia begin to clash, the iron fist of the proletariat from both countries must smash in between [the combatants]."[9]

On March 20, the day after the police occupation had gone into effect, the *Rote Fahne* carried the banner line: "Hörsing orders his gang of murderers to march in!" The days of the Bloodhound Noske had returned. The workers in central Germany had decided to offer resistance and thus had set an example which should be followed by workers throughout the country. SPD and Independents came in

[8] *Die Rote Fahne*, No. 131, March 19, 1921.
[9] *ibid.*, No. 132, March 19, 1921.

141

for a sharp attack because they supported Hörsing, and Severing and Weismann were labeled "henchmen of the *Orgesch*." Once again the *Rote Fahne* demanded: "Weapons into the hands of the workers!" And the entire German working class was urged to come to the assistance of their embattled brothers in central Germany.[10]

This frantic appeal to the German working class at large was neutralized by an editorial in the same issue, entitled, "He Who Is Not For Me, Is Against Me! A Word to the Social Democratic and Independent Workers." This editorial, instead of addressing the Socialists as potential allies, told them that they, and the rest of the German proletariat, were on the wrong road; only the Communist Party knew where it was going. After a lengthy enumeration of the virtues inherent in the Communist cause, the *Rote Fahne* listed a number of conditions under which the misled workers might join the Communist ranks, one of which was a barely concealed suggestion that the Socialists should string their own leaders from the lamp posts.[11] It was, in Levi's words, "a declaration of war against four-fifths of the German workers at the beginning of the *Aktion*."[12] The ineptness of the Communist propaganda effort was succinctly expressed by *Vorwärts* when it told its readers: "Moscow needs corpses .... We warn the working class. ... Do not let yourselves be provoked!"[13]

Although slogan after slogan rolled off the Communist presses, no serious unrest accompanied Hörsing's appeal in Prussian Saxony.[14] The *Zentrale*, which gradually realized that it was illusory to rely on the spontaneity of the population, decided that some outside help was needed to arouse the masses, and acted accordingly. On March 18, the Communist district executive for Halle-Merseburg received orders from the *Zentrale* to start a revolutionary action at once. The directives stipulated that Hörsing's police measures were to serve as an excuse for the insurrection. Two local party leaders, Lemck and

---

[10] *ibid*., No. 133, March 20, 1921.
[11] *ibid*., No. 133, March 20, 1921; Levi, *Unser Weg*, p. 30.
[12] Levi, *Unser Weg*, p. 31.
[13] *Vorwärts*, No. 133, March 20, 1921.
[14] Despite their often repeated assertion of the immediate violent reaction by the population to Hörsing's announced occupation plans, the Communists mention in two of their principal accounts that open fighting in central Germany erupted only on March 23. See M.E.L.S.I., *Märzkämpfe 1921*, p. 27; *Taktik und Organisation*, p. 38.

Bowitzki, were entrusted with the direction of the operations (*Aufstandsleitung*), with headquarters to be situated at Halle.[15] The next day, March 19, the Halle district committee of the KPD met for a conference to determine the line of action which the party was to take in the region. Representatives from various subdistricts and individual towns attended the conference, which was chaired by a leading official of the Halle district, Fred Oelssner. Oelssner started out by giving a brief summary of the domestic and foreign political problems which Germany faced, a résumé that followed closely the familiar arguments of Kun. The situation in Upper Silesia, according to the speaker, was tense, and in Bavaria the *Orgesch* was on the move. Large-scale strikes by farm workers in Germany's eastern provinces were assuming political overtones. In view of these circumstances the KPD had to decide on how best to exploit the situation to produce revolutionary action. The problem, thus stated, was then thrown open for discussion. The prevailing atmosphere at the conference was later described by a participant: "We were all convinced that Hörsing's decree would never suffice to produce an *Aktion* in Germany, but that we had to resort to provocation . . . the first shot,

[15] *Vorwärts*, No. 556, November 25, 1921; No. 558, November 26, 1921. Kommunistische Partei Deutschlands, *Die Enthüllungen zu den Märzkämpfen: Enthülltes und Verschwiegenes* (Halle, 1922), p. 7. This, and much of the following account of events that took place in Halle, the strategic KPD headquarters for the March uprising, is largely based on Communist material which was first published in November 1921 by *Vorwärts*. The material consisted primarily of affidavits from party functionaries who participated in one way or other in the events described. The information was collected by the Levi faction which intended to use it at the Third World Congress of the C.I. as evidence that the *Zentrale* had acted irresponsibly when it provoked the disastrous uprising. Clara Zetkin, an opposition delegate, was entrusted with the material when the German delegation left for Moscow in the summer of 1921. At the frontier, customs guards discovered it, confiscated it, and turned it over to the Prussian government. In November, the contents were made available to *Vorwärts*, which proceeded to publish extracts. The KPD, taken by surprise, was forced to admit that the affidavits were genuine but resorted to the desperate device of impugning the veracity of the top Communist functionaries in central Germany, most of whom were still party members at the time. The equivocal attitude which the *Zentrale* adopted on this matter led to another leadership crisis involving, among others, Ernst Reuter-Friesland. The nature and consequences of the crisis will be discussed below, Ch. VII. Eventually, with an air of bravado, the *Zentrale* thought it wisest to publish the statements of the party functionaries who had participated in the uprising, and whose testimony had been published in part by *Vorwärts*, in their entirety in *Die Enthüllungen zu den Märzkämpfen*, hereafter cited as *Enthüllungen*. See also Borkenau, *The Communist International* (London, 1938), p. 220. Aside from the issues of *Vorwärts* cited above, additional material was published in the following issues of this newspaper: No. 560, November 27, 1921, and No. 563, November 29, 1921.

The "Unauthorized" Bid for Power

the notorious first shot, had to come from the side of the enemy."[16]
It was suggested in the course of the discussion that favorable results
might be achieved by harassing the police, who sooner or later were
bound to open fire. Some of the members present were less than
enthusiastic, but all indications of faintheartedness were speedily
quashed from the chair. Oelssner terminated the conference by stating, contrary to the facts, that fighting had already begun and that
it was now the duty of the party to increase the intensity of the struggle. The immediate objective was to arm the workers, then to capture political power.[17]

During the session of the district executive at Halle came the first
reports that the police occupation was already in progress. Another
conference was called in Halle for March 20, this time by the regional executive, and all central German districts sent representatives who gave their individual situation reports. The conference
was overcast by a cloud of deep depression. It was the general consensus that the spirit among the population was anything but revolutionary, and that artificial means would have to be used in order
to bring matters to a head (*um die Sache hochzubringen*).[18]

Indeed, all was not well with the revolutionary spirit of the
masses, which had figured so prominently in the calculations of the
party leaders. The proletarians in Prussian Saxony, who according to
subsequent Communist claims were so desperately in need of assistance, behaved initially with unforeseen timidity in the face of the
Prussian police uniforms. Despite some ripples of discontent and
attempts by agitators to stir up the workers and get them to stage
walkouts, everything remained calm throughout March 19 and 20
(the latter being a Sunday) in the Eisleben area which had been the
first to be occupied.[19] Only on Monday, March 21, had agitation
progressed sufficiently to encourage the Communist district executive of Mansfeld to call for a general strike, and on that day leaflets
were distributed throughout the mining region which, in part, read
as follows:

"Mansfeld workers! The reactionaries have carried out their
threats and have turned your peaceful homes into a staging area for

16 *Enthüllungen*, p. 10. *Vorwärts*, No. 556, November 25, 1921. Until he was
purged in 1957-58, Oelssner was a member of the East German *Politbüro*.
17 *Enthüllungen*, p. 19. *Vorwärts*, No. 558, November 26, 1921.
18 *Enthüllungen*, p. 11. *Vorwärts*, No. 556, November 25, 1921.
19 Drobnig, *Der mitteldeutsche Aufstand 1921* (Lübeck, 1929), p. 9.

the White Guards. . . . They did not come with the ordinary weapons of the police forces but armed with machine guns and handgrenades . . . . Mansfeld workers! Show that you are not slaves and use your power to repulse this onslaught. A general strike must be called. All wheels must stop turning . . . . Workers! you hold the power in your hands. Use it in proper time and be prepared for all eventualities [*seid gewappnet für alle Fälle*]."[20] The appeal was reproduced the same day in the *Mansfelder Volkszeitung*, the local Communist paper, and the strike began to spread, with moderate success, in the heart of this mining area. Yet outside of the immediate Mansfeld district most factories went on working, and there was still no sign of open violence.[21]

Up to this point the *Zentrale* had been content to sit back and grind revolutionary tunes on the propaganda organ. But when the proclamation of the general strike failed to have the desired effect, Hugo Eberlein, who had recently been put in charge of the party's military-political organization (*MP-Apparat*), was dispatched to central Germany on March 22.[22] Eberlein was a Spartacist veteran who had participated in the founding of the KPD, and who in March 1919 represented the young party at the Founding Congress of the Communist International. He was a member of the *Zentrale* from the founding of the party up to the unification with the USPD, and it is conceivable that he was not elected into the Levi-Däumig *Zentrale* because of his delicate position as chief of the *MP-Apparat*. Eberlein enjoyed in party circles a reputation as an experienced saboteur, and was known among the rank and file as "*Hugo mit der Zündschnur* (Hugo with the fuse)."[23]

As soon as Eberlein arrived in Halle he conferred with the local party functionaries. He told them that the *Zentrale* had ordered him to direct strategy in the region and to do his utmost to accelerate the pace of the projected operation. When some scepticism was ex-

[20] Full text in *Taktik und Organisation*, p. 36; also M.E.L.S.I., *Märzkämpfe 1921*, p. 137, and *Die Rote Fahne*, No. 135, March 22, 1921.

[21] Brandt and Lowenthal, p. 156; Drobnig, p. 9. Cf. *Taktik und Organisation*, p. 36.

[22] *Enthüllungen*, pp. 8, 11. *Vorwärts*, No. 556, March 25, 1921. The witnesses do not agree on which date Eberlein made his appearance: one has him arrive on March 22, the other on March 23. The earlier date appears to be the correct one. See also Brandt and Lowenthal, p. 156, who have accepted March 22.

[23] Fischer, p. 175. Eberlein eventually fell victim to the Stalin purges of the thirties (Borkenau, *Der europäische Kommunismus* [Bern, 1952], p. 44).

pressed by two local leaders, Eberlein left no doubt that he intended to carry out the uprising under any circumstances. He rejected all talk of calling off the general strike, and then proceeded to develop his plans. It was essential, Eberlein argued, to win mass support, first in central Germany and ultimately in the rest of the Reich. Artificial means would have to be used to arouse the workers from their passive attitude. He suggested that trusted comrades were to commit acts of violence which could be blamed on the police—in this manner, even the most reluctant of workers would be provoked into action. But Eberlein's fertile imagination provided a number of additional suggestions. He wanted to stage a mock-kidnapping of the two regional Communist leaders, Lemck and Bowitzki, who were nominally in charge of directing the *Aktion.* Other popular leaders should disappear for a day or two, only to re-emerge with fairy tales about how they had been liberated from the reactionaries. Another scheme was to blow up an ammunition train of the police and then to charge in the *Klassenkampf,* the Communist newspaper in Halle, that carelessness on the part of the reactionaries had ruined the homes of numerous workers, and had caused the death of hundreds of victims. Once it became known that the report was false, the paper could print a correction a few days later. Two more targets for Eberlein's store of dynamite were an ammunition factory at Seesen, and a workers' producers' cooperative (*Produktivgenossenschaft*) in Halle.[24]

None of these projects was carried out successfully, although several abortive attempts were made to blow up both the ammunition factory and the producers' cooperative. Eberlein's reaction to the initial failure of the dynamiting exercises was a blast at the inefficiency of the local illegal apparatus which, he complained, did not even own a decent piece of fuse to do a reliable job.[25] Yet before the day (March 23) was over, Eberlein's tactics were largely overshadowed by the activities of a less sophisticated, albeit more renowned, revolutionary figure who had appeared in the Mansfeld district—Max Hoelz.

Hoelz was no unknown to the revolutionary movement. He had

[24] *Enthüllungen,* pp. 8, 9, 11, 12, 16. *Vorwärts,* No. 556, November 25; No. 558, November 26, 1921. The accounts of the witnesses vary slightly with respect to dates and details of events, but are in agreement on the principal facts.

[25] *Enthüllungen,* pp. 8-9. *Vorwärts,* No. 556, November 25, 1921.

first won prominence in 1918, when he organized the unemployed in his Saxon home-town of Falkenstein in the Voigtland during the revolution. His activism and initiative attracted the attention of the entire region at the time, and he won nationwide fame during the Kapp Putsch by his talented organization of workers' brigades, which he led in guerilla warfare all over Saxony. In the course of the fighting he came into conflict with the leader of the Communist Chemnitz branch, Heinrich Brandler, who resented what he termed Hoelz's undisciplined inroads on Brandler's territory. The grudge continued, and after the Kapp Putsch Brandler had Hoelz expelled from the party, which he had joined in 1919. His expulsion from the KPD did not discourage Hoelz from continuing in his role of a German Robin Hood, a "*condottiere* with a social conscience and the temperament of a rebel fighting for the poor and oppressed."[26]

When Hoelz learned on March 21 that a general strike had been called in the Mansfeld district, he left Berlin, where he had lived underground ever since the spring of 1920, and journeyed into the industrial region of Prussian Saxony. He arrived at Kloster-Mansfeld late at night, but still in time to attend a meeting on the general strike. There was, as yet, no mention of armed insurrection. The situation changed on the following day, March 22, when walkouts increased in the Mansfeld-Eisleben mining district, and armed

[26] Anderson, *Hammer or Anvil* (London, 1945), p. 80. For accounts of Hoelz see Fischer, pp. 128-129, incl. n. 11; M.E.L.S.I., *Märzkämpfe 1921*, pp. 105-111; and *Bericht über den 5. Parteitag der K. P. D. (Sektion der K. I.) vom 1. bis 3. November 1920 in Berlin* (Berlin, 1921), pp. 55-59, on the party's debate concerning Hoelz's readmission, which was offered to him, but which Hoelz ultimately turned down. Hoelz's autobiography, *From White Cross to Red Flag* (London-Toronto, 1930), is valuable because it reveals the author's personality and ideas, and also throws light on his movements during the uprising. His criticism of the KPD is particularly interesting in this connection and goes far to explain Hoelz's actions during the March days. He retained his independence throughout the uprising and only cooperated with the local KPD organizations if and when it was convenient for him to do so. He preferred to work with the KAPD with which he was then associated. The tone of his narrative is exceedingly naïve. Hoelz's account is essentially that of a revolutionary idealist to whom political realities were profound mysteries. The social ideas which he expresses are primitive and reminiscent of medieval peasant revolts. The same impression is conveyed by *Max Hoelz, Briefe aus dem Zuchthaus*, ed. Egon Erwin Kisch (Berlin, 1927).

Hoelz was apprehended in the wave of arrests which followed the March uprising. He was tried, convicted, and received a life sentence, but was released in 1928. He went to Moscow where he reportedly was "liquidated" by the OGPU in 1933; Krivitsky, *In Stalin's Secret Service* (New York-London, 1939), p. 35; Fischer, p. 129, note 11; Buber-Neumann, *Von Potsdam nach Moskau* (Stuttgart, 1957), p. 412.

bands prevented non-striking mining crews from entering the pits. During the day Hoelz addressed strike meetings at Hettstedt, Mansfeld and Eisleben, and it was as a result of his Eisleben speech that the situation got out of hand. According to a Prussian police major, Hoelz spoke in support of the general strike, urged his audience to arm themselves, and allegedly incited them to beat up police patrols. His suggestion was followed immediately after the meeting was over, when a group of his listeners marched to Eisleben's market square and attacked four policemen who were out shopping, armed only with dress bayonets. The policemen were rescued before long, but the incident encouraged many unruly elements in the neighborhood, and from the night of March 22-23 on the strike movement began to turn into an open, and spreading, insurrection.[27] Incited by Hoelz and his "adjutant" Josef Schneider, the editor of the *Mansfelder Volkszeitung,* a growing number of persons among the local population provided themselves with rifles, machine guns, and large amounts of explosives, which were easily obtained in a mining area. Some of the weapons came from secret depots which dated from the days of the Kapp Putsch and its aftermath; others were either captured or stolen from the police. Hoelz then began to form shock troops. He recruited strikers and unemployed miners most of whom were in possession of arms, organized them into units, and then descended with his motley troops upon the region around Mansfeld, Eisleben, and Hettstedt. For the next ten days Hoelz's "army" terrorized the countryside by arson, looting, bank robberies, and the dynamiting of buildings, trains, and other suitable targets. Aimless though most of these activities were, Hoelz nevertheless succeeded where the KPD, Eberlein's exertions notwithstanding, had so far failed: only two days after he came to the region, Hoelz had transformed the strike movement into a bloody insurrection.[28]

[27] Drobnig, pp. 9-10. Hoelz has presented a different version of this incident. According to his account (pp. 139-140), he had only urged the workers to support the general strike. Trouble started when the police, following his Eisleben speech, arrested and maltreated several strikers who had attended the meeting. When their comrades tried to liberate them by force, fighting broke out. The incident convinced the workers and Hoelz that it was time to seize weapons and organize fighting units.

[28] Hoelz, pp. 134-143, and 144-164, *passim; Taktik und Organisation,* p. 38. *Vorwärts,* No. 556, November 25, 1921, quotes the report of one witness, Lemck, according to which Hoelz was in Halle as early as March 18, although Lemck did not claim that he saw Hoelz. The account of events pertaining to Hoelz as related

The March Uprising and Its Failure

From March 23 on, the situation in central Germany was extremely confused. Although the strike was spreading, and resistance to Hörsing's police was gathering momentum, the SPD, Independents and unions continued their initial opposition to what they felt was an irresponsible Communist adventure, and made every effort to prevent the workers in Prussian Saxony and elsewhere in Germany from lending support to the movement.[29] There was, moreover, little or no coordination among the various proletarian groups that participated in the insurrection. Communist headquarters at Halle lacked effective control over the operation as a whole, and in particular over developments in the vital mining district around Mansfeld, Hettstedt and Eisleben.[30] Eberlein's presence in Halle could not change this fact. He was given but lukewarm cooperation from the local party leaders, and most of the attempts to extend the scope of the uprising in accordance with Eberlein's unorthodox directives were either bungled, or they actually backfired. For example, the repeated dynamiting and derailing of passenger trains alienated railroad personnel, whose support of the insurrection would have been of vital importance for its success.[31]

Most of the actual fighting took place in the Mansfeld district, the heart of the insurgent region, where Hoelz and his guerilla bands

---

in M.E.L.S.I., *Märzkämpfe 1921*, relies largely on Hoelz's own account, including errors. For a view from the government's side see *Preussischer Untersuchungsausschuss* (see Ch. IV, note 13), *passim*, and Severing, *Mein Lebensweg*, I (Cologne, 1950), pp. 322-323. For a contemporary profile of "General" Hoelz at the "headquarters" of his "army" see a journalist's account in *Vorwärts*, No. 155, April 3, 1921. I was unable to secure either the *Denkschrift über die Märzunruhen im Jahre 1921*, herausgegeben vom Reichskommissar für Überwachung der öffentlichen Ordnung (Berlin, 1921), or *Die Märzunruhen 1921 und die preussische Schutzpolizei. Amtliche Denkschrift des Ministeriums des Innern* (Berlin, 1921), but have consulted excerpts from these documents in M.E.L.S.I., *Märzkämpfe 1921*, and H. M. Meyer, *Die politischen Hintergründe* . . . (diss. Friedrich-Wilhelms-Universität zu Berlin, 1935).

[29] According to Heinrich Malzahn, a Communist functionary in charge of the party's trade-union activities, at most 120,000 workers struck in the central German region at the peak of the insurrection, and at most 200,000 throughout the entire country (*Protokoll des III. Kongresses der K.I.*, pp. 250, 251); cf. Radek's unconvincing attempt to challenge these figures *ibid.*, p. 465). See also Hörsing's estimate on the support which the uprising received (*Preussischer Untersuchungsausschuss*, p. 117).

[30] *Taktik und Organisation*, pp. 71-73; M.E.L.S.I., *Märzkämpfe 1921*, p. 92.

[31] *Enthüllungen*, *passim*; Drobnig, p. 10; Levi, *Unser Weg*, pp. 39-40. Paul Frölich's account in *Taktik und Organisation* denies on page 39 that railway installations were dynamited by insurgents, but contradicts himself on p. 49. For a veiled criticism of these "artificial means" see M.E.L.S.I., *Märzkämpfe 1921*, p. 85.

wreaked havoc and stole the Communists' thunder. Supported by scattered contingents from the KAPD, hordes of unemployed, and the inevitable sprinkling of undefinable drifters who participated in the uprising for reasons of their own, this latter-day Schinderhannes[32] battled police and ransacked the countryside, all in the name of social justice. There was little system to his burning, dynamiting and plundering, but no one, least of all the local KPD, could control him or gain his cooperation. Stubborn and self-righteous, he did not accept advice, much less orders, from anyone. Whoever joined his forces became subject to his command: this happened to a few impatient hotheads from the KPD organization in Halle who, without authorization from headquarters, collected six thousand men during a street demonstration, marched them to the Mansfeld district, and there joined Hoelz.[33]

Relations between KPD and KAPD were also poor during the entire course of the uprising. The radical KAPD men admired Hoelz and hardly disguised their contempt for the KPD. Hoelz rewarded this admiration by handing over to the war chest of the KAPD the money that his desperados robbed from the local banks, and this incurred the jealousy of the rival party.[34] Lack of cooperation between the two Communist organizations was prominently displayed in the "defense" of the chemical works at Leuna, south of Merseburg. This large industrial complex, which employed roughly twenty thousand workers, would have been eminently suited as a strongpoint for the entire insurrection, but the potential strength of the

[32] The "Schinderhannes" was a highwayman by the name of Johann Bückler who terrorized the Rhineland with a band of thugs during the Napoleonic wars. Bückler, like Robin Hood, is purported to have robbed the rich merchants and to have distributed his loot to the poor. Unlike Robin Hood, however, he frequently murdered his victims, hence his nickname. See Carl Zuckmayer's play, *Der Schinderhannes*.

[33] *Taktik und Organisation*, pp. 38, 46, 73-74, and *passim*. *Enthüllungen, passim*. Cf. Hoelz's own account of this particular incident, p. 146. During the Third World Congress, Radek paid Hoelz some very back-handed compliments (*Protokoll des III. Kongresses der K.I.*, pp. 216-220). See also the official, slightly ambiguous, resolution which the congress adopted in honoring Hoelz: Exekutivkommittee der Kommunistischen Internationale, *Thesen und Resolutionen des III. Weltkongresses der Kommunistischen Internationale* (Moskau, 22. Juni bis 12. Juli, 1921) (Hamburg, 1921), p. 68; hereafter cited as *Thesen und Resolutionen des III. Weltkongresses*.

[34] Hoelz, p. 140, and *passim*; see pp. 132-133 for his self-critical comments concerning the acts of individual terror and bank robberies. *Vorwärts*, No. 556, November 25, 1921. See also Levi, *Was ist das Verbrechen?*, pp. 14-15, on the criticism by the KAPD of the KPD, and Frölich's comments on the KAPD activities during the uprising. *Protokoll des III. Kongresses der K.I.*, pp. 227-229. Further, M.E.L.S.I., *Märzkämpfe 1921*, p. 85 and *passim*.

The March Uprising and Its Failure

Leuna works was never effectively utilized.[35] A mammoth protest meeting, attended by an alleged eighteen thousand employees, was held on March 21, and an action committee was elected. Two days later, the Leuna works joined the regional general strike. The majority of workers went home, either to stay there and await the resumption of work, or to join battle against the police. At Leuna proper, a garrison, consisting of an estimated two thousand armed strikers, barricaded themselves inside the works and prepared to defend the compound against a police assault.[36] But the defenders were neither unified nor well organized. The action committee which had been elected on March 21 was dominated by KAPD men who quarrelled incessantly with their comrades from the KPD. No agreement was reached on the essential question of whether they should remain on the defensive, or take the initiative and partake in the regional fighting. A further reason for controversy was the problem of emergency maintenance of the plant's most vital installations, a measure which the KAPD opposed. Mutual recriminations among the members of the action committee, coupled with the failure of KPD headquarters to maintain contact with the garrison, left Leuna an isolated, albeit armed, citadel.[37]

Thus Hoelz's excessive violence, the ineffective efforts of the KPD to gain control over the movement, and the factional rivalries, all combined to jeopardize the chances of the uprising from the outset. Yet, for a few days after the outbreak of fighting, the fate of the insurrection hung in the balance; success or failure depended on whether the government could suppress it before the *Zentrale* extended it beyond central Germany.

On March 23, news of the radical turn of events in Prussian Saxony reached Berlin and was discussed by the cabinets of the Reich and Prussia. Additional bad news came from Hamburg, where labor trouble had erupted the same day, and the authorities had to find means of protecting the country from possible civil war. After some deliberations, which concentrated on central Germany, it was de-

[35] Drobnig, p. 96, calls Leuna the "principal stronghold of the entire insurrection," but indicates that its danger remained primarily potential in nature.
[36] *ibid.*, pp. 45-46. Estimated armaments: 800 rifles, 14 machine guns. But only three machine guns were subsequently captured (p. 107).
[37] H. M. Meyer, p. 73; M.E.L.S.I., *Märzkämpfe 1921*, pp. 29-31, 34, 78-82, 89-92, 98-99. See also the somewhat inconsistent references in *Taktik und Organisation*, pp. 39, 49-50, 54-55, 74-75.

cided not to declare martial law in the insurgent region unless such a step should become unavoidable.[38] Probably at this point, or very shortly thereafter, a decision was reached to rely primarily on police forces, but to keep several army units in readiness. They were to be employed only in case of emergency. The question of whether these Reichswehr contingents would then come under the command of the police or would act independently was temporarily left open.[39]

Meanwhile, disturbing reports continued to reach the capital. Toward evening it became known that fighting around Eisleben had grown more intense, that the Leuna works had been hit by a general strike, and that the insurrection threatened to spread to the state of Saxony, where bomb plots against law courts had been discovered in Dresden, Leipzig and Freiberg. In Halle, where Communist headquarters in charge of regional operations was located, no strikes had developed so far, but the insurgents had distributed pamphlets with the following text: "On to the barricades, long live Soviet Russia! The revolutionary Ruhr district has been cut off by imperialist designs of the *Entente* powers, and central Germany has therefore become the heart of the German revolution. On to the barricades! Conquer the world!"[40]

Equally somber was the news from Hamburg, where the senate had imposed a state of emergency that day at 4 P.M.[41] Under the im-

[38] *Frankfurter Zeitung*, No. 222, March 24, 1921. On Hamburg, see below.

[39] The question of when and how army contingents were to be used was discussed on March 28 and 29, 1921, during two joint meetings held by the cabinets of the Reich and Prussia ("Reichskabinett-Protokolle," Auswärtiges Amt und Reichskanzlei, Germany, microfilm T-120, container 1672, frame D 747640; container 1673, frames D 747642-747643, National Archives, Washington, D.C.). No reference to a discussion of either the central German crisis or the military question is extant in the protocols of the Reich cabinet, but it is evident from the protocols of the meetings on March 28 and 29 that prior deliberations on the use of troops had taken place. The account of the army problem in Otto Braun, *Von Weimar zu Hitler* (New York, 1940), pp. 105-106, conflicts with that of Severing, *Mein Lebensweg*, I, pp. 323-324. Otto Gessler, *Reichswehrpolitik in der Weimarer Zeit*, ed. Kurt Sendtner, introduction by Theodor Heuss (Stuttgart, 1958), omits mention of the March interlude altogether.

For the eventual disposition and use of police units see especially Drobnig, pp. 115-116. For the testimonies of Severing and Hörsing on the issue see *Preussischer Untersuchungsausschuss* (see Ch. IV, n. 13), pp. 98-99, 117-118. For the employments of army artillery units, formally under police command, see Severing, *Mein Lebensweg*, I, p. 323, and Drobnig, p. 112. See also Gordon, *The Reichswehr and the German Republic* (Princeton, 1957), pp. 225-226, and Rabenau, ed., *Seeckt, Aus seinem Leben 1918-1936* (Leipzig, 1940), pp. 257-258.

[40] *Frankfurter Zeitung*, No. 221, March 24, 1921.

[41] *ibid.*, No. 223, March 25, 1921; *Schulthess' Europäischer Geschichtskalender*, N. F., LXII, 1921 (Munich, 1926), p. 107.

pact of these reports, President Ebert became convinced that drastic measures were needed. During the night he consulted with federal and Prussian officials and, still shying away from a declaration of martial law, proclaimed on the morning of March 24 a non-military state of emergency for Hamburg and the province of Saxony. Hörsing was appointed (federal) civilian commissioner and entrusted with the execution of all measures which he deemed necessary for the restoration of order.[42]

As the government was trying to find ways and means to quell the insurrection, the Communist *Zentrale* in Berlin made every effort to spread it beyond central Germany. Placards all over Berlin announced that in Prussian Saxony the (legal) factory councils had been replaced by revolutionary workers' councils, an example which proletarians everywhere should follow. On March 22, the morning edition of the *Rote Fahne* called for mass demonstrations, to be held in the evening of March 24 at four points in the capital. The demonstrators were urged to protest Hörsing's police action and to express their solidarity with their comrades in central Germany. To add some local color, the Berlin workers were also asked to register a protest against the arrest of Ernst Reuter-Friesland by the police.[43] In the course of the day the *Zentrale* changed its mind and scheduled the demonstrations for the same evening, March 22, presumably because somebody had realized that to hold a mass meeting on Maundy Thursday, shortly before the Easter holidays, was inpropitious. Despite the short notice the meetings were well attended, but revolutionary fervor was strikingly absent. Some wind had been taken out of the Communist sails when Reuter-Friesland was released shortly before the demonstrations were held—after he had spent two days in jail the police revealed that his arrest was a case of mistaken identity. His return deprived the *Zentrale* of an effective local slogan and made it necessary to concentrate solely on central Germany. Party spokesmen addressing the crowds urged all workers to stand by and be prepared to come to the aid of their imperiled comrades. The audience listened attentively but without any display of emotion. When some hecklers from the KAPD registered their dissatisfaction with mere preparedness, and demanded that a general strike be called at once, they elicited hardly any response.[44]

[42] Text in Drobnig, "Anlage" 7.   [43] *Die Rote Fahne*, No. 135, March 22, 1921.
[44] *Frankfurter Zeitung*, No. 220, March 24, 1921; Brandt and Lowenthal, pp. 157-158.

The evening edition of the *Rote Fahne* that day was likewise devoted to the situation in central Germany. The editorial emphasized, with unconcealed gratification, that this was the third time since the end of the war that the workers in the Mansfeld district were attracting everyone's attention. This time, however, neither Hörsing nor the *Orgesch* would succeed in provoking the workers to dissipate their collective strength in isolated skirmishes. Nor would the German labor movement as a whole be misled again by so-called anti-putschist phrases which had bred so much cowardice and passiveness in the past. The general strike called by the workers in central Germany was no putsch. It was the beginning of a collective action (*Gesamtaktion*), essential for the German proletariat if it was to prevent in time the disastrous consequences of the inevitable collapse of capitalism. The editorial ended with the usual revolutionary ruffles and flourishes: "The proletarian battalions in central Germany stand ready to fight. German workers, show your revolutionary solidarity, join your brothers, cast off your indifference, get rid of your cowardly and treacherous leaders, and fight—or you will perish!"[45]

Despite all inflammatory slogans the Berliners did not stir. Not even the Communist-sponsored mass demonstrations elicited as yet more than polite curiosity, mixed with the traditional scepticism for which the population of the capital was famous. But on March 23 the *Zentrale* was compensated by encouraging news from Hamburg, Germany's second largest city, where the propaganda efforts of the Red press had fallen on fruitful ground. Widespread unemployment had created a dangerous atmosphere which the KPD skillfully exploited. Communist agitation became noticeable in Hamburg on March 22. On that day the city's Communist leaders, Ernst Thälmann among them, held a conference in the business office of the KPD in order to determine how the Hamburg workers could render immediate assistance to the proletariat in central Germany. It was resolved, among other things, to make use of the unemployed in any mass actions taken.[46]

[45] *Die Rote Fahne*, No. 136, March 22, 1921. Excerpts of various inflammatory Communist appeals which the *Zentrale* issued during the uprising are in *Vorwärts*, No. 563, November 29, 1921.
[46] M.E.L.S.I., *Märzkämpfe 1921*, pp. 57-58. Ernst Thälmann, who moved to the KPD from the USPD in December 1920, joined the Left Opposition faction until his break with Fischer and Maslow in 1924-25. He became chairman of the *Zentrale*

The March Uprising and Its Failure

The local party organ, *Hamburger Volksblatt*, set the tone in an impassioned report on events in central Germany, and called on the workers of Hamburg to prove their solidarity with their comrades in Prussian Saxony. The paper demanded that the government disarm the *Orgesch*, arm the proletarians, create jobs for the unemployed, and call off Hörsing's police action in central Germany. The paper threatened a general strike by Hamburg's proletariat if the government should reject these demands. In order to lend some substance to their threats, the Communists scheduled a protest meeting for March 23 at the Heiligengeistfeld, a fair-ground not far from the waterfront.[47]

Radical Communist agitation proved more effective in "red" Hamburg than in Berlin.[48] On the morning of March 23 a large crowd of unemployed, led by the KPD, marched to the waterfront and invaded three of Hamburg's largest shipyards, Blohm & Voss, Vulkan, and Deutsche Werft. The plant managers tried to order the crowd off the premises by threatening to close down the yards unless they were obeyed. The unemployed shouted back that they wanted jobs and urged the workers in the shipyards to support them. Support was not forthcoming, nor could it have been expected, since most shipyard workers were loyal supporters of the Social Democratic Party. The issue did not long remain in doubt. Arguments led to threats of force, and strong-arm tactics eventually succeeded in dislodging from the yards all opponents of the Communist-led mob. The managers retreated along with the Socialist personnel, and the invaders occupied the premises. Once in possession, they elected *ad hoc* action committees and hoisted red flags. The KPD had attained its objective of infusing revolutionary spirit into a section of Hamburg's labor movement, although this was done at the expense of unemployed desperate enough to act as shock troops for the "revolutionary vanguard." Nothing constructive could have been accomplished in the long run by the forceful occupation of the yards, as the Communist leaders undoubtedly knew.

---

in 1925, and retained this position as the most popular Communist leader of the German party since the deaths of Luxemburg and Liebknecht until his arrest by the National Socialist regime in 1933. He died in a concentration camp in 1944. For Thälmann's activities during the period covered by this study see below, *passim*.

[47] The text of the appeal is in M.E.L.S.I., *Märzkämpfe 1921*, pp. 146-147.

[48] *Enthüllungen*, pp. 23-24.

And the occupation proved of short duration. The KPD had issued instructions to keep the yards occupied, but the crowd within
the gates, the group which occupied the Vulkan wharf, left the
yards in the early afternoon perhaps through some misunderstanding, and marched into the city, presumably to attend the protest
demonstration at the Heiligengeistfeld which was scheduled for 5
P.M. They were met by police forces, who tried to break up the formation, and after heavy street fighting succeeded in dispersing the
would-be demonstrators, including those who had already reached
the Heiligengeistfeld. The police then surrounded the wharves of
Blohm & Voss, firing into courtyards and buildings. By early afternoon the shipyards were cleared, but Hamburg remained dangerous-
ly restless. Street battles between unemployed and police continued
throughout the rest of the day in various parts of the city, and at 4
P.M. the senate proclaimed a state of emergency, which was given
full backing the following day by the federal emergency decree of
President Ebert.[49]

The president's proclamation of a state of emergency for Hamburg
and Prussian Saxony on March 24 posed a challenge to the Communist leaders which they decided to meet head on. With the Easter
holidays just ahead, the *Zentrale* had to do something to sustain
the movement and, if possible, to accelerate its intensity. For this
purpose the KPD called a nationwide general strike on March 24,
urged the proletarians to seize arms, to get organized, and to join the

---

[49] *Taktik und Organisation*, pp. 39-42, 80-81; M.E.L.S.I., *Märzkämpfe 1921*, pp.
58-59; *Schulthess'*, 1921, p. 107; *Frankfurter Zeitung*, Nos. 220, 221, March 24,
1921. The use of unemployed workers as shock troops was not restricted to Hamburg,
but was Communist practice everywhere throughout the March risings. Factories
which continued to work after a general strike had been called were frequently attacked by Communist-led mobs of unemployed and strikers, in an effort to dislodge
those who were unwilling to join the walkout. The ensuing pitched battles heightened the state of confusion but did not substantially further Communist objectives.
In some cases the owners closed down the plants, thereby creating more unemployed.
Those who lost their jobs in this way harbored no tender feelings for the Communists who were responsible for their misfortune. More often, however, the employers refused to shut down, and with their employees defended the premises
against assaults from the outside. They also used the disturbances to discharge
workers who were suspected of being Communists or Communist sympathizers. In
such a case the party was deprived of the opportunity to agitate from within the
factory. Finally, the assault troops of unemployed were easily demoralized, after they
were beaten up by the defenders of the plants, and cursed the Communists for
having led them into trouble. See Levi, *Unser Weg*, pp. 32-33; *Was ist das Verbrechen?*, p. 23; Brandt and Lowenthal, p. 158; *Protokoll des III. Kongresses der
K. I.*, pp. 553-554 (Heinrich Malzahn's report).

struggle against the counterrevolution.[50] It was a desperate step, for all plants closed down anyway from Good Friday (March 25) through Easter Monday. But the response to the Communist appeal was negligible. Both Socialist parties countered the call for a general strike by instructing their members to ignore it. In Berlin, the seat of the *Zentrale*, the strike movement was a total fiasco. Most workers reported to their jobs on the 24th, and only a few factories were idle, despite the aforementioned attempts by the KPD to enforce the shutdown of working plants through attempted invasions by unemployed. These methods aroused sharp criticism even from within the party. Ernst Däumig, for instance, sent a furious letter to the *Zentrale* in which he protested the practice of pitting proletarians against proletarians. Equally indignant were the party officials in charge of trade-union activities, who complained that the tactics employed by the *Zentrale* were wrecking their influence within the unions.[51]

The *Zentrale* scored slightly better in the Ruhr region and the Rhineland. In the Communist *Ruhrecho*, and through handbills, the regional KPD organizations followed the lead of the *Zentrale* by exhorting the population to join the general strike. Throughout March 24 and 25, the Communists kept up an untiring propaganda barrage by calling for demonstrations, for support of the embattled comrades in Prussian Saxony, and for support of the general strike. Party leaders recommended "Easter promenades" through the streets, especially in the working-class districts. They hoped in this way to keep the issue alive over the holidays, and to win support from non-Communist labor for the intensified struggle which they expected in the days ahead. On Easter Monday, armed clashes between workers and police occurred in Essen. During the next few days similar incidents took place in a number of mines, and in nearly every sizable city of the Rhenish region. Only a fraction of the population, however, supported the general strike, most walkouts that were staged were of short duration and, by March 30, order was restored to the region except for some isolated pockets. Germany's

[50] *Die Rote Fahne*, No. 140, March 24, 1921, as quoted in M.E.L.S.I., *Märzkämpfe 1921*, pp. 138-141. A slightly different version of the appeal was printed by the *Rote Fahne* on March 26 (No. 142).

[51] Brandt and Lowenthal, pp. 158-160; H. M. Meyer, p. 72; M.E.L.S.I., *Märzkämpfe 1921*, pp. 64-65; *Taktik und Organisation*, pp. 46-48, 51; *Protokoll des III. Kongresses der K.I.*, p. 249 (Malzahn).

largest industrial area, traditionally a radical stronghold, had proven of little help to the KPD.[52]

Equally unspectacular was the impact of the insurrection on southern Germany, the northern plains, and the East Elbian region. Only token strikes and isolated minor riots briefly disturbed these otherwise quiet areas.[53] Thus, in the last analysis, success or failure of the uprising hinged on developments in central Germany, where the fighting had taken a more violent turn after President Ebert's decree had become known. Because Hörsing's police forces were restricted in numbers, and the Reichswehr units continued to stand by without participating in the fighting, the operations of the government proceeded at first at a rather slow pace.[54] On March 24, insurgent forces held Eisleben and Hettstedt against the police, and Halle and Merseburg were affected by the strike movement. There were reports that in the area around Leuna, now occupied by armed strikers, every male between the ages of fifteen and fifty had become eligible for "conscription" into the ranks of the insurgent proletariat, and that compulsion was used on some occasions to enlist unwilling recruits.[55]

Heavy fighting continued for several days. On March 25, government forces gradually won the upper hand in Eisleben and Hettstedt, and on the following day took Mansfeld, Helbra, and Sangershausen. At the same time, however, they suffered some setbacks

[52] H. M. Meyer, pp. 73-74; Frankfurter Zeitung, Nos. 225, 227, 232, 233, March 26, 27, and 30, 1921; Taktik und Organisation, pp. 49-51; M.E.L.S.I., Märzkämpfe 1921, pp. 61-62; Protokoll des III. Kongresses der K.I., pp. 249-250 (Malzahn). See also Radek's tacit admission that the general strike, on the whole, had not been a success (ibid., p. 465). For a nationalist account of Communist disturbances in the Rhenish region see Hans Spethmann, Zwölf Jahre Ruhrbergbau. Aus seiner Geschichte von Kriegsanfang bis zum Franzosenabmarsch, 1914-1925, II, Aufstand und Ausstand vor und nach dem Kapp-Putsch bis zur Ruhrbesetzung (Berlin, 1928), pp. 288-300.

[53] M.E.L.S.I., Märzkämpfe 1921, pp. 60, 64; cf. Taktik und Organisation, pp. 87-97, where Remmele, on the basis of a few isolated incidents, attempts to portray southern Germany as a veritable hotbed of revolution.

[54] Contemporary critics, notably right-wing newspapers, complained at the time that the police action lacked speed, vigor, and efficiency. Both Hörsing and Severing rejected these charges and maintained that the available forces did their best under very trying circumstances: Preussischer Untersuchungsausschuss (see Ch. IV, n. 13), pp. 98-99, 117-118; Severing, Mein Lebensweg, I, pp. 323-324; Frankfurter Zeitung, No. 234, March 31, 1921. Drobnig's account is not entirely uncritical of the way in which the operations were conducted; see especially his summary, pp. 159-180, and passim.

[55] Schulthess', 1921, p. 106; Frankfurter Zeitung, No. 225, March 25, 1921.

when new riots broke out in such peripherally situated towns as Wittenberg, Delitzsch, and Bitterfeld, which until then had not been affected by the insurrection.

On Good Friday, some confusion was thrown into the ranks of the insurgents when rumors circulated throughout the region that Hörsing had offered immunity from punishment to anyone willing to surrender and to hand his weapons over to the police. Whatever substance there may have been to this rumor, it was quickly quashed. On March 26, Severing sent a telegraphic order to the government forces, forbidding all negotiations with the fighting workers, and instructing the police to proceed without leniency.[56]

The attitude of Communist headquarters in Halle was equally uncompromising, as was evident from the instructions issued by this body on Good Friday: "Provocation at any price! Overturn street cars, throw handgrenades . . . !"[57] But in spite of these desperate exhortations, from March 27 on the *Aktion* turned gradually into a rout, as bands of insurgents, varying in size, engaged in desperate and usually fruitless rearguard skirmishes with the police. Hoelz's account of his own movements during these last hectic days constitutes a very representative description of the collapse.[58] He and some of his men spent Easter Sunday (March 27) at Schraplau, a small town roughly ten kilometers southeast of Eisleben, where he paid his "troops" for the first time. Hoelz has recounted this momentous occasion with customary modesty: "The finance and commissariat department of the troops was entrusted with the payment. Each man received fifty marks."[59] He does not indicate the source of the money.

At Schraplau he met Lemck (Hoelz calls him "Lembke") and Bowitzki, nominally the *Aufstandsleiter* appointed by the KPD, who had, however, lost contact with their own headquarters. Hoelz planned originally to march to the Leuna works and reinforce the garrison there, but changed his mind and set out for Halle, by way of Ammendorf. He intended to launch a surprise attack upon Halle

---

[56] A copy of the telegram is in M.E.L.S.I., *Märzkämpfe 1921*, p. 175. See also *Taktik und Organisation*, pp. 45-46, and *Frankfurter Zeitung*, No. 227, March 27, 1921. According to *Schulthess'*, 1921, p. 106, the government had actually intended to grant an amnesty but reconsidered when violence flared up again in Eisleben after police occupied the town.

[57] *Enthüllungen*, pp. 18, 20; *Vorwärts*, No. 558, November 26, 1921.

[58] Hoelz, pp. 151-164.

[59] *ibid.*, p. 151.

in the hope of capturing some artillery pieces. In the night from March 27 to 28, Hoelz led his men in a belated Easter parade from Schraplau to Ammendorf, a distance of roughly twenty-five kilometers. On the following day he advanced on Halle with two thousand men, but ran into police who surrounded his force before he reached the city. Hoelz sent Lemck to the garrison of the Leuna works with the urgent request for immediate reinforcements, and ordered his men to hold the line until the expected relief arrived. It never came, although Lemck returned, after two hours, in a car with one thousand rounds of ammunition and the promise of speedy aid from Leuna.[60] After waiting in vain for some time, while the police were tightening their ring, Hoelz's troops began to disperse in an effort to escape from the trap before it was too late. In the ensuing confusion Hoelz became separated from his men and hid in a mineshaft. When he emerged from his concealment, his troops had disappeared. During the next few days he wandered north, sometimes alone, sometimes accompanying small groups of stragglers and participating in running fights with police, in the hope of eventually reaching Mansfeld where he expected to find the remnants of his troops. But he never reached his destination. On March 31 he found himself in Beesenstedt, a village halfway between Halle and Mansfeld, and here on April 1 he joined in the last sizable battle of the insurrection. The outcome of the workers' last stand at Beesenstedt was never in doubt. Hoelz was captured after the police closed in, but got away two days later when he successfully fooled his captors with false identity papers and the brazen tale that he was unjustly arrested while peacefully buying eggs from a local farmer. With a price of 185,000 marks on his head, Hoelz made his way to Berlin where he was soon arrested, tried, and sentenced to life imprisonment. His revolutionary career was over for good when the March uprising, in which he had played such a prominent part, collapsed before his eyes.

The backbone of the insurrection as a whole was, in effect, broken

[60] Hoelz does not tell us why Lemck submitted to his command, nor how he managed to get the ammunition through the police cordon.

According to M.E.L.S.I., *Märzkämpfe 1921*, pp. 31, 109, the dispatch of relief troops was contemplated, but execution of the plan was sabotaged by a KAPD member of the Leuna plant's action committee. For a Communist evaluation of Lemck (Lembck) and Bowitzki see *ibid.*, p. 92, and *Vorwärts*, No. 556, November 25, 1921.

several days before Hoelz saw its last dying spasms at Beesenstedt. Hamburg was the first area where order was restored. The riots which had broken out on March 23 were quelled three days later, and by March 29 most shipyards began to resume full operations. On that day the insurrection suffered another blow, as police forces, reinforced by one battalion of Reichswehr artillery, captured the Leuna works and took most of the defenders prisoner.[61] Although Leuna had played a rather undistinguished role in the regional struggle, the mere fact that the famous chemical works were in the hands of proletarian fighters had been played up for days by the Communist press as a symbol of revolutionary triumph.

With Hamburg pacified, the rumblings in the Rhineland subsiding, and the Leuna works captured, the *Zentrale* could see the handwriting on the wall. Everywhere the movement was collapsing; everywhere the Communists found themselves isolated. The majority of German labor followed the lead of the two Socialist parties and the trade-unions, whose spokesmen were denouncing the putschism of the KPD in no uncertain terms.[62] In view of these circumstances the *Zentrale* called a high-level conference on March 30 to deliberate on whether or not to continue the uprising. An emissary, just arrived from the Rhineland, reported on the situation in western Germany and demanded that the *Aktion* be called off at once. His bleak account prompted four leading members of the *Zentrale*, Brandler, Heckert, Thalheimer and Stoecker, to speak in favor of ending the fighting, and one unidentified member sighed that he wished the police in Berlin would lose their nerve and start antagonizing the workers. The pessimistic mood which permeated the conference was dispelled, however, when another participant in the conference rose, banged the table, and asserted that contrary to prevailing opinion the uprising was still gathering force and should be allowed to continue, at least for a few more days. Clinging tenaciously to the belief that the tide might yet turn in favor of the Communists, the speaker cited a number of encouraging examples from various parts of the country in support of his position. Although we

---

[61] *Schulthess'*, 1921, pp. 106-107; cf. M.E.L.S.I., *Märzkämpfe 1921*, p. 102; and *Taktik und Organisation*, p. 50. By far the most detailed account of this event is in Drobnig, pp. 96-112.

[62] See Paul Frölich's chapter "Demaskierung" in *Taktik und Organisation*, pp. 103-117. The attitude of non-Communist labor during the entire period is well reflected by *Vorwärts*, and *Freiheit*, the principal organ of the USPD.

know no further details of the ensuing debate, its outcome was a resolution to hold out for another two or three days. During this period of grace the *Zentrale* was to prepare a suitable plan for ending the struggle as uniformly as possible.[63]

Thus, a day after Leuna was taken and Hörsing's control of the insurgent region virtually assured, the *Zentrale* made a last desperate effort, against the better judgment of some of its members, to postpone the inevitable. On the same day the *Rote Fahne* appealed once more to the German workers to support the uprising. But in doing so, the paper hurled one vituperative insult after another against the leaders of the same Social Democratic and Independent rank and file whom the Communists were trying so hard to win as allies. All the setbacks which the Communists had just suffered the *Rote Fahne* blamed on the Socialist leadership, and the paper ended the appeal on a note of "revolutionary solidarity" with "all workers." Finally, the attempt to win friends was topped by the last sentence of the editorial which appeared in the same issue of the paper: "Shame [*Schmach und Schande*] upon the worker who at this moment still stands aside; shame upon the worker who still does not know where his place is."[64]

The decision to prolong needlessly the agony of those who did the fighting, taken by a few party functionaries in Berlin, introduced to the KPD a pattern of thinking which in the years ahead was to become primary law for over one-third of the world's population: the individual is nothing, the party everything. "For the movement was without scruples," writes Arthur Koestler in *Darkness at Noon*, "she rolled toward her goal unconcernedly and deposed the corpses of the drowned in the windings of her course."[65] But the proletarians who in March 1921 manned picket lines, were wounded or killed, or lost their jobs, did not realize that in the eyes of their leaders they were expendable. The rank and file, whether party members or sympa-

---

[63] The account of the meeting on March 30 is based on the verbal duel between Paul Neumann and August Thalheimer during the Third World Congress (*Protokoll des III. Kongresses der K.I.*, pp. 584-585, 594-595). The unidentified speaker who wanted to postpone termination of the *Aktion* appears to have been Eberlein (*ibid.*, 595). The reference to the remark on the Berlin police is in Levi, *Unser Weg*, p. 33. It is not quite clear whether Levi's account of the *Zentrale's* indecision on whether to call the uprising off pertains to the conference of March 30, or to an earlier meeting (*ibid.*, pp. 34-35).

[64] *Die Rote Fahne*, No. 145, March 30, 1921; Levi, *Unser Weg*, pp. 33-34.

[65] Arthur Koestler, *Darkness at Noon* (Signet Classics, New York, 1961), p. 72.

thizers, knew nothing of Comrade Bela Kun. They did not know that Brandler's theory about an existing revolutionary situation had been imparted to him by a few ill-informed and reckless individuals. The rank and file joined in the insurrection because their press told them that Hörsing had attacked the German workers; that they must show their solidarity with their brothers in Mansfeld and Eisleben; that the *Orgesch* was about to slaughter the "defenseless" workers; and that the capitalists everywhere were plotting a new war for which the proletariat would have to foot the bill. Deceived and poorly led, they fought and died for the most part in good faith, the victims of what Levi came to call the "greatest Bakunist putsch in history."[66]

For two more days, following the conference of March 30, the *Zentrale* waited in vain for a miracle. Rumors of growing unrest among the farm workers of three eastern provinces briefly rekindled sparks of hope, only to prove another disappointment when no uprisings materialized.[67] On April 1, even the most stubborn die-hards among the Communist leaders had to recognize the futility of further waiting, and the *Zentrale* resolved to end the insurrection by calling off the "nationwide" general strike. The proclamation by which this decision was communicated to the party at large blamed the defeat on the counterrevolutionaries, ranging from Ludendorff to Hilferding, and culminated in the promise that the Communists would fight another day: "The strike and the insurrectionist movement have been crushed. Hundreds of proletarians lie murdered on the battlefield. Thousands remain out on the streets, punished by their employers. . . ." Despite the defeat, however, the party's spirit had remained unshaken, and its members were looking forward to new challenges ahead. "Let us not waste time. Close ranks for the coming fight. Be prepared. Soon we shall hear again: tighten chin straps! Forward, against the enemies. . . . Long live the German Revolution! Long live the World Revolution!"[68] On this note of defiance the *März Aktion* ended.

In view of the facts, the self-righteous attitude which the *Zentrale* assumed in blaming others for the failure of the uprising was, to say

[66] Levi, *Unser Weg*, p. 31.
[67] *Taktik und Organisation*, pp. 52, 98-103.
[68] The appeal of April 1 was reprinted in its entirety in *Die Rote Fahne*, No. 190, April 4, 1921.

the least, inappropriate. From the moment of its conception until the final call for retreat on April 1, the entire operation, with its grandiose scheme of capturing the power of state, was conducted by a few Communist leaders who approached it in a spirit of recklessness and irresponsibility. Without a careful appraisal of the situation, these men proceeded from the premise that a revolutionary opportunity was shaping up and should be exploited by the party. This was a misconception, as no less a person than Trotsky was to tell them later on at the Third World Congress.[69] Based, as it was, on a contrived analysis of the national and international situations, the project was then pushed down the throats of an unenthusiastic and sceptical assembly of party officials who were left with the impression that the enterprise in question would be undertaken only when the time was ripe, and in any case not prior to the Easter holidays. To all appearances, this original plan was to be adhered to even in the face of Hörsing's announcement that a police occupation of Prussian Saxony was impending. But appearances proved deceptive. The decision to postpone any overt action by the KPD until after Easter was quietly dropped in favor of interference in central Germany, and strenuous efforts were made to utilize Hörsing's so-called provocation for triggering all the other anticipated crises, mostly mythical in nature, on which the original plans had been based. There is good reason to assume that the party reversed itself on this issue primarily because of Kun, and because of the support he received from those members of the *Zentrale* who had advocated a more aggressive course even before the arrival of the Comintern agents. But neither Kun nor his German disciples took the trouble to assess the chances for a Communist-led revolution at this particular moment; nor did they give any serious consideration to the party's state of preparedness, an omission which in view of the stakes involved bordered on criminal neglect. Impulsive, ignorant of the true political situation, and without a clear conception of the risks involved, the Communist leaders plunged the party into a disastrous adventure.

Everything went wrong from the beginning. Contrary to later legends, the Mansfeld workers and miners did not rise "spontaneously" after Hörsing's appeal had been published, not even when the

[69] *Protokoll des III. Kongresses der K.I.*, pp. 641-643.

local Communist organization proclaimed a general strike. It took Max Hoelz with his revolutionary experience and his personal magnetism to get the workers to move. But neither Hoelz's ends nor Hoelz's means were those of the KPD. He came to the Mansfeld region on his own initiative, because he wanted to render whatever assistance he could to the local proletariat.[70] Hoelz had his own ideas on how to be helpful, and he did not want anyone to tell him what to do. Once he was on the scene, the old revolutionary zeal carried him away, and he succeeded in transforming what began as a strike movement into a bloody orgy. The haphazardly recruited insurgent bands under his command terrorized the mining district without a clearly defined aim, without a strategic plan, and with a minimum of discipline.

It was bad enough for the KPD that Hoelz usurped control and leadership over the mounting insurrectionist movement. But in addition to this sizable handicap, the party's own organizational efficiency proved none too adequate. Confusion and poor coordination bedeviled operations from the first to the last day. Communications between the *Zentrale* in Berlin and the party organizations in central Germany were never effectively established. Despite the presence of Hugo Eberlein, Communist headquarters in Halle dragged its feet. Chemnitz waited for Halle to take decisive measures, Leipzig felt altogether too weak to do anything, and other local KPD organizations wanted to be assured of a successful outcome before taking any initiative. And so it went everywhere.[71]

The party's failure to provide adequate direction and purpose to the insurrection in central Germany was also evident in other trouble spots in the nation. The sporadic strikes in the Rhineland and Ruhr, the protest demonstrations in south Germany and Berlin, the unrest among East Elbian farm laborers, and the abortive riots in Hamburg remained isolated and relatively ineffective incidents. Although they all possessed some nuisance value, they never developed into the strong, coordinated revolutionary movement on which the initial plans of the *Zentrale* were based. But the most decisive factor in the defeat of the March uprising was the lack of mass support. The KPD proved incapable of rallying the millions of non-Communist workers

[70] Hoelz, p. 34.
[71] For an acid criticism of the party's shortcomings see *Taktik und Organisation*, pp. 71-78.

behind the revolutionary banner. "The March struggle broke on the passiveness of the German workers," a Communist leader subsequently complained;[72] he might have added that such passiveness was inevitable because no genuine revolutionary situation existed on a nationwide basis. Whatever the party did to create such a situation, whether by "artificial means" or by clumsy and tactless propaganda, only repelled the majority of German workers, and without their backing and participation any revolution in Germany was doomed from the outset. In short, the March uprising was an undeniable fiasco, the aftereffects of which were to haunt the KPD for the remainder of the year.

[72] *ibid.*, p. 119. It is very difficult to obtain reliable figures of either the number of insurgents who participated in the fighting in central Germany, or of those who, on a nationwide basis, supported the general strike. The Communists have confused the issue by speaking of "hundreds of thousands" who participated in the uprising, an estimate which fails to distinguish between fighters and mere strikers; see, for instance, Lenin's remarks at the Third World Congress (*Protokoll des III. Kongresses der K.I.*, p. 518; also M.E.L.S.I., *Märzkämpfe 1921*, p. 32). A more reasonable estimate is Malzahn's figure of approximately 200,000 strikers in the entire country (*Protokoll des III. Kongresses der K.I.*, p. 251). Flechtheim (p. 74) sets the number of strikers at a maximum of 300,000, whereas Brandler (*War die März Aktion ein Bakunisten-Putsch?*, p. 22), gives the fantastic figure of one million strikers.

Drobnig (Appendix 13, no page) does not give the over-all fighting strength of the insurgents in central Germany, but lists only the number of prisoners taken, and casualties counted. He lists 3,470 prisoners, 145 killed, 2 missing, and an undetermined number of wounded. He states that 1,346 rifles were captured, 34 machine guns (not all in working condition), and miscellaneous gear. M.E.L.S.I., *Märzkämpfe 1921*, p. 33, gives the number of fighting workers in central Germany as approximately 4,000, with at most 2,000 rifles and 40 machine guns. These figures, which have been slightly enlarged, are taken from Drobnig, whose book is cited as the source. Drobnig, however, gives only the number of prisoners and casualties. The number of insurgents actually engaged in the fighting may well have been higher than the estimates given in the East German publication, perhaps because the authors were trying to prove that the insurgents were vastly outnumbered by the police.

More accurate figures are available for the number of police forces in central Germany. Drobnig (pp. 120-123, and Appendix 9) gives their strength, committed by March 28, as 38 *Hundertschaften* (hundreds), plus special units; and as 39 *Hundertschaften* by March 31. Of these, he lists 35 as killed, 53 wounded, and one missing (*ibid.*, Appendix 13).

Flechtheim's statement (p. 75) that 40,000 (!) disorganized (*zersplitterte*) insurgents faced 17,000 police appears to be way off on both counts.

CHAPTER VI

RETRIBUTION, RECRIMINATIONS, AND CRITIQUE

THE BATTLE was over, the party counted its losses, and the victors proceeded to punish the vanquished. Public opinion was bitterly hostile to the Communists, particularly because, during the last stages of the uprising, the fighting in Prussian Saxony had been ferocious, and charges of atrocities were raised by both sides.[1] On March 29 the Prussian government established special courts for the prosecution of captured agitators,[2] and for weeks after the end of hostilities the legal mills ground out sentences which altogether amounted to an estimated 3000 years of prison and penitentiary terms for 4000 insurgents.[3] Five years earlier, when the British under somewhat similar circumstances crushed another Easter rebellion, that of the Sinn Feiners, they executed Sir Roger Casement and fifteen other leaders, but showed marked restraint in dealing with the rank and file of the Irish Volunteers and the Citizen Army. In Germany, on the other hand, only two prominent leaders, Max Hoelz and Heinrich Brandler, were tried and convicted, whereas on the rank and file, who had borne the brunt of the fighting, fell most of the retribution that followed. It was therefore hardly surprising

[1] For Communist charges of atrocities: KPD, Taktik und Organisation der revolutionären Offensive (Leipzig-Berlin, 1921), pp. 52-71, including a criticism of the special courts; also passim, for alleged local incidents involving government forces. Hörsing claimed in his testimony that most of the atrocities were committed by insurgents, but under cross examination admitted that isolated cases of irregularities may have occurred among the police forces as well (Preussischer Untersuchungsausschuss [see Ch. IV, n.13], pp. 118-119). Severing concurs with the general picture established by the committee's inquiry that atrocities were committed by both sides (Mein Lebensweg, I [Cologne, 1950], p. 324). Cf. Noske's acid comments on this issue (Erlebtes aus Aufstieg und Niedergang einer Demokratie [Offenbach-Main, 1947], pp. 204-208).

[2] Text in Drobnig, Der mitteldeutsche Aufstand 1921 (Lübeck, 1929), Appendix 12.

[3] These figures are a Communist estimate (Bericht über die Verhandlungen des III. (8.) Parteitages der K.P.D., Sektion der K.I., abgehalten in Leipzig vom 28. Januar bis 1. Februar 1923 [Berlin, 1923], p. 103). According to this estimate, approximately 6,000 insurgents were arrested for their participation in the uprising. Of these, 1,500 were released after a few weeks of confinement; 4,500 were tried by special courts which acquitted 500 and sentenced the remaining 4,000. I was unable to verify these figures. The majority of those convicted in 1921 were released again in 1922 under two laws of amnesty, one passed by the Reich on July 21, one by Prussia on July 26, 1922 (ibid., p. 104).

that the membership of the Communist Party, which at the beginning of the uprising had numbered about 350,000, dropped to a mere 180,443 by the summer of 1921.[4]

As soon as the insurrection had collapsed, the Communist Party underwent a grave internal crisis, set off by Paul Levi. News of the *Aktion* had reached him in Vienna, on his way to Italy, and he returned at once to Germany. As he was no longer a leading official, Levi had to gather his information from friends and acquaintances who had participated in the various decisive conferences held by the party prior to and during the initial stages of the uprising. On March 29 he sent a summary of his findings to Lenin in a confidential letter in which he made it quite clear that he felt in no way responsible for what had occurred, but that he would not interfere while the uprising was in progress.[5]

The first Central Committee meeting after the debacle was held on April 7 and 8. The new leadership failed to invite Levi, presumably because they did not care to have him state his views on their conduct of the party's affairs.[6] But they could not very well exclude Clara Zetkin, then in her sixties. After Brandler had given his version of the recent developments, the old lady proceeded to castigate the *Zentrale* for having recklessly precipitated an *Aktion*. She criticized the use of extreme and unrealistic political slogans which, she said, had turned the masses against the KPD. She called for an end to "revolutionary calisthenics" and for a return of concern for the interests of the masses; she concluded her speech with a motion for a vote of censure of the *Zentrale's* policy and asked for a special party congress (*ausserordentlicher Parteitag*) in the near future to air all problems in open debate. After a brief discussion, Clara Zetkin's motion was put to the vote and defeated 43 to 6, with three abstentions.[7] Encouraged by this initial victory, the *Zentrale* introduced a resolu-

---

[4] *ibid.*, p. 63. Flechtheim, *Die K.P.D. in der Weimarer Republik* (Offenbach, 1948), p. 76, gives an estimated membership of approximately 150,000 after the uprising.

[5] Brandt and Lowenthal, *Ernst Reuter* (Munich, 1957), p. 160; Degras, ed. *The Communist International 1919-1943, Documents*, I, Royal Institute of International Affairs (London-New York-Toronto, 1956), p. 218. Radek, *Soll die Vereinigte Kommunistische Partei Deutschlands eine Massenpartei der revolutionären Aktion oder eine zentristische Partei des Wartens sein?* (Hamburg, n.d.), pp. 107-108.

[6] Levi, *Was ist das Verbrechen?* (Berlin, 1921), pp. 31, 44.

[7] Brandt and Lowenthal, p. 160; KPD, *Bericht über die Verhandlungen des 2. Parteitages der K.P.D. (Sektion der K.I.), abgehalten in Jena vom 22. bis 26. August 1921* (Berlin, 1922), p. 62.

tion of its own which turned into a lengthy and involved justification of the revolutionary offensive, presenting it as the only proper revolutionary approach in the face of counterrevolutionary provocation and assault: "The over-all situation . . . required . . . the sharpest class struggles; it demanded that the working class seize the revolutionary initiative . . . , resolve upon independent action, and meet the counterrevolution in a powerful counterattack. . . ."[8] In answer to Zetkin's criticism that faulty tactics had alienated the masses, the *Zentrale* produced the excuse that the German workers had remained passive as a result of unemployment and Socialist demagoguery. Under the circumstances the KPD could not afford to wait until the reluctant workers took courage, and the party chose to risk defeat rather than to do nothing. The resolution, meandering on through twelve paragraphs, praised the fighting spirit displayed by the party, re-emphasized that revolution was the ultimate duty of every Communist, and consigned responsibility for defeat to the counterrevolutionaries and their Socialist lackeys. It concluded in the same tone of self-righteousness with which it began: "Therefore the Central Committee approves of the political and tactical attitude taken by the *Zentrale*; condemns in the strongest terms the passive and active opposition of individual comrades during the *Aktion*; and calls upon the *Zentrale* to put the organization into top fighting condition by introducing all measures required to do so."[9]

The resolution was voted upon and passed 26 to 14. A number of additional motions, dealing primarily with organizational improvements, enforcement of discipline, and the right of the *Zentrale* to expel any individual who was found unworthy of remaining a party member, passed equally handsomely and enhanced the triumph of the *Zentrale*. One of its members, Max Sievers, was deprived of his office because he had broken party discipline during the uprising, and the Central Committee adjourned.[10]

The failure of Clara Zetkin's criticism prompted Paul Levi to address himself directly to the public. As soon as he was informed of the outcome of the Central Committee meeting, he sent to press a polemical pamphlet on the *Aktion* which he had written a few days earlier, April 3 and 4.[11] *Unser Weg* was a blistering attack on the

[8] *Taktik und Organisation*, p. 140.   [9] *ibid.*, p. 145.
[10] *Bericht über die Verhandlungen des 2. Parteitages*, 1921, p. 62.
[11] Levi, *Was ist das Verbrechen?*, p. 31.

methods and errors of the *Zentrale*, interspersed with several oblique references to Kun and his colleagues. Levi wrote the pamphlet with a lawyer's touch and the pathos of a thwarted lover. He had been forced to watch the party, which he had helped to found, fall into the hands of incompetents, adventurers, and misguided idealists who, within the short span of a week, had almost succeeded in thoroughly discrediting the Communist cause. All the bitterness, the disappointment, the indignation of the author were reflected in the sharp and aggressive tone of the pamphlet. Levi revealed, sometimes openly, sometimes by insinuation, that the initial plan for an uprising did not originate within the KPD;[12] that the theory of the revolutionary offensive dominated the thinking of party leaders, thus belying the insistent use of the word "defensive"; and that provocations were employed as a means of creating mass action. At the Central Committee meeting on March 16, Frölich had said that the proposed course of action was "a complete break with the past." Levi commented sarcastically: "It is indeed an innovation in the history of the party which Rosa Luxemburg has founded; it is a complete break with the past that the Communists should labor like juvenile male prostitutes [*Achtgroschenjungen*] to provoke the murder of their brothers."[13] But Levi reserved the highest pitch of his angry eloquence for the manner in which the *Zentrale* had ordered the rank and file into battle, while the leaders themselves stayed in Berlin.

"The *Zentrale* accelerated the action [*steigerte die Aktion*]. Squad upon squad rose. . . . Heroic and disdainful of death, the comrades got ready. . . . Squad upon squad prepared for the assault—as the *Zentrale* ordered. Squad upon squad moved up into battle—as the *Zentrale* ordered. Squad upon squad met with death—as the *Zentrale* ordered. [Fähnlein um Fähnlein ging in den Tod—wie es die Zentrale gebot.] *Ave morituri te salutant!*"[14] This passage contained the gist of Levi's argument: the *Zentrale*, acting with criminal irresponsibility, had needlessly caused the death of many of its followers. Levi demanded that the guilty ones resign from the leadership of the party.[15]

The pamphlet was published on April 12 and caused a sensation

12 Levi, *Unser Weg* (Berlin, 1921), pp. 43-48, and *passim*.
13 *ibid.*, pp. 23, 25.
14 *ibid.*, p. 34.
15 *ibid.*, p. 35.

in party circles. The *Zentrale* was outraged, not only because a former chairman washed the party's dirty linen in public, but also because he revealed secrets which most Communist leaders were not eager to see in print. The only ray of light was the receipt of a congratulatory message from the Communist International, dated April 6, 1921, which was printed in the *Rote Fahne* immediately after the appearance of Levi's accusations. Its closing words read: "The Communist International says to you: You acted rightly! The working class can never win victory by a single blow. You have turned a new page in the history of the German working class. Prepare for new struggles. Study the lessons of your past struggles. Learn from your experience. Close your ranks, strengthen your organization, legal and illegal, strengthen proletarian discipline and Communist unity in struggle . . . .

> Long live the Communist proletariat of Germany!
> Long live the proletarian revolution in Germany!
> Long live the Communist International!"[16]

Encouraged by the emphatic slap on the back, the *Zentrale* prepared to deal with Levi, whose exposé made him liable to disciplinary action. But Levi did not stand alone. Many of his friends, some still in leading positions, shared his views. One of them, a former leader of the Revolutionary Shop Stewards, Richard Müller, had gone at the height of the uprising from one Berlin factory to the next in order to dissuade the metal workers from supporting the general strike.[17] Others, too, had made no secret of their disapproval. In short, the *Zentrale* knew that the party faced a crisis. But most of its members, irritated by the defeat and stung to the quick by Levi's public exposure of their actions, were eager to turn on the rebel and his supporters. On April 15, 1921, he was formally expelled from the party on the grounds that he had violated party discipline and solidarity. Upon being asked to surrender his Reichstag seat,

[16] *Die Rote Fahne*, No. 165, April 14, 1921. English translation in Degras, ed., *The Communist International, Documents*, I, pp. 219-220.

[17] Brandt and Lowenthal, p. 160. The issue of alleged "sabotage" of the *Aktion* by Levi supporters was acrimoniously debated by Heckert and Malzahn at the Third World Congress (*Protokoll des III. Kongresses der K.I.*, Moskau, 22. Juni bis 12. Juli 1921 [Hamburg, 1921], pp. 538-539, 556-558). The recorded interjections and the arguments of the two protagonists, though revealing, are inconclusive. Ruth Fischer's statement, *Stalin and German Communism* (Cambridge, Mass., 1948), p. 176, that Neumann and Malzahn also toured the Berlin factories is unsubstantiated.

Levi refused and appealed to the Central Committee for a hearing.

Levi's expulsion had immediate repercussions. Eight prominent Communists sided with him by affirming their solidarity with his aims and endorsing his charges against the *Zentrale*.[18] Four of the *frondeurs*, Clara Zetkin, Adolf Hoffmann, Ernst Däumig, and Otto Brass, were former members of the *Zentrale*; one, Curt Geyer, was a member of the Brandler *Zentrale*, and the remaining three, Heinrich Malzahn, Paul Neumann, and Eckert, were members of the party's *Reichsgewerkschaftszentrale*, a subdivision of the *Zentrale* in charge of union affairs. Yet the majority of the Communist leaders remained unimpressed. Neither Levi's criticism nor the demonstrative attitude of his supporters could shake their conviction that they had done the right thing. By way of emphasis they put themselves on record when in mid-April they published a defense of the March uprising under the title *Taktik und Organisation der Revolutionären Offensive: Die Lehren der März Aktion*.[19]

The Central Committee held another meeting from May 3 to 5, and on May 4 invited Levi to appeal his expulsion.[20] Since Brandler had been arrested by the police on April 18, Wilhelm Pieck presided as acting chairman. It had been Pieck's intention to restrict the discussion of the "Case Levi" to the question of whether or not Levi had committed a breach of party discipline. To the chairman's chagrin, Levi shifted the issue by asking whether the March uprising was justifiable or not. He answered this question in the negative and proceeded to repeat the charges which he had made earlier in his pamphlet *Unser Weg*. Taking issue with such terms as "offensive," "defensive," "transition from agitation to action," all of which were being bandied about indiscriminately by the *Zentrale*, Levi pointed out that the use of these terms amounted to hairsplitting because throughout the uprising the party leadership had exhibited an offensive spirit. Only necessity had eventually transformed the *Aktion*

[18] *Bericht über die Verhandlungen des 2. Parteitages, 1921*, p. 64.

[19] The brochure contains an introduction and ten articles. The theses which the Central Committee of the KPD adopted on April 8 are appended. Thalheimer and Frölich contributed two articles each, Hermann Remmele one. All three were members of the *Zentrale*. The brochure was officially disavowed by the party after its thesis had been rejected and condemned by the Third World Congress of the Communist International.

[20] The following account is based on *Bericht über die Verhandlungen des 2. Parteitages, 1921*, pp. 63-64, and Levi, *Was ist das Verbrechen?*, *passim*.

into a defensive struggle. Furthermore, the party's policy during those fatal March days had been full of irresponsible decisions, faulty judgments, inadequate preparation, and poor organization. Terrorist measures—the responsibility for which Levi ascribed, by implication, to Kun—and ill-conceived strategy had ruined the party's hold on a district which had been one of the foremost Communist strongholds in Germany. In addition, the *Zentrale* had given no thought to public opinion and had grossly overestimated the influence and strength of the KPD.

In this context Levi said: "And now, comrades, another matter. . . . It is now being said that it is the duty of the vanguard to engage in an *Aktion* in order 'to speed up the [coming of the] revolution.' Let me read you the following passage: 'The most important thing is the ideological conquest of the vanguard. Without it even the first step toward victory becomes impossible. Yet from there to the final victory is still quite a distance. One cannot win with only the vanguard. To engage the vanguard in a decisive struggle before the entire class . . . and the broad masses have taken a position by which they can either support the vanguard directly, or at least express their benevolent neutrality . . . would not be merely folly, but a crime as well.'

"The man who wrote this is fortunate that he has not yet been labeled a 'Levite,' though he still has every chance to become one. He is Lenin."[21]

If Levi had any illusions that he could achieve a reversal of the original decision to expel him, he was disappointed. The Central Committee was unimpressed by his eloquence. Reuter-Friesland voiced his regret that Levi's expulsion was to be based solely on his breach of discipline. Presumably he was more concerned with the heresy of Levi's behavior, a sentiment quite in line with the fiery defense of the *Aktion* which Reuter-Friesland had offered at a meeting of Berlin's KPD leaders a few days earlier. At that meeting, Levi had watched with dismay the enthusiastic reaction of the audience and had commented resignedly with a pun on a line from Schiller's *Wallenstein*, "It must be night where Friesland's [*Friedland's*] stars are shining!"[22] The night did not lift at the meeting of the

[21] Levi, *Was ist das Verbrechen?*, pp. 25-26.
[22] Brandt and Lowenthal, pp. 165-166.

Central Committee which, by a roll call vote, upheld Levi's expulsion 36 to 7.[23]

With the "Case Levi" apparently closed, the Central Committee got ready to deal with Levi's supporters. On April 20 the *Zentrale* had notified the eight principal "Levites" that those of them holding Communist seats in the Reichstag must surrender them to the party at once. Following Levi's example, they refused, and they persisted in their refusal when the Central Committee reiterated the order on May 4. Faced with what amounted to open rebellion, the committee resorted to a half-measure by passing a vote of censure (31 to 8) against the recalcitrant group, probably in the expectation that the matter would be taken up anyway at the Third Congress of the Communist International which was scheduled to meet in June. There remained one piece of business, a reshuffling of the *Zentrale*. Max Sievers had been already expelled from his post. Now Paul Wegmann and Curt Geyer joined his fate. The three openings were filled by Jakob Walcher, Emil Höllein and Hugo Eberlein, all old party hands who could be trusted to support the present *Zentrale*.[24]

The first leader purge conducted by the German Communist Party war over.[25] A renowned party member, a protégé of Rosa Luxemburg, and a man who for a crucial year had occupied the highest office the KPD could bestow, had been driven from the party in disgrace. In addition, eight of Levi's supporters faced the prospect of sharing his fate before long. It would be wrong to assume, however, that the "Right Opposition," as the group came to be called at the Comintern Congress, had rejected Communism. Levi and his friends were still loyal adherents to the cause, and some of them, notably Clara Zetkin, remained so to their death. They were up in arms because they felt that the new *Zentrale* had abandoned the course which Rosa Luxemburg had laid down for the party. The *Zentrale*, with the full support of the left wing, indignantly denied this charge. Neither faction perceived that the fundamental issue was not whether the Levites or the Brandlerites had followed the right course, but to what extent both had failed, and what conse-

[23] *Bericht über die Verhandlungen des 2. Parteitages, 1921*, p. 63.
[24] *ibid.*, p. 64.
[25] At the party congress at Heidelberg, in the fall of 1919, Levi did not conduct a purge, but maneuvered the left-wing extremists into such an untenable position that they seceded on their own account.

quences this would have for the future. None of them, in fact, realized that the KPD had arrived at a major crossroad.

The split within the party remained unresolved during the preparations for the Third Comintern Congress. The official delegation of the KPD, all firm champions of the March action, was led by Thalheimer and Frölich. Together with the Communist youth group, it numbered thirty-three delegates. Clara Zetkin, virtually constituting a delegation of her own, went as representative of the Communist Women's League and also acted as the unofficial spokesman of the Right Opposition. In addition, and by special request from Lenin, Heinrich Malzahn and Paul Neumann attended the congress to state the views of the opposition. As they had not received a mandate from the *Zentrale* to speak for the party, they had only an advisory vote, and attended to all intents and purposes as a disenfranchised grievance committee. Finally, the KAPD sent four delegates, which put the Germans, divided though they were among themselves, in second place as far as numerical strength at the congress was concerned. But they, and everyone else, were dwarfed by the Russian delegation of seventy-four voting members.[26]

The German delegation left for Moscow with the expectation that the Russian leaders would receive them as heroes, especially after the ECCI, on April 29, had endorsed Paul Levi's expulsion from the party in a letter bristling with expressions of disgust and contempt for "the traitor."[27] They were to be disappointed. The Russians had in the meantime "reinterpreted" the March uprising. The process had been accompanied by severe factional struggles, because the debate on the uprising was only part of a more fundamental problem, the future of world revolution. Ever since the Russo-Polish War of 1920, the revolutionary wave in Europe had subsided, a development which Lenin, at least, was unwilling to ignore. During the winter of 1920-1921, when general unrest all over

[26] *Protokoll des III. Kongresses der K.I.*, pp. 1068, 1070; Brandt and Lowenthal, p. 167. The following account concentrates on those aspects of the debates which bear directly on the March uprising. Readers interested in the over-all significance of the Third World Congress will find an excellent analysis in Carr, *The Bolshevik Revolution*, III (New York, 1953), pp. 383-392. Summaries of the proceedings, and extracts from the resolutions and theses adopted, are in Degras, ed., *The Communist International, Documents*, I, pp. 224-285. The number of KAPD delegates is based on Degras (p. 226); the official record of the congress lists five delegates, which appears to be an error.

[27] Text in Degras, ed., *The Communist International, Documents*, I, pp. 219-220.

Russia culminated in the Kronstadt mutiny and made it abundantly clear that the Bolshevik government could strengthen its hold on the people only by giving the country a chance to recover from the civil war, Lenin decided to buy time by making concessions at home and abroad. The first of these was the introduction of the New Economic Policy, which included vigorous efforts to improve trade relations with Western capitalist countries. The German March uprising was thus completely out of tune with the trend that was developing in the fatherland of the revolution. On March 16, the day that Hörsing's appeal was published, and the German Central Committee listened to Brandler's variations on a theme by Kun, Russia signed a trade agreement with Great Britain. The Kronstadt mutiny was crushed on March 17, and Lenin had officially introduced N.E.P. on March 15. No wonder that Lenin was unenthusiastic about the German events, that he was hardly surprised when the uprising failed, and that he profoundly disapproved of the whole adventure.

Since the KPD was the strongest Communist party outside Russia, its fortunes and misfortunes served as a useful gauge to assess the chances for further revolutions in Europe.[28] The recent fiasco, therefore, confirmed Lenin's view that a temporary retreat on the revolutionary front was necessary, and he wanted to impress this view on the congress by making the German debacle a starting point for a change in over-all Comintern strategy. In order to be effective, Lenin had to secure prior unanimity among the Russian leaders, which was not easy. Trotsky and Kamenev sided with Lenin in condemning the German putsch, but Zinoviev, Bukharin, and Radek defended it. We do not know the details of these factional struggles which preceded the opening of the congress; nor do we know whether a personal report by Clara Zetkin to Lenin was made before or after the Russians had settled the matter.[29] It is very likely, however, that Zetkin's detailed description of what had occurred in Germany strengthened Lenin's determination to disavow the Kun-Brandler-Thalheimer-Frölich theory of the revolutionary offensive, especially after Zetkin's report was confirmed and elaborated by Malzahn and

---

[28] For a general survey of Bolshevik policies during this period see Carr, *The Bolshevik Revolution*, III, pp. 271-304; for Germany in particular, *ibid.*, pp. 330-331, 337-338. See also Eudin and Fisher, *Soviet Russia and the West 1920-1927* (Stanford, 1957), pp. 3-34, and appended documents, pp. 37-66.

[29] The report is in Zetkin, *Reminiscences of Lenin* (London, 1929), pp. 23-35.

Neumann, who were likewise questioned by Lenin.[30] Whatever the exact sequence of events may have been, by the time the congress was about to convene the Russians presented a united front on the German question. The Lenin-Trotsky faction overruled Zinoviev and Bukharin after Radek, always a flexible man, abandoned the latter, an action which netted him their angry abuse.[31]

News of the latest official Russian position came as a shock to the German delegates. After the initial congratulatory message from the ECCI they had counted on full Comintern endorsement of their policy. Now, on the eve of the congress, they were informed that they had blundered, and that they must under no circumstances embark on a similar unprepared venture in the future.[32] Although the Russians upheld the German party in the matter of Levi's expulsion, Lenin let it be known that he basically agreed with Levi's criticisms, and only objected to the methods which the former party chairman had employed in making them.

"The Congress will condemn Paul Levi, will be hard on him. . . . But his condemnation will be only on account of breach of discipline, not of his basic political principles. How could it be otherwise at the very moment when those principles will be recognized as correct? The way is open for Paul Levi to find his way back to us, if he himself does not block the road. His political future lies in his own hands."[33]

[30] *ibid.*, pp. 34-35.

[31] Whatever we know of the Russian intraparty struggle is based on Trotsky's account which he gave to the Russian Politburo on March 18, 1926. It is reproduced in Leon Trotsky, *The Stalin School of Falsification*, ed. Max Shachtman, trans. John G. Wright (New York, 1937), pp. 33-35. Carr, *The Bolshevik Revolution*, III, p. 383, n.1, cites the identical passage, but gives as his source Leon Trotsky, *The Real Situation in Russia* (1928), which is also correct. Trotsky mentions in his account a clash between himself and Bela Kun, but does not reveal the nature of their disagreement.

[32] Brandt and Lowenthal, p. 169.

[33] Zetkin, *Reminiscences of Lenin*, pp. 32-33. Lenin's willingness to readmit Levi if he acted the role of the prodigal son and repented is also borne out by Wilhelm Pieck, "Die Partei- und Führerkrisen in der KPD," *Die Kommunistische Internationale*, VI, No. 11 (November, 1925), pp. 1199-1200; also by Ruth Fischer, who states (pp. 177-178) that after Lenin's initial defense of Levi he dropped him once Levi drifted openly into opposition to Communism. For Lenin's own evaluation of the Levi crisis see "On Fox Hunting; on Levi; on Serrati," *The Communist International*, English edition, No. 2, New Series (n.d.), pp. 7-8. Lenin states in this article that he made a mistake at the Third World Congress, but only from extreme caution. He defended Levi at the time because he agreed with his criticism. He also wanted to correct the position of the "Left" whose immoderate and incorrect ideas Lenin considered dangerous. Meanwhile, however, he had come to realize that Levi had

By the time the proceedings began, Lenin and Trotsky were assured of the unconditional, though not entirely enthusiastic, support of their Russian colleagues. They had whipped the ECCI into line and had duly warned the German delegation to prepare for some rough treatment. With these preliminaries out of the way, they could entrust the issue to the congress, confident that their views would prevail. And so they did. Despite occasional fierce verbal duels, indignant interjections, and angry charges and countercharges, an air of unreality pervaded the debates whenever the March uprising was on the agenda. The Russians had set the stage very well. Any direct references to such precarious subjects as the role of the ECCI, especially as far as the Kun mission and Zinoviev's share in it were concerned, and the *Zentrale's* attempts to create a revolutionary spirit artificially, were excluded from open debate. These topical taboos benefited the ECCI and the Bolshevik leadership, and restricted both German factions in their arguments. The critics of the uprising had to couch their charges in carefully worded insinuations, and the proponents of the revolutionary offensive could not invoke Kun, Zinoviev, or any other member of the Executive Committee in their defense. Nor does it seem a coincidence that on the Russian side the principal speakers were Radek and Trotsky rather than Zinoviev, who would have been the logical person to place the "German question" before the congress, since he was chairman of the ECCI. Zinoviev had evidently been too deeply implicated in the German imbroglio,[34] and was moreover too reluctant a convert to the official Russian position to serve as its most suitable spokesman. His references to this explosive topic in his official report on the activities of the Executive Committee were accordingly brief and rather innocuous. He complimented the German party for having fought bravely in a struggle imposed from the outside, but when he touched upon the crucial problem of the revolutionary offensive, he skilfully spouted commonplaces with great oratorical emphasis while dodging the issue.

"Too much loose talk has been wasted on the revolutionary offensive. May God preserve us from a repetition of such foolishness.

---

become a full-fledged Menshevik. Lenin wrote the article eight months after the Third World Congress.

[34] This theory is advanced in Carr, *The Bolshevik Revolution*, iii, p. 386, n.2.

. . . The enemy attacked us. You need not lament about the mis-conceived offensive. Many mistakes were made, many organizational weaknesses were revealed. Our comrades in the German *Zentrale* have not shut their eyes to them; they want to correct their mistakes."

After posing the rhetorical question whether the past struggle constituted a step forward or should be labeled a putsch, Zinoviev said emphatically: "The Executive is of the opinion *that the March action was not a putsch.* It would be ludicrous to talk of a putsch when half a million [sic] workers have fought. . . . We must clearly point out the mistakes [committed by the KPD] and learn from them. We conceal nothing, we don't conduct . . . secret diplomacy. And we are of the opinion that, *by and large, the German party need not be ashamed of this struggle,* quite the contrary."[35]

Zinoviev delivered his report on June 25. The following five days were taken up by discussions of the report, with the Comintern bosses presiding from the bench rather than sitting in the dock. They had, moreover, used their privileged position to help formulate the "Resolution to the Report of the ECCI," Article II of which dealt with the German question. In its relevant part it read as follows: "The Congress . . . sanctions completely the attitude of the Executive in regard to the further developments within the V.K.P.D. The Congress expresses its expectation that the Executive will apply in the future these principles of international revolutionary discipline with equal strictness."[36]

The resolution, including its Article II, was scheduled for a vote of adoption at the end of the discussion period. In spite of its deceptive vagueness its significance could hardly be missed. Its wording clearly expressed the right of the ECCI, retroactively as well as for the future, to interfere in the affairs of a member party. In this particular instance, the interference to be sanctioned by the congress referred to the approval by the ECCI of Paul Levi's expulsion from the KPD. In this respect, therefore, it appeared to be intended primarily as a chastisement of the so-called Right Opposition, but at the same time the phrasing provided sufficient leeway to allow for its application to any other faction. That the resolution made no men-

[35] *Protokoll des III. Kongresses der K.I.*, pp. 183-185; emphasis in the original.
[36] EKKI, *Thesen und Resolutionen des III. Weltkongresses der K.I.* (Moskau, 22. Juni bis 12. Juli, 1921) (Hamburg, 1921), p. 5.

tion at all of any possible connection between the March uprising and Comintern was hardly surprising.

The discussion which preceded the vote on the first vital resolution also touched on the German insurrection, even though this topic was officially scheduled for later debate. Ostensibly the arguments centered around Paul Levi's role, since the pending vote would determine once and for all his status as a Communist. But actually the charges and countercharges hinged on the larger question of principles and thereby constituted a continuation of the German intraparty feud, only now being fought *coram populo*. The high point of these preliminary skirmishes was a debate between Clara Zetkin and Ernst Reuter-Friesland, each expressing the point of view of his own faction with great frankness. Zetkin put up a spirited defense of Paul Levi. With her usual bluntness the old lady lashed out against all her opponents in the KPD and the ECCI, and even included the German police who had confiscated all her documentary ammunition.[37] Her principal point was that both the ECCI and the apologists of the March action were trying to make Paul Levi the scapegoat for their own blunders and, while she was careful not to endorse *Unser Weg*,[38] in essence she repeated many of the charges Levi had raised in his brochure.

"It remains a fact . . . that representatives of the Executive bear indeed a large share of responsibility for the way in which the *Märzaktion* was conducted, [and] that representatives of the Executive bear a large share of responsibility for the wrong slogans, the wrong political attitude of the party, or, more correctly, of the *Zentrale*."

Equally outspoken was her opinion on the attitude of the Brandler *Zentrale*: "If Paul Levi is going to be severely punished for his criticism . . . and for mistakes which he has undeniably committed, what punishment, then, deserve those who are really guilty? The putschism against which we have raised our charges did not consist of the actions of the fighting masses . . . but was endemic in the heads of the *Zentrale* who led the masses in this manner into battle. . . ."[39]

Measured by the limited degree of free speech which prevails

[37] These papers were to turn up again a few months later, to the great embarrassment of the German Communists. See below, Ch. vii.

[38] *Protokoll des III. Kongresses der K.I.*, p. 296.

[39] *ibid.*, p. 298.

Retribution, Recriminations, and Critique

nowadays at Communist conferences, Zetkin's performance was indeed daring. It must be remembered, however, that in the early twenties, before the days of Stalin, debates among Communists were still relatively unimpeded by fear of retribution. Moreover, Clara Zetkin knew that Lenin was in agreement with her on this question. For this reason she made hardly any effort to defend Levi against the charge of having broken party discipline but concentrated instead on the substance of his criticism, which coincided with her own views and Lenin's. From the lengthy talk she had with Lenin before the congress opened, she knew that he was less concerned with crushing the right wing of the KPD than he was with labeling as harmful the principles underlying the *Märzaktion*.[40] It was a foregone conclusion that once the "Case Levi" had been settled by the vote on the "Executive Report," attention would be focused on the uprising proper, during the "Debate on Tactics." Then the Bolshevik leaders would be free to bear down on the Brandlerite errors, since they had successfully barred any further debate on the role of the ECCI by means of the innocuously phrased "Resolution to the Report of the ECCI."

Zetkin's attack on the errors of the *Zentrale* were met by a no less fiery counterattack from Ernst Reuter-Friesland. The man who only six months later was to share Paul Levi's fate now directed all his indignation against Levi and his supporters, notably against Clara Zetkin whom he accused of intellectual dishonesty.[41] While admitting that the March uprising had suffered from mistakes committed by the party leadership, he made it clear that *"we shall talk about these mistakes only with those comrades who fought alongside us, and not with those who systematically sabotaged the Aktion."*[42] After a lengthy diatribe against Levi, whom he accused of having persistently undermined the reputation and influence of the ECCI ever since the Second Comintern Congress, Friesland invited Levi's followers at the congress to take an unequivocal stand condemning him, or forfeit the right to call themselves Communists and members of the Communist International.[43]

Shortly before the vote on the "Resolution on the Report of

[40] Zetkin, *Reminiscences of Lenin*, pp. 23-34.
[41] *Protokoll des III. Kongresses der K.I.*, p. 301.
[42] *ibid.*, p. 302; italics in the original.
[43] *ibid.*, pp. 302-306.

the Executive," Malzahn and Neumann, the two right-wing opposition delegates who had only an advisory vote, requested that a final
vote on the resolution be postponed until after the full-fledged
debate on the uprising. They argued that only at the conclusion of
this debate could the members of the congress properly judge whether or not Levi ought to be definitely excluded from the Communist
movement.[44] Radek employed all the biting sarcasm for which he
was famous to discredit the two hapless Levites, badgering them
mercilessly.

When he had finished, Malzahn and Neumann asked the congress
once again, this time formally, to postpone voting on the resolution
until after the discussion on the March uprising. Their plea was read
aloud and then ignored.[45] Five minutes later the "Resolution on the
Report of the Executive Committee of the Communist International" was adopted. The only delegation which abstained from voting
on Article II was that of Yugoslavia. No one voted against, but
Clara Zetkin stated publicly that the "Case Levi" had been settled
"over our protest."[46] It was a clear-cut victory for the ECCI, though
not for the Brandlerites, as they were soon to find out.

Now that the Executive had effectively removed itself from the
sphere of controversy, the Bolshevik leaders felt free to encourage
wide-open discussion of the March *Aktion* on the floor. Up to this
point the debate had centered around Levi's attitude, with special
reference to his criticism of KPD and ECCI. From then on the uprising proper became the chief issue and was discussed within the
framework of the "Tactics of the Communist International." By
the time this phase of the congress began, the behind-the-scenes
efforts of the Russians had succeeded in noticeably narrowing the
gap which divided the views of the Right Opposition from those of
the *Zentrale*, although many important points of conflict were still
unresolved.[47]

The vital debate on tactics was introduced by a lengthy speech by
Radek, who was the first member of the ECCI to criticize the mistakes of the *Zentrale* publicly and in detail. But the part of his
speech that dealt with the German party lacked force and convic-

[44] *ibid.*, pp. 418-420.
[45] *ibid.*, p. 428.
[46] *ibid.*, p. 598.
[47] Brandt and Lowenthal, p. 171.

tion; his heart apparently was not in it. His introductory remarks amounted to a virtual apology to those whose mistakes he was about to discuss, and one wonders whether this unusual civility was not partly due to the realization that his own role in the March events had not been free of ambiguity.[48]

Radek's criticism of the March uprising included most of the major points later to be incorporated in the official theses of the congress, e.g., the need for capturing the masses prior to any revolution; the need for better party organization and discipline; and the dogma that the uprising had been a defensive action which in spite of its failure constituted "one step forward." He carefully concealed how many arguments he had borrowed from the opposition. Moreover, he did not mention that without the constant pressure for "greater activity" which the Executive had applied to the German party, and which culminated in the Kun mission, many of the "errors" would never have been committed in the first place.[49] He was not challenged on these omissions, due to the "oratorical taboos" so prudently devised by the ECCI.

Although Radek's arguments were couched in the deceptively optimistic phrases so peculiar to Marxist rhetoric, the underlying call for a strategic retreat on the revolutionary front was unmistakable. Even when read today, his sophistries sound hollow and they must have impressed his listeners in that way on the afternoon of June 30, 1921. With capitalism inevitably on the decline, he argued, Communism is moving forward to great struggles. However, the decline of capitalism does not proceed in a straight line; nor does revolution, which has its ebb and flow. If Communists want to fight and win, they must prepare for the struggle—which does not mean

[48] *Protokoll des III. Kongresses der K.I.*, p. 455. A letter which Radek wrote from Moscow on March 14 to the *Zentrale* reveals that his ideas on what the KPD should do in the event of a national or international crisis did not altogether rule out the possibility of an *Aktion* (see Carr, *The Bolshevik Revolution*, iii, p. 338, n.1, and also Freund, *Unholy Alliance* [New York, 1957], p. 65, whose use and interpretation of Carr's account are generally misleading, and in some instances incorrect). However, Radek's letter could not have possibly arrived in time to have influenced the decisions of the Brandler *Zentrale* one way or another. Radek's reaction after the uprising as expressed in his pamphlet *Soll die Vereinigte Kommunistische Partei . . . ,* written between April 18 and May 21, 1921, emphasized already the "defensive" nature of the uprising. But his language was still violent enough in its condemnation of Levi to obscure the fact that the men in the Kremlin were then in the process of "rethinking" the March uprising. See especially "Der Fall Levi," *ibid.*, pp. 89-119.
[49] Brandt and Lowenthal, p. 171.

that preparation and propaganda should become a substitute for action. But action lies still in the future, and in the meantime the Communists must be the bell which calls the living to battle. The watchword of universal Communism must be, *"first and foremost, to the masses, with all means."* The Communists must actively prepare the masses for the eventual struggle by means of propaganda and agitation.

"Prepare yourselves and the proletariat for the [coming] struggles . . . , lead it into the struggles which history will produce. It will not be necessary to look for these struggles; they will come to us. And we shall fight the better if we prepare for them. The mistakes we make always mean a step backward, and there is no doubt that we have suffered such a setback . . . in Germany. . . . If the left comrades have made mistakes . . . during the March *Aktion*, then I say that these mistakes speak in favor of them [as] they demonstrate the will to fight. For this reason we were with them, their mistakes notwithstanding. But it is better to win than merely to prove that one wanted to win. And therefore, comrades, *our tactical line is focused on world revolution.* We see the road toward world revolution in the conquest of the great masses. These masses we want to lead into the great struggles which history has decreed for us. . . . We stand at the threshold of a historical turning point, and there is no power . . . which can save capitalism. We want to hasten its death, and this can only be done if we unify the great masses under the Communist banner. We are but the heralds, the organizers. The proletariat will bury capitalism. The proletariat will also be the hammer driving the nail into its coffin."[50]

Radek's report heralded a decisive swing to the right, but, as was to be expected, this projected shift of policy was promptly challenged from the left. On the following day a speaker of the KAPD, Hempel, agreed with Radek on only one point, the impending decline of capitalism. The rest of the report he rejected, with all its implications, defending in particular the justification of the revolutionary offensive and partial actions (*Teilaktionen*), which must precede the all-out revolution.[51] Since the KAPD was not affiliated with the Comintern and its delegates attended merely as guests, this

[50] *Protokoll des III. Kongresses der K.I.*, pp. 479-483; italics in the original.
[51] *ibid.*, pp. 485-497.

first assault could be ignored by the ECCI. It was a more serious matter, however, when Ernst Reuter-Friesland requested in the name of the German delegation that the next speaker, Comrade Terracini from the Italian Communist Party, be granted a longer speaking time than was customary to justify a number of suggested amendments to the theses developed by Radek. He added that these amendments had been drafted by the German, Italian, and Austrian delegations, and that additional delegations would most probably endorse them at a later time.[52] The request was granted.

Terracini, like the KAPD speaker before him, criticized Radek's report from a radical point of view. He took issue with the condemnation of the theory of the offensive and charged that Radek's theses were too pronouncedly directed against the radical left wing of the Comintern and its affiliates. As he was probably unaware of the hectic behind-the-scene struggles among the Bolsheviks which had preceded the congress, Terracini said naïvely, "Comrade Zinoviev has spoken at length in his Report on the Executive against rightist tendencies. If we now suggest amendments to the theses on tactics, we herewith merely endorse once again the arguments of Comrade Zinoviev. We do not think that Comrade Radek will raise objections to our amendments."[53]

It was not Radek who raised objections, but Lenin. In a brief speech, delivered in a mildly ironic vein which barely concealed the underlying intensity of his arguments, Lenin tore into the leftists by ridiculing their charges and amendments. He stated bluntly that all future feuds against the so-called "centrists" within the various Communist parties would have to cease, as the real centrists (meaning Levi) had been expelled. Violations of this injunction would be fought ruthlessly by the Comintern. He reiterated the necessity to win the masses prior to any future Communist revolution, and defended those passages in the draft which bore on this question and which had become subject to a leftist amendment.

Lenin said, "Whoever does not understand that we must conquer the majority of the working class in Europe, where nearly all proletarians are organized, is lost to the Communist movement. . . . Comrade Terracini has not understood the Russian Revolution very well. We in Russia were a small party, but we had a majority

[52] *ibid.*, p. 498.   [53] *ibid.*, p. 503.

185

in the workers' and peasants' councils throughout the country. Where do you have anything like it? We had at least half of the army, which then numbered at least ten million men. Have you the majority of the army? Show me such a country. If these intentions [to make amendments] of Comrade Terracini are supported by three delegations, then something is rotten [*krank*] in the International. Then we must say: Stop! Fight to the bone! [*entschiedener Kampf*] otherwise the Communist International is lost."[54]

After he had repeated in no uncertain terms that the theory of the offensive, as applied in the March uprising, was wrong, Lenin gave his definition of "the masses" as "not only the labor movement, but also the majority of the working and exploited rural population." Then he came back to intraparty feuds: "We have not only condemned the centrists, but also chased them away. Now we must turn against the other side, which we also deem dangerous. We must tell the comrades the truth in the politest possible way. Our theses are also held in a congenial and polite form, and nobody can feel hurt by our theses. We must tell them: we now have other tasks than to hunt centrists. Enough of this sport. It is already getting a little boring."[55]

Lenin's unequivocal defense of the theses, and his equally unequivocal rejection of the attempts by the left to amend them, did not end the debate on tactics in general, nor on the tactics of the *Märzaktion* in particular. One German speaker after the other, Heckert, Reuter-Friesland, Thalheimer and Ernst ("Teddy") Thälmann, the future idol of the German proletariat, tried to salvage as much of their point of view as was possible. Ignoring Lenin's warning not to prolong the feud with the former Levites, the spokesmen for the *Zentrale,* and especially the extreme left-wingers of the German delegation, Reuter-Friesland and Thälmann, persisted in hurling charges at Zetkin, Malzahn, *et al.*[56] Their bitterness increased the more they realized that they were fighting a losing battle. Their colleagues of the Right Opposition had won a significant advantage when they signed a statement that they were now willing to go along with the general interpretation which the Comintern had given to the March uprising.[57] This left the German majority delegation in

54 *ibid.,* pp. 511-512.   55 *ibid.,* p. 518.
56 *ibid.,* pp. 528-543; 574-578; 594-597; 633-637.
57 *ibid.,* pp. 627-628.

the uncomfortable position of obstructionists who held up a generally desired settlement of their intraparty feud, not to mention their
reluctance to bow to the ECCI on the crucial issue of tactics.

The last speaker on the question of "Tactics of the Comintern"
was Trotsky. He had angered those who defended the *Märzaktion*
on principle by an earlier report, "The World Economic Crisis and
the New Tasks of the Communist International," delivered at the
beginning of the congress. In this report he had given an estimate of
the worldwide economic situation and its probable effect on revolution. While predicting the inevitable collapse of capitalism in the
long run, he had been outspokenly sceptical with regard to revolution in the near future: ". . . In a word, the situation now at the
time of the Third Congress of the Communist International is not
the same as at the time of the First and Second Congresses. . . . Now
for the first time we see and feel that we are not so immediately near
to the goal, to the conquest of power, to the world revolution. At
the time, in 1919, we said to ourselves: 'It is a question of months.'
Now we say: 'It is perhaps a question of years.' "[58]

It was under the shadow of Trotsky's essentially pessimistic evaluation that the debates on the March action took place. The left-
wingers at the congress, and not only the Germans, proved rather
unwilling to accept his perspectives at face value. Most of them did
not see, or did not want to see, that the debate on the uprising served
essentially as a rallying point for two opposing schools of thought
concerned with the most fundamental issue confronting the congress, namely what course the Communist movement was to take in
the days ahead. Trotsky alluded to this point when he again addressed the congress, prior to Radek's summary, to wind up the
debate on the German question.[59] After a few brief and rather con-
descending remarks directed at Thälmann, who had been the last
of the *enragés* to defend the leftist position, Trotsky turned his at-

[58] *ibid.*, pp. 87-90. Before he delivered his report, Trotsky had distributed copies
of it to the delegates for study. The actual report which he gave orally was briefer
than the written version subsequently printed. See Trotsky, *The First Five Years of
the Communist International*, I, (New York, 1945), pp. ix, 174-226; cf. *Protokoll
des III. Kongresses der K.I.*, pp. 48-90.

[59] Trotsky's speech on which this summary is based, including the quoted passages,
can be found in *Protokoll des III. Kongresses der K.I.*, pp. 637-650. I have used, in
part, the English translation in Trotsky, *The First Five Years of the Communist
International*, I, pp. 269-281, but have made minor changes whenever I felt that the
translation was lacking in accuracy.

tention to the essence of the March action. Many delegates, he said, had complained to him that the German delegation took up so much of the congress' time in discussing its internal affairs. Such an impatient attitude on the part of these critics was unwarranted. The March action was the main issue under discussion. The congress had to choose between two tendencies. One was represented by Lenin, Zinoviev, Radek, and himself. The other tendency was expressed by the various amendments to the theses on tactics that were soon to be submitted for a vote.

Trotsky granted the German delegation that the March action, as compared to the past history of the party, constituted a step forward, "but it does not mean that the first action, this first attempt to play an independent leading role, has proved successful." With considerable sarcasm Trotsky then leveled his guns at the Brandlerites: "They tell us that they have learned a great deal from it [the March action] and, moreover, precisely from their own mistakes. That is what their own amendments say. . . . They state that the major merit of the March action consists precisely in this, that it provided an opportunity for clarifying the mistakes committed therein, only in order to eliminate them subsequently. Isn't it a little too audacious to seek for special merits in this connection?"

Trotsky proceeded to expose the errors of the March action, and to enumerate the contradictory reports on the uprising which members of the German delegation had given at the congress. All these reports, he thought, served primarily to confuse and becloud the issue. "From all this one gets the impression that the members of the German delegation still approach the issue as if it had to be defended at all costs, but not studied nor analyzed. . . . I think that for your situation in Germany it is best to introduce clarity into this question. I don't believe what Levi has said, that is, that the party will perish from it. However, the congress must say to the German workers that a mistake was committed, and that the party's attempt to assume the leading role in a great mass movement was not a fortunate one. We must admit that this attempt was completely unsuccessful in this sense—that were it repeated, it might actually ruin this splendid party. . . . It is our duty to say clearly and precisely to the German workers that we consider this philosophy of the offensive to be the greatest danger: and in its practical application to be the greatest political crime."

As soon as Trotsky had finished, a motion was made by the American delegation to close the debate and to let Radek give his summary. But Trotsky's speech, in which he had expressed the attitude of the Bolshevik leaders more plainly than any of the preceding speakers, including Lenin, had stirred up the emotions of many delegates. Bela Kun rose to protest against the motion to terminate the debate: "Comrade Trotsky has just spoken for one hour against the so-called Left; he has done so in such a tone that we must absolutely [*unbedingt*] reply to his speech. . . . In my estimation this motion . . . is a low political trick [*Schiebung*] and against this . . . trick I firmly protest."[60] But the motion was passed, and Radek made a summarizing speech which was remarkable for its conciliatory tone. When he had finished, the congress prepared to vote on whether the theses on tactics, in their existing draft form, were acceptable to the delegates in principle. If the vote was in the affirmative, the draft was to go to a committee where the final version would be worked out for subsequent approval by the congress. However, a few minutes before the vote, the left die-hards made what can only be called a demonstration against Trotsky, in the form of a "declaration."

"The undersigned delegations, Poland, Germany, Youth International, Hungary (majority), '*Deutschböhmen*,' and Austria declare that they will accept, in principle, the tactical theses suggested by the Russian delegation, but that they make express reservations concerning the interpretation which Trotsky has given to the theses in his speech."[61] Thalheimer and Kun were among the signers. The congress then voted to send the draft of the theses to the committee. The great debate on the March uprising was over.

While the congress moved to less controversial issues, such as the trade-union question, the economic question, the women question, etc., the committee which worked on the definitive version of the theses on tactics made every effort to eliminate all remaining differences between the two German factions, in order to secure una-

---

[60] *Protokoll des III. Kongresses der K.I.*, pp. 650-651. The speaker for the American delegation, Marshall, hastened to explain that no political trickery was intended when his delegation moved to terminate the debate. The Americans were simply tired of the whole sordid mess, and they made this quite plain when their spokesman stated: "And we should like very much to see an end [to the debate] and not have to listen to the same arguments over and over again" (*ibid.*, pp. 651-652).

[61] *ibid.*, p. 671.

nimity in the final vote. The Russian leaders were clearly worried by the possibility of a further split within the KPD. During the debate on tactics, Zinoviev had said, "There can be only one answer: under no circumstances must there be a further split in the ranks of the German Communist Party. . . . Therefore the congress must press for an agreement."[62] On the surface at least such an agreement was reached. On July 9, three days before the theses on tactics were adopted, the congress passed a special "Resolution on the March Action and the Internal Situation in the V.K.P.D.," which bore all the earmarks of compromise inasmuch as its tone was conciliatory toward the defenders of the uprising, although the congress had rejected their policy.[63] The resolution, proposed by Zinoviev in the name of the Russian delegation, reemphasized that "The congress considers any further disintegration of forces within the VKPD, any factionalism—not to mention a split—as the greatest danger for the entire movement." The congress, the resolution continued, expected that the *Zentrale* and the party majority would treat the former opposition with tolerance, and expected from the members of the opposition that they would loyally carry out the decisions reached at the Third Congress. The resolution concluded with a warning.

"The congress demands of the former opposition . . . the immediate cessation of any political collaboration with persons expelled from the party and the Communist International. . . .

"The congress instructs the Executive to observe carefully the further development of the German movement, and in the event of the slightest breach of discipline to take immediately the most energetic steps."[64]

Before the congress voted on this resolution, Malzahn presented in the name of the former opposition an alternate version.[65] Thalheimer immediately protested because Malzahn's version, signed by Malzahn himself, Clara Zetkin, Paul Neumann, and Paul Franken, was too vague in form and content. Zinoviev supported Thalheimer and suggested that the former opposition offer their draft as a mere

[62] *ibid.*, pp. 628-629.
[63] Degras, ed., *The Communist International, Documents*, I, p. 239.
[64] English text *ibid.*, pp. 240-241; *Protokoll des III. Kongresses der K.I.*, pp. 945-946.
[65] *Protokoll des III. Kongresses der K.I.*, p. 948.

declaration rather than as a formal countermotion. The suggestion was accepted, and the Russian-sponsored resolution was unanimously adopted a few minutes later.

The adoption of the theses on tactics on July 12, the final day of the congress, presented no more difficulties. They expressed with meticulous conciseness the principal tenets which the Russian leaders had previously developed in their speeches. Although they bristled with militant expressions, the call for a retreat from an aggressive revolutionary policy was too plain to be missed. "The world revolution, that is, the downfall of capitalism . . . will require a fairly long period of revolutionary struggle," read the first sentence of the second section. The third section began with the statement that "The most important question before the Communist International today is how to win predominating influence over the majority of the working class, and to bring its decisive strata into the struggle." The fourth one warned that "The attempts of impatient and politically inexperienced revolutionary elements to resort to the most extreme methods . . . frustrate for a long time the genuinely revolutionary preparation of the proletariat for the seizure of power." All parties were admonished to reject "these extremely dangerous methods."[66]

Section seven, "The Lessons of the March Action," was a document the tone of which was on the whole rather unenthusiastic.[67] Perhaps its most important statement was the first sentence, which roundly asserted that "The March action was a struggle forced on the VKPD by the Government's attack on the proletariat of central Germany." This statement became a Communist dogma from which no party publication has deviated since. There followed an enumeration of the mistakes committed by the party, with special emphasis on the fact that the mistake of not having clearly defined the "defensive" nature of the struggle "was aggravated by a number of party comrades who represented the offensive as the primary method of struggle. . . ." Despite the errors, however, the congress was willing to grant that it considered the uprising "as a step forward." The

[66] *Thesen und Resolutionen des III. Weltkongresses*, pp. 32, 35, 41; English version in Degras, ed., *The Communist International, Documents*, I, pp. 242-243, 246.
[67] *Thesen und Resolutionen des III. Weltkongresses*, pp. 52-53; English version in Degras, ed., *The Communist International, Documents*, I, p. 252.

Russian leaders had been initially content with letting the matter stand at that, but in the process of formulating the final draft in committee had decided to elaborate on the meaning of this phrase.[68] The uprising constituted one step forward because "it was a heroic struggle by hundreds of thousands of proletarians against the bourgeoisie," and because the KPD, "by assuming leadership . . . showed that it was the party of the revolutionary German proletariat." With these sparse compliments the German party had to rest satisfied. The balance of the section on the March action contained once again the look-before-you-leap sort of warning with regard to future revolutionary situations, although the congress stated explicitly that once the party had decided on action, everyone must obey and cooperate to the best of his ability. Criticism of an action was to be allowed only after the action was over, and then only within the framework of the party organization. The congress pointedly reminded all potential future critics that Levi had been expelled for having violated this basic principle of party discipline.

On that same day, July 12, 1921, the "Theses on the Communist International and the Red International of Labor Unions" were also adopted.[69] The gist of what the Bolsheviks envisaged in the foreseeable future as the principal task of all Communist parties was contained in section IV: "In the forthcoming period the chief task of Communists is to work steadily . . . to win a majority of the workers in all unions . . . to win the unions for Communism by the most active participation in their day-to-day struggles. The best measure of the strength of any Communist party is the influence it really exercises over the working masses in the trade-unions. *The party must learn to exercise decisive influence in the unions without subjecting them to petty control.* It is the union cell, not the union as such, which is under the authority of the party."[70]

Here was spelled out in very practical terms the new party line which all the member organizations of the Comintern were expected to follow. They were not to engage in putsches, but were to talk softly and persuasively to their fellow proletarians in the unions and

[68] *Protokoll des III. Kongresses der K.I.*, pp. 936-937.

[69] *Thesen und Resolutionen des III. Weltkongresses*, pp. 70-86; excerpts, in English, in Degras, ed., *The Communist International, Documents*, I, pp. 274-281.

[70] *Thesen und Resolutionen des III. Weltkongresses*, p. 75; English version in Degras, ed., *The Communist International, Documents*, I, p. 277. Italics in the original.

Socialist parties. Direct action had dismally failed in the German March uprising. Capitalism was dying much more slowly than had been anticipated. Finally, since the Russians needed that breathing space which the Bolshevik leaders so tenaciously pursued, and so manifestly expressed by NEP and international trade agreements, the Communist International switched its emphasis at the Third Congress from crusading to missionary work. "For the power of capital can only be broken if the idea of Communism is embodied in the stormy pressure of the great majority of the proletariat, led by mass Communist parties which must form the iron clamp holding together the fighting proletarian class. *To the Masses*—that is the first battle-cry of the Third Congress to the Communists of all countries."[71]

The congress was over. Before the German delegation left for home to devote itself to its new tasks, the Russian leaders arranged for one more meeting with both German factions. The purpose of this get-together was to confirm the "treaty of peace" that had been concluded so laboriously and, as time was to show, so superficially, between the majority delegation and its Right Opposition. Harmony seemed to have been established. Significantly, Reuter-Friesland, who had held many private conversations with Lenin and other leading Bolsheviks, had been won over to the newest shift in policy, as expressed in the slogan "To the Masses!"[72] Thus the Russians had every reason to be pleased with the outcome of the Third Comintern Congress.

This peace treaty marked a turning point in the development of German Communism. A distinct phase had come to a close. For when the conflict which divided the KPD after the March uprising was settled by the Russian-dominated Third World Congress, the German party unwittingly surrendered to Moscow a large share of its former independence which it was never to regain. Luxemburg's maxim of friendly aloofness was buried for good, and its place was taken by Leninist centralization and discipline. The spirit of independence which Rosa Luxemburg had infused into the KPD had still been very pronounced during the first two Comintern congresses. The *Zentrale* had then felt free to weigh any advice the Bolshe-

[71] *Thesen und Resolutionen des III. Weltkongresses*, p. 184; English version in Degras, ed., *The Communist International, Documents*, 1, pp. 282-283.
[72] Brandt and Lowenthal, p. 172.

viks gave, had argued with the Russian leaders from a position of strength and confidence, and in the end had made its own decisions. True, as an affiliate of the Comintern, the party had been bound by the over-all policy adopted at the first two congresses, especially by the twenty-one conditions of the Second Congress. But as long as Levi was chairman of the *Zentrale*, these policies had been interpreted liberally and with discretion. The Third Congress, where the intraparty feud over the March uprising became the key issue of debate, put an end to all this. The change came about for a number of reasons. In the summer of 1921 the Soviet Union, for the first time since the revolution, was in a position to exert more than a nominal influence over the Communist parties of Europe. Foreign and civil war, and Allied intervention, were past, making physical contact with the West easier, and at the same time giving Russia time to recover. Lenin was eager to utilize the relatively favorable situation to stabilize Bolshevik gains at home, and to strengthen the Communist movement abroad. As far as Lenin was concerned, the latter task could only be accomplished if the Russian Communist Party strengthened its control over the various European parties, something which he had always thought necessary and which now, for the first time, had become possible of realization. It was done at the Third Congress by tightening the bonds of organization and discipline within the Comintern. Special emphasis was placed on the authority of the ECCI over the member parties, thereby ensuring a better control over the Communist movement than had been possible in the past.[73]

The KPD, second in strength and importance only to the Russian party, facilitated the task of the Bolsheviks in no small measure. In their effort to change the general course of Communist strategy, Lenin and Trotsky in particular made the German question a key issue at the congress, incorporated the specific lessons learned from the March uprising into the theses and resolutions, and thus turned the German disaster into a Bolshevik asset. What was more, in the process of making the March action a convenient vehicle for imple-

[73] See Carr, *The Bolshevik Revolution*, III, pp. 392-397, for further details on this issue. Despite repeated protestations by prominent Bolshevik leaders that the Russians did not intend to dominate the Comintern (e.g., *Protokoll des III. Kongresses der K.I.*, pp. 214-215, 455-456), the theses and resolutions which were drafted under Lenin's close personal supervision, and were pushed through the proceedings of the congress with only minor changes and concessions, belied these protestations.

menting a major shift in policy, the Russians effectively destroyed most of the still remaining sparks of independence among the KPD leadership. Both factions of the German delegation had gone to Moscow in the hope of winning approbation for their respective stands on the uprising, and they were so deeply involved in their intraparty feud that they failed to see how much their disunity benefited the Russians. Without the coarse dictatorial manner which Stalin was to employ on similar occasions in later years, Lenin, Trotsky, Radek, and Zinoviev displayed excellent teamwork in their handling of the German delegates. In private talks and on the floor of the congress, both factions were subjected to unsparing criticism, but with the exception of Levi no one was punished for his or her past errors. After the Russians had censored the Right Opposition for having abetted Levi, they turned around and used many of Levi's and Zetkin's arguments to chastise the *Zentrale* and its left-wing supporters. When it was all over, the German delegates could not help but agree that the Kremlin knew best. So strong was the prestige and personal magnetism of the Bolshevik leaders that the Germans submitted, however reluctantly in some cases, to the demands made of them. They let themselves be maneuvered into accepting theses and resolutions which, at least in part, were distasteful to them. Clara Zetkin was honored by the congress on her sixty-fifth birthday, and the Russians scored a minor triumph when Heckert delivered the principal ovation in the name of the German delegation, and showered the old lady with good wishes. Only four days earlier he had been one of her most outspoken critics.[74] Finally, after Lenin had persuaded both Zetkin and Reuter-Friesland of the rightness of the Russian position, the way was clear to a general reconciliation, and in the interest of the common cause both German factions buried their differences, at least on the surface.

Thus, as far as the KPD was concerned, the most significant result of the Third Congress was the increase of Russian influence over the affairs of the party. This was a notable achievement by Lenin and Trotsky, whose dialectical skill and singleness of purpose were not matched by the divided German leadership. The old argument between Lenin and Luxemburg over the tactical questions of discipline and centralization had been finally won, for all practical purposes,

[74] *Protokoll des III. Kongresses der K.I.*, pp. 541-542, 741-743.

by Lenin. The victory had been made easier by the default of the KPD, which no longer had a Luxemburg to defend its independence, and which had now lost in Levi the last strong champion of the Luxemburg tradition. The position of the Comintern had been immeasurably strengthened. Not only had the congress expressly endorsed that body's recent interference in the affairs of member parties, notably those of the KPD, but had also voted to give it enlarged and additional powers for the future. Thus the right of the ECCI to dispatch meddling *Turkestaner* to the member parties remained unimpaired; this was a distinct victory over the western organizations by what Levi had sarcastically called "the mullahs of Khiva and Bokhara."

Essentially, then, strong Russian influence over the affairs of the KPD dates from the Third Congress rather than from a later date.[75] To be sure, it was initially neither as noticeable nor as rigid and oppressive as it was to become in Stalin's time; yet it was there. Its foundation had been firmly laid by Lenin and his colleagues, firm enough for Stalin to build on and to make more effective. This is not to say that there was henceforth no more opposition to Russian interference in the German party. But what opposition there was never had a chance to restore the original spirit of independence, after Lenin had so successfully disposed of the Luxemburg tradition.

In March 1922 Lenin wrote: "Paul Levi now wants to get into the good graces of the bourgeoisie . . . by publishing precisely those works of Rosa Luxemburg in which she was wrong. . . . Rosa Luxemburg was mistaken on the independence of Poland; she was mistaken in 1903 in her appraisal of Menshevism; she was mistaken in July 1914. . . . She was mistaken in the works she wrote in prison in 1918, especially her book on the Russian Revolution. . . . But in spite of her mistakes she was and remains for us—an eagle."[76]

Indeed, Lenin was by then quite safe in calling her that. He did not need to add that the wings of this eagle had been securely nailed to the wall, to serve as decoration for Communist meeting-halls and party offices—and that it was a very dead eagle.

---

[75] This is also the opinion of Rosenberg. *Entstehung und Geschichte der Weimarer Republik* (Frankfurt am Main, 1955), p. 392. Cf. Flechtheim, p. 80, who disagrees with Rosenberg but fails to marshal convincing evidence for his point of view.

[76] Vladimir Ilich Lenin, *Selected Works*, x (New York, 1938), pp. 312-313.

CHAPTER VII

REPERCUSSIONS: THE
"FRIESLAND CRISIS"

AS SOON as the German delegates returned from Moscow it became apparent that the "peace treaty" between the factions, concluded with the aid of the Russians, rested on very shaky foundations. The intraparty feud continued behind the façade of solidarity.[1] The fact that Levi and several fellow "renegades" now published a periodical, containing polemical articles against the *Zentrale* and the ECCI, kept resentment in party circles alive, especially among the left-wingers.[2] Strong suspicion persisted against the former Levites who had remained in the party and at the Third Congress had adopted its theses. This became clear at the first meeting of the Central Committee after the return of the delegates from Moscow, held in Berlin on August 2 and 3, 1921. Both factions gave reports on the congress. Wilhelm Koenen, Bertha Braunthal and Ernst Reuter-Friesland spoke for the majority delegation, Heinrich Malzahn for the Right Opposition. The discussion showed that no real harmony existed, and that the old antagonism lingered on. The Central Committee, with four opposing votes, reaffirmed its full acceptance of the theses and resolutions passed by the congress, and in addition pledged its support of the "peace treaty" which had been made under Lenin's auspices. But further concessions to the former Right Opposition were rejected. This was true of Zetkin's demand for a new election of delegates to the impending party congress.[3] It was also true of a motion, made by the *Zentrale*, to enlarge that body by two seats, one each for Zetkin and Malzahn, in order to give the right wing a voice in party affairs.[4] In the course of the

[1] Wilhelm Pieck, "Der Parteikonflikt in der Vereinigten Kommunistischen Partei Deutschlands," *Die Kommunistische Internationale*, II, No. 18 (1921), pp. 99-100.

[2] The periodical was first called *Sowjet*, then *Unser Weg*. Two contributors to the periodical, Curt Geyer and Bernhard Düwell, were expelled from the party at the Jena congress (*ibid.*; *Bericht über die Verhandlungen des III. (8.) Parteitages der K.P.D., Sektion der K.I., abgehalten in Leipzig vom 28. Januar bis 1. Februar 1923* [Berlin, 1923], p. 48).

[3] An earlier election had been held shortly after the March uprising. No representatives of the Right Opposition were voted into the delegation, largely because of the atmosphere of mutual distrust which then prevailed within the party.

[4] *Bericht über die Verhandlungen des 2. Parteitages der K.P.D. (Sektion der*

197

debate on this last motion, Reuter-Friesland clashed with fellow members of the Left, notably with Arkadi Maslow, over the party's future relationship with the Right. Reuter, who at the end of the congress had wholeheartedly subscribed to Lenin's new course, pleaded for cooperation with Zetkin, Malzahn, *et al.*, whereas the Left wanted to curtail, if not altogether eliminate, their influence. The argument was continued a few days later, during a district meeting of the Berlin-Brandenburg party section. There it became quite obvious that the Left, Reuter-Friesland excluded, wanted to gain control of the party, even if this meant acting in opposition to the wishes of the ECCI. Ruth Fischer and Arkadi Maslow, in fact, spoke openly against several resolutions passed by the congress which affected the KPD, and in a final vote carried the day against Reuter-Friesland, still nominally the leader of the party's left wing, who had tried to win a special endorsement of the new Comintern policy from his Berlin organization.[5]

The mounting confusion over the proper attitude which the various groups within the German party were to take on the problems arising out of the March action and the Third World Congress increased when another party congress convened in Jena from August 22 to 26, 1921.[6] The congress was confronted by no less than three separate communications from Moscow: an official letter from the ECCI, a personal letter from Lenin, and another from Radek.

The letter from the Executive started with a reiteration of the main lines adopted at the Third World Congress, especially the rejection of the theory of the revolutionary offensive and the endorsement of the new battle cry, "To the Masses!" The ECCI then turned to the recent "deviationist" movements within the KPD and launched a surprisingly vehement attack against the Berlin Left. Its members were called *"leere Schreihälse"* (meaning, approximately, "idle shouters") whose every word was either an error or an empty phrase. The party was urged to keep a watchful eye on this group, which the letter compared to a similar Russian faction during the

---

K.I.), *abgehalten in Jena vom 22. bis 26. August 1921* (Berlin, 1922), p. 64; Brandt and Lowenthal, *Ernst Reuter* (Munich, 1957), p. 175.

[5] Brandt and Lowenthal, pp. 175-176.

[6] The congress at Jena was officially the Second Congress of the KPD, counting from the Unification Congress of December, 1920. Actually, if counted from the founding of the KPD, it was the seventh congress. See above, Ch. III, n.51.

early revolutionary period at the turn of the century, the "Otsovich-niks." To strike a balance, the letter included a renewed condemnation of the Levite deviationists, who were labeled "Mensheviks." The ECCI urged that any party member who contributed to Levi's publication should be expelled from the party at once.[7]

Lenin's letter stressed that the party was now facing many difficulties, not the least of which was the desertion of the "bad Communists of the Left . . . and of the Right,"[8] meaning the KAPD, which had cut its last remaining tie with the Comintern subsequent to the Third World Congress, and Paul Levi. After dismissing the desertion of the KAPD as a blessing in disguise, Lenin turned once more to the vexing problem of the Right. Abstaining from the diatribes which marked the letter of the ECCI, he censured Radek for having recently published an article in the *Rote Fahne*. Radek's article, Lenin thought, violated the unanimously adopted decisions of the Third Congress by sharp attacks, "not only against Paul Levi . . . but also against Clara Zetkin,"[9] despite the fact that Zetkin had signed a "peace treaty" with the Central Committee of the KPD. Radek's misplaced polemical zeal, he stated, merely helped the cause of Paul Levi, who would like nothing better than to stir up new trouble within the ranks of the party. Lenin then explained why he defended Levi's views at the Third Congress, stating that "Levi's criticism of the March uprising in Germany in 1921 was *right* (not, of course, when he said that the uprising was a 'putsch'; that assertion was absurd)."[10] To be sure, Levi's criticism suffered from many weaknesses, especially in form and approach, but the essence of what he said was correct and therefore had been embodied in the resolutions of the Third Congress. "I defended and had to defend

[7] Brandt and Lowenthal, p. 176. *Bericht über die Verhandlungen des 2. Parteitages, 1921,* pp. 150-151.

Moscow's new toughness against the German Left was not accidental. Before and during the Third World Congress, members of this faction had established contact with the Russian Left, the so-called "Workers' Opposition," which was at odds with the Russian party's politburo, and antagonistic toward many measures which Lenin had introduced in connection with NEP. See Fischer, *Stalin and German Communism* (Cambridge, Mass., 1948), pp. 181-182. On the Workers' Opposition see Carr, *The Bolshevik Revolution* (New York, 1953), I, pp. 196-200; II, pp. 223-227, 293-294; also Deutscher, *The Prophet Armed: Trotsky 1879-1921* (New York and London, 1954), pp. 507-510, 518-520.

[8] Lenin, *Selected Works,* x (New York, 1938), pp. 290-291.

[9] *ibid.*, p. 292.

[10] *ibid.*, p. 293; Lenin's italics.

Levi, insofar as I saw before me opponents of his who merely shouted about 'Menshevism' and 'Centrism' and who refused to see the mistakes committed during the March uprising and the necessity of explaining and rectifying them."[11] Levi nevertheless had to be expelled for breach of discipline, and meanwhile had adequately justified this decision by his general attitude toward his former party. Lenin advised the German party to ignore Levi from now on, just as the KAPD ought to be ignored. "In cases of extreme necessity the controversy could be conducted in weekly or monthly magazines. . . , and as far as possible care must be taken not to afford the K.A.P.D.-ists and Paul Levi the pleasure they feel when they are mentioned by name; they should simply be referred to as 'certain not very clever critics who at all costs desire to regard themselves as Communists.' "[12] Having thus dealt with the problem of the Right, Lenin, equally bluntly, dealt with the Berlin organization.

"I am informed that at the last meeting of the enlarged C[entral] C[ommittee] even the left-winger Friesland was compelled sharply to attack Maslow, who is playing at Leftism. . . . Maslow displayed his unwise (to put it mildly) conduct here in Moscow. It would be a good thing if the German Party sent Maslow, and two or three of his overzealous supporters. . . , who obviously do not wish to observe the 'peace treaty,' to Soviet Russia for a year or two. We would find useful work for them. . . . And the International and German movement would gain a great deal by it.

"The German Communists must at all costs put a stop to the internal conflict; they must curb the quarrelsome elements on both sides . . . and engage in real work. There is plenty of real work to be done."[13]

In comparison to the ECCI letter with its blustering party jargon, Lenin's was a model of precision, balance, and perspective. He had written it hurriedly, as he himself admitted,[14] and it revealed the worried urgency of an ailing man trying to make his ideas painstakingly clear, lest foolish minds should again misunderstand the simple but vital lessons which he was trying to impress on the movement.

The third letter, Radek's, was the most ambiguous of the three,

[11] *ibid.*, p. 294.   [12] *ibid.*, p. 295.
[13] *ibid.*, pp. 295-296.
[14] *ibid.*, p. 289.

not surprisingly so, if one considers the character of its author. Radek, too, went through the motions of condemning once again the mistakes made during the March uprising, especially the theory of the revolutionary offensive. But then he turned his attention to the practical aspects of the new line which the congress had adopted and which, to judge from Lenin's scathing remarks, Radek either misunderstood, or, more likely, disapproved of. Radek's emphasis in this letter was still not in tune with Lenin's, for Radek expressed grave concern over the danger of "opportunism" in the German party, and not the opportunism of the past but of the future. He was afraid that the Communists, in their effort to win the masses, would identify the party too closely with the humdrum bread-and-butter struggles of the German proletariat at large; that they would lose in consequence their revolutionary *élan*, and eventually might become indistinguishable from the Social Democrats. He warned that the effort to win the masses must under no circumstances lead to a true alliance with the SPD, and that the party must never forget that the "proletarian traitors," i.e., Socialists and Independents, remained the enemies of the Communists. In short, Radek, who in conjunction with Levi had initiated the policy of the "Open Letter," was at least for the moment emphasizing the arguments of the Left, just when his own former policy had become official Communist doctrine. What were his reasons? Presumably Radek, who knew the German party better than Lenin, Trotsky, or Zinoviev, was afraid that, after the recent fiasco brought about by the activist segments within the KPD, the pendulum might now swing the other way, especially since the right wing could always fall back upon the resolutions of the Third Congress to justify any conciliatory move toward non-Communist labor which they might plan to make. To Radek, the prospect of a revolutionary party working closely together with semi- or non-revolutionary parties in a non-revolutionary situation was fraught with danger.[15]

In order to make quite sure that the German party leaders had really understood what the Comintern wanted them to do, the Executive Committee, in addition to its letter, sent a special delegate. He was Vasil B. Kolarov, a Bulgarian. Kolarov addressed the congress at length, but said nothing that had not been said before.

[15] For the discussion of Radek's letter I am in part indebted to Brandt and Lowenthal, pp. 177-178.

The theory of the revolutionary offensive was once more criticized and rejected by him, and he again cautioned the KPD never to start another great struggle without mass support and without careful preparations. In the end he urged the delegates to accept the decisions reached at the Third Congress, ". . . not for the sake of discipline, but because it must be understood that these decisions constitute the only correct line which the Communists of all countries must take."[16]

The debates that followed revealed that most of the delegates present were much too concerned with the immediate past to grasp the complexity of the problems ahead, Radek's letter notwithstanding. Right, Center (*Zentrale*), and Left still argued basically along the same old lines that they had held ever since the March uprising; the only difference was that now most speakers were trying to give the impression that their ideas were in accord with the officially adopted interpretation of the Third Congress. An exception to this general pattern was Ruth Fischer, the chief spokesman for the Left. She, at least, had understood the meaning of Radek's letter, and she agreed with him. She argued that since the German bourgeoisie was the most class-conscious and the most aggressive in Europe, it met every demand made by the workers with force of arms. This, in turn, made it possible for the right wing of the party to counsel passivity, on the basis that every step taken by the Communists which extended beyond propaganda measures increased the danger of bloody encounters with the counterrevolutionaries. Yet the possibility, implied in the new party doctrine, that the unions and Socialist parties could be won over to the revolutionary cause before the beginning of an armed struggle was, she said, an illusion. She felt that it was the real job of the Communists to increase the pressure on these organizations during a struggle already in progress, thereby either forcing them to go along with the Communists and whatever portion of the proletariat supported them, or to eliminate their influence altogether.[17]

Although Ruth Fischer was careful throughout her speech to play down the theory of the revolutionary offensive, the implication of her statements left little doubt that she was still an unregenerate

[16] *Bericht über die Verhandlungen des 2. Parteitages*, 1921, p. 212.
[17] *ibid.*, pp. 262-265.

believer in Communist *Teilaktionen* (partial actions, or actions with limited objectives), not so much because she believed that such glorified putsches could be successful, but because she deemed it essential for the preservation of the revolutionary spirit of the KPD that the Communists should distinguish themselves from the rest of the proletariat by constant and unflagging radicalism.[18] Her attitude at the party congress was quite in keeping with her statement, made earlier in the month, that the resolutions of the Third Congress were a misfortune for the German party.[19]

Less incisive were the arguments of Ruth Fischer's fellow left-wingers, Ernst Thälmann and Arkadi Maslow. "Teddy" Thälmann had become confused by the three letters from Moscow which had been read to the delegates, and he proceeded to argue against what he thought was Lenin's point of view, when he really meant the official ECCI letter which the other Leftists prudently and contemptuously ignored.[20] Maslow tried to convince his audience that the theory of the revolutionary offensive was in fact the product of the Levi supporters, whereas the Left had been trying to restrain them. Not satisfied with the absurdity of his argument, he crowned it with the remark that the March uprising had been a "defensive offensive."[21] It was apparently not Maslow's day, perhaps because Lenin's suggestion that he be sent to Moscow to be re-educated had momentarily upset his mental equilibrium.

Despite these minor mishaps, the left point of view was strongly presented at the Jena Congress.[22] But it was Ruth Fischer rather than Reuter-Friesland who took the initiative in presenting it. She evidently understood better than most of her comrades that Moscow's new policy was a step away from the revolutionary mission of the KPD. Reuter-Friesland adopted a much more conciliatory attitude. Although he revealed at the congress that he shared the sentiments of his faction concerning Trotsky's statements at the Third Congress, his objections were more moderate, and he concluded his speech with an appeal for unity and cooperation on the basis of the theses adopted by the Third Congress.[23] In view of his

---

[18] Brandt and Lowenthal, p. 178.   [19] *ibid.*, p. 176.

[20] *Bericht über die Verhandlungen des 2. Parteitages, 1921*, p. 252.

[21] *ibid.*, pp. 269-271.

[22] F[ritz] H[eckert], "Der Parteitag der Kommunistischen Partei Deutschlands," EKKI, *Die Kommunistische Internationale*, II, No. 18 (Hamburg, 1921), p. 92.

[23] Brandt and Lowenthal, p. 179.

open resolve to adhere loyally to the intraparty peace treaty, Reuter-Friesland's moderation was undoubtedly warranted. Nevertheless, it represented a marked change from the attitude which he held prior to, and during, the Third Congress, a change which was soon to culminate in his complete break with Communism. But that moment in his career had not yet come. When the new slate of party officers was elected, Reuter-Friesland found himself general secretary of the KPD. The congress then accepted the resolutions of the Third Congress, but included an amendment, introduced by Thälmann, by which the KPD explicitly took exception to Trotsky's criticism of the German March uprising.[24]

In spite of the active left-wing influence of the *Parteitag*, the composition of the new *Zentrale* and the trend revealed by some of the resolutions passed reflected the basic acceptance of the new party line by the German leadership. The new chairman was Dr. Ernst Meyer, an old Spartacist and former editor of the Social Democratic *Vorwärts*. Like Paul Levi, Meyer was an intellectual, interested in art and literature, who had studied psychology, philosophy, and economics at the universities of Königsberg and Berlin. Like Paul Levi, Meyer was ill at ease whenever he was in contact with the proletarian element of the party.[25] Unlike Levi, however, he allowed himself to be guided by Moscow even though he, too, had been a close associate of Rosa Luxemburg. With the exception of Stoecker, Koenen, Frölich (and Brandler, who was in prison), all former leading members of the Brandler *Zentrale* were re-elected, together with Clara Zetkin, the only representative of the former Levi faction, and Reuter-Friesland, the only representative of the Berlin Left.[26] Since

[24] *ibid.*; *Bericht über die Verhandlungen des 2. Parteitages,* 1921, p. 408. The resolution was accepted against the votes of the Right Opposition members, excluding Clara Zetkin.

[25] *Wer Ists?* ed. H. A. L. Degener, 9th ed. (Berlin, 1928), p. 1045; Fischer, p. 180.

[26] *Bericht über die Verhandlungen des 2. Parteitages,* 1921, pp. 382, 406, 438. The following members were elected to the *Zentrale* on August 26, 1921: Ernst Meyer, Wilhelm Pieck, Paul Böttcher, Fritz Heckert, Hugo Eberlein, Edwin Hörnle, Jakob Walcher, Ernst Friesland (Reuter), August Thalheimer, Bertha Braunthal, Clara Zetkin, Hermann Remmele, Rosi Wolffstein, and Felix Schmidt. The district Berlin-Brandenburg was represented in the Central Committee by Ruth Fischer and Otto Geschke; Arkadi Maslow and Hans Pfeiffer were alternates. Brandler was still in prison at the time of the election, and Paul Frölich was not a candidate for office. The delegates also decided to restore the original name of the party, *Kommunistische Partei Deutschlands,* in place of *Vereinigte Kommunistische Partei Deutschlands* (F[ritz] H[eckert], *Die Kommunistische Internationale,* II, No. 18, p. 94).

both Zetkin and Reuter-Friesland had been won over by Lenin toward an attitude of cooperation and conciliation, the new setup promised to be a harmonious one.

The resolutions of the KPD congress went beyond those adopted by the Third Comintern Congress. They included the open advocacy of a "united front" with the rest of the German proletariat. The congress also drafted a program for the party's domestic policy which asked for the confiscation by the republic of all property held by the former ruling dynasties, the control of production by factory councils, and transfer of the major burden of the reparations to the capitalists.[27] Coupled with this was the demand for close political and economic relations between Germany and the USSR. In short, the Jena *Parteitag* ended with a decisive victory of the right and middle-of-the-road factions of the KPD over the militant left wing, although the latter, its determination and fighting spirit strengthened rather than diminished, was soon to develop into a more formidable headache for the party than Levi and his faction had ever been. Furthermore, all the principal former spokesmen of the theory of the revolutionary offensive whose views had until recently coincided with, and largely been determined by, the left wing of the party, henceforth became the strongest exponents of a cautious and moderate party policy.[28] The combination of the March fiasco and the subsequent tongue-lashing that they had received at the Third World Congress drove men like Thalheimer, Meyer, Pieck, and others, further toward the "right," and also made them less prone than ever before to question the authority of the Kremlin.

By the time the Jena party congress concluded its business, the recent crisis which the March uprising had set off within the KPD seemed to be over. The party prepared to carry out with vigor the new policy which had been laid down in Moscow, and confirmed at Jena. The first opportunity to do so arose when Matthias Erzberger, the most prominent leader of the Center Party, was killed by nationalist assassins on August 26, the day the Jena Congress adjourned. The murder caused a wave of public indignation which was particularly pronounced among the working class. The KPD used this emotionally charged atmosphere to issue a proclamation to the

---

[27] Carr, *The Bolshevik Revolution*, III, p. 413.
[28] Borkenau, *The Communist International* (London, 1938), p. 220.

workers, calling for a number of practical measures to strengthen the German labor movement vis-à-vis the "reactionaries." August 31 saw a number of proletarian protest demonstrations throughout Germany which were supported by the Communists.[29] In Thuringia, where elections to the local diet on September 10 had resulted in a combined majority of the three principal working-class parties (SPD, USPD, KPD), the Communists stated their qualified readiness to support, though not to participate in, a government formed by the two Socialist parties.[30]

But the most ambitious party project was concerned with the financial crisis which Germany was approaching in the fall of 1921. Inflationary trends increased rapidly. In July, 1921, the mark stood 76.7 (monthly average) to the dollar. In the fall of the year, trade-unions and the Social Democratic Party demanded that the Reich cover a substantial part of the reparations payments by a partial confiscation of all real values (*Erfassung der Sachwerte*, or *Goldwerte*), including bank assets, stocks, bonds, real estate, factories, mines, and so on. At the end of October, the *Zentrale* decided to back this demand and, going beyond the original formulation, asked for a confiscation of real values by means of state participation in industry, agriculture, trade, and transportation. The measures were to be controlled and administered by the factory councils. The intention was to cover the reparation payments with the profits thus obtained by the state, and to make it unnecessary to tax the laboring classes.[31]

These developments created new controversies within the KPD. The left wing of the party, now no longer controlled by Reuter-Friesland but increasingly by Ruth Fischer, Maslow, and Thälmann, wanted the workers rather than the state to carry out the confiscation of real values, in a bid for mass support of the party. The Left was also opposed to all negotiations with other labor parties concerning the formation of Socialist governments in any German *Land*. In Thuringia, for instance, such a development seemed to be possible.

Another Central Committee meeting was held on November 16

[29] *Bericht über die Verhandlungen des III. (8.) Parteitages*, p. 10.
[30] Ulbricht, *Zur Geschichte der deutschen Arbeiterbewegung* (Berlin, 1953), pp. 54-56.
[31] Brandt and Lowenthal, p. 184.

and 17, 1921, to discuss these issues. Once again the *Zentrale* won its point over the opposition from the Left, and once again with strong backing from Moscow. Radek, who in August had expressed sentiments very close to the left-wing point of view, had since undergone a change of heart and supported the "moderate" stand of the *Zentrale* against the Left.[32] He stated in an article that confiscation of real values in Germany could best be accomplished by the creation of "workers' governments," i.e., coalition governments formed by the working-class parties. Thus the realization of the KPD's financial program should not be attempted through mobilization of the masses, as the militant Left advocated, but rather by Communist participation in government wherever and whenever possible. "The Communist Party can join any government which is sincerely willing to fight capitalism."[33] Indeed, within a few months Radek and the KPD had traveled a long way from the path of revolution.

When the *Allgemeiner Deutscher Gewerkschaftsbund*, Germany's strongest trade-union federation, urged the German government and the Reichstag on November 19 to affect a speedy resolution of labor's fiscal and economic demands, including the confiscation of real values (*Sachwerte*), the KPD endorsed the appeal along with other German working-class organizations.[34] And at the end of the month August Thalheimer stated in an article in *International Press Correspondence* that the KPD was ready to support any Socialist or workers' government which was prepared to carry out the demands of the masses. Thalheimer assured the workers in the SPD and the USPD that they could count on full Communist

[32] According to Borkenau, *The Communist International*, p. 224, and *Der europäische Kommunismus* (Bern, 1952), p. 45, the conduct of German affairs by the Comintern passed after the Third World Congress from Kun to Radek. Radek was allegedly chosen because he was regarded as an exponent of the "Right," and thus a suitable person to supervise the correct application of the new party line which soon came to be known as "united front" policy. Borkenau's statement, however, requires some qualification. In the first place, Radek had been in touch with German affairs for years, whereas Kun had played no significant part in directing them except for the brief interlude in March 1921. Furthermore, Radek's position kept on shifting, and it is virtually impossible to label it at any time with even a modicum of precision. Finally, "right" and "left" were very tentative terms in this period when applied to the position adopted by a Communist functionary. See also Flechtheim, *Die K.P.D. in der Weimarer Republik* (Offenbach, 1948), p. 80, who follows Borkenau.

[33] Brandt and Lowenthal, pp. 184-185; see also Borkenau, *The Communist International*, pp. 224-228.

[34] *Bericht über die Verhandlungen des III. (8.) Parteitages*, pp. 12-13.

support in their struggle to capture new positions of power for the working classes.[35]

One of the most energetic and enthusiastic exponents of the new party line was Ernst Reuter-Friesland, general secretary of the KPD. And yet, not long after he had assumed office, he found himself in conflict with the ECCI. His admiration for the Russian leaders had always been sincere, but, in contrast to most of his colleagues in the *Zentrale*, he did not credit the Bolsheviks with infallibility, political or otherwise. He had only reluctantly accepted Lenin's dictum that the March uprising had been a mistake. In the end, however, he let himself be persuaded and returned to Berlin with the firm intention of helping to steer the course of the party along the lines agreed upon in Moscow. It will be recalled that prior to the March uprising Reuter-Friesland and the other left-wingers had been as wary of a Russian-oriented policy as had been the Levi faction, although for different reasons. Whereas the Right had resented the reckless interference in internal party affairs by agents of the Comintern, the Left had been worried that the revolutionary mission of the German party would be sidetracked, or even subverted, in the national interest of Soviet Russia.[36] Now, after the Third Congress had corrected most of Reuter-Friesland's earlier views, and since he himself was no longer in opposition but a responsible member of the *Zentrale*, he arrived before long at a position closely resembling that which Levi had held as party chairman.

As early as September 1921, the *Zentrale* had instructed the two German representatives to the ECCI in Moscow, Wilhelm Pieck and Fritz Heckert, to tell the Executive not to send so many public appeals and "open letters" to the KPD. The *Zentrale* suggested instead that a more frequent personal exchange of ideas would be more conducive to strengthening the authority of the German leadership over the rank and file. The German envoys were also to transmit the request that the newly-founded Communist Trade Union International, led by the Russian Lozovsky, should cease its continuous attacks on the non-Communist unions. The *Zentrale* saw in Lozovsky's methods a perhaps involuntary, yet in practice

[35] August Thalheimer, "The Central Committee of the KPD," *International Press Correspondence*, 1, No. 12 (November 29, 1921), pp. 98-99; hereafter cited as *Inprecorr*.

[36] Brandt and Lowenthal, pp. 147-149.

exceedingly harmful, sabotage of the new united front tactics which the German Communists were trying to promote.[37]

The ECCI and Lozovsky ignored the German requests. All kinds of pamphlets, brochures, and other publications continued to be distributed both by the West European Secretary's Office of the Comintern, and the Central European Bureau of the *Rote Gewerkschafts Internationale* (Red Trade-Union International, or RGI), usually without prior clearance with the *Zentrale*. In addition, "free-floating" Comintern agents such as Lenin's former secretary, Jelena Stassova, made themselves at home in the central office of the KPD and interfered with the conduct of party business.[38] Friction resulted as a matter of course, and Reuter-Friesland did not hide his irritation with what he considered an intolerable state of affairs. His constant altercations with those who fondly thought of themselves as a *"Nebenregierung"* were duly reported to Moscow, where the Bolshevik leaders did not take kindly to this display of independence and perpetual criticism. They saw a close affinity between Reuter-Friesland's current attitude and that of Paul Levi. Once this specter had been raised, further suspicions began to arise.[39] For Paul Levi was still very much in evidence, and his little band of renegades had grown. Curt and Anna Geyer, together with Bernhard Düwell and one other former official, had joined Levi after they had been expelled at the Jena Congress. Three more left the party at the end of September to join Levi's group: old Adolf Hoffmann, Levi's former co-chairman Ernst Däumig, and a Marie Mackwitz. As most of them held Reichstag seats when they broke with the KPD, they formed a rival parliamentary delegation (*Fraktion*), the *Kommunistische Arbeitsgemeinschaft* (literally: Communist Working Cooperative), or KAG. The KAG ignored all demands from the *Zentrale* to surrender their Reichstag seats, and also continued to publish a brochure, *Unser Weg*, which frequently contained critical articles on the KPD and the ECCI.[40]

[37] *ibid.*, pp. 185-186. Pieck and Heckert represented the German party with the ECCI in Moscow from September to November, 1921. They were replaced by Remmele and Brandler, after the latter was prematurely released from prison. Remmele served from December, 1921, until January, 1922, Brandler from November, 1921, to August, 1922 (*Bericht über die Verhandlungen des III. (8.) Parteitages*, pp. 57-58).
[38] Brandt and Lowenthal, p. 187.
[39] *ibid.*
[40] *Bericht über die Verhandlungen des III. (8.) Parteitages*, pp. 48, 51. See also

Reuter-Friesland's handling of the problem posed by the KAG enhanced Moscow's suspicions concerning his political reliability. The Russian leaders might have been willing to overlook even his querulous attitude toward the Comintern agents in Germany if he had taken energetic steps to combat Levi's splinter group. Instead, Reuter-Friesland saw to it that the *Zentrale* conscientiously followed Lenin's recent advice to ignore Levi as much as possible.[41] But this was not all. Gradually Reuter-Friesland's concepts concerning the nature, strategy, and objectives of German Communism came to resemble more and more those of Paul Levi and his friends. Although he prudently refrained from establishing even indirect contact with the KAG, his subsequent behavior indicated that he had not given up hope of seeing most of the lost sheep around Levi return to the Communist fold. Such a development he desired less from personal preference—the Levites had never been friends of his—but because his views had come very close to theirs in the few months that he had been general secretary of the party. This marked trend away from his erstwhile radical position was encouraged by members of the former Right Opposition within the KPD, men like Malzahn and Neumann, who had remained in the party without having abandoned their long-standing misgivings regarding ECCI machinations. Reuter-Friesland's continuous resistance to Comintern interference won him their friendship and confidence. While they favored a close alliance with the forces of the Russian revolution, they maintained at the same time that only a free party with an independent policy could hope to win mass support in Germany. As Malzahn and his friends were in charge of the party's union policy and, as former Independents, were in a position to re-establish contact with old acquaintances in the USPD, their efforts constituted a vital aspect of the united front tactics.[42]

During the first part of November, the ECCI prepared to move against Reuter-Friesland, whose extensive influence in the *Zentrale* was thought to be dangerous, both in view of his obstinate stand on the matter of Comintern publications and of his ambiguous attitude

---

Clara Zetkin's less than kind remarks about her former friends in the KAG: "On the Situation in the German Party," *Inprecorr*, I, No. 2 (October 17, 1921), p. 17.

[41] Brandt and Lowenthal, p. 187.

[42] Brandt and Lowenthal, pp. 188-189; *Bericht über die Verhandlungen des III. (8.) Parteitages*, p. 48; Pieck, *Die Kommunistische Internationale*, VI, No. 11, pp. 1200-1201.

toward the KAG. Radek sent a letter with the following warning: "Whoever fails to unmask the character of the KAG. . . , whoever does not fight them politically as enemies of Communism, is working for them, is their exponent within the party."[43] Then, in an effort to isolate Reuter-Friesland within the party, the Executive let it be known that it held him primarily responsible for the various tactical errors which the KPD had lately committed. Pieck and Heckert, the two party representatives to the ECCI, made a surprise appearance in Berlin and delivered the message during a conference of the *Zentrale*. After they had given their report, Eberlein moved that the implicated general secretary, Ernst Reuter-Friesland, be replaced by Wilhelm Pieck. The motion was defeated. What was more, the Central Committee, which met shortly after, endorsed Reuter-Friesland's handling of party affairs. In a resolution concerning the attitude of the KPD toward the KAG, the Central Committee expressed the intention "to further henceforth the objective debate over existing party-political differences" with the KAG, but to oppose sharply any possible attempts which this group might undertake to split the German Communist Party.[44] This formulation was a clear rebuff of Radek.

A few days after the Central Committee meeting, on November 20, the KAG held a conference at which the Levites in their turn defined their attitude toward the KPD. The conference was attended by Otto Brass, a former member of the Levi *Zentrale* who had remained in the party as a Communist Reichstag delegate, and who now reported to his former colleagues on the decisions reached at the last Central Committee meeting. The reaction of the KAG to these decisions was embodied in a resolution. It rejected the creation of a rival party, approved of the recently adopted course of the KPD which it recognized as the future core of a growing revolutionary mass movement, but listed five stipulations as the basis for future cooperation with the KPD. The five conditions were: complete financial independence from the Comintern; parity of control between the *Zentrale* and the ECCI over all publications of foreign Communist organizations; guarantees against open or covert organizational interference of the ECCI into the affairs of the German party; a well-defined Communist policy to which all revolutionary

[43] Quoted in Brandt and Lowenthal, p. 187.
[44] *ibid.*, p. 188.

workers in Germany could subscribe, and which would rule out such putschist adventures as the March uprising; a sane policy with regard to the labor unions.[45]

The position of the KAG on all vital questions of Communist policy conformed to an appreciable extent with Reuter-Friesland's own. This rapport, established without any personal discussions between the leaders of the two camps, gave promise of a possible future reconciliation of aims. Both sides saw eye to eye on the nature and mission of German Communism; both favored a united front policy; and both resented the tactics of the ECCI. Thus encouraged by the over-all outlook, the general secretary sat down (some time between November 20 and 25) and wrote an article for *Die Internationale*,[46] in which he analyzed the situation of the KPD and its interpretation of the meaning and objectives of the united front tactics. At the end of the article, adopting the arguments made by the KAG a few days earlier, he demanded that in the best interest of the KPD the influence of the ECCI on the party should henceforth be restricted to political authority and solidarity; financial and organizational influences were harmful and should be discontinued.[47]

A few days after the article was written, the Social Democratic *Vorwärts* published the first installment of a series of revelations concerning the fostering of violence by Eberlein and others during the March uprising.[48] Based on the documents confiscated from Clara Zetkin by border officials on July 8, 1921, at Eydtkunen, the charges had such a ring of authenticity that they at once threw the KPD into another severe crisis. The lame attempts to deny the veracity of the *Vorwärts* articles by those party leaders most directly affected by the revelations only enhanced the general clamor for explanations and clarification. Party functionaries throughout Germany, and many segments of the rank and file, insisted on being told the truth. And the KAG demanded that the Communist Party

45 *ibid.*, pp. 189-190.
46 *Die Internationale*, No. 17 (December 1, 1921), as cited in Brandt and Lowenthal, p. 727.
47 Brandt and Lowenthal, pp. 190-192.
48 *Vorwärts*, No. 556, November 25, 1921. The account of the Friesland crisis, as it became known, is largely based on the excellent treatment of this episode in Brandt and Lowenthal. The authors had access to material and surviving witnesses not available to me. For documentation see *ibid.*, pp. 727-728. I have also made use of the following: *Bericht über die Verhandlungen des III. (8.) Parteitages*, pp. 14-15, 49, 126; and *Die Kommunistische Internationale*, VI, No. 11, pp. 1200-1201.

expel at once all those whose responsibility for the unsavory by-products of the March uprising could be established. The same demands were raised within the narrower circle of the Communist top command. On November 30, Malzahn and his colleagues in the party's central trade-union section (*zentrale Gewerkschaftsabteilung*), supported by the general secretary Reuter-Friesland, asked categorically for the resignation of the implicated persons. In a joint memorandum they urged every member of the *Zentrale* who was in any way familiar with the exact circumstances surrounding the excesses of the March action to stop hedging, and to speak "Yea, yea" or "Nay, nay." "The Communist Party would have a much stronger appearance, and would offer less of a target, if the comrades concerned would state: Yes, we made at the time certain mistakes and shall draw the obvious conclusions."[49]

How far Reuter-Friesland had moved toward the right became evident during a meeting of the *Zentrale* on December 13. Pieck, who chaired the discussion, invited Reuter-Friesland to give his opinion on the acute political questions of the moment. Friesland began by recalling how successful the KPD had been in recent months on the labor front. The KAG had been forced to take the defensive, and inroads had been made in the USPD. More and more proletarians began to look toward the Communist Party for guidance. Then came the *Vorwärts* articles, accompanied by an equivocal attitude of the *Zentrale*. For example, the *Zentrale* ruled against the expulsion of Eberlein, and in general handled the charges that were leveled against the party in a very cavalier manner. As a result of this, the position of the KAG was strengthened. He then discussed the program of the KAG, and concentrated especially on its demand that the KPD be financially independent from the Comintern, a demand with which he agreed completely. Again he emphasized that financial strings meant organizational strings which could only lead to the German party's complete dependence on Russia.

"In Russia, the course of development is away from Communism. As far as centralism is concerned, it arose in Russia in conjunction with the conquest of political power and the [establishment of the] dictatorship [of the proletariat]. The German working class has accepted it only because it sensed that it was facing decisive struggles.

[49] Quoted in Brandt and Lowenthal, p. 194.

Now we have entered another phase. The ideological independence of our party . . . is absolutely necessary. This does not mean that we reject the use of the experiences of the Russian revolution. But we need intellectual elbow room [*geistige Bewegungsfreiheit*]. . . ."[50] He added that the only negative aspect of the demands made by the KAG was that they originated with this group rather than with the KPD.

Reuter-Friesland's pronounced identification with a deviationist sect caused deep consternation among his audience. True, his attitude during the past few weeks had been highly critical of his fellow leaders, but never before had he stated in so many words that he, the "left" Friesland, saw virtually eye to eye with the renegade Paul Levi. The discussion which followed Reuter-Friesland's startling speech was accordingly painful. Party chairman Ernst Meyer, personally on very cordial terms with the general secretary, was the first to defend centralism and the intellectual dependence of the party on the Russian revolutionary tradition. Reuter-Friesland was accused—unjustifiedly—of having secretly collaborated with the KAG. His position in the party was obviously becoming problematic, a fact which Wilhelm Pieck stated in so many words. Yet Pieck was in a peculiarly embarrassing position. Only a few weeks earlier he had been mentioned as a possible replacement for Reuter-Friesland as general secretary of the party. How could he now propose that this replacement be carried out? Pieck solved the dilemma by offering the unique suggestion that the office of general secretary be abolished altogether in the German Communist Party, because of Friesland's admittedly deviationist attitude. Pieck's solution was accepted in lieu of a stiffer recommendation, made by implication in the course of debate by the chief editor of the *Rote Fahne*, Heinrich Süsskind, that Reuter-Friesland be expelled from the party. Pieck and some of his colleagues were at the moment unwilling to go that far and settled on a compromise by which the ousted general secretary was to be sent to Moscow, presumably for purposes of re-education.

Reuter-Friesland did not go to Moscow, nor did he plan to do so. He braced himself instead for a fight with the *Zentrale*, his last fight within the ranks of the German Communist Party. Once again he

[50] Quoted, *ibid.*, pp. 195-196.

became the spokesman of "the opposition," only this time not of the left, but of the right. Supported by his friends in the party's central trade-union section, notably by Malzahn and Brass, he collected signatures for a declaration which he had drafted subsequent to his removal as general secretary. The declaration called the denials of the *Vorwärts* revelations by the *Zentrale* harmful to the party, and demanded once more the resignation of all party officials who had been involved in any dubious activities during the March uprising. The declaration with 128 signatures was submitted to the *Zentrale* on December 22.[51]

The final step that led to Reuter-Friesland's break with the party was brought about by a printed appeal which he directed to the membership of the KPD. In it the same demands that he had just made in his declaration to the *Zentrale* were repeated and amplified for the benefit of the rank and file. For one who was still technically a member of the *Zentrale* (his removal as general secretary had not affected his other office), this was clearly open rebellion. The appeal, signed by himself, Malzahn, and Brass, could have been written by Paul Levi. It concluded with a blast against the ECCI.

"The crisis which is overtaking our party at present has been partly brought on by the pernicious influence which individual members of the Executive have exercised over our party since its foundation; [they have done so] uncontrolled by, and without the knowledge of, the membership [of the KPD]. . . . The Communist International, and the idea of international centralized leadership of the revolutionary proletariat will be hopelessly compromised if such methods as smelling out deviations (*Tendenzenriecherei*), snooping, uncontrollable side influences and . . . interferences into the affairs of the German party are not ruthlessly exposed and eliminated."[52]

Simultaneously with the appeal, Reuter-Friesland published a small brochure, in an edition of only 500 copies. Entitled *On the Crisis in Our Party*, it covered the same ground as the appeal, criticizing the *Zentrale* in the matter of the *Vorwärts* articles, and the ECCI for its dangerous meddling in German affairs. Only this time Reuter-Friesland singled out Radek as one of the chief culprits, and demanded genuine guarantees from the Executive that its agents would henceforth mend their ways. He warned in conclusion that

[51] *ibid.*, p. 198.
[52] *ibid.*

any attempt to purge the party of its so-called "rightist" elements would lead eventually to the capture of leadership by the sectarian "Left," a development which in his opinion would spell the end of the party. With this open attack on his former friends, Reuter-Friesland's career as a Communist had run full circle. There was no other place for him to go within the party; inevitably the next step had to lead away from it.

On December 22 the various polemical pamphlets were submitted to the *Zentrale,* which answered the challenge by a series of counter-measures. The demands made in the declaration and the appeal were rejected. Their authors were branded as fellow-travelers of the KAG, as "Party wreckers," and charged with conspiracy. Reuter-Friesland was expelled from the *Zentrale* on December 27, and the co-signers of the appeal were deprived of whatever official party functions they held. The final decision on how to deal with the mutiny was postponed until the next meeting of the Central Committee, scheduled for January 22, 1922. Reuter-Friesland utilized the weeks between his expulsion from the *Zentrale* and the meeting of the Central Committee to travel around the country and address party meetings in behalf of his cause. In the majority of cases the local party leaders opposed his point of view, but he retained the support of the most important Communist union officers. His whirlwind campaign forced the party leadership to partake in what threatened to become a "great debate." In so doing, the *Zentrale* played down its opponent's charges against the ECCI, a subject pregnant with hidden dangers, and tried instead to identify the Reuter-Friesland rebels with the KAG rebels.[53]

Once again a small group of German Communists fought a losing battle in an attempt to save the independence of their party. The issue, although beclouded by the usual Marxist-Leninist jargon, was essentially the right of the party to run its affairs free from outside interference. The rebels knew that their objectives were prejudiced by the fact that the KAG had also made them their own, and that the KAG was anathema to all those who had been implicated by

[53] Reuter-Friesland may have given occasion for this charge when he met Paul Levi for a private conference shortly after his ouster as general secretary, but before his dismissal from the *Zentrale.* The meeting had no practical consequences, perhaps because Reuter-Friesland realized that the KAG was an isolated faction without any political future (Brandt and Lowenthal, p. 202). Levi reached the same conclusion before long, for he eventually became a member of the SPD, as Reuter did.

their use of rather dubious tactics during the March uprising. Chances for winning support on the question of greater independence from Moscow were slightly better, but whereas most members of the *Zentrale* admitted in private the desirability of such an achievement they lacked the courage to say so in public. The excuse which they offered was always that they did not want to give the appearance of turning against the ECCI.[54]

Two weeks before the Central Committee was to meet, the leaders of the party revolt issued another appeal, signed by twenty-eight prominent members outside the *Zentrale* proper. This appeal pointed out that party membership, subsequent to the March uprising, had declined to a mere 200,000,[55] and warned that the need of the hour was not a new split, but the rallying of all revolutionary forces.

Could another split be avoided? The decision, as was to be expected, was made in Moscow. Four days prior to the crucial meeting, the *Zentrale* received an "open letter" from the ECCI which demanded a break with the "agents of the KAG" within the party. Reuter-Friesland, Brass, Malzahn, and everyone else who had violated the resolutions of the Third World Congress were to be expelled. A second letter, this time from the leaders of the Russian Communist Party, and signed by Lenin, Trotsky, Zinoviev, Radek and Bukharin, arrived shortly after and was published in the *Rote Fahne* on the day of the Central Committee meeting. Although it contained a conciliatory clause in which all erring comrades, not mentioned by name, were asked to "rally at the last moment around the flag of the party," the original threat remained: "Whoever abets this group [the KAG] violates the resolutions of the Third Congress and the Moscow peace treaty, [and] he is against the Communist International."[56]

The Central Committee of the German Communist Party met on January 22. Reuter-Friesland attended and gave the views of his faction on the political and economic outlook for the future as far as it affected party policy. Was capitalism on the decline, or was it

<hr/>

[54] *ibid.*, p. 200.

[55] This was a charitable estimate. The official party record gives the membership of the KPD in the summer of 1921 as 180,443 (*Bericht über die Verhandlungen des III. (8.) Parteitages*, pp. 63-64).

[56] *Die Rote Fahne*, No. 37, January 22, 1922.

holding its own? Reuter-Friesland upheld that the latter was the case, and drew two conclusions. First, in the prevailing "unrevolutionary" period the rigid centralism advocated and practiced by the Comintern no longer corresponded with existing conditions and should be abolished. Second, under the circumstances the party line would have to be adjusted so that it would become meaningful for workers now in the Socialist camp. Logically, this would necessitate at least the revision of the twenty-one conditions adopted by the Comintern, and accepted by the KPD, at the Second World Congress. The party would have to choose whether it wanted to remain a relatively small, sectarian organization of the "Bolshevik" type, or whether it was to become a strong, democratically run, mass party which could act as a focus for all revolutionary-minded forces in Germany.

Although the united front policy had been the official party line for the past five months, Reuter-Friesland's interpretation of it aroused angry protest from the *Zentrale*. His analysis of existing political and economic conditions was rejected as "revisionist." It was argued that an acute revolutionary situation could recur at any moment in view of the decline of Germany's productive strength, a decline only temporarily obscured by a fake boom. The party gave its verdict the following day. The Central Committee voted 41 to 4 to expel Reuter-Friesland and twenty-seven co-signers of the latest appeal from the Communist Party. The reason given was that they had violated discipline, and had voiced opinions which conflicted with the basic principles of Communism.[57]

And so the party conducted its second major purge within the short span of nine months. Once more the aftereffects of the March uprising rocked the KPD, and in the process reduced the quality of leadership still further as the party deprived itself of political talent it could ill afford to lose. The second purge completed in effect what the earlier one had begun: the elimination of the old right wing with its independent-minded spokesmen who had embarrassed the *Zentrale* with their often savage criticism of party affairs and their running feuds with the Comintern. Taken together with Clara Zetkin's return to the fold—a remarkable triumph of Lenin's persuasive powers—the destruction of the old right-wing faction with

[57] *Bericht über die Verhandlungen des III. (8.) Parteitages*, pp. 49, 126; Brandt and Lowenthal, pp. 203-204.

their one left-wing convert all but invited future Russian encroach-ments. Furthermore, the expulsion of Brass, Malzahn, and other leading officials in charge of the party's trade-union affairs placed the success of the united front program in jeopardy. In Reuter-Friesland, finally, the Communist Party lost one of its ablest, most devoted, and most honest leaders. He dropped "Friesland" from his name, and as Ernst Reuter eventually joined the Social Democratic Party after a brief interlude in the USPD. After the Second World War, as Lord Mayor of beleaguered West Berlin, he devoted the last years of his life to a resumption of his struggle against Communism, a movement which he joined in his youth with great expectations, and with which he broke when he found it wanting.

PART THREE
RETRENCHMENT

CHAPTER VIII

UNITED FRONT POLICY IN
THEORY AND PRACTICE

THROUGHOUT the greater part of 1921 the German Communists had been preoccupied with the ramifications of their ill-fated March uprising. Their attempt at revolution had miscarried, and the ensuing internecine recriminations had come close to wrecking the party. The purges which followed left the KPD subject to the control of men who favored compliance with Moscow's wishes. The grueling criticism to which the Bolshevik leaders had subjected them after the March fiasco goes far to explain why the members of the *Zentrale*, many of them "pre-March" activists, from then on preferred caution to heroics, reliance on Moscow to their own judgment and initiative. It was under this leadership that the German Communists pursued their united front policy throughout 1922.

It will be recalled that the initial step to create a united workers' front was taken in Germany with Paul Levi's "Open Letter," a device which at the time, early in 1921, had the full support of Radek. The idea behind this approach was to win the allegiance of the masses, and especially to convince workers organized in non-Communist labor organizations that the KPD alone was willing and able to promote the general welfare of the working class by leading the fight for better living conditions, for better hours and wages, and against unfair taxation. Closely connected with this objective was the desire to drive a wedge between the rank and file and their leaders, both within the unions and within the two Socialist parties. The workers were to be told that only the Communists had their immediate interests at heart, whereas the union and party *Bonzen* (bosses) would not procure for them so much as a piece of bread.[1]

The "Open Letter" campaign failed to meet with the desired response. What its chances might have been in the long run if

[1] See Radek's comments on this point, *Protokoll des III. Kongresses der K.I.* (Moskau, 22. Juni bis 12. Juli, 1921) (Hamburg, 1921), p. 460.

Levi had remained in the *Zentrale,* and if the March uprising had not discredited the KPD in the eyes of many German workers is, of course, impossible to say. During the intraparty wrangles that followed the uprising, any thought of continuing the "Open Letter" approach was out of the question; the fact that it was closely identified with the "traitor" Levi inhibited its immediate resumption. The idea was only revived after the Third World Congress had instructed Communist parties everywhere to go "to the masses." At the Jena party congress the pursuit of united front tactics was formally accepted by the KPD, which thereby became the first Communist party to give form and substance to the vague directives of the Third World Congress.

The policy had hardly been adopted when its execution led to new complications. Reuter-Friesland's liberal interpretation of what constituted a united front campaign exposed him to the charge of right deviationism and paved the way for his expulsion and that of his like-minded friends. At this point the *Zentrale* might have been expected to learn from the bitter experiences of its dangerous political pioneering project and to drop it. But such a solution was no longer open to the KPD when it conducted its second purge. A few weeks earlier, in December 1921, the ECCI had made the united front policy, hitherto strictly a German experiment, an integral part of official worldwide Communist strategy.[2]

This decision of the Comintern marked the culmination of a major shift in Bolshevik strategy. It had begun with the introduction of NEP, had led to the resolution of the Third World Congress to go "to the masses," and was paralleled by Russian attempts to establish economic and diplomatic contacts with other powers. Like all preceding changes in policy, from the stage when world revolution seemed just around the corner to that of the "breathing space," the latest change was also dictated by necessity and not by conviction. As long as Soviet Russia was in need of political and economic consolidation at home, and therefore not in a position to challenge the hostile capitalist world abroad, concessions were

[2] For the texts of the several manifestos, and for a discussion of their origins see Degras, ed., *The Communist International 1919-1943, Documents,* I, Royal Institute of International Affairs (London-New York-Toronto, 1956), pp. 307-320; also Carr, *The Bolshevik Revolution, 1917-1923,* III, (New York, 1953) pp. 412-413.

necessary. In what spirit these concessions were meant Lenin made perfectly clear in December 1920.

"Our task is to maintain the existence of our isolated socialist republic . . . which is so much weaker than the capitalist enemies who surround it; to remove the opportunity for the enemies to create an alliance among themselves for a struggle against us; to keep on interfering with their policies; to prevent them from winning. . . . We do not for a moment believe in lasting trade relations with the imperialist powers; what we shall obtain will be simply a breathing space."[3]

In essence, then, the Bolsheviks viewed the concessions they made on any level and in any sphere as temporary expedients, designed to meet the needs of the moment. The same spirit motivated the united front policy which the Communists adopted for universal use in December 1921. The approach had suggested itself to the ECCI as a result of the German experience which, despite its shortcomings, served as a model for the entire non-Russian world.[4]

The project with all its implications was as ambiguous as it was ambitious. The Bolsheviks visualized a dual policy: every attempt was to be made to arouse mass support for the Communists in the capitalist countries, preparatory to the ultimate overthrow of capitalist society, but this attempt was to be accompanied by diplomatic maneuvers designed to pit the capitalist nations against one another. As the latter policy demanded the establishment of at least tolerable relations with one, or even several, capitalist countries in order to set them against other states, the first policy was hardly conducive to furthering the second. Both policies, their inner contradictions notwithstanding, were to be initiated simul-

---

[3] Quoted in Eudin and Fisher, *Soviet Russia and the West* (Stanford, 1957), p. 6. Excerpts from Lenin's report to the Communist Party faction at the Eighth Congress of Soviets of the R.S.F.S.R. in December 1920, *ibid.*, pp. 44-48.

[4] Carr, *The Bolshevik Revolution*, III, p. 412. Borkenau, *Der europäische Kommunismus* (Bern, 1952), p. 43. Borkenau writes in this connection (*ibid.*) that during this particular phase of Comintern history all experiments, shifts in tactics, and methods of organization began in Germany, so that for this reason the history of the KPD during this period became the quintessence of the history of western Communism.

The following discussion of the united front policy owes much to the studies of Carr and Borkenau.

taneously as part of the temporary strategic retreat which the Bolsheviks in 1921 deemed necessary.[5]

The incompatibility of this dual approach was paralleled by a number of inherent contradictions in the united front policy. In order to win mass support for the Communists in capitalist countries, it would have been essential, as Carr says, to "relax the rigidities not only of doctrine, but also of discipline, and to concede to national parties and their leaders a far wider discretion in the framing of policies and tactics suited to local conditions, which would never be well enough or promptly enough appreciated in Moscow."[6] Such powers of discretion the Comintern was unwilling to allow its member parties, and, instead of relaxing control, the Comintern leaders saw to it that the Third World Congress devoted a great deal of time, energy, and printer's ink to strengthening centralization and tightening organization and discipline.[7] These discrepancies between aims and methods, between the desire for mass support and the requirement to work under Moscow's ever-suspicious tutelage made the united front policy a perilous enterprise for any Communist party that embarked on it. The entire approach was essentially dishonest, at least as far as the Bolshevik leaders were concerned. While one can agree with Carr's statement that "the leaders of [the] Comintern . . . sincerely desired to modify their tactics in such a way as to win the allegiance of the masses," it is much harder to accept his subsequent conclusion that "they did not understand the conditions which would have been necessary to make this policy a success."[8]

It is very likely that just because the Bolsheviks understood the conditions which would have been necessary to make united front tactics successful, they insisted on imposing a stricter measure of discipline and control to safeguard the Communist movement from future "deviationists" such as Levi and Reuter-Friesland. Both men, Levi in January 1921, and Reuter-Friesland in the fall

[5] For a fuller discussion of this issue see Carr, *The Bolshevik Revolution*, III, pp. 394-397.

[6] *ibid.*, p. 392.

[7] For a useful and concise discussion of the organization, methods of approach, and historical development of the Comintern, see Nollau, *Die Internationale* (Cologne, 1959), pp. 45-147.

[8] Carr, *The Bolshevik Revolution*, III, p. 392. The author's afterthought, ". . . nor would they have been willing to accept these conditions" appears to be a more realistic appraisal.

of that year, had made serious efforts to establish closer relations with the non-Communist labor movement. The too literal interpretation of their mission proved their undoing. They had failed to understand, or had simply ignored, the fact that the leaders of the Comintern were only willing to modify their tactics to the extent that any resulting rapprochement with non-Communist labor groups would not be made at the expense of Communist revolutionary *élan*. As Borkenau has pointed out, the underlying dishonesty which marked and marred the united front approach during this period had already been expounded by Lenin, in his brochure *"Left-Wing" Communism*. The relevant passage pertains to Lenin's advice that British Communists should, for mere tactical reasons, vote for Henderson's Socialist Party against the Coalition Government of Lloyd George, but that they should support Henderson with their vote "in the same way as a rope supports one who is hanged."[9] Implicit in Lenin's metaphor was the dictum that a Communist offer of cooperation with non-Communist labor organizations for any stated purpose must never be anything but a tactical maneuver. As soon as a Communist leader took such cooperation seriously (as Levi and Reuter-Friesland eventually did), he became a traitor to his party and its ideology.

How precarious the policy was is apparent from a speech which Zinoviev delivered in December 1922, at the Fourth World Congress of the Communist International. On that occasion, after a year's experience, he made a not altogether successful attempt to define what the ECCI understood by the term "united front."

"What should the united front be, and what should it not be? Under no circumstances must it become what the French call an 'electoral combination.' . . . It should, as already said, not be an electoral combination, and, of course, no organizational union with the Social Democrats either. . . . This would be the greatest crime which we could commit. Every one of us would rather have his hand cut off than to underwrite a union with the greatest traitors of the working class, who are now our enemies and the last prop of the bourgeoisie. This is by no means a united front. The united front is the common struggle of the laboring masses in their day-

[9] Lenin, *"Left-Wing" Communism* (New York, 1934), p. 68; Borkenau, *Der europäische Kommunismus*, pp. 45-46.

by-day demands vis-à-vis capitalism. The united front is to mean that we are prepared to fight, together with all workers, be they Anarchists, Syndicalists, Christian-Socialists, Social Democrats, or whatever they may call themselves, against capitalism and the capitalists in the daily struggle for a piece of bread, in the daily struggle against wage reductions and the abolition of the eight-hour day [meaning presumably wherever this hard-won proletarian achievement was in effect but under attack]. In return we have to put up with the fact that on occasions we shall have to sit at one table with the traitorous leaders. This, and nothing else, is meant by the united front."[10]

The glaring ambiguities which are evident in this brief "definition" illustrate that the margin for error which the ECCI left its member parties was narrow indeed. For who could ever say beforehand whether Moscow would look at any given attempt at cooperation with, for instance, Social Democrats, as a necessary tactical measure to fight capitalism, or as collaboration with the "greatest traitors of the working class"?

In order to walk the thin line which separated Bolshevik-approved united front tactics from political heresy, Communist party leaders in the individual countries either had to be infallible, or were forced to rely on precarious, and often indeterminate, political maneuvers. Since no man is infallible, the second alternative became mandatory for any party functionary who wanted to avoid courting trouble with Moscow. A good example of how to conduct united front policy with a minimum of risk was provided, in September 1921, by the KPD in Thuringia. The local Landtag elections of that month had returned 13 deputies from the SPD, 9 from the USPD, and 6 from the KPD—a slim parliamentary majority of 28 deputies from the Left against 26 from the middle-class parties. The outcome of the election posed a problem to the Communists: were they to join the two Socialist parties in forming a genuine workers' government, or were they to content themselves with merely supporting a Socialist government in the diet? As the party was unable to reach a decision on this point, but at the same time

[10] Exekutivkommitee der Kommunistischen Internationale, *Protokoll des Vierten Kongresses der Kommunistischen Internationale, Petrograd-Moskau vom 5. November bis 5. Dezember 1922* (Hamburg, 1923), pp. 64-65; hereafter cited as *Protokoll des Vierten Kongresses der K.I.*

could not very well allow this fact to become known to the Socialists with whom they planned to negotiate, a joint strategy was worked out beforehand by the Communist Landtag delegation and district leaders on how to conduct the talks. The result of these dress rehearsals was what the official party report describes as a display of "clever tactical mobility" during the subsequent conferences: the Communists maneuvered to avoid committing themselves either way. "This succeeded so well that the two Social Democratic parties were forced to form a Socialist government without committing our delegation to accept any obligation whatever, except for the promise that our delegates would vote for them [the Socialist delegates] at the first election of ministers."[11] This promise the KPD kept, and on October 7, 1921, the Social Democrats and Independents formed a government in Thuringia under Minister President August Frölich (SPD). With one minor exception the composition of the Frölich government remained unchanged until October 1923.[12]

Thuringia, however, was but one of many areas where the KPD conducted united front policy. When the excitement accompanying the Reuter-Friesland purge had died down, and the inconvenient right-wingers with their constant insistence on independence and principles had been banished, the party, led by Ernst Meyer, who in turn relied on the guiding hand of Radek, searched the German scene for further opportunities to shower the non-Communist workers with brotherly love.

The most immediate problems to which the united front policy could be applied lay in the economic sphere. By the end of 1921 the inflationary trend began to work severe hardships on that portion of German labor that was in the employ of the Reich, the

---

[11] *Bericht über die Verhandlungen des III. (8.) Parteitages der K.P.D. (Sektion der K.I.) abgehalten in Leipzig vom 28. Januar bis 1. Februar 1923* (Berlin, 1923), p. 52.

The vexing questions of what constituted a workers' government, what it should accomplish, and when to form one, or not, were to haunt the KPD from the fall of 1921 to the fall of 1923 (see below, especially Chs. x-xiii). See also Borkenau's analysis in *The Communist International* (London, 1938), pp. 226-227, and *Der europäische Kommunismus*, p. 45.

[12] On the Thuringian situation in the fall of 1921 see Thalheimer, *Inprecorr*, i, No. 12, pp. 98-99; Ulbricht, *Zur Geschichte der deutschen Arbeitergewegung*, i (Berlin, 1953), pp. 60-63; Georg Witzmann, *Thüringen von 1918-1933: Erinnerungen eines Politikers* (Meissenheim am Glain, 1958), pp. 55-56; *Schulthess' Europäischer Geschichtskalender*, N.F., lxii, 1921 (Munich, 1926), p. 287.

states, or the municipalities. The dwindling value of the mark did not as yet affect the industrial workers to any serious extent. German industry was replacing the backlog of consumer goods and capital goods that had been depleted during the war, and the demand for reparation deliveries also helped to keep the plants busy. Unemployment had steadily receded throughout 1921 and continued to do so during the first half of 1922.[13] Industry was therefore better equipped to meet wage demands—made as a result of rising prices—than was any branch of government, because increases in salaries and wages of public officials and employees had to be met by raising fees and taxes. It was this consideration which prompted the German national government, in December 1921, to reject a cost-of-living wage increase demanded by the Federal Association of Railway Employees. After a series of fruitless negotiations which continued throughout January 1922, the railway workers called a strike on February 1. President Ebert, invoking Article 48 of the Constitution, issued an injunction against the strike on the basis that railway employees were public officials. The government urged the strikers to return to their jobs or face disciplinary action. But the strike continued. To make matters worse, on February 5 the municipal workers of the city of Berlin staged an unauthorized walkout which deprived the German capital of electricity, gas, and water.[14]

Here was a splendid chance for the KPD to demonstrate its recently acquired concern for the interests of non-Communist labor organizations. Unmindful of the fact that not only the government but also the majority of workers condemned the strikes, the party resolved to support them. As soon as the railway strike had been called, the *Zentrale* contacted union officials and leaders of both Socialist parties and suggested that they consult together on measures to resist the strike ban of the government. But neither the union officials (ADGB) nor the Socialist party leaders were interested. The SPD, unwilling to defy the government injunction, published an appeal to the railway men and the municipal workers

[13] *Jahrbuch für Politik, Wirtschaft, Arbeiterbewegung 1922-23* (Hamburg, n.d.), p. 635.
[14] *Schulthess'*, 1922, pp. 11-12, 15-16; Flechtheim, *Die K.P.D. in der Weimarer Republik* (Offenbach, 1948), pp. 77-79; Stampfer, *Die vierzehn Jahre der ersten deutschen Republik*, 3rd ed. (Hamburg, 1947), pp. 258-261.

of Berlin, urging them to call off the strikes. *Freiheit*, the party news-paper of the Independents, adopted a similar, though somewhat less determined, position. The Communists found themselves alone in their support of the walkouts, which collapsed on February 8 without having netted any concessions for the strikers.[15]

Apart from the fact that the episode ended in total failure, the KPD had once again suffered an unmistakable rebuff from or-ganized labor. Official party reaction, however, remained undis-mayed and emphasized the few rays of sunshine in an otherwise cloudy sky. August Thalheimer claimed that during the strikes the lower and middle strata of government employees had entered the arena of class warfare, and that the most active among them had been drawn closer to the industrial proletariat.[16] The party as a whole expressed pride in having been the only labor organization which had stood by the strikers in their hour of need.[17]

The February strikes had been entirely a German affair, but the next united front offensive in which the KPD participated was on a much larger scale. The project in question was an attempt to establish closer contacts and better understanding throughout the entire European labor movement, and the initiative did not come from the Communists, but from the International Working Union of Socialist Parties. This organization, known more familiarly as the "Vienna Union" or, among its foes, as the "Two-and-a-Half Inter-national," had been founded in Vienna in February 1921.[18] Politi-cally it stood between the Second and Third Internationals, and included the German USPD, the British Independent Labour Party, a French Socialist faction under Longuet, the Austrian Socialist groups led by Otto Bauer and Friedrich Adler, Russian Mensheviks, and some less well-known organizations. Sandwiched, as it was, between the Comintern and the Second International, and without a clear-cut policy or philosophy of its own save for a pronounced pacifism, the Vienna Union was in an awkward, and

[15] *Bericht über die Verhandlungen des III. (8.) Parteitages*, pp. 18-19; Stampfer, p. 261; *Schulthess'*, 1922, p. 16; Severing, *Mein Lebensweg*, 1 (Cologne, 1950), pp. 339-346, gives a detailed account of the strike as he saw it.
[16] August Thalheimer, "Der proletarische Klassenkampf in Deutschland im Jahre 1922," *Jahrbuch für Politik, Wirtschaft, Arbeiterbewegung 1922-23*, p. 608.
[17] *Bericht über die Verhandlungen des III. (8.) Parteitages*, p. 19.
[18] Carr, *The Bolshevik Revolution*, III, p. 407; Sender, *The Autobiography of a German Rebel* (New York, 1939), pp. 180-181. Miss Sender attended the found-ing of the Union.

politically precarious, position. The realization of this fact may well have been the reason for the suggestion, made by its spokesmen early in 1922, to improve cooperation among the three international proletarian organizations. The original plan was to call a world conference of all workers' organizations, a proposal which was accepted with alacrity by the Comintern during the enlarged session of the ECCI on February 24. Moscow suggested that all trade-unions be invited regardless of their affiliation. The plan of a world conference was opposed by the Second International, representatives of which met with those of the Vienna Union at Frankfurt am Main from February 24 to 27. There it was resolved to hold, not a world conference, but a preliminary meeting restricted to representatives from the executive committees of all three Internationals. The stated purpose of the meeting was to determine the extent to which the international labor movement was able to cooperate in solving pressing issues common to all. The most important issue on the agenda was the coming conference of the Powers, scheduled to convene at Genoa on April 10, 1922. The meeting of the representatives for the Internationals, to be held in Berlin, was accordingly arranged for April 2.[19]

Since the proposed preconference fitted in well with the policy of the united front, the readiness of the Comintern to participate was hardly surprising. There were, moreover, additional considerations. From the statement which the ECCI sent to the meeting it is apparent that the Russians hoped to gain specific advantages for the Soviet Union from their Socialist "allies," in particular, support for their country at the impending Genoa conference. The statement lists, among other items, the desire for recognition of the Soviet Union, for trade relations with the West, and for aid in Russia's economic reconstruction.[20]

The meeting convened on April 2 in the Reichstag building in Berlin. The German hosts were the only participants with repre-

[19] Christo Kabaktschieff, *Die Entstehung und Entwicklung der Komintern: Kurzer Abriss der Geschichte der Komintern* (Berlin, 1929), pp. 105-106; *Schulthess'*, 1922, pp. 320-321; Carr, *The Bolshevik Revolution*, III, pp. 407-408; Degras, ed., *The Communist International, Documents*, I, pp. 333-337.

[20] Degras, ed., *The Communist International, Documents*, I, p. 335; Borkenau (*The Communist International*, p. 233) suggests that the Bolsheviks intended to use the conference also to discredit the Socialist leadership. This they did, but it is impossible to say whether they acted with premeditation, or from habit.

sentatives in all three delegations: Otto Wels for the SPD, Arthur Crispien for the Independents, and Clara Zetkin for the KPD. Deliberations began after Clara Zetkin read the ECCI's previously mentioned statement of aims to the assembled delegates at the opening session. The details, which have been treated elsewhere, need not concern us here.[21] The meeting soon developed into a verbal duel between Karl Radek, the spokesman for the Comintern, and the Belgian minister, Emile Vandervelde, who was ably supported by England's Ramsay MacDonald, as spokesmen for the Second International. Vandervelde, after flatly refusing to sanction either a discussion of reparations or of the Versailles treaty, demanded three guarantees from the Comintern before the Second International would consent to a conference. The Communists must desist from cell building in workers' organizations; they must give fair treatment to the Georgian Republic, where in February 1921 a Menshevik government had been overthrown by Red Army troops under the direction of Stalin; and they must free the Social Revolutionary leaders whose trial was impending, but who had been held in prison by the Bolsheviks ever since the civil war period. Radek, apart from insisting on a joint denunciation of the Versailles treaty, refused to make any concessions to Vandervelde or other Socialist speakers—at least while he addressed them in public. Behind the scenes, Radek proved amenable to mild compromises, because he was eager to avoid an open split just a few days before the conference of the Powers at Genoa. Nevertheless, the achievements of the meeting were negligible. Most important was the decision, embedded in a joint resolution of April 5, to form an organizational committee of nine, three from each International, to lay plans for further conferences, and for possible discussions between the "Red" and "Yellow" Trade-Union Internationals. The Comintern delegates gave some reassuring promises concerning the trial of the Social Revolutionaries, and authorized the organizational committee to receive information on the Georgian question from all three executives. The joint resolution ended with a general appeal to the workers of every country to stage demonstrations for the eight-hour day, for the Russian revolution, for the re-establish-

[21] See in particular Borkenau, *The Communist International*, pp. 233-234; Carr, *The Bolshevik Revolution*, III, pp. 408-412; and Kabaktschieff, p. 106.

ment of a proletarian united front everywhere, and against unemployment and the "capitalist offensive."

Reaction in Moscow to the outcome of the meeting was less than enthusiastic. Lenin, in a *Pravda* article of April 11, 1922, entitled "We Have Paid Too Dear," repudiated Radek's concessions made in regard to the trial of the Social Revolutionaries, and noted pointedly that no concessions had come forth from the delegates of the two Socialist Internationals. The attitude of the Socialists to the Berlin meeting was equally chilly, and in mid-May the Socialist parties of England, France, and Belgium prepared the way for a reunion of the Second and Two-and-a-Half Internationals, without the Comintern. Thus ended a most ambitious experiment —the first, though not the last of its kind—the attempt to rally the international proletariat behind the united front slogan. Although the move had not originated with the Comintern, the Bolshevik leaders eagerly seized upon the idea once it had been proposed. That the experiment failed was hardly surprising in view of the uncompromising attitude of all factions. But the fact that such an attempt had been made at all, and that Moscow had participated in it, gave added incentive to the various Communist parties outside Russia, including the KPD, for a vigorous resumption of united front policies in their own countries.

Despite the inconclusive note on which the meeting of delegates had ended, the Communists of Berlin joined with the Independents on April 20 in staging a mass demonstration which was attended by a crowd estimated at between 20,000 and 30,000. Long columns of men and women marched behind red banners—those of the Communists with hammer and sickle or Soviet star emblems, those of the Independents without them—and assembled at the meeting place. Speakers from both parties reiterated the principal demands raised by the recent conference in its concluding joint resolution: the eight-hour day; a unified stand of all proletarians against the "capitalist offensive"; and the formation of a united labor front. With a cheer for the latter the demonstration ended, and the columns marched back home. Representatives of the SPD had been conspicuously absent.[22]

[22] *Frankfurter Zeitung*, No. 297, April 22, 1922; *Vossische Zeitung*, No. 187, April 21, 1922.

According to the official annals of the KPD, the Communists alone had organized

United Front Policy

Communist May Day speakers were also conspicuously silent on the spectacular Russo-German agreement which had been concluded a few days earlier in Rapallo.[23] The German press abounded with detailed reports and editorials on this surprising turn of events, but the Communist newspapers acted with rare restraint. Two days after the Rapallo agreement had been signed, the *Rote Fahne* commented favorably on how the French and British had been outwitted at Genoa, but refrained from returning to the subject for another six weeks.[24] As far as is known today, the initial Communist reaction to the treaty was a mixture of bewilderment and embarrassment. Apparently only a few initiated leaders had been informed beforehand by Radek. The rank and file were taken by surprise.[25] Although friendship between

---

the demonstration, without cooperation from any other party. This claim seems unjustified in view of the fact that the USPD furnished speakers and participants. See *Bericht über die Verhandlungen des III. (8.) Parteitages*, p. 22. Subsequent demonstrations, which were attended by both Socialist parties, trade-unions, and Communists were held throughout Germany on May 1, the traditional holiday of international labor. Demands for the eight-hour day again dominated the themes of the speakers. Only in Hamburg did the Communists refuse to join the demonstrations because the Socialists included in this city's program a public avowal of faith in the republic (*Frankfurter Zeitung*, Nos. 323, 324, May 2, 1922).

[23] The well-known event whereby the two pariah nations absented themselves from the Genoa conference on April 16, 1922, and at nearby Rapallo concluded an agreement by which they resumed diplomatic relations, cancelled each other's war debts, and laid the basis for closer economic relations need not be retold. For literature on this agreement see Schieder, *Die Probleme des Rapallo-Vertrags*, Arbeitsgemeinschaft für Forschung des Landes Nordheim-Westfalen, Heft 43 (Cologne and Opladen, 1956), pp. 30-50, and *passim*; Hilger and Meyer, *The Incompatible Allies* (New York, 1953), pp. 76-83, and *passim*; Kochan, *Russia and the Weimar Republic* (Cambridge, 1954), pp. 35-59; Freund, *Unholy Alliance* (New York, 1957), pp. 84-140; Blücher, *Deutschlands Weg nach Rapallo* (Wiesbaden, 1951), pp. 153-165; Carr, *The Bolshevik Revolution*, III, 339-382, and the same author's earlier study, *German-Soviet Relations between the Two World Wars 1919-1939* (Baltimore, 1951), pp. 48-66; see also the East German interpretation in Rosenfeld, *Sowjetrussland und Deutschland, 1917-1922* (Berlin, 1960), pp. 355-398.

[24] *Die Rote Fahne*, No. 180, April 18, 1922. Carr, *The Bolshevik Revolution*, III, 414.
Three days later, however, the *Rote Fahne* printed a speech which Pieck had delivered at a mass demonstration of workers in the Berlin Lustgarten. He was quoted as having said that "if the German bourgeoisie has . . . concluded a treaty with Soviet Russia at Genoa [sic], then [the bourgeoisie] acted not from friendship, but from cogent necessity, i.e., the kicks of the Entente. German labor must do everything to breathe life into that paper treaty" (*Die Rote Fahne*, No. 185, April 21, 1922).

[25] Fischer, *Stalin and German Communism* (Cambridge, Mass., 1948), pp. 192-193.

Germany and Soviet Russia had been for years a constant Communist propaganda slogan, once this demand seemed on the verge of realization the new situation posed more problems for the KPD than it solved. It must have been obvious to every thinking party member that the Rapallo agreement severely complicated Communist policy in Germany. How could the KPD continue to preach revolution against a state which had just formally committed itself to improving its relations with the fatherland of the proletariat? Was there not bound to be further restriction of independent action in relation to the state, and increased dependence on Bolshevik guidance and direction, since the interests of Soviet foreign policy would be from now on closely affected by any move made by the KPD?[26]

To complicate matters further, it was difficult for the German Communists to ascertain with any degree of certainty Moscow's true interpretation of the Rapallo treaty. The official formula which the Central Committee of the Russian Communist Party adopted on May 18, and which Trotsky in essence reiterated the following day in *Izvestia*, seemed primarily designed to conceal a divergence of views held by the Soviet leaders in the evaluation of Rapallo.[27] According to this formula, the treaty signified merely the re-establishment of normal relations between Soviet Russia and another capitalist state; it was not an alliance, intended to counterbalance other powers.

". . . The All-Russian Central Executive Committee welcomes the Russo-German treaty concluded at Rapallo as the only correct way out of the difficulties, chaos, and threats of war; accepts this treaty as a normal form for treaties in the relationship between the R.S.F.S.R. and the capitalist states; and instructs the Council of People's Commissars and the Commissariat of Foreign Affairs to pursue their policy in the future in a similar vein, and to allow deviation from the format of the Rapallo treaty only under exceptional circumstances. . . ."[28]

Trotsky commented the same day, May 18, that on "the principles of the Rapallo Treaty, Soviet Russia is ready to sign today a

---

[26] This theme is more fully developed in Carr, *The Bolshevik Revolution*, III, 415.
[27] Schieder, p. 49.
[28] Quoted in Eudin and Fisher, p. 169; this work gives the date of the resolution as May 18, whereas Schieder, p. 49, dates it May 17.

treaty with any other country."[29] The language employed, both by Trotsky and the Central Committee of the Russian C.P., was in line with the realistic approach to Soviet foreign policy which Lenin had inaugurated early in 1921, although Lenin himself did not draft the official statement. He was seriously ill, having suffered a stroke some time during May 1922.[30]

At the same time, the pronounced reserve of the wording, which seemed intended to reduce the significance of the Russo-German agreement, could not but satisfy that faction in the ECCI which under no circumstances wanted to close the door to future revolutionary agitation in Germany.[31] This was made perfectly clear in a statement which the ECCI issued on May 19, 1922. The key passages of this document are worth quoting.

". . . The treaty between Russia and Germany signed at Rapallo is of enormous historical importance. . . . On the German side the treaty was signed by the present bourgeois-Menshevik government, but everybody understands that while the position of the bourgeois-Menshevik German government is a temporary thing, the German working class remains. The German working class will one day inevitably conquer power in their own country. Germany will become a Soviet Republic. And then, when the German-Russian treaty brings together two great Soviet republics, it will provide such unshakable foundations for real Communist construction that the old and outworn Europe will not be able to withstand it for even a few years. In this sense the fate of humanity in the next few years will be determined by the successes of the German working class. The victory of the German proletariat over 'its' bourgeoisie will involve unprecedented changes in the social structure of the whole of Europe. When the German proletariat destroys in its country the influence of the Second and Two-and-a-Half Internationals a new chapter will open in the history of mankind."[32]

[29] Quoted in Kochan, p. 55.

[30] Schieder, p. 49. Lenin's illness was reported to Berlin by the German Embassy in Moscow on May 31, 1922. The wording implied that Lenin had fallen ill only a few days before the message was sent ("German Embassy to Foreign Office," Auswärtiges Amt, Germany, microfilm, container 1405, frame D 552572, National Archives, Washington, D.C.). Schieder, basing himself on Leo Trotski, *Mein Leben* (Berlin, 1930), pp. 454ff., dates Lenin's stroke early in May.

[31] Schieder, p. 49.

[32] The statement appeared in *Inprecorr*, II, No. 73 (May 22, 1922), p. 563, and is quoted in Degras, ed., *The Communist International, Documents*, I, p. 347.

The reaction of the ECCI to Rapallo was thus as uncompromising a reaffirmation of its revolutionary aims as the statement of the Central Executive Committee of the Russian C.P. was reserved and noncommittal. If this discrepancy of views sowed confusion in the minds of outsiders, such confusion was further compounded by still another viewpoint, espoused by Radek, who saw Rapallo primarily as a convenient means of changing the European constellation of powers. Radek, who in the spring of 1922 spent a good deal of time in Berlin, between trips from Genoa to Moscow and back, propagated the idea of an alliance between the activist elements among the German nationalists and the equally activist Communists. Such an alliance, he explained to Ernst Troeltsch, was essential for an eventual all-out struggle against western European capitalism.[33] According to Ruth Fischer, Radek went even further and maintained that a national front of all classes in Germany was imperative in the coming struggle against the Entente. In conjunction with Professor Eugen Varga, noted Soviet economist, and Bukharin, Radek developed the theory that the western powers, notably England and France, intended to turn Germany into an "industrial colony," a policy which would victimize the German bourgeoisie almost as much as the German worker.[34] Hence the need, not only of cooperation between German patriots and Communists, but of an equally active cooperation between Germany and Soviet Russia against Versailles and its henchmen, the capitalist exploiters of the West.

The views Radek stated in the late spring of 1922 not only foreshadowed his National-Bolshevist policy of a year later,[35] but also

[33] Troeltsch, *Spektator-Briefe* (Tübingen, 1924), p. 269; Eudin and Fisher, p. 171.
Radek received official German permission to stay in Berlin between his trips after he promised that he would refrain from all propagandist activities (Troeltsch, *loc.cit.*). He apparently kept this promise, in part, one may assume, because restraint was at this time in accordance with his views on Russo-German relations. This is borne out by a letter from Hans von Raumer, an expert on Russian affairs, and the official observer of the German People's Party at Genoa. The letter, addressed to Foreign Minister Walther Rathenau, who was still in Genoa after Raumer had returned to Berlin, is dated May 5, 1922. Raumer passed on a piece of information, according to which Radek was allegedly using his influence with the KPD to keep the party quiet. When Raumer asked Radek point blank whether this was true, Radek answered in the affirmative. "He had explained to these people [the German Communists] why they could not now string up fellows like Scheidemann [a prominent Social Democratic leader]"; ("Raumer to Rathenau," Auswärtiges Amt, Germany, microfilm, container 1405, frame D 552545).
[34] Fischer, pp. 198-199.   [35] See below, Ch. xi.

offered a third interpretation of Rapallo which visualized an alliance between revisionist Soviet Russia and Germany against the Entente and the Versailles settlement.[36]

In the absence of a clear and decisive Russian line on Rapallo, the KPD exercised prudence and restraint in dealing with the issue. Thalheimer wrote an article attacking the SPD because it was the only German party opposed to the treaty; he admonished the workers that it was their "duty to see that this step is not followed by a step back, but by further steps in the direction of *Anschluss* with Soviet Russia."[37] Frölich spoke on the matter at length during the Reichstag session of March 30, 1922, when the treaty was submitted for debate. He favorably contrasted the Russian delegates at Genoa with the Germans, because the Russians had shown more backbone during the negotiations with the western powers. He claimed that Rapallo merely confirmed a situation which had already existed for some time, i.e., the fact that Russia and Germany had been living peacefully side by side. "It must be further stated that whatever this treaty of Rapallo may contain in addition [to the confirmation of already existing facts?], up to now it is nothing else but fine phrases which, for the time being, lack any real content."[38]

[36] Later in the year, Radek wrote in a report to the Fourth World Congress of the Comintern that "the policy of throttling Germany implies as a matter of fact the destruction of Russia as a great power, for no matter how Russia is governed it is always her interest to see that Germany exists. A Russia which has been weakened . . . by the war could neither have continued as a great power nor acquired the economic and technical means for her industrial reconstruction unless she had in the existence of Germany a counter-balance against the supremacy of the Allies" (Karl Radek, *The Winding-Up of the Versailles Treaty: Report to the Fourth Congress of the Communist International,* English translation [Hamburg, 1922], p. 16, as quoted in Kochan, pp. 55-56). Contrary to the statements made by Kochan (p. 55) and by Freund (p. 143), Radek did not deliver this speech at the Fourth World Congress, where the only reference to Rapallo was made, obliquely, by Bukharin on November 18, 1922. Bukharin asked: "From the standpoint of strategic usefulness to the proletariat as a whole, can a proletarian state sign military alliances with bourgeois states?" And he answered his own question: "There is no difference in principle between a loan and a military alliance; and I affirm that we have already grown up enough to conclude a military alliance with the bourgeoisie of one country so as to be able, with its help, to crush the bourgeoisie of another country" (*Protokoll des Vierten Kongresses der K.I.,* p. 420). I have used the translation of Eudin and Fisher, pp. 209-210. See also Degras, ed., *The Communist International, Documents,* I, pp. 343-344, for references to Radek and Bukharin's respective positions; also Carr, *The Bolshevik Revolution,* III, p. 447.

[37] Quoted in Degras, ed., *The Communist International, Documents,* I, p. 343. The original source is not given.

[38] *Stenographische Berichte des Reichstags, Verhandlungen,* vol. 355, p. 7738.

A similar note of scepticism was sounded on July 4, 1922, by Walter Stoecker, during the combined second and third reading of the bill prior to the final vote of adoption. Although he conceded grudgingly that the rapprochement with Russia was a good omen for the future of German foreign policy, he warned that the conclusion of the agreement as such meant very little, and that it would remain a paper treaty unless the German working class succeeded in giving it content as well as life. "For our petty bourgeois government is vacillating to and fro . . . ," and will be so afraid of the Entente that it will never execute the treaty properly, but will conduct a capitalist policy in its relations with Russia. Any real and effective alliance with Russia, according to Stoecker, could and would be concluded only by a German workers' government.[39]

The party's less than enthusiastic approach to Rapallo was also reflected by the remarkably brief comments on the treaty in the official record: "The party utilized the negotiations in Genoa and the Russo-German Rapallo treaty, which was concluded at the time, to show the workers the advantages of such a liaison with Soviet Russia, and also the dangers of the coalition policy [with middle-class parties] conducted by the Social Democrats, [a policy] which was hostile to the execution of the Rapallo treaty."[40]

While the German Communists were still trying to adjust their political bearings with regard to the Russo-German rapprochement, they were confronted by a new and complicating situation on June 24, 1922. On that day nationalist fanatics assassinated Foreign Minister Walther Rathenau, one of the architects—albeit a reluctant one—of Rapallo. The murder caused an outburst of shock and indignation throughout the country. It was still fresh in most people's minds that less than a year before Matthias Erzberger had suffered the same fate. On June 4, 1922, an attempt had been made to kill Philipp Scheidemann, a veteran Social Democrat and mayor of Cassel, by throwing prussic acid into his face. And now, only three weeks after that outrage, Rathenau became another victim of an organized nationalist murder gang. The latest assassination was widely interpreted as preliminary to a right-wing putsch.[41] For aside from the more prominent statesmen against whom rightist assas-

[39] *ibid.*, vol. 356, pp. 8269-8271.
[40] *Bericht über die Verhandlungen des III. (8.) Parteitages*, pp. 22-23.
[41] Troeltsch, p. 282; Sender, pp. 196-198.

sins had struck, 354 murders of less well-known persons had been perpetrated by nationalists between 1918 and 1922.[42] Thus Chancellor Joseph Wirth, a close personal friend of Rathenau, expressed the sentiments of most fair-minded citizens when he charged in the Reichstag on June 25 that "the enemy . . . stands on the right!"[43]

With the chancellor's conclusion that the enemy stood on the right German labor was in general agreement. The question now was what could be done about it. The KPD was quick to seize the initiative. That the party was moved by genuine grief for the "capitalist" Rathenau is doubtful, although Rathenau had shown a genuine interest in Socialist experiments. He had exchanged ideas on political and economic questions with Radek when the latter had been a prisoner of the German government in the fall and winter of 1919. He was intimately associated with the Rapallo agreement, although his consent to the pact had been given with serious misgivings.[44] None of these facts, however, would have weighed heavily enough to elicit from the Communists even a stir of sympathy if Rathenau had died a natural death. He became useful to the party only because he was killed by nationalists, an event which could be exploited in connection with the united front policy.

When the news of Rathenau's death reached the *Zentrale*, the Communist leaders contacted the SPD and the labor unions and suggested a joint conference to deliberate on how to deal with this latest right-wing provocation. The Communists also outlined a number of demands to be submitted to the government. The most important of these called for drastic measures against all counter-revolutionaries, the dismissal of all public officials suspected of reactionary sentiments, immediate amnesty for all imprisoned pro-

[42] Emil J. Gumbel, *Vier Jahre politischer Mord* (Berlin, 1922), pp. 73-78; see also Waite, *Vanguard of Nazism* (Cambridge, Mass., 1952), pp. 218-220, and *passim*.

[43] *Stenographische Berichte des Reichstags, Verhandlungen*, vol. 356, p. 8058.

Joseph Wirth, a liberal and a leading member of the Center Party headed two consecutive cabinets from May 1921 until November 1922. The "Era Wirth" saw the first, and generally unsuccessful, effort of the republican government to carry out a "policy of fulfillment" with regard to the stipulations of the peace treaty. The attempt failed to pacify the Allies at the time, and made Wirth and his colleagues, including Rathenau, special targets for the hatred of the political Right.

[44] Blücher, p. 161; Harry Graf Kessler, *Walther Rathenau, Sein Leben und sein Werk* (Berlin, 1928), pp. 333-334, 343.

letarians, and arms for the working class. To these were added demands for the creation of labor courts and proletarian control commissions. Finally, the Communists urged the proclamation of a general strike which was to last until all demands were granted.[45]

The KPD was not alone in calling for drastic curbs on nationalist violence. Public indignation was widespread, and many of the demands suggested by the Communists were made simultaneously by labor organizations and by spokesmen of the middle class. On June 25 the SPD summoned a mass demonstration in the Berlin Lustgarten, which met with wide and spontaneous response. On the following day the Reich government issued a decree for the Protection of the Republic, a stopgap measure designed to preserve order until a proper law could be enacted by the Reichstag. During the next few days, protest meetings and street marches of those who condemned the Rathenau murder were staged all over Germany, and in several instances led to acts of violence against known representatives of right-wing parties.[46] In short, the "Rathenau campaign" seemed to lend itself ideally to the propagandist purposes of the KPD.

Representatives of the SPD, the Independents, the KPD, and the independent labor unions met in Berlin on June 28 against a background of mass demonstrations and political tension. The joint conference agreed on a resolution demanding the passage of a law for the protection of the republic. Some of the points which the Communists had advanced were incorporated into the resolution, but not all of them. The most notable omissions were those pertaining to the arming of the working class, the creation of labor courts and proletarian control commissions, and the proclamation of a general strike.[47]

[45] *Bericht über die Verhandlungen des III. (8.) Parteitages*, p. 27.

[46] For public reaction to the Rathenau murder see Stampfer, pp. 283, 286-288; Sender, pp. 196-198; Troeltsch, p. 282; *Schulthess'*, 1922, pp. 80-81; Anderson, *Hammer or Anvil* (London, 1945), p. 86; Wilhelm Keil, *Erlebnisse eines Sozialdemokraten*, II (Stuttgart, 1948), pp. 257-258; Severing, *Mein Lebensweg*, I, pp. 349-352.

A Law for the Protection of the Republic was passed by the Reichstag on July 18, 1922.

[47] The Communist records are not explicit on which of their specific demands were omitted (*Bericht über die Verhandlungen des III. (8.) Parteitages*, pp. 27-28), but these can be deduced from the demands which were actually presented to the government by the ADGB on June 28, 1922; see *Schulthess'*, 1922, pp. 81-82; Stampfer, p. 287.

Despite these omissions the Communists decided to sign the resolution, together with the other labor representatives, hoping that a further radicalization of the masses would follow. But the party soon realized that the Socialist parties and the unions had no intention of pressing for the demands agreed upon outside the established democratic-parliamentary framework, and the Communists decided to "concentrate on stirring up the masses against the parliamentary maneuvers of their leaders and against the government."[48] This was a strange performance for a party which had just signed a resolution calling for a law to protect the republic against violence and abuse. The Communist attitude led to an acrimonious exchange of letters between the two Socialist parties and the unions on the one hand, the Communists on the other. A final break between the partners of the "Berlin Agreement" of June 28 occurred on July 8, when the KPD was informed that by its actions it had forfeited the right to remain within the *Aktionsgemeinschaft* established only a week earlier.[49]

Once again the party's united front tactics had miscarried, but this was not surprising, in view of the basic dilemma which the Communists faced. Could they sincerely rally to the defense of the republic? They could not; but in the interest of day-to-day tactics they had to give the appearance of doing so. Thus they signed the initial resolution calling for a law to protect the republic, and then quarreled with the other signatories over the implications of this step, trying to stir up the masses simultaneously against the leaders with whom they negotiated and against the republic which they allegedly wanted to protect. Presumably they acted from a desire to reconcile two essentially irreconcilable aims: acquisition of greater influence over the labor movement, and unremitting pursuit of the party's revolutionary ideals. In view of the political conditions then prevailing such a venture was highly unrealistic and amounted to an attempt to square the circle. But as they had little choice in the matter they went ahead and tried anyway. In the end they succeeded only in intensifying German labor's traditional distrust of the KPD. The party's growing isolation became painfully clear when the other partners of the abortive Berlin Agreement drew closer together. Both Socialist parties agreed on July 14 to

[48] *Bericht über die Verhandlungen des III. (8.) Parteitages*, p. 28.
[49] *loc.cit.*

pool their forces in the Reichstag by forming a parliamentary bloc, an *Arbeitsgemeinschaft der sozialdemokratischen Reichstagsfraktion.* It was a preliminary step toward the eventual fusion of SPD and USPD which materialized a few months later, on September 24, 1922.[50] Simultaneously with their decision to work as a parliamentary bloc, the two Socialist parties announced that they wanted to cooperate with the middle-class parties in a common effort to pass the bill for "the Protection of the Republic." This they did. On July 18 the bill was passed by a vote of 303 to 102, despite the fact that many of its supporters, especially the Independents, were unhappy about some of the changes which the bill had undergone in the course of debate. Conversely the KPD, which only a few weeks earlier had clamored for such a law and had signed a resolution calling for one, joined with the Nationalist Party, the Bavarian People's Party, and the Bavarian Peasant League in voting against the measure. The KPD explained its stand by claiming that the law, which was originally intended to curb the counterrevolution, had been transformed into a weapon directed against the political Left.[51]

To what extent the Communist position on the bill was influenced by Moscow is not known, but there is little doubt that the party's final vote was in accordance with the views of the Russian leaders. From a confidential communication which the ECCI sent to the German party it is apparent that the Bolsheviks were less than enthusiastic about the way in which the KPD had handled the Rathenau campaign.

". . . As far as can be judged from the *Rote Fahne,* the tactics [of the KPD] during the first days [following Rathenau's assassination]

---

[50] *Schulthess',* 1922, pp. 92, 122; Severing, *Mein Lebensweg,* I, p. 358.

[51] Koenen, speaking for the Communists in the Reichstag on July 18, 1922, explained his party's position in a long-winded and unconvincing speech. His basic argument was that the bill, as amended during the preceding sessions, had been deprived of all clauses which would have provided for effective protection from the Right, thus turning the projected law instead into a potential weapon of the bourgeoisie against the Left (*Stenographische Berichte des Reichstags, Verhandlungen,* vol. 356, pp. 8712-8720); see also *Bericht über die Verhandlungen des III. (8.) Parteitages,* p. 28, and Wilhelm Pieck, *Reden und Aufsätze, Auswahlband* (Berlin, 1948), p. 246.
Flechtheim (p. 83) accepts the Communist interpretation at face value, citing in support of his position an article by Thalheimer in *Jahrbuch für Politik, Wirtschaft, Arbeiterbewegung 1922-23,* pp. 607-611. Apart from the fact that Flechtheim's page reference to Thalheimer's article is wrong, the article itself does not mention the issue at all.

seem to all of us rather weak. One should not cry 'Republic! Republic!' in a situation such as [then] existed. . . . In this moment of excitement one ought to show the broad masses of workers . . . not only that the republic offers no guarantees to the proletarian class interests, but that, under the circumstances, it constitutes on the contrary the best opportunity for suppressing the masses of workers. One should not blow into the same horn with the Social Democrats and the USP [Independents]; the united front should never, never, never preclude the independence of our agitation. This is . . . a *conditio sine qua non.*

"We are prepared to negotiate with the gentlemen from the SPD and USP, though not as poor relations, but as an independent force. . . ."[52]

An official letter from the ECCI dated July 8, and addressed to the German workers as well as to the German Communist Party, expressed essentially similar ideas, but was couched in more diplomatic language. In contrast to the confidential letter, this one contained no open criticism of the KPD, but rather complimented the party for having "nobly" overcome its erstwhile misgivings about joining the German workers in the defense of the republic. The letter expressed regrets concerning the deterioration of this initial cooperation, putting the blame for this development on the two Socialist parties which, the ECCI charged, were threatening to wreck the united front by their efforts to come to terms with the bourgeoisie. The Communists, it stated, could hardly be expected to join a united front with bankers, industrialists, and middle-class politicians. The letter ended with an appeal to the German workers to impose their collective will on their leaders, and prevent a rupture of the united front policy. The republic could not be saved by a coalition of

---

[52] The letter was referred to, and parts of it read, by Zinoviev at the Fourth World Congress of the Comintern. Zinoviev stated before the delegates that "we sent the German party a confidential communication at the moment when the Rathenau murder occurred, [thus] at the moment of the *Aktion* proper." He added that the letter was dated "June 18, that is, still written in the heat of battle" (*Protokoll des Vierten Kongresses der K.I.*, p. 198). It is highly unlikely that the letter was written on June 18 because Rathenau was only assassinated on June 24. For this reason Carr, *The Bolshevik Revolution*, III, p. 416, n. 1 (where the citation ought to read p. 198, not 98), assumed that "its correct date was presumably July (not June) 18, 1922." But from the context of the letter it seems to be much more likely that the proper date was June 28, a day when the first relevant issues of *Rote Fahne* would have reached Moscow, and when negotiations between the KPD and the Socialist parties were still going on—as they were not on July 18.

workers with bourgeois parties and their reactionary friends, but only by a united front of the proletariat.[53]

Although Moscow publicly pinned all the blame for the unsatisfactory developments on the Socialist parties, the Bolsheviks did not absolve the German Communists from having mismanaged their latest propaganda campaign. Shortly after the adoption of the Law for the Protection of the Republic, the party's failure to exploit the Rathenau crisis effectively was analyzed by Radek in an article written at the end of July. He pointed out that the party had resisted the temptation of independent action and had maintained the united front but, being in a minority position, it had been unable to take up the fight alone. Although the party was stronger now than it had been in March 1921, it had not yet won enough converts from the working masses. The Communists would have to step up their efforts in order to speed the day when they could enter the coming struggle with hope of success. Radek predicted, however, that with the bourgeois offensive against the proletariat growing stronger, and with economic conditions rapidly deteriorating, the influence and the size of the KPD would increase accordingly.[54]

Although the article was written with greater restraint and tact than was customary for the author, it contained both a barely concealed criticism of, and an open challenge to, the KPD. Radek said in effect that the united front tactics, as the German Communists had conducted them, had failed to yield enough dividends. Whereas the two Socialist parties had continued to improve their political position, the Communists had only suffered setbacks. The task of the party was to win mass support and, as long as the Socialist parties remained strong enough to snub the Communists publicly whenever they chose to do so, the KPD was not doing a good job. The united front tactics had to be conducted more ener-

[53] ECCI, "To the German Workers! To the German Communist Party!" *Inprecorr*, II, No. 57 (July 17, 1922), pp. 426-427.

[54] Karl Radek, "The Class Struggle in Germany after the Rathenau Murder," *Inprecorr*, II, No. 62 (July 28, 1922), pp. 465-466. The parliamentary bloc of the middle-class parties to which Radek referred consisted of the People's Party, the Center Party, and the Democratic Party. It was formed on July 19, 1922, and its declared purpose was to stabilize German politics at home and abroad, and to improve cooperation among the middle-class parties in the Reichstag. The bloc took the name *Arbeitsgemeinschaft der verfassungstreuen Mitte* (literally: working community of the middle [parties] loyal to the constitution). See *Schulthess'*, 1922, p. 96.

getically if the party wanted to attract the masses to the Communist cause.

With the Rathenau campaign ended, Communist propaganda efforts were shifted to advocacy of the formation of workers' governments, an issue closely interwoven with the party's united front policy. The signal, as had become customary by now, was given from Moscow. On August 3, 1922, the ECCI issued another appeal to "the international proletariat and to the German workers."[55] After the usual recital of "crimes" which the SPD had committed in the eyes of the Communists from 1914 on, the appeal warned German workers that the threat from Bavaria had increased ever since the Socialist parties had helped to pass the Law for the Protection of the Republic.[56] To defend themselves against the monarchist reactionaries, the German proletarians must follow the leadership of the KPD and, if necessary, disown their Socialist leaders. Then, with a fanfare, came the cue for the new line: "Down with the [bourgeois-socialist] coalition government! ... Long live the fight for the workers' government! Long live the united battlefront of the revolutionary working class!"

As has been shown earlier, the issue of workers' governments as a Communist propaganda device was not new, but dated back to 1921.[57] Since 1918 in Saxony, and since the fall of 1921 in Thuringia, the Social Democrats, together with the Independents, had formed Socialist governments which, however, frequently depended on Communist votes for a majority in the diets. This situation put the Communists in a very favorable position. They

[55] ECCI, "To the International Proletariat! To the German Workers!" *Inprecorr*, II, No. 69 (August 15, 1922), pp. 516-517.

[56] Bavaria opposed the federal Law for the Protection of the Republic, and the Bavarian People's Party voted against its adoption in the Reichstag on July 18, 1922. Six days later, on July 24, Bavaria passed a special state Emergency Decree for the Protection of the Republic which contained a number of provisions from the federal law. However, the execution of the Bavarian decree was specifically left to the state authorities. Berlin strongly resented the particularist Bavarian attitude, and it looked as if another conflict was in the offing. This time, however, a breakdown of relations between Munich and Berlin was averted, and after the Reich granted a number of concessions to Bavaria a *détente* was reached. That a conflict had been avoided had been largely due to the sensible attitude of Bavaria's Minister President Count Lerchenfeld. In gratitude for his achievements, a combination of nationalists and Bavarian monarchists made life so difficult for him that he resigned on November 2, 1922. From then on, the trend toward the Right in Bavaria proceeded rapidly and virtually unchecked throughout the better part of the crisis year 1923. See Schwend, *Bayern zwischen Monarchie und Diktatur* (Munich, 1954), pp. 191-198.

[57] See above, Ch. VII.

could either lend their support in return for concessions from the Socialist government or withhold it when they were dissatisfied with any measure.

In view of their peculiar situation in Saxony and Thuringia the Communists had to decide whether to join the government of one, or even both, of these states. From the late fall of 1921 and throughout 1922 this problem was repeatedly debated at sessions of the Central Committee, and in the Communist press.[58] On several occasions negotiations were conducted with the Social Democrats and Independents, but every time the demands of the Communists proved so excessive that they were rejected by the potential coalition partners.[59] Once again the party's tactics were determined by the ambiguous united front policy. While the *Zentrale* continued to call for the formation of workers' governments, it refused the concessions in Saxony and Thuringia which were necessary to make an understanding with the Socialists possible.[60] A number of party leaders undoubtedly took the issue seriously, but the *Zentrale* also realized the undeniable propaganda value inherent in the workers' government campaign. From this realization Communist tactics developed a pattern. The party continued to call on the Socialists to form a coalition with the Communists and, when the SPD refused to agree to the terms, the *Zentrale* exploited such refusals for propaganda purposes. The leaders of the Social Democrats were "exposed" as traitors, who preferred to make deals with middle-class parties rather than with the real friend of the workers, the KPD. This policy was maintained until the spring of 1923, when a series of national crises prompted the Communists to revise their tactics and to think more seriously in terms of forming coalition governments in Saxony and Thuringia.[61]

In addition to its preoccupation with workers' governments, the KPD improved and expanded its organization. A propaganda de-

[58] *Bericht über die Verhandlungen des III. (8.) Parteitages*, pp. 52-53; also Thalheimer, *Inprecorr*, I, No. 12, pp. 98-99; Paul Böttcher, "The United Front and the Government Crisis in Saxony," *Inprecorr*, II, No. 44 (June 2, 1922), pp. 331-332; and Borkenau, *The Communist International*, pp. 226-227.

[59] *Bericht über die Verhandlungen des III. (8.) Parteitages*, pp. 52-53.

[60] Between August 28, 1922, and December 8, 1922, the KPD published twenty-seven appeals to the German workers, most of them pertaining to united front activities, including demands for the formation of workers' governments (*Bericht über die Verhandlungen des III. (8.) Parteitages*, pp. 35, 45-46).

[61] See below, Chs. XII-XIII.

partment had been created as early as March 1921, though too late to become effective during the uprising. The department's principal function was to train party members for specific tasks, and to see to it that the party apparatus would continue to function even if the government should outlaw the KPD. The department's additional responsibilities consisted of maintaining contact with the various party cells under all conditions, normal or adverse; of distributing propaganda leaflets to members of the army, the police, and the Allied occupation forces; and, finally, of establishing a special section which was to check on "counterrevolutionary" activities conducted by the *Orgesch* and other rightist organizations.[62] After the party congress at Jena in August 1921, the *Zentrale* itself was divided into a political and an organization section, the *Polbüro* and the *Orbüro*, in order to achieve greater efficiency in dealing with the party's diverse tasks. At the same time a central agency for the coordination of parliamentary activities (*parlamentarische Zentralstelle*) was formed. Its purpose was to exercise control over the party's deputies in the Reichstag and the various state diets; to coordinate whatever campaigns the Communists happened to be conducting at the moment, outside of the parliamentary sphere; to make better use of parliamentary procedure for propaganda purposes; and to advise the Communist delegates on any special issues.[63]

In view of the party's negative attitude toward parliamentary institutions as such, its participation in the Reichstag and the individual state diets was prompted entirely by expediency. The parliaments, according to Communist doctrine, were mere "platforms for the revolutionary enlightenment of the working class."[64] As a consequence it had become standard practice for the Communist *Fraktion* to oppose virtually every measure on the floor which was not sponsored by the KPD, even if the measure was designed to benefit the working class.[65] By imitating Goethe's *Geist, der stets verneint* (the spirit who always negates), they set an example

---

[62] *Bericht über die Verhandlungen des 2. Parteitages der K.P.D.* (Sektion der K.I.), *abgehalten in Jena vom 22. bis 26. August 1921* (Berlin, 1922), pp. 22-23.
[63] *Bericht über die Verhandlungen des III. (8.) Parteitages*, pp. 51-52, 57.
[64] Germany, Reichstag, *Handbuch der kommunistischen Reichstagsfraktion* (Berlin, 1928), pp. 21ff, as cited by Wenzel, "Die K.P.D. im Jahre 1923" (unpubl. diss., Freie Universität Berlin, 1955), p. 40.
[65] Wenzel, p. 40.

which the National Socialists in later years followed with alacrity.

The most vital objective of the KPD's united front policy was to increase the party's influence within the German labor movement in an effort to win mass support. Party membership in the summer of 1921 had numbered 180,443. In September 1922 the KPD had, in its twenty-six German districts, 2,481 local organizations, and an official membership of 224,389.[66] These figures, which were computed on the basis of membership fees, included only card-carrying members—the party's electoral strength was much greater. For instance, in the election to the Thuringian diet in September 1921, the KPD polled 73,686 votes as compared to 8,131 the preceding year.[67] In the election to the Saxon diet on November 5, 1922, the KPD polled 266,864 votes as compared to 117,359 in November 1920, and increased its parliamentary strength by one seat, from nine to ten.[68] Adverse economic conditions and very active propaganda helped the Communists to recover gradually from the setback they had suffered after the March uprising. The party conducted an intensive membership drive in September 1922, aiming its propaganda especially toward those workers who were dissatisfied with the accomplishments of their unions and the SPD.[69] Although no figures on the results of this drive are extant, the party continued to grow slowly and to increase its electoral strength throughout the better part of 1923. In the fall of that year, Communist membership stood at 294,230.[70]

But numbers were not everything. In its drive for mass support and influence, the party made a special effort to infiltrate the strongholds of German labor, the unions and the factories. When the

[66] *Bericht über die Verhandlungen des III. (8.) Parteitages*, pp. 63-64. It must be noted, though, that after the majority of the Independents rejoined the SPD on September 24, 1922, the Communists faced a strengthened Social Democratic Party with over 1,300,000 members.

[67] *ibid.*, pp. 40-41.

[68] Saxony, Statistisches Landesamt, *Statistisches Jahrbuch für den Freistaat Sachsen, 1929* (Dresden, 1930), pp. 302-303.

[69] *Bericht über die Verhandlungen des III. (8.) Parteitages*, p. 33.

[70] Kommunistische Partei Deutschlands, *Bericht über die Verhandlungen des IX. Parteitages der Kommunistischen Partei Deutschlands (Sektion der Kommunistischen Internationale), abgehalten in Frankfurt am Main vom 7. bis 10. April 1924* (Berlin, 1924), p. 57; hereafter cited as *Bericht über die Verhandlungen des IX. Parteitages.* At this point the KPD apparently decided to renumber its congresses from the beginning and adopted Roman numerals in place of the Arabic ones which heretofore appeared in parentheses.

largest German labor union, the *Allgemeiner deutscher Gewerk-schaftsbund*, convened at Leipzig in June 1922, Communists comprised one-eighth of the delegates.[71] This was a relatively high percentage and indicated the party's growing strength in an essentially hostile organization. But before the KPD could hope to capture the German labor unions, traditionally strong supporters of the Social Democrats, the party had to win control over the workers in the individual factories. "The more or less firm foothold of the Communist party in the factories [*Betriebe*] is the measure of the party's capacity for action [*Aktionsfähikeit*]," wrote Walther Ulbricht on November 22, 1922,[72] With this idea in mind, the KPD worked hard to infiltrate the factory councils. The intention was to capture control of them and to use them eventually to undermine the influence of the established trade-unions.[73] In September 1922 the party launched a campaign for a national congress of factory councils, at which the delegates could discuss ways and means of dealing with the deteriorating economic conditions. The Communists hoped to muster enough strength at such a congress to influence its decisions and resolutions and, perhaps, to make the resolutions binding for all participating unions and political parties.[74] A conference of factory councils from Berlin and surrounding areas tentatively designated October 22 as the day when the national congress should meet. A national committee of factory councils met in Berlin on September 17, and asked the principal unions whether they would agree to hold such a congress on the scheduled date. The unions were urged to reply by September 24. Meanwhile the party urged the workers to stage demonstrations throughout the country in protest against high food prices, and to demand price controls over food, fuel, and clothing. The entire scheme met with the disapproval of the unions, which considered it mere propaganda for the Communist-sponsored congress of factory councils,

[71] Schürer, *Die politische Arbeiterbewegung Deutschlands* (diss. Leipzig, 1933), p. 51.

[72] Ulbricht, *Zur Geschichte der deutschen Arbeiterbewegung*, I, p. 72; see also Karl Marchionini, *Bürgerkrieg und Bolschewismus in Deutschland* (Leipzig, 1924), p. 18.

[73] For details on Communist tactics vis-à-vis the factory councils and unions at the height of the party's united front campaign in 1923, see Ch. x.

[74] Marchionini, p. 18.

and threatened to expel every worker who participated in such demonstrations. The threat proved effective. The demonstrations were held on October 1 but were poorly attended. The national committee of factory councils therefore postponed the congress until November 23, in order to gain additional time for mobilizing the masses, and on this date the congress met in Berlin. It was obvious from its composition who had organized it: out of a total of 846 delegates, 674 were Communists, including 17 from the Communist Youth Organization. Thus it was not surprising that the resolutions adopted by the congress included demands for workers' governments, and for the creation of proletarian defense units and proletarian control commissions. Although the congress could hardly be called representative of German labor as a whole, it still had an undeniable propaganda value for the KPD, which prided itself upon its success.[75]

Such pride was to some extent justified. By the end of 1922 the KPD had overcome in many ways the setback it had suffered through the March uprising, and its political position was improving. But although the German Communists seemed to have every reason to face the future with confidence, all was not smooth sailing. Factionalism, the traditional Achilles' heel of the KPD, had been in evidence throughout 1922. The issue in question was the united front policy, which had met with opposition from the party's radical left wing, notably from its spokesmen Ruth Fischer and Arkadi Maslow. They charged that the new tactics threatened to degrade Communism to the level of "reformism" and would weaken the movement. Cooperation with the Socialists, in whatever form, was bound to turn the Communists eventually into the same kind of traitors to the working class which the Social Democrats had long since become. The Left Opposition believed that the workers would join the Communists anyway, once they had suffered enough. Such cheerful optimism was rejected by the party leadership, which maintained that the masses would have to be won over first, gradually, peacefully, and through hard work—only then could they be expected to support a revolution. This conflict over means had hampered party unity ever since the united front policy had

[75] *Bericht über die Verhandlungen des III. (8.) Parteitages*, pp. 30-36.

been adopted.[76] It became a major issue of debate at the Fourth World Congress of the Communist International, which met at Petrograd and Moscow from November 7 to December 3, 1922, and which was attended by representatives of the *Zentrale* and the Left Opposition.

[76] Borkenau, *The Communist International*, pp. 224-226.

CHAPTER IX

EMERGENCE OF THE "LEFT OPPOSITION"

DISCORD between the party's left wing (the "Berlin" or "Left" Opposition) and the *Zentrale* dated back to the beginning of 1921. When Reuter-Friesland, later that year, disassociated himself from this faction, leadership of the Left had fallen largely to a group of young intellectuals: Ruth Fischer, Arkadi Maslow, Werner Scholem, and Arthur Rosenberg in Berlin; Iwan Katz in Hanover; and Hugo Urbahns in Hamburg. They were considerably younger (ten years at an average) than the leaders of the *Zentrale*, nearly all of them came from a middle-class background against which they had rebelled, and Fischer and Maslow were foreign born. They also lacked the political experience, the pride, and the maturity of their class-conscious older comrades, who had grown up in the school of militant labor struggles with strikes, lockouts, and often imprisonment. Far from being impressed by a revolutionary tradition in which they had not shared, however, the younger party leaders were self-confident, and impatient with what they considered the excessive caution of the old-timers. Under the circumstances they might well have become an isolated clique within the party, had they not received support from such genuine proletarians as Ernst "Teddy" Thälmann, Arthur König, and others.[1]

The best-known and most colorful member of this group was Thälmann. A former transport worker who had won his spurs during the war as an activist on the docks of the Hamburg waterfront, he was an uncouth, heavy-set, tempestuous man. He had joined the KPD after the split of the Independents at Halle in 1920, and soon acquired popularity among the Communist rank and file of northern Germany. Thälmann was a powerful speaker at proletarian mass meetings, despite his notorious predilection for mixed metaphors (e.g., "in the hour of the moment," or "like a stillborn child which has lost its way in the sand"), and an equally unfortunate habit of leaving bombastic sentences unfinished.[2] What he

[1] Wenzel, "Die K.P.D. im Jahre 1923" (unpubl. diss. Freie Universität Berlin, 1955), pp. 33-34.
[2] Buber-Neumann, *Von Potsdam nach Moskau* (Stuttgart, 1957), pp. 266-267; Fischer, *Stalin and German Communism* (Cambridge, Mass., 1948), pp. 422-423.

lacked in grammatical precision he made up by forceful delivery, radical phraseology, and emphatic gestures such as hitting the rostrum with his huge fists whenever he wanted to make a point. With the help of Thälmann and like-minded, nonintellectual labor leaders, the Left Opposition gained grass-roots support along the northern coast, in the Ruhr region, Berlin, and the area around Frankfurt am Main. It is difficult to determine why men like Thälmann were drawn to the Fischer-Maslow group. That it was opportunism pure and simple, as has been suggested, is not convincing.[3] It appears more plausible that Thälmann and other such unsophisticated labor leaders, men who by inclination and from conviction were impatient with the pedestrian approach which the *Zentrale* had adopted toward revolution, were eager to support the radical demands of the young and articulate newcomers with whose aims they could fully agree. Whatever the reason, the Left Opposition consisted after 1921 of an alliance between the most boisterous segments of the party's rank and file and the Fischer-Maslow group, many of whom already occupied key positions in various party districts.

Although the controversy over Paul Levi had forced them temporarily into the background during and after the March uprising, the Left resumed the initiative at the Jena Party Congress, where Ruth Fischer voiced her disapproval of the contemplated united front policy and advocated a return to a more dynamic course.[4] Throughout the following period, until the meeting of the Fourth World Congress of the Communist International in November and December 1922, the Left remained consistently and vociferously critical of the course charted for the KPD by the *Zentrale*.[5] Ruth Fischer, Arkadi Maslow, and their supporters were particularly incensed over what Ernst Meyer called the "German NEP," a program which repudiated the methods of "War Communism"—expropriation by violence, and the like—and instead stressed a gradual approach toward the seizure of power. Ruth Fischer claimed later that Meyer hoped to create a united front of all workers and (presumably some) middle-class groups in an effort to shift taxes exclusively to the wealthy segment of the German population. The

[3] For this theory see Wenzel, p. 34.
[4] See above, Ch. VII.
[5] Borkenau, *Der europäische Kommunismus* (Bern, 1952), p. 47.

255

government—though what kind of government is not indicated—was to seize control of all key industries, the proceeds of which were to be used for reparations payments. These and related measures would then result in a Socialist state economy which would make the violent overthrow of the government unnecessary.[6] Another irritant was the party's Rathenau campaign which, according to the Left, had been grievously mismanaged by the *Zentrale*.[7] Shortly before the opening of the Fourth Comintern Congress, three thousand delegates of the KPD's Berlin organization held a meeting in the *Kliems Festsäle*. The delegates drafted a program which opposed Ernst Meyer's concept of a German NEP, elected Ruth Fischer to represent them at the coming World Congress of the Comintern, and several speakers made some very critical remarks about Comintern policies. Ernst Meyer, who was angered by the fact that the Opposition had convoked a conference in the first place, decided to fight out the issue at the World Congress and urged the Bolsheviks to take disciplinary measures against the intransigent Left Opposition.[8] Thus once again a divided German delegation went to a Comintern congress, but this time it was the Left rather than the Right which had incurred the displeasure of the *Zentrale*.

The atmosphere at the congress was not favorable to the radicalism espoused by the Fischer faction.[9] The great retreat from the path of world revolution which had been sounded at the Third Congress over a year before was still in progress, with no indication of when and how it would end. Soviet Russia was the living symbol of this development. NEP had made great strides toward restoring economic and political stability to the country. Russia had re-entered the European community of nations at the Genoa conference, had concluded the Rapallo treaty with Germany and, in November 1922, shortly before the opening of the Comintern Congress, had accepted the credentials of Count Ulrich von Brock-

---

[6] Fischer, pp. 180-181. Considering the author's point of view, her account of Meyer's ideas may well be overdrawn.

[7] Arkadi Maslow, "Tactical Differences in the KPD in the Light of the Theses brought up at the Leipsic Conference," *The Communist International*, No. 2, New Series (London, n.d.), pp. 82-83.

[8] Fischer, p. 181.

[9] *ibid.*, pp. 183-184.

dorff-Rantzau, the first regular German ambassador since the assassination of Count Mirbach in 1918.

This course of events had a profound effect on the prestige of the Comintern. The continued absence of a revolutionary climate outside Russia, and especially in Germany, was the measure of the Comintern's failure and, momentarily at least, its influence receded before the pressing need to strengthen the power of the Soviet state. It was the sober realization of this fact which set the tone of the Fourth Comintern Congress.[10]

The addresses delivered by the two main speakers of the ECCI, Zinoviev and Radek, were permeated by a note of pessimism, only barely concealed behind the usual bravado.[11] Lenin's short, and only, speech was even more subdued than were those of Zinoviev and Radek. Weak as he was after his severe illness,[12] Lenin directed his attention almost exclusively to a defense of NEP. He ended by exhorting his audience to recognize that the first duty of Communists everywhere was to make use of the temporary calm for study, in order to gain a real understanding of the organization, structure, method, and content of revolution—if this was done, the prospects of world revolution would be not only good, but excellent.[13]

Yet this final expression of hope for the future was overshadowed by an earlier statement which reflected Lenin's sober appraisal of the present. He suggested that the congress should not draw up a final program for the Comintern, but should restrict itself to the drafting of a tentative outline, because ". . . we have given scarcely any thought to the possibility of retreat, and of securing

---

[10] Carr, *The Bolshevik Revolution*, III (New York, 1953), pp. 441-443.

[11] See *Protokoll des Vierten Kongresses der K.I., Petrograd-Moskau vom 5. November bis 5. Dezember 1922* (Hamburg, 1923), pp. 1-12, 29-54, for Zinoviev's; pp. 296-329, 388-401, for Radek's main speeches. For an excellent summary of the principal points made by the speakers see Carr, *The Bolshevik Revolution*, III, pp. 443-444ff.

[12] That Lenin was not in good physical condition is borne out by his introductory remarks, an apology for the briefness of his speech because of his convalescence (*Protokoll des Vierten Kongresses der K.I.*, p. 219). Carr mentions Zinoviev's subsesequent description of Lenin's state of exhaustion at the end of his speech which "was the occasion for his last public appearance but one" (*The Bolshevik Revolution*, III, pp. 444, 445, n.1). Cf. Zetkin, *Reminiscences of Lenin* (London, 1929), p. 42, who quotes Lenin as having said: "Don't worry. . . , I feel quite well, quite strong. I have even become 'reasonable,' or what the doctors call such. I work, but spare myself. Many thanks, but I don't want to be ill again! It's a dreadful thing."

[13] *Protokoll des Vierten Kongresses der K.I.*, pp. 230-231.

this retreat. In view of the fundamental change that has taken place in the world . . . we cannot absolutely ignore the question. We must not only know how to act when we are passing to the offensive and are victorious. . . . If the enemy possesses sufficient power of endurance, he can rally his forces, and so forth; he can easily provoke us to attack him, and then throw us back for many years. That is why I think that the idea that we must prepare for the possibility of retreat is very important. . . ."[14]

Continued revolutionary retrenchment, then, was the theme which dominated the debates at the congress, including the discussions of the German question. For although no special resolution on Germany was passed by the Fourth Congress, the KPD remained "the nerve-centre of Comintern and the focal point of all its controversies."[15] Ernst Meyer was the first member of his delegation who spoke on the activities of the German party, with special emphasis on the united front policy and that troublesome problem child of German Communism, the workers' government. After agreeing with Zinoviev that the question of the united front was not a mere episode, but an extended process within the framework of Communist tactics (*eine Periode der kommunistischen Taktik*), Meyer assured his audience that the KPD had no intention of amalgamating its organization with the Social Democrats or any other party. Although such an idea had on occasion taken root in the minds of individual German workers, among them some Communists, it was based on a misunderstanding. On the other hand, it was inescapable that the *Zentrale* would have to negotiate from time to time with the leaders of the Social Democrats and of labor unions in order to coordinate common operations. Such contacts were necessary if the policy of establishing a united front of workers was to be successful. As to the workers' government, Meyer pointed out that this was a concept which differed from a Social Democratic government inasmuch as only the former would conduct genuine labor policies, and that it would rest on mass support rather than on a parliamentary majority. Was the workers' government a necessary stage on the road to ultimate conquest, or was it merely a his-

14 *ibid.*, pp. 221-222; I have used the translation in Degras, ed., *The Communist International 1919-1943, Documents,* I, Royal Institute of International Affairs (London-New York-Toronto, 1956), p. 375.
15 Carr, *The Bolshevik Revolution,* III, p. 452.

torical possibility? Meyer, basing his argument on an earlier reference to the same question raised by Zinoviev, came out in favor of the latter alternative. But at the same time he took issue with another statement made by Zinoviev, who had equated the workers' government with the dictatorship of the proletariat. This Meyer rejected. He argued that the creation of a workers' government would have to start out as a program, formulated with the objective of winning over the workers and of convincing them that it was necessary for the proletarian class to organize against the bourgeois class. Once this program (*Losung*) was accepted by the majority of labor, the attempt to realize it in countries with a strong proletarian population would either lead immediately to the proletarian dictatorship, or at least culminate in heightened class struggle, i.e., in civil war.[16]

Meyer's speech had been moderate and slightly defensive. As chairman of the *Zentrale* he was understandably eager to present the German delegation to the assembled congress in as unified a light as possible, a fact which may explain why he made no direct reference to the views of the Berlin Opposition. Ruth Fischer, the principal representative of this faction, refrained on her part from openly attacking the *Zentrale,* but directed her criticism chiefly against shortcomings and misconceptions which she thought she had discovered, both in the KPD as a whole and in the policies of the ECCI. In contrast to Meyer, however, she took the offensive and hurled charge after charge at the audience. She began by taking the Third Comintern Congress to task for having failed to settle, clearly and unequivocally, the then acute split within the German party. The Friesland crisis could have been avoided, she argued, had there been less shilly-shallying, less of an attempt to compromise in the Levi affair, all of which had cost the party precious months of work. With regard to the united front policy, Ruth Fischer deplored the existence of too many definitions concerning these tactics, and then singled out as insufficient Radek's "piece of bread" theory, i.e., Communist support of day-by-day bread-and-butter demands on the part of German labor. Agitation as such, she continued, was not enough; it was essential to go beyond agita-

---

[16] *Protokoll des Vierten Kongresses der K.I.,* pp. 73-76. The debate on the German question was part of a general discussion following Zinoviev's "Report of the ECCI."

tion and to create organizational bases among the masses from which the fight for the demands of the workers could proceed. Then, without mentioning Meyer by name, she asserted that the practice of dealing with Socialist leaders in conjunction with united front policy had become a shibboleth with many German comrades. It was a policy fraught with dangers because it evoked illusions, weakened the revolutionary *élan* of the party, and threatened to transform Communism into a revisionist movement. Not the leaders, but the masses must be convinced. This did not mean, however, that the German Communists should wait until the Socialist masses were firmly allied with the KPD. This, too, was a dangerous theory, bound to culminate in revisionism.

After she had thus expressed herself on general principles, Ruth Fischer subjected the party's Rathenau campaign to very specific criticism. Toward the end of her speech she suggested that greater emphasis should be placed on the German factory council movement (*Betriebsräte*), as potentially the most useful labor organization with which to conduct united front tactics. She finally closed on this, somewhat pretentious, note: ". . . I am now enunciating here, in accordance with my mandate [received] from the Berlin organization, our wish that the Fourth Congress may make it its business [*möge darüber wachen*] to free the Communist International from any opportunism."[17]

A rebuttal to Miss Fischer's charges was lamely and laboriously advanced by Karl Becker, a delegate from Bremen, and a close friend of Radek. Following by and large the line of arguments already developed by Meyer, Becker said little that had not been said before, and his speech made no impression on his listeners.[18] It was for Radek to take issue with the champion of the Berlin Opposition, and he did so with his customary aplomb, and not without graciousness. Comrade Fischer's speech, he said, had dealt with the mistakes of the party. "Comrade Fischer may or may not have analyzed these mistakes correctly, but nobody listening to the speech gained the impression that here spoke a comrade who did not belong to the party."[19] He supported her criticism of the party's Rathenau campaign as having been indecisive and tactically wrong. "As soon

[17] *ibid.*, pp. 80-84.
[18] Fischer, p. 184; *Protokoll des Vierten Kongresses der K.I.*, pp. 92-95.
[19] *Protokoll des Vierten Kongresses der K.I.*, p. 96.

as we here got a look at the *Rote Fahne,* Comrade Zinoviev said repeatedly: 'To Hell with them, what concern of theirs is the republic, why do they worry about that Rathenau! Not a single critical word on these issues.' And this was our general sentiment."[20] Comrade Fischer's criticism, however, also contained some errors. Whenever it became necessary to negotiate with non-Communist leaders, the Berlin Opposition, with Comrade Ruth Fischer at the head, grew terribly nervous. Radek cited as an example the conference of the executive committees of the three Internationals. "Every day which passed, and on which we had not broken with the others, appeared to Comrade Fischer and the Opposition a day lost; and when negotiations began during the Rathenau crisis, the Opposition sent daily a motion to the *Zentrale:* [either] an ultimatum, or a break. Why? Because of the purely mechanical conception on the part of the Left comrades."[21] The gist of Radek's argument was that by their impetuousness Ruth Fischer and her friends were hamstringing united front policies in Germany. And although he warned the KPD that a wrong interpretation of these policies could easily lead to revisionism, he censured the exaggerated emphasis which the Left was putting upon this danger. Turning next to the concept of the workers' government, Radek defined it as a possible transition stage on the road to the dictatorship of the proletariat, thus endorsing Meyer's stand on this issue. But on no account, Radek warned, must the idea of a workers' government be permitted to become what it apparently already was to a number of German Communists—an excuse for inactivity.

"They say: Dictatorship—the Devil knows when it will come; anyhow, it is very difficult to agitate with the slogan of dictatorship [of the proletariat]; then I would rather say 'workers' government,' which sounds very moderate and innocent. Nobody knows what it is. Perhaps it may become something, and, in any case, it does not look dangerous."

Such an attitude, Radek said, must be eliminated by a proper approach toward Communist agitation. Then he pleaded, in summing up, that "If we conceive of the workers' government as an excuse for inactivity, it will not only mean the bankruptcy of the workers' government, but we shall be beaten politically. . . . If we

[20] *ibid.,* p. 99.
[21] *ibid.,* p. 100.

keep alive among the masses the consciousness that the workers' government is muck unless it is backed by workers who seize weapons, form factory councils, nudge the government, and do not permit it to make compromises toward the Right—then the workers' government will become a starting point of the struggle for the dictatorship of the proletariat, and eventually will be replaced by a soviet government. . . ."[22]

Radek's comments did not terminate the general debate on the united front policy and the workers' government, in their specifically German context. Additional references were made on and off at later stages of the proceedings, especially during a heated debate between the second speaker for the Left Opposition, Hugo Urbahns from the Hamburg organization, and Radek, over the latter's "Report on the Capitalist Offensive." But the principal lines of argument had been drawn during the initial sessions of the congress, and no startling new points were subsequently raised by any of the speakers.[23]

In contrast to the bitterness which had marked the tone of the German factions at the preceding Comintern Congress, the debates at this one were conducted on the whole with great restraint and moderation. This was probably due in part to the subdued atmosphere which prevailed among the delegates, and to the conviction of the Germans that their internal party conflict had better be settled in a restricted special meeting with the Bolshevik leaders rather than *coram populo*. Such a meeting was accordingly arranged between the Russian Politburo and the German delegation, and was held in one of the salons of the Kremlin, near St. Andrew's Hall. On the Russian side, the meeting was attended by Zinoviev, Trotsky, Radek, Bukharin and, his weak state of health notwithstanding, Lenin. According to Ruth Fischer, the debate between Meyer and Becker on the one side, herself and Urbahns on the other, centered on Meyer's concept of a German NEP, which the Left rejected. Ruth Fischer argued that whereas a program of gradual transformation was appropriate for Soviet Russia under the prevailing conditions, it was totally unfeasible and downright dangerous to transfer such a program to Germany. Applied to that

---

[22] *ibid.*, pp. 101-102.
[23] *ibid.*, pp. 296-329 (Radek), pp. 358-361 (Urbahns), pp. 383-386 (Hörnle, Zentrale), and pp. 388-401 (Radek again).

country it would destroy the militant spirit of the young Communist Party and would pave the way for the eventual victory of the counterrevolution. At the conclusion of the meeting Lenin, who had listened to the debate in silence, demolished Meyer's theories concerning a German NEP. In the opinion of Ruth Fischer, he thereby rejected by implication any disciplinary action against the German Left, much to the chagrin of the *Zentrale*.[24] Was Lenin really as impressed with the Left Opposition as Ruth Fischer's account of the meeting would indicate? Not according to Clara Zetkin, who tells us that Lenin, although he agreed with many of the arguments advanced by the Fischer faction, had a low opinion of the aims, tactics, and caliber of its adherents. "Such 'leftists,' " Zetkin quotes him, "are like the Bourbons. They have learnt nothing and forgotten nothing. As far as I can see, there is behind the 'left' criticism of the mistakes in carrying out the united front tactics the desire to do away with those tactics altogether."[25] He referred to Ruth Fischer as a "personal accident" who was politically unstable and uncertain, and whose faction did not impress him. But neither was he impressed by the *Zentrale* which, he asserted, "does not understand, [and] . . . hasn't the energy to have done with such petty demagogues."[26]

Despite the special session of the Russian and German leaders, the underlying differences within the KPD were not eliminated at Moscow. The officially adopted theses which bore most directly on that controversy were a compromise which settled nothing.[27] The united front tactic was reaffirmed as being "more than ever appropriate." Yet the definition of what this approach was to mean was still ambiguous. "The united front tactic means that the Communist vanguard must take the lead in the day-to-day struggles of the broad working masses for their most vital interests. In these struggles the Communists are even ready to negotiate with the treacherous Social Democratic and Amsterdam leaders."

This statement was entirely in accordance with the views of the Meyer *Zentrale*. The resolution then stressed the need for independence of action on the part of Communist parties, repudiated

[24] Fischer, pp. 183-186. See Carr, *The Bolshevik Revolution*, III, p. 453, n.2, on Ruth Fischer's exaggerated claim that Lenin had to save the Left from expulsion.
[25] Zetkin, *Reminiscences of Lenin*, p. 44.
[26] *ibid.*, p. 45.
[27] Carr, *The Bolshevik Revolution*, III, p. 453.

electoral alliances with other working-class representatives in the parliamentary sphere, emphasized the importance of agitational and organizational work, and, in this connection, took into account the grievances of the Left: "The most important thing in the united front tactic is and remains agitational and *organizational* rallying of the working masses. Its true realization can come only 'from below,' from the depths of the working classes themselves. Communists however must not refuse in certain circumstances to negotiate with the leaders of the hostile workers' parties, but the masses must be kept fully and constantly informed of the course of these negotiations. Nor must the Communist parties' freedom to agitate be circumscribed in any way during these negotiations with the leaders."[28]

To the German delegation the theses dealing with the formation of workers' governments were as important as those pertaining to the united front. Here the congress tried to devise directions geared to meet well-nigh every possible situation, with the result that the finished product took on the appearance of a menu specializing in revolutionary fare. The individual customer was encouraged to pick and choose on the basis of the particular conditions prevailing in his part of the world. The theses listed five possible combinations and pointed out that "not every workers' government is a really proletarian government, that is, a revolutionary instrument of power." The first possibility visualized was a liberal workers' government such as existed in Australia. The second was a Social Democratic government, suitable for Germany as a whole. The third was a government of workers and poorer peasants as envisaged for the Balkan region. The fourth, which coincided with the situation which the KPD had been contemplating for months in regard to Saxony and Thuringia, considered a workers' government in which Communists would participate alongside Social Democrats. Finally, there was the ideal proletarian workers' government, composed only of Communists. This alone represented the real dictatorship of the proletariat.[29]

<hr>

[28] *Protokoll des Vierten Kongresses der K.I.*, pp. 1014-1015; italics in the original. I have used the translation in Degras, ed., *The Communist International, Documents,* I, pp. 424-425.
[29] *Protokoll des Vierten Kongresses der K.I.*, pp. 1015-1017.

Emergence of the "Left Opposition"

As far as the German delegates were concerned, the generous choice of models and methods provided by these theses contained convenient features both for the *Zentrale* and for the Left Opposition. To the former it held out the prospect of forming a coalition with Socialists, a step which would avoid a risky upheaval. The Fischer faction could seek comfort in the clauses which demanded continued party control over any Communist cabinet members, and those which guaranteed complete independence of agitation. To be sure, on the surface the theses dealing with the united front and the formation of a workers' government, in the words of Professor Carr, "left the [German] Right in possession, but allowed the Left to fight again another day on the same ground. Within the Russian party, it upheld Radek . . . against the attacks of Zinoviev, whose exclusive identification of the 'workers' government' with the dictatorship of the proletariat was rejected, but not emphatically enough to prevent a renewal of the same attack at a later date."[30]

When the congress came to an official close on the evening of December 5, 1922, not much more had been accomplished during a month of deliberations than to reaffirm and strengthen the resolutions of the Third World Congress. Moreover, there had been an air of unreality about the proceedings, created partly by the concealed but unresolved contrast between the immediate interests of the Soviet Union and the stubborn revolutionary aims of the Comintern. This contrast had been heightened by tense awareness, in the Bolshevik leaders at least, that Lenin, the man who in the past had always been able to reconcile these differences, was now very ill. The crucial sessions dealing with the international situation concentrated on the "capitalist offensive," which was depicted as constituting the death throes of capitalism. The Communist answer to the "capitalist offensive" was the retention of united front tactics.

Enclosed as they were by the ancient Kremlin walls, most delegates seemed to have been oblivious to the rapidly changing events in the outside world, events which rendered obsolete the premises for most of the debates. In Germany, the slightly left-of-center government of Chancellor Joseph Wirth had been replaced in mid-November by a right-of-center government headed by a businessman, Dr. Wilhelm Cuno. The nation as a whole began to brace

[30] Carr, *The Bolshevik Revolution*, III, pp. 453-454.

itself for a threatened French occupation of the Ruhr region which France's premier, Raymond Poincaré, openly advocated, because of Germany's default in meeting her reparations payment to the Allies. These developments, which throughout the late fall of 1922 clouded the political horizon of Europe, were treated at the Fourth World Congress with a remarkable lack of insight.[31]

The only direct reference to a possible French occupation of the Ruhr region was made by the French delegate Cachin during one of the debates. Furthermore, in the "Resolution . . . on the Versailles Peace Treaty," this possibility was briefly and obliquely mentioned twice, once in connection with the German situation, and the second time by way of instructing the French Communist Party to prevent any such scheme on the part of the French bourgeoisie.[32]

Thus, the German representatives at the congress left Moscow early in December with their fundamental disagreements over united front tactics still unresolved, and without any clear idea as to the nature of the international crisis which had been shaping up for weeks. For all they had gained from their four weeks in Russia, they might as well have stayed at home.

The extent to which tactical differences over united front tactics preoccupied the leadership of the KPD to the exclusion of nearly

[31] Section III of the Theses on Tactics which the congress adopted on December 5, 1922, analyzed the international situation as follows: "The international political situation also reflects the continuing breakdown of capitalism.

"The reparations question is still unsettled. While one conference of the Entente states after another is held, Germany's economic collapse is proceeding unchecked and threatens the existence of capitalism throughout central Europe. The catastrophic deterioration in Germany's economic situation will either force the Entente to renounce reparations, which will aggravate the economic and political crisis in France, or it will lead to the creation of a Franco-German industrial bloc on the continent, and this will make England's economic situation . . . worse; it will place England and the continent in political opposition to each other . . . .

"The *Versailles treaty* is being liquidated by events. It is not, however, being replaced by a general understanding among the capitalist states, by the abandonment of imperialism, but by new contraditions, new imperialist alignments, and new armaments. . . . Capitalist America watches like a vulture the breakdown of capitalism in Europe . . . [and] will enslave capitalist Europe if the European working class does not seize political power and set about . . . beginning the construction of a federal Soviet republic of Europe" (*Protokoll des Vierten Kongresses der K.I.*, pp. 1008-1009; I have used the translation in Degras, ed., *The Communist International, Documents*, I, pp. 418-419; italics in the original).

[32] *Protokoll des Vierten Kongresses der K.I.*, pp. 772-773, 1005-1006; see also Carr, *The Bolshevik Revolution*, III, p. 455, for an analysis of the "Resolution . . . on the Versailles Treaty."

every other problem became very evident during the Eighth Party Congress, held at Leipzig from January 28 to February 1, 1923. When the congress opened, the French occupation of the Ruhr had already begun, and with all its ramifications should have posed a most acute and pressing challenge to the party. This was correctly perceived by the Left Opposition. During the opening debate on the agenda five delegations, all from strongholds of the Left, moved that the first item of business should be a debate on the political situation and the tasks of the KPD. Pieck, speaking for the *Zentrale,* tried to shrug off the motion with the dry remark that a separate debate on this issue would unnecessarily prolong the deliberations of the congress. But then he decided after all to put the motion to a vote, and it was defeated 122 to 89.[33]

The majority apparently felt that the Ruhr invasion had been adequately treated in the opening address which Clara Zetkin had delivered the previous afternoon. The old lady had given a general picture of the situation, but beyond her reiteration of the *Zentrale's* rather vague slogan that the party should "smite Poincaré and Cuno on the Ruhr and on the Spree,"[34] she had offered no specific suggestion on how the KPD was to react to the newest international crisis. The German chancellor, she told her audience, could only be smitten on the Spree if the French premier were smitten by German workers in the Ruhr region. "Wherever we meet with capitalism we shall say, like the poet: 'Where stands the foe? Here stands he pat! Let's mark the spot! We'll beat him yet!' "[35]

Behind the fiery oratory of the venerable Zetkin, however, was no concise program, no clearly defined policy. Nor did subsequent speakers who referred to the Ruhr imbroglio treat the event in practical terms. Most of the speeches expressed a general attitude which amounted to a denunciation of capitalism on both sides of the Rhine, a rather vague declaration of war without an order of

[33] *Bericht über die Verhandlungen des III. (8.) Parteitages der K.P.D. (Sektion der K.I.) abgehalten in Leipzig vom 28. Januar bis 1. Februar 1923* (Berlin, 1923), p. 187. The five districts where the Left had strong support were Berlin-Brandenburg, *Wasserkante* (Hamburg and the surrounding coastal region), Middle-Rhine, Lusatia, and Hesse-Frankfurt.

[34] The slogan appeared first a week earlier in *Die Rote Fahne,* No. 18, January 23, 1923.

[35] *Bericht über die Verhandlungen des III. (8.) Parteitages,* p. 178. "Wo steht der Feind? Der Feind steht hier! Den Finger drauf! Den schlagen wir!" These lines, slightly misquoted by Zetkin, are from August Kopisch's poem "Blücher am Rhein."

mobilization, in short, noncommittal rhetoric. At no time during the congress did anyone advance a definite plan on how to smite Cuno and Poincaré in their respective bailiwicks. According to Ruth Fischer, this evasion of the major issue of the day was intentional and originated with Narkomindel, the Soviet Foreign Office, which wanted to create a common front of German labor, German nationalists, and the German government against France; furthermore, Narkomindel had informed Radek of these plans when he went to Leipzig, though he went not as an official participant in the congress, but incognito. It now became Radek's mission, according to Miss Fischer, to steer the attention of the congress away from the Ruhr problem, since Narkomindel anticipated opposition to its National-Bolshevist schemes from the delegates. Such opposition would have deprived Russian foreign policy of flexibility in the anticipated negotiations with the German government, and also would have intensified competition between Narkomindel and the Zinoviev-led Comintern.[36] This theory is not convincing. While it is correct that official Russian foreign policy adopted a strong line in favor of Germany and against the Franco-Belgian occupation of the Ruhr, and while Radek actually was in Leipzig during the congress, there is no evidence for either a Narkomindel-sponsored policy of National Bolshevism at this time, or for Radek's role as its secret agent.[37]

National Bolshevism was to become an important factor in Soviet policy later in the year, and Radek became its spiritual father—but as the agent of the Comintern as well as of Narkomindel. On the other hand, a vote on the motion to discuss the Ruhr conflict thoroughly had been defeated. It is highly unlikely that Radek could have manipulated the vote beforehand, as it was taken on the spur of the moment. A lengthy debate on the issue was

[36] Fischer, p. 230.

[37] For Russia's initial reaction to the French occupation of the Ruhr see Hilger and Meyer, *The Incompatible Allies* (New York, 1953), p. 120. According to Hilger, rumors of Russian plans to support Germany in case of a Ruhr occupation dated back to September 1922. If true, the evasion of this topic during the Fourth World Congress appears in an even stranger light. See also Kochan, *Russia and the Weimar Republic* (Cambridge, 1954), pp. 67-68; Freund, *Unholy Alliance* (New York, 1957), p. 152, on Russian reactions. On Radek's presence at Leipzig see Edward Hallett Carr, *A History of Soviet Russia: The Interregnum 1923-1924* (New York, 1954), p. 158, including note 5; hereafter cited as *The Interregnum*. Also Fischer, pp. 229-230, and Flechtheim, *Die K.P.D. in der Weimarer Republik* (Offenbach, 1948), p. 87.

probably rejected only because too many delegates were primarily concerned with the settlement of the united front dispute which threatened party unity.

During the Leipzig Congress all the unresolved party squabbles, which had occupied so much time at the Fourth World Congress, received another airing. At the bottom of this dispute lay the haunting memory of the 1921 March uprising, a memory which particularly affected Brandler and Thalheimer, the men who were to guide the party through the stormy year of 1923. As has been pointed out before, Brandler and Thalheimer became very cautious and prudent after their advocacy of the ill-fated theory of the revolutionary offensive had been subjected to severe criticism during the Third World Congress. There were to be no more adventures, no putsches, and there was to be strict adherence to directives from Moscow. Thus when the united front approach became the worldwide Communist line, the leadership of the KPD accepted it gladly because this policy retained the revolutionary theory without making it obligatory, at least for the immediate future, to man the barricades. In short, after the summer of 1921 the German *Zentrale* moved to the right, and was to stay there until the late summer of 1923.

That Moscow had entrusted Radek, after the Third World Congress, with the supervision and guidance of the KPD proved increasingly comforting to the *Zentrale*. With Lenin ill—he had retired to the country after the congress was over and lived virtually in isolation—the German Communists stood in need of a guardian angel.[38] They could hardly avoid being apprehensive as to who among the Bolsheviks would emerge as Lenin's possible successor, but it is unlikely that they were as yet aware of the Russian intra-

[38] On January 6, 1923, the German Ambassador to the Soviet Union, Count von Brockdorff-Rantzau, cabled to the German Foreign Office that Lenin was undergoing treatment by Professor Foerster, a German, who had arrived in Moscow on December 20, 1922. The ambassador mentioned one appearance of Lenin before the All Russian Central Executive Committee on November 20, 1922, when Lenin spoke "on a lower level than usual." Soon thereafter Lenin moved into virtual seclusion to the countryside. The ambassador also reported that according to confidential medical reports Lenin suffered from sclerosis of the central nervous system. The cable concluded with a report that Stalin was allegedly preparing to become Lenin's successor ("Brockdorff-Rantzau to German Foreign Office," Auswärtiges Amt, Germany, microfilm, container 1405, frame D 552717, National Archives, Washington, D.C.).

party struggle, which had begun, quietly and unobtrusively, shortly
after Lenin had suffered his first stroke in May 1922.[39]

Radek's clandestine presence at the Leipzig congress discomfited
the Left Opposition because he acted essentially as a supporter of
the party majority.[40] The Left had remained dissatisfied with the
course of the party after the German delegation had returned from
Russia. The Opposition members were disturbed by what they
considered a growing trend of the KPD toward the right. Their
principal accusation was that the party neglected its ultimate goal
of revolution by employing tactics which concentrated on short-
range objectives. To the Left, this smacked too much of "reformism." They differed with the *Zentrale* and the majority of the KPD
over the party's chief aim: to bring the SPD from the left wing of
the bourgeoisie over to the right wing of the working classes. The
Zentrale hoped to accomplish this by negotiating with Socialist
leaders, forming workers' governments whenever feasible in individual states—especially Saxony and Thuringia—and by using the
factory council movement for putting pressure on the trade-unions
to open their ranks to Communists. The Opposition rejected as
illusory both the objectives and the methods of approach advocated by the party majority. Instead of negotiating with the Socialist
leaders, the Left supported a "united front from below." By this
they understood an attempt to revolutionize the rank and file of the
non-Communist labor movement and to win them for the forces
of revolution. As far as the formation of workers' governments was
concerned, the Left had no faith in the effectiveness of such a move
under existing circumstances. Finally, the faction resented the use
of the factory councils as a pressure group. They maintained that
the councils had an independent value and should be supported in
order to offer competition to the Socialist-dominated trade-unions,
presumably with the idea of eventually supplanting the latter by
the councils.[41]

The principal debates at the Leipzig Congress centered around
these differences over tactics and short-range objectives, but it soon
became quite obvious that neither side was willing to depart from

[39] Trotski, *Mein Leben* (Berlin, 1930), p. 459, and *passim*.
[40] Fischer, p. 229; Flechtheim, p. 87; Carr, *The Interregnum*, p. 157.
[41] Fischer, pp. 225-227; Flechtheim, pp. 85-86; Carr, *The Interregnum*, pp. 157-
158.

its original premises. The arguments advanced by the spokesmen of the Right were dull and uninspiring even when the speakers resorted to polemics. Meyer, in a lengthy and learned dissertation on tactics, outlined the position of the *Zentrale* with emphasis on those divisive issues within the KPD which the Fourth World Congress had so singularly failed to settle. Once again the past was reviewed, the Rathenau campaign scrutinized and defended, and the criticism of the Left ridiculed and condemned. Meyer presented the party's negotiations with the leaders of the trade-unions and the Social Democrats as a sound and vital aspect of united front policy. He argued that whenever the KPD invited any non-Communist labor organization to partake in a common campaign or a common struggle (the word *Kampf* occurred repeatedly in Meyer's speech, although it evidently referred to struggles for wages and hours rather than to actual fighting, a difference which Meyer prudently left unclear), the party exercised pressure upon its negotiation partners either to join the Communists, or face exposure as lackeys of the bourgeoisie. This approach, according to Meyer, prevented Communist isolation, increased the reputation of the KPD with the Socialist rank and file, and eventually would either detach the non-Communist workers from their leaders, or force the latter to cooperate with the Communists.[42]

Brandler's speech, although it meandered along similar lines, camouflaged the speaker's earnest plea for closer cooperation with non-Communist labor organizations behind brave revolutionary phrases. The main enemy, according to Brandler, was not Social Democracy, not even the bourgeoisie as such, but the rising "Fascist" movement, which especially in Bavaria was making inroads into the ranks of the middle classes. "If we do not succeed in crushing Fascism, if [Fascism] succeeds in crushing us, then we shall be chastised with scorpions," Brandler warned his listeners.[43] How was the party to fight Fascism? By means of united front tactics.

"The united front tactic is not a mere propaganda slogan, but decidedly a fighting tactic [*Kampftaktik*]. . . . We are convinced that we can fight the final struggle for the overthrow of the bour-

[42] *Bericht über die Verhandlungen des III. (8.) Parteitages,* pp. 206-208; the entire speech, pp. 197-219.

[43] *ibid.,* p. 317. After Mussolini's "March on Rome" in October 1922, the Communists began to bestow the term "Fascist" indiscriminately on any right-wing movement.

geoisie and the establishment of the proletarian dictatorship only if we struggle daily, at every opportunity, to alleviate misery, [and] to eliminate the troubles of the day. . . . Although we know that the fight for higher wages, for lower rents, for lower prices will not suffice to render secure the existence [*Existenz*] of the proletariat within this period of capitalist decay even for a brief period, we shall nevertheless conduct the struggle against the troubles of the day [*Tagesnöte*] for small results, . . . train and increase the fighting spirit and fighting strength of the working class, and train them for the great fights [ahead] which we shall not be spared."[44]

These words summarized Brandler's point of view concerning united front tactics. His was decidedly a moderate approach, but hardly a revolutionary one, despite the frequent use of the word *Kampf*. He crowned his plea for a sane party policy by telling his audience that just as the Communists had always been there whenever German proletarians were manning the barricades, weapons in hand, "so shall we be there when . . . the Social Democratic leaders under the pressure of the masses will finally be ready to dissociate themselves from the left wing of the bourgeoisie and become the right wing of the workers (very good!)."[45]

In the course of his speech Brandler, the veteran trade-union leader, could not resist the temptation to lash out at the "intellectuals" in the party, a term by which he meant the Left Opposition. The intellectuals in most radical movements, Brandler charged, tended to create unrest among the rank and file by turning the workers' heads with wild phrases and irresponsible criticism. He warned the intellectuals within the KPD not to undermine the party by exploiting the understandable impatience of the suffering proletariat. Did not the entire history of the labor movement show that most contemporary opportunists such as Briand, Millerand and Hervé had started out as "bloody radicals"? Of course, it would be grotesque to assume that anyone wanted to reject the intellectuals, but the party must demand of them that they, who had come to the party by a road different from that of most of its members, did not make their confused state of mind the starting point for demoralizing discussions.[46]

44 *ibid.*, p. 318.
45 *ibid.*, p. 328.
46 *ibid.*, pp. 325-326; the entire speech, pp. 314-333.

Brandler's warning was undoubtedly directed against Ruth Fischer, who had taken the floor three times earlier in the proceedings, and on each occasion had attacked the *Zentrale* and the entire right wing of the party.[47] The *Zentrale*, she charged, was mismanaging the party's policies with regard to the Ruhr crisis, the growing counterrevolutionary activities in Bavaria, and the thorny reparations problem. Although progress had been made in the preceding years, the KPD was not yet a real revolutionary party. She criticized once again the way in which the *Zentrale* handled the Rathenau murder, and characterized the prevailing trends within the KPD as passive, opportunist, and revisionist.[48] She condemned the party's attempts to form workers' governments as halfhearted efforts to reconcile democracy with dictatorship [of the proletariat], and contemptuously referred to such a form of government as a "connecting link between ape and man." When she finished her second speech with the words: "We shall fight on, you may yell as [much as] you will," there was applause as well as dissent.[49]

The second principal speaker for the Left Opposition was Arkadi Maslow, whose argumentation was less acid than Ruth Fischer's but had more substance. Going over the same ground which every preceding speaker had already covered from his or her respective point of view, he singled out for special criticism the party's neglect of the factory council movement and the fallacious concept of the workers' government. The two problems, Maslow stated, were closely connected. Only after a dynamic and activist factory council movement had been carefully nurtured, trained, and armed by the Communists, could any workers' government which contained Social Democratic ministers hope to stay in power, particularly if the bourgeoisie should try to overthrow it, and the SPD ministers should defect.[50] Toward the end of his speech he succinctly stated the position of the Left Opposition.

"In closing I want to offer this summary: the creation of a workers' government does not depend on rigid conditions, but in

[47] Brandler may have been particularly irked by the fact that Ruth Fischer was fourteen years his junior, and eight years younger than Meyer; Fischer was born in 1895, Brandler in 1881, Meyer in 1887. See also Wenzel, p. 33, on the age differences among the leaders.

[48] *Bericht über die Verhandlungen des III. (8.) Parteitages*, pp. 238-240.

[49] *ibid.*, p. 287.

[50] *ibid.*, pp. 339-343.

each given situation unquestionably on the mass movement which poses the power question [*die die Machtfrage stellt*]; on the existence, the possibility of expansion, the fighting ability, and fighting spirit of proletarian fighting organizations (workers' councils, control committees); on the demand for weapons on the part of the working class and . . . [its] shift from the defensive toward the offensive. These are the points which divide us from the views of many of our party comrades."[51]

Maslow's preoccupation with the problem of when and under what conditions to form a workers' government in coalition with Social Democrats was no longer merely a matter of theory. The question had taken on new significance when it was announced, in the midst of the proceedings on January 30, that the Saxon government of the Social Democratic premier, Buck, had been forced to resign after a combination of Communists and middle-class parties had passed a vote of "no confidence" against the SPD.[52] Although the congress took no immediate steps to pursue the matter further, the new situation in Saxony sharpened the contrast between the two opposing wings more than ever.

How irreconcilable their views were became evident when the congress had to choose between two sets of theses and resolutions, one drafted by the *Zentrale*, the other by the Left Opposition. Read side by side, the theses at first glance look very much alike, partly because the Left made an effort to couch their proposals in terms which, superficially at least, seemed to constitute concessions to the majority point of view. But upon closer scrutiny it becomes apparent that the members of the Opposition had preserved the substance of their radical proposals intact. All the familiar demands were embedded in the draft: the emphasis on control commissions, factory councils, confiscation of real values (a euphemism for expropriation of the propertied classes), the need for arming the workers, and, above all, the creation of a workers' government based exclusively on the bayonets of an armed proletariat as a preliminary step to the seizure of power by the workers. Although propaganda was accepted as essential, the draft stressed explicitly that propa-

[51] *ibid.*, p. 345.
[52] *ibid.*, pp. 268-269; *Schulthess' Europäischer Geschichtskalender*, 1923 (Munich, 1928), p. 22. See also Fischer's rather misleading account, p. 228.

ganda must be accompanied by active organization of the masses, and must be followed up by real struggles involving the Communist-led mass of the German working class.[53]

In contrast to the proposals presented by the Opposition, the draft of the party's majority, sponsored by Radek and the *Zentrale*, was not only wordier, but also much more obscure. Although these resolutions contained the same revolutionary terminology employed by the Left, the wording served the primary purpose of concealing the majority's unwillingness to depart one iota from its course. Whereas the Left placed the emphasis on action, organization, initiative, and armament of the workers, the majority theses stressed defense against "Fascist" aggression, and a policy of attrition vis-à-vis the Social Democrats. They proposed that the seizure of power be accomplished by gradual stages, through constant struggles for improved positions of the workers in the political arena. Although the majority theses paid lip service to the importance of factory councils, the creation of workers' councils and related proletarian institutions, the clauses pertaining to these items were, significantly enough, put in parentheses.[54] When the vote was taken, the draft of the *Zentrale* was adopted 118 to 59.[55] The party had clearly opted for continuation of the united front policy.

Toward the end of the congress the delegates prepared to elect a new *Zentrale* and a new Central Committee, a procedure which frayed tempers even further. Trouble began when the outgoing *Zentrale* announced that the new one would consist from then on of twenty-one rather than fourteen officers, and then placed twenty-one names in nomination, every one of them from districts where the Right had a safe majority. No candidate of the Left Opposition was on the proposed slate. In a huff, the members of the Left announced that their delegates would abstain from participating in the election. The move was designed as a threat to deprive a slate thus elected of the confidence of the strongest party districts— Berlin-Brandenburg, the Ruhr, and Hamburg.[56] According to Ruth

[53] The text of the Left resolutions is given in *Bericht über die Verhandlungen des III. (8.) Parteitages*, pp. 142-150.

[54] *ibid.*, p. 417; the relevant passages of these theses and resolutions are on pp. 392-397, 415-424.

[55] *ibid.*, p. 375.

[56] Fischer, p. 229. The Ruhr region, which belonged to the party district Rhineland-Westphalia North, was strictly speaking not a stronghold of the Left Opposition, at least not to the same extent as Berlin-Brandenburg and Hamburg. Al-

Fischer, this strategy forced Radek, allegedly the instigator of the blue-ribbon slate, to beat a hasty retreat. He called for a secret night session, probably held from January 31 to February 1, and suggested a compromise. Although the exact nature of this compromise may never be established with certainty, it appears that Radek used the nocturnal session mainly for mediating between *Zentrale* and Opposition, throwing all his weight as ECCI emissary into the scales to prevent a party split.[57] In any case, on the following day the congress was presented with a new slate which this time included the names of three members from the Opposition. One of them, Arthur Ewert, was Radek's personal choice. None of them, however, was a prominent Leftist, and Ewert was actually distrusted by the Fischer faction. Under the circumstances it was hardly surprising that even the revised slate failed to satisfy the Opposition members. They manifested their displeasure by putting up four additional candidates, Ruth Fischer, Otto Geschke, Iwan Katz, and Arthur König, who were sponsored, respectively, by the districts of Berlin-Brandenburg, *Wasserkante* (Hamburg and surrounding areas), Hesse-Frankfurt, and Middle Rhine. Furthermore, the district East Prussia insisted on running Ernst Meyer as a favorite son. When the ballots were counted, only those on the *Zentrale's* "revised" slate received enough votes to be elected; Ruth Fischer, her three running mates, and Ernst Meyer suffered defeat.[58]

---

though the Opposition had strong grass-roots support among the Communist rank and file in the Ruhr, the local organizations were firmly in the hands of functionaries who supported the party majority and its views. The only party district in the Rhineland which the Opposition controlled was Middle-Rhine, situated to the south of the Ruhr region (*Bericht über die Verhandlungen des IX. Parteitages der K.P.D.* [*Sektion der K.I.*], *abgehalten in Frankfurt am Main vom 7. bis 10. April 1924* [Berlin, 1924], pp. 382, 445-448, and *passim*).

[57] Carr, *The Interregnum*, p. 158.

[58] The following members were elected to the *Zentrale*: Carl Becker, Paul Böttcher, Heinrich Brandler, Arthur Ewert, Hugo Eberlein, Paul Frölich, Fritz Heckert, Erwin Hörnle, August Kleine, Wilhelm Koenen, Rudolf Lindau, Hans Pfeiffer, Wilhelm Pieck, Hermann Remmele, Felix Schmidt, Georg Schumann, Walter Stoecker, August Thalheimer, Walter Ulbricht, Jacob Walcher, and Clara Zetkin (*Bericht über die Verhandlungen des III.* [8.] *Parteitages*, p. 382).

Ruth Fischer's description of the election (pp. 225, 229-230) is exceedingly muddled. She claims that four rather than three representatives of the Left were taken into the *Zentrale*, but identifies only Ewert (cf. Flechtheim, p. 87, and Carr, *The Interregnum*, p. 158, who mentions three Opposition candidates elected. So does Wenzel, p. 70, who adds that all three broke with the Left in the spring of 1923). She further claims that Radek, by means of dubious maneuvers, eliminated Thälmann and Maslow from running for office. This is indeed very probable, but whereas she depicts Radek in her book as a sinister intriguer, back in 1924 she

Emergence of the "Left Opposition"

With the election of the new *Zentrale*, party leadership fell once again to Heinrich Brandler, former bricklayer, trade-union official, and co-founder of the KPD. He was closely assisted by August Thalheimer, the party's principal theoretician, who tended in turn to rely on Radek's advice.[59] Among the other more prominent members of the new *Zentrale* were a number of tried and dedicated veterans: Zetkin, Pieck, and Eberlein, all old Spartacists; Heckert and Walcher, trade-union functionaries of long experience; Koenen, Stoecker, and Remmele, who had held leading positions in the USPD before joining the Communist Party; and Paul Frölich, house-painter by trade, who had gained a reputation for his thorough knowledge of Marxist theory. Of the newcomers to the *Zentrale*, two deserve special mention. One was Walter Ulbricht, a young (thirty years old) member from Thuringia and, like Pieck, originally a cabinet maker.[60] The other was August Guralski, of March 1921 fame, who for the moment preferred to be known by his alias, Kleine. Zinoviev had sent him to Germany as a watchdog

credited him, though without mentioning him by name, with having prevented a party split (Carr, *The Interregnum*, p. 159, n.5). Nor can her assertion be upheld that the delegates of the Opposition abstained from voting in the election. The total number of delegates at the congress numbered 219; of these, 203 cast their ballots, among them roughly 70 representatives of the Opposition. Thus at most 16 representatives of the Left could have abstained from voting (see Fischer's own statement in *Die Rote Fahne*, No. 76, April 1, 1923, where she gives the number of Opposition members at Leipzig as "between 60 and 80"). Finally, she does not mention her own unsuccessful candidacy or that of her three running mates. Her account of the election must be read against the official stenographic record of the proceedings, *Bericht über die Verhandlungen des III. (8.) Parteitages*, pp. 187, 375, 382, 445-448, and *Die Rote Fahne*, No. 27, February 2, 1923.

[59] Flechtheim, p. 85; Carr, *The Interregnum*, pp. 157, 159; Borkenau, *Der europäische Kommunismus*, p. 47; Fischer, pp. 225, 278, and *passim*. The stenographic record of the Eighth Party Congress does not indicate who the new chairman was.

[60] Johannes R. Becher, *Walter Ulbricht, ein deutscher Arbeitersohn* (Berlin, 1958), pp. 20, 86; Becher errs in that Ulbricht was elected to the *Zentrale*, not the *Zentralausschuss* (Central Committee). See also Wenzel, pp. 36-38.

Thirty years after the event, Ulbricht wrote the following slanted account of the Eighth Party Congress: "The debates at the party congress centered around the questions of the united front and the workers' government. The debates were caused by the pronounced opportunist attitude of the party leaders . . . of the time—Brandler, Thalheimer, and others. They misled the party with the aid of the Trotskyite Radek. . . . The position taken by the Brandlerite leadership of the KPD amounted to a rejection of the Marxist dogma [*Lehre*] of proletarian revolution and armed insurrection. Comrade Ernst Thälmann, who throughout the congress stood at the head of the party's revolutionary faction [sic], led the fight against this anti-party position . . . *in conjunction with the Comrades Wilhelm Pieck, Clara Zetkin, Walter Ulbricht, Walter Stoecker*, and others. . . ." (*Zur Geschichte der deutschen Arbeiterbewegung*, 1 [Berlin, 1953], pp. 112-113; my italics). This version is too preposterous to merit further comment.

for the ECCI, and Kleine was duly "elected" into the *Zentrale*.[61]

Most of the veteran party leaders, Brandler, Thalheimer, Zetkin, and so forth, whatever their individual shortcomings, had acquired a sense of responsibility and proportion. Raised in the tradition of the German labor movement with its ups and downs, its relentless, slow, and frequently precarious struggles, they had been taught through hard experience, including the *Märzaktion* fiasco, to accept disappointments, setbacks, and defeats. What was more, they had learned patience and prudence.[62] Although revolution remained their ultimate objective, they did not believe that it could be achieved under existing circumstances, certainly not without widespread and active mass support. It was as evident to Brandler and his colleagues as it had been to Meyer before them that the united front policy offered the only suitable approach toward winning such support. This conviction they expressed at the Leipzig congress, both in the debates and the final resolutions, and the majority of the party endorsed their position.

Their victory netted the moderates the undisguised resentment of the Left Opposition. Ambitious, impatient and intolerant, Ruth Fischer and her following had expressed their dissent on the floor of the congress with their usual vehemence. Whether they were really as eager to mount the barricades as they pretended to be, then and on subsequent occasions, is at least questionable. But so long as they were "The Opposition," so long as control of the party was still in the hands of their less impetuous elders, they stood to gain in influence and supporters by their radical approach, and they needed both to climb to the top of the party. For the young hotheads of the Left were "on the make," and they lost no opportunity of advocating a dynamic, daring, and resolute party policy, especially for the benefit of the rank and file.

The outcome of the Eighth Party Congress essentially confirmed the results of the Fourth World Congress: the alignment of the factions within the KPD remained unchanged. Divided within, and vastly outnumbered without, the German Communist Party approached the challenges of the crisis year 1923.

[61] Fischer, p. 392; Nollau, *Die Internationale* (Cologne, 1959), pp. 127-128, 263. Nollau states (p. 263) that Guralski-Kleine stayed in Germany from 1921 to 1923, but does not substantiate his claim. It is exceedingly doubtful that Guralski had remained in Germany after the March uprising in 1921 had failed.
[62] Wenzel, p. 38.

PART FOUR
THE "AUTHORIZED" BID
FOR POWER (1923)

CHAPTER X

INTENSIFIED UNITED FRONT POLICY

☭ 1923 was for the Weimar Republic a year of perpetual crisis, and each phase of this crisis affected the plans and activities of the KPD. The key problem around which all subsidiary difficulties revolved was the occupation of the Ruhr region by French and Belgian forces on January 11, 1923.[1] The occupation grew out of a dispute between Germany and France over the former country's lagging reparations payments. The legal basis for the application of sanctions, i.e., the occupation of the Ruhr, was provided by the Inter-Allied Reparations Commission, which on December 28, 1923, sent a note to the German government in which it specified the amount of German arrears in timber and coal deliveries to the Allies.[2] When Germany pleaded inability to deliver the outstanding goods, the French government, basing itself on Articles 17 and 18, Part VII, Appendix II of the Versailles treaty, ordered General Degoutte to occupy the highly industrialized Ruhr region. The French were reinforced by Belgian contingents and a number of Italian officials.

This action, inspired by the French Premier, Raymond Poincaré, evoked an intense wave of bitterness among the Germans and led initially to a spirit of unity such as the nation had not known since 1914. On January 20, 1923, the Cuno government issued the following proclamation to all German officials of the newly occupied territory: "The action of the French and Belgian governments in the Ruhr district constitutes a grave violation of international law

[1] The literature on the Ruhr occupation is extensive. The following titles constitute only a few selected works which are useful for further reference: Paul Wentzke, *Ruhrkampf*, 2 vols. (Berlin, 1930-1931); Hans Spethmann, *Zwölf Jahre Ruhrbergbau. Aus seiner Geschichte von Kriegsanfang bis zum Franzosenabmarsch, 1914-1925: Der Ruhrkampf, 1923-1925, Das Ringen um die Kohle*, vol. IV of 4 vols. (Berlin, 1930); Hannes Pyszka, *Der Ruhrkrieg* (Munich, 1923); Friedrich Grimm, *Vom Ruhrkrieg zur Rheinlandräumung: Erinnerungen eines deutschen Verteidigers vor französischen und belgischen Kriegsgerichten* (Hamburg, 1930); United States Army, *American Representation in Occupied Germany*, compiled by the Assistant Chief of Staff, G-2, American Forces in Germany (Coblenz, 1923); Viscount D'Abernon, *The Diary of an Ambassador: II, Rapallo to Dawes, 1922-1924* (New York, 1930).

[2] Legally, sanctions could only be imposed in case of deliberate default. The Reparations Commission had phrased its note of December 28, 1922, in such a way that it could be construed to imply deliberate failure on Germany's part, thereby providing a legal excuse for the imposition of sanctions.

and of the Versailles treaty. By reason of this, all orders and instructions issued to German officials in the execution of this action are legally of no effect. The national government . . . therefore directs that orders of the occupying powers are not to be followed, but that the orders of our own government are to be adhered to exclusively.[3]

This proclamation may be considered the official beginning of what has become known as Germany's "policy of passive resistance." Its main characteristic was non-cooperation of German workers, employers, and officials with the occupying forces. In some cases the population resorted to strikes and slowdowns after the French took over the local systems of transportation and communication. When the military authorities retaliated by arresting a number of prominent German mine owners and fining them for having sabotaged coal deliveries to the Allies, the majority of workers backed up their employers by refusing to dig coal. On January 29 the French authorities proclaimed a state of intensified siege (verschärfter Belagerungszustand) in the region, and on the following day the German government issued orders to the German railway workers in the Ruhr to stop all foreign trains which were used to transport coal to France and Belgium. The French in turn began to arrest German officials, charged them with disobedience to the occupation forces, and expelled them to the unoccupied part of Germany. This measure increased the bitterness of German resistance, multiplied the financial burdens of the Reich, but did little to benefit the French. For many months to come, the whole occupation process moved in a vicious circle: France demanded compliance and was answered by defiance. Thereupon French measures grew stricter, the methods of dealing with violators became more arbitrary and, at times, amounted to outright brutality. Inevitably, the consequence was again an increase of German resistance, ranging from strikes to acts of sabotage. While the French demanded that Germany pay her reparations and terminate passive resistance, the German government declared that passive resistance would not cease as long as foreign troops remained in the Ruhr. In short, recrimination was answered by recrimination, leading neither side to its goal.

[3] Quoted in Major General Henry T. Allen, U.S.A., The Rhineland Occupation (Indianapolis, 1927), pp. 275-276.

Intensified United Front Policy

While inconclusive diplomatic attempts to settle the conflict continued throughout the spring and summer of 1923, the Cuno government felt compelled to take steps for the protection of the German borders, both in the West and the East. An invasion along the eastern frontier was held to be possible, as it was suspected in leading German military circles that Poland would exploit the international tension to obtain a "rectification" of her borders. Lithuania had already taken advantage of the Ruhr crisis by seizing the city of Memel.[4] In order to be prepared for any emergency, the German government resorted to the desperate measure of secretly strengthening the defenses of the republic. To do so without arousing the suspicion of either the Allies or anti-military circles within the country, the government authorized the army to train *Zeitfreiwillige* (short-term volunteers), many of whom were students, and so-called *Arbeitskommandos* (labor units), made up mostly of men who had seen war service. The enterprise was financed from army funds and from voluntary contributions by industrialists and conservative agrarian interest groups. Training was conducted throughout the summer and fall of 1923.[5]

At the time that the government permitted the creation of these auxiliaries, some of the freecorps, which had been disbanded in 1921, decided to reactivate on their own. These extra-legal and unruly organizations reassembled shortly after the occupation of the Ruhr began, and freebooter commanders such as Rossbach, Hauenstein, and Heydebreck once again became active recruiting agents. Much has been written on the freecorps, and this is not the place to add more to this topic.[6] Of immediate importance, how-

[4] Ludwig Zimmermann, *Deutsche Aussenpolitik in der Ära der Weimarer Republik* (Göttingen-Berlin-Frankfurt, 1958), p. 152; *Schulthess' Europäischer Geschichstkalender*, 1923 (Munich, 1928), p. 238.

[5] For this and the following information concerning the government's defense measures and the role of the freecorps I am indebted to Professor Harold J. Gordon, Jr., letter dated April 2, 1962. Professor Gordon's information is based on his own latest research.

[6] Waite, *Vanguard of Nazism* (Cambridge, Mass., 1952), pp. 239-247; Rabenau, *Seeckt* (Leipzig, 1940), pp. 323-328; Gordon A. Craig, *The Politics of the Prussian Army, 1640-1945* (New York and Oxford, 1956), pp. 401-403; Hans Buchrucker, *Im Schatten Seeckts. Die Geschichte der "Schwarzen Reichswehr"* (Berlin, 1928), *passim*; Otto-Ernst Schüddekopf, *Heer und Republik: Quellen zur Politik der Reichswehrführung 1918-1933* (Hannover and Frankfurt am Main, 1955), pp. 122-128; Gordon, *The Reichswehr and the German Republic 1919-1926* (Princeton, 1957), pp. 233-234, 256; George W. F. Hallgarten, *Hitler, Reichswehr und Industrie: Zur Geschichte der Jahre 1918-1933* (Frankfurt am Main, 1955), pp. 23-28.

ever, is the effect which the freecorps had on the political scene. Eager for action, the freebooters infiltrated into the occupied Ruhr region to harass the French, and thereby helped to transform Germany's passive resistance into active resistance. Although some members of the Reich Cabinet were not averse to some measure of secret and limited active resistance, neither the government nor the army command was able effectively to control the many fighting groups which were sprouting up overnight, particularly since they operated in an area which the occupation forces had just removed from the jurisdiction of the republic. The most famous incident perpetrated by the freebooters was the destruction of a railway bridge at Calcum, a point between Düsseldorf and Duisburg, on March 15, 1923. The undertaking was led by Albert Leo Schlageter, a lieutenant in the freecorps unit *Organisation Heinz*. The action as such was not of great significance; in fact, the actual damage caused at Calcum was less extensive than the dynamiting of the Rhine-Herne canal embankment by another freecorps unit a few weeks later. But it was significant that Schlageter was caught, tried, and executed by a French firing squad on May 26, 1923, which made him at once a national hero, a martyr, and a symbol of active resistance. What was more, his death was shortly to be exploited by the Communists for their own purposes.[7]

The guerilla war in the Ruhr proved extremely detrimental to the German cause. It brought added misery to the population of the Ruhr region where the occupation troops, provoked and often frightened by repeated assaults, resorted to reprisals. Embitterment mounted in France also, and enhanced the difficulties of solving the conflict by a compromise acceptable to both sides. The irresponsible acts of violence weakened the initially strong sympathy which Great Britain and the United States had shown for Germany's position. Finally, German labor watched with growing suspicion the rise of intense nationalism which the freecorps aroused within the nation, a trend indicative of a possible right-wing resurgence.

Since the Ruhr region was economically disrupted and, in addition, virtually cut off from the rest of Germany by a newly established customs line, the government was deprived of the area's

[7] See below, Ch. XI.

normal production, but it still had to support the population with money and food and take care of the numerous refugees and expellees as well. Such a burden would have put a great financial strain on the country at any time, but it was particularly heavy in 1923, on account of the mounting inflation which wrought havoc with the value of the mark. The Cuno government had succeeded, in the middle of February, in temporarily halting the inflation by pegging the rate of exchange at approximately 18,000-20,000 marks to the U.S. dollar. The currency then remained relatively stable for two months, but in the second half of April the dam gave way, and the paper mark literally rushed into the void.[8] In May, the rate of exchange stood (roughly) at 48,000 marks to the dollar; in June, 110,000 marks; in July, 349,000 marks; and in August, 4,600,000 marks. In July, after six months of Ruhr occupation, the government published statistical data on the effects of the struggle. The occupation forces numbered altogether 87,000 men, to which had to be added 10,000 French and 1,000 Belgian railway employees sent into the Ruhr to take over the transportation system which German officials had abandoned, in accordance with the policy of passive resistance. The upkeep of these forces was Germany's financial responsibility. The government also had to provide relief for 71,145 persons who had been expelled from the region and were homeless, thus becoming the responsibility of the state.[9] The strain on German finances was indeed enormous.

Even more damaging than the technical difficulties which the financial crisis imposed on the government was the toll which the inflation took in human terms. The middle-class citizens, especially those in the lower income brackets, were hit hardest. Men and women, who had all their lives thought of the ownership of money as a basis for present and future security, saw this concept destroyed before their eyes. Savings accounts melted into nothing; pensions became worthless; heirlooms had to be sold for worthless paper marks, with denominations in billions stamped upon them, in order to buy food for the family. Respectable old civil servants living on retirement pay found themselves paupers overnight. Salaried em-

[8] Bresciani-Turroni, *The Economics of Inflation* (London, 1937), pp. 62-63; Rosenberg, *Entstehung und Geschichte der Weimarer Republik* (Frankfurt am Main, 1955), p. 398.
[9] *Schulthess'*, 1923, p. 130.

ployees and wage earners were paid several times a day during the height of this cataclysm, collecting the money in burlap bags. With these, their waiting spouses rushed to the grocer to buy bread before the store owner scribbled the new, always more astronomical exchange rate, on the blackboard which had become a necessary fixture in every retail business. Bewildered, shocked, and helpless, an entire generation found itself deprived of the modest possessions of the present, and its hopes for security in the future. Gone was all confidence in the established order of things. If a man could no longer rely on the money he earned, or had saved, what could he believe in? Loss of even modest means meant loss of status, meant poverty, and this in turn dealt fierce blows to pride and dignity. At the same time the impoverished *rentier*, the salaried white-collar worker, the worker whose government-regulated wage increase did not keep step with the dwindling value of the mark—all these could observe how a privileged few were benefiting from their misery. Speculators who had got hold of dollars; industrialists who paid worthless paper wages for the production of goods which, if sold abroad, brought in foreign currency; and profiteers who bought up real estate and other valuable property cheaply from desperate owners, and then sold again at a high profit to foreigners or Germans with non-German currency—these prospered.[10]

While the inflation fostered tension, discontent, and despair throughout the entire nation, the growing embitterment of labor was due also to Germany's leading industrialists. As early as October 1922, Hugo Stinnes, Rhenish steel, coal and oil magnate, had proposed in a speech before the National Economic Council the abolition of the eight-hour day in order to increase production. There was to be no overtime pay for overtime work, and no strikes or other forms of wage struggle.[11] Stinnes reiterated this suggestion in March 1923 during a conversation with Gustav Stresemann, leader of the German People's Party.[12] Nothing came of these proposals, but in May Stinnes, this time in the company of his

---

[10] For a discussion on the influence which speculation had on the value of the mark during this period see Bresciani-Turroni, pp. 100-103; for the role of special interest groups, especially industrial ones, see *ibid.*, pp. 103-106.

[11] Anderson, *Hammer or Anvil* (London, 1945), p. 87.

[12] Gustav Stresemann, *Vermächtnis: Der Nachlass in drei Bänden*, ed. Henry Bernhard, 1: *Vom Ruhrkrieg bis London* (Berlin, 1932), p. 43.

peers, launched another effort to curb labor. The powerful *Reichs-verband der deutschen Industrie* (National Association of German Industries) offered the government a guarantee to the amount of 500 million gold marks for payment of Germany's annual economic obligation. The association suggested that the sum was to be raised by the country's economic interests as a whole (*Gesamtwirtschaft*), including labor, with industry alone pledging 200 million gold marks of the total sum. In return for this offer the association demanded that the government should cease to interfere with the production and distribution of goods; that it remove all remaining economic controls; that it revise the taxation system, free the economy of all unproductive burdens and, finally, that employers be given full freedom to draw up labor contracts, whereby the eight-hour day was to be maintained "in principle." The offer—or was it an ultimatum—was signed by von Sorge, Bücher, von Borsig, Bosch, Duisberg, Klöckner, Thyssen, Stinnes, Silverberg and Siemens, every one of them an influential magnate. The labor unions, however, registered their strong objections to the scheme, and Chancellor Cuno felt obliged to reject the offer.[13]

The combined effects of the runaway inflation and the disputes between labor and industry inevitably affected the domestic political climate. The situation in the Ruhr strengthened extremist forces on the Right, largely because of the government's hesitancy to wage the struggle more boldy. At the same time the deterioration on the economic front, coupled with labor's mounting distrust of big industry and of the vociferous right-wing elements, strengthened

[13] Stampfer, *Die vierzehn Jahre der ersten deutschen Republik*, 3rd ed. (Hamburg, 1947), pp. 330-331; *Schulthess'*, 1923, p. 106.

For the reaction of the KPD to this offer see Franz Dahlem, "The Communist 'Putsch' in the Ruhr," *Inprecorr*, III, No. 41 (June 7, 1923), p. 389.

In *Hugo Stinnes* (Tübingen, 1958), a recent biography by Gert von Klaas, the attempt has been made to demonstrate that Stinnes was a big-hearted, lovable philanthropist.

Aside from Bresciani-Turroni's book, the reader interested in additional material on the inflation period may profitably consult the following works: James W. Angell, *The Recovery of Germany* (New Haven, 1929); Kuno Francke, *German After-War Problems* (Cambridge, Mass., 1927); John Maynard Keynes, *A Revision of the Treaty, Being a Sequel to the Economic Consequences of the Peace* (New York, 1922); Sir Andrew McFadyean, *Reparation Reviewed* (London, 1930); Gustav Stolper, *Deutsche Wirtschaft 1870-1940: Kaiserreich, Republik, Drittes Reich* (Stuttgart, 1950), pp. 92-103; Heinrich Bechtel, *Wirtschaftsgeschichte Deutschlands*, III (Munich, 1956), pp. 387-394; Heinrich Zimmermann, *Die deutsche Inflation* (Berlin, 1926).

the extremists on the Left. Not since 1918 had the country been so ripe for a major political and social upheaval as in that fateful year, 1923.

In view of the immense problems which the republic faced, it would appear that the KPD now stood an excellent chance of realizing its objective, i.e., to launch a revolution in Germany which would culminate in the seizure of power by the proletariat. High expectations to this effect were indeed held by party leaders as well as by the rank and file, but even under the prevailing favorable conditions the revolution was to remain an unfulfilled hope. Communist policy during the first seven months of 1923, from the occupation of the Ruhr to the resignation of the Cuno government, lacked cohesion, coordination, and clear direction. The party majority, including the *Zentrale*, continued to differ with the Left Opposition on tactics, and on more than one occasion the two sides worked at cross purposes. Both factions agreed on the necessity of winning mass support from the German labor movement as a whole, but they could agree on little else. Although these divergences of views were not always operative, they were frequent and strong enough to hinder unity of purpose. Furthermore, the party found it difficult effectively to combine its opposition to the German "bourgeois" government with its opposition to the "imperialist" French occupation forces in the Ruhr. This, in turn, was due in part to insufficient guidance from Moscow, where the Boleshevik leaders already stood in the shadow of Lenin's sickness and approaching death. The beginning struggles for the succession within the Russian hierarchy were reflected in the fact that orders from Moscow often lacked clarity and became subject to different interpretations within the KPD. Only late in the summer did the various Communist contingents reach an agreement on "What is to be done," and by then the most favorable moment for a revolution had passed.

The party's first and most energetic response to the Ruhr occupation was to infuse the united front policy with fresh vigor, and the *Zentrale* adhered consistently to this revitalized course until the summer. Aside from the long-standing demands to form workers' governments, other aspects of the united front approach, which so far had played a subordinate role, were now given added attention, notably the factory council movement, proletarian control commissions, and armed proletarian hundreds (*Hundertschaften*).[14]

The factory councils, legally instituted under Article 165 of the Weimar Constitution and the Factory Council Law of February 4, 1920, had been designed to give employees within any given plant the right to deliberate, together with management, on questions affecting working conditions, personnel changes, and policy decisions.[15] As the councils were elected by the totality of the employees, the composition of their membership posed a strong challenge to the Communists, who tried hard and persistently to capture as many seats on the councils as possible. In addition to such local efforts, the party tried to turn the councils as such into effective rivals of the trade-unions, which were less easily infiltrated and manipulated. Finally, the councils were a convenient vehicle for Communist propaganda. The repeated efforts of the KPD to sponsor periodic factory council congresses, on a regional or national level, were mainly for this purpose. Although few of these congresses were representative of German labor, in view of the fact that most of the participating delegations were either partly or completely Communist-controlled, the party tried hard to attract non-Communist council members to them.[16]

Another device by which the party displayed its concern for the welfare of the workers was the formation of control commissions. A recent definition of these extra-legal agencies has been given by an East German writer: "The control commissions were the self-help organs of the suffering population . . . in [their] struggle against price speculation [*Preiswucher*] and black market activities. The commissions moved resolutely against hoarders, speculators and swindlers. They enforced the sale of hoarded foodstuffs, both

[14] *Bericht über die Verhandlungen des III. (8.) Parteitages der K.P.D. (Sektion der K.I.) abgehalten in Leipzig vom 28. Januar bis 1. Februar 1923* (Berlin, 1923), pp. 414-415; Ulbricht, *Zur Geschichte der deutschen Arbeiterbewegung,* I (Berlin, 1953), pp. 116-117.

[15] Ernst Fränkel and Karl Dietrich Bracher, *Staat und Politik* (Frankfurt am Main, 1957), pp. 29, 106-107.

[16] Wenzel, "Die K.P.D. im Jahre 1923" (unpubl. diss. Freie Universität Berlin, 1955), pp. 23-26, including n.25 on pp. 24-25; Flechtheim, *Die K.P.D. in der Weimarer Republik* (Offenbach, 1948), p. 91; Flechtheim's assumption, based on his discussion of the factory councils, that in 1923 "the KPD had at least a strong minority of unionized, and perhaps the majority of unorganized workers, behind it," is difficult to believe, impossible to substantiate.

from the prosperous peasant in the village and from the merchant in town."[17] Just as in the case of the factory councils, the KPD tried to camouflage its influence on the commissions by presenting them as *ad hoc* organs, created by customers for the protection of consumers. The members of these commissions were elected by delegates from factory councils, unions, and other labor organizations at conferences specially called for the purpose. Sometimes local consumers' meetings were hastily convoked to elect a control commission. Yet the participants at such meetings were carefully selected by the KPD, and to no one's surprise tended to vote predominantly for Communists. Although the commissions actually did attempt to control food prices, frequently by intimidating merchants who had raised prices in response to the rapidly declining value of the currency, their primary purpose was to extend the scope of Communist influence among the non-Communist workers.[18]

The most drastic measure which the party took in boosting the effectiveness of its united front campaign was the creation of armed shock troops, the "proletarian" or "red hundreds." Demands to give weapons to the workers had been part and parcel of the party propaganda ever since Rathenau's assassination,[19] but in the spring of 1923 these demands were not only stepped up, but positive measures were taken to organize such a workers' militia. The party justified the need for proletarian "defense" units with the argument that the "Fascists" were well-armed and organized throughout Germany, and that the workers would have to do likewise in order to protect themselves against the constant and growing threat from rightist forces. On the surface, this argument had much to recommend it. It was common knowledge at the time that many clandestine right-wing organizations existed, well-armed, in every part of the republic—concentrated mostly in Bavaria, and lately in the Ruhr region as well. The Communist case for arming the workers began to sound even more convincing after the French, in February 1923, dissolved the Prussian state police in the newly occupied territory, and German freecorps fighters started to infiltrate

[17] Helmut Gast, "Die proletarischen Hundertschaften als Organe der Einheitsfront im Jahre 1923," *Zeitschrift für Geschichtswissenschaft*, IV, No. 3 (1956), p. 441.

[18] Wenzel, pp. 26-27; Ulbricht, *Zur Geschichte der deutschen Arbeiterbewegung*, I, pp. 117-118.

[19] Gast, *Zeitschrift für Geschichtswissenschaft*, IV, No. 3 (1956), p. 441.

across the demarcation line. Finally, by stressing the common interest of all workers in mutual defense, the KPD tried to avoid the application of the Communist label to the proletarian hundreds. The real motive of the party was to utilize the existing tensions for building revolutionary cadres which, at the proper moment, could be employed to overthrow the existing German government. As the formation of fighting units could be accomplished most easily in those parts of Germany where the authority of the central government was momentarily weakest, the KPD concentrated its efforts first in the Ruhr region, and subsequently in Saxony and Thuringia.[20]

Less dramatic, though ranking in importance with the party's above-mentioned activities, were its attempts to infiltrate the trade-unions. This process was furthered and supervised by special sections for union activities (*Gewerkschaftsabteilungen*), which on the national and regional levels formed part of the organizational apparatus of the KPD. Party members were instructed to run for office on the lower and intermediary levels, especially in unions affiliated with the German Federation of Unions, the *Allgemeiner Deutscher Gewerkschaftsbund* (ADGB).[21] As the majority of the seven million members organized in the ADGB did not belong to any political party—although many of them tended to vote for the Social Democrats in elections—the Communists could hope to win supporters among them with relative ease. These expectations proved in part justified. In the first six months of 1923 the economic situation deteriorated rapidly, and an increasing number of workers, especially from unions belonging to the ADGB, turned in despair to the KPD.[22]

---

[20] *ibid.*, p. 443; Wenzel, pp. 27-28; Severing, *Mein Lebensweg*, I (Cologne, 1950), pp. 385-386; Spethmann, IV, 100. For the special role assigned the proletarian hundreds in the late summer of 1923, see below, Ch. XII.

[21] Wenzel, pp. 41-42. The ADGB and the *Allgemeiner freier Angestelltenbund* (Independent Federation of Employees), or AfA, constituted Germany's so-called "*freie Gewerkschaften*" (independent trade-unions). Besides these independent trade-unions, which worked closely with the Social Democrats, there existed during this period trade-unions that were organized along denominational lines, the so-called Christian unions, which together formed the *Deutscher Gewerkschaftsbund*, or DGB. See Theodor Leipart, "Die Arbeitnehmer in Deutschland," *Zehn Jahre deutsche Geschichte*, 1918-1928 (Berlin, 1928), p. 340; Fränkel and Bracher, p. 106.

[22] It is nearly impossible to determine how many union members the Communists were able to control within the various trade-unions. The party claimed in the summer of 1923 that 2.4 million members of the ADGB were under Communist influence

It might have been expected that the party's next move would be to use this mounting discontent to split the German trade-unions. It could then have created separate Communist unions which would have become affiliated with the Red Trade-Union International, the Profintern. But the KPD rejected this approach, deeming it more profitable and prudent to infiltrate instead the existing German trade-unions, and to strengthen Communist influence from within their ranks. For this reason, only an insignificant number of trade-union organizations in Germany were affiliated with the Profintern. Of these, the most notable was the "Union of Manual and Brain Workers (*Union der Hand- und Kopfarbeiter*)" which the KPD had founded in 1919, and which by 1923 numbered approximately 120,000 members. Despite its name, it was almost entirely composed of miners from the Ruhr region and, because of its strong syndicalist tendencies, gave the party a good deal of trouble. Ordinarily, Communist workers expelled from one of the regular trade-unions were not allowed to join the *Union*, but were encouraged to work their way back into the organization which had expelled them.[23]

All these attempts to revitalize the party's united front policy remained fairly constant during the first half of 1923. In addition, however, the KPD faced the thorny problem of how to deal with the Ruhr crisis. On the one hand, the Fourth World Congress had reaffirmed the long-standing opposition of international Communism to the treaty of Versailles and all it implied,[24] and the Ruhr occupation was, after all, based on the assumption that Germany had violated certain terms of this treaty. It was therefore quite in line with Communist doctrine to condemn the combined Franco-Belgian operation as a prime example of western imperialism. On the other hand, the KPD was a revolutionary party, dedicated to

---

(*organisatorisch beeinflusst*) in the spring of that year (Wenzel, p. 42; see also Flechtheim, p. 91).

There is no doubt that the trade-unions were in desperate straits in 1923. This is discernible from the following figures: On December 1, 1923, 23.4% of all German workers organized in trade-unions were unemployed, and 47.3% worked only part-time. Thus only 29.3% of the total German labor force was fully employed. It is hardly surprising that membership of the ADGB, which in the early part of 1923 had numbered seven million, dropped to four million by 1924 (Leipart, *Zehn Jahre deutsche Geschichte*, p. 343).

[23] Wenzel, pp. 41-43.

[24] *Protokoll des Vierten Kongresses der K.I., Petrograd-Moskau vom 5. November bis 5. Dezember 1922* (Hamburg, 1923), pp. 1002-1006.

the destruction of the existing order in Germany. How was the party to reconcile its opposition to the Ruhr occupation, an opposition which placed the party alongside the German government and the nation, with its ultimate objective of overthrowing this same government by a revolution? Here was a dilemma which defied any simple solution and caused the KPD leadership to adopt a tortuous, often contradictory, line of action.

A few days before the occupation of the Ruhr, on January 6 and 7, 1923, representatives of the Communist parties of France, Germany, Great Britain, Belgium, Holland, Italy, and Czechoslovakia met for a conference in Essen, to deliberate on how to meet the approaching crisis brought on by the conflict between Germany and the Allies over reparations. Brandler and Thalheimer represented the KPD. The chief topic was the approaching "imperialist conflict," and the debate centered on the question of how the parties most directly concerned, the KPD and the French C.P., were to conduct themselves in this coming struggle. Two areas of agreement were reached at once: to fight "imperialist aggression," regardless of what side advocated it, and to do so by close cooperation between the German and French proletariat. Marcel Cachin, speaking for the 52,000 members of the French Communist Party, promised that the French workers were resolved to offer fierce resistance to the intended occupation of the Ruhr. The conference adjourned after its delegates had passed a resolution condemning the treaty of Versailles and the imperialist designs of France.[25]

As soon as Brandler and Thalheimer had returned from Essen, the *Zentrale*, on January 10, directed an open letter to the SPD and the principal German trade-unions, calling for a united stand on the Ruhr occupation. The letter suggested that a nationwide general strike be called to demonstrate labor's protest against the projected French move, and demanded simultaneously that the burden of reparation payments be shifted exclusively to the German propertied classes. Finally, the strike was to serve as an appeal for the resignation of the Cuno government. Although nothing came of these suggestions, the KPD seemed satisfied to have gone on record that the party was ready to fight the enemies of the working class at home and abroad. In lieu of the contemplated general

[25] *Die Rote Fahne*, No. 5, January 7, 1923; No. 6, January 9, 1923; Wenzel, p. 55.

strike, which the SPD and the unions rejected, and which the Communists could not hope to launch by themselves, the KPD participated very patriotically in a government-sponsored half-hour work stoppage which, as a protest, was carried out in the occupied region on January 15.[26]

The search for an attitude which would express both antagonism to French "imperialism" and to German "capitalist exploitation" led the Communists repeatedly into positions of near-absurdity. On January 11, the day the occupation began, the *Rote Fahne* published a proclamation by the *Zentrale* which bluntly accused the Cuno government of sharing with the French the responsibility for the German dilemma in the Ruhr.[27] This approach differed markedly from the official position adopted by Soviet Russia. On January 13, 1923, the All Russian Central Executive Committee issued "To the Peoples of the World," a strongly worded protest against the French action, but did not abuse the German government, Russia's Rapallo partner.[28]

The same day that Moscow let it be known how Soviet Russia felt about the Ruhr occupation, the German Reichstag met for an emergency session to debate the situation. Just before the opening of the session, the deputies rose from their seats, thereby marking the solemnity of the moment. Only the Communist representatives remained seated.[29] In the course of the day, Paul Frölich took the floor and delivered an inflammatory speech—not against the French occupation policy, but against the projected adoption of "passive resistance," against the Cuno government, and against German big industry. "We live at war," he exclaimed, "and Karl Liebknecht has taught us how the working class must carry on war policy. He called for class struggle against war! That will be our slogan. No *Burgfrieden*, but *Burgkrieg*. . . . In this hour, we consider ourselves brothers of our French comrades, the French proletariat." Frölich

[26] *Bericht über die Verhandlungen des III. (8.) Parteitages*, pp. 38-39; Wenzel, p. 57; Anderson, p. 90.

[27] *Die Rote Fahne*, No. 8, January 11, 1923.

[28] Jane Degras, ed., *Soviet Documents on Foreign Policy*, 1 (London-New York-Toronto, 1951), pp. 368-370. See also Carr, *The Interregnum 1923-1924* (New York, 1954), pp. 155-156, for an analysis of Soviet Russia's position on this question.

[29] Germany, *Stenographische Berichte des Reichstags, Verhandlungen*, vol. 357, p. 9417.

then rejected a united national front, and when the house terminated the session by a vote of solemn protest against the events in the Ruhr, the Communist delegates registered their votes as "nays."[30] Four days later, during another debate in the Reichstag, Communist delegate Höllein delivered a speech in which he referred to the Ruhr crisis as a "nationalist swindle," perpetrated by the French and German governments to deceive their respective peoples. He charged that the industrialist Stinnes was in the process of initiating secret negotiations with M. Poincaré in order to deliver the people into the hands of the French. Then, turning to the delegates of the middle-class parties, Höllein warned them that there were men in Moscow who some day would exterminate them (the delegates), root and branch.[31]

The official party line received overt expression on January 23, 1923. On that day, the *Zentrale* published a leading article in the *Rote Fahne* under the banner line "Smite Poincaré and Cuno on the Ruhr and on the Spree." The article, addressed to the men and women of the German working class, informed its readers that the struggle over the Ruhr was essentially one between the German and French bourgeoisie, though it was fought on the "backs of the German working class." Underlying the struggle, according to the party pundits, was a disagreement among the French and German industrialists, who were eager to form a common trust for the exploitation of coal and iron ore deposits on both sides of the frontier, but were unable to come to terms on particulars. The French, claimed the *Rote Fahne*, wanted 60% of the common shares, leaving Krupp, Thyssen and Stinnes only 40%. Caught between two fires, the German proletariat now had to engage in a two-front war, against the "foreign capitalist invaders" protected by the bayonets of the French occupation forces in the Ruhr, and against the oppressive capitalist exploiters at home. In practical terms, the article explained, this meant working-class opposition to the occupation forces in the Ruhr, accompanied at home by continuous demands

[30] *ibid.*, pp. 9429-9434, 9437-9438.
[31] *ibid.*, pp. 9480-9483. Shortly after he made this speech, Höllein was arrested by the French when he tried to cross the frontier illegally on his way to attend a Communist conference in Paris, and spent several months in prison. Upon his return to Germany he was greeted like a national hero, and his seat in the Reichstag was decked out with flowers (Wenzel, p. 60).

for wage increases, for the cessation of oppressive police measures, and for the liberation of imprisoned proletarians.[32]

As has been shown earlier,[33] the entire complex of the Ruhr occupation was largely ignored by the Eighth Party Congress at Leipzig, though whether this was done intentionally or not is difficult to determine. Quite possibly the *Zentrale* wanted to sidestep debate on the issue, and to settle first the various outstanding differences on over-all policy which divided the party. But since it proved impossible to reach a genuine agreement on fundamentals, the problem of the Ruhr occupation was left in abeyance, much to the detriment of subsequent party policy.

From the first, the Janus-faced Communist slogan of smiting Poincaré and Cuno on the Ruhr and on the Spree presented difficulties. Perhaps the clearest directive of how the slogan was to be applied in practice was written early in the struggle by Paul Frölich. The Ruhr war, according to his view, had led to the first international Communist operation. French and German party members were working and fighting side by side for the same goal and on the same front, though manning different sectors and facing different tasks. The slogan along the French sector was: "Against Poincaré, the *Comité des Forges*, and Imperialism"; along the German sector: "Against French Imperialism, Cuno, and the German Industrial Magnates." The fight against Poincaré was fought because French imperialism did violence to the German proletariat; because it was the mainstay of the Versailles treaty; because bourgeois France was the most powerful military force on the continent; because France was now the stronghold of reactionary, counterrevolutionary forces, the like of which would make Noske and Mussolini look tame by comparison; and because France was an enemy of Soviet Russia and had lent assistance to the Whites. On the other hand, Cuno had to be fought because he represented heavy industry's dominion over German labor; because his policies benefited im-

---

[32] *Die Rote Fahne*, No. 18, January 23, 1923. The slogan "Smite Poincaré. . . ," etc., had already appeared the day before, though in a slightly different version, on Communist propaganda handbills which were circulated in the streets (*Bericht über die Verhandlungen des IX. Parteitages der K.P.D. (Sektion der K.I.) abgehalten in Frankfurt am Main vom 7. bis 10. April 1924* (Berlin, 1924), p. 41; cf. the discussions on the origins of this slogan in Carr, *The Interregnum*, p. 156, n.2; and Wenzel, p. 58, incl. n.17).

[33] See above, Ch. IX.

perialists and exploiters and were inevitably leading toward catastrophe; because he not only failed to prevent the occupation of the Ruhr but had actually provoked it, and now did nothing to alleviate the suffering of the masses. The article closed with the following injunction.

"The fight against Poincaré is to be carried on by systematic sabotage in the Ruhr district, as a proletarian action, and by the revolutionary permeation of the imperialist army. Against Cuno, by combating nationalism as an ideology, by taking advantage of the present situation to lead the working class in its defensive struggles, and to mobilize the masses for the general strike."[34]

Frölich's lucidly expressed formula notwithstanding, the task which the party faced in the Ruhr was much harder than it looked on paper. The Ruhr population's initial reaction to the occupation was one of outrage and hostility. Labor and management suffered alike from the stringent measures of the invaders, and spontaneously supported the national policy of passive resistance. A fierce patriotism gripped the people and grew in intensity as right-wing freecorps fighters began to infiltrate across the newly erected demarcation line. The Communists were likewise committed to oppose the occupation authorities, but they could not very well identify themselves with either the aims or the actions of government and bourgeoisie, not to mention the freecorps. Their principal objective, as far as can be discerned, was to gain a maximum of political influence among the Ruhr proletariat, an objective which was in full accord with the party's united front policy. But in the process the Communists had to compete with the Social Democrats, and with anarchist and syndicalist splinter groups, and whereas the overwhelming majority of Social Democratic workers supported the policy of passive resistance, the syndicalist elements cooperated openly with the French.[35] The KPD had to balance between these two camps while trying to win converts in both.

[34] Paul Frölich, "The Ruhr War and the German Communists," *Inprecorr*, III, No. 24 (March 8, 1923), pp. 183-184. A similar, though somewhat less incisive analysis of the situation had been written a few weeks earlier by Franz Dahlem, today a leading SED functionary in East Germany: Franz Dahlem, "The Occupation of the Ruhr and the Proletariat," *ibid.*, No. 12 (February 1, 1923), p. 92.

[35] Wenzel, p. 59. The Syndicalists should not be confused with the Separatists who, contrary to Ruth Fischer's account, *Stalin and German Communism* (Cambridge, Mass., 1948), p. 254, did not become active until late in the summer of 1923; see Spethmann, IV, pp. 216-217.

As it turned out, this approach was not an altogether happy one. Communist resistance to the French, ranging from intensive propaganda among the occupation forces to isolated acts of sabotage, was initially frustrated by the preferential treatment which the French allotted to labor, including the KPD, in order to split the German forces of opposition in the Ruhr.[36] To what length the party went by way of demonstrating its zeal is evident from the following episode. At the end of February, when all non-Communist newspapers were temporarily banned, the regional party paper *Ruhr Echo* provoked the occupation authorities by printing deliberate insults, in order to be included under the ban.[37] But lest the KPD be suspected of nationalist tendencies or hidden sympathies with the bourgeois class enemy, local party organizations missed no opportunity to pit workers against employers by staging demonstrations for wage increases, and by asserting that the proletariat rather than government and bourgeoisie constituted the true forces of resistance in the Ruhr.[38] This line was warmly supported by Radek, who wrote toward the latter part of March in a Moscow paper that only the German proletariat seemed to be in a position to defend Germany's national independence. Pointing to acts of brutality which French officials had committed in the Ruhr, Radek erroneously predicted that the occupation was about to collapse, and asked sarcastically whether Poincaré really hoped to get coal this way.[39]

An incident which occurred in Essen on March 31 seemed to justify Radek's rhetorical question. On that day, the Saturday before Easter, French troops moved into a plant of the Krupp works with the intention of requisitioning trucks. Members of the plant personnel, provoked by the soldiers, staged an *ad hoc* demonstration in the course of which the troops were pelted with lumps of coal. During the ensuing melee the French opened fire, leaving thirteen workers dead and forty-one wounded. Among those who were killed was a Communist. The whole incident caused widespread concern throughout Germany, and the KPD duly exploited the

[36] Wenzel, pp. 56-57, 60; *Bericht über die Verhandlungen des IX. Parteitages*, p. 10; see also D'Abernon, II, pp. 186-188, on this aspect of French occupation policy.

[37] Wenzel, p. 60. *Die Rote Fahne*, No. 49, February 28, 1923, reported the ban on the front page.

[38] Wenzel, p. 59.

[39] "Brockdorff-Rantzau to German Foreign Office, March 20, 1923"; Auswärtiges Amt, Germany, microfilm, container 1406, frame D 552863, National Archives, Washington, D.C.

"Essen massacre" in strict accordance with the party line. Under the headline "Proletariat Murdered in Essen; Krupp Workers the Victims of French Militarism and German Nationalist Provocateurs," the *Rote Fahne* put the blame for the tragedy on German nationalist trouble-makers who sang *"Siegreich wollen wir Frankreich schlagen* (victoriously we want to beat France)," and one of whom, a "paunchy one with a silver-handled cane," allegedly told workers not to let the soldiers get away alive. The French troops who had done the shooting, and especially the lieutenant in charge, were depicted as ruthless butchers firing repeatedly into the densest part of the fleeing crowd. There was one hero, Josef Zander, the KPD member who was among those killed. The *Rote Fahne* credited him with having tried to "restrain the mad nationalists in order to prevent a blood bath."[40] The same theme, with minor variations, was treated on the front page of the paper in four additional issues, one of which, on April 5, carried a full page proclamation by the ECCI on the matter.[41]

Despite incidents such as this, despite the progressive deterioration of the German economy in the occupied as well as in the unoccupied part of the republic, the first three months of Ruhr occupation netted the Communists few, if any, tangible advantages. The party press stuck closely to the line agreed upon in January, but the consistent double-track policy did little more than keep the KPD isolated, and cast suspicion on Communist motives.[42] In the absence of directives from Moscow,[43] the Brandler *Zentrale* apparently had no plans for the time being other than to follow the established united front policy. If as a result of national and international tensions a revolutionary situation developed in Germany, the Communists, if they were reasonably certain of massive support, could always revise their course. But short of such a contingency, the party, allowing for minor local adjustments, preferred to plod over the same familiar ground.

[40] *Die Rote Fahne*, No. 76, April 1, 1923.

[41] *ibid.*, Nos. 77 to 80, April 3 to 6, 1923. See also Stampfer, p. 321; Fischer, p. 257, and Spethmann, IV, pp. 266-268; although there is agreement on the essential points, details of the Krupp incident vary from account to account.

[42] An echo of these suspicions is still discernible in Carl Severing's recollections of this period, *Mein Lebensweg*, I, pp. 380, 385-390.

[43] Carr, *The Interregnum*, p. 161.

This "wait and see" attitude was very much in evidence during several Communist-dominated conferences which were held in March in the Ruhr region. On March 1 a "Committee of Twenty-Three" of the Rhenish-Westphalian factory councils issued invitations to various labor organizations of sixteen European countries to meet on March 17 for an international conference at Cologne. The purpose of the conference was to discuss the Ruhr crisis and to appraise its effects on international labor.[44] But before the international meeting convened, the factory councils of Rhineland-Westphalia decided to hold a preliminary conference of their own in Essen on March 11, to discuss "what measures were to be taken against French imperialism and German capitalism."[45] The Essen meeting was attended by 669 delegates, of whom 462 belonged to the KPD, 36 to the SPD, 46 to the Independents, a splinter group of ten thousand members who in the fall of 1922 had refused to merge with the SPD,[46] 11 to the virtually defunct KAPD, 24 to the Syndicalists, and 89 to no party at all. The principal speaker was Karl Becker, a member of the *Zentrale*, who said nothing that had not been said or printed time and again in the preceding three months. There was to be no cooperation and no coalition with the bourgeoisie; a mass struggle was to be waged against the Versailles treaty and for the evacuation of the Ruhr, with the German bourgeoisie footing the bill for all damages that had occurred during the occupation; troops and "other organizations of the ruling class" were to be "enlightened" by systematic agitation. To these points Becker added demands for the disarmament of bourgeois-controlled "White Guards," the arming of the workers, creation of workers' governments, and the perfection of such proletarian organs as control commissions, armed red hundreds, and factory councils.[47] Becker apparently had very little to do with the draft of his speech which, according to the *Rote Fahne*, followed the outlines of a manifesto drawn up by the conference, and of which each delegate had a copy.

[44] *Die Rote Fahne*, No. 50, March 1, 1923. An earlier invitation had been extended on February 10, setting the date of the meeting for March 4, but without designating a place (*ibid.*, No. 35, February 11, 1923).

[45] Karl Becker, "The Ruhr Proletariat Holds Its Council of War," *Inprecorr*, III, No. 27 (March 29, 1923), p. 210.

[46] Wenzel, p. 71, n.1.

[47] *Die Rote Fahne*, No. 60, March 13, 1923.

For all practical purposes, then, the meeting had not produced much more than a routine recital of very familiar objectives.[48]

On March 15, two days before it was to convene, the international conference to which the Rhenish-Westphalian factory councils had been invited was banned in Cologne by the British occupation authorities.[49] Without delay the conference was transferred to Frankfurt am Main, where it opened according to schedule on March 17. Once again, Communist delegates were in the majority (213 of 243). Fifty delegates represented foreign countries. Clara Zetkin, the Bulgarian Comintern representative Vasil P. Kolarov, and A. Lozovsky, chairman of Profintern, were elected to the presidium of the conference and eventually addressed the delegates. The tone was set by the inevitable proclamation of the ECCI which, under the circumstances, sounded rather restrained. It urged that another invitation be sent to the Second International and the Amsterdam Trade-Union International to join the united front of the international proletariat.[50] The advice was particularly apropos since neither of these two organizations sent delegates to Frankfurt. The small group of Socialists who participated in the proceedings had come as individuals and against the orders of the SPD.[51]

The purpose of the conference, according to Moscow, was to ready the working classes everywhere in Europe for common action, to coordinate their fighting methods, and to prepare them for the general struggles ahead. Significantly enough, the ECCI stated quite pointedly that the chief enemy of the moment was French imperialism, and added that in the fight against this enemy so far only the Communist parties of France and Germany had done their duty.[52] The gist of this proclamation was faithfully echoed by the principal speakers, though with minor embellishments. Kolarov, the spokesman for Comintern, stressed the need for a united front

[48] Cf. the more sensational but entirely unsubstantiated account given in Spethmann, IV, p. 139. Among other obvious errors in Spethmann's account, he confused the Essen conference with the international conference at Frankfurt.

[49] *Die Rote Fahne*, No. 62, March 15, 1923. According to Wenzel (p. 71), the Communists had anticipated this move and had hoped thereby to destroy the widespread belief among German labor that Great Britain would protect German interests. They also hoped to prove that the British were hostile to labor. The first allegation, at least, seems far-fetched.

[50] *Die Rote Fahne*, No. 63, March 18, and No. 66, March 20, 1923.

[51] *ibid.*, No. 67, March 21, 1923; Wenzel, p. 72.

[52] The ECCI proclamation, dated March 16, 1923, is in *Die Rote Fahne*, No. 66, March 20, 1923.

of workers on a national and international basis in order to break capitalist class domination. Lozovsky told his audience that "if you want peace, you must wage class warfare." To do so effectively, the proletariat must form a revolutionary bloc against the forces of imperialism and must prepare for the struggles ahead. Moving from the general to the specific, he suggested, as a war-preventive measure, the designation of a propaganda week with slogans calling for opposition to Versailles, for a rejection of coalitions with the bourgeoisie, and for an international front of the proletariat.

Heinrich Brandler's report on the situation in Germany is revealing because of its essentially pessimistic tone. Brandler blamed the calamities which had befallen the nation since 1918 on the Socialists because, as he put it, they obstructed the process of transforming society from a capitalist into a Socialist one. When the Socialists helped the bourgeoisie into the saddle they created the basis for the present conditions. "While we experienced then [in 1918] a rising revolutionary tide on account of the Russian Revolution, we face today a receding tide because of the seizure of power by the bourgeoisie, and now our primary task is to rally [sammeln] the proletariat."[53] The closing address was delivered by Clara Zetkin, who stressed the need for defense against international Fascism by means of organized revolutionary mass struggles. All the points made by the speakers were incorporated into the resolutions taken by the conference: French imperialism was to be fought through cooperation between French and German workers and through active agitation among the occupation troops; Fascism, notably German Fascism, was to be combated by an anti-Fascist week, and the week from April 5 to 12 was designated for this purpose. Finally, the resolutions called for a united front of the international proletariat, condemned war and Versailles, and demanded that Germany make an alliance with Soviet Russia.[54]

Neither the Frankfurt conference nor the earlier one held in Essen presented a new departure, offered any surprises, or indicated an intended change in the Communist party line. The speeches and resolutions reflected the familiar pattern of united front policies, which, since they were geared to meet the needs of a special

[53] ibid.
[54] Die Rote Fahne, No. 66, March 20, 1923; No. 67, March 21, 1923; and No. 68, March 22, 1923; Bericht über die Verhandlungen des IX. Parteitages, p. 10.

situation, had been somewhat extended in scope, and in some instances were more specifically defined than during the preceding period. At no time during the proceedings did the tone of the debates indicate that the Communists had a definite plan for revolutionary action in the foreseeable future. That the speakers used revolutionary jargon was only to be expected. No Communist conference, regardless how routine, could do without it. Even the occasional outbursts of inflammatory rhetoric were no more pronounced than similar ones at past Comintern and KPD congresses. If there was anything remarkable in the tenor of the ECCI proclamation, the content of the speeches, or the emphasis of the resolutions in the midst of an unprecedented political and economic crisis, it was the sameness, the inflexibility of Communist thinking which they expressed.[55]

Shortly after the international conference at Frankfurt, the party was confronted with another controversy over tactics in the Ruhr. The conflict, once again caused by the Left Opposition, had been smouldering ever since the Leipzig Congress. It was brought on by the Fischer faction, which was dissatisfied with the pedestrian course charted by the *Zentrale*, whereas the *Zentrale* was deeply disturbed by Ruth Fischer's activities in the Ruhr.

The ire of the Opposition was aroused when the party's chief theorist, August Thalheimer, published in mid-February a series of articles in several Communist publications.[56] In an assessment of what was involved in the Ruhr struggle, Thalheimer drew a distinction between the roles of the German bourgeoisie on the one

[55] Dr. Wenzel, who in his dissertation expounds the thesis that from the beginning of 1923 the KPD was systematically preparing for a revolution, sees in the Frankfurt conference an important stage on the road toward this objective (pp. 72-73). While the KPD undoubtedly wanted to make a revolution in Germany *at the proper moment*, there is no evidence to show that during the first half of 1923 the *Zentrale* believed this proper moment to have arrived, or even expected it to arrive in the near future. If anything, the party's rigid adherence to the united front policy, the absence of active encouragement from Moscow, and the (subsequently discussed) quarrel within the party over tactics are all indications that the KPD was marking time, and that it did, indeed, very little which can be interpreted as an active and systematic preparation for armed insurrection. See also Carr, *The Interregnum*, p. 163, with whose interpretation I am essentially in agreement.

[56] Ruth Fischer (pp. 281-282) gives a very one-sided and distorted picture, both of the one article on which she bases her arguments, and of the conclusion which she draws concerning the origins of Communist reaction to the Thalheimer line outside Germany. Cf. Carr, *The Interregnum*, pp. 159-160, incl. n.2 on p. 160, and Wenzel, pp. 66-69, on this particular issue.

hand, and French imperialism on the other. Without denying that the policy of passive resistance, advocated and backed by the German bourgeoisie and the Cuno government, was in the last analysis "reactionary," he asserted that in the present struggle the German bourgeoisie played at times an "objectively revolutionary role," though it did so involuntarily. He compared present German foreign policy with that which Bismarck conducted between 1864 and 1870, a policy which Marx and Engels had characterized at the time as revolutionary. Bismarck's role became "openly reactionary" only after the battle of Sedan, and this spirit of reaction lasted until 1918. At that time, Germany's international position changed, and German nationalism once more became a potentially revolutionary force. Thus when Thalheimer concluded that "the defeat of French imperialism . . . in the Ruhr is a Communist aim," he implied that this aim happened to coincide at the moment with the objectives of the German ruling class. Yet Thalheimer qualified his approval of the German bourgeoisie by pointing out that its resistance showed signs of wavering. If and when the bourgeoisie should thus betray its mission by giving in to the French, the burden of resistance would fall exclusively on the proletariat, which then would have to continue its struggle against French imperialism and, at the same time, would have to fight its enemies at home. The objective of this second task would be, first, to make the German bourgeoisie pay for the damages of the Ruhr occupation; then to overthrow the government, after which the revolutionary proletariat would conclude the struggle against the foreign invaders. But before any of these goals could be reached, the Communists would have to eliminate the strong influence which the Social Democrats and the trade-unions were still exercising over the masses.[57]

Thalheimer's arguments were a neatly balanced interpretation of the *Zentrale's* point of view on the Ruhr question. It justified Communist opposition to the French without identifying the aims of the party with German bourgeois nationalism. At the same time, this interpretation accepted German nationalism as a useful, though incidental, ally of Communism, but predicted that this incidental

[57] This summary of Thalheimer's theory is based on Carr, *The Interregnum*, p. 159; Fischer, pp. 281-282; and Wenzel, pp. 66-67. When Thalheimer was later on attacked for his views by non-German Communists he modified his original position (Carr, *The Interregnum*, p. 160, n.2).

ally would betray the nationalist cause. It would then be overthrown by the proletariat, which would proceed to combine revolution at home with the destruction of French imperialism. In order to emphasize that all these momentous events were still a long way off, Thalheimer pointed out, very subtly, that nothing decisive could be accomplished before the masses of German labor had been wooed away from the SPD and the unions. This was in line with what Brandler stated at Frankfurt a few weeks later. It was also expressed by Radek who, of all the Russian leaders, was most closely identified with the position of the Brandler *Zentrale*. Writing in a British Communist publication in March, Radek had this to say.

"Even today the Social Democratic Party is the strongest party of the proletariat in Germany. This may cause disappointment and uneasiness, but it is nevertheless a fact to which one attitude or another has to be taken. One might follow Levi . . . or one might take up arms against the traitors and be defeated, as happened to the German Communist Party in March, 1921. One may also fight against this infamous fact day by day by educating the proletariat, mobilizing the proletarian ranks. Preliminary spade work must be done before the word of command, 'Forward to the assault,' is given to the troops. When the supreme moment arrives the Social Democratic banner can be hauled down and torn to shreds."[58] There was no doubt which of the three alternatives Radek wanted to see adopted.

While Thalheimer, Brandler, and Radek urged the party to work harder to overcome the obstacles which still obstructed the road to victory, the Left Opposition tried to turn the Ruhr conflict into a shortcut to revolution.

Sometime after the Leipzig Congress, presumably in mid-March, Ruth Fischer went to the Rhenish industrial region and "was very active . . . between Hamm and Cologne."[59] She went there as an emissary of the party's Berlin organization with the mission to maintain liaison. Why did the Berlin organization send one of its

[58] Karl Radek, "The Crucible of Revolution," *Communist Review*, III, No. 11 (March 1923), p. 533.
[59] Fischer, p. 254. Her account does not make it clear when exactly she was in the occupied region. She spoke in Berlin twice in public meetings, once on February 8, and again on March 7, 1923 (*Die Rote Fahne*, No. 33, February 11, 1923; and No. 55, March 7, 1923). Whether she went west between these two meetings, or after the second one, cannot be established.

most prominent members into the occupied territory? There were a number of excellent reasons for such a move. In the first place, the Opposition had strong rank and file support in the Ruhr, although the local party organizations were predominantly in the hands of men who adhered to the directives and wishes of the *Zentrale*. Furthermore, the newly established demarcation line made it just as difficult for the *Zentrale* to maintain effective control over party affairs in the Ruhr as it was for the German government to restrain the freecorps in that region. But of even greater import was the fact that the Opposition detected favorable opportunities for left-wing missionary work among the Ruhr population at large. There was some justification for such a belief.

It has already been mentioned that political radicalism in this part of Germany had been endemic for some years. Syndicalist tendencies existed here to a stronger degree than anywhere else in the country.[60] The Communist "Union of Manual and Brain Workers," which had syndicalist sympathies, was more strongly represented in this area than elsewhere. Thus it was not surprising that, shortly after the military occupation had begun, radical segments among the Ruhr proletariat, including a sizable Communist minority, advocated the seizure of mines and factories by the workers. These sentiments were actively encouraged by the Left Opposition, notably by Ruth Fischer, who on this and other issues did not hesitate to attack the official party line in public speeches.[61] In taking this approach, she not only flouted the wishes of the *Zentrale*, but she also antagonized the local KPD leaders, who were not prepared to yield to the radical demands of the least disciplined elements among the Ruhr proletariat, Communist or non-Communist. These men believed that the French, who gave their underhanded support to demands for seizure of the mines, acted only from selfish motives; once the workers were in possession of mines and factories, the occupation forces would confiscate them, and the workers would have only exchanged German for French exploiters.[62]

The differences over tactics in the Ruhr, which existed between the party majority and the Left Opposition, constituted the chief

[60] Fischer, p. 254.
[61] *Die Rote Fahne*, No. 75, March 30, 1923; Wenzel, p. 64.
[62] Wenzel, p. 64.

topic at a regional party congress held by the district Rhineland-Westphalia North in Essen on March 25.[63] Although the Opposition was well represented, it lacked a working majority, and the Fischer faction suffered a first defeat before the deliberation had even begun. Ruth Fischer, Ernst Thälmann, and a certain Eugen Epstein from Cologne had arranged to have themselves elected delegates for the district Rhineland-Westphalia North. This maneuver was invalidated by an adverse vote of the assembled congress, and the would-be Rhinelanders were only allowed to participate as representatives of their respective home districts. The *Zentrale* was represented by Walter Stoecker and Clara Zetkin.

As there was no love lost between the two women, it was only fitting that Zetkin and Fischer were the principal speakers. The former, speaking for the party majority, stated once again the chief points of the official line: united front tactics, workers' governments, fight against Cuno and Poincaré, fight against French imperialism. Then Ruth Fischer gave her rebuttal. She began by attacking the tactics which the party had applied since the Leipzig convention. She rejected the *Zentrale's* concept of the workers' government, especially in its projected application in Saxony, and condemned the prevailing policy in the Ruhr. The KPD, Ruth Fischer charged, was moving closer and closer to the SPD. A coalition government with the Socialists she called unacceptable. After she was through saying what she did *not* want, Ruth Fischer gave her own version of how the Communists should conduct the struggle in the Ruhr. She advocated control of production by the workers, in conjunction with the seizure of factories, and the formation of local (workers') defense units throughout those parts of the occupied zone where the French had expelled the German police forces. These demands the Left incorporated into a written resolution, together with a very unrealistic description of the situation in Germany, urging the party to commence the struggle for political power, crush all Fascist

[63] Unless otherwise indicated, the following account of the congress at Essen is based on the report given in *Die Rote Fahne*, No. 74, March 29, 1923.

Ruth Fischer's assertion (p. 255) that the congress was called to "draft a program for the seizure of factories and . . . local power" is not supported by the available evidence. Periodic party congresses on the regional level were routine, as was this one. No doubt, the Opposition delegates at the Essen congress would have liked to see such a program adopted, but they were not in control of the congress.

enemies, overthrow the Cuno government, and establish a revolutionary workers' government.[64]

The proposals of the Left were severely criticized. Spokesmen for the party majority pointed out that the policies suggested by the Left could only lead to unnecessary defeat and isolation of the Communist cause, apart from the fact that the measures advocated would also play into the hands of the French occupation authorities, whose agents had repeatedly approached local party leaders with similar propositions. When the majority presented a counter resolution which reaffirmed the official party line adopted at Leipzig, it was carried by a vote of 68 to 55. Undoubtedly Ruth Fischer did not help her cause when she indulged in threats and abuse. She could hardly expect to make converts by referring to the majority delegates as "friends of democracy" (in the Communist lingo of the time a hideous insult), or when she said that "the day will come when all comrades will stand behind us, and chuck out those who support democracy and ogle with the Weimar Constitution."

When the Essen Congress was over, the dispute within the party was not. The *Zentrale* was clearly worried, and with justification. The strength of the Opposition in the Ruhr was formidable, as the final vote at Essen had shown. The party's entire political course would be jeopardized if this vital region fell into the hands of the Fischer faction. The *Zentrale* expressed its apprehension in a notice which the *Rote Fahne* printed on March 30 under the heading: "It can't go on this way!" (*So geht es nicht weiter!*) Occurrences such as marked the proceedings at Essen, the notice stated, were damaging to party unity. By following a line directly opposed to that adopted at the Fourth Comintern Congress, and affirmed at Leipzig by the majority of the KPD, the Opposition was in effect sabotaging the party's Ruhr struggle. The notice contained the promise that the problems raised at Essen would be further debated; it expressed the hope that an understanding would be reached; and it threatened that the *Zentrale* would "under all circumstances" prevent any move designed to undermine party unity.[65]

The *Zentrale* kept its promise as to further debate. On April 1, the *Rote Fahne* carried two articles, one which Ruth Fischer had

---

[64] Fischer, p. 256; *Bericht über die Verhandlungen des IX. Parteitages*, pp. 132-135.
[65] *Die Rote Fahne*, No. 75, March 30, 1923.

published in the *Internationale Presse Korrespondenz* of March 23, 1923, and Brandler's reply to it. Although Fischer's article had been written before the Essen congress, it expressed her fundamental position, and foreshadowed most of the arguments which she advanced on that occasion. Neither side said anything strikingly new, and the debate centered as usual around the old question of how to win mass support for the KPD. Brandler maintained that this objective could only be accomplished by the persistent application of united front tactics in order to cure the masses of their "democratic illusions" (i.e., the belief that their interests were best safeguarded within the framework of a democratic republic). Fischer denied the existence of "democratic illusions" and claimed that the workers were merely scared of the bourgeoisie. It was up to the Communists to cure them of their fear. "The masses will join us if we stand untiringly in the forefront of the daily struggles, provided we accompany these by Communist propaganda and policy." She explained that "Communist propaganda and policy" simply meant that the ultimate goal of the party, seizure of power, had to find unmistakable expression even in these day-to-day struggles.[66]

The most interesting aspect of this journalistic duel was the light which it cast upon the two protagonists. Ruth Fischer's language was cutting and, in spots, presumptuous. She repeatedly quoted members of the *Zentrale* out of context, or even distorted their statements. Her impetuous nature was revealed throughout the article; many of her sentences, figuratively speaking, expressed snarls and sneers. In contrast, Brandler wrote with a mixture of didactic pedantry and barely concealed anger. The old trade-unionist was obviously stung by the reckless charges which were hurled against him and the *Zentrale* by this "radical party savior," as he called Ruth Fischer in the headline of his article. Brandler also gave vent to his feelings when he referred to the recent controversy in addressing the Seventh Congress of the German Communist Youth organization in Chemnitz on March 31.

". . . the *Zentrale* will make one more attempt to reach an understanding with the Opposition. We hope that the overwhelming majority of our comrades in the Opposition camp will join us in an honest effort to find a way in which we can protect the party

[66] *ibid.*, No. 76, April 1, 1923.

309

from harm. However, as a revolutionary . . . party we cannot tolerate that such incidents as occurred at the regional party congress . . . will be repeated. We can not permit a second attempt to oppose the practical party slogans during combat [*Aktion*], and to replace them by others which were rejected [by the majority]. It would spell death to the revolutionary fighting discipline. Whoever should undermine this [discipline] is an enemy of the party and must be prevented from doing harm [*muss unschädlich gemacht werden*]."[67]

The newspaper debate might have continued beyond the first week of April, but only two more articles by Ruth Fischer, defending her stand at Essen, appeared on April 6. On the following day the police president of Berlin temporarily banned the *Rote Fahne*, and the paper did not resume publication until April 15. Negotiations between the *Zentrale* and the Fischer faction during the press ban led to a *détente* in the second half of April.[68] Though the fundamental differences remained unresolved, the *Zentrale* promised not to apply any sanctions against the Opposition. Its views, moreover, were to be given more space than before in the party press. In addition the Left had demanded that a special party congress be held in the fall. This the *Zentrale* rejected. It also turned down a suggestion that the Opposition send a delegation to Moscow. The suggestion was presumably made by the Left in the hope of winning some influential support for the projected special party congress.[69] It is quite possible that the Opposition communicated its proposal to the ECCI as well, because on April 22, 1923, Zinoviev wrote a letter to the KPD in which he invited the *Zentrale* and the Opposition to send representatives to Moscow for a joint conference with the Bolshevik leaders.[70]

[67] *ibid.*, No. 78, April 4, 1923.

[68] The *détente*, which had been reached between *Zentrale* and Opposition at a special conference, was mentioned in an article by Maslow, written with unusual restraint; and by a report of the Hamburg party organization, a Left stronghold, which expressed in a resolution its collective satisfaction over the recent agreement (*Die Rote Fahne*, No. 86, April 19; and No. 89, April 22, 1923).

[69] Wenzel, p. 69. Wenzel speculates that the leaders of the Left made the proposal in the hope that the ECCI would oust the Brandler *Zentrale* and turn the party leadership over to the Opposition. This appears unlikely. Such highhanded measures were not yet customary, even among the Bolsheviks, in 1923. Nor were Fischer and Maslow as naïve as Wenzel's speculation would lead one to believe.

[70] Carr, *The Interregnum*, p. 162. According to Carr, the ECCI was so thoroughly alarmed by the activities of the Left that it summoned delegates of both factions to Moscow. He refers in this connection to Communist revolts in Mühlheim and Gelsenkirchen, which will be discussed below. The Mühlheim riots occurred on

Zinoviev wrote his letter while the Twelfth Annual Congress of the Russian Communist Party was in session (April 17-25, 1923). The proceedings took place in an atmosphere both somber and tense. Lenin had suffered a third stroke on March 9, and the delegates knew that news of his death might come at any moment. Every speaker referred with awe to "Vladimir Ilyich," but behind the cloud of oratorical incense factions began to form, to intrigue, to maneuver. Lenin was not yet dead, but while everyone waited for the inevitable, all major decisions remained suspended in the balance. It was under these circumstances that the two KPD delegations arrived in Moscow, either at the end of April or in the first days of May, to call once again on the Bolshevik leaders to arbitrate between them.[71]

It was practically a foregone conclusion that the special conference in Moscow could offer no satisfactory solution to either of the German delegations. The ECCI was represented by Trotsky, Radek, Bukharin, and Zinoviev. Trotsky and Radek faced in Zinoviev a potential political antagonist and, in view of the uneasiness which prevailed at this juncture among the Bolshevik leaders, they could hardly be expected to risk a dispute over the German question. Radek acted as the champion of the *Zentrale*, Trotsky was at odds with Zinoviev, and Zinoviev sympathized with the Left Opposition. Under these circumstances the Russians had to try for a compromise, in order to forestall open conflict in their own camp. In this attempt they apparently succeeded, though what exactly happened at the sessions may never be fully known.[72] The *Zentrale* had sent Brandler and Böttcher; the Opposition, Fischer, Maslow and Thälmann, and it can be assumed that the preliminary armistice, reached prior to their departure from Berlin, facilitated the work

---

April 18, and involved unemployed who were led by anarcho-syndicalist agitators. On this point both the Communist and Social Democratic press agreed. The Gelsenkirchen riots occurred only on May 23, thus after the conference in Moscow had taken place. Furthermore, the feuding factions within the KPD had reached at least a tentative reconciliation of views before Zinoviev sent his letter of invitation. In view of these facts, Carr's argument that the ECCI acted from undue alarm is difficult to accept.

[71] For a full report on the Twelfth Annual Congress of the Russian C.P. see *ibid.*, pp. 268-285.

[72] The only personal account of the conference is that of Ruth Fischer (p. 260). It is brief, inaccurate on some minor points which can be checked against the official resolution adopted at the end of the conference, and contains the statement, made earlier in a different context (p. 184), that Brandler was trying to get the Opposition

of the ECCI representatives. There is a near-ludicrous quality about the final resolution in which the conference for the "liquidation of party differences" culminated.[73] With Solomonic wisdom, the Russians carefully meted out praise and demerits among the Germans. The course taken by the *Zentrale* was found essentially sound, although some errors in tactics and some misleading theories such as the "democratic illusions" of the German working class were condemned. "The . . . erroneous phrases . . . [of] the *Zentrale* stem from its desire to penetrate into the broadest masses of the proletariat . . . (which are) not yet Communistic. . . . Nothing in the activities of the *Zentrale* gives cause for the assumption and fear that it is conducting a policy of rapprochement with the bourgeoisie. . . . [But] because of such phrases the *Zentrale* has aroused the distrust among those circles within the party which tend toward left deviations." The Opposition, in turn, was censured for its recent obstructionist tactics, especially in the Ruhr, though the ECCI allowed for extenuating circumstances in view of the misleading, albeit provocative, errors which had crept into the *Zentrale's* united front policy. After the Russians enjoined the Left to refrain from proselytizing outside those districts in which its faction held control, they suggested that four Left Opposition members be admitted to the *Zentrale*. This ended the conference, and the Germans returned to Berlin.

The compromise resolution reached in Moscow was submitted to, and accepted by, the *Zentrale* and the Left Opposition on May 11.[74] On May 16, at a meeting of the Central Committee, this acceptance was confirmed and acted upon by the election of Ruth Fischer, Ernst Thälmann, Otto Geschke, and Arthur König into the *Zentrale*. It meant that three strongholds of the Left were now represented in the party's top command, Berlin by Fischer and

---

leaders expelled from the party. Although Brandler had implied on one occasion that such a measure might have to be taken *if* the Left continued to sabotage official party policy, it is unlikely that he continued to harbor such an intention after the two factions had reached a preliminary agreement to bury the hatchet. See also Carr, *The Interregnum*, pp. 162-163. On the growing rift among the Bolsheviks see Deutscher, *Stalin* (London-New York-Toronto, 1949), pp. 255ff, and *passim*.

[73] *Die Rote Fahne*, No. 107, May 13, 1923.

[74] *ibid.*; a declaration accepting the compromise solution, signed by Fischer, Maslow, and Thälmann, was printed in *Die Rote Fahne*, No. 108, May 15, 1923. The dateline read: "Moscow, May 4, 1923."

Geschke, Hamburg by Thälmann, and the Ruhr by König.[75] The election of König amounted to a tacit recognition by the *Zentrale* that the Left had gained strength in the occupied region.

The inclusion of the Opposition members into the *Zentrale* had a salutary effect on party unity, at least for the next crucial months ahead. Ruth Fischer is probably right when she says that "the crisis in the German party was by no means healed."[76] But the mere fact that she and three of her associates shared responsibility for conducting party affairs with their recent antagonists greatly reduced their former obstreperous attitude. In addition, new crises which developed in Germany and abroad revived hopes within the KPD that a revolutionary situation might be shaping up after all. With the vision of barricades looming larger, the Left now deigned to cooperate with the *Zentrale* in an effort to speed "The Day."

[75] *Die Rote Fahne,* No. 110, May 17, 1923.
[76] Fischer, p. 260.

CHAPTER XI

IN SEARCH OF A COURSE AT THE HEIGHT
OF THE RUHR CRISIS

✤ IN MAY 1923 the pace of events quickened everywhere, in Europe, in Germany, and in the Ruhr region; and each new development had its impact on the KPD. The most serious crisis, which, for a few hectic days at least, conjured up the danger of war, arose over Anglo-Soviet relations. On May 8 the British representative in Moscow handed to the Soviet government a memorandum which, on account of its contents and its signatory, has become known as the "Curzon Ultimatum." Lord Curzon, the British Foreign Secretary, charged the Soviet Union in the memorandum with flagrant violation of the Anglo-Russian Trade Agreement of 1921. He specifically mentioned anti-British operations conducted by Soviet agents, in the form of hostile propaganda in Afghanistan, Persia, and along the Indian border. The memorandum demanded of the Soviet Union that these activities be discontinued, and that an official apology be made for them. Otherwise, the agreement between the two countries would be abrogated at once by His Majesty's Government.[1]

The Curzon note brought to a head a conflict which had been brewing for months. It also caused a great deal of concern to the Bolshevik leaders, who had no intention of adding a war with Great Britain to their already sizable problems. Even worse was the prospect that Russia might have additional enemies if an armed conflict arose. On May 2, Marshal Foch had arrived in Poland for a state visit and had spent much of his time reviewing Polish army parades.[2] The specter of an Anglo-French-Polish coalition against the Soviet Union revived bitter memories of the Allied interventions at the close of the great war.

No doubt the Bolsheviks were worried. But they were also angry, a sentiment which was heightened when news reached Moscow of

[1] A succinct and recent account of the Anglo-Soviet conflict is in Carr, *The Interregnum 1923-1924* (New York, 1954), pp. 165-173. See also Eudin and Fisher, *Soviet Russia and the West 1920-1927* (Stanford, 1957), pp. 184-189, 222-228; and Georg von Rauch, *Geschichte des bolschewistischen Russland* (Wiesbaden, 1955), pp. 270-271.
[2] Carr, *The Interregnum*, p. 169.

the assassination of Vatslav V. Vorovsky, Soviet delegate to the Lausanne conference, by a "White" Russian on May 10. The murder, while heightening the outraged feelings of the Russian leaders, also intensified their growing sense of danger. "The shots fired at Comrade Vorovsky light up the situation," wrote Zinoviev in *Pravda* on May 16. "What the most irreconcilable sections of international imperialism are now planning is nothing less than a new campaign against the Russian revolution. The Ruhr events, the ultimatum sent by Curzon, the murder of Comrade Vorovsky, the triumphal visit by General Foch to Poland . . . all these are links in the same chain."[3]

"May this cup pass from us,"[4] Trotsky had said in a speech on May 13, and pass it did. The first Russian reply to Great Britain, on May 11, had been conciliatory in tone, and the same was true of the second memorandum of May 23. But the international situation remained tense, and only by June 18, after the Russians had complied with the Curzon note in all essential points, was this particular incident closed.[5]

During the height of this crisis Karl Radek came to Berlin and stayed there until the early part of June.[6] As his departure from

[3] Eudin and Fisher, p. 223.

[4] Quoted Carr, *The Interregnum*, p. 171.

[5] For the texts of these diplomatic exchanges see *Soviet Documents on Foreign Affairs*, ed. Jane Degras, 1 (London-New York-Toronto, 1951), pp. 384-392, 396-398, 399-403, 405-406.

[6] Ruth Fischer claims, in *Stalin and German Communism* (Cambridge, Mass., 1948), pp. 259, 261, that Radek was in Berlin throughout the spring of 1923, implying that he was there as early as March. Carr (*The Interregnum*, p. 163) accepts Miss Fischer's statement on face value. Several factors, however, cast doubt on the accuracy of Miss Fischer's recollections. On May 6, 1923, Ambassador Brockdorff-Rantzau wired the German Foreign Office that Radek was scheduled to depart for Berlin on May 7, and that he had asked the German Embassy for an official letter to the German border officials. On May 9, 1923, Brockdorff-Rantzau sent another, more detailed wire to Berlin, stating that Radek's trip was not connected with political affairs on the German domestic scene but with delicate negotiations between himself and non-Communist labor leaders in connection with the Russo-British dispute ("Brockdorff-Rantzau to Foreign Office, May 6 and 9, 1923," Auswärtiges Amt, Germany, microfilm, container 1406, frames D 552062 and 552965, National Archives, Washington, D.C.).

Although Rantzau's good faith in the harmless nature of Radek's mission proved to be unjustified, the two wires indicate that Radek's movements were closely watched by the German Embassy in Moscow, and that his departure for Germany had attracted special notice. In view of Radek's important position and the interest which his movements held for German officials in Moscow and Berlin, it is unlikely that he could have spent months in the German capital, installed in the Russian Embassy and working in the offices of the *Rote Fahne*, without his presence being noted

Moscow occurred immediately after the joint conference between the ECCI and the two KPD delegations, it is conceivable that he was sent to Germany to make sure that the provisions of the recent agreement were observed. The KPD was indeed in need of some guidance. For one, the party had run afoul of the Prussian government. This particular trouble began on May 4, during a session of the Prussian diet. The German Nationalist Party moved a vote of "no confidence" against the Prussian Minister of the Interior, Carl Severing, on the grounds that he was "soft on Communism." The motion was defeated. After the vote, a Communist deputy asked to be recognized in order to issue a formal statement explaining why the KPD *Fraktion* had not supported the motion. When the chair refused to recognize the Communist deputy, a scuffle ensued which soon deteriorated into a Communist demonstration. The session was adjourned until the following Monday, May 7, when the Communists continued to stage demonstrations on the floor of the diet. The result was that twelve KPD deputies were expelled from the building, and the rest of the *Fraktion* followed in a walkout. They were back again the following day, causing further disturbances. Finally the entire delegation was excluded from participation in all sessions of the diet for a fortnight. A formal protest against this exclusion which the party made on May 11 was to no avail; the ban remained in effect. But the worst blow fell on May 12, when Minister Severing banned all proletarian hundreds in existence on Prussian territory, a measure which, at least in theory, applied to the Ruhr region as well.[7]

---

and eliciting correspondence on the matter between the Embassy in Moscow and the always suspicious German Foreign Office in Berlin.

If one considers further that Radek was not likely to leave Moscow for a prolonged period of time in the midst of the heightened intraparty struggle following Lenin's third stroke on March 9; that his mistress, Larissa Reissner, had returned to Moscow sometime in the spring of 1923 after a long absence (Karl Radek, *Portraits and Pamphlets*, introd. by A. J. Cummings, note by Alec Brown [New York, n.d.], pp. 267-268); and that he attended the Twelfth Party Congress of the Russian C.P. early in April, as well as the ECCI conference with the two German delegations early in May, the "almost continuous presence of Radek in Berlin during this time" (the first four months of the Ruhr occupation), which Carr mentions, could not have been very continuous. In fact, it is very likely that Radek's trip to Berlin in May was actually the first since his clandestine appearance at the Leipzig Congress, at the end of January 1923.

[7] *Schulthess' Europäischer Geschichtskalender*, 1923 (Munich, 1928), pp. 97-98, 101; cf. the rather one-sided accounts in *Die Rote Fahne*, No. 100, May 5; No.

Radek, who arrived in Berlin sometime during the first two weeks of May, could do nothing about these mishaps, but he could, and did, step up the party's propaganda efforts. The corpse of the murdered Vorovsky, which conveniently was routed through Berlin on its way to Moscow, provided the opportunity for a splendid show. Despite the fact that the Berlin proletariat had demonstrated three days earlier, on May 13, in protest against Vorovsky's murder, the Curzon note, and the exclusion of Communist delegates from the Prussian diet, another monster-demonstration was staged on May 16. Under a banner line "Vatslav Vorovsky's Last Journey," Karl Radek wrote an obituary, bordered in black, in the *Rote Fahne*. It was probably the worst bit of purple prose that he ever wrote. Vorovsky, whose lithographed picture appeared in the center of the front page, was depicted as a paragon of every imaginable revolutionary virtue. But it was not the man who was Radek's primary concern, it was his value as a symbol.

"We shall carry Vorovsky's corpse to Russia, and we shall carry him across Russia, and we shall ask the masses of workers and the masses of peasants in Russia: do you want to be treated like pariahs? And we shall ask the proletariat of the world: do you workers of the world want to permit the representatives of the first proletarian state to become fair game [*Freiwild*] for every capitalist canaille? We have no doubt what the answer . . . will be.[8]

Radek also participated in the ceremonies by addressing the crowds in the *Lustgarten* square, and by walking behind the coffin with two other prominent mourners, Deputy Chairman of the Council of People's Commissars, Alexis Rykov, and Soviet Ambassador Nikolai Krestinsky. Behind these dignitaries marched the members of the *Zentrale* and of the Central Committee. On the following day, Radek had another lead article on the front page of the *Rote Fahne*. Entitled "The Proletarian Wall Around Soviet

---

101, May 6; No. 102, May 8; No. 103, May 9; No. 105, May 11; No. 109, May 16, 1923.

[8] *Die Rote Fahne*, No. 109, May 16, 1923.

Radek's efforts at dramatization played him a neat trick in that he actually had Vorovsky die twice; this, at least, is the impression the following lines give: ". . . sogar im Antlitz des Todes verliess ihn nicht dieser Humor und er reizte das Geschick mit seinem blanken Witz. Als er nach dem Überstehen eines Typhus, von anderen Krankheiten geplagt, auf dem Sterbebett lag und ich ihn besuchte, um ihn zum letzten mal zu sehen . . . hauchte er noch den Scherz aus: 'Wollt ihr mich zum Vertreter Sowjetrusslands im Himmel ernennen?' " *ibid.*

Russia," it praised the Berlin workers for the solidarity with Russia which they had expressed at Vorovsky's bier, and urged the proletariat of the world to rally likewise around the Soviet Union.[9] At this point even Radek's remarkable ability to get the most out of a corpse was finally exhausted, and he was free to attend to specific German problems.

On May 16 and 17, the Central Committee of the KPD held a meeting in Berlin. The first day's session—presumably held in the evening, after the ceremonies for Vorovsky were over—dealt mostly with organizational and tactical questions. Specifically, the committee resolved to concentrate the party's efforts on forming more Communist cells within individual industrial plants. In this way the party's agitation potential was to be coordinated and strengthened.[10] The following day was devoted to a thorough discussion of the political situation in Germany and of the attitude which the party should take in response to it. It is very likely that Radek attended this day's session, although there is no record of his presence. He was, however, the author of the committee's principal resolution which, in the form of a manifesto, was published in the *Rote Fahne* on May 18.[11]

The main speech was delivered by Brandler. He carefully followed the outlines of this resolution, which he submitted to the committee for approval at the end of the session. Brandler dealt first with the international situation, which he depicted as explosive. Turning to domestic problems, he pointed to the bankrupt policies of the Cuno government, which he represented as impotent. Government-sponsored nationalism led nowhere, Brandler charged, predicting that Cuno, virtually a captive of German big industry, might sell out to the French at any moment. Only if the German working class assumed control of the government could such a development be prevented. An interesting nuance which Brandler introduced at this point was a reference to the Fascists, a term which the KPD applied indiscriminately to every political group with "bourgeois-nationalist" leanings. "We must distinguish in our fight against Fascism between capitalist-paid Pinkerton gangs and

[9] *ibid.*, No. 110, May 17, 1923.
[10] *ibid.*

[11] Carr, *The Interregnum*, p. 176, note 2. The manifesto appeared on the front page of *Die Rote Fahne*, No. 111, May 18, 1923, under the bannerline "To The Party!"

those petty bourgeois who have joined the [Fascist] movement from genuine nationalist disappointment."[12] Brandler did not elaborate upon this theme at the meeting, but in the manifesto party members were urged "to go to the suffering, misled, stirred-up masses of the proletarianized petty bourgeoisie." These remarks were not mere phrases. Within a few weeks after this meeting it was shown that the references to the Fascist petty bourgeoisie heralded the beginning of an intensive, though short-lived, campaign to split the nationalist forces in Germany, and among them to win supporters for the KPD.

In view of the gaudy banner line under which the manifesto appeared, it is easy to attach undue importance to the significance of the Central Committee meeting and the resolution it adopted. But outside of the reference to the Fascists, and of a somewhat overdrawn picture concerning the imminence of danger on the international scene, no strikingly new ideas were in evidence. The usual slogans were employed, calling for workers' governments on the state and federal level, confiscation of real values by the state, weapons in the hands of the workers, and an alliance with the Soviet Union. Only a slight shift of emphasis in Communist strategy, giving the struggles at the Spree priority over those at the Ruhr, emerged from the discussion which followed Brandler's speech, and from some passages in the manifesto.[13] The main outlines of party policy did not change. All that Radek seems to have desired, and what Brandler faithfully communicated to the Central Committee, was to increase Communist agitation within the framework of the united front. Moreover, such agitation was to be geared from then on toward a wider audience, through a readjustment of united front tactics. Radek made this point very clear when he wrote, following the standard prophecy of "momentous battles" ahead: "Today we are not yet in a position to establish the proletarian dictatorship, because the pre-conditions, the revolutionary will among the majority of proletarians for it, are missing."[14]

[12] *Die Rote Fahne*, No. 111, May 18, 1923; also Carr, *The Interregnum*, p. 176.
[13] This, as Carr points out, may have been a concession to the Left (*The Interregnum*, p. 176).
[14] *Die Rote Fahne*, No. 111, May 18, 1923. For a summary of the meeting and the decisions taken, see also *Bericht über die Verhandlungen des IX. Parteitages der K.P.D. (Sektion der K.I.) Abgehalten in Frankfurt am Main vom 7. bis 10. April 1924* (Berlin, 1924), pp. 64/73-64/74 (double pagination).

The "Authorized" Bid for Power

Just when Radek's cautious, if not pessimistic, estimate appeared in print, it seemed to be invalidated by a mass strike movement which gripped the Ruhr region. The causes of this movement were economic rather than political. Until the middle of April, the government had succeeded in keeping the exchange rate of the mark at roughly 20,000 marks to the dollar. To prevent the mark from dropping further, the government depended on the cooperation of business and industry. The big concerns, many of which received extensive loans from the *Reichsbank*, were expected to refrain from purchasing foreign currency on the stock market in order not to destroy the precarious financial equilibrium. The captains of industry adhered to this gentlemen's agreement until the afternoon of April 18. At this time, agents of the powerful Stinnes concern purchased, within a few hours, extensive amounts of foreign currency. This action at once sent the mark on a new downward trend which, after a short period of time, reached catastrophic proportions.[15]

The end of the so-called *Markstützungsaktion* (loosely, governmental action to peg the mark at a given rate) had particularly detrimental effects on the Ruhr region, where the economy was already badly dislocated by the occupation.[16] When retail merchants disregarded the injunction of the German government not to adjust prices to the dollar exchange rate, the cost of merchandise, and notably food, rose consistently. In order to adjust wages to the rising cost of living, the government negotiated with employers a 39.65% increase of the average wage, to become effective on May 1. Labor's reaction to this agreement was negative, as the increase lagged far behind the rising costs. Bitterness increased, and even a

---

[15] Hallgarten, *Hitler, Reichswehr und Industrie* (Frankfurt am Main, 1955), p. 30.

Hallgarten explains the process as follows: The official rate of 20,000 marks to the dollar, fixed by the government ". . . leads to an economic setback which threatens especially the giant combines which have contracted huge debts in marks [from *Reichsbank* loans]. Stinnes knows that the unwieldy monster structure he has built up cannot be held together without either a continuation of the inflation or, by way of an alternative, extensive (and for the moment unavailable) foreign credits, plus overtime work [without overtime pay] . . . . Thus his combine gives the signal for an attack on the currency and his own political friends within the industry."

[16] Unless otherwise indicated, the following account of the strike movement in the Ruhr during the second half of May is based on Wenzel, "Die K.P.D. im Jahre 1923" (unpubl. diss. Freie Universität Berlin, 1955), pp. 87-97.

promise for new wage negotiations which the government announced for May 27, did not lessen the discontent of the workers. On May 16, the first major strike was called in the "Kaiserstuhl" mine near Dortmund. The strikers demanded wage increases of 50% for the period between May 1 to 15, and periodic additional adjustments thereafter. When management moved in strike-breakers, clashes occurred between them and the pickets, and both sides suffered casualties. Spontaneous protest demonstrations of striking miners increased tensions still further.

These developments caught the KPD by surprise. During the first four days, while the strikes spread through the mines in the vicinity of Dortmund, the party did nothing to capture control of the movement. The Communists did not interfere until May 20, and then only indirectly, through a hastily summoned regional conference of factory councils. Two hundred delegates represented altogether sixty plants, twenty-nine from Dortmund and thirty-one from outlying districts. Although not all delegates were Communists, party members dominated the conference and the resolution it passed, which was directed in the form of an appeal to the workers in the Rhine-Ruhr region. It expressed solidarity of the councils with the strikers, backed their demands in full, and added that the employers should pay to every single worker a lump sum of 150,000 marks, to every family 200,000 marks. The appeal closed with the threat of a general strike if the just claims of labor went unheeded, and called on the entire German working class to support their striking brothers in the Ruhr.[17]

During the following week the strike movement spread within the occupied region. On May 22 it reached Bochum; on the 24th, Gelsenkirchen; on the 26th, Hamborn; and Essen on the 27th. It is doubtful, however, that the appeal of the factory council conference had anything to do with this westward spread of the movement. Much as the Communists welcomed the walkouts, they neither controlled them effectively, nor did they substantially benefit by them. No general strike materialized. The most heavily affected area was that between Dortmund and Essen, while the peripheral part of the region remained relatively undisturbed, as did the unoccupied part of Germany. The total number of workers out on

---

[17] Text in Spethmann, *Zwölf Jahre Ruhrbergbau 1914-1925: Der Ruhrkampf 1923-1925,* vol. IV of 4 vols. (Berlin, 1930), p. 168.

strike apparently did not exceed 310,000, although Communist estimates were higher.[18] And only on May 26 did the Communists form a central strike command, headed by the *Union der Hand-und Kopfarbeiter*, in the comparatively quiet atmosphere of Essen, just in time to prepare for the liquidation of the movement. It was a far cry from the subsequent party claim that "this giant strike movement . . . succeeded in delivering several cities into the controlling hands of the Communist-led proletariat."[19]

As usual, lack of unity hampered the ranks of the Communists. The *Zentrale*, mindful of the party's united front policy, instructed its organizations in the Ruhr to conduct the strikes as an economic rather than a political struggle, and to refrain from acts of violence.[20] This had been the party's official attitude from the beginning of the disturbances. But the injunctions of the *Zentrale* met with opposition, and in some quarters with outright rejection. Apart from the anarcho-syndicalist groups which did not take their orders from the KPD, some of the proletarian hundreds in the region also proved refractory. Among many of these units were radicals who felt no allegiance toward any political party, including the KPD, and the Communist leaders were frequently unable to enforce discipline. To what extent individual local party organizations likewise sabotaged the instructions of the *Zentrale* is difficult to determine, but in view of the strong left-wing sympathies in the region, disobedience in these quarters may have occurred as well. Whatever the number of non-conformists may have been, Communists did participate in street fighting, especially in Bochum and Gelsenkirchen. And although their participation in acts of violence may have been small in relation to the total number of unemployed, anarcho-syndicalist elements, and rioting miners and metal workers out on strike, they were generally blamed for all disturbances.[21]

Nor was the *Zentrale* very skillful in refuting charges that the Ruhr Communists were fighting a political rather than an economic battle. The party press wrote in as aggressive a tone as ever, but

[18] *Frankfurter Zeitung*, No. 248, May 28, 1923; *Die Rote Fahne*, No. 121, May 30, 1923.
[19] *Bericht über die Verhandlungen des IX. Parteitages*, p. 11. The phrasing reflects the views and interpretation of the Left whose leaders were in control of the KPD when the report was written.
[20] *Die Rote Fahne*, No. 117, May 25; No. 119, May 27, 1923.
[21] This view is prominently represented in Spethmann, IV, pp. 166-181.

insisted that the Communists were maintaining order in the Ruhr. When the acting governmental representative of the province Rhineland-Westphalia, Dr. Lutterbeck, asked the French occupation authorities at the end of May to permit the dispatch of Prussian police forces back into Gelsenkirchen to help quell the riots there, the *Rote Fahne* protested angrily: "Down with the government of national shame and treason!"[22]

The riots in Bochum, Gelsenkirchen, and other parts of the occupied region aroused German public opinion not only against the KPD, but also against Soviet Russia. Rumors that Russian agents were actively fanning the riots in the Ruhr circulated in the German press, among Reichstag delegates, and inside the government. Radek in particular was suspected of masterminding the disturbances.[23] The basis for these reports had been laid by the Russians themselves earlier in the year. At the beginning of March, the Soviet Union had announced that the Russian workers were going to send twenty million pounds of grain to the Ruhr for free distribution among the population.[24] Radek used the occasion to write a long article in the *Rote Fahne,* in which he compared the generosity of the Soviet Union with the German government's rejection of a similar Russian offer of free grain back in 1918.[25] The first transport arrived in Hamburg on March 29, and from there was sent to the Ruhr. A small delegation of Russians accompanying the grain transport used the occasion for propaganda speeches, and this incident caused a great deal of apprehension in official German circles.[26] It was remembered a few weeks later when the riotous strikes broke out in the Ruhr, and gave rise to renewed suspicions and recriminations.

Radek, following the maxim that attack was the best defense, had a conversation with State Secretary Ago von Maltzan at the German Foreign Office on May 26. When Radek complained about

---

[22] *Die Rote Fahne,* No. 120, May 29, 1923. For a typical example of the official Communist attitude to the Ruhr riots see also Anon., "The Struggle in the Ruhr Area and the German Communist Party," *Inprecorr,* III, No. 43 (June 14, 1923), pp. 412-413.

[23] Auswärtiges Amt, Germany, microfilm, container 1406, frames D 553037; D 553040; D 553041; D 553044.

[24] *ibid.,* frames D 552819; D 552820. *Die Rote Fahne,* No. 56, March 8, 1923.

[25] *Die Rote Fahne,* No. 63, March 16, 1923.

[26] Auswärtiges Amt, Germany, microfilm, container 1406, frames D 552845; D 552929; D 552930.

the charges leveled against the Soviet Union in connection with the disturbances in the Ruhr,[27] Maltzan was sufficiently impressed by his visitor to send a personal wire to Brockdorff-Rantzau in Moscow. He told the ambassador of the difficulties he had had in preventing Radek's expulsion from Germany, and added that so far none of the reports which linked the riots in the Ruhr with Russian agitators had been substantiated. He closed with the interesting suggestion that the Soviet government be asked "to demand from us [the German Foreign Office] categorical proof for the—in my opinion groundless—charges."[28]

The Russian Foreign Office unwittingly concurred with Maltzan's opinion and vigorously denied that any Soviet agents were operating in the Ruhr.[29] However, Narkomindel was telling the German ambassador a half-truth. Soviet agents were indeed in the occupied region, and had been there ever since February 7. They were in all likelihood technical advisers to the Communist military underground apparatus, which at the time was not in active operation. These Russian specialists had been instructed not to get involved in acts of agitation, so as to avoid any possible diplomatic

---

[27] *ibid.*, frame D 553038.

[28] "Maltzan to Rantzau, May 31, 1923," *ibid.*, frame D 553044. See also D'Abernon, *Diary of an Ambassador: II, Rapallo to Dawes, 1922-1924* (New York, 1930), pp. 229-230, for his entry after a conversation with Maltzan on May 21, 1923.

Maltzan was the head of the Eastern Division of the German Foreign Office, and the chief architect of the Rapallo agreement. Throughout 1923 he and Brockdorff-Rantzau tried hard to prevent any incident which could have threatened the very delicate relations between Germany and the Soviet Union. On May 7, 1923, Brockdorff-Rantzau wrote a lengthy and secret letter to the Foreign Office in Berlin in which he outlined his basic views on this matter. Germany, he argued, was defeated and isolated, and thus needed Russian friendship. In the West, Germany faced only humiliations and enslavement, whereas the road to the East lay wide open. Russia depended on good relations with Germany. She did not want to see Germany weak, nor was she interested in creating chaos on the German domestic scene. The danger of Communist contagion, according to Brockdorff-Rantzau, was not very great as long as a sound relationship existed between the two countries. The ambassador conceded that he did not like the Communist form of government, but pointed out that under the prevailing circumstances such a dislike was hardly a relevant consideration for German diplomacy ("Rantzau to Foreign Office, May 7, 1923," Auswärtiges Amt, Germany, microfilm, container 1406, frames D 552950-552952).

Brockdorff-Rantzau's fundamental attitude toward German-Russian relations was also revealed in a letter to Maltzan on June 5, 1923. The ambassador wrote that, in his opinion, the present disturbances in the Ruhr were stirred up by Poincaré rather than by the Bolsheviks (*ibid.*, frame D 553062).

[29] "Rantzau to Foreign Office, June 4 and 8, 1923," *ibid.*, frames D 553060 and D 553065.

complications.[30] In contrast to many German Communists in the region, the Russians obeyed their instructions, and none were apprehended at this time.

The dispute between Germany and the Soviet Union over this issue, which continued into June, became rather academic because by then the strike was over. The KPD did not start the strike movement, did not effectively control it while it lasted, but was instrumental in its liquidation. During the last days of May the *Zentrale* realized that the Communists were gaining very little from the disturbances while risking very much. The walkouts had not culminated in a general strike; they had not even spread throughout the Rhenish-Westphalian industrial region, let alone the rest of the country; the miners and the steel and metal workers out on strike between Dortmund and Essen could not hold out indefinitely without either strike funds or the moral stimulus of nationwide support. If the movement collapsed of its own accord, the prestige of the KPD was bound to suffer; to prevent such a setback, the *Zentrale* decided to call it off. On May 28, at the height of tumultuous scenes in Bochum and Gelsenkirchen, arbitration talks were conducted in the Reich Labor Ministry at Berlin. The central strike command was represented at these talks, which resulted in a 52.3% wage increase. The *Zentrale*, which had joined the strike command in Essen, thereupon summoned the local party functionaries, together with the commanders of the red hundreds, and informed them that the strike would be called off. It was resolved to ground all arms on May 29, and to resume work on the following day. The central strike command was empowered to announce these decisions to the strikers. Despite the dismay of the red hundreds, the issue was not disputed. Brandler left no doubt that this time the *Zentrale* expected to be obeyed, and even Ruth Fischer assented. By the last of the month, most strikers had returned to their jobs.[31]

As the party had suffered a defeat which it was loath to admit, the anticlimactic end of the disturbances in the Ruhr had to be rationalized. While taking full credit for the smooth break-up of

[30] Wenzel, pp. 96-97. The author bases his information on documents which were captured by the police in August, 1923, and deposited at the State Archive in Düsseldorf under the number 16923, B1. 47. On the military apparatus of the KPD in 1923 see below, Ch. XII.
[31] Wenzel, pp. 92-96; Fischer, p. 259; Spethmann, IV, pp. 179-181.

the strike (the word "termination" was intentionally avoided),[32] and for the wage increase gained, the party developed the thesis that the German bourgeoisie had been planning to massacre the strikers in order to lay the blame for such a bloodbath upon the KPD. In the face of these provocations the Ruhr proletariat had maintained iron discipline, and in the end had obtained some of the demands for which the strike had been fought. Although these concessions were inadequate, they nevertheless constituted a greater success than had all previous wage negotiations. Better results could have been achieved if the striking Ruhr proletariat had been adequately supported by the entire German labor movement, but efforts towards this end had been sabotaged by the "reformist" union bosses and Socialist leaders. Once a united front of the German working class was a reality, the Ruhr proletariat would fight another day.[33]

There remains the question whether the KPD had hoped to utilize the Ruhr strikes for starting a revolution. To this, no unequivocal answer can be given. Had circumstances been more favorable, the party might have decided to press whatever advantage they seemed to offer. But circumstances were not favorable. The strike movement, initially spontaneous in nature, arose largely over economic grievances aggravated by conditions prevailing in a region under foreign occupation. Whatever political overtones the movement subsequently assumed lacked clearness of purpose and direction. Communist leadership never attained complete control of the situation. But, worst of all, the movement did not spread sufficiently to warrant any hopes that it might touch off a genuine, mass-supported revolution.

There is in any case no indication that the *Zentrale* harbored such hopes at any time during the May strikes. Radek, the eye of the Comintern, and chief adviser to the German party, busied himself with defending the Soviet Union against what he called "unjustified" charges of meddling in the Ruhr. Brandler and other members of the *Zentrale* went into the region only for the purpose of liquidating the strikes. The *Rote Fahne* warned repeatedly that

[32] Wenzel, p. 95.

[33] *Die Rote Fahne*, No. 120, May 29; No. 121, May 30, 1923; Franz Dahlem, "The Communist 'Putsch' in the Ruhr," *Inprecorr*, III, No. 41 (June 7, 1923), p. 398; A. Pragemer, "After the Mass Strikes in the Ruhr Area," *ibid.*, No. 43 (June 14, 1923), p. 413.

the Ruhr Communists must not let themselves be provoked into open fighting, a timely warning since the Communist leaders proved unable to prevent whatever riots did take place. The only advantages which the KPD reaped from the disturbances during the second half of May were the propagandist uses to which it put the red hundreds, the factory councils, and the control commissions. All three agencies were used propagandistically throughout the period, and the Communist press gave full coverage to their activities. Of course, only such aspects as the maintenance of order and discipline, and the protection given to the population against the "Fascist" and "imperialist" enemies were mentioned. But this was good united front policy, and was intended as such.

Shortly after the termination of the Ruhr strikes the KPD caused widespread bewilderment in Germany, when this traditionally internationalist-minded party adopted a propaganda line with a decidedly nationalist tinge. The speculations which this phenomenon aroused among contemporary observers have continued among historians ever since the summer of 1923. The first wave of National Bolshevism, as this particular policy was called, ran its brief course shortly after the KPD was founded. It was then roundly condemned and rejected by Lenin.[34] Its reappearance in 1923, if it was a reap-

---

[34] See above, Ch. II, and *passim*.
Whoever employs the term "National Bolshevism" must specify to what period he is referring. The need to draw distinctions has been realized by some, but by no means all, writers concerned with this phenomenon. Professor Carr states: "Understanding of the somewhat tortuous tactics adopted by Comintern and . . . KPD under Radek's inspiration in the summer of 1923 has been obscured both by a popular confusion of these tactics with the old programme of 'national Bolshevism' and by the hindsight derived from knowledge of much later events in Germany. The program of national Bolshevism was . . . [in 1923] an amalgam of nationalist and Bolshevist aims; from the nationalists it took the call for a union of all Germans to liberate the nation from the yoke of the imperialist Powers, from the Bolsheviks it took the conception of revolution, shorn, however, of its international framework" (*The Interregnum*, pp. 183-184). It is due to his justified fear of adding to this "popular confusion" that Professor Carr refrained from using "National Bolshevism" as an all-inclusive term descriptive of Communist tactics in 1923.
A similar procedure has been adopted by Dr. Wenzel who refers to this interlude as "nationalist united front tactics." Other authors have been less discriminating. Ruth Fischer (pp. 189-287) has entitled an entire part of her book "National Bolshevism." Klemperer (*Germany's New Conservatism*, Princeton, 1957) calls one of his chapters "National Bolshevism and the Neo-Conservatives." Mohler (*Die Konservative Revolution in Deutschland 1918-1932*, Stuttgart, 1950) also employs this term both for the 1919 and 1923 periods (pp. 59-65, and *passim*). So do Erich Müller, *Nationalbolschewismus* (Hamburg, 1933), and Karl O. Paetel, "Der deutsche Nationalbolschewismus 1918-1932, ein Bericht," *Aussenpolitik*, III, No. 4

pearance, occurred in very different circumstances from those which prevailed in 1919, and differed also in form and objective. Laufenberg and Wolffheim, the advocates of the earlier version, had visualized an alliance between the German proletariat and the nationalist bourgeoisie for a war against the victorious Entente. No such plans were contemplated by the KPD in 1923. The slogan "against Poincaré *and* Cuno" ruled out any cooperation between the proletariat and the "capitalist exploiters" with their "racist murder gangs." The new "nationalist" line of 1923 was rather a variation on the united front theme, and was intended to win new Communist allies outside the ranks of the German labor movement. It is in this light that the nationalist interlude must be examined.

It will be recalled that Thalheimer, as early as February 1923, opened the issue of German nationalism for discussion. His thesis, although qualified then, and strongly modified later, represented the German bourgeoisie as playing a revolutionary role, at least for the moment, in its struggle against French imperialism.[35] But even at this early stage Thalheimer voiced doubts concerning the sincerity of the middle class in offering resistance to the French. He suggested that the German government and its bourgeois supporters might at any moment surrender to the French, at the expense of the nation as a whole and the proletariat in particular, and that then the burden of resistance would fall exclusively upon the shoulders of the German working class. This theme became more pronounced in the Communist press as the struggle in the Ruhr continued, and the *Rote Fahne*, throughout the second half of May, printed scathing predictions that the "Cuno gang" was about to capitulate to Poincaré.[36] The party's Cassandra line was always accompanied by the assertion that the working class alone took the struggle against the French seriously, and that for this reason only a government of workers could save Germany from foreign enslavement.

Did the Communist leaders really believe that Cuno would yield to the French? There is strong indication that they did not, and

---

(April, 1952), pp. 229-242. More precise in his definition is Schüddekopf in *Linke Leute von Rechts* (Stuttgart, 1960), pp. 138-164, *passim*.

[35] See above, Ch. x; also Carr, *The Interregnum*, pp. 159-160.

[36] See, for instance, *Die Rote Fahne*, No. 115, May 23; No. 117, May 25; No. 120, May 29, 1923.

that despite all their propaganda to the contrary they actually preferred him to remain in office. They knew that Cuno and his cabinet were committed to passive resistance. They also knew that the prospects for forming a workers' government on the national level were not very good for the time being. Thus, while they continued to clamor for Cuno's scalp, they had no real desire to see him go. He was much too useful as a whipping boy, and his bungling conduct of national affairs drove the country closer to that stage of chaos which the KPD so eagerly awaited. The *Rote Fahne* revealed in an unguarded moment the real state of mind of the party leadership: "As long as the Social Democratic workers do not fight with us side by side for a workers' government, the Communist Party is not interested in seeing this confused [*kopflose*] government replaced by another bourgeois one."[37]

For the moment, at least, this statement was meant sincerely, although it did not express the party's apprehension concerning another, more dangerous, political alternative. This was the specter of a "Great Coalition," a government composed of middle-class parties and the Social Democrats. Such a political constellation could conceivably muster sufficient popular backing to risk negotiations for ending passive resistance in the Ruhr. References to this possibility appeared in the party press throughout May and were indicative of Communist uneasiness.[38] The termination of passive resistance would deprive the party of valuable propaganda material, would ease the tension both in Germany and abroad and, worst of all, would diminish Communist chances of profiting from the ills of the nation by winning converts. The KPD had only recently suffered a considerable setback in this connection when on May 23 the Second and Two-and-a-Half Internationals merged forces at a unification congress in Hamburg and formed the Socialist Workers' International.[39] Radek, with his customary irreverence, ridiculed both the idea of a Great Coalition in Germany and

[37] *ibid.*, No. 119, May 27, 1923.

[38] Open and implied references to a possible "Great Coalition" can be found in the following issues of *Die Rote Fahne*: No. 100, May 5; No. 101, May 6; No. 102, May 8; No. 103, May 9; No. 113, May 20; No. 119, May 27; No. 122, May 31; No. 123, June 1, 1923.

[39] *Schulthess'*, 1923, p. 432. The unification of the two Internationals had been preceded in the fall of 1922 by the merger of the SPD and that faction of the USPD which had not joined the KPD in December, 1920.

the unification of the two internationals, in an article entitled "Without Sail and Rudder."

"To write 'coalition with the bourgeoisie' upon the banner of the Second International is at the moment ridiculous. It needs two to form a coalition, just as with love, and the bourgeoisie wields the club of Fascism and tells the coalition-hungry Social Democrats: 'Here is your coalition; my club will unite with you.' What is there left of reforms . . . , what remains of the skinny democratic horse? They [the two internationals] sat down at the Alster [lake within Hamburg] and cried, like the Jews at the shores of Babylon: 'Reaction everywhere! Bad times—*nebbich*! Let's wait . . . for better days!' "[40]

But Radek was whistling in the dark. The party needed support, needed it badly, and it was slow in coming. The Ruhr strikes had collapsed, and the masses had watched the collapse without acting. New ideas were wanted to offset this reverse. Thus it seems more than a coincidence that by the end of May Communist propaganda efforts were directed with mounting intensity toward a new target, the lower strata of the pauperized and embittered German middle class.

Strictly speaking, the party's decision to extend the united front policy beyond the ranks of the proletariat did not come without preparation. On March 25 Radek had written, in an article entitled "Powerless Germany," that the German Communists had so far neglected to "fight in the name of the people," an omission which had driven large segments of the population to the nationalist side, even though many of those affected belonged to a social class which ultimately stood to gain more than it would lose by a proletarian victory.[41] A similar idea was expressed in the resolution drafted early in May by the ECCI and the two KPD delegations after the "reconciliation talks" in Moscow.

"The German bourgeoisie, in view of the hopelessness of its attempts at compromise [with the Entente], is compelled to carry on a . . . revolutionizing policy, but is unable in its struggle against the Entente to rely on the masses of the people. On the contrary, it is doomed by history to repel the masses. . . . For this reason, the

[40] *Die Rote Fahne*, No. 119, May 27, 1923.
[41] *ibid.*, No. 71, March 25, 1923.

national and nationalist sentiments let loose by it are bound in the long run to turn against it. The Communist Party of Germany must make it clear to the nationalist masses of the petty bourgeoisie and the intellectuals that the working class alone, once it achieves victory, will be able to defend German soil, the treasures of German culture, and the future of the nation."[42]

At the height of the mass strike movement in the Ruhr, toward the end of May, the KPD issued a joint appeal with the National Committee of German Shop Stewards. One section of this appeal was directed toward the lower middle class. With reference to Dr. Lutterbeck's request that the occupation authorities should permit him to send police forces into riotous Gelsenkirchen, the appeal read: "We ask the nationally-minded petty bourgeois masses, the masses of German officials and intellectuals: what do you intend doing against a government which dares, with the shamelessness of a courtesan, to apply openly to the French generals for permission to butcher [your] German fellow-countrymen? We are fully convinced that the nationalist masses of the people consist, in the great majority, of persons of sincere and honest convictions, but who are misled, and unaware that the Entente is not their sole enemy. . . . Can you not recognize that you are mere tools in the hands of the greediest plunderers of the German people? Will you help the German people . . . to fight against this government of this profiteering rabble, which delivers Germany over to French capital. . . ?"[43]

These very tentative feelers which the KPD extended during the first five months of 1923 elicited hardly any response from the nationalist side, and none whatever from the Communist rank and file. Only the right-wing magazine *Gewissen*, organ of the neo-conservative June Club, was in the habit of tossing occasional bouquets in the direction of the KPD. Thus on February 12 *Gewissen* wrote: "We have always been of the opinion that the KPD contains more active forces than the United Socialists and the middle class combined."[44] And the same magazine wrote in June that the KPD was

---

[42] *ibid.*, No. 107, May 13, 1923. I have used the English translation in Eudin and Fisher, p. 171.

[43] This passage from the appeal is quoted in Anon., "The Struggle in the Ruhr Area and the German Communist Party," *Inprecorr*, III, No. 43 (June 14, 1923), pp. 412-413.

[44] Quoted in Wenzel, p. 107.

"a fighting party . . . which day by day becomes more 'national-Bolshevik.' "[45]

It was Radek who gave real impetus to Communist attempts in Germany to win sympathizers, if not allies, from the political Right, especially from the nationalist-minded lower middle class. The occasion arose when the enlarged Executive Committee of the Communist International met for a regular session in Moscow from June 12 to 23, 1923. During the first four days of the session, Radek spoke no less than three times, and in each of his speeches touched on the problem of nationalism in Germany. None of the ideas which Radek advanced were startling. In essence, and with a semantic virtuosity of which he was a past master, he merely repeated the main points of a policy which the German Communists had followed for months. His fine distinction between "national" and "revolutionary-national" interests may have puzzled his audience, but his meaning was actually quite clear: to smite Poincaré at the Ruhr was the demand of the hour for the German proletariat. The German bourgeoisie, from pure self-interest, had initially held the same objective, and to this end had fostered a wave of extreme patriotism. But the bourgeoisie was ready to capitulate to France, at the expense of the German working class. It therefore fell to the latter to rally the masses to the defense of the nation, and in this endeavor the KPD had to lead the way. Once the masses, including the misled segments of the petty bourgeoisie, now still in the nationalist camp, came to realize that their interests were better represented by the proletariat than by the "corrupt capitalist classes," the moment would arrive when the old order would be overthrown and replaced by a workers' government. That such a government would then be in a position to conclude a firm and binding alliance with Soviet Russia went without saying.

It was toward the end of the proceedings, on June 20, that Radek delivered his most sensational speech. It was sensational because of its unabashed bid for nationalist support in Germany, and, beyond

---

[45] Quoted in Carr, *The Interregnum*, p. 177. Two regular contributors to *Gewissen* were well-known nationalist writers, Eduard Stadtler and Arthur Moeller van den Bruck, the latter the author of *Das dritte Reich* (Berlin, 1923). Stadtler, ironically enough, also headed the *Antibolschewistische Bewegung*, the north German counterpart of the *Orgesch*, until his resignation in March 1919 (Klemperer, pp. 105-107). For an excellent discussion of the June Club, its membership, objectives, and publications see *ibid.*, pp. 102-11, and *passim*.

that, for what Radek himself called "Fascist" support. As in the case of Vorovsky a few weeks earlier, Radek made use of another convenient martyr, this time the freecorps fighter Albert Leo Schlageter who had died on May 26 before a French firing squad.

Immediately before Radek gave his address, Clara Zetkin had delivered a report on international Fascism. In the report she denounced Fascism as an "extremely dangerous and terrible enemy," doubly dangerous because it had become the "refuge of the politically homeless," including workers who had lost faith in their own class. She warned her audience that these uprooted, disillusioned people, many of whom had embraced Fascism in despair, had to be either won over "to our side," or, at least, neutralized as social forces.[46] Radek skillfully picked up his cue from there and expanded it along his own lines. He started his speech by referring to Zetkin's "comprehensive and impressive" report, but added that he could not always follow her words because he saw in his mind the dead body of a German Fascist, a class enemy, who was executed by the henchmen of French imperialism. "Throughout the speech of Comrade Zetkin . . . the name of Schlageter and his tragic fate was in my head." He should be remembered, Radek said, "when we are defining our attitude toward Fascism." His story, his martyrdom for German nationalism must neither be forgotten nor dismissed "with a mere phrase." Schlageter's tragic death "has much to tell us and . . . the German people." At this point Radek waxed eloquent.

"We are not sentimental romanticists . . . , nor are we diplomats, who say: By the graveside say nothing but good, or remain silent. Schlageter, a courageous soldier of the counterrevolution, deserves to be sincerely honored by us, the soldiers of the revolution. Freksa [a nationalist writer], who shared his views, published in 1920 a novel in which he described the life of an officer who fell in the fight against Spartacus. Freksa named his novel 'The Wanderer into the Void.'

"If those German Fascisti, who honestly thought to serve the German people, failed to understand the significance of Schlageter's fate, Schlageter died in vain, and on his tombstone should indeed be inscribed: 'The Wanderer into the Void.' "[47]

[46] Carr, *The Interregnum*, p. 179, including quoted lines.
[47] "Schlageter, 'The Wanderer into the Void' (A Speech delivered by Karl

Radek briefly traced the career of the dead freecorps fighter. With baffling objectivity, he omitted neither the fact that Schlageter had fought the Bolsheviks in the *Baltikum* at the end of the war, nor that he "regarded the working class as the mob that must be governed." And yet, Radek pointed out, Schlageter acted in good faith, and although he was serving the wrong cause proved willing to die for it. How gravely Schlageter and all those like him have been deceived by the capitalist bourgeoisie was recently proven by Herr Dr. Lutterbeck, who "turned to his [Schlageter's] executioners with the request that they should permit the iron and steel kings to shoot down sons of Germany . . . with machine guns." He then contrasted the contemporary German ruling class, which had enslaved the workers, with the Prussian military reformers Scharnhorst and Gneisenau, whom he credited, somewhat overgenerously, with the emancipation of the peasants (Freiherr vom Stein was not mentioned). Then came the moral of his story. The German people, one and all, must break with the existing order and must become a truly unified nation. Old prejudices must be brushed aside. The brain workers and hand workers must form a solid phalanx. "United into a fighting nation of workers, it [Germany] will gain the assistance of other people who are also fighting for their existence." With this clarion call Radek had reached the point where he felt it necessary to spell out the Communist position vis-à-vis the German nationalists.

"This is what the German Communist Party and the Communist International have to say at Schlageter's graveside. . . . The German Communist Party must declare openly to the nationalist petty bourgeois masses: Whoever is working in the service of the profiteers . . . will meet with the resistance of the German Communist Workers. They will oppose violence by violence. . . . But we believe that the great majority of the nationalist minded masses belong not to the camp of the capitalists but to the camp of the Workers. . . . We shall do all in our power to make men like Schlageter . . . not wanderers into the void, but wanderers into a better future. . . . Schlageter himself cannot now hear this declara-

---

Radek at the session of the Enlarged Executive of the Comintern on June 20, 1923)," *Inprecorr*, III, No. 47 (June 28, 1923), pp. 460-461. The faulty punctuation and poor diction are in the original.

tion, but we are convinced that there are hundreds of Schlageters who will hear it and understand it."[48]

The "Schlageter speech" undoubtedly marked the apex of Radek's career as German expert in the Comintern. It was a good speech, and it was a clever speech. No other Bolshevik leader, not even Lenin, possessed Radek's feeling for the mode of language and the imagery that would appeal most effectively to a German nationalist. Unlike his funeral oration for Vorovsky, Radek's Schlageter speech was logically constructed, was free of cheap sentimentality, and carried a sense of conviction even in those passages where the pathos was a little heavy.

What were Radek's motives for giving the speech? No doubt he had composed it himself, but before delivering it he had sought, and received, Zinoviev's approval.[49] His listeners, the members of the Enlarged Executive, apparently did not conceive of the ideas Radek expressed as a radical new departure. Although they applauded him when he had finished, nobody returned to the topic or offered to debate it further. Zinoviev did not even mention Germany at all in his closing address.[50]

Thus it would appear that the Communist leadership conceived of Radek's "Schlageter line" merely as a tactical maneuver, and not as a fundamental revision of policy. It was certainly not designed to promote a military alliance between Germany and the Soviet Union; nor was it expected to foster a political alliance between the German Communists and the nationalist Right, including the German "Fascists," against Versailles and the Entente. Both theories have been variously suggested as possible explanations for the Schlageter line, and both are unconvincing.[51] Though the

[48] *ibid.* A German version of the speech is in *Deutsche Geschichte seit 1918 in Dokumenten*, ed. Ernst Forsthoff, 2nd ed. (Stuttgart, 1938), pp. 142-148. Also *Die Rote Fahne*, No. 144, June 26, 1923.

[49] *Fifth Congress of the Communist International: Abridged Report of Meetings Held at Moscow June 17th to July 8th, 1924* (London, n.d.), p. 210; hereafter cited as *Fifth Congress of the Communist International, Abridged Report.*

[50] Carr, *The Interregnum*, pp. 180-181.

[51] Both theories have been advanced by a number of authors, usually in an implied form and depicted as subtly interrelated policies. Thus Ruth Fischer emphasizes Radek's alleged close relations with the German officer corps during the spring and summer of 1923 (pp. 261-266), and states that, "the secret discussions of a German-Russian alliance became more concrete in 1923" (p. 265). She says in connection with the Schlageter speech that "Radek crusaded for the necessary alliance between the Soviet power and German nationalism" (p. 272), and then

Bolsheviks and the KPD would have found the idea of a Russo-German military alliance tempting, it was held to be premature and dangerous in German diplomatic, and even military, circles.[52] A possible alliance between the KPD and the Right was even less feasible. It would have been unworkable, because it was fundamentally unacceptable to both sides. By far the most persuasive explanation for Radek's "Schlageter line" has been presented by

---

claims that "Radek had been assigned . . . the Schlageter speech because of growing Soviet-British tension in the Near East" (p. 272), although this incident was virtually closed when Radek delivered his speech. She cites (p. 261, n.4) Grigory Bessedovsky, *Revelations of a Soviet Diplomat* (London, 1931), p. 100, as evidence for Radek's alleged close ties with the Reichswehr, but Radek's name is neither mentioned on the page she cites, nor does it appear in the index of Bessedovsky's book. Freund (*Unholy Alliance* [New York, 1957] p. 150) states that "the 'Schlageter line' was to create an alliance between the Communists and the Right-wing parties," though he virtually contradicts his own statement on p. 159. Flechtheim begs the question when he writes that "Diese nationalbolschewistische Taktik sollte sowohl den Interessen der deutschen Revolution wie auch denen der russischen Aussenpolitik dienen" (*Die K.P.D. in der Weimarer Republik* [Offenbach, 1948], p. 89). Rauch, following Fischer, speaks of the "Notwendigkeit eines deutschen 'Nationalbolschewismus' oder eines Blocks mit dem Bürgertum . . ." (p. 263). Much more persuasive is Schieder's suggestion (*Die Probleme des Rapallo-Vertrags*, Arbeitsgemeinschaft für Forschung des Landes Nordrhein-Westfalen, Heft 43 [Cologne and Opladen, 1956], p. 51) that Radek's speech, made at the height of national excitement in Germany during the Ruhr struggle, was designed to tempt the German government into closer diplomatic relations with the Soviet Union by holding out the possibility of a common Russo-German revolutionary war on the Rhine as a bait.

52 For an excellent up-to-date survey of Russo-German military relations see the article by Hans W. Gatzke, "Russo-German Military Collaboration During the Weimar Republic," *The American Historical Review*, LXIII, No. 3 (April, 1958), pp. 565-597. Especially pertinent for the 1923 period are pages 569-576. It appears from the documents consulted by Professor Gatzke that Brockdorff-Rantzau accepted the post as German Ambassador to Soviet Russia with the understanding that the German government did not contemplate a military alliance with the Soviet Union. The ambassador was primarily interested in strengthening the economic and political ties between the two countries, and he even thought in terms of a possible informal Russian promise to render aid to Germany if the republic should be attacked by either France or Poland, or both. But an alliance, especially a military one, the ambassador considered dangerous and premature. Although he did have knowledge of, and tolerated, a certain degree of secret and restricted military collaboration of a technical nature between the Reichswehr and the Red Army, both in 1923 and after he clung to his initial standpoint that an outright military alliance was not in the interest of Germany. The basis on which Russo-German relations rested, then and during the decade following 1923, remained the Rapallo agreement which was not, and never developed into, a military alliance between the two states.

Radek could not have been unaware of the official German attitude on this matter. When in Moscow he was always in touch with Brockdorff-Rantzau, and in Berlin with Maltzan. He probably knew also of the secret talks which were conducted between representatives of both armies, but there is no evidence to show that in 1923 Radek either had an active part in these talks, or that he could have harbored any illusions concerning their tentative and restrictive nature.

Professor Carr, who sees it as an attempt to split the ranks of the various nationalist groups, especially of the lower middle class, by "proving that effective opposition to the Versailles treaty could in the long run be offered only by the Communists."[53] It is this emphasis on the role of Communism which holds the key to the motives behind Radek's words. All Germans unwilling to subscribe to the Communist objectives, all those who continued to support the existing regime and bourgeois class structure were and remained enemies who had to be vigorously fought. In addition, the session of the Enlarged Executive showed no indication that any concessions to the Fascist movement as such were contemplated. A resolution calling for an all-out struggle against international Fascism was adopted without modifications,[54] and the same issue of the *International Press Correspondence* which printed Radek's Schlageter speech also carried an article by Paul Böttcher, a member of the *Zentrale*, who stressed the need to fight Fascism as a dangerous foe of the working class.[55] In brief, the Comintern leadership did not think in terms of forming a united front between KPD and the German Right, but rather aimed at splitting the nationalist camp by applying traditional united front tactics to this particular problem.

It is evident from Radek's speech that he appealed to two categories of nationalists in particular. The first included those men and women of the lower middle class who were adversely affected by the economic chaos, and who in addition were embittered by the humiliating Ruhr imbroglio. By offering "solutions" to both problems, Radek could hope that many of the dispossessed and disillusioned would in their despair clutch at the Communist straw he held out to them. The second category consisted of the numerous "Schlageters," the wild and undisciplined freebooters, who stood

[53] Carr, *The Interregnum*, p. 181.

[54] *ibid.*, pp. 180-181.

[55] Paul Böttcher, "The Struggle against Fascism, and New Experiences of the United Front in Germany; II: The Defense Units and Their Tasks," *Inprecorr*, III, No. 47 (June 28, 1923), p. 465. Two weeks later, Radek recapitulated in the same publication the main points which he had made in the Schlageter speech, and reemphasized the need for fighting Fascism while simultaneously trying to split the Fascist ranks in an effort to win the lower middle class for the Communist cause. See Karl Radek, "Fascism, Ourselves, and the German Social-Democrats," *ibid.*, No. 50 (July 12, 1923), pp. 527-528. As Wenzel has pointed out (pp. 109-110), this aspect of Radek's speech has been omitted in Ruth Fischer's account of the event.

in the nationalist camp because they detested the democratic and "pacifist" republic. Ironically enough, many of these same men, who during the past years had variously participated in the suppression of left-wing riots or uprisings, had developed a genuine respect for their Communist opponents.[56] Expressions of open appreciation for the fighting spirit, though not for the political objectives, of the "Reds" were not uncommon in the ranks of the right extremists, and in all likelihood Radek was aware of this fact.

Radek's speech was the cue for the KPD to embark upon a nationalist propaganda campaign, which at the time aroused much attention but netted the party few, if any, tangible advantages. The most sensational aspect of the Schlageter line was that it provided the public for a few weeks with the unprecedented spectacle of nationalist and Communist writers engaged in a series of intellectual exchanges on the feasibility of political cooperation between Right and Left.[57]

The civilized tone which marked the exchange of ideas on the Schlageter line among the literati of both camps was generally absent from the party's street-corner debates. The "man on the street" was rarely susceptible to lofty ideas, the nature of which contrasted with his own concepts of what a nationalist and a Communist had or had not in common. This was as true for the "Fascists," whom the party tried to convert, as it was for the Communist rank and file who were more accustomed to exchanging bullets with the Fascists than to engaging them in public discussions.[58] Nevertheless, the street-corner approach was tried, at first especially with the academic youth. Oratorically gifted Communist functionaries ventured into such hostile strongholds of nationalism

[56] Waite, Vanguard of Nazism (Cambridge, Mass., 1952), pp. 271-275; Ernst Röhm, Die Geschichte eines Hochverräters (München, 1928), pp. 239-240, 288; Adolf Ehrt and Julius Schweickert, Entfesselung der Unterwelt: Ein Querschnitt durch die Bolschewisierung Deutschlands (Berlin, 1933), p. 273; Müller, Nationalbolschewismus, p. 21, claims that in 1923 nationalists fought side by side with Communist shock troops against Rhenish Separatists.

[57] This episode has been variously treated in relatively recent publications and need not be repeated here. The interested reader may want to consult the following accounts: Von Klemperer, pp. 145-147; Fischer, pp. 282-284; Mohler, pp. 61-62; Karl Radek, Paul Frölich, Graf Ernst Reventlow, Arthur Möller van den Bruck, Schlageter: Eine Auseinandersetzung (Berlin, 1923); Hans Schwarz, ed., Das Recht der Jungen Völker, Sammlung politischer Aufsätze (Berlin, 1932), pp. 81-100; Schüddekopf, Linke Leute von Rechts, pp. 149-156, 445-447.

[58] Fischer, pp. 286-287.

as university campuses and student eating-houses to do missionary work. Early in July a Comrade Schneider, KPD member from Hannover, addressed students at Göttingen University, or, as the *Rote Fahne* put it, penetrated the sticky atmosphere of the small universities. He spoke on the subject: "For What Did Schlageter Die?" The same topic was used as a basis for discussion at Jena, and toward the middle of the month in Berlin as well.[59] There the party distributed handbills in various restaurants, frequented mostly by students, with this announcement:

> Wednesday, July 25, 1923, 7 P.M.
> Auditorium of the Dorotheenstädtisches Realgymnasium
> Dorotheenstrasse 12
> AGENDA:
> "For What Did Schlageter Die? Communism, Fascism, and the Political Decision of the Students."
> Speaker: Comrade Ruth Fischer
> Students: Gain an understanding of the ways of the revolutionary fight for freedom. We want to point out especially to our *völkischen* opponents that unlimited opportunities for discussion will be maintained.[60]

According to the report of the *Rote Fahne*, the discussion at this particular gathering lasted several hours without leading to any incidents. Ruth Fischer stated that "the giant, who is going to liberate Germany, is here. . . . The giant is the German proletariat, to which you belong, and with which you should align yourselves." This was greeted, so the paper says, with "loud applause." Then the meeting broke up, and the opposing groups separated "not exactly conciliated, but with a feeling of mutual respect."[61] The Social Democratic organ, *Vorwärts*, threw an interesting sidelight on this particular performance of Comrade Ruth Fischer. Quoting an eyewitness account, the paper claimed that the Communist speaker appealed openly to the anti-Semitic sentiments of her audience. "Whoever cries out against Jewish capital . . . is already a fighter

[59] *Die Rote Fahne*, No. 159, July 13, 1923.
[60] The handbill was reprinted in 1923 by the SPD to show how the Communists betrayed the German workers. A copy of the original pamphlet is part of the "Duke Library Collection," deposited with the Hoover Institution on War, Revolution, and Peace, Stanford, California, Folder No. 232.
[61] *Die Rote Fahne*, No. 173, July 29, 1923.

for his class [*Klassenkämpfer*], even though he may not know it. You are against the stock market jobbers. Fine. Trample the Jewish capitalists down, hang them from the lampposts. . . . But . . . how do you feel about the big capitalists, the Stinnes, Klöckner? . . . Only in alliance with Russia, Gentlemen of the *völkische* side, can the German people expel French capitalism from the Ruhr region."[62]

Anti-Semitic remarks, innuendos rather than open expressions, occasionally cropped up during this period in the Communist press. Thus the *Rote Fahne* printed on August 7 a little item on "Stresemann's Jewish *Kommerzienräte*" (councilors of commerce, a title conferred on distinguished financiers), in which the paper drew attention to the fact that such prominent Social Democrats as Friedrich Stampfer, the editor of *Vorwärts*, Carl Severing and Hermann Müller were closely connected with these Jewish capitalists.[63] Although the Communists tried on the whole to stay clear of the anti-Semitic issue, they could not always avoid it, especially when it was raised by nationalist hecklers during joint discussion meetings. This was clearly demonstrated in the case of Hermann Remmele, who on August 2 addressed a mixed audience of Com-

[62] *Vorwärts*, No. 390, August 22, 1923, as cited by Wenzel, p. 117, n.29. Twenty-five years after the event Ruth Fischer denied that she ever made such a statement and claims that she had said instead: "Communism was for fighting Jewish capitalists only if all capitalists, Jewish and gentile, were the object of the same attack" (p. 283, n.16). As Wenzel points out (p. 118), Miss Fischer failed at the time to issue a denial in *Die Rote Fahne*, although she did so a week later (*ibid.*, No. 200, August 30, 1923) in connection with another *Vorwärts* article of August 29 which had allegedly misquoted her on a far less controversial issue. See also Klemperer (p. 146 and n.19), who calls Miss Fischer's explanation of the episode "unsubstantiated and unconvincing."

[63] Another example of anti-Semitism in the party press occurred earlier, in the beginning of July, during the "Circus Busch" trial. Three Communists were tried for their part in disturbing a nationalist meeting which had been held on the premises of the Circus Busch in Berlin. One of the witnesses for the prosecution was *Oberregierungsrat* Dr. Bernhard Weiss, then head of the political department in the Prussian Ministry of the Interior, subsequently deputy police president of Berlin. In referring to Dr. Weiss, *Die Rote Fahne* (No. 152, July 5, 1923) called him "Isidor," considered in Germany a typically Jewish name. This practice was normally reserved to the National Socialists. In addition, a little poem appeared in the same issue, signed by "Havelok." Its first stanza ran as follows:

> Herr Weiss
> Urgermanisch! Keine Phrase
> Dieser Weiss! Geschwung'ne Nase!
> Sass und blätterte in Akten,
> Als ihn die Verteid'ger zwackten.

munists and National Socialists in Stuttgart. When he told his listeners that anti-Semitism was an age-old device which those in power employed to distract the attention of the blind and ignorant masses from the real causes of their misery, he was interrupted by shouts of contradiction from the floor.

Remmele continued: "How such anti-Semitism arises I can easily understand. One merely needs to go down to the Stuttgart cattle market in order to see how the cattle dealers, most of whom belong to Jewry, buy up cattle at any price, while the Stuttgart butchers have to go home again, empty-handed, because they just don't have enough money to buy cattle. ('Quite right!' from the Fascists.)"[64]

A little later in his speech, Remmele again touched on this subject, and again with the apparent purpose of appeasing the audience in order to put his own point across: "You, the Fascists, now say [that you want] to fight the Jewish finance capital. All right. Go ahead! Agreed! (Stormy applause from the Fascists.) But you must not forget one thing, industrial capital! (Interjections from the Fascists: 'We fight that too!') For finance capital is really nothing else but industrial capital."[65]

How eager the party was to use any expedient to reach some common ground with the nationalists was evident from another public debate in which Remmele participated on August 10. Besides Remmele, one speaker each from the National Socialists and the Social Democrats had been invited by the Communists to participate in the discussion. The SPD, however, turned down the invitation. In his eagerness to win the sympathies of the Nazis, Remmele made a number of statements which were in flagrant violation of the party's official united front policy. Thus he told his 8,000 listeners that he considered an alliance with the National Socialists less objectionable than one with the Social Democrats, and then added that the Communists would even be willing to cooperate with the murderers of Liebknecht and Luxemburg.[66]

[64] *ibid.*, No. 183, August 10, 1923.
[65] *ibid.*
[66] Wenzel, p. 116 and n.21. *Die Rote Fahne*, No. 190, August 18, 1923, charged that Remmele had been misquoted in the Social Democratic press, and claimed that the passage should have read: "Even with people who have murdered Liebknecht and Rosa Luxemburg we shall go together, if they want to join our ranks. We offer our hand daily to the Social Democratic Party . . . [in the interest of] the united

Aside from engaging in literary debates and holding joint meetings with nationalists, the party concentrated in the summer of 1923 on winning converts among the Reichswehr and the police forces throughout Germany. Two different avenues of approach were used for making inroads into these organizations. One was designed for officers, either active or retired, and another for enlisted men.

Early in August, the Social Democratic newspaper *Vorwärts* published a "Blueprint for the Solicitation [*Gewinnung*] of Officers," copies of which had been found on two Communists arrested by the police. The blueprint outlined various means of establishing contact with officers, such as propaganda literature and the use of Communist officers or ex-officers as intermediaries, and also specified the manner of properly addressing men of military rank. The instructions stressed that ideological differences should be minimized in the arguments used by party members, and common interests should be emphasized, for instance, mutual hostility to France and the German republic. Furthermore, promises of high army positions "after the revolution" were to be given to prospective collaborators.[67]

Another instance of this campaign was a circular letter which a "Group of Communist Officers of Germany" [*Gruppe kommunistischer Offiziere Deutschlands*] sent to officers in the Reichswehr and the police. This eight-page communication, adorned with quotations from Clausewitz and Trotsky, contrasted the Communist struggle against the Entente with the attitude of the "Social Democratic traitors." The party membership was portrayed as constituting the "most splendid human material among the German working

---

front. . . , even though Scheidemann and Noske, who have murdered Liebknecht and Luxemburg [sic], are still in [that party's] ranks." This version appeared also in the Communist pamphlet *Sowjetstern oder Hakenkreuz? Deutschlands Weg-Deutschlands Rettung: Ein Waffengang zwischen Faschisten und Kommunisten* (Berlin, 1923). Wenzel, who bases his account of Remmele's two speeches exclusively on this pamphlet, as does Carr (*The Interregnum*, p. 183, n.1), points out that *Vorwärts*, No. 388, August 21, 1923, accused the KPD of having distorted Remmele's original statement which had been taken down during the speech by Social Democratic stenographers. In view of the fact that neither Wenzel nor Carr have made reference to Remmele's anti-Semitic statements of August 2, it appears that the pamphlet (which was not available to me) may well have been an expurgated version of Remmele's speeches.

[67] *Vorwärts*, No. 368, August 8, 1923, as cited by Wenzel, p. 121 and n.3.

class." Eighty percent of the KPD, claimed the letter, were former soldiers. The circular then depicted the future national liberation movement as an extensive guerilla war which would follow in the wake of a proletarian revolution. To make the latter acceptable to members of the officers' corps, the letter invoked Oswald Spengler as a means of affirming that "Prussianism is Socialism," and claimed that the system of councils (*Rätesystem*) was by no means an alien institution but a "Prussian idea, based on the concepts of elite, co-responsibility, and *esprit de corps* among colleagues [*Kollegiali-tät*]."[68]

It is doubtful that the KPD had any illusions as to the effectiveness of its ambitious recruiting drive. However, one retired officer from Munich, a world war veteran by the name of Hans von Hentig, responded to the Communist efforts with a letter to the *Rote Fahne*, which appeared under the heading "Worker and Soldier." Herr von Hentig lamented Germany's present condition, and the demoralizing effects of political and economic chaos on the population, in particular on the educated youth. After the enigmatic statement that "petty-bourgeois masses and intellectual strata [*Schichten*] will soon exist only as displays in museums," he wrote that ". . . the working class, . . . [especially] Communism, shall know that hundreds of veteran frontline officers, who really put Germany *über alles*, will march by its [Communism's] side through every social upheaval, through every political change, unmindful of their own treasured concepts, *im gleichen Schritt und Tritt*, once the drum has sounded the call to battle."[69]

The propaganda approach to the non-commissioned personnel of the Reichswehr and the police forces was similar to that applied to the officers. The same methods of dissemination were used, personal contacts and the illicit distribution of leaflets, pamphlets, and newspapers. The emphasis, however, was different. The material designed for the soldiers and policemen concentrated on what the Communists assumed were perennial grievances among the lower ranks in every military or paramilitary organization. Soldiers

[68] Staatsarchiv Düsseldorf, No. 16964, B1. 83-86, as cited by Wenzel, p. 122, n.4.
[69] *Die Rote Fahne*, No. 192, August 21, 1923. The italicized words are fragments from the German national anthem and the famous funeral march, "Ich hatt' einen Kameraden. . . ." On the strange career of Hans von Hentig, including his earlier involvement with Communists, see Schüddekopf, *Linke Leute von Rechts*, pp. 95-96, 160, 448, and *passim*.

were encouraged to report to the party any incidents of ill-treatment by superiors. They were reminded of the privileges which the officers enjoyed over the men, and in some instances were encouraged to disobey unpopular orders *en masse*.[70] Similar instructions were deposited in the hallways of police headquarters, though here the party faced some very thorny problems. The policemen were those agents of the "bourgeois" state with whom the Communists collided most frequently. The party press referred to them usually as "henchmen of capitalism," or applied other, equally unflattering terms to them. On the other hand, most policemen, unlike the majority of Reichswehr soldiers, were city-bred and normally lived on a modest, lower middle-class level. For this reason the party leadership encouraged the Communist rank and file in the summer of 1923 to fraternize with the guardians of the law, and to persuade them that they were, after all, merely exploited proletarians in uniform.[71]

The efforts to win sympathizers among the lower echelons of Reichswehr and police forces proved on the whole as unsuccessful as did those to convert the officers. This was not surprising. Reichswehr soldiers were very carefully selected. The military authorities took great care to concentrate the recruiting drives primarily in the traditionally conservative rural regions of Germany, and as a rule excluded from the army Jews, Socialists, Communists, or even men of outspoken democratic leanings.[72] In addition, the soldiers were not conscripts but volunteers, career men who generally had nothing but contempt for the Communist "rabble." The police forces, especially the hand-picked and strictly disciplined Prussian police, were equally immune to Communist propaganda.[73]

[70] A detailed, although slanted, account of Communist efforts to subvert army and police is given in Ehrt and Schweickert, pp. 256-262, and Adolf Ehrt, *Bewaffneter Aufstand! Enthüllungen über den kommunistischen Umsturzversuch am Vorabend der nationalen Revolution* (Berlin-Leipzig, 1933), pp. 74-98. Although the examples given pertain mostly to a later period, and although the authors approach their subject from a National Socialist viewpoint, the documents, liberally inserted, provide a vivid picture of Communist propaganda methods. These may have been less widespread and perfected in 1923, but probably differed little in essence from those used in the early thirties. See also Wenzel, pp. 123-124.

[71] Wenzel, p. 124.

[72] Craig, *The Politics of the Prussian Army 1640-1945* (New York and Oxford, 1956), pp. 394-395; Gordon, *The Reichswehr and the German Republic 1919-1926* (Princeton, 1957), pp. 206-207.

[73] Gordon, p. 366; Wenzel, p. 124. August Thalheimer, *1923: Eine Verpasste*

Parallel to the party's attempt to undermine the enemy's camp went efforts to win friends among the German intelligentsia, efforts which netted the Communists a reasonable measure of success.[74] To many liberal intellectuals at the time, the Communists were first of all workers whom one admired for the strength of their political convictions, even if one did not share these convictions sufficiently to join the KPD. The fact that the Communists were underdogs, but proud and class-conscious underdogs, heightened their appeal. The "prolcult," i.e. the glorification of the proletarian toiler by those who work with their brains, made its debut in the early twenties. The proletarian who was caught in the crucible of inflation, reduced to living on a bare subsistence level, and yet refused to grovel and submit, became aesthetically attractive to members of the intelligentsia and acquired in their eyes a nimbus of dignity, simplicity, and strength. This picture fitted the uncompromising Communists much better than it did the Social Democrats with their trade-union mentality and bread-and-butter consciousness. It was Rousseau's Noble Savage all over again, only in a different setting. A typical representative of this kind of thinking was Kurt Tucholsky, a contributor to the left-wing, pacifist, but non-Communist weekly, *Die Weltbühne,* which was widely read in German liberal circles. Tucholsky never joined the party, nor did he ever hesitate to criticize the Communists if he disagreed with any of their aims or tactics. But he shared their distaste for the SPD, especially its party bureaucracy, and frequently sympathized with them to the extent of adopting their arguments, ascribing all of Germany's ills to a number of select scapegoats, notably businessmen, army officers, and Junkers. For in the fight against the Right the Communists were allies, a fact which outweighed many of their objectionable features in the eyes of their liberal friends.[75]

Part of the fascination which Communism held for many German intellectuals resulted from genuine admiration for the Soviet

---

Revolution? Die deutsche Oktoberlegende und die wirkliche Geschichte von 1923 (Berlin, 1931), pp. 17-18. On the Prussian police see Severing, *Mein Lebensweg,* I (Cologne, 1950), pp. 312-317.

[74] *Bericht über die Verhandlungen des IX. Parteitages,* p. 64/35 (double pagination).

[75] For a more detailed discussion of the relations between liberals and Communists in this period see Jürgen Rühle, *Literatur und Revolution—Die Schriftsteller und der Kommunismus* (Cologne-Berlin, 1960), pp. 167-191 and *passim.*

Union with its planned economy, its promise of progress, its complete break with the past, and its proud revolutionary legend. The "discovery" of Soviet Russia by the intelligentsia was aided by post-revolutionary Russian literature, which had become readily accessible in translation to a wide circle of readers. Both translation and distribution were frequently the work of German Communists, but advertisements of new publications by the *Malik Verlag*, the *Pionier Verlag*, and other publishing houses specializing in proletarian, and particularly Russian, literature appeared not only in the *Rote Fahne*, but also in the *Weltbühne* and other liberal periodicals. Students, physicians, writers, teachers, scientists and others read German translations of the novels of Vsevolod Ivanov, P. E. Dybenko, and Pawel Dorochow. They flocked to John Reed's *Ten Days that Shook the World*, and were inspired by Vladimir Mayakovsky, poet of the Russian Revolution, who had written the lines:

> We shall commit heroic deeds,
> three times harder
> than the deeds of God.
> He bestowed things upon emptiness,
> but we must not merely indulge in reveries,
> but must dynamite that which is old.[76]

It was often by way of their admiration for Soviet Russia, seen through the books they read about it, that German intellectuals grew interested in the German Communists. But few of these admirers became party members, either then or later. Theirs was a Platonic love, and they usually were content to sympathize with, and admire, the vanguard of the German proletariat at home, and the pioneering spirit of the Soviet Union abroad. Thus when on March 16, 1923, the "League of the Friends of the International Workers' Aid" (*Bund der Freunde der Internationalen Arbeiterhilfe*) was founded, the sponsors included such prominent figures as Albert Einstein, Käte Kollwitz, Maximilian Harden, the writers Arthur Holitscher and Leonhard Frank, the actor Alexander Moissi, the painters Heinrich Vogeler and George Grosz, and the educator and author Professor Paul Oestreich.[77] Of these, only Vogeler

[76] Quoted, in German, in Heinrich Euler, *Die Aussenpolitik der Weimarer Republik 1918-1923* (Aschaffenburg, 1957), pp. 122-123.

[77] Ehrt and Schweickert, p. 239. The German branch of International Workers' Aid (Internationale Arbeiterhilfe, or IAH) was founded in 1921 by Willy Münzen-

joined the KPD. In June, a similarly constituted group founded the "Society of the Friends of the New Russia" (*Gesellschaft der Freunde des neuen Russland*). Its charter members included persons as distinguished as the sponsors of the League; some names, for instance those of Albert Einstein and Professor Paul Oestreich, appeared on the rosters of both organizations.[78]

In the summer of 1923 the KPD began to reciprocate the sympathies which representatives of the German intelligentsia had bestowed upon them during the past years. Many students, writers, and artists, but also professional men, especially doctors of medicine, were suffering from the effects of the inflation. Over a thousand physicians held a meeting in Berlin on July 13 and deliberated on their near-desperate plight and that of their colleagues elsewhere in the Reich. In the course of the meeting a representative of the *Arbeitsgemeinschaft* (approximately "study and work group") of Communist physicians rose to announce, "in the midst of enthusiastic cheers from the assembly," that the Communists considered it their duty to help the impoverished physicians who "have finally come to realize their situation."[79] References to the deteriorating economic condition of the educated and professional middle classes continued to appear in the Communist press. On July 22, the *Rote Fahne* carried an article entitled "The Growing Impoverishment [*Verelendung*] of the Intellectual Proletariat," again with emphasis on the physicians.[80] And four days later, the same paper carried a special report on "The Fate of the German Intelligentsia." It presented a devastating picture.

". . . Libraries are becoming desolate: the most ordinary foreign literature is missing. Clinics can no longer operate . . . [because] of lacking funds. . . . The German intelligentsia faces a void. Doctors become suicide candidates; professors die miserably in institutions

---

berg, subsequently known as the "Red Hugenberg" on account of the network of publishing houses, theaters, and newspapers which he controlled. Originally the IAH was an organization created to sponsor relief action for victims of the Russian famine. It then branched out and aided strikers, women and children of working-class families in need of medical aid, and related hardship cases. See Margarete Buber-Neumann, "Schiksale Deutscher Kommunisten in der Sowjet Union," *Aus Politik und Zeitgeschichte*, Beilage zur Wochenzeitung *Das Parlament*, Beilage xxii (June 4, 1958), p. 281. Also Fischer, p. 611.

[78] Wenzel, p. 125; *Die Rote Fahne*, No. 148, June 30, 1923.

[79] *Die Rote Fahne*, No. 161, July 15, 1923.

[80] *ibid.*, No. 167, July 22, 1923.

for the ailing; widows of privy councilors starve while renting out rooms. . . . Shamefaced poverty has long since become evident misery."[81] The report closed with the prediction that "without the German working class the German intelligentsia will perish. The fate of the German working class is the fate of the German intelligentsia."[82]

The party employed very similar arguments in seeking support from German officials. Like all salaried employees, members of the governmental bureaucracy were particularly hard hit by the rapid devaluation of the currency. Whereas wage earners were somewhat protected by escalator clauses in their contracts, and in addition could resort to strikes in order to press for higher pay, governmental salaries, never very generous even in normal times, increased very slowly, and state employees were not allowed to go on strike.[83] Between July 25 and September 18, the Communist press devoted one article after another to the sad lot of the German officials, especially those in the lower echelons of the bureaucratic hierarchy. The most sustained effort in this direction was made from the middle of August to the middle of September, when the Reichstag debated a legislative measure by which all officials were to be paid on a weekly basis rather than receive their salaries in advance four times a year. When this proposal (which was eventually adopted on September 27) met with the disapproval of the government employees, the Communists hastily created a special committee, a *Beamtenwerbeausschuss*, designed to widen the breach between salaried employees and the government. Although these efforts had no lasting effect, the party had at least the satisfaction of receiving some letters protesting the projected law, some of them from members of such conservative organizations as the "Federation of Higher Officials" (*Reichsbund der höheren Beamten*) and the "German Federation of Officials" (*Deutscher Beamtenbund*). These letters were printed in the *Rote Fahne*.[84]

---

[81] *ibid.*, No. 170, July 26, 1923.   [82] *ibid.*

[83] The only substantial salary increase for federal employees was granted in 1923 on June 19 (*Schulthess'*, 1923, p. 118).

[84] Wenzel, p. 127. *Die Rote Fahne*, No. 203, September 2, 1923. For the party's additional efforts to enlist the support of government officials see *ibid.*, No. 169, July 25; No. 190, August 18; No. 200, August 30; No. 201, August 31; No. 202, September 1; No. 206, September 13; No. 210, September 18, 1923. Also *Schulthess'*, 1923, p. 182.

It appears that the principal reason why state employees opposed a measure which,

The Schlageter line with its several facets was ultimately a failure. Desperate though the bulk of the lower middle classes had become in the course of the summer months, few of them could be convinced that the German Communists held the answer to their troubles. The Hitler movement in southern Germany, and the *Völkischen* behind Reinhold Wulle and Albrecht von Graefe in the North, remained aloof. They distrusted the nationalist slogans of the KPD.[85] The same was true of the Reichswehr, the police, and the governmental bureaucracy, all fundamentally conservative organizations composed of loyal and disciplined civil servants. Only from among the liberal intellectuals could the Communists elicit some favorable response, but in practical terms the intelligentsia constituted the party's least important, because least useful, ally.

Under these circumstances, why did the Communists pursue this unpromising line until well into September of 1923? For one thing, party policy during this period did not consist solely of the Schlageter line. In its effort to win mass support, the KPD simultaneously applied several tactics which the *Zentrale* attempted to coordinate as best it could. The Schlageter line was merely one of these tactical moves; it was not considered an all-or-nothing proposition, but was held to serve a useful purpose even if it achieved no more than the neutralization of certain segments of the population ordinarily hostile to Communism.[86] As an adjunct to the united front policy, specifically designed by Radek to appeal to the lower middle class, it was deemed profitable as long as it did not jeopardize the party's paramount objective—the mobilization of the German labor movement against the state. It was this objective which determined general party policy during the entire summer, and every tactical move was directed toward it. And only because the Schlageter line was a matter of tactics rather than of doctrine was it supported throughout the party, even including the Left Opposition.[87] On the

at the height of the inflation, could have only worked to their advantage, was that of prestige. As salaried employees the officials considered it their "well-earned right" (*Die Rote Fahne*, No. 203, September 3, 1923) to be paid three months in advance, a method of remuneration which implied trust, and which set them apart from the wage earners who were paid on a weekly basis.

[85] Paetel, *Aussenpolitik*, III, No. 4 (April, 1952), p. 231; Borkenau, *The Communist International* (London, 1938), p. 236.

[86] *Bericht über die Verhandlungen des IX. Parteitages*, pp. 11-12.

[87] Carr, *The Interregnum*, p. 185; for Ruth Fischer's *ex post facto* criticism of this approach see *Bericht über die Verhandlungen des IX. Parteitages*, p. 227.

other hand, even with these qualifications the nationalist campaign
had its pitfalls, because of the suspicions it aroused among the Social
Democratic workers whom the KPD was trying to enlist.[88] In order
to offset this danger, the Schlageter line had to be constantly balanced by an unremitting fight against Fascism as a movement, and
by an equally strong effort to support wage struggles conducted by
non-Communist labor. It is to these aspects of party policy that we
must now turn.

From the beginning of June until nearly the middle of August,
the unoccupied part of Germany was the scene of a series of strikes
which threatened to shake the republic to its foundations. Like the
strike movement in the Ruhr a month earlier, the constantly shifting walkouts during the summer occurred as a result of the runaway
inflation. The monthly average of the dollar in relation to the mark
tells its own story:[89]

January 1923	17,972,00	marks
July 1923	353,412,00	"
August 1923	4,620,455,00	"
September 1923	98,860,000,00	"
October 1923	25,260,208,000,00	"
November 1923	4,200,000,000,000,00	"

Demands for an adjustment of the wage scale to the rapidly declining value of the mark prompted most of the strikes. During the first
half of June, large-scale walkouts were called by the labor unions in
Upper Silesia, affecting thousands of industrial workers and miners.
The Communists had taken no part in the initial decision to strike,
but once the workers left their jobs, the local party organizations,
with the assistance of the Communist "Union of Manual and Brain
Workers," attempted to seize control of the movement and to
spread it. These attempts failed. Only six Communists were included in the central strike command, which consisted of twenty-
seven members, and when the labor unions decided on calling the
strikes off, the resolution to this effect was adopted over Communist protests.[90]

[88] Carr, *The Interregnum*, p. 185.
[89] Cited in Stolper, *Deutsche Wirtschaft 1870-1940* (Stuttgart, 1950), p. 96.
[90] Unless otherwise indicated, my discussion of the summer strikes is based on
Wenzel, pp. 135-139, the only detailed account of these events that was available

While trying hard to capture control of the movement in Upper Silesia, the party simultaneously stirred up strikes among the merchant seamen in the northern harbor cities, notably Hamburg, Bremen, and Emden. Jan Valtin, who saw his first action as a party member during this operation, writes that the motive of the KPD in promoting unrest along the waterfront was explained to him in these words: "You know that Germany is an industrial country dependent on industrial exports and raw material imports. So shipping is a jugular vein of German capitalism. Should we succeed in making harbors and ships into fortresses of the Communist Party—we've got that jugular vein in our grip. We can break it and the bourgeoisie will bleed to death."[91]

Communist agents roamed the docks distributing leaflets, selling party newspapers, and trying to enlist young merchant seamen into the KPD.[92] In some places strong-arm tactics were employed. Special party detachments led unemployed sailors and strikers onto the ships in order to set them against strike breakers, or to extinguish the fires under the boilers. Even so, the strikes collapsed after six days because they lacked union backing. Again according to Valtin, the Communists anticipated this early collapse, and ordered seamen who were party members to hire on board before the strikes were over, so as to prevent the ship owners from excluding Communists later on. "While the action committees still issued manifestoes exhorting the seamen to continue to strike, ships stealthily manned by Communists steamed seaward at dawn."[93]

Isolated strikes of metal workers broke out during June in Saxony, in the Prussian province of Brandenburg, and in Mecklenburg, and early in July spread to the vast metal industry in the Berlin region. Over a hundred thousand workers were idle. Here the Communists employed the same tactics they had used in Upper Silesia, and with the same lack of success. The strike had not been called by them, but by the metal workers' union, the *Metallarbeiterverband*. Its sole purpose was to obtain a more adequate wage for the

---

to me. For the Communist version, in which the role and success of the party are grossly exaggerated, see *Bericht über die Verhandlungen des IX. Parteitages*, pp. 11-13.

[91] Jan Valtin, *Out of the Night* (New York, 1941), p. 38.

[92] *ibid.*, p. 39.

[93] *ibid.*, p. 44. The strikes were called off by the Transport Workers Union after a wage increase was granted; *Inprecorr*, III, No. 50 (July 12, 1923), p. 517.

workers whose take home pay diminished daily in purchasing power as the mark declined further in value. The central strike command had altogether forty-three members, of whom ten were Communists. When the employers offered a raise of basic wages, and promised in addition a weekly adjustment allowance to offset the sinking purchasing power of the mark, the ten Communists on the central strike command moved that the offer be rejected, and demanded a doubling of the prevailing wage. The matter was referred to the union membership at large, who voted overwhelmingly for ending the strike.

In supporting striking miners, industrial workers, and seamen, the KPD moved on firm and familiar ground. But in the sultry and explosive political atmosphere of the summer of 1923 the Communists, encouraged by the growing discontent which was sweeping the country, ventured along untried paths.[94] One such novel excursion was the Schlageter line. Another was a sudden and unprecedented interest in Germany's rural population. Like Radek's Schlageter line, this interest was not home-grown but had been promoted by another Bolshevik leader, Zinoviev. During the session of the Enlarged Executive Committee of the Comintern, in June, Zinoviev had launched a new slogan which forthwith became official doctrine for all Communist parties affiliated with the Comintern: the demand for the creation of "Workers' and Peasants' Governments."[95]

The new slogan posed something of a problem to the KPD. The German peasants were traditionally conservative. As a rule, they did not dabble in politics unless their economic interests were directly affected, and the Communist Party could hardly affect these interests except in a negative fashion. Furthermore, the German inflation, which was wreaking havoc with that part of the population which relied for income on wages, salaries, pensions, dividends, and the like, proved a boon to the German landholders, irrespective of the size of their holdings. The farmer's debts dwindled with the declining value of the mark and, as a contemporary observer

[94] Apart from the numerous strikes during the summer, unrest manifested itself also by demonstrations staged by the unemployed in several large German cities. The demonstrations culminated frequently in looting of stores and clashes with the police. The KPD, which tried to control the demonstrations but rarely succeeded in doing so, adopted by and large an attitude of sympathetic disapproval, notably in regard to the looting of stores. For a more detailed discussion of this relatively obscure phase of Communist activities in 1923 see Wenzel, pp. 139-141.

[95] *Inprecorr*, III, No. 45 (June 22, 1923), p. 439.

commented with some bitterness, they "bought pianos which nobody played."[96] But quite apart from these considerations, Germany was a predominantly industrial country, and only a fraction of its population, roughly 25%, was engaged in agriculture. Under these circumstances, the new slogan was pathetically unrealistic, and required a special interpretation in its application to Germany. Thus the Communists adopted a propaganda line which was geared toward the small, marginal farmers and the farm workers. It was hoped that this approach would divide the farm front and rally the lowest agricultural income groups behind Communist banners. Throughout July and August, the *Rote Fahne* carried articles on the peasant question, the dominant theme being the need for a reapportioning of the land and the expropriation of the large landholders, especially the East Elbian Junkers.[97] Although the whole venture was viewed with misgivings by the Left Opposition, whose leaders raised doubts concerning the desirability of promoting the creation of numerous small farm-holdings instead of large communal farms, the line was maintained and actually brought a few results. Some local farm organizations, representing the small, marginal peasants (*Kleinbauern*), among them the "League of Producing Farmers" (*Bund schaffender Landwirte*), reacted favorably to the Communist overtures and applauded the party's offers to help them. This, however, was all the party achieved as far as the peasantry was concerned.[98]

Potentially more promising for the Communists was a series of mass strikes among agricultural laborers in various parts of the Reich during the crucial harvest period. The strikes began in Silesia at the end of May over wage disputes. They gathered mo-

[96] Stampfer, *Die vierzehn Jahre der ersten deutschen Republik*, 3rd ed. (Hamburg, 1947), p. 325; Thalheimer, *1923: Eine verpasste Revolution?*, p. 18.

[97] *Die Rote Fahne*, No. 152, July 5; No. 160, July 14; No. 169, July 25; No. 171, July 27; No. 179, August 5; No. 190, August 18; No. 191, August 19, 1923.

[98] Wenzel, pp. 129-132. For the criticism of the slogan "Workers' and Peasants' Government" by the Left Opposition see *Die Rote Fahne*, No. 179, August 5, 1923.

An interesting sidelight was thrown on the debate over the workers' and peasants' government by Leon Trotsky, who published an article entitled "Is the Time Ripe for the Slogan 'The United States of Europe'?" in *Pravda* on June 30, 1923. In the article Trotsky expounded the idea that Europe, ruined by capitalism and especially American capitalism, would sooner or later form a "United States of Workers and Peasants," created, of course, through the combined revolutionary actions of the urban and rural proletariat in the various national states. The article was reprinted in the German Communist press. An English version appears in Leon Trotsky, *The First Five Years of the Communist International*, II (New York, 1953), pp. 341-346.

mentum in June, collapsed at the end of that month in Silesia, but flared up again intermittently in several other agricultural regions during July and August. Here, presumably, was a golden opportunity for the KPD to champion the cause of that part of the rural population which could be called truly proletarian. Interestingly enough, however, the party's reaction to the rural strikes was slow in coming. For the first three weeks the party press ignored them altogether, whereas the strike movement of the miners and industrial workers in Upper Silesia received ample coverage. On June 15, the *Rote Fahne* finally reported to its readers that the farm laborers in Silesia had been on strike for three weeks, and then explained why this was so. A follow-up, consisting of a few brief paragraphs, appeared on June 21 in one of the back pages, and an even smaller notice, equally well hidden, two days later.[99] It was quite apparent that the KPD was not vitally interested in the lot of the farm workers, nor in rural affairs in general. Only after Zinoviev's speech on the "workers' and peasants' governments" was prominently printed in the *Rote Fahne* on July 5 did the party dutifully turn its attention to the rural regions, and for the following weeks the topic of agriculture received due attention from the Communist press. But it came too late to benefit the Silesian farm workers, who had gone on strike before the new line took effect, and the scattered agricultural strikes that were staged during July and August in other rural areas of Germany did not reach sufficiently large proportions to receive more than cursory attention from the KPD.[100]

All the party's multifarious activities so far considered were aspects of the united front policy. That the KPD supported striking proletarians who were struggling for Radek's proverbial piece of bread had been an acknowledged practice ever since the united front policy was formally adopted by the Comintern. At the same time, their manner of going about their business precluded any notion that the Communists were exerting themselves simply because of proletarian solidarity. It was their avowed aim to broaden

[99] *Die Rote Fahne*, No. 135, June 15; No. 140, June 21; No. 142, June 23, 1923. Seven lines were devoted by the paper to the same event on June 24, and on June 30 *Die Rote Fahne* reported on the last page that the strike in Silesia was over (Nos. 143, 148).
[100] Ruth Fischer's account of the farm laborers' strike (pp. 296-297) is misleading and inaccurate. Cf. Wenzel, pp. 133-135, including note 6, on this point and on the strikes as such.

the front of the discontented in an effort to mobilize the masses for "The Day." They said as much with disarming frankness. "As the extent of the strike grows, so must its objectives . . . the 'purely economic' strike [must become] political and seek to apply pressure upon the machinery of state." And analogous to this statement was the prediction that the working class would "continue the struggle until the bourgeois government in Germany will be overthrown."[101] On the other hand, it would be fallacious to attribute to the German Communists more unity of purpose, more wisdom and foresight than they actually possessed. Much of the time the *Zentrale* improvised the next move in an attempt to apply the proper tactic to a constantly shifting political scene. A case in point is the party's decision to organize an "anti-Fascist day," which was scheduled to be held on Sunday, July 29.

Throughout 1923, Communist outcries against "Fascism" never ceased, despite the Schlageter line. On the contrary, at the height of the party's nationalist campaign the tone of the party press toward the political Right became progressively shriller, and for several reasons. First of all, the Communists interpreted the term "Fascism" to include a wide spectrum of the German Right, roughly from Hitler's National Socialists through the German People's Party. As the Cuno government rested on a coalition ranging from the German Nationalist Party to the Democratic Party, the Communists tried to discredit the government by dwelling on its alleged links with big industry, freecorps, Black Reichswehr, and Hitler's Nazis. Furthermore, anti-Fascist propaganda served to counteract the unfavorable reaction which the Schlageter line had aroused among the non-Communist sections of the German labor movement. Finally, and probably most important, the *Zentrale* believed, and not without cause, that the activities in the nationalist camp indeed warranted countermeasures on the part of labor.

Nationalist extremism, on the rise ever since 1920, had received a new boost with the Ruhr occupation. In Prussia, where the National Socialists and the "League of Nationalist-Minded Soldiers" (*Verband nationalgesinnter Soldaten*) had already been outlawed before the Ruhr occupation began, Minister of the Interior Carl

[101] Quoted in Wenzel, p. 137.

Severing banned the *Deutschvölkische Freiheitspartei* by a decree of March 22. The step was taken because it was felt that the *Völkischen* posed a threat to the republic.[102] On April 29, the Nationalist Socialist Party was banned in Hesse for the same reason.[103] But the strongest concentration of right-wing extremists was in Bavaria, a state which granted them political asylum and permitted all nationalist organizations, banned elsewhere in the Reich, to carry on as they pleased. That this attitude was not without risk was driven home to the Bavarian government on May 1, when Hitler and his storm troopers staged a parade at Munich's Oberwiesenfeld which gave all the appearances of an intended putsch. Although the scheme was forestalled by army and police, the political atmosphere in this state remained tense and, throughout the summer, "Bavaria was a witches' cauldron of conspiracy, terror, and treason."[104]

Until the end of June, the KPD had reacted to the noticeable growth of nationalist extremism in a manner to which the German public had long been accustomed. The party press regularly printed articles which denounced the "Fascist" threat, and urged the workers to be on their guard. In essence, Communist treatment of this issue had taken on a well-established and rarely varying pattern, which was taken for granted, like snow at Christmas.[105] This pattern changed abruptly on July 12, when the *Rote Fahne* published on its front page an appeal "To the Party!," the tenor of which was disquieting, if not ominous.

The appeal began with the statement that Cuno's government was bankrupt, and that an "internal and external" crisis was imminent. In the occupied regions, i.e. the Rhenish-Westphalian province, France was supporting a Separatist movement which was expected to create an independent buffer state between France and Germany before the end of the summer.[106] This event would be

---

[102] Severing, *Mein Lebensweg*, I, p. 383.

[103] *Schulthess'*, 1923, p. 91.

[104] Landauer, *The Journal of Modern History*, XVI, No. 3 (September, 1944), p. 213; see also pp. 211-212.

[105] The campaign against the "Fascist threat" received new impetus when *Die Rote Fahne* (No. 148) on June 30 printed Clara Zetkin's "Report on Fascism" which she had delivered before the Enlarged Executive of the Comintern. On July 3, *Die Rote Fahne* (No. 150) ran a front page article under the caption "The Fascists Arm."

[106] The Separatist movement, which lies outside the framework of this study, was

used as a pretext by the south German Fascists to unleash a civil war "after the harvest was in." In Bavaria and also in the northern part of Germany, Fascist organizations were making feverish preparations for a large-scale uprising, primarily directed against the German proletariat. The Fascists were actively supported by high-ranking Reichswehr officers and by the bourgeois parties. The plans were well known to government officials and deputies to the Reichstag and the various state diets, including the Social Democrats among them. But the latter were too cowardly to inform the workers of the impending danger.

After this introductory passage, the appeal urged party members to prepare for the struggles ahead. "We must develop supreme readiness for action." When and how the Fascist onslaught would come was unknown. No reliance could be placed on either the SPD or the unions. On the contrary, "we Communists can only win the battle against the counterrevolution if we succeed in leading the Social Democratic and unaffiliated [*parteilose*] workers' masses together with us into the fight," which must be accomplished without, or even against, the treacherous Social Democratic leaders and union bureaucrats. Then followed detailed instructions on how to prepare for action in "open civil war." To emphasize the urgency of the situation, the appeal pointed out that the Fascists were known to have resolved upon the execution of every worker they captured who had offered armed resistance. The Fascist uprising could only be put down if White Terror was met by Red Terror.

"If the Fascists, who are armed to the teeth, slay the proletarian fighters, then the latter must ruthlessly liquidate all Fascists. If the Fascists put every tenth striker to the wall, then the revolutionary workers must put every fifth member of the Fascist organizations against the wall."

As the Fascists were armed and the workers were not, the latter would have to rely initially on their superior numbers, and in the course of combat would have to conquer weapons from the enemy. After reminding the party that the Communists might have to

---

indeed gaining strength in the summer of 1923. Contrary to widespread belief which was held by contemporaries, the Communists persistently opposed the Separatists. See, for instance, *Bericht über die Verhandlungen des IX. Parteitages*, p. 13; *Die Rote Fahne*, No. 152, July 5, 1923; No. 161, July 13, 1923; and M.E.L.S.I., *Zur Geschichte der Kommunistischen Partei Deutschlands* (Berlin, 1955), pp. 144-145.

open and lead the defensive struggle alone, especially in the occupied regions of Germany, the appeal exhorted the rank and file
to double their efforts in winning as many non-Communist workers
as possible for the fight ahead. "The party is ready to fight shoulder
to shoulder with everybody who is sincerely prepared to fight . . .
under proletarian leadership. Onward, close the ranks of the vanguard of the German proletariat. In the spirit of Karl Liebknecht
and Rosa Luxemburg, let us fight. Berlin, July 11, 1923. The *Zentrale* of the German Communist Party. . . ."[107]

The appeal was, to use a German saying, "strong tobacco." How
did it originate? According to an account which Heinrich Brandler
gave to Dr. Otto Wenzel in 1952, the appeal owed its existence to
a rumor. Shortly before Brandler intended to go on vacation in
July 1923, he received news of a nationalist meeting recently held
at Karlsruhe. In the course of this meeting, in which the former
left-wing Communist Fritz Wolffheim was supposed to have actively participated, a motion was said to have been made, according
to which every tenth striking worker was to be executed in case of
a right-wing putsch. Brandler, outraged at the report, and perhaps
particularly infuriated by Wolffheim's renegade behavior, sat down
and drafted this appeal to the party, which caused surprise and some
consternation even among the other *Zentrale* members. Yet it was
approved unanimously, and on the next day, July 12, was printed in
the party press.[108] In the same issue of the *Rote Fahne* a notice appeared announcing that proletarian "anti-Fascist day" demonstrations would be led by the KPD throughout Germany on Sunday,
July 29.

If one accepts Brandler's version of the story—and there is much
to recommend it[109]—the decision to alert the party for civil war was
taken on impulse. It was done even though the party was not pre-

[107] *Die Rote Fahne*, No. 158, July 12, 1961.

[108] Wenzel, p. 148. See also Brandler's reference to this issue in Exekutivkomitee
der Kommunistischen Internationale, *Die Lehren der deutschen Ereignisse* (Hamburg, 1924), p. 31.

[109] Both Dr. Wenzel and Professor Carr talked to Brandler after World War II
(see Wenzel, p. 36, n.14; Professor Carr talked to me about Brandler in the summer
of 1959). Both agree that his recollections are valuable and, on the whole, appear to
be trustworthy. However, we do not know to what extent Brandler's recollections
are colored by a desire for self-justification. Moreover, he has made it clear (in a
conversation with Dr. Wenzel) that he considers himself still bound by Communist
discipline, despite the fact that the KPD expelled him in 1929, and that, because
of his sense of loyalty, he does not yet feel free to reveal everything he remembers.

pared for such an event, a fact of which the *Zentrale* could not have been unaware. Why, then, did Brandler's colleagues agree to publish the appeal? Two interacting factors seem to have prompted the decision: one, that the party leaders really believed in the existence of nationalist plans to strike a blow against the working class, and especially the KPD; the other, that the deepening crisis in Germany led them to believe that Communist influence on the masses was growing more rapidly than it actually was. This belief encouraged the *Zentrale* to try the party's strength in large-scale demonstrations which, they hoped, would reveal that the balance of forces had shifted in favor of the Communists.

The party was soon to discover that the support it commanded was not nearly as strong as its leadership tended to believe. Much has been written about Communist strength in the summer of 1923, and statistics have been marshaled to prove that the KPD possessed at the time "the backing of at least a strong minority of [workers] organized in unions, and perhaps even the majority of the unorganized workers."[110] Another account claims blandly that "the KPD undoubtedly was backed in the summer of 1923 by the majority of the German proletariat."[111] Both authors have based their assertions on an increase of Communist strength in elections to several state diets and municipal councils, in a number of labor unions, notably those of the metal workers, and among the factory councils. Moreover, they have placed great stress upon the fact that in the Reichstag elections of May 1924 the KPD polled nearly 3,700,000 votes to the 6,008,713 of the Social Democrats.

There can be no arguing the fact that the KPD was gaining strength in the summer months of 1923, in actual membership as well as through sympathizers not affiliated with the party.[112] This was hardly surprising in view of the growing political and economic crisis which sharpened discontent throughout the country, and particularly among the working class. To turn toward Communism, either by joining the party, or by supporting its views without seeking membership, was one of several means by which a disgruntled or desperate worker could register his protest against the disquiet-

[110] Flechtheim, p. 91; see also p. 90.

[111] Rosenberg, *Entstehung und Geschichte der Weimarer Republik* (Frankfurt am Main, 1955) p. 406.

[112] See Wenzel's detailed discussion, pp. 156-164.

ing developments of a time out of joint. But to back the KPD in elections, and to support Communist motions at meetings held by trade-union locals and factory councils, did not necessarily mean that those who did so were also prepared to man the barricades whenever the party should give the signal. Furthermore, most of the estimates as to the party's influence on German labor at the time have been based largely on Communist sources. These have to be used with great caution, because exact figures were usually impossible to obtain. Since those who compiled the estimates often had to rely on inconclusive and scattered reports from local party organizations, since it was in the interest of the Communists to present as favorable a picture as possible, and, finally, since they inclined to believe in their growing influence, it is rather safe to assume that in case of doubt they tended toward overestimation rather than the reverse. Conversely, the figures easily available to them, such as those pertaining to party membership, were far from impressive. Whereas the KPD had in September 1922 a membership of 224,389 in 2,481 local organizations (*Ortsgruppen*), the count a year later was 294,230 members in 3,321 local organizations.[113] Thus out of a labor force (workers only) which the Communists themselves estimated as close to 23 million,[114] only about 70,000 actually committed themselves to Communist party membership in this very turbulent year.

The inference drawn from the 1924 election results, that the strength of the party's appeal in summer and fall of 1923 must have been still greater than it was in the spring of 1924, is inconclusive, if not fallacious.[115] The party's relatively strong showing in this election stemmed in all likelihood from the side effects of the stabi-

---

[113] *Bericht über die Verhandlungen des III. (8.) Parteitages der K.P.D. (Sektion der K.I.) abgehalten in Leipzig vom 28. Januar bis 1. Februar 1923* (Berlin, 1923), pp. 63-64; *Bericht über die Verhandlungen des IX. Parteitages*, pp. 57-58. Of 294,230 members, 32,856 were women. According to an estimate given by Remmele, the Communists controlled only 5,000 out of a total of 370,000 factory councils in Germany; and even among the 5,000 councils there were many which lacked a Communist majority (*Die Lehren der deutschen Ereignisse*, pp. 44-45).

[114] *Jahrbuch für Politik, Wirtschaft, Arbeiterbewegung 1922-23* (Hamburg, n.d.), p. 614.

[115] Leon Trotsky, *The Third International After Lenin*, transl. by John G. Wright (New York, 1936), p. 93. Trotsky quotes *Pravda*, May 25, 1923; see also Trotsky, *The First Five Years of the Communist International*, I (New York, 1945), p. 5; Flechtheim, p. 90; and Rosenberg, p. 407.

lization of the mark, especially the growth of unemployment, which set in with full force only during the winter of 1923-1924.[116]

In the absence of any conclusive evidence available on the actual strength of the party in the summer of 1923, it can only be said that its influence grew as Germany drifted further toward a crisis. But it grew neither as fast nor as extensively as its leaders were wont to believe. Their optimistic outlook was colored by the mounting resignations of workers from trade-unions, and by the diminishing hold which the Social Democratic Party was able to exert on its rank and file. The Communist leaders failed to take into account that only some of the workers who defected from the unions and the SPD embraced Communism. Most of them, disillusioned and apathetic in the face of economic and political chaos, lost their faith in democracy, in the republic, and in labor organizations, and withdrew from politics altogether.[117] It seems, moreover, that the Communists did not fully appreciate the fact that the ranks of the political Right, in particular the National Socialists and other extremist organizations, were growing in strength and determination, while the German labor movement as a whole became daily more divided and ineffective.[118] To be sure, the Communists were aware of the threat from the Right, as their anti-Fascist propaganda showed. But they had at the same time an exaggerated image of their own growing strength, and failed to see that the German labor movement, which they had helped to split, was in no way prepared seriously to challenge either the government or the nationalist forces on the Right, and certainly not both simultaneously. These facts were made amply clear by events during the last days of July and the first half of August.

Once the signal for staging an anti-Fascist day had been given, the party concentrated all its efforts on mobilizing the masses in support of it. Propaganda efforts were directed more emphatically than ever toward segments of society which had only lately been included in the united front approach. Thus office employees, of-

---

[116] Wenzel, p. 161; Leipart, in *Zehn Jahre deutsche Geschichte, 1918-1928* (Berlin, 1928), p. 343.

[117] Borkenau, *The Communist International*, p. 247; on the decline of union membership see also Leipart, in *Zehn Jahre deutsche Geschichte*, p. 343; and Kessler, in *Strukturwandlungen der deutschen Volkswirtschaft*, 1, ed. Bernhard Harms (Berlin, 1928), pp. 447-448.

[118] Borkenau, *The Communist International*, pp. 246, 248.

ficials, and peasants were urged to close ranks with the workers, and join the KPD on July 29 in holding mass demonstrations. It was indicative of the political atmosphere of those days that some of the proclamations were signed by representatives of non-Communist trade-union locals, whose names appeared side by side with those of Communists.[119]

The appeal "To the Party" and the propaganda barrage which followed in its wake created apprehension in government circles and among the public that a Communist coup was imminent.[120] The KPD denied and ridiculed the charges, but did so in such an equivocal manner that its denials carried little conviction. Ever since July 12 the tone of the Communist press had become unusually sharp and aggressive. Nor was it apt to inspire confidence that the *Rote Fahne*, in its edition of June 10, introduced in its Sunday supplement a series of articles dealing with civil war, guerilla tactics, experiences gained from the Russian Revolution, and related topics. These articles continued to appear at irregular intervals until September 2, 1923.[121] Sharp-eyed security agents might also have found a disturbing item in the paper's advertisement section. For months prior to July 12, a Herr Rose, Gollnowstrasse 16, had indicated in the "Wanted" section that he was prepared to pay record prices for field glasses. On July 12, and for weeks afterwards, Herr Rose included "pistols of all makes" among the items for which he advertised.[122]

The Communist language in regard to the anti-Fascist day demonstrations remained ambivalent and unclear throughout July. The general theme was that the Fascists were ready to strike and would have to be opposed by a united front of workers, peasants, employees, and other decent people. But there were variations on this theme which did not always agree with each other, either in aims or in emphasis. Some party spokesmen, while protesting against allegations that the KPD intended to unleash a civil war on

[119] See, for instance, *Die Rote Fahne*, No. 167, July 22; No. 172, July 28, 1923.

[120] Wenzel, pp. 154-155; Thalheimer, 1923: *Eine verpasste Revolution?*, p. 21; Severing, *Mein Lebensweg*, I, p. 420.

[121] *Die Rote Fahne*, No. 131, June 10; No. 143, June 24; No. 167, July 22; No. 191, August 19; No. 198, August 28; No. 203, September 2, 1923.

[122] Cf., for instance, *ibid.*, No. 103, May 9; and No. 151, July 4, 1923 with No. 158, July 12, 1923. Wenzel (p. 150) attributes in my estimation too much importance to these advertisements.

July 29, also let it be known that they expected such an event to transpire in the near future. "Our moment has not yet come! But it is much closer than many believe!" said the *Rote Fahne*.[123] August Thalheimer warned that "everyone in Germany feels that we are on the eve of a decisive combat between the bourgeoisie and the proletariat."[124] A somewhat different line was taken by Ernst Meyer. He said that even the Social Democratic press knew the KPD did not expect, at this present moment, to realize its desire for establishing a dictatorship, least of all on July 29. What the KPD wanted to achieve was "the formation of a Workers' and Peasants' Government in cooperation with the Social Democrats." If the Communists intended to make July 29 the day on which to start a civil war, he maintained, no one could prevent them from doing so. But all the party wanted was to test and strengthen Communist power. The Communists "have no idea of venturing into battle at a moment chosen by their enemies. Even the open attempt of the government and the Fascisti to provoke an armed struggle on July 29 will not have the desired effect."[125]

Meyer's explanation probably came closest to the truth. The anti-Fascist day was primarily intended to test the strength of the nationalist forces, of the government, and of Communist influence over the masses. There is no evidence to show that the *Zentrale* was then seriously considering the possibility of an early bid for power.[126] Brandler may have lost his temper, but he had not lost his mind. He and his colleagues in the *Zentrale*, except for the members of the Opposition, were still firm believers in the united front policy, although they were quite willing to step up the pace.[127] To an outsider, however, the KPD presented the picture of a party ap-

---

[123] *Die Rote Fahne*, No. 172, July 28, 1923.

[124] August Thalheimer, "What Is Brewing in Germany?" *Inprecorr*, III, No. 53 (July 26, 1923), p. 552.

[125] Ernst Meyer, "The Situation in Germany," *ibid.*, No. 54 (August 2, 1923), p. 571; the article was written prior to July 29, but after the demonstrations had been banned by the government.

[126] Brandler said as much at the Fifth World Congress of the Comintern: "We issued the slogan [pertaining to the Anti-Fascist day] in order to see what we could do ourselves, without the aid of the Social Democrats. . . . Naturally, at the first trial demonstration we did not want to fight, since the organizational conditions for it [sic] were still lacking" (*Fifth Congress of the Communist International, Abridged Report*, p. 65).

[127] On Brandler's position see Carr, *The Interregnum*, p. 188; and *Die Rote Fahne*, No. 181, August 8, 1923.

parently preparing for an armed upheaval. This impression was heightened by Communist demonstrations held in Frankfurt am Main on July 23. Though staged jointly with Social Democrats, the demonstrations were dominated by Communist slogans such as "Without Blood no Justice," and "The Exploiters to the Gallows." Stores were closed, streetcars stopped running, and some middle-class citizens caught unawares by the demonstrators were forced to carry banners and placards with revolutionary slogans. The day ended on a note of violence when demonstrators clashed with police.[128]

The Frankfurt incidents gave the Reich government an excuse to advise all individual states to prohibit the scheduled demonstrations on July 29. Hannover, where Gustav Noske was *Oberpräsident* (approx.: governor), had already done so on July 23. Now nearly every German state followed Hannover's example and banned all open-air demonstrations and street processions on anti-Fascist day. Only Saxony and Thuringia, which had governments controlled by left-wing Social Democrats, and Baden ignored the advice of the Reich government.

The ban posed an immediate problem for the *Zentrale*. Were the Communists to yield without a struggle? And if not, what form should and could this struggle take? Brandler suggested a compromise: demonstrations were to be held in Saxony, Thuringia, and Baden, where no ban existed, and in Prussian Saxony, the Ruhr region, and Upper Silesia, where the authority of the state was momentarily weak and the proletariat strong.[129] All demonstrations were to be protected by escorts of armed proletarian hundreds. Thereupon Ruth Fischer demanded that demonstrations be held in Berlin as well, despite the ban. This was obviously not a good idea. The German capital was protected by Severing's well-trained Prussian police, quite aside from the fact that the Communists in Berlin were decisively outnumbered by the Social Democrats. Brandler told her as much, and insisted that the party could permit demonstrations in Berlin only if they received adequate protection from armed escorts. This suggestion caused Ruth Fischer to lose her temper, and to call the chairman of the *Zentrale* an ad-

[128] *Die Rote Fahne*, No. 168, July 24, 1923; *Schulthess'*, 1923, p. 137.
[129] *Fifth Congress of the Communist International, Abridged Report*, p. 65; Wenzel, pp. 153-154.

venturer and a Fascist. Brandler, eager to temporize, next suggested that a strike be called to protest the ban, but this idea she also rejected.[130]

The decision to hold outdoor demonstrations only in places where the Communists could protect them, and to rely on indoor protest meetings in the rest of the country, had the backing of the ECCI. Exactly when and how this backing was obtained is still obscure, and may never be cleared up satisfactorily. It appears that the prime mover in opposing street processions was Radek, one of the few members of the ECCI who was not on vacation but had remained in Moscow. Zinoviev and Bukharin were taking a holiday, but had indicated their approval of the demonstrations by telegram. Radek apparently secured the advice of the secretary of the Russian party, Joseph Stalin, who agreed with him that the German Communists should not, at present, be encouraged to challenge the Fascists. A telegram to this effect was sent on July 26, in the name of the president of Comintern, to the German *Zentrale*, with Radek still acting on his own responsibility in the absence of Zinoviev and Bukharin. He had, however, informed the two vacationers that if the Comintern should grant permission to the KPD to stage demonstrations, the German party might be pushed into a "July defeat."[131]

[130] Brandler's and Fischer's respective versions of this quarrel are in *Die Lehren der deutschen Ereignisse*, pp. 32, 55.

[131] Carr, *The Interregnum*, pp. 186-187; Wenzel, pp. 153-154.

The accounts of Carr and Wenzel do not agree. Carr, basing his on a statement made by Zinoviev at the Thirteenth Congress of the Russian Communist Party in January, 1924, infers that the ECCI entered the scene only after the German *Zentrale* discussed, and disagreed on, the problem of outdoor demonstrations. Carr also has Radek hurry to Moscow, presumably from Berlin, though this point is as obscure as is the destination of the telegrams of approval sent by Zinoviev and Bukharin. Equally puzzling is the date of the final telegram. According to Carr, Radek sent it on July 26, 1923, thus only a day or two after the various state governments had begun to issue bans against the scheduled demonstrations.

Carr's account thus raises a number of questions: when did the *Zentrale* first discuss the matter of the ban? How was Radek able to travel from Berlin to Moscow, contact Zinoviev and Bukharin in the Caucasus, have Stalin write him a letter, and still send a telegram on July 26, advising the cancellation of the demonstrations? Carr also errs on the date when Prussia announced her ban; he gives July 23, but the announcement was made on July 24, 1923.

Wenzel, basing his account on two articles in the *Internationale Presse Korrespondenz* (*Inprekorr*) and a private interview with Brandler in 1952, states that Radek sent his telegram before the matter had been taken up by the German *Zentrale*. Neither Wenzel nor Brandler (see *Die Lehren der deutschen Ereignisse*, p. 32) indicate that Radek was in Berlin at any time during July, 1923. In fact, there is no evidence to show that Radek returned to Germany after his departure

Owing to the neat arrangement by which demonstrations were conducted according to local distribution of strength between the authorities and the proletariat, the anti-Fascist day passed without major incidents. The Berlin organization staged a series of indoor rallies. Estimates as to the number of participants vary between 150,000 and 250,000, the latter being the Communist figure. In Saxony and Thuringia, two areas where the Communists were not only relatively strong, but where they were also allowed to hold outdoor processions, party estimates claimed the participation of 180,000 demonstrators in nine cities.[132] This turnout, which constituted a test of the party's mass appeal, was far from overwhelming, even if allowances were made for the effect of local bans.

As usual, it was left to Radek to pick up the pieces. An article of his entitled "The Approaching Bankruptcy of the German Bourgeoisie and the Tasks of the German Communist Party" appeared on the front page of the *Rote Fahne* on August 2. Although written before he could have known the results (the article carried a Moscow dateline of July 29), Radek's lengthy analysis of the political situation indicated that he, for one, harbored no illusions concerning the party's present position. Behind the customary bluster and inevitable dire predictions concerning the future of the bourgeoisie, the Fascists, and the Social Democrats, Radek's sobering criticism could hardly be missed. The Bolsheviks, he said, could seize power with 70,000 people because the Russian bourgeoisie was not organized, and the Bolsheviks controlled the army. To emulate the Bolshevik example in Germany required a Communist party with a minimum of a million members. Once again he emphasized the importance of the united front. The growing strength of the KPD made it even more obligatory than in the past to persuade the Socialist workers to join with the Communists as a team. To carry out

---

in June, when he left for Moscow to attend a meeting of the Enlarged Executive of the Comintern.

Wenzel's account seems to be the more convincing, especially in regard to the time sequence. Radek may well have sent his telegram as soon as he learned of the ban, and after having communicated with Zinoviev, Bukharin, and Stalin.

Zinoviev mentioned Radek's opposition to the anti-Fascist day at the Fifth World Congress of the Comintern (*Fifth Congress of the Communist International, Abridged Report,* p. 107); Fischer's brief reference to this issue (p. 287) is misleading.

[132] Wenzel, p. 156.

united front tactics meant a doubling of effort, harder work, more drive. But it was not sufficient to enlist merely the proletariat. The petty bourgeoisie had to be won over as well, and here the work had just begun. Radek's article closed on a note of cautious optimism. The moment for the all-out assault had not yet come, though it was drawing closer. The bourgeoisie, divided as it was, was proving itself unable to handle the critical situation which the nation faced. The strength of the Social Democrats was waning, and that of the KPD growing. It was the strategic mission of the Communists to further the ripening process of the revolution. This revolution would come—in time.

"We must fight the battles to which we are destined by history, but we must always keep in mind that we are at the moment still the weaker. We cannot as yet offer a general battle, and we must avoid everything which would enable the enemy to beat us piecemeal."[133]

A few days later, Brandler expressed very similar ideas, though he phrased them more belligerently. The party, wrote the chairman of the *Zentrale*, had to prepare for a "defensive revolutionary struggle." The bourgeoisie, utterly bankrupt, was preparing to wage a class war for which the proletariat had to get ready unless it wished to be massacred. Class war could only be avoided if the KPD succeeded in forming a united front with the Social Democrats and the labor unions. This would lead to the overthrow of the Cuno government and the establishment of a workers' and peasants' government in Germany. To this end the party had to double its efforts, win the workers now still in the Socialist camp, and continue its campaign of gaining the sympathy, or at least the benevolent neutrality, of the lower middle class. The latter, Brandler claimed, was no tactical maneuver but "strategic necessity."[134]

Brandler's formula for victory was in essence the gist of the "Resolution on the Political Situation," which had just been adopted by the party's Central Committee meeting on August 6.[135] The resolution bore all the marks of compromise—the revolutionary mission of the party was stressed in strong words, while the

[133] *Die Rote Fahne*, No. 176, August 2, 1923.
[134] *ibid.*, No. 181, August 8, 1923.
[135] *Bericht über die Verhandlungen des IX. Parteitages*, p. 64/74 (double pagination). The conference lasted from August 5 to 6, 1923.

fundamental course was not changed one iota. Such a compromise had become necessary because the Central Committee meeting had led to a renewal of the long-standing dispute between the majority and the Left Opposition. Ruth Fischer, ably assisted by several of her left-wing colleagues, denounced the united front policy, the party's stress on the workers' government, and Brandler's rejection of the slogan "proletarian dictatorship." And Hugo Urbahns, from Hamburg, complained that "according to north German notions, a peasant is a capitalist. Therefore the slogan workers' and peasants' government is wrong." In the final vote, however, the Central Committee adopted without dissent the "Resolution on the Political Situation" which the *Zentrale* had introduced. The fact that nine members of the Opposition merely abstained, without submitting a minority resolution of their own, was interpreted by Brandler as a healthy sign, but his public statement that the party was "uniform [in its views] and united" still rang rather hollow.[136]

The barely restrained bitterness which accompanied the debates of the Central Committee reflected a mounting impatience and irritation among the Communists, intensified by dissatisfaction with the meager results of the anti-Fascist day demonstrations. Events appeared to be perpetually mocking them. Ever since the onset of the Ruhr occupation they had watched the prospects for a revolution grow brighter. The steady disintegration of the existing order had time after time aroused and sustained their hopes. But throughout the spring and summer the moment for which they were waiting always evaded them.

It has been said that the party had only its own indecisions to blame for its failure to profit from the chaotic conditions which then prevailed in Germany: that by the first week of August "the KPD had exhausted its repertory of words and ideas, and was not equipped, or not ready, for action"; and although it had "every provocation to revolt . . . [the party] shrank back half-heartedly, when the moment came, from the decisive step."[137] This argument presupposes that the Communists could have made a successful revolution at the time. The fact remains, however, that Radek, Brandler, and the majority of the *Zentrale* members were not con-

[136] *Die Rote Fahne*, No. 181, August 8, 1923.
[137] Carr, *The Interregnum*, p. 188.

vinced that the KPD could make a successful bid for power until there was a reasonable assurance of substantial mass support. This assurance they thought was lacking, and the historian, surveying the period nearly four decades later, cannot help but concur. Whenever the party had tested its public appeal—during the Ruhr strikes in May, during the July strikes throughout the republic, and on the anti-Fascist day—the results had not been sufficiently encouraging to persuade a group of party functionaries, still haunted by the fiasco of March 1921, to risk another defeat. This does not mean that they rejected a revolution altogether, or that they were unaffected by the undeniable progress the party had made since 1921, both in terms of growing strength and the self-confidence that went with it. But one gains the impression that Radek and Brandler, at least, maintained their sense of proportion and were unwilling to rush the party into a premature revolutionary action. They evidently put their faith in what may be called a policy of attrition which, if properly applied and manipulated, was bound to lead either to a revolution in which the odds would be overwhelmingly in favor of the proletariat, or even to the formation of a workers' and peasants' government by non-violent means. In either case, they were convinced that time was working for the Communists, and therefore urged all party members to increase their efforts to explore and exploit every weak spot in the socio-political fabric of the state, and for the rest let bourgeois society dig its own grave. At the proper moment the KPD, supported by the rest of German labor, would be on hand to bury the capitalists along with all their cohorts.

A few days after the Central Committee meeting, during what has come to be known as the "Cuno strike," the party had one more opportunity to put the policy of attrition to work. It was to be the last time. By an ironic twist of fate, the repercussions of the Cuno strike not only put an end to this policy, but in addition helped to end a distinct phase in the history of the KPD.

The Cuno strike originated in Berlin and began as a protest movement against the new catastrophic economic situation in the face of which the Reich government seemed helpless. Runaway inflation played havoc with the ratio between wages and prices. Undernourishment, sometimes approaching starvation, became more and more common among low income groups. On August 8 Chancellor

Wilhelm Cuno, a well-meaning but ineffectual man, addressed the Reichstag in a lengthy speech. It was supposed to be a justification of his policies, but amounted in effect to a public admission of failure. On the same day, the Berlin printers' union voted to strike on August 10 unless the printers were granted higher wages. The decision had received the endorsement of the union's mother organization, the ADGB. Only the labor newspapers and printing houses were to remain unaffected by the strike. Efforts on the part of the ADGB executive to exempt also the government printing presses from being struck failed. For this the Communists were responsible.[138] They knew that stopping the machine which produced the paper money, on which the inflation-ridden economy so sadly depended, would produce a shortage of banknotes within a few hours, and would contribute to unrest and tension.

Friday, August 10, turned the German capital into a veritable madhouse. The printers struck, including those working for the government, and precipitated the shortage of paper money. A Communist-dominated Factory Council Committee of Fifteen dispatched agitators into the city's industrial and public utilities plants. These agents succeeded in drawing the operators of the power plants into the strike, thereby causing a partial disruption of Berlin's electricity service. In addition, the construction workers walked off their jobs; the employees of the municipal transportation systems struck; and in several districts hospital personnel became affected by the mushrooming work stoppage.[139] However, there was not yet a general strike. The government hoped to avert one by issuing, that same day, a decree "for the protection of public order," by which all printed material designed to incite anyone to disturb the peace, or to advocate the violent overthrow of the existing form of state, became subject to immediate confiscation.[140]

But a general strike was exactly what the Communists hoped to bring about. An opportunity to realize this intention arose when on the same day the Berlin Trade-Union Commission invited the heads of the local labor unions, together with representatives of the SPD, the rump USPD, and the KPD, to a joint consultative meeting. In the ensuing discussion the Communist delegation, of

[138] *Die Rote Fahne*, No. 184, August 11, 1923.
[139] Wenzel, p. 165.
[140] *Schulthess'*, 1923, pp. 149-150.

which Ruth Fischer was a member, moved to call a three-day general strike to obtain the following main objectives: a minimum hourly wage of 0.60 gold marks; the overthrow of the Cuno government; and the establishment of a workers' and peasants' government. Considering the tense circumstances under which the meeting was held, it is at least conceivable that a majority of delegates might have declared in favor of such a strike. But before a vote on the Communist motion was taken, a Social Democratic functionary told the meeting that his party's Reichstag delegation had just secured assurances from the government that fifty million gold marks, pledged by a combine of leading business firms, industries, and other economic groups, would be spent for immediate food imports. Moreover, two hundred million gold marks would be used to stem the inflationary trend. Finally, he reminded the meeting that the Reichstag that day had passed a law to raise income and corporation taxes. The law, which had been supported by all parties, including the KPD, offered promise of a rapid economic improvement. This optimistic appraisal of the situation accomplished its purpose; the Communist motion was defeated.[141]

The party was unwilling to accept the verdict of the joint meeting as final. The rejection of their motion by a majority of non-Communist labor leaders only confirmed the Communists in their long standing conviction that the labor bureaucracy was corrupt, and that the party must appeal directly to the rank and file of the SPD and the unions. On August 11, "Constitution Day" for the Weimar Republic, a hastily summoned conference of the city's factory councils proclaimed a general strike in Berlin and urged the working class throughout the rest of the country to join the strike. The proclamation was carried by a special edition of the *Rote Fahne*, but the entire issue was promptly confiscated by the authorities, who invoked the one-day-old government decree "for the protection of public order." Despite this handicap, the Communists succeeded at first in eliciting a surprisingly strong response from several occupational groups within the city. Moreover, sporadic wildcat strikes erupted on this and subsequent days in various parts of the country.[142] There was a distinct possibility that these

[141] *Die Rote Fahne*, No. 184, August 11, 1923; Wenzel, p. 165; *Bericht über die Verhandlungen des IX. Parteitages*, pp. 12-13, 21.
[142] *Die Rote Fahne*, No. 185, August 12; No. 186, August 14, 1923.

intermittent strikes might have turned into a general one, as had happened in March 1920 during the Kapp putsch. But before the Communists were able to fan these brush-fires into a major conflagration, their designs were thwarted by the announcement, on August 12, that Chancellor Cuno and his cabinet had resigned.[143]

Cuno's resignation had become mandatory after the Social Democratic Reichstag delegation had informed the chancellor on August 11 that he no longer possessed the confidence of their party. The next day, President Ebert invited the leader of the German People's Party, Gustav Stresemann, to form a new government. By August 13, Stresemann had filled most of the cabinet posts, four of which were held by Social Democrats. The Great Coalition government, for months the bugbear of the KPD, was now an undisputable fact.

The disappearance of the Cuno government was undoubtedly the most significant factor in calming the turbulent political scene; when the Cuno government collapsed, the general strike did too. The effect of the appointment of Stresemann cannot be so easily evaluated. He was certainly respected as a political leader, and his energy and sincerity inspired confidence. But these and other positive characteristics of Stresemann were neatly balanced in the public mind by the fact that he held essentially conservative views, and that he had been an outspoken annexationist during the war. As far as German labor was concerned, however, what weighed heaviest in the scales was the inclusion of the SPD in the government. Although there had been considerable opposition to joining the cabinet when the Reichstag delegation had caucused on August 11

[143] Ruth Fischer's suggestive treatment of Cuno's resignation is misleading. She writes (p. 301) that "On August 10, the Communists in the Reichstag moved a vote of no confidence [which they did]. On the 11th, Cuno resigned. Now the strike in Berlin spread like wildfire . . . ." The implication is plainly that the Communist motion in the Reichstag prompted the resignation of Cuno and his cabinet. But Cuno did not resign because of this particular motion. He did so only after the SPD had informed him that he no longer enjoyed the confidence of that party. Cuno could well afford to ignore the KPD, but he could not govern after he had forfeited the confidence of the SPD, the strongest single party in Germany.

Another distorted version of this event is in Ulbricht, *Zur Geschichte der deutschen Arbeiterbewegung*, I (Berlin, 1953), p. 125. The author claims that the general strike had such an overwhelming impact, and spread so rapidly, that it swept the Cuno government away on its first day. A similar view is given in Flechtheim, p. 89 (based on Thalheimer's account), and in Rosenberg, p. 409; cf. Severing, *Mein Lebensweg*, I, pp. 423-424.

(forty-three Social Democratic delegates had voted against the proposal), the majority of workers were not unaffected by the fact that four out of twelve ministerial posts were held by Social Democrats. Thus the psychological impact of the change in government, and a surprising readiness of the affected industries and public services to grant generous wage increases, deprived the strike movement of both its political and economic motives.[144]

When the movement began to collapse the party tried to keep it going. On August 12, a Sunday, the *Rote Fahne* printed a censored version of the original strike appeal and reported proudly that the strike had begun. There was no issue on Monday. The morning issue of the paper on August 14 carried the banner line "Millions [Engaged] in Struggle!", and another heading read "The Fight Goes On." Before the day was over, however, the paper issued a special edition which surprised its readers with the statement that the strike was over. "Simultaneous, Unified End of the Strike!", read the headline, and the paper explained that the anti-strike propaganda of the unions and Socialists threatened to unleash a "fraternal struggle" within the working class which could only be avoided by calling off the strike. The same information was repeated the following day in an appeal "To the Working Population of Germany!" in which the unions and Social Democrats were blamed for having stabbed the fighting proletariat in the back. The party gave notice, however, that the Communists intended to resume the struggle at the next opportunity. "The Struggle Has Been Broken Off—Let Us Prepare for the Next One" was the title of the unsigned editorial. And another caption read: "An Interruption, Not a Conclusion of the Struggle" [*Kampfpause, nicht Kampfabschluss*]![145]

Why did the KPD call off the strike after such a relatively short trial period? According to Ruth Fischer, Brandler insisted on it "since it was not officially endorsed by the German Federation of Labor [ADGB]."[146] Walter Ulbricht blames the "opportunists and

[144] Wenzel, p. 170; Thalheimer, 1923: *Eine verpasste Revolution?*, p. 20.

[145] *Die Rote Fahne*, No. 185, August 12; No. 186, August 14; "Extra," August 14; No. 187, August 15, 1923.

[146] Fischer, p. 302. Ruth Fischer further maintains that the Left Opposition joined with the factory councils in objecting to the termination of the strike, but that the *Zentrale* issued a formal order on August 13, 1923, to break off the strike the next day. If this was so, why did the *Rote Fahne* insist on August 14 that the strike would go on, and only late that night issue a special edition calling it off? Furthermore, Miss Fischer implies that she was unconnected with the decision,

traitors in the *Zentrale* . . . , Brandler, Thalheimer and others, who had neglected to give [the strike] clear political aims and had failed to call for the creation of a workers' government."[147] Neither explanation is convincing. Brandler knew beforehand that the strike was not backed by the ADGB; in fact, the *Zentrale* was forced to turn to the factory councils, which the party controlled, to find an effective vehicle for launching the strike which the trade-unions had voted the day before. Ulbricht's charges are equally untenable. Among the announced political aims of the *Zentrale* were Cuno's resignation and the creation of a workers' and peasants' government. The first objective was accomplished. The second objective was not accomplished, nor could it have been in the absence of unequivocal mass support for such a demand.

In the last analysis, it was exactly the absence of mass support which led the party to call off the strike. Impressive though its initial impact had been in Berlin, even there it never developed into a "general" strike, and it lost whatever force it had once Cuno had resigned. The response in the provinces was even less encouraging. Outside of a few isolated and insignificant demonstrations, the whole of southern Germany and the Ruhr region remained unaffected. The movement was strongest in central Germany, especially the Halle-Merseburg district; but as soon as the Social Democrats

---

treating the *Zentrale* as a kind of outside force. But she was a member of it, too. What is more, she was chosen from among twenty-odd members of the *Zentrale* to represent the KPD on August 14 at the meeting of Berlin's factory councils, and it was she who told the delegates to this meeting that the strike would have to be called off, and why. (*Die Rote Fahne*, No. 187, August 15, 1923.) If she was really as opposed to the decision as she later claimed, why did she act as the official representative of her party on this occasion? Had this event occurred five years later, at a time when the KPD had developed into a thoroughly bolshevized party, it could be argued that she was probably chosen for this unpleasant task just because she was opposed to the decision which her party had taken. But in 1923 the discipline in the German party had not yet reached that state of rigidity whereby a reluctant party member could be required, on general principles, to carry out orders of which he or she disapproved. Finally, it appears that Maslow also favored the decision to call off the strike (Wenzel, p. 170).

    [147] Ulbricht, *Zur Geschichte der deutschen Arbeiterbewegung*, I, p. 126. Ulbricht's charge that the *Zentrale* failed to call for the creation of a workers' (and peasants') government is unfair. The author neglects to mention that the official strike proclamation which appeared in *Die Rote Fahne* (No. 185) on August 12, 1923, was censored. Item No. 4 was left blank, carrying only the numeral. The empty space had contained the appeal for the creation of a workers' and peasants' government, a demand which violated the governmental decree of August 10, 1923, in letter and spirit.

gained control of it, the strikes began to die down. Even in Dresden and Chemnitz, cities in a state with a left-wing Social Democratic government, the strike movement was hardly in evidence. Hamburg, in the north, a traditional stronghold of radicalism, saw two days of violence and required the imposition of a state of emergency on August 13. Lübeck and Stettin, in contrast, remained relatively quiet.[148]

And so it went, region by region, city by city. Enough unrest had been stirred up throughout the country to give the Communists a feeling of accomplishment, but they failed to turn these scattered outbursts of protest and despair into a genuine nationwide mass movement. This failure was not merely the result of faulty coordination and related incidental shortcomings, although these factors entered in: its ultimate cause must be sought in the party's inherent approach and attitude to non-Communist labor. Even with a more capable and resolute *Zentrale* it is unlikely that the KPD would have done much better than it did, as long as it insisted on alternately wooing and insulting other labor organizations, and calling this method a united front policy.

Ruth Fischer has claimed that "if the union leaders had supported the strike, the successor to Cuno would have been a trade-union man," and also that the trade-union leaders "were on the verge of supporting the strike," but were restrained from doing so by a Social Democratic official.[149] The validity of her argument is doubtful and, moreover, misses the point. Could it have been that the unions and Social Democrats were wary of Communist intentions and refused to trust them? Ruth Fischer's own contribution to the crucial discussion at the joint labor organizations meeting on August 10 may throw some light on this question. In the course of the deliberations on whether labor should call a general strike in Berlin, she spoke plainly.

[148] Wenzel, pp. 169, 171; *Schulthess'*, 1923, p. 153. Brandler stated a few months later that after Cuno's resignation the strike virtually collapsed, despite efforts of the *Zentrale* to keep it going for a fourth day, at least in Berlin. He added that the Berlin organization was likewise unable to prolong the strike (*Die Lehren der deutschen Ereignisse*, pp. 30-31). See also the official party criticism of the Cuno strike, written by the Fischer faction in 1924, in *Bericht über die Verhandlungen des IX. Parteitages*, pp. 21-22. Both the extent and violence of the strike have been vastly exaggerated in a recent East German study; see Heinz Habedank, *Zur Geschichte des Hamburger Aufstandes* 1923 (Berlin, 1958), pp. 42-45.

[149] Fischer, p. 301.

"I only wish that the workers could see and hear your noble union commission. You have no idea of what is going on outside, or you would not spout such lame [*lendenlahme*] phrases. The movement is here; it is strong; and the question is simply whether it can be led in a unified manner with you, without you, or against you."[150] Even if one takes into consideration the tense atmosphere in which the meeting was conducted, even if one makes allowances for Ruth Fischer's impatient temperament, and even if one assumes, giving her the benefit of the doubt, that all she wanted was to prod the meeting into making a decision—this was hardly the way to win allies.

Ruth Fischer's attitude was typical of the way in which the Communists generally went about soliciting non-Communist labor support in 1923. Nothing portrays better the limitations of a closed political system than the party's pursuit of tactics which in the face of experience had proven inadequate, if not harmful. Here was a real dilemma. It had haunted the party in the past, and was to haunt it in the future. The KPD called itself a revolutionary party. Revolution was its final objective and its sole *raison d'être*. When the party leadership and the Russian Bolsheviks began to realize that revolution in Germany could only be attempted if and when the Communists commanded support from a majority of labor, they instituted the united front policy as a means to attain this end. But the party could not afford to, and never did, conduct this policy in good faith. To have done so would have meant a compromise with revolutionary principles. Thus the united front policy was turned into a policy of attrition, designed to undermine the state as well as the rival working-class organizations which the Communists professed to want to convert to their side. Had they been sincere in their ceaseless advocacy of a working-class alliance during the crucial months preceding the Cuno strike, they could have made an honest and convincing offer to the Social Democrats, suggesting in effect that both parties cooperate with each other and with the unions in striving for the establishment of a labor government. Certainly the workers, and probably the nation as a whole, would have benefited in 1923 from a genuinely united labor front, even if a workers' government had not immediately materialized.

[150] *Die Rote Fahne*, No. 184, August 11, 1923.

But the Communists were barred from making such a move because it would have constituted a concession to the "reformists"—according to Communist dogma a cardinal sin.

One may argue that the Communist position was illogical and self-defeating, since the SPD and the unions, despite some setbacks, still commanded between them the allegiance of a majority of German workers. This was not a matter of logic, however, but of doctrine, faith, and discipline. As long as the German party was a section of the Communist International, and bound by the decisions of this organization, such a left-handed approach to the project of winning mass support was inescapable. Perhaps a Rosa Luxemburg, had she lived, would have had the courage and foresight to cut the umbilical cord which connected the KPD to the Comintern, in order to secure for German Communism freedom of movement and decision. But Brandler and his colleagues lacked the vision and the courage to risk open violation of the norms which the Comintern had established for the conduct of united front policies. Thus for many months, while Germany was subject to unprecedented stresses and strains, the Communists proceeded along the same narrow path which they had trodden for the last two years, and which had netted them, politically speaking, small change but no fortune. How long they might have continued to pursue this course it is impossible to say. That they changed it after the Cuno strike, however, was none of their doing. The decision was made for them by the men in the Kremlin.

CHAPTER XII

REVOLUTION IN PREPARATION

⟨⟩ THE DECISION of the Comintern to engineer a Communist revolution in Germany was largely based on faulty premises. In their eagerness to revive the revolutionary wave in Europe, the Bolshevik leaders succumbed to wishful thinking, to a misjudgment of the true situation in Germany, and to the temptation to sponsor a "German October" uprising.

That the situation in Germany remained grave even after Cuno's resignation cannot be disputed. Nevertheless, the apex of the 1923 crisis had been passed on August 12, although few contemporaries realized this fact at the time. With the collapse of the Cuno government, which had demonstrated a nearly unprecedented incompetence in dealing with problems both at home and abroad, the confused and embittered nation, except for extremists on the right and left, rallied hopefully behind the new chancellor and the Great Coalition cabinet which he headed.

Gustav Stresemann had several important advantages over his predecessor. His economic knowledge, acquired early in life during his years of apprenticeship in industry, was more profound than Cuno's. He was also politically more astute, particularly with respect to foreign policy, and, unlike his predecessor, he possessed the courage to make necessary, though unpopular, decisions. Finally, he commanded greater confidence from German labor than had Cuno. All these were factors in Stresemann's favor, but the new chancellor was fully aware of the enormous difficulties which his government would have to overcome in the immediate future.[1]

The seriousness of the over-all situation was clearly enunciated by the participating ministers at a cabinet meeting on August 20. The exchange rate to the dollar, which on August 13 had stood at 3,700,000 marks, had risen within a week to six million marks. Prices kept rising everywhere. Most parts of the country were faced by economic strikes, and the food problem grew daily more difficult. Radicalism on the right and the left grew in intensity as Bavaria,

[1] For an astute and recent appraisal of Stresemann see Annelise Thimme, *Gustav Stresemann: Eine politische Biographie zur Geschichte der Weimarer Republik* (Hannover and Frankfurt, 1957).

378

Saxony, and Thuringia seemed to be drifting into open rebellion against the Reich. In short, the home front was in need of drastic emergency measures.[2]

The international picture looked equally somber. A brief ray of hope had been provided by the Curzon Note of August 11, in which His Majesty's Government informed France and Belgium that Great Britain held the occupation of the Ruhr to have been in violation of international law. The note made it plain that the British government would not back France and Belgium in their contemplated move to demand from Germany the unconditional cessation of passive resistance in the Ruhr. The note was polite, assured the two continental powers of England's good will, but left no doubt that France and Belgium would receive no British support for any future *démarches* to Germany in connection with the Ruhr.[3]

This British demonstration of sympathy for Germany's position might have boosted German morale had it been issued earlier. As it was, the effect was largely lost in the turmoil which accompanied Cuno's resignation, although the note did achieve a temporary relaxation of tension. On August 21 the French Premier, Raymond Poincaré, issued the statement that France would be willing to abandon her occupation of the Ruhr, gradually and by stages, if Germany would end her policy of passive resistance. Poincaré's gambit led to a series of statements and counterstatements on both sides of the Rhine, without, however, bringing the two countries closer to a satisfactory solution. Meanwhile the inflation reached astronomical proportions. On September 1, the dollar rate stood at 98,800,000 marks. Passive resistance proved an ever increasing burden on the German treasury, and made it mandatory for the government to terminate the hopeless struggle in the Ruhr. On September 24 Stresemann announced in a cabinet meeting that passive resistance would have to be abandoned. To do so was the only way out of a serious dilemma. A continuation of this policy could offer the nation no advantages, and there was no alternative solution to the problem which had not been tried. On September

---

[2] Stresemann, *Vermächtnis*, 1: *Vom Ruhrkrieg bis London* (Berlin, 1932), pp. 93-94.
[3] L. Zimmermann, *Deutsche Aussenpolitik in der . . . Weimarer Republik* (Göttingen-Berlin-Frankfurt, 1958), pp. 182, 183.

26 passive resistance was officially ended by a joint proclamation of the Reich President and the government.[4]

On the same day, President Ebert declared a state of emergency in Germany and transferred the executive power to Minister of Defense Otto Gessler. The decree announced stiffer penalties for all crimes pertaining to high treason, or violence vis-à-vis the state. The minister of defense received the right to transfer his executive power to the military district commanders whenever the need arose; he also had the power to appoint governmental commissioners to assist the military commanders in the field of civil administration. Gessler lost no time: he at once appointed the commanders of the seven military defense districts as regional executives.[5]

These drastic measures had become necessary in the face of growing disturbances in several parts of the Reich. One very critical problem was that of Bavaria, which throughout the summer of 1923 seethed with conspiracy and terror, and where political tension led to Hitler's beerhall putsch on November 9.[6] Thuringia presented another trouble spot. There a Socialist government, ever since its formation in October 1921, had had to rely for support and for its very existence on Communist backing in the diet. Although the cabinet tried to steer a moderate course, under the leadership of Minister-President August Frölich, distrust of the

---

[4] *ibid.*, pp. 185-193; Stresemann, *Vermächtnis*, I, pp. 98, 100-128.

[5] *Schulthess' Europäischer Geschichtskalender*, 1923 (Munich, 1928), pp. 177-179; Gessler, *Reichswehrpolitik in der Weimarer Zeit*, ed. Kurt Sendtner (Stuttgart, 1958), pp. 260-262.

[6] The story of Bavaria during 1923 has been told many times, and for the purpose of this study it will suffice to recapitulate briefly the principal problem. The Bavarian Right was divided into two main groups: the "black-white-red" (old imperial colors) nationalists, who wanted to see a strong, centralized, right-wing nationalist government in Berlin; and the "white-blue" (Bavarian colors) Bavarian monarchists, who wanted to break with Berlin and establish an independent Bavarian state under a Wittelsbach king. The two forces were only united by their common dislike for the Weimar Republic, a sentiment which, at least temporarily, concealed their very real and fundamental differences of aims and political philosophy.

For more detailed accounts see the following works: Karl Schwend, *Bayern zwischen Monarchie und Diktatur* (Munich, 1954), pp. 199-260. Werner G. Zimmermann, *Bayern und das Reich* (Munich, 1953), pp. 134-149, and *passim*. Carl Landauer, "The Bavarian Problem in the Weimar Republic, 1918-1923," *The Journal of Modern History*, XVI, No. 2 (June 1944), pp. 93-115; and No. 3 (September 1944), pp. 205-223. Alan Bullock, *Hitler, a Study in Tyranny* (London, 1952), pp. 77-101. Ernst Röhm, *Die Geschichte eines Hochverräters* (Munich, 1928), pp. 158-229. Ernst Deuerlein, *Der Hitler-Putsch; Bayerische Dokumente zum 9. November 1923* (Stuttgart, 1961).

Socialists by the middle-class parties, and constant Communist pressure, combined to drive Thuringia steadily toward the left. By 1923 the state began to drift into open opposition to the central government in Berlin. In March, Frölich justified in the diet the formation of proletarian defense organizations which, he said, were necessary as long as right-wing fighting leagues were permitted to operate freely.[7] During the month of May the Socialist ministers entered into negotiations with the Communists in an attempt to form a coalition government, but the negotiations collapsed on May 26 because Communist demands proved unacceptable to the government. Five days later the KPD moved a vote of no confidence which was defeated only after the middle-class parties refused to support the motion, although they expressly declared that the government did not possess their confidence either.[8]

Throughout the subsequent weeks, Communist pressure to force the resignation of the Frölich government increased. By August 4, the middle-class parties decided to force the issue, and in their turn introduced in the diet a motion of no confidence against the Frölich ministry. A vote on this motion was postponed until September 11, however, presumably because the diet adjourned for summer vacation. The Socialists attempted during this period of grace to regain Communist support, but their efforts were in vain. When the day of decision approached, the KPD delegation joined with the middle-class parties in voting the Frölich government out of office. The Socialist government resigned, but it proved impossible to form a new one. Frölich and his colleagues continued to take care of the affairs of state and at the same time resumed their negotiations with the Communists, whose primary objective it was to impose a proletarian dictatorship upon Thuringia. This was to be a first step toward the creation of a "red bloc" in central Germany, consisting of Saxony, Thuringia, and Brunswick. The Socialist ministers faced a serious dilemma. None of the three party-blocs could form a government without support from one of the other two. The middle-class parties had initiated the ouster of the Frölich cabinet, with the aid of the Communists; in addition, the middle-class parties had moved to dissolve the diet, although no vote on that motion was taken. As it was quite unlikely that the

[7] *Schulthess'*, 1923, p. 65.   [8] *ibid.*, p. 103.

Socialists could come to terms with the middle-class parties, their only remaining hope was an agreement with the Communists with whom they had likewise been feuding for months, and who had just secured the downfall of their government. A deadlock ensued which continued for weeks. That it was eventually broken was largely due to the presidential decree of September 26, by which Thuringia was placed under the jurisdiction of General Walther Reinhardt, commander of the Fifth German military district. Constant altercations arose between the general and the caretaker government of Frölich. The ministers protested because Reinhardt insisted on his own prior approval of any political demonstrations and the publication of any new newspapers. He also forbade Communist mass meetings, and repeatedly banned KPD publications, measures which the ministry resented. In turn, the general did not take kindly to the government's hostile attitude in regard to all so-called patriotic activities in Thuringia. He resented particularly the fact that the acting chief of the state police, *Ministerialdirektor* Brill, referred to patriotic organizations which had expressed a desire to celebrate a "German Day" as "national-socialist rabble." In short, though he too had justified grievances, there is little doubt that General Reinhardt's paternalism contributed, by mid-October, to the reconciliation of Frölich and his friends with the Thuringian Communists.[9]

Saxony was an even thornier problem than Thuringia. At the end of January 1923 the Saxon government, which was headed by right-wing Social Democrat Johann Wilhelm Buck, was compelled to resign after a vote of no confidence had been passed by a coalition of middle-class parties and Communists.[10] To justify their action the KPD charged that the Saxon Social Democrats had betrayed the workers by clandestine arrangements with the "counter-revolutionaries."[11] The entire maneuver was an obvious move to drive a wedge between the rank and file of the Saxon SPD and their leaders. A subsidiary motive seems to have been to split the Saxon Social Democrats, whose left wing was stronger than their

[9] Witzmann, *Thüringen von 1918-1933* (Meissenheim am Glain, 1958), pp. 88-94; *Schulthess'*, 1923, pp. 116, 167.

[10] *Schulthess'*, 1923, p. 22.

[11] *Bericht über die Verhandlungen des III. (8.) Parteitages der K.P.D. (Sektion der K.I.) abgehalten in Leipzig vom 28. Januar bis 1. Februar 1923* (Berlin, 1923), pp. 278, 407-408.

right one, in the hope of reaching a working agreement with the left wing, preliminary to the formation of a joint workers' government. The SPD held its regional party convention at Dresden on March 4 and 5. A majority rejected a right-wing motion to form a new government with the Democratic Party, and resolved to continue negotiations with the Communists in the hope of finding a basis for future cooperation. A mixed commission of the two workers' parties met on March 17 to work out directives for a common program, and two days later they announced the main points of a preliminary agreement. A new Saxon government would strengthen the power of the proletarian control commissions and would establish a chamber of labor. Furthermore, such a government would sponsor the formation of proletarian defense units which were to protect demonstrations, assemblies, and the property of the workers against "Fascist" attacks. Although the Communists declared that they would not join a new Saxon cabinet, they promised their support to a Socialist government if it followed the directive worked out and agreed upon by the joint commission. On March 21 the Saxon diet voted 49 to 46 to make Dr. Erich Zeigner, a left-wing Socialist, the new minister-president.[12]

Zeigner, formerly minister of justice in the Buck ministry, formed his new cabinet on April 10, and outlined his program in an address to the diet the same day. The speech, like the composition of the cabinet, showed a decided trend toward the left. The new Saxon minister-president criticized the central government's Ruhr policy and suggested to Berlin a course of moderation, and negotiations conducted on a reasonable basis. The German propertied classes would have to make sacrifices, and would have to pay their share of the costs which the French were liable to demand as a price for settlement of the Ruhr conflict. Zeigner announced that his government would do everything to speed up the transformation from private to collectivized economy. He followed up this promise with a bitter attack on the propertied classes, which fostered Fascist organizations in order to use them in their exploitation of German labor. To protect their lives and their interests, the working class would have to form defense units. Another blast was directed against the Reichswehr which, according to Zeigner, was turning

[12] *Schulthess'*, 1923, pp. 44, 54-55, 57.

into a threat to the republic, as were the numerous clandestine paramilitary organizations which the Reichswehr protected.[13]

Although Zeigner ended his speech with a profession of loyalty to the republic and a promise to keep his oath of office, in which he had sworn to defend the Saxon constitution, his accusations and veiled threats weighed heavier in the scales than did his closing statement, both inside and outside Saxony. But the tenor of his address went a long way toward pleasing the Communists. They could hardly help being overjoyed when the Saxon SPD leaders resolved on May 17, with the approval of the Zeigner government, to form joint proletarian defense organizations with the KPD.[14]

In the course of the summer, Zeigner's attacks against the central government became more frequent and progressively less restrained. On June 16, in a speech delivered at Niederplanitz, he repeated his charges against the Reichswehr, accused German industrialists of corrupt practices and profiteering, and lashed out sharply against the Cuno government. When this speech was debated in the Saxon diet on June 28, the chairman of the Democratic Party delegation, Dr. Seyfert, accused the minister-president of having talked treason, having incited the masses to class warfare, and having lowered German prestige in foreign states. But a motion of no confidence, introduced by the middle-class parties, was defeated 48 to 43.[15]

On July 11 the diet accepted a new communal administration for Saxony, by which the existing order was drastically changed. A new political "standard community" was created, former differences between large and small communities were eliminated, and the executive power, formerly held by mayors and city councilors, was transferred to the communal representatives. This reorganization was plainly designed to strengthen the political influence of the lower classes in the communities.[16]

Despite Zeigner's numerous concessions to the extreme left, he was not immune to attacks from that quarter. This was demon-

[13] *Verhandlungen des Sächsischen Landtages 1923*, 2. Wahlperiode, 1. Band, 29. Sitzung (April 10, 1923), 717-720; hereafter cited as *Verhandlungen des Sächsischen Landtages 1923*.
[14] *Schulthess'*, 1923, p. 103.
[15] *ibid.*, pp. 116, 122; *Verhandlungen des Sächsischen Landtages 1923*, II, pp. 1235-1237, 1243.
[16] *Schulthess'*, 1923, p. 130.

strated a day after the communal reorganization law was adopted, when Paul Böttcher, speaking for the KPD, called a recent visit which Zeigner had paid to Cuno a "walk to Canossa." Zeigner replied with dignity that, despite the differences of opinion which existed between the central government and that of Saxony, Saxon policies could not and would not be divorced from those of the republic as a whole. But he also repudiated charges, raised by the middle-class parties, that certain measures which his government had taken violated the spirit of the Weimar constitution. His entire speech reflected the precarious course which his government was pursuing. In trying to strike a balance between the demands of the workers and the middle class on the one hand, the interests of Saxony and those of the Reich on the other, Zeigner risked alienating all sides.[17]

With the beginning of August, as the national crisis was approaching its height, relations between Saxony and the Reich reached a new low. In a public speech on August 7, Zeigner repeated his assertion that a number of Reichswehr officers were anti-republican and a threat to the nation, because the Reichswehr maintained close relations with extreme right-wing organizations which had large arms depots at their disposal. These charges were reiterated a few days later in an article which he wrote for the *Sächsische Staatszeitung*. In response to Zeigner's attacks on the Reichswehr, the ministry for defense issued orders to the troops stationed in Saxony not to participate in any celebrations which the Saxon government planned to conduct on August 11, Constitution Day. The ministry also instructed all military personnel to refrain from maintaining direct contact, in any form, with the Saxon government, except in case of a public emergency. And on September 5 the ministry, in an official announcement, condemned and rejected Zeigner's charges against the military.[18]

Contrary to what might have been expected, the creation of a Great Coalition government after Cuno's resignation did not improve relations between Saxony and Berlin. Zeigner prohibited all celebrations of Sedan Day, which patriotic organizations in Saxony had scheduled for September 2. But on September 9 eight thousand workers gathered in Dresden for a muster of the proletarian de-

[17] *Verhandlungen des Sächsischen Landtages 1923*, II, pp. 1541, 1549-1551.
[18] *Schulthess'*, 1923, p. 161; Gessler, p. 257.

fense units. The formations drilled for two hours under the command of a minor Social Democratic official, who then addressed the workers' militia, telling them that the immediate future would show whether the republic could be saved. It was quite possible, he said, that very soon a decisive struggle would begin between the political right and left, a struggle in which each side would try to establish a dictatorship. If this showdown should come, it would be the task of the proletarian defense forces to fight in behalf of a dictatorship of the left. The muster ended with the units avowing, in chorus: "We all shall stand firmly together, as comrades united, come what may!"[19]

The Saxon question was discussed during a Reichstag caucus of the People's Party delegation on September 11. Chancellor Stresemann attended the meeting. A representative from Saxony described the local political conditions, and claimed that Saxon industries no longer received any business from outside the state on account of Zeigner's radicalism. If businessmen elsewhere in Germany considered it too risky to entrust the manufacture of their goods to Saxon factories, half of the working population of this state would soon be unemployed. He predicted that both Saxony and Thuringia would turn to Communism unless the federal government soon took some energetic measures to counter this dangerous trend. A representative from Thuringia fully endorsed the opinion of his Saxon colleague, emphasizing especially that the economy of his state was being terrorized by the proletarian hundreds.[20]

Throughout the spring and summer of 1923, the German Communists had watched the Saxon situation closely. The arrangement between the party and the Zeigner government proved on the whole satisfactory to the KPD. In contrast to the situation in Prussia, Bavaria, and most other German states, the party's freedom of movement was unrestricted in Saxony. Here the Communists

[19] *Schulthess'*, 1923, pp. 162, 166-167.
[20] Stresemann, *Vermächtnis*, I, p. 117. That Stresemann received at the time similar complaints from Saxon citizens, notably from members of the German People's Party, is evident from the correspondence found in his *Nachlass*. See Stresemann Nachlass, "Dieckmann to Stresemann, August 24, 1923," Auswärtiges Amt, Germany, microfilm, container 3158, frames H 171288-171292, National Archives, Washington, D.C.; "Stresemann's secretary (Henry Bernhard?) to Ernst S. Clauss, September 5, 1923," *ibid.*, container 3099, frames H 145890-145891; "Moras to Stresemann, September 22, 1923," *ibid.*, container 3104, frames H 154097-154098.

could train their proletarian hundreds unhampered by suspicious, or even hostile, police forces. But they were not blind to the dangers which their Saxon sanctuary posed. Before the formation of the Zeigner cabinet, Communist activities had been largely confined to the parliamentary arena. After their agreement with the new government in March, however, their activities extended beyond this sphere and included, for instance, the formation of joint proletarian defense corps. From then on they were, so to speak, on parade. Every move which they made in Saxony was open to the scrutiny of a suspicious public, a watchful central government, and a hostile array of nationalist organizations throughout the country.[21]

The unique position which the party faced in Saxony (and to a lesser extent in Thuringia as well) remained a disputed issue within the KPD during the better part of 1923. The majority of the *Zentrale* believed that if constant Communist pressure were brought against the Zeigner government and the left wing of the SPD, on which the government was largely based, the Saxon Social Democratic Party would eventually disintegrate. The Communists could speed up this process by leading and intensifying the pressure for a change in the social order—a pressure already emanating from the desperate masses. At the decisive moment, the Saxon government would have to decide whether to join the masses in an all-out struggle against the bourgeoisie, or to draw back and thereby to destroy the last illusions still harbored by Socialist workers about the sincerity of their leaders. This view was rejected by the Left Opposition, whose members demanded the overthrow of the Zeigner government whenever the party came into conflict with the Saxon Social Democrats. The dispute over this issue lasted throughout the summer and part of autumn. It was only settled in October and, like most of the fundamental differences which divided the party at the time, it was settled from and by Moscow.[22]

Foreign political difficulties, the paper mark still falling in value, ominous developments in Bavaria, Thuringia, and Saxony—these were the principal problems which Stresemann faced during his

[21] See Paul Böttcher, "The Attack on the Strategic Positions of the Saxon Proletariat," *Inprecorr*, III, No. 36 (May 9, 1923), pp. 322-333, for a contemporary assessment of these dangers.

[22] *Bericht über die Verhandlungen des IX. Parteitages der K.P.D. (Sektion der K.I.) abgehalten in Frankfurt am Main vom 7. bis 10. April 1924* (Berlin, 1924), p. 20.

first weeks in office. And these were not all. From September 14 to 24 the southwestern part of Baden was rocked by a series of wage riots, which for a while threatened to spread throughout the entire state. The upper-Badensian Wiesental, close to the Swiss border, was part of the demilitarized zone which lacked adequate police protection. The region was also suffering from large-scale unemployment. The KPD in upper Baden had been able to enlist many new members during the summer of 1923, but had not succeeded in organizing its new recruits, or in controlling them adequately. On September 14 an action committee of factory workers, with the blessings of the local Communist organization, called a general strike at Lörrach which led to demonstrations in the streets and demands for higher wages. These were granted, and the movement might have died down had not the Baden government grown panicky. The state's ministry of the interior despatched a special police force to Lörrach on September 17, a move which at once rekindled violence and led to armed clashes between demonstrators and police. New strikes, called in Lörrach proper and in the surrounding towns, soon led to street fights. What had started as a largely spontaneous movement, set off by economic grievances, threatened to turn into serious riots which were encouraged and supported by local Communist organizations. The *Zentrale*, however, had no desire to have an isolated uprising in a remote corner of Germany jeopardize the Communist party as a whole, merely because some of its local branches were lacking in discipline. Thus when the party's Baden organization called a statewide general strike, which had not been authorized beforehand by the *Zentrale*, the latter sent orders from Berlin to avoid every act which could conceivably lead to any further clashes with the police. This interference by the *Zentrale*, coupled with the promise of the Baden government to withdraw its forces as soon as quiet and order were restored, brought the upheaval in Baden to a halt. By September 25 the strikes and demonstrations were over.[23]

Nearly simultaneously with the Baden uprising, the Separatist

[23] Germany, Kriegsgeschichtliche Forschungsanstalt des Heeres, *Darstellungen aus den Nachkriegskämpfen deutscher Truppen und Freikorps*, v, *Die Kämpfe in Südwestdeutschland, 1919-1923* (Berlin, 1939), pp. 110-118; Habedank, *Zur Geschichte des Hamburger Aufstandes 1923* (Berlin, 1958), pp. 45-48; Wenzel, "Die K.P.D. im Jahre 1923" (unpubl. diss. Freie Universität Berlin, 1955), pp. 203-205.

movement in the Rhineland threatened to erupt in full force. Public meetings, protected by the French occupation forces, were held by the Separatists toward the middle of the month in Aachen. Large-scale demonstrations in Cologne, Trier, Wiesbaden, and Aachen on September 23 and 24, under the leadership of Adam Dorten, Joseph Matthes, and Joseph Smeets, led to street fighting with the local population. The Separatist movement, though frequently violent and enjoying underhanded French support, never became strong enough to pose a serious threat to the republic. Its followers were rather confused; they were led by what an American scholar has called "an assorted group of criminals,"[24] and their cause found little sympathy among the Rhenish population.[25] But during the last two weeks of September the disturbances in the Rhineland added to the dangers which the central government faced, and therefore contributed to the pressures which finally prompted Stresemann to terminate passive resistance, and to impose a state of emergency throughout Germany.[26]

The positive factors at work in this period seem at first sight to have been eclipsed by the more obvious calamities. Nevertheless, positive aspects there were. They operated very subtly, and it is difficult to gauge their influence on the nation with any accuracy. Probably the most important factor, and one which was recognized by the Communists several months later, was the impact of the Great Coalition on the mass of Social Democratic workers:[27] the fact that their party was prominently represented in the cabinet undoubtedly strengthened their confidence in the government of the Great Coalition.

Closely connected with this factor was the stormy relationship between Bavaria and the Reich, which in its effects on the nation was not entirely negative. Whereas the Communists were trying

[24] Waite, *Vanguard of Nazism* (Cambridge, Mass., 1952), p. 234.

[25] Severing, *Mein Lebensweg*, I (Cologne, 1950), pp. 435-436; *Schulthess'*, 1923, pp. 171, 176; for a longer, though biased account see Spethmann, *Zwölf Jahre Ruhrbergbau 1914-1925: Der Ruhrkampf 1923-1925*, vol. IV of 4 vols. (Berlin, 1930), pp. 212-238. Ulbricht, *Zur Geschichte der deutschen Arbeiterbewegung*, I (Berlin, 1953), pp. 131-132, claims that the Separatists were led by Dr. Konrad Adenauer, and defeated by the Communists.

[26] Stresemann, *Vermächtnis*, I, 113-114; this reference to the Separatist threat was made as early as September 7, 1923, and reflects Stresemann's genuine concern even at this early stage.

[27] See EKKI, *Die Lehren der deutschen Ereignisse* (Hamburg, 1924), pp. 40-41; Thalheimer, *1923: Eine verpasste Revolution?*, (Berlin, 1931), p. 10.

to create the impression that the Bavarian "Fascists," the enemies of the working class, were in some sinister way connected with the national government and the entire German "ruling class," events in Bavaria clearly invalidated this view. It did not require superior intelligence on the part of the public, including the by no means insensitive or illiterate German workers, to notice that the most vitriolic attacks emanating from Bavaria were reserved for the national government and the republic as such. As the majority of German labor either belonged to, or at least supported, the SPD, which, in turn, was in the Great Coalition, only devoted Communists could fail to realize that the national government and the workers stood side by side in defense of the republic against the various anti-republican forces in the south.[28]

Hopeful signs appeared also on the economic front. The grain harvest proved to be above average in yield, thereby alleviating fears of an insufficient bread supply.[29] With regard to the most pressing problem, the monetary inflation, the Stresemann government displayed more imagination and initiative than had the Cuno administration. As early as August 14, one day after the new chancellor had formed his cabinet, a law was passed to float "a loan of fixed value" (*wertbeständige Anleihe*), designed to make the sum of five hundred million gold marks available for public expenditure.[30] To be sure, this step had no immediate effect on the inflation, for the value of the paper mark continued to drop at an alarming rate. But the measure demonstrated that the government was resolutely trying to stop the devaluation of the currency. In the meantime, while various schemes to that effect were investigated and tried, one of the most pressing problems was the adjustment of wages to the cost of living. Here an agreement, concluded on August 23 between representatives of the working class and of employers, proved at least temporarily beneficial. The agreement attempted to establish a method of payment by which the falling

[28] One devoted Communist who did not share his party's view on this matter was Heinrich Brandler; see *Die Lehren der deutschen Ereignisse*, p. 33.

[29] *Schulthess'*, 1923, p. 192. The announcement was made by the Prussian Minister of Agriculture in the diet on October 12, 1923; but the abundant yield must have been apparent earlier, during harvest time, in July and August. It should be noted, though, that the reluctance of the peasants to sell their potatoes for nearly worthless paper money somewhat offset the good grain harvest. Information Gordon, letter of April 2, 1962.

[30] Rolf E. Lüke, *Von der Stabilisierung zur Krise* (Zürich, 1959), p. 9.

value of the mark was taken into account: wages were to be fixed on the basis of the prices expected to exist in the week when these wages would be spent. For this purpose a "multiplier," deduced from the exchange rate of the dollar at Berlin on the day the wages were paid, had to be calculated on the basis of forecast prices. If a forecast proved inaccurate, it could be corrected by either supplementing the wages, or deducting from them, the following week. Unfortunately, the system proved to be far from foolproof but, uneven though it was in practice, it had a salutary effect on the morale of wage earners.[31] On September 2 Stresemann announced in a public speech his intention of creating a new and sound currency, and from then on the government devoted its energies to this problem.[32] In mid-October it issued a decree for the creation of a *Rentenbank*, and with it a *Rentenmark*, a measure signifying the definite and final assault upon the inflation.[33]

Germany, then, presented a complex and confusing picture in the fall of 1923. Hopes and fears, loyalties and defections, unifying and particularist trends, revolutionary threats from right- and left-wing extremists—all appeared to be operative at the same time, intermixing and bewildering, without providing any clue as to where the nation was going in the days ahead. Under these circumstances it is easy to see why the Bolshevik leaders mistook Cuno's resignation for a sign of Germany's impending collapse, and laid their plans accordingly.[34]

Bolshevik leaders had watched the troubled country for months without having made any decisive move in the direction of a Communist revolution. Preoccupied as they were with their own factional strifes and the anticipation of Lenin's death, they had been marking time and, at the meeting of the Enlarged Executive in June, had not even bothered to discuss the situation in Germany except in very general terms.[35] After the meeting was over, most of the top-

[31] Bresciani-Turroni, *The Economics of Inflation* (London, 1937), p. 310; Wenzel, pp. 211-212.

[32] *Schulthess'*, 1923, p. 164.

[33] Lüke, pp. 16-20; Hjalmar Horace Greeley Schacht, *Confessions of "The Old Wizard"* (Boston, 1956), pp. 162-166; Bresciani-Turroni, pp. 334-349.

[34] For an excellent study of Stresemann's policies during the crucial months of his chancellorship see Erich Heinz Schlottner, *Stresemann, der Kapp Putsch und die Ereignisse in Mitteldeutschland und in Bayern im Herbst 1923; ein Beitrag zur Geschichte der Weimarer Republik* (diss. Frankfurt am Main, 1948).

[35] Thalheimer, *1923: Eine verpasste Revolution?*, p. 20; Hermann Remmele, "The

ranking members of the Politburo and the ECCI had gone on vacation.

It was at their remote retreats in southern Russia that Zinoviev and Trotsky learned about the apparently mounting crisis in Germany. Zinoviev, it will be recalled, had already been stirred in the latter part of July by the plans for the anti-Fascist day. Now, only a fortnight later, he learned of the Cuno strike and of the formation of Stresemann's Great Coalition government. Whatever the exact source or the nature of his information may have been, the news prompted Zinoviev on August 15 to communicate to Moscow that the KPD should take stock of the approaching revolutionary crisis, because "a new and decisive chapter is beginning in the activity of the German Communist Party and, with it, the Comintern."[36]

Equally enthusiastic was Trotsky's reaction to the news from Germany. In the written exchanges which preceded the anti-Fascist day, Trotsky had refused to commit himself because he lacked sufficient information at his holiday retreat to make a decision.[37] But after he learned about the Cuno strike and the new Stresemann government, he reached the conclusion that developments in Germany were, indeed, pointing toward a domestic crisis which the KPD ought to exploit. Eager to receive additional information, he invited two members of the German party, August Enderle and Jakob Walcher, to visit him at once in southern Russia. The two men were then serving as KPD delegates to the executive committee of the Profintern, and were for this reason stationed in Moscow. At the end of the conversation Trotsky sent one of the two men, probably Walcher, back to Berlin, presumably to act as his contact man and on-the-spot observer.[38]

Proletarian Struggle for Power in Germany," *The Communist International*, New Series, I, No. 2 (n.d.), p. 29.

[36] Quoted in Carr, *The Interregnum 1923-1924* (New York, 1954), p. 201.

[37] *ibid.*, pp. 186-187; Issac Deutscher, *The Prophet Unarmed: Trotsky 1921-1929* (London-New York-Toronto, 1959), p. 142.

[38] The events of this visit are given by Wenzel (p. 179) whose account is based on personal information which he obtained from Enderle in 1952. While one may accept the fact that the visit as such occurred, Enderle's version of it sounds unconvincing. According to his story, Trotsky sent instructions to the German *Zentrale*, demanding that the German leaders prepare the party for an impending insurrection. Trotsky also promised the *Zentrale* that he would send the Red Army to assist the KPD as soon as a revolution in Germany was under way. This story does not ring true. First of all, even if Trotsky should have initially toyed with the idea of a

Revolution in Preparation

During the following week the Russian leaders broke off their vacations and returned to Moscow. On August 23 the Politburo met for a secret session which was also attended by Radek, Pyatakov—then deputy chairman of the economic supreme council—and possibly Tsyurupa, subsequently president of the Gosplan.[39]

---

possible military intervention by Russian forces, it is very doubtful that he would have committed himself to such a course of action on the spur of the moment, and in front of two visiting delegates from another country. It is equally hard to believe that he would have "alerted" the KPD for an *Aktion* without having discussed the matter first with his colleagues in the ECCI and the Politburo. Furthermore, Trotsky's subsequent attitude indicates that he did not intend to risk a war with Poland, and possibly with the Western Allies as well, by sending Russian troops into Germany (Carr, *The Interregnum*, pp. 215-219; cf. Wenzel, p. 189, who holds the opposite view but has given no substantiating evidence to back it up). Finally, according to an unsigned, undated, and unfortunately unsubstantiated report which the German Embassy in Moscow sent to Berlin, Trotsky expressed his opposition to Russian military interference, in case of a German revolution, in the course of a meeting held by a group of Bolshevik leaders in Trotsky's home on September 22, 1923. According to this report, Trotsky was only prepared to support such a revolution indirectly, by propaganda, money, and grain deliveries ("German Embassy to Foreign Office," Auswärtiges Amt, Germany, microfilm, container 911, frames 378974-378975; the incident is also mentioned in Hilger and Meyer, *The Incompatible Allies* [New York, 1953], pp. 122-123, n. 13).

For Walcher's report concerning his stay in Moscow see *Die Rote Fahne*, No. 207, September 14, 1923. In the report Walcher made it a point to deny rumors to the effect that Radek had been in Germany during the summer months of 1923. Radek, according to the report, had been the only one in charge of handling the affairs of the Comintern since mid-July because Zinoviev and Bukharin were then on vacation. Walcher's statement concerning Radek's whereabouts during the summer of 1923 is in general agreement with whatever other sources of information are extant on this matter. Thus, according to a communication which Prussian Minister of the Interior Carl Severing sent to the German Embassy in Moscow on September 5, 1923, Radek had been in Germany in December 1922, and at the time had incurred the displeasure of the Prussian government. Severing complained that Radek nevertheless was granted another visa from the German Embassy in Moscow. It was valid from May 5 through August 6, 1923. Radek returned to Berlin early in May, stayed for about a month, and departed for Moscow sometime during the first half of June. Severing added that he did not know whether or not Radek had since returned to Germany, but implored the German Embassy in Moscow not to grant him another visa. A similar request was made by the Federal Minister of the Interior Wilhelm Sollmann on September 19, 1923 ("Severing to Foreign Office, with copy to German Embassy in Moscow, September 5, 1923," Auswärtiges Amt, Germany, microfilm, container 911, frames 378942-378944; "Sollmann to Foreign Office, with copy to German Embassy, Moscow, September 19, 1923," *ibid.*, frames 378945-378946).

For some unknown reason, the official party record lists only Enderle as a delegate to the Profintern during this period. See *Bericht über die Verhandlungen des IX. Parteitages*, p. 45.

[39] The only known eyewitness account of this session is in Boris Bajanov, *Avec Staline dans le Kremlin* (Paris, 1930), pp. 190-198. Bajanov was at the time secretary to the Politburo, and while his judgments "are of little value . . . his facts generally fit in with what is otherwise known" (Carr, *The Interregnum*, p. 201, n.3).

According to the only existing account of this session, Radek, the ECCI expert on Germany, presented what appears to have been an optimistic report on the rapid increase of revolutionary sentiment in that country, and asked the members of the Politburo for their comments. If this story is true—and we have only one man's record of it—it again throws a peculiar light on Radek's character. He may have sounded optimistic, but his subsequent behavior would indicate that his heart was not in the report he presented. During the weeks of negotiations that followed, he generally favored a cautious approach to the German problem, an attitude indicative of barely concealed scepticism as to the chances of a successful revolution.[40] Such a position was indeed well in line with his article of August 2, in which he told the German Communists that the time for revolution had not yet come.[41] On the other hand, Radek was not the man openly to oppose the general consensus of opinion, especially at a moment when the Bolshevik leaders, under the shadow of Lenin's illness, were engaged in a bitter, though still subdued and premature, struggle for power. Thus it is conceivable that when he realized how strong an impression the Cuno strike had made, especially on Trotsky and Zinoviev, two men otherwise unable to agree on virtually anything, Radek would not have been Radek had he tried openly to oppose them. His forte was equivocation and subtle maneuver rather than frontal assault, and it is quite likely that at this session Radek presented a report which expressed the beliefs of his audience rather than his own, hidden, viewpoint.

In the ensuing discussion Trotsky spoke first, and warmly advocated that the KPD be encouraged to prepare for revolution. To the inventor and chief exponent of "permanent revolution," the allegedly mounting revolutionary tide in Germany promised to justify the theory, which he had always maintained, of the close interrelation between the Russian and German revolutions. This theory he briefly reiterated at the meeting, and he closed with the

---

Both Carr and Wenzel (p. 180, n.26) accept Bajanov's account, and so do I, although with some misgivings. As to Tsyurupa's presence, Bajanov writes (p. 191): "Outre les membres titulaires et suppléants du Politburo, il y avait à cette séance trois membres du Comité central, Radek, Piatakov, et, si je ne me trompe, Tsiouroupa, qui, modestement, n'ouvrit pas la bouche."

[40] Carr, *The Interregnum*, p. 205.
[41] See above, Ch. XI.

prediction that a showdown in Germany was now only a matter of weeks.[42]

Zinoviev generally concurred with Trotsky's views, but did not share his optimism in regard to the time factor. Counseling prudence and soberness, he suggested that it would be safer to think in terms of months rather than weeks. Only Stalin, who spoke very briefly, voiced scepticism as to the imminence of a German upheaval. He doubted that it would occur in the fall, and was even dubious about its chances in the following spring.

Despite these differences of opinion, the Politburo decided to proceed without delay to a number of measures designed to stimulate the nascent revolutionary movement in Germany. A committee of four was appointed by the Politburo and charged with the preparations for, and subsequent supervision of, the German *Aktion*. It consisted of Radek, who as the representative of the ECCI was to keep in close touch with the *Zentrale* of the KPD; Pyatakov, who was put in charge of "agitation" and was also to maintain contact with Moscow; Unshlikht, then a high-ranking official of the secret police (later deputy commissar for war), whose task it was to supervise the formation of "red army" detachments in Germany; and finally Vasilij Shmidt, commissar of labor, who was commissioned with the organization of revolutionary cells in the German trade-unions.[43]

A fifth, though apparently "informal," member of the committee, who was added to the original four shortly after the secret session, was Nikolai Krestinsky, the Soviet Union's Ambassador to Germany. He was entrusted with the management of secret funds which were channeled into Germany during this period to finance the preparations for revolution.[44]

The reasons for this abrupt about-face on the part of the Russian leaders have puzzled historians ever since the autumn of 1923. It

[42] On Trotsky's inherent faith in the coming of the German revolution see also Carr, *The Interregnum*, pp. 201-202.

[43] Bajanov, pp. 195-196; Wenzel, pp. 193-194. Wenzel's account is based in part on personal information received from Erich Wollenberg, who in 1923 was in command of one of the six military districts which the KPD established prior to the projected insurrection. Fischer, *Stalin and German Communism* (Cambridge, Mass., 1948), p. 323, mentions Radek and Shmidt, but substitutes August Guralsky-Kleine and Alexis Skoblevsky for Pyatakov and Unshlikht. Boris Souvarine, *Staline* (Paris, 1935), p. 316, mentions only Radek and Pyatakov.

[44] Bajanov, pp. 195, 199-200.

has been suggested that Stresemann's appointment to the chancellorship was interpreted in Moscow as a possible German move to come to terms with the West, at the expense of her still very recent and tenuous ties with Soviet Russia.[45] This may well have been an important consideration, but the most decisive factor seems to have been the encouraging news from Germany, with its prospects of a "second October."[46] Throughout the weeks of deliberation which followed the initial decision to support an uprising of the German Communist party, the Bolshevik leaders inevitably invoked their own revolution, drew comparisons from it, and set it up as an example.[47] The historical parallel which they thought they had detected kept them spellbound, and blinded them to the fact that Germany was not Russia, that 1923 was not 1917, and that the German *Zentrale* had neither a Lenin nor a Trotsky. Hard realists though they were in every other respect, they turned into sentimental dreamers at the thought that the greatest event of their lives might soon be re-enacted under their experienced guidance, marking another milestone on the road to worldwide Socialism.

The excitement stimulated among the Bolshevik leaders by their anticipation of the German revolution also communicated itself to the Russian people. Meetings were held throughout the country by Russian labor organizations and workers in local factories to debate the importance of the coming German events, and to vote resolutions to support their proletarian brothers in the West. Such resolutions, moreover, were not mere formalities. Russian workers were expected by the government to make genuine sacrifices in behalf of the German revolution. Thus, according to the records of the ECCI, "the Russian working-classes agreed to suspend the increase of their wages and to submit to reductions if it were necessary in the interest of the German revolution."[48] The workers were told that a defeat of the German proletariat would constitute a defeat of the

[45] Carr, *The Interregnum*, p. 203; Fischer, pp. 312, 316; Eudin and Fisher, *Soviet Russia and the West 1920-1927* (Stanford, 1957), pp. 179-180.

[46] See Wenzel, pp. 175-176, 178, 182; however, Wenzel's subsidiary thesis that the Russians tried to divert attention from their own economic difficulties by trying to foster a revolution in Germany is a specious argument. See also Thalheimer, *1923: Eine verpasste Revolution?*, pp. 12-13.

[47] Thalheimer, *1923: Eine verpasste Revolution?*, p. 21.

[48] Communist Party of Great Britain, *From the Fourth to the Fifth World Congress: Report of the Executive Committee of the Communist International* (London, 1924), p. 12.

Russian workers as well. Women were asked at public meetings to donate their wedding rings and other valuables for the German cause.[49] The Trade Commissariat distributed circulars which stated that "the advent of the German revolution confronted the Trade Commissariat with new problems; the present routine of trading must be replaced by the establishment of two German reserves: gold and corn, for the benefit of the victorious German proletariat"; and the various agencies of this Commissariat within the individual soviet republics were ordered to send altogether sixty million *pud* of grain toward Russia's western frontiers.[50] The Russian Communist Party, by orders of the Politburo, drew up lists of members who spoke German, in order to create a Communist-trained reserve corps which could, at the appropriate moment, be transferred to Germany where it would assist the revolution.[51] Special attention was paid to the mobilization of Russia's Communist youth organizations, whose members were told that they might have to risk their lives on behalf of the German proletariat and the cause of revolution.[52] In October, revolutionary slogans were coined: "Workers' Germany and our Workers' and Peasants' Union Are the Bulwark of Peace and Labor," and "German Steam Hammer and Soviet Bread Will Conquer the World." And Soviet newspapers wrote that, if the German workers were successful, the new German government would join with Soviet Russia and thereby "unite in Europe the tremendous power of 200 million people, against which no war in Europe will be possible . . . because no one would be able to face such a force."[53]

It was to this scene of ebullition and fantasy that Heinrich Brandler, a man not easily given to romantic illusions, was summoned—for discussions of a German revolution which his Bolshevik hosts not only expected him to launch, but which to their minds was already as good as won. Brandler arrived in Moscow sometime during the latter part of August or the first part of September—the exact date has never been determined, and probably never will be.[54] He was

---

[49] Wenzel, p. 192.

[50] Bessedovsky, *Revelations of a Soviet Diplomat* (London, 1931), p. 62. One *pud* = 36.113 lbs.

[51] *ibid.*, p. 63; Bajanov, p. 200.

[52] Wenzel, p. 192.

[53] Quotes in Eudin and Fisher, p. 180.

[54] Brandler stated at the Fifth World Congress of the Comintern that he spent four weeks in Moscow. Since he returned to Germany sometime during the first

followed in due course by Maslow, Thälmann, and Ruth Fischer. In addition, Edwin Hoernle and Clara Zetkin, two members of the *Zentrale* who belonged to the Brandler faction, were stationed in Moscow at the time as delegates of the KPD to the Executive Committee of the Comintern.[55]

Brandler was in a peculiar and difficult position.[56] He had been called to Moscow for consultations in connection with the projected German revolution. Another man might have cherished the idea that he was to be cast in the role of a martial people's tribune. But the role did not fit Brandler, and he knew it. The greatest virtue of this sober, cautious, and essentially shrewd ex-union official was his sense of responsibility and proportion. This quality had failed him only once, in March 1921, and the memory of that fiasco had served to strengthen his aversion to gambling. And now, only two and a half years after the abortive March uprising, he was in Moscow to prepare for what he was convinced would be another gamble, with the odds stacked once more against the party to which he was dedicated. On the other hand, Moscow was the capital of the revolutionary motherland, and here, for weeks on end, Brandler was exposed to the pressure and influence of men whom every Communist in the world acknowledged as prophets and veterans of the revolutionary cause. When he stepped out of the Kremlin he found the streets bedecked with slogans welcoming the German revolution.[57] No wonder that he was torn between the demands made upon him and his own bitter forebodings, that he began to act inconsistently, and that he eventually faltered.

During the drawn-out negotiations which lasted until the first week of October, Brandler was gradually worn down by the arguments of the Bolshevik leaders and by his own colleagues, the members of the Left Opposition. The latter presented the German situation in a light which reflected their own wishful thinking rather than reality. Conditions in Germany, according to their estimates, favored a Communist revolution in the near future. Their views on this mat-

---

week of October 1923, he must have arrived in Moscow early in September. However, Brandler may have used the term "four weeks" loosely, and may have stayed a month, or even longer (*Fifth Congress of the Communist International, Abridged Report of Meetings Held at Moscow June 17th to July 8th, 1924* [London, n.d.], p. 65).

[55] *Bericht über die Verhandlungen des IX. Parteitages*, p. 45.

[56] *ibid.*

[57] Fischer, p. 312.

ter were shared to varying degrees by Trotsky, Zinoviev, and the majority of the Politburo.[58] The decisive factor which determined their views was not so much the political uncertainties which the Stresemann government had to face, though these, of course, entered into their calculations, but rather their optimism in regard to the influence which the Communists would be able to exert over German labor in a revolutionary situation. It was Zinoviev in particular who played a rather curious numbers' game. He wrote, in October 1923, "in the cities the workers are definitely numerically superior [to the rest of the population]," and "the forthcoming German revolution will be a proletarian class revolution. The *twenty-two million* German workers who make up its army represent the cornerstone of the international proletariat." Finally, in a euphoric lapse of all commonsense, he stated that "in the forthcoming decisive events, *seven million* agricultural workers will exercise a great influence on the countryside."[59]

Overwhelmed by such buoyant confidence in the chances for a successful German revolution, Brandler began to yield. He did so despite his secret doubts as to the wisdom of the projected uprising. Only a few weeks earlier he had warned the party that the distribution of strength was not yet in favor of the Communists, and that they must work harder than ever to tip the scales in their direction. Now, under duress, he bowed before the superior knowledge and experience of the Bolshevik veterans who, moreover, were strengthened in their optimism by the members of the Left Opposition. Brandler acknowledged that a revolution could and should be attempted, and that seizure of power by the Communists would be "a fully practicable task," though he added that it would be "more complicated and difficult" to retain power.[60]

[58] Carr, *The Interregnum*, p. 204.

[59] The quotes are extracts from a series of articles entitled "Problems of the German Revolution," reproduced in Eudin and Fisher, p. 214. The italics are mine.

[60] Quoted in Carr, *The Interregnum*, p. 205. The account of Brandler's attitude is based on *ibid.*, pp. 204-205; Wenzel, pp. 181-182; Deutscher, *The Prophet Unarmed*, pp. 142-143. All three authors have interviewed Brandler and have received the identical information. Brandler's reluctance has also been confirmed by Paul Frölich, in a letter to Dr. Wenzel in June 1952 (Wenzel, p. 181, n.29). Thalheimer (*1923: Eine verpasste Revolution?*, pp. 21, 29) also confirms Brandler's stand, with particular reference to the question concerning the entry of Communists into the Saxon government. Finally, Brandler publicly voiced his regret over ever having consented to enter the Saxon cabinet (*Fifth Congress of the Communist International, Abridged Report*, p. 65).

These accounts are contradicted by Wilhelm Pieck who charged, in 1925, that

But although Brandler consented to the feasibility of a revolution in principle, he remained a stumbling-block whenever the planning reached a point where a practical, concrete issue was involved. Of these there were several, all interrelated, and every one led to heated arguments.

The point of departure for the revolution was to be Saxony. Here was a government which for months had cooperated with the Communists, had tolerated, and even actively supported, the formation of proletarian hundreds, and which was not averse to a workable government coalition with the KPD. Zeigner was a left-wing Social Democrat, suspect to the right wing of his party, but he enjoyed popular support in his state. The Russians, and notably Zinoviev, believed that the Communists should enter this government, and from their strategic position lay the groundwork for an armed uprising. The problem was subsequently put most succinctly by Radek.

"The proletariat concentrates its strength [*marschiert auf*] in Saxony, taking its start from the defense of the workers' government, into which we enter; and it will attempt in Saxony to use the state power in order to arm itself and to form, in this restricted proletarian province of central Germany, a wall between the southern counter-revolution in Bavaria and the Fascism of the north. At the same time the party throughout the Reich will step in and mobilize the masses."[61]

The key words emphasized by the Russians were "[the proletariat] will attempt in Saxony to use the state power in order to arm itself." This, according to Brandler, was putting the cart before the horse. Brandler argued that it would be a mistake to enter the Saxon cabinet before the country, including Saxony, was politically prepared for an uprising which a Communist-infiltrated government in Sax-

---

"Brandler, during his stay in Moscow, in September [1923], made the mistake of giving a wrong picture of the German situation, and of the forces and possibilities of a revolutionary rising (*Die Kommunistische Internationale*, vi, No. 11, [1925], p. 1203). Ruth Fischer, writing in a similar vein (p. 314), has charged that Brandler misrepresented the German situation to the Russians, as a result of which the Left Opposition had "to modify his picture with a more sober survey." But as late as January 11, 1924, Ruth Fischer defended the theory that the situation in the fall of 1923 was uniquely suited for a revolution, and she did so before the assembled presidium of the ECCI (*Die Lehren der deutschen Ereignisse*, pp. 52-53). Both Freund (*Unholy Alliance* [New York, 1957], p. 176) and Wenzel (pp. 180-181) have challenged Ruth Fischer's subsequent interpretation of Brandler's motives.

[61] *Die Lehren der deutschen Ereignisse*, p. 5; I have used, with minor changes, the translation given in Carr, *The Interregnum*, p. 207.

ony might bring on much sooner than was desirable or prudent. The weapons, which such a coalition government was to obtain, would be useless if the masses were not yet properly prepared politically for a revolution, and, Brandler argued, such a government might not even have sufficient time for the procurement of arms if the Communists should enter the Saxon government prematurely. In short, Brandler disagreed with the Russians on the tactical purpose of entry into the Saxon government. The Russians saw only the weapons, while Brandler saw primarily the absence of the political and psychological preparedness of the masses prerequisite for a successful uprising. Entry into the Saxon government, in the opinion of Brandler, should not be undertaken on a coalition basis, and was not to serve primarily as a convenient means for the procurement of arms. Rather, the Communists should enter the Saxon cabinet only when they could be assured that such a step would have popular backing, which would make it possible to create a genuine workers' government. Once Saxony had a genuine workers' government, this could serve as a signal for revolution. By then the party could be reasonably sure of receiving substantial mass support, in Saxony as well as in Thuringia, and beyond, in the rest of the Reich.[62]

The problem of when the revolution was to be attempted proved equally knotty. Should a date be fixed, or should the proper moment be left to the discretion of the KPD? The foremost proponent for fixing an exact date was Trotsky, and his attitude seems to have been determined in part by his intense preoccupation with historical parallels. On September 23, 1923, Trotsky published an article in *Pravda* which he entitled "Is It Possible to Fix a Definite Schedule for a Counterrevolution or a Revolution?" Trotsky thought that it was.

"Obviously, it is not possible to create artificially a political situation favorable for a . . . coup, much less to bring it off at a fixed date. But when the basic elements of such a situation are at hand, then the leading party does . . . choose beforehand a favorable moment, and synchronizes accordingly its political, organizational, and

[62] The above account is based on Brandler's own analysis of the uprising as given in *Die Lehren der deutschen Ereignisse*, pp. 24-25; in *Bericht über die Verhandlungen des IX. Parteitages*, p. 246; and in *Fifth Congress of the Communist International, Abridged Report*, p. 65. See also Wenzel (pp. 181-182), whose account is based on an interview with Brandler in 1952, and *Die Lehren der deutschen Ereignisse*, pp. 42, 61-62, for Remmele's and Zinoviev's respective comments.

technical forces, and—if it has not miscalculated—deals the victorious blow. . . .

"Let us take our own October Revolution as an example. . . . From the moment that the Bolsheviks were in the majority in the Petrograd Soviet . . . our party was faced with the question—not of the struggle for power in general, but of preparing for the seizure of power according to a definite plan, and at a fixed date. The chosen day, as is well known, was the day upon which the All-Russian Congress of the Soviets was to convene. . . ."[63]

Armed with these arguments, the Father of the Red Army insisted on fixing a date for the outbreak of the German revolution. Over the protests of Brandler, whose misgivings were apparently shared by Radek, November 9 was chosen. It was a fine historical landmark. On November 7, 1917, the Russian Revolution began, and on November 9, 1918, the German revolution. At this point, however, Brandler balked and refused to be bound by any definite date. What resulted, judging from the very confusing and inconclusive evidence available, was a compromise. Zinoviev, who was then engaged in a fierce intraparty fight with Trotsky in connection with the struggle for succession to Lenin, stipulated that the date was to serve merely "for orientation," and that the uprising was to take place sometime during the next four to six weeks. As the deliberations took place at the end of September, early November remained, in principle, the target date. But no specific day was named—in this matter Brandler had been given some leeway.[64]

[63] Trotsky, *The First Five Years of the Communist International*, II (New York, 1953), pp. 347, 349-350.
[64] For the Russian intraparty struggle see Deutscher, *The Prophet Unarmed*, pp. 111-112, and *passim*; Leonard Schapiro, *The Communist Party of the Soviet Union* (New York, 1959), pp. 277-280. It appears from everything that is known about the fixing of a target date that the matter was never fully resolved even in the minds of those most directly affected. Ruth Fischer (pp. 316-317) claims that "Trotsky . . . proposed a time-table of events up to a climax on the 7th or 8th of November." Zinoviev then stepped in and, according to Miss Fischer, asked Brandler whether he objected on "principled grounds." When Brandler protested that he was "for the revolution," Trotsky's more rigid proposal was dropped, and the KPD was permitted to fix its own time for the uprising which, however, was expected to take place sometime during the following four to six weeks. Wenzel (pp. 182, incl. n.34, and 188, incl. n.1), basing his account on his personal interview with Brandler and on a letter from Paul Frölich, states that the date was and remained November 9, 1923, and that the KPD laid all its plans accordingly. But the date was known to only a few select members of the KPD leadership. Radek (in *Die Lehren der deutschen Ereignisse*, pp. 15-16) argued after the events that while it had been perfectly proper to set a target date for the projected uprising, such a date should not

Revolution in Preparation

Three additional questions had to be settled before the deliberations could be ended. The first one was raised by Brandler and concerned the supreme command of the projected German revolution. Brandler, as he himself put it, was not "a German Lenin," and he asked both Trotsky and Zinoviev whether the former could not be assigned to take charge of the German operations—to come incognito and establish himself either in Saxony or Berlin. Trotsky was tempted to go. He was at the time thoroughly disgusted by the infighting which took place, day after day and behind closed doors, among the Bolshevik leaders. But Brandler's request was rejected, presumably because Trotsky's enemies, notably Zinoviev and Stalin, preferred to hold him at home where he could be kept under surveillance. The commission of four which had originally been appointed remained in charge.[65]

The second question revolved around another historical parallel: should the outbreak of the revolution in Germany be accompanied by the immediate formation of soviets, on the Russian model, or should the movement rely instead on the factory councils which were already in existence and did not require special organizational efforts? Zinoviev argued in favor of soviets, but he was opposed by Trotsky and Brandler who, on this issue at least, won their point. Trotsky argued that the organization of soviets in the midst of revolutionary activities would merely handicap operations; their creation prior to the revolution would be a "dead giveaway" to the govern-

---

have been set in Moscow. He added that he had opposed this procedure at the time. Hermann Remmele (*ibid.*, pp. 41-42) stated that the "fixed date for the uprising could not be observed" because the entire scheme was upset by the entry of the Communists into the Saxon government. And Zinoviev said at the same occasion, i.e., the post-mortem of the "German October" by the presidium of the ECCI on January 11, 1924: "As to the question of fixing a date, Trotsky wrote an article in which he set up a timetable. That was a mistake. Radek, I have to admit, was opposed to it (Brandler: 'So was I'). Brandler, too. We decided that the date should serve only as a general guide, and should be definitely fixed [only] in Germany. Thus the Executive made no mistake in the question of fixing a date; [there was] no mistake on the part of the Russian party" (*Die Lehren der deutschen Ereignisse*, p. 60). Thus the principal framers of policy disagreed on what exactly had been decided in Moscow, and everyone ultimately felt inclined to defend his own interpretation of the issue.

[65] Deutscher, *The Prophet Unarmed*, pp. 111-112, 143. Brandler related this incident to Deutscher, and gave the identical information to Wenzel (p. 193). Both authors have made additional use of a report given in Bajanov (pp. 74-75), according to which Zinoviev also volunteered his services, but that both were turned down, on Stalin's instigation, by the Central Committee of the Russian C.P. Souvarine (p. 316) gives a briefer and less sensational account of the same incident. Mention of Trotsky's candidacy is also in Bessedovsky, p. 61.

ment that the Communists were planning an insurrection. It was resolved that after the revolution had succeeded a special congress of factory councils should be called, which was to proclaim a German soviet republic and thereby sanction the *fait accompli.*[66]

One unpleasant detail still remained; it concerned another of the many intraparty squabbles among the Left Opposition members and Brandler. The constant disagreements and disputes within the German delegation during its stay in Moscow aroused Trotsky's apprehensions. Although he could not have been unaware of Brandler's sceptical approach to an undertaking which the Bolshevik veteran anticipated with something approaching gusto, Trotsky shared Brandler's distrust of his Left Opposition colleagues. They had acted irresponsibly in the past. They had repeatedly come close to an open violation of party discipline. It was safer to keep at least Maslow and Ruth Fischer in Moscow. But this led to another row between Trotsky and Zinoviev and ended once again in a compromise. Ruth Fischer was permitted to return to Berlin, but Maslow was retained. He had to submit to an investigation, conducted by a special commission of the Comintern, in connection with his past party record, and returned to Germany only at the end of the year. Interestingly enough, no one seems to have thought of retaining Thälmann as well. "Teddy" was not yet taken seriously by either the Russians or Brandler.[67]

By the end of September, all the decisions had been made. Brandler had yielded, "in principle," on most points of controversy: the entry of the Communists into the Saxon cabinet, himself included; the launching of the uprising within the next four to six weeks; and the appointment of a commission, headed by Radek rather than Trotsky, to supervise the coming operations. Overawed by the enthusiasm which he encountered in Moscow, Brandler set aside his own misgivings, and even became affected by the spirit of optimism which reigned among the Bolshevik leaders. In the end he seems to have gone so far as to claim that the Communists could count on the

[66] Leon Trotsky, *The Lessons of October 1917*, transl. by Susan Lawrence and I. Olshan (London, 1925), pp. 72-74; Bajanov, pp. 202-203; Wenzel, pp. 182-183; Thalheimer, *1923: Eine verpasste Revolution?*, p. 21.

[67] The best account of this episode is in Carr, *The Interregnum*, pp. 208-209, including notes. Wenzel (p. 181, n.27), basing his account on that of Ernst Böse, *Wahnsinn oder Verbrechen?* (Bernburg, n.d.), p. 14, mentions as a possibility that Maslow was suspected of disloyalty. See also Fischer (pp. 322-323, 361-362), who attributes Maslow's detainment to Brandler's intrigues.

active support of from 50,000 to 60,000 proletarians in Saxony, an estimate which was to prove woefully wrong.[68]

On October 1, 1923, Zinoviev, in the name of the ECCI, sent the following telegram to the *Zentrale* of the KPD: "Since we estimate the situation in such a way that the decisive moment will arrive not later than in four–five–six weeks, we think it necessary to occupy at once every position which can be of immediate use [to our purposes]. On the basis of the [present] situation we must approach the question of our entry into the Saxon government in practical terms. We must enter [the Saxon government] on the condition that the Zeigner people are actually willing to defend Saxony against Bavaria and the Fascists. 50,000 to 60,000 [workers] have to be immediately armed; ignore General Müller. The same in Thuringia."[69]

This telegram signified the end of the deliberations in Moscow. The decision to start a revolution was made, the blueprints were drawn, and Russian hopes were high. Brandler left Moscow sometime during the first week of October. He arrived in Germany on October 8 and, if we can trust Ruth Fischer's description of his departure, he carried with him the trust and good wishes of at least Leon Trotsky: "As I left the Kremlin, I saw Trotsky bidding farewell to Brandler, whom he had accompanied from his residence inside the Kremlin to the Troitski gate—an unusual gesture of extreme politeness. There they stood, in the sharp light of an autumn afternoon, the stocky Brandler, in his unpressed civilian suit, and the elegant Trotsky in his well-cut Red Army uniform. After the last words, Trotsky kissed Brandler tenderly on both cheeks in the usual

[68] Brandler's estimate was mentioned by Zinoviev in January 1924 (*Die Lehren der deutschen Ereignisse*, p. 60).

[69] *ibid.*; *Bericht über die Verhandlungen des IX. Parteitages*, p. 30. As already mentioned, Brandler was at first opposed to the wording of the telegram, and objected particularly to its emphasis on the immediate arming of the Saxon workers. Radek, who shared Brandler's misgivings, had suggested an alternate version which Zinoviev, however, rejected (*Die Lehren der deutschen Ereignisse*, pp. 24-25). Zinoviev's enigmatic instruction to "ignore General Müller" (the commander of the Fourth German military district, who had been invested with the executive power over Saxony under the provisions of the national state of emergency decree of September 16, 1923) was another example of Russian preoccupation with historical parallels, then a very pronounced trait among veterans of the Russian Revolution. General Müller's position, Zinoviev related several months later, had reminded him of "the example of Kronstadt in 1917, when the Provisional Government appointed as commissar the Kadet Pepelyaev, though power was really in the hands of the Kronstadt Soviet, and the Kronstadt Soviet ignored Pepelyaev and made him ridiculous, and then in our own good time we arrested him." Quoted in Carr, *The Interregnum*, p. 208, n.1.

Russian manner. Knowing both men well, I could see that Trotsky was really moved; he felt that he was wishing well the leader of the German revolution on the eve of great events."[70]

The period between the Cuno strike and Brandler's return from Moscow proved rather trying for the KPD. For several weeks, while Brandler and his colleagues were deliberating with the Bolshevik leaders in the Kremlin, the *Zentrale* in Berlin continued to work toward the capture of mass support, the party's most pressing objective. Although the Communists did not know what decisions would be taken in Moscow, they had to count on the possibility that they would be ordered to act while the situation in Germany seemed favorable for an insurrection. And they did not doubt that the situation was indeed favorable. The Cuno strike, its inconclusive results for the KPD notwithstanding, had raised expectations within the party that a revolutionary situation might soon be shaping up. But since no one knew when or how it would come, nor what directives Brandler would bring home from Moscow, all the party could do was to keep political agitation at a high pitch, without setting off isolated and premature incidents which could easily lead to drastic and possibly disastrous countermeasures by the authorities. It was a difficult task, which required more skill than either Thalheimer or the other members of the caretaker *Zentrale* could muster.[71]

The increasingly aggressive tone of the Communist press, from mid-July on, did not escape the attention of the German authorities. Not very much had been done about it until the day of Cuno's resignation, but from that moment on the attitude of the national government and of the individual states toward the Communists became noticeably more determined. In a discussion on August 13

[70] Fischer, p. 323. Fischer places the date of departure on October 9 or 10, 1923. Brandler said in January, 1924, that he arrived in Germany on October 8, 1923, in time to participate in the last stages of discussion concerning his own entry and that of two of his colleagues into the Saxon cabinet (*Die Lehren der deutschen Ereignisse*, p. 24). This statement of Brandler conflicts with what he told Isaac Deutscher a quarter of a century later, i.e., that he learned of his appointment as Saxon minister from a newspaper which he bought in a Warsaw railway station (Deutscher, *The Prophet Unarmed*, p. 143, including n.2).

[71] Brandler later complained that the conduct of party affairs in his absence had been disappointingly inept. It is doubtful, though, that he would have done a much better job under the circumstances (*Die Lehren der deutschen Ereignisse*, p. 34; *Fifth Congress of the Communist International, Abridged Report*, p. 65).

between Stresemann and Lord D'Abernon, the British ambassador, the new chancellor left no doubt that he was aware of the Communist threat, and that he was fully prepared to meet it.[72] On August 16, the *Rote Fahne* printed a little poem, signed by one Mally Resso, which expressed the Communist spirit of the day very neatly, and thus seemed to justify the apprehensions of the government: Entitled: "It Approaches!" (*Sie naht!*), the poem ran as follows:

Tough, like ivy creepers	Zäh wie *Efeuranken*
Our thoughts are twisting	Winden sich unsere Gedanken
Around the goal!	Um das Ziel!
Many	Viele
Have run ashore on the way	Sind auf dem Weg dorthin
to it,	gestrandet,
Landed	Gelandet
Have in spirit already the	Sind im Geiste bereits die
prophets,	Propheten,
They have seen the proletarians	Sie sahn die Proleten
Depending on their own	Auf eigene Kraft gestellt
strength	
As Lords of the World.	Als Herren der Welt.
Pioneers, what you envisioned,	Bahnbrechende, was Ihr saht,
For the freeing of the slaves,	Zur Befreiung der Knechte,
The deed,	Die Tat,
Fighters for justice,	Kämpfer im Rechte,
It approaches!	Sie naht![73]

The poem marked the beginning of a tug of war between the German Communists, with their "thoughts twisting around the goal," and the republic, which was threatened by the "approaching deed." One day after the poem appeared, the Prussian Minister of the Interior Carl Severing announced that the Federal Committee of Factory Councils and its subcommittees, all situated in Berlin, were dissolved and banned. The KPD was outraged. "The first act of the Great Coalition," jeered the *Rote Fahne*, and put the entire blame for the measure on the Social Democrats, who were now represented in the federal as well as in the Prussian government. The Communists charged that the Social Democratic ministers in Stresemann's

---

[72] D'Abernon, *The Diary of an Ambassador*, II (New York, 1930), pp. 247-248.
[73] *Die Rote Fahne*, No. 188, August 16, 1923.

cabinet were the spiritual fathers of the blow against the factory councils, duly executed by the Prussian Social Democrat Severing. "We shall take up the challenge of the Social Democrats," wrote the *Rote Fahne*, "but the consequences they will have to bear themselves."[74]

Severing's move against the Federal Committee of Factory Councils was a severe setback for the KPD. Although the agency was not officially connected with the party, the Communists controlled it well enough to allow them considerable influence over the important German Factory Council movement. The ban, against which the party press protested vociferously but ineffectively for days, made it necessary to move the Committee from its strategically located position in the German capital to the more congenial, but also more remote, regions of Thuringia.[75]

The days which followed the ban saw the party in a defiant mood. Its press on August 19 depicted the country as a passenger taking a "ride into the abyss," predicted new struggles ahead, and reprinted a chapter from S. J. Gussev's brochure, *Lessons of the Civil War*, entitled "Let the Proletariat Prepare Itself."[76] Two days later, under the heading of "Preparations for a New Struggle," the *Rote Fahne* told its readers that new and difficult struggles lay ahead for which the proletariat must arm. "Workers' control and workers' government, these are our aims. . . . Workers! Employees! Officials! Arm for battle!"[77] On August 22 the same paper carried an appeal by the *Zentrale* "To the Workers of the SPD and USP," in which the two parties were violently condemned and their members invited to "get out of the SPD . . . the accomplice of the class enemy . . . and the harmful, illusory . . . impotent USP. . . . Join the KPD, that is the demand of the hour! Long live the proletarian class struggle!. . . the dictatorship of the proletariat! . . . the Communist International!"[78]

The last week of August brought a series of repressive measures directed against the Communists. On the 22nd, the government of Württemberg banned the regional party convention which was

---

[74] *ibid.*, No. 189, August 17, 1923.

[75] *ibid.*, No. 195, August 24, 1923. Thalheimer (in 1923: *Eine verpasste Revolution?*, p. 24) charges that the KPD failed to protest the ban in any form. This is an unjustified charge. Protests were made, although only in the form of resolutions passed by some factory councils, and in the Communist press.

[76] *Die Rote Fahne*, No. 191, August 19, 1923.

[77] *ibid.*, No. 192, August 21, 1923.

[78] *ibid.*, No. 193, August 23, 1923.

scheduled to meet in Stuttgart on the 25th and 26th. On the 24th, the French occupation forces prohibited the publication of every Communist newspaper—five altogether—in the Ruhr region. The *Rote Fahne* of August 26 was seized in the early morning hours by orders of the police president of Berlin. No reasons for this act were given. August 28 was an especially black day. The police once again raided the editorial offices of the *Rote Fahne* in Berlin, confiscated a number of files, and arrested five party functionaries who happened to be on the scene. In Hamburg, the local party organ *Hamburger Volkszeitung* was banned for three days. And Carl Severing outlawed the Central Committee of the Factory Councils of Greater Berlin which, his decree pointed out, had become a front organization for one of the subcommittees of the Federal Committee of Factory Councils that had been banned two weeks earlier. The Prussian Minister of the Interior explained that it had become apparent, on the basis of material seized from the offices of the *Rote Fahne* a few days earlier, that the Central Committee of Berlin's factory councils was actually run by the Communist district command of Berlin-Brandenburg, notably by Ruth Fischer and Arkadi Maslow. On August 29, presumably as a result of this incriminating information (some of which must have been known beforehand to the local authorities), the police raided the offices of the party's Berlin district command. The apartments of party leaders were also searched by police officers who had warrants for the arrest of the entire Communist hierarchy of the district Berlin-Brandenburg. But since five leading functionaries had been apprehended the day before in the office of the *Rote Fahne*, and a number of others were apparently "unavailable," only two additional party leaders were actually arrested that day. A warrant against Ruth Fischer was issued, but could not be served, because she was by then already on her way to Moscow.[79]

Far from being intimidated, the Communists continued their propaganda offensive throughout the better part of September. They now concentrated with increasing tenacity on the exploitation of grievances held by segments of the population outside the ranks of labor. Peasants with marginal holdings, farm workers, and especially government officials became targets of their agitation.[80] "The *Rote*

[79] *ibid.*, No. 195, August 24; No. 196, August 25; No. 197, August 26; No. 199, August 29; No. 200, August 30, 1923; Severing, *Mein Lebensweg*, I, p. 426.

[80] Habedank, pp. 72-73; *Die Rote Fahne*, No. 201, August 31; No. 202, September 1; No. 210, September 18, 1923.

Fahne has virtually become an officials' newspaper," noted the recorder of the chancellery for the information of Stresemann on September 11.[81]

But the party's chief concern and principal propaganda target remained the mass of non-Communist workers. To demonstrate the alleged gap between the words and deeds of the Socialist leaders, the KPD demanded, in the parliaments of the states and in the individual communities throughout the country, that communal efforts be made to aid the starving poor. To accomplish this, the Communists proposed a redistribution of goods. They suggested, in practical terms, that communal stores of provisions and goods be given free of charge to wounded war veterans, the unemployed, and those on the rolls of the social welfare department. These goods should be sold at reduced prices to all low-income groups. They further suggested a graduated charge for public utilities according to the income and the number of children of each family, to "soak the rich and spare the poor." Homeless proletarian families were to be given quarters in the large apartments of the bourgeoisie, while all wealthy and childless middle class families were to be resettled in the "cave dwellings" of the proletariat. Finally, they demanded the immediate institution of public food kitchens where pregnant proletarian women, nursing mothers, and working-class children would be able to receive a balanced diet free of charge and at public expense. These were the principal items of the Communist program to alleviate the worst effects of the economic crisis.[82]

Such positive suggestions could not help but appeal to workers even if they did not agree with the Communists on other matters. It is revealing that the circulation of the Communist press increased in the summer and fall of 1923, at a time when the rising cost of living caused a decline of subscriptions among most other German newspapers.[83] Nor could the government and the captains of industry and business fail to notice the benefits which the Communists derived from the critical economic situation. They could not deny

[81] Max von Stockhausen, *Sechs Jahre Reichskanzlei: Von Rapallo bis Locarno, Erinnerungen und Tagebuchnotizen 1922-1927,* ed. Walter Görlitz (Bonn, 1954), p. 77.

[82] Habedank, p. 73; *Bericht über die Verhandlungen des IX. Parteitages,* pp. 64/39-64/40 (double pagination).

[83] Wenzel, pp. 13, 157; Habedank, p. 75.

the truth when the *Rote Fahne* claimed on August 31 that the mark stood at two million to the dollar, that there was a shortage of food, and that queues were forming in front of stores.[84] And one copy of the *Rote Fahne* itself cost 100,000 marks. The seriousness of the situation was frankly admitted by Stresemann who met in conference with the members of the People's Party's Reichstag delegation on September 11. One participant, Siegfried von Kardorff, pointed to the importance of keeping the nation's food supply steady, and added, with reference to the conditions in Saxony: "One cannot shoot at starving women." Hugo Stinnes predicted at the same conference that the country could expect civil war to break out within a fortnight.[85]

The appeals in the *Rote Fahne* became more ominous in tone and content. On September 1, the *Zentrale* published a proclamation to "Workers, Employees, Officials!" in which the party reviled the government, the middle class, and the Social Democratic ministers—these last were called the figleaves of the bourgeoisie. The proclamation repeated the Communist demands for the control of production by the workers, the confiscation of real values [*Sachwerte*], and the creation of a government of workers and "small" peasants. The appeal ended with the slogan: "Let us fight—then victory will be certain!"[86] The same issue carried an article by Zinoviev, written for the occasion of the 9th International Youth Day, in which the chairman of the ECCI predicted that the German proletariat was moving rapidly toward decisive struggles. "There is no power on earth that can defeat twenty million proletarians! Twenty million proletarians, . . . every man able to read and write. . . ." But the *non sequitur* paled beside the magic figure of twenty million! Finally, the issue carried an unsigned article which was headlined "Onward to the Decisive Battle!"

On the following day the paper outdid itself. The front page carried a joint appeal to the workers of all countries by the executive

[84] *Die Rote Fahne*, No. 201, August 31, 1923.

[85] Stresemann, *Vermächtnis*, I, pp. 116-118. Stinnes revised his estimate somewhat ten days later, during a conversation with the American Ambassador Alanson B. Houghton. Stinnes told the ambassador that since by mid-October three, or perhaps four million men would be out of work, the Communists would take advantage of the situation and would start a revolution (Hallgarten, *Hitler, Reichswehr und Industrie* [Frankfurt am Main, 1955], pp. 65-66).

[86] *Die Rote Fahne*, No. 202, September 1, 1923.

committees of the Comintern and the Profintern, as well as an article by Radek entitled "Hands off Germany!" The former urged world-wide support for the German proletariat and, in effect, urged the international working class to prevent foreign interference if and when the German proletariat engaged in a revolutionary struggle with the German bourgeoisie. Such a struggle was seen to be approaching, and the appeal contained a note of concern that it might come prematurely: "The [German] working class is to be driven to despair, is to be provoked into battle, before it has put its ranks in order." The joint appeal was directed at the international labor movement, but Radek addressed himself to the governments of the western nations, warning them that Soviet Russia would not take it lightly should any nation interfere with the affairs of Germany while that country was engaged in a revolutionary struggle.

"Soviet diplomacy will do everything to make it clear to all concerned that it would be best for the capitalist part of the world to leave the decision of Germany's fate to the mass of the German people rather than to throw the sword into the scales of history; for not only the capitalist powers hold a sword, but also the first proletarian state, Soviet Russia."[87]

No government could afford to ignore such an array of cold-blooded affronts, and from such formidable quarters. On September 4, the German Minister of Interior, the Social Democrat Wilhelm Sollmann, banned the *Rote Fahne* and another Communist paper, the *Volkswacht*, for a period of eight days. In his explanation of the reasons for the ban, which the paper printed in full before closing down, the minister presented a long list of offenses which the Communist papers had committed in violation of the presidential decree of August 10, 1923. Quoting chapter and verse from a series of utterances designed to incite the population to revolution, Sollmann's list was impressive and disturbing. Apparently from a sense of diplomatic delicacy the explanation omitted mention of the Russian contributions of September 2, and instead closed with the quotation of a little verse by one Hardy Worm [sic] which had appeared the previous day.

---

[87] *ibid.*, No. 203, September 2, 1923. An article held in a similar vein was published by the president of the Profintern, Lozovsky, in the September issue of *Die Rote Gewerkschaftsinternationale*, No. 9 (32), September, 1923, pp. 785ff, as cited in Carr, *The Interregnum*, p. 203.

Proudly form ranks for final strife!	Formiert Euch stolz zum letz- ten Krieg!
Unite, be brave, till victory's here!	Seid einig, tapfer bis zum Sieg!
Unfold the flags, as red as life,	Entfaltet Fahnen, rot in rot,
And sacrificial death don't fear!	Und fürchtet nicht den Opfer- tod![88]

It was quite appropriate, therefore, that the *Rote Fahne* printed another poem on the first day of its reappearance, September 11. It was entitled: "You Cannot Force Us!" [*Ihr zwingt uns nicht!*], the text of which the reader shall be spared. But it soon became evident that the poem's title expressed the attitude of the German Communists. Issue after issue of the *Rote Fahne* contained incendiary headlines, articles, appeals, and "theoretical" discussions of Russian civil war tactics. "Down with the Regiment of Blood and Hunger!" read the headline on September 15. On September 19, the paper printed a resolution taken by the Moscow Soviet on August 28. The resolution, which pledged the support of the Russian workers and soldiers to the German proletariat, had been adopted after an address by Radek. The meeting had been attended by representatives of the Russian labor unions and the Red Army. On September 21, the *Zentrale* published another proclamation, "To the Working Population of Germany!", this time to protest against the rumored termination of passive resistance in the Ruhr. The document contained the usual diatribes against the government, together with the customary gamut of Communist objectives. It ended by calling on the workers, employees, officials, "small" peasants, and members of the (lower) middle class to hold mass meetings and demonstrations, and to prepare for a political mass strike, the principal aims of which were the overthrow of the Stresemann government, creation of a workers' and peasants' government, and "closest" alliance with Soviet Russia. Two days later, when the paper carried on its front page an article headed "The Road to the Proletarian Dictatorship in Germany (An Additional Word to the Social Democratic Worker)," the government decided to step in again. The next day, September 24, the *Rote Fahne* was banned once more, and this time for a fortnight. As on the previous occasion, the agency from which the ban emanated—this time the police president of Berlin—pre-

[88] *Die Rote Fahne*, No. 204, September 4, 1923.

sented a bill of particulars.[89] Thus for two crucial weeks the central organ of the Communist party was not published, depriving the party of its principal mouthpiece just at the moment when the *Zentrale* received word from Moscow to prepare for revolution in from four to six weeks' time.

This two-weeks' ban coincided with a series of portentous developments. On the day after the central government announced the end of passive resistance in the Ruhr and proclaimed a national decree of emergency, the National Socialist newspaper *Völkischer Beobachter,* in Munich, printed an unrestrained attack on President Ebert, Chancellor Stresemann, and the commander of the Reichswehr, General von Seeckt. This led to an exchange of communications between Seeckt and General Otto von Lossow, the Reichswehr general in command of the army contingents stationed in Bavaria, centering around Seeckt's order to Lossow to proceed at once against the *Völkischer Beobachter.* Lossow, backed by the newly appointed general commissioner for the state, Gustav von Kahr, refused to obey, with the result that the Bavarian army contingents virtually "seceded" from the rest of the Reichswehr and, under Lossow's leadership, took an oath of allegiance to the state of Bavaria on October 22. The extremely belligerent attitude which Bavaria adopted toward the central government was paralleled by a series of repressive measures which von Kahr applied against the Bavarian labor movement, such as the outlawing of strikes and the banning of Socialist paramilitary defense organizations.

The Bavarian problem, combined with controversies between the SPD and the People's Party over the nature of a contemplated Enabling Act and over the eight-hour working day, threatened to break up the Great Coalition and led to a government crisis. On October 3 the cabinet resigned. A number of compromises, including the continued inviolability of the eight-hour day (a concession to the SPD), the chancellor's decision for the time being not to interfere actively in Bavaria (partly as a concession to the People's Party), and a change of ministerial appointments for the posts of Finance and

---

[89] *ibid.,* No. 204, September 11; No. 208, September 15; No. 213, September 21; No. 215, September 23; No. 216, September 24, 1923. The paper was banned the first time for one week. Its issue of September 4 had carried the number 204, and the same number was given to the first issue which appeared after the ban, September 11, 1923.

Economy saved the Great Coalition. On October 6 Stresemann was able to form his second cabinet.[90]

The government crisis had been accompanied by an abortive right-wing putsch which a Major Bruno Buchrucker staged against the Reichswehr garrison of Küstrin on October 1. Buchrucker, who commanded five hundred members of the clandestine *Arbeitskommandos*, or Black Reichswehr troops, seems to have had only the vaguest concept of his ultimate objective. The putsch was unsuccessful, and led to Buchrucker's arrest and subsequent trial and conviction. But its occurrence at this particular time further aggravated the prevailing political tension.[91]

In this troubled atmosphere the KPD approached the moment of decision. On September 27 the party issued another proclamation to the German working class in those of its publications not banned by the government. The proclamation took issue with the cessation of passive resistance and warned that the "German imperialists" were now preparing to move against the proletariat. To counter this threat, the workers were urged to arm themselves and stand together. The document ended with the battle cry: "Long live the mass strike! Long live the struggle!"[92]

A day before the party received Zinoviev's telegram, presumably on September 30, the *Zentrale* held a meeting to discuss what action the situation required. One unidentified member of the *Zentrale* suggested that if circumstances in Saxony were "ripe," the party ought to start an uprising [*losschlagen*]. The suggestion was rejected out of hand because it was considered to smack of putschism. Then, as Remmele, the source of this information, has related, the telegram arrived and "the whole policy of the party became focussed on what had been rejected the day before."[93]

[90] The Bavarian crisis of October, 1923, has been variously treated in recent historical studies. For further reference see Schwend, pp. 217-227; Schlottner, pp. 52-58, and *passim*; Stresemann, *Vermächtnis*, I, pp. 131-146. Interesting new material is also in the microfilmed Stresemann Nachlass, Auswärtiges Amt, Germany, microfilm, container 3099, frames H 146003-146007, H 146017-146023, H 146026-146028; and container 3105, frames H 154123, H 154158-154160.

[91] For the Buchrucker Putsch see Waite, pp. 248-253; Gordon, *The Reichswehr and the German Republic 1919-1926* (Princeton, 1957), pp. 233-235; Schüddekopf, *Heer und Republik* (Hannover and Frankfurt am Main, 1955), pp. 167-169; Bruno Ernst Buchrucker, *Im Schatten Seeckts: Die Geschichte der "Schwarzen Reichswehr"* (Berlin, 1928); Rabenau, *Seeckt* (Leipzig, 1940), p. 354; Gessler, p. 265.

[92] *Der Kämpfer*, September 29, 1923, as cited in Habedank, p. 71.

[93] *Die Lehren der deutschen Ereignisse*, p. 41.

The "Authorized" Bid for Power

The German Communists threw themselves into preparations for the contemplated uprising with feverish intensity. The target date, according to party calculations based on Zinoviev's telegram, was to be sometime in the first half of November. The remaining six weeks had to be used to mobilize the party for action, to coordinate the political and military preparations, and to draw up a strategic plan for revolutionary conquest. From the inconclusive and often vague evidence available, it appears that the party gave most of these measures its wholehearted and undivided attention only after October 1.[94] Whatever was done prior to this date—as far as can be established at all—consisted of conspiratorial work conducted by the military-political *Apparat*. But in the absence of definite plans and clearly defined objectives, these activities were restricted to preliminaries, and seem to have suffered from a multiplicity of frequently overlapping and poorly coordinated secret agencies.[95]

A great deal has been written about the technical preparations for the projected uprising, notably on their so-called "military" aspects. Much of the information has been provided by former Communist agents who in one way or other participated in the work of the clandestine party *Apparat*. Unfortunately, the reliability of most of these accounts is open to serious doubts,[96] so that any historical treatment

[94] The existing accounts concerning the actual beginning of serious preparations for the uprising differ on virtually every detail, and the only element all of them have in common is a tendency toward vagueness. Brandler stated in January 1924 that serious preparations for civil war began only after the Cuno strike; then he corrected himself and said that preparations began after July 11, 1923, but gave no further clues (*Die Lehren der deutschen Ereignisse*, p. 31). Remmele said on the same occasion that after the arrival of Zinoviev's telegram "the party and the entire party apparatus were alerted and mobilized for the armed uprising" (*ibid.*, p. 41). But in his article "The Proletarian Struggle for Power," *The Communist International*, I, New Series, No. 2, 29-30, Remmele places the first moves for mobilizing the party at sometime after the mass strikes in July. However, his few references to details, and especially to the target date, indicate that no very significant steps were taken prior to October 1, 1923, i.e., the day when Zinoviev's telegram was sent. Thalheimer implies that technical preparations did not begin until after the Cuno strike, but fails to say how soon after this event (*1923: Eine verpasste Revolution?*, p. 24). Borkenau claims that orders to prepare for the rising reached the lower echelons of the party early in September, but he adds that when Brandler returned from Moscow there were no weapons, and the party was weak (*The Communist International* [London, 1938], p. 250). Fischer (p. 324) places the beginnings of military preparations on the part of the Communists at mid-September; Gast, *Zeitschrift für Geschichtswissenschaft*, IV, No. 3 (1956), p. 445, mentions "September-October," and Flechtheim, *Die K.P.D. in der Weimarer Republik* (Offenbach, 1948), pp. 92-93, evades the issue altogether.

[95] Carr, *The Interregnum*, p. 211.

[96] The most notable of these are Walter G. Krivitsky, *In Stalin's Secret Service*

of this particular phase of Communist activities must remain, in part, conjectural.

It has been mentioned earlier that, after the Second World Congress of the Comintern, the KPD and all other Communist parties affiliated with the Comintern were expected to create an illegal party apparatus.[97] At that time, the haphazard organization which had existed in Germany prior to the summer of 1920 was scrapped, and a new one established in its place. This is when the military apparatus (*M-Apparat*) and intelligence apparatus (*N- or Nachrichten-Apparat*) were created. For the next two and a half years these agencies played a very subordinate role, though the exact extent of their effectiveness, or lack of it, cannot be established with any certainty. But while the party was preoccupied with winning mass support, i.e., while the united front policy dominated the tactics of the German Communist Party, cloak and dagger activities could serve no useful purpose, and we have seen that even during the March uprising of 1921 the role of the *Apparat* was negligible.

The situation changed after the Ruhr occupation in January 1923. Soon after this event a group of twenty-four Russian "civil war" experts arrived secretly in Germany and apparently acted for several months mainly as observers.[98] There is no reliable indication, however, that any decisive steps to prepare the party for the anticipated fighting were taken before the late summer, or even early autumn, of 1923.[99] Initiation of the most elementary measures required for

---

(New York and London, 1939), pp. 38-47, 54-55; Walter Zeutschel, *Im Dienst der Kommunistischen Terror-Organisation: Tscheka Arbeit in Deutschland* (Berlin, 1931); Jan Valtin, *Out of the Night* (New York, 1941), pp. 56-87, *passim*. Somewhat more trustworthy than the preceding accounts appears to be Erich Wollenberg, *Der Apparat: Stalins Fünfte Kolonne* (Bonn, 1952), pp. 9-12. David J. Dallin, *Soviet Espionage* (New Haven, 1955), pp. 71-92, *passim*, has used all the aforementioned books, Ruth Fischer's account, and a collection of documents identified only as "D papers XYZ." Some of the papers of "X" and "Y" were published under the pseudonym "Ypsilon" with the title *Pattern for World Conquest* (Chicago-New York, 1947). After having consulted all of these "revelations" I can only underscore Carr's advice to use them with extreme caution (see *The Interregnum*, p. 210, n.1).

[97] See above, Ch. IV.

[98] Wenzel, p. 37, who received his information from Brandler in 1954. Brandler also claimed at that time that Alexis Skoblevsky (see below, note 100) was sent to Germany as early as December 1922, although Brandler had told Carr on another occasion that Skoblevsky arrived in Germany only in the autumn of 1923 (*The Interregnum*, p. 209 and n.3). The latter date seems to be more probable; it would, incidentally, agree with Ruth Fischer's statement that the "general" arrived in September (pp. 324-325).

[99] Carr, *The Interregnum*, pp. 209-210, including n.4.

the contemplated revolution came in the course of negotiations between the Bolsheviks and representatives of the German party in September. On Brandler's request the Russians agreed to send one of their civil war generals, Rose, alias Gorev, but most commonly known as Pëtr Aleksandrovich (or Alexis) Skoblevsky, reputedly a Lett by birth, to assist the KPD on questions of military organization.[100] Shortly after this decision was taken, the actual build-up of the German *Apparat* began in earnest.

What emerged, at least in skeleton form, was an elaborate network of organizations.[101] The "general staff" of the planned uprising was a "Revolutionary Committee," abbreviated to *REVKO*. It was headed by August Guralsky-Kleine, of March 1921 fame, and since January 1923 a member of the *Zentrale*. *REVKO* had to prepare and organize the party for the coming struggle, which was conceived primarily in terms of partisan warfare. But the committee was not in charge of military operations. These were entrusted to General Skoblevsky, supreme commander (*Reichsleiter*) of the party's military-political (MP) organization. He was assisted by a military council (*Militärrat*), headed by Ernst Schneller (later a member of the party's organizational bureau, or *Orgbüro*) and composed of leading party members, including Walter Ulbricht, who was then a member of the *Zentrale*. Subordinate to Skoblevsky and his military council were six regional military-political commanders (*MP-Oberleiter*), each of them responsible for the military organization and the anticipated operations of the KPD in his region. The regions approximated the military defense districts of the German Reichswehr: West, North-West, Central Germany, Berlin, South-West and East Prussia. Bavaria, for obvious reasons, was for the time omitted from the strategic calculations of the KPD. The regional commanders were trusted party leaders, each of them assisted by a

---

[100] No agreement exists on Skoblevsky's origins, or even his real name. But since the matter is not of vital importance I shall not pursue it further. For additional, though widely differing theories on this point see Wollenberg, p. 10, including n.1; Dallin, p. 73; Nollau, *Die Internationale* (Cologne, 1959), pp. 73, 251; Valtin, pp. 63-69; Hilger and Meyer, pp. 140-141.

[101] Unless otherwise indicated, the subsequent account of the party's preparations for an uprising is based on Wenzel, pp. 194-203. Dr. Wenzel had access to archival material, notably the Staatsarchiv Düsseldorf, and had the opportunity to interview Brandler, Wollenberg, and other, less well-known, persons who participated in the events. Wherever possible I have tried to check Wenzel's story against other accounts, some of which were not yet available to him when he wrote his dissertation.

Russian military adviser who functioned as chief of staff, but had no command position.[102]

A corresponding setup to that of the regional *MP-Oberleitung* existed on the district and sub-district levels. The latter were combat commands (*Kampfleitungen*) which were expected to organize and train the proletarian hundreds, and eventually lead them into battle.[103]

Parallel to the *MP*-organization the Communists created, or in some cases merely revitalized, auxiliary agencies designed to aid and supplement the work of the military-political *Apparat*. To these belonged the *T-* (for *Terror*) and *Z-* (for *Zersetzung*, i.e. infiltration and subversion) groups, as well as the highly important Office for the Procurement of Weapons and Ammunition (*Waffen-und Munitionsbeschaffungsamt*, abbreviated as WUMBA). These were apparently coordinated by the chairman of the party's organizational bureau (*Orgbüro*), mild-mannered and quiet Leo Flieg, who was also in charge of administering the secret funds which, in dollar currency, flowed from Moscow to Germany via the Russian Embassy in Berlin. The connecting links in these transactions, which Ruth Fischer used to call the Russian water-pipe line (*russische Wasserleitung*), were the Soviet Ambassador Krestinsky and the representative of the Comintern's Department for International Liaison (*Otdel Mezhdunarodnoy Syvazi*, or OMS), Jacob Mirov-Abramov, who resided in the Russian Embassy where he nominally belonged to the press department.[104] Finally, it must be remembered that all

---

[102] Besides Wenzel, see Carr, *The Interregnum*, pp. 209-211; Flechtheim, p. 92; Wollenberg, p. 10; Ulbricht, *Zur Geschichte der deutschen Arbeiterbewegung*, I, p. 135; Becher, *Walter Ulbricht* (Berlin, 1958), p. 90; Nollau, p. 134, and *passim*. No reliable estimate exists as to the number of Russian agents, military or civilian, who were operating in Germany during this period. The usual mythical figure of "several hundred," given by Fischer (p. 319, and, more vaguely, p. 324), and copied from her by other authors appears a gross exaggeration.

[103] For details on the "proletarian hundreds" see Gast, *Zeitschrift für Geschichtswissenschaft*, IV, No. 3 (1956), pp. 452-457, and *passim*.

[104] Nollau, pp. 112-113, 133, 136, and *passim*; Buber-Neumann, *Von Potsdam nach Moskau* (Stuttgart, 1957), pp. 201-202; Dallin, pp. 73-74, 94, and *passim*; Flechtheim, pp. 92-93; Fischer, pp. 319-320, 324-327, 442, 444-445. To what extent the Russian Ambassador Krestinsky was directly implicated in the clandestine transactions concerning funds and the purchase of weapons, which were conducted with the aid of the Embassy, has never been cleared up. Bajanov (pp. 199-200) is convinced that he played a key role. The German government seems to have suspected Krestinsky but was so eager to maintain the Rapallo agreement—even in the face of a threatening Communist uprising—that the officials concerned avoided a showdown. The delicate position of the German authorities with regard to the

these different agencies were expected to function, when the time came, under the supervision of Radek and his three fellow representatives of the ECCI.

The formation of conspiratorial agencies was accompanied by training and mobilization of the party's rank and file, including the communist youth groups. Military training was largely left to the proletarian hundreds, who drilled, paraded, and conducted secret tactical maneuvers in isolated parts of the country, where they were protected against detection by police or political enemies by rigid security measures, such as outposts and patrols. Practice alerts were conducted, and special courses given on the handling and use of weapons. Consumption of alcoholic beverages during training sessions was strictly forbidden.[105]

Local party headquarters throughout Germany drew up lists of places where vitally needed goods were stored, such as food, fuel, and clothing, and special *Erfassungsgruppen* (procurement squads) were appointed to secure these goods as soon as the revolution broke out. Everywhere party cadres were formed to take over local administrative duties, a process which involved a preliminary screening of those officials who would be allowed to stay on their jobs, and those who were subsequently to be arrested or liquidated. To this must be added the pinpointing of special targets such as power plants, telephone exchanges, and centers of communication and transportation, all of which were to be secured when "The Day" came.[106]

These preparations (and this account does not pretend to have exhaustively covered them) looked impressive and formidable. In practice, however, the whole plan, including the preparatory measures, suffered from a variety of shortcomings and inefficiencies. There was, in the first place, the strategic blueprint for the uprising,

---

dubious activities of the Russian Embassy is reflected by the diplomatic correspondence between the German Foreign Office and the German Embassy in Moscow. See, for instance, "Foreign Office to Embassy, September 25, 1923," Auswärtiges Amt, Germany, microfilm, container 1406, frame D 553229; "Brockdorff-Rantzau to Foreign Office, October 6, 1923," *ibid.*, frames D 553247-553248; "Maltzan to German Embassy, October 11, 1923," *ibid.*, frame D 553257; "Brockdorff-Rantzau to Foreign Office, October 11, 1923," *ibid.*, frame D 553260. Of particular interest concerning official German estimates of Communist activities is a memorandum by Minister of the Interior Sollmann, dated October 17, 1923, *ibid.*, frames D 553279-553282.

[105] Gast, *Zeitschrift für Geschichtswissenschaft*, IV, No. 3 (1956), pp. 455-456; Wenzel, pp. 200-201.

[106] Wenzel, pp. 201-202.

which had been drawn up by the regional military supreme commanders. On the day of the uprising, the signal for which was to be either the proclamation of a general strike or an important conference of labor groups, the Communist-led red hundreds were to rise in every part of Germany except the occupied Ruhr region. There the proletarian formations were to march in closed formations into unoccupied territory and arm themselves at once. The Communist forces in southwestern and central Germany were to take over power, secure their positions, and then dispatch all available units to Berlin where the decisive battle was expected to take place. Bavaria was to be sealed off, and in northern and northeastern Germany, where the rural population was hostile to Communism, the proletarian hundreds were to wage partisan warfare to prevent the enemy from rallying his forces, and were also to capture arms, ammunition, vehicles, and other needed equipment.[107] Skoblevsky had calculated that in order to carry out this plan successfully it would be necessary to confront each unit of the Reichswehr and police with Communist forces three times as strong, and he had given his orders accordingly.

The "plan" had a number of evident loopholes. To outnumber every "enemy" unit three to one would have required a minimum of 750,000 well-armed Communist fighters. Furthermore, the 100,-000 men who composed the Reichswehr and the 150,000 police were not only superbly trained, but were in possession of weapons and equipment such as the Communists could only hope to capture in the process of revolution. Finally, the plan left out of account the paramilitary right-wing organizations, many of which had never been effectively disarmed, and most of which were strategically concentrated in Bavaria which the Communists hoped to "seal off."[108]

This raises the questions of Communist strength and procurement of arms. According to party estimates, total membership of the KPD amounted in the fall of 1923 to 294,230, including women and, presumably, older persons unfit for combat.[109] According to a recent

---

[107] *ibid.*; cf. Habedank, pp. 68, 82, 85.

[108] Wenzel, pp. 112, 196-197, 199-200. According to Wenzel, who bases his account on information received from Brandler and Wollenberg and on documents from the Staatsarchiv Düsseldorf, this plan was drawn up "at the end of September." As it was essentially an amplified version of the plan which had been drafted in Moscow earlier that month, it is conceivable that it was submitted to the German *Apparat* either prior to Zinoviev's telegram of October 1, 1923, or that it was actually worked out early in October rather than at the end of September.

[109] *Bericht über die Verhandlungen des IX. Parteitages*, p. 57.

East German estimate, the total number of proletarian hundreds in October 1923 amounted to eight hundred, with an over-all strength of 100,000 fighters.[110] These, however, are paper figures and we can only guess at the true effective strength. The fact that some members of these organizations did not participate in training exercises with the excuse, "We'll be there for the real thing,"[111] casts a dubious light on the discipline of the troops. In some areas, local party organizations apparently submitted lists of proletarian hundreds which had been compiled from the files without notifying the persons concerned that they were now members of a Communist fighting unit. And occasionally a simple resolution voted on by a Communist-infiltrated union local or factory council sufficed to "create" a proletarian hundred, although presumably the process began and ended with the vote and a report submitted to higher echelons.[112]

To make a revolution, men alone are not enough. They have to be armed, and the KPD tried hard to meet this requirement. Like the question of strength, estimates as to how many weapons were at the disposal of the German Communists vary widely, ranging from six hundred to fifty thousand rifles.[113] How many there really were is impossible to establish, and judging from the way in which the party proceeded to arm its members it is very doubtful that anyone, including the *Zentrale* or the Communist military high command, knew even remotely the approximate number of weapons available.

A number of schemes for the procurement of weapons existed. By far the easiest was a "do-it-yourself" system which was used to produce hand grenades and explosives. All that was needed was dy-

[110] Gast, *Zeitschrift für Geschichtswissenschaft*, IV, No. 3 (1956), p. 452. Some proletarian hundreds were SPD-controlled, though whether or not these have been included in Communist estimates cannot be established.

[111] *ibid.*, p. 456.

[112] *ibid.*, p. 455; Wenzel, p. 196. Gast mentions the formation of hundreds by women, both in Thuringia and the Rhineland, but does not indicate whether or not he has included these Amazon units in his estimate of eight hundred "hundreds." Wenzel (pp. 195-196), basing himself on captured documents, gives a slightly higher estimate of the total strength of the Communist forces, i.e., 113,600, but points out that this figure may well be too high.

[113] Borkenau, *The Communist International*, p. 251, gives the number as 600; Flechtheim, p. 93, n.1, gives 11,000; this was the figure named at a Central Committee meeting in November, 1923. Zeutschel, p. 13, claims that Brandler stated in Moscow that the party possessed 500,000 rifles, whereas it had in fact only 50,000. Gast, *Zeitschrift für Geschichtswissenschaft*, IV, No. 3 (1956), p. 457, is vague and gives no figures at all.

namite, usually stolen from stone quarries and construction projects, old tin cans, and fuses. Production of such homemade weapons was entrusted to the proletarian hundreds.[114] For the purpose of blowing up trains, power stations, and other targets, the party also manufactured makeshift bombs, such as sticks of dynamite placed in a small paper carton, which was then made to look like a piece of commercial pressed coal (briquette).[115] Home production of weapons was limited, however, and had to be supplemented by other means of procurement. Theft was one of these. Apart from stealing explosives, the party had plans to pilfer secret arms caches of right-wing organizations, armories of the Reichswehr and the police, gun stores, and weapons of individual, non-Communist, citizens, especially the guns of farmers. It was in the nature of these ventures that they could not be carried out on a large scale, and in many cases the thefts remained projects. This meant that "intelligence reports" were compiled by the local party organizations as to where weapons could be easily and quickly obtained once the signal for the uprising had been given. At that moment, special squads ("action committees") were to raid the places previously earmarked, and the weapons and vehicles thus obtained were to be quickly distributed among the Communist troops. It appears that under this scheme many a party member came to look at the pistols, guns, and rubber truncheons hanging from the belts of the local police force as future booty. In some cases, weapons were "confiscated" from private persons by party members posing as plain-clothes police officers.[116]

Finally, there was the method of buying weapons. Ample funds for this purpose were available to the German party through the Russian Embassy. WUMBA's purchasing agents, usually equipped with U.S. dollars, roamed the country in quest of arms. It soon became apparent, however, that the Communists were not too well suited to the capitalist game of doing business. As all purchases had

[114] Gast, *Zeitschrift für Geschichtswissenschaft*, IV, No. 3 (1956), p. 457.

[115] Wenzel, p. 199.

[116] *ibid.*, pp. 197-199; see also pp. 297-301, where the author reproduces a "Report of the District Command of Silesia to the KPD *Zentrale*," dated October 8, 1923. The report dealt with the party's state of preparedness in Silesia, concentrating on the weapons already secured and on those potentially available once the signal for the uprising would be given. Most of the weapons listed were rifles and pistols, and an occasional machine gun. The report, arranged by townships and villages, also included evaluations of Communist morale, the state of readiness of "action committees" formed, and similar data.

to be conducted in a conspiratorial manner, the process allowed for all kinds of shady dealings. Despite the fact that the party tried to control its own buyers through special control agents, usually members of the *Terror-Apparat,* some comrades succumbed to the temptation of filling their own pockets while conducting transactions with corrupt police officers, army quartermasters, and even members of paramilitary right-wing organizations. After all, it sufficed to list in the party's accounts a figure higher than the actual price, a procedure which was easy to suspect, but virtually impossible to prove. It also happened that weapons, which had been painstakingly obtained and hidden, were detected by right-wingers and stolen, only to be bought a second time by Communist agents. On some occasions, the party's buyers were deceived, and purchased boxes of rocks, carefully hidden beneath a top layer of rifles.[117]

All these preparations were conducted intensively and, it appears, with a real sense of anticipation. And yet one cannot escape the impression that much of what was done was amateurish, and carried out in a spirit of juvenile, if not frivolous, exuberance. Granted that the young men of the proletarian hundreds probably enjoyed the war games with improvised or simulated weapons in the depths of the German forests, that the cloak and dagger activities of mapping targets, ferreting out hidden arms caches, and stealing shotguns from isolated farmhouses at night provided excitement as well as a sense of importance. The fact remains that these activities failed to take into account the real odds which the party would be facing in the case of an armed uprising. Besides their unbelievably naïve disregard for the excellently trained and equipped forces at the disposal of the government, the party leaders also failed to give their attention to the popular support they could expect in a revolution. Throughout the preceding months the German masses, restless and irritated though they were, had at no time given any clear indication that they were prepared to follow the lead of the KPD. The May strikes in the Ruhr, the mass strikes during the height of the summer, the anti-Fascist day, the Cuno strike, all these occasions had shown that the Communists were unable to wrest the allegiance of the working class as a whole away from the SPD and the unions. Nor had the Schlageter line been a glowing success. True, the party had made inroads here and there, had captured control of many factory

[117] *ibid.,* pp. 198, 202-203; Flechtheim, p. 93.

councils, and had grown in numbers. But all these factors did not establish the KPD as a leading force in the German labor movement, the only position from which it could hope to carry the proletariat to victory.[118] Moreover, nothing had happened since the Cuno strike to change this picture materially—nothing, that is, but the minds of the Russian leaders. The men in the Kremlin thought they detected a growing revolutionary spirit in Germany after Cuno's resignation. They thought in terms of twenty million proletarians poised for action and eager to do battle. They held illusions with regard to the "working-class elements" in the Reichswehr "which at a decisive moment will not defend the bourgeoisie very stoutly."[119] They believed that arming the German workers required merely the presence of a few Communist ministers in the government of a medium-sized German state, and for this purpose transferred sizable sums to the Russian Embassy in Berlin. In short, Moscow was steeped in illusions, and on the basis of these illusions the German party prepared itself for an uprising.[120]

[118] This was quite frankly admitted by Radek, who said in January, 1924, that "even though [we are] a good worker's party, we are nowhere yet a good Communist party. . . . We Communists are still a minority among the masses; the masses sympathize with us, but were nowhere ready to fight with us to the finish. Our German brother party . . . is still an unfinished [*unfertig*] Communist party" (*Die Lehren der deutschen Ereignisse*, p. 13).

[119] Trotsky in *Izvestya*, October 21, 1923, as quoted in Carr, *The Interregnum*, p. 212. According to Carr, the leaders of the KPD shared the Russian illusions with regard to the attitude of the Reichswehr in case of a Communist rising. But neither the post-mortem held in Moscow in January 1924, nor the apologias of Remmele and Thalheimer bear out Carr's statement. What did exist among the German Communist leaders was the hope that despite the forces arraigned against them—Reichswehr, police, and right-wing organizations—the Communists would still be able to make some progress, enough to lay the basis for a final conquest of power in the not too distant future. See especially Remmele's statements in *Die Lehren der deutschen Ereignisse*, pp. 42-47. Thalheimer (*1923: Eine verpasste Revolution?*, p. 18) refers only to rumors concerning pro-Communist sympathies among the Reichswehr, but claims that these rumors were intentionally planted by army intelligence in order to mislead the workers. Thalheimer's account does not give the impression that these rumors were either widespread, or that they were believed by the leaders of the KPD.

[120] Carr, *The Interregnum*, pp. 213-214.

CHAPTER XIII

THE ABORTIVE "GERMAN OCTOBER"

⚓ DESPITE THE FACT that the Communists were not at all sure of the mass support on which their projected enterprise entirely depended, the party did very little during the weeks immediately after Zinoviev's telegram either to sound out the sentiment of the workers, or to prepare the masses psychologically for the struggle in which the KPD expected them to play an important part. The KPD concentrated all its efforts on mobilizing and arming its own members, without paying much attention to what went on outside the party. Where strikes or other signs of unrest erupted anywhere in the country, as for instance in Baden, the *Zentrale* saw to it that such movements did not receive Communist encouragement lest they interfere with the preparations for the uprising.[1] The rationale behind this attitude is easy to understand, but one cannot help wondering why the party decided to stake everything on the rigid plan based on the entry of Communists into the Saxon government, a plan in whose wisdom the majority of the *Zentrale* did not even believe.

What little was done by way of political preparation was done haphazardly. This was, at least to some extent, because the chief organ of the party, the *Rote Fahne*, was banned throughout most of the crucial period of preparation.[2] The only means of communication which remained at the disposal of the KPD was leaflets and the Communist press in some of the provinces. One such leaflet, headed "Mobilization," was distributed by the Communist-controlled Federal Committee of Factory Councils (then in Thuringia) on October 7, the day before Brandler returned from Moscow. The leaflet announced that any counterrevolutionary attack on the workers

[1] EKKI, *Die Lehren der deutschen Ereignisse* (Hamburg, 1924), pp. 34, 41; Thalheimer, *1923: Eine verpasste Revolution?*, (Berlin, 1931), p. 24; Remmele, *The Communist International*, I, New Series, No. 2 (n.d.), pp. 29, 36-38; *Bericht über die Verhandlungen des IX. Parteitages der K.P.D. (Sektion der K.I.) abgehalten in Frankfurt am Main vom 7. bis 10. April 1924* (Berlin, 1924), pp. 22-29, 56; Fischer, *Stalin and German Communism* (Cambridge, Mass., 1948), p. 327; Wenzel, "Die K.P.D. im Jahre 1923" (unpubl. diss. Freie Universität Berlin, 1955), p. 216.

[2] *Die Rote Fahne* was published again on October 9 and 10, 1923; on the 10th, the paper was banned again "until further notice," this time by the army. Publication resumed on October 20, 1923.

would be met by a general strike, and urged all proletarians to form action committees and defense organizations within the next week, and to meet daily in the factories and other places of work for discussions of the situation.[3]

On October 8 Hermann Remmele, a member of the *Zentrale* and of the party's Reichstag delegation, delivered a speech in the Reichstag which said in so many words that the KPD was contemplating civil war. After a furious attack on the Stresemann government, the presidential emergency decree of September 26, and the industrial leaders of the country, Remmele pointed to the threat which the "reactionary forces of the Whites" posed to German labor.

"We do know exactly: the White dictatorship which rules in Germany today can only be destroyed by the Red dictatorship. . . . The working classes have no other choice but to recognize that the rule of force can only be abolished through the same means and methods employed by you. (Very true! from the Communists.) . . . And if you make the workers conscious [of the fact] that hand grenades and machine guns are better weapons than all the speeches made in parliament, that the weapons of the White dictatorship are more effective than votes, then you only create the conditions by which you will liquidate [*erledigen*] yourselves. (Very true! from the Communists.)"[4]

On the following day, the *Rote Fahne* made the first of its two appearances before it was banned again for two weeks. The paper carried a poem by "a worker," entitled "Before the Battle"; an appeal from the KPD in Thuringia, which began with the words "We must act!"; and another poem, "That Reichstag . . . ," which ended with the words "Ours must be the country! Ours the Power!" It also again advocated a general strike and, in a little "interest story," reproduced a conversation, allegedly held in a machine shop, which contained lines reminiscent of the opening scene of Macbeth:

"And the Social Democrats?" . . . "Their hour of decision!". . .
"Everything is at stake!—The demand is: Stand together!". . .
"Are you willing?" "Will you fight with us?"

[3] Habedank, *Zur Geschichte des Hamburger Aufstandes 1923* (Berlin, 1958), p. 72.
[4] *Stenographische Berichte des Reichstags, Verhandlungen*, vol. 361, p. 12004. A barely recognizable version of Remmele's pedestrian prose was reprinted in *Die Rote Fahne*, No. 218, October 10, 1923.

"Everything is at stake—yes, indeed! We must stick together."
"Bravo—Then we can fight—and win!"[5]

Still more provocative than the revolutionary threats made by the German Communists was a letter which Joseph Stalin, General Secretary of the Russian Communist party, wrote to Thalheimer, the editor of the *Rote Fahne*. The letter, handwritten in Russian, appeared in facsimile form and with a German translation in the paper on October 10.

"Dear Comrade Thalheimer!

The approaching revolution in Germany is the most important world event in our time. The victory of the revolution in Germany will have a greater importance for the proletariat of Europe and America than the victory of the Russian Revolution six years ago. The victory of the German proletariat will undoubtedly shift the center of world revolution from Moscow to Berlin. The *Rote Fahne* can congratulate itself on a genuine success, because it has been the steadfast beacon which has shown the German proletariat the road to victory and which has helped it to regain the leadership of the European proletariat. From the bottom of my heart I wish the *Rote Fahne* new, decisive successes in the struggles ahead, for the conquest of power by the proletariat, for the unity and independence of a Germany about to be born. J. Stalin."[6]

Letters from Bukharin and Zinoviev, written in German and rather innocuous in tone and content, had appeared in the paper the previous day. But it was the letter from Stalin, the man who only a month earlier had been most outspokenly sceptical of a revolution in Germany, which aroused the apprehensions of the German authorities.[7] Alerted by the tumult and the shouting of the KPD, the German central government prepared to meet the challenge. It decided to do so in Saxony, the very part of the country which the Communists had selected for their revolutionary staging area.

Negotiations between the KPD and the Zeigner government of

---

[5] *Die Rote Fahne*, No. 217, October 9, 1923. The ellipsis is in the original.
[6] *ibid.*, No. 218, October 10, 1923.
[7] This is evident from the communications which the Prussian Ministry of the Interior sent to the German Foreign Office and to the German Embassy in Moscow. See Auswärtiges Amt, Germany, microfilm, container 911, frames 378970-378971, National Archives, Washington, D.C.; they are dated October 15, 1923.

Saxony had commenced immediately after the receipt of Zinoviev's telegram. The party's intention of joining the Saxon and Thuringian governments had been publicized by the *Zentrale* as early as October 5, and Hermann Remmele had shouted it to the assembled Reichstag delegates three days later.[8] His ostentatious demonstration, however, was premature. The talks were still going on, and Brandler, who had just that day arrived in Germany, proceeded at once to Dresden where he joined the negotiations the next morning, October 9.

Both sides were in a peculiar position. They needed each other's cooperation, but for very different reasons. Zeigner was still feuding with Berlin. He was also genuinely concerned about the ominous situation in Bavaria, about the recent Küstrin putsch, and other manifestations of a resurgent nationalism.[9] Although he was neither a Communist nor a believer in revolutionary action, Zeigner was determined to turn Saxony into a bastion of the Left. During his first months in office he had done everything possible to mollify the KPD in order to retain its vitally needed support in the diet. Now, faced by what he considered a serious threat from right-wing Bavaria, he was prepared to form a coalition government with the Communists in order to assure himself of their further cooperation, so that at least in Saxony the working class would be in a position to repulse any attacks made upon it by the Right.

The Communists, on the other hand, were under orders to enter the Saxon government, though they could not admit this in public. Whereas Zeigner wanted to strengthen the defensive position of the working class in his state, the KPD wanted to use the projected coalition to turn Saxony into an armory for their revolutionary designs. Thus the Communists were committed to join Zeigner's cabinet regardless of the outcome of negotiations. For this reason they proved to be much more yielding and conciliatory than they had been in the past, and accepted in advance most of Zeigner's government program. They used the "Fascist danger" to explain their eagerness to come to terms, but they did drive a hard bargain on points of detail. One of these was that a Communist should be appointed to

[8] *Schulthess', Europäischer Geschichtskalender,* 1923 (Munich, 1928), pp. 185-186. *Stenographische Berichte des Reichstags, Verhandlungen,* vol. 361, p. 12005.

[9] In the night from October 9 to 10, 1923, Bavarian National Socialists and proletarian hundreds from Thuringia clashed at the border between Thuringia and Bavaria (*Vossische Zeitung,* No. 491, October 17, 1923).

head the ministry of the interior, which controlled the police. This Zeigner would not grant, and the Communists had to be satisfied with seeing one of their number—it happened to be Brandler, the party chairman—appointed *Ministerialdirektor* (approx.: Assistant Secretary) in charge of the state chancellery, an office which allowed at least an indirect influence over the police. It was agreed in addition that the former Communist delegate to the Saxon diet, Paul Böttcher, should become Minister of Finance, while Fritz Heckert became Minister of the Economy. Both were members of the *Zentrale*. All these preliminary agreements were concluded on October 10, and two days later the new Saxon government was officially formed.[10]

On this day, the diet convened to hear Zeigner announce his government's program. The session began on a note of unrest when the chairman of the KPD delegation, Siewert, staged a one-man demonstration under the pretext of making a point of order: "Prepare everywhere for a general strike! Make provisions for tying up every transport designed to move Reichswehr and armed gangs [hired to] crush the workers. Now I have finished."[11]

After the house had quieted down, Zeigner was able to speak. He introduced the new ministers who, he stated, had sworn an oath to protect the constitutions of the Reich and of Saxony, and then called his reconstituted government one of "republican and proletarian defense." The program which he outlined was phrased in rather general terms and contained three major points: Saxony, based on an alliance of all the workers and those sincerely dedicated to the republic, would form a bulwark against the combined forces of reaction, which ranged from the big industrialists to the rabble-rousers in Bavaria. Saxony would stand loyally by the Reich and would fight to the utmost to preserve its unity. Finally, the new government pledged itself to do everything possible to help the poor, the downtrodden, the dispossessed.[12]

The entry of two Communist ministers and one *Ministerialdirektor* into the Saxon government was a distinct tactical achievement by the KPD. Since three members of the *Zentrale*, including the

[10] *Schulthess'*, 1923, p. 190; Wenzel, pp. 217-218; Habedank, pp. 76-77; Remmele, *The Communist International*, I, New Series, No. 2 (n.d.), pp. 30-31, 34; Carr, *The Interregnum 1923-1924* (New York, 1954), p. 220.

[11] *Verhandlungen des Sächsischen Landtages 1923*, II, p. 1577.

[12] *ibid.*, p. 1578.

chairman, were now permanently stationed in Dresden, it was found convenient to move the rest of the *Zentrale* also to the Saxon capital. In theory, at least, it was a perfect setup: the leaders of the KPD, some as cabinet ministers, were safely situated in a state which sympathized with many of the party's views; proletarian "defense" forces were still operating freely in the open, "ignoring" General Müller, and the Communists seemed justified in anticipating that at least in Saxony their plans for an uprising early in November would meet with few obstacles. Thus, as soon as they were sworn in, Brandler, Böttcher, and Heckert settled down to their various offices, Brandler to peruse the files in search of information concerning secret arms caches, Böttcher and Heckert respectively to wrestle with the state's financial difficulties and an acute food shortage.[13]

Up to the moment when the new Saxon government took office, everything had gone well for the Communists. But the next day, October 13, the political horizon began to cloud over. General Müller, Commander of the Fourth German Military District, issued an order which banned all proletarian hundreds "or similar organizations."[14] The Saxon government launched an immediate and strong protest in which it stated that the proletarian hundreds were loyal to the constitution and would defend the republic against any attacks.[15] It became apparent at once that neither side was prepared to give in. On the same day that General Müller published his order, Finance Minister Paul Böttcher made a speech in Leipzig and demanded that all proletarian hundreds be armed at once.[16] A congress of Saxony's proletarian hundreds, scheduled in September to convene on October 14, was now moved up a day and met illegally in a suburb of Chemnitz during October 13 and 14. The police proved unable to locate the meeting place where representatives of the SPD, KPD, and the unions deliberated for two days. The pro-

---

[13] Gast, *Zeitschrift für Geschichtswissenschaft*, IV, No. 3 (1956), p. 458; Wenzel, p. 218. The three Communist government officials tried to combine two different jobs. They used their positions to obtain information, especially information pertaining to the location of weapons; their findings they would then pass on to the party's *Apparat*. But at the same time they applied themselves seriously and sincerely to their task as ministers of a workers' government, an attitude which eventually earned them disapproval and acid criticism from the Comintern and the Opposition within the KPD. See, for instance, Habedank, pp. 77-78; Fischer, pp. 332-333; Ulbricht, *Zur Geschichte der deutschen Arbeiterbewegung*, I (Berlin, 1953), pp. 136-138.

[14] *Schulthess'*, 1923, p. 192.

[15] *ibid.*, p. 193.

[16] *ibid.*; *Frankfurter Zeitung*, Nos. 772 and 774, both October 18, 1923.

ceedings were published a few days later in the Communist press.[17]

But October 13 was a black day for the Communists in other respects. On that day the Reichstag passed a hotly debated Enabling Act which empowered the government to take all measures necessary to meet any emergencies in the fields of finance, economics, or social welfare.[18] Stresemann had asked for this Act in order to give the government a chance to work out the most urgent domestic problems without interference from political or other pressure groups.[19] All parties, except for the Nationalists and the KPD, had voted for the Act. Only the extremes on the left and right were not interested in strengthening the hand of a government which both sides would have liked to see disappear. At the same time, however, the passage of the Enabling Act held some advantages for the Communists because it proved a very unpopular measure with German labor as a whole. Although the Reichstag delegation of the SPD had supported the Act, that party's rank and file by and large opposed it. There had been too much talk about abolishing the eight-hour day, and the workers were also concerned by the repeated demands of the big industrialists for a "dictatorship," i.e. a dictatorship of the Right. There were numerous demonstrations against the high cost of living, especially by the unemployed, and the mood of the working class in general, by the middle of October, was by no means uncritical of the government, so much so that many Social Democratic party members objected to General Müller's decree outlawing the proletarian hundreds in Saxony.[20] It was probably due to this dissatisfaction with economic and social conditions that the

[17] Gast, *Zeitschrift für Geschichtswissenschaft*, IV, No. 3 (1956), pp. 461-462; Habedank, p. 67; *Vossische Zeitung*, No. 493, October 18, 1923.

[18] *Stenographische Berichte des Reichstags, Verhandlungen*, vol. 361, pp. 12148-12149, 12152-12154.

[19] Stresemann, *Vermächtnis*, I: *Vom Ruhrkrieg bis London* (Berlin, 1932), pp. 155-158.

[20] *Vossische Zeitung*, No. 489, October 16, 1923. The mood of labor is reflected in the daily press of the period, and is probably most succinctly expressed in a report on a conference of trade-unionists held in Berlin on October 17, 1923. Many of labor's grievances were aired at this conference. See *Frankfurter Zeitung*, Nos. 772, 773, both October 18, 1923.

The eight-hour day, labor's most important post-war achievement, was not abolished, but was tampered with: it was retained "in principle," but for a number of occupational groups a longer working day—nine and ten hours—was authorized, though with overtime pay. See *ibid.*, No. 776, October 19, 1923; on plans for a "dictatorship" see Schlottner, *Stresemann* (diss. Frankfurt am Main, 1948), pp. 62-63; Stockhausen, *Sechs Jahre Reichskanzlei* (Bonn, 1954), p. 84; Hallgarten, *Hitler, Reichswehr und Industrie* (Frankfurt am Main, 1955), pp. 65-66.

KPD's Berlin organization felt encouraged to initiate talks with the Social Democrats in the capital. The Communists were trying to form a common front and draw up a common program of action, ostensibly to defend labor against any possible attacks from the "reactionaries," in reality to mobilize the non-Communist workers for a revolution which the latter did not know was in the offing. But the Berlin organization, led by Ruth Fischer, overplayed its hand by demanding too much, and creating what the papers called a "general strike atmosphere."[21] The negotiations broke down, and non-Communist labor in Berlin worked out an agreement without the KPD.[22]

Meanwhile in Saxony the reaction on the part of the KPD and the Saxon government to General Müller's ban of the hundreds, and to the passage of the Enabling Act in the Reichstag, was defiance. The Communists were heartened by the fact that on October 13 they had come to terms with the Thuringian government. Here, too, a coalition of left-wing Socialists and Communists was agreed upon, and three days later the Communists Dr. Karl Korsch and Albin Tenner joined the Thuringian government. They were appointed as Ministers of Education (*Volksbildung*) and Economy, respectively.[23] Thus encouraged, the *Zentrale* circulated a proclamation on October 14 which called on the workers to arm themselves and to prepare for "a battle to establish a government of all working people in the Reich and abroad."[24] The party organ in Chemnitz, *Der Kämpfer*, wrote on October 15 that the working class ". . . was not prepared to tolerate the policy of suppression [which was practiced] by the government of Stresemann-Sollmann. It will defend German unity and its own existence as a class against the great-capitalistic-military

[21] *Frankfurter Zeitung*, No. 771, October 17, 1923.

[22] *Die Lehren der deutschen Ereignisse*, p. 63. Similar talks were held in Hamburg during the same period (*Schulthess'*, 1923, p. 196). With reference to such negotiations in general, Ruth Fischer said in June, 1924: "We do not reject negotiations with [Social Democratic] leaders on principle, but . . . as Communists, our object in entering into negotiations with leaders is to separate the masses from these very leaders, and not to form treaties with them. The Right [within the KPD], however, actually reproached us with [sic] entering into negotiations solely in order to break them off!" (*Fifth Congress of the Communist International, Abridged Report of Meetings Held at Moscow June 17th to July 8th, 1924* [London, n.d.], p. 59).

[23] Witzmann, *Thüringen von 1918-1933* (Meissenheim am Glain, 1958), p. 95; *Vossische Zeitung*, No. 487, October 14, Nos. 491, 492, both October 17, 1923; *Schulthess'*, 1923, pp. 194, 196.

[24] Quoted in Marchionini, *Bürgerkrieg und Bolschewismus in Deutschland* (Leipzig, 1924), p. 23.

counterrevolution by means of economic pressure and, if need be, by arms."[25]

If the KPD was not prepared to tolerate the government's policy of suppression, Stresemann was equally averse to tolerating the Communist threat of civil war. He had enough troubles already. There was the situation in Bavaria, where nationalist agitation was on the increase, and where the local Reichswehr commander was in open conflict with his superiors in Berlin. The economic crisis was still acute, and while the government was hopeful that it would be alleviated by the creation of the *Rentenmark*, which had just been announced, as yet there was more hope than actual success. As early as October 6, during a cabinet meeting, the Reich Defense Minister Gessler had suggested with his customary bluntness that if conditions in Saxony should deteriorate any further, the central government would be forced to depose the government of that state, and to appoint a civilian Reich commissioner. In short, Gessler proposed to apply a *Reichsexekutive* (federal executive action, as authorized by Article 48 of the constitution) against Saxony.[26] During the following days, the chancellor's initial reluctance to accept Gessler's advice was effectively worn down by the conduct of the Communists and the Saxon government, as well as by pleas for help from regional organizations of Stresemann's own People's Party in various parts of central Germany.[27]

But before the central government had reached a decision on this point, General Müller in Saxony, acting after consultation with the *Reichswehrminister*, resumed the initiative on the local level. On October 16 he informed the Zeigner government that from that date the Saxon police were to be placed under the immediate authority of the Reichswehr.[28] As the KPD deputy Siewert said the same day in the diet, this was in effect the *Reichsexekutive* and, in practical terms, amounted to the deposition of the Saxon government.[29] With the police removed from his control, Zeigner was

[25] Quoted in Habedank, p. 62. Sollmann, the Reich Minister of the Interior, was a Social Democrat.

[26] Stresemann, *Vermächtnis*, i, pp. 166-167; Schlottner, p. 58.

[27] See, for instance, the "Resolution of the *Landesverband* of the People's Party in Halle-Merseburg," dated October 9, 1923, Stresemann Nachlass, Auswärtiges Amt, Germany, microfilm, container 3195, frames 171378-171379, National Archives, Washington, D.C.

[28] *Verhandlungen des Sächsischen Landtages 1923*, ii, pp. 1606-1607.

[29] *ibid.*, p. 1596.

powerless, and Brandler became a *Ministerialdirektor* in charge of meaningless police files.

Having once resumed the offensive, General Müller continued to press his advantage. The day after he put the Saxon police under his command he sent the Zeigner government an ultimatum, demanding submission to his orders. After a sharp condemnation of Paul Böttcher's Leipzig speech on October 13, the general's communication read as follows: "In all my previous measures I have proceeded on the assumption that I possessed the cooperation of the Saxon government. . . . I ask you, Herr Minister-President, to comment on Minister Böttcher's statements, and to let me know unequivocally by 11 A.M. on October 18 whether the ministry as a whole agrees with the letter and spirit of Minister Böttcher's statements, and whether it intends to conduct the affairs of government further along these lines, or whether it is willing . . . to act according to my instructions.

"Should the latter be the case I must demand, in order to clarify matters, that the Saxon government publish a declaration to this effect in the press. I furthermore ask to be informed of what measures the government is contemplating to prevent in the future a repetition of incidents [*Entgleisungen*, literally, derailments], such as the speech of Minister Böttcher undoubtedly constitutes."[30]

Zeigner's response to General Müller's ultimatum was a resounding and uncompromising "No." The minister-president declared in the diet that he was not going to honor the general with a reply. The Saxon government, he exclaimed, stood on constitutional ground, whereas the general did not. He demanded that the Reich government take immediate steps to rectify the humiliating position in which the Saxon government had been placed.[31] During the same session, Finance Minister Böttcher announced that preliminary talks were at present being held with Soviet Russia about a trade agreement between Saxony and the Soviet Union. Russia was prepared to send grain shipments to Saxony to help alleviate the food shortage, and in return Saxony was to send industrial goods to Russia. Böttcher expressed hopes that the negotiations would be concluded by October 19, in which case 20,000 tons of grain would reach Saxony by the end of the month.[32]

[30] *ibid.*, p. 1622. [31] *ibid.*, pp. 1647-1649.
[32] *ibid.*, p. 1646.

Saxony's decision to turn to Russia for food supplies was not a mere gesture of protest, but arose from real necessity. The military commanders of East Prussia and Silesia had prohibited the transport of potatoes from their respective military districts to any part of the republic, a measure which affected especially the densely populated central German industrial region, including Saxony.[33] When Böttcher had turned to the banking concerns in Dresden and asked for a loan of 150 million gold marks to provide the state with food supplies, the banks had refused to loan any money to the Saxon government, but had offered to advance the needed sum to General Müller.[34] A similar situation existed in Thuringia, where the Communist International Workers' Aid made the new workers' government a present of 788 tons of grain. Here, too, the state drifted into conflict with the regional military commander, General Reinhardt, who on October 17 issued a decree forbidding labor to call a general strike.[35]

The growing tension in central Germany as a whole, and in Saxony in particular, was discussed on October 17 during a cabinet meeting of the Stresemann government. General Müller's ultimatum of that day to Minister-President Zeigner had been delivered with the prior consent of Ebert and Stresemann. Its form and content aroused the concern of Social Democratic Reich Minister of the Interior Sollmann, who told Stresemann that General Müller's measure constituted an open provocation of the SPD. When the chancellor defended the general and pointed to the very disturbing situation which existed in Saxony, Sollmann replied that he had received assurances that the Communist ministers in Zeigner's cabinet intended to remain quiet and orderly. But Stresemann was not convinced, and expressed lack of confidence in Zeigner's ability as a politician. He stated that if the Saxon government failed to take energetic measures to cope with mounting radicalism, those circles in Saxony that felt themselves threatened might turn to Bavaria for aid. Such a move, Stresemann said, would mean civil war and the collapse of the republic.[36]

Sollmann and his two Social Democratic colleagues in the cabinet,

[33] Habedank, p. 78.
[34] Stresemann, *Vermächtnis*, 1, p. 167.
[35] Habedank, pp. 80-81.
[36] Stresemann, *Vermächtnis*, 1, pp. 167-168; "Reichskabinett-Protokolle," Auswärtiges Amt und Reichskanzlei, Germany, microfilm T-120, container 1749, frames D 757226-757227.

Gustav Radbruch and Robert Schmidt (Rudolf Hilferding, the fourth Social Democrat, had resigned when the cabinet was reconstituted early in the month), found themselves in a difficult position. Zeigner was a fellow Social Democrat, and as such warranted their support. But the three Reich ministers were also fully aware of his shortcomings. They knew that he was basically a weak person who tried to conceal this fact behind a show of ruthlessness; they knew that he was easily influenced, and that he was one person when they met him in Berlin and another in the radical atmosphere of Dresden. But since they were unaware of the role which the KPD was playing in Saxony behind Zeigner's back, and since they felt obligated to defend their party comrade, they tended to make light of Zeigner's unorthodox ways as head of state, and pretended to consider his behavior simply as the "antics of a silly child."[37]

On October 18 the Saxon crisis grew sharper. Around noon, Zeigner received the following letter from General Müller: "As you have thought it proper not to reply to my communication of October 17, 1923, I am respectfully informing you that I have passed on the matter to the Reich Defense Minister for further action. With the assurance of my highest esteem, (signed) Müller, Lieutenant-General."[38]

During the morning session, before he received General Müller's letter, Zeigner had taken a step which was bound to infuriate Reich Defense Minister Otto Gessler, and the entire Stresemann cabinet as well. For that morning Zeigner delivered in the diet what came to be known as his "Black Reichswehr Speech." He began by saying that his speech would undoubtedly have repercussions in France, and that although he regretted the necessity to speak out, he was also convinced that he had nothing to say which was not already known to the French intelligence service. Then he delivered a sharp attack on the Reich government's induction and training of illegal troops, men whose training was so brief that they could not possibly be a threat to another nation, but would be an acute threat at home, notably to the workers. Zeigner charged that the government defended the formation of irregular units with the argument that they were needed to protect the republic, while those organizations sin-

[37] Stockhausen, p. 86; Gustav Radbruch, *Der Innere Weg: Aufriss meines Lebens* (Stuttgart, 1951), pp. 171-172.
[38] *Verhandlungen des Sächsischen Landtages 1923*, II, p. 1724.

cerely dedicated to just this purpose (i.e. the proletarian hundreds) were officially banned. The question was not, he said, "whether or not my procedure is formally correct, the question is, whether there is the will and the possibility to smash [*zerschlagen*] these organizations within a few weeks, because they are a tremendous danger to the continuance of the Reich and to the smooth functioning of administration and justice."[39]

However sincere, honorable, and even patriotic Zeigner's intentions may have been, in making this speech he rendered a disservice to his own cause and to the security of the republic. Undoubtedly he wanted to embarrass the Stresemann government and the army, but he completely miscalculated the consequences. Rather than striking a blow against the irregulars, he antagonized the regular army, the Reichswehr, and played into the hands of Defense Minister Gessler, who now had an excellent pretext for carrying out his projected *Reichsexekutive* against Saxony. In fact, Berlin could justify such a step on more than one count. The government faced a difficult political situation both in central Germany and Bavaria. The nascent rebellion in the latter state was much more serious and dangerous than was the threat from either Saxony or Thuringia. Thus logic would have required the government to proceed at once against Bavaria, but in this case logic yielded to expediency. Armed intervention in Bavaria would have been by far the greater risk, and for several reasons. Under the circumstances it could easily have led to civil war, which Stresemann was determined to avoid. Furthermore, the Reichswehr could be trusted to intervene in Saxony and Thuringia, two states with Communist-Socialist coalition governments, whereas the reliability of the troops in case of open conflict with Bavaria was doubtful. Sentiments similar to those of the Reichswehr were held by many middle-class nationalists, sentiments which weighed heavier with Stresemann and the majority of his cabinet than the opinions of the Social Democrats. Nor could the government overlook the practical advantages of sending troops into central Germany. The presence of the Reichswehr in this region would effectively forestall any putsches which the Communists might want to stage in Saxony and Thuringia. It was hoped, moreover, that such a move would create a military barrier against Bavaria, and at the

[39] *ibid.*, p. 1683.

same time would deprive this state of an excuse for sending armed bands of nationalists into central Germany, and from there possibly toward Berlin. Rumors concerning the existence of such plans were circulating widely at the time.[40]

Consequently, during a cabinet meeting on October 19, the Chancellor mentioned briefly that he had been told about illegal bands, suspected of planning to interfere in Saxony and Thuringia, and that for this reason Reichswehr formations would be concentrated at several points in that region. Stresemann said that he expected this measure "to intimidate radical elements, and to restore public order and security."[41]

On October 20 Zeigner received a letter from Berlin which informed him that movements of Reichswehr troops into Saxony were not intended to constitute a "hostile act." The purpose of these troop movements was rather to protect Saxony against any possible attacks from "right-radical Bavarian forces."[42] This communication, the sender of which Zeigner failed to reveal, seems to have been the first indication he received concerning the central government's decision to intervene in his state. But if he still had illusions about the intentions of Berlin, they were destroyed a few hours later by another communication from General Müller, as clipped, correct, and concise as the earlier ones. The most crucial passage in it read as follows: ". . . I have been instructed [by the Reich Defense Minister] to restore and maintain constitutional and orderly conditions in the Free State of Saxony with those means of enforcement . . . at my disposal. I shall communicate the reasons for the interference by the Reichswehr to the population. . . ."[43]

This General Müller proceeded to do forthwith, by publishing his letter to Zeigner with an official commentary on his action, and by posting it in the streets. Without knowing it, the general thereby gave official notice to the KPD that the Reichswehr, as Professor

[40] Schüddekopf, *Heer und Republik* (Hannover and Frankfurt am Main, 1955), p. 169; Schlottner, pp. 79-81, 116-117; Thimme, *Gustav Stresemann* (Hannover and Frankfurt, 1957), pp. 58-60; Schwend, *Bayern zwischen Monarchie und Diktatur* (Munich, 1954), pp. 234-239; Gessler, *Reichswehrpolitik in der Weimarer Zeit*, ed. Kurt Sendtner (Stuttgart, 1958), pp. 269-270; Severing, *Mein Lebensweg*, I (Cologne, 1950), pp. 441-442.
[41] Stresemann, *Vermächtnis*, I, p. 171; "Reichskabinett-Protokolle," Auswärtiges Amt und Reichskanzlei, Germany, microfilm T-120, container 1749, frame D 757256.
[42] *Verhandlungen des Sächsischen Landtages 1923*, II, p. 1760.
[43] *ibid.*; Habedank, p. 81; *Die Rote Fahne*, No. 221, October 21, 1923.

Carr puts it, "had fixed the date on which the Communists must either act, or confess their impotence."[44]

Reports of the army's impending march into Saxony apparently reached the party shortly before General Müller announced it publicly. During the night from October 19 to 20 the KPD had circulated a leaflet, 150,000 copies of it, which instructed party members to seize all available weapons. For unknown reasons, this order was almost completely ignored.[45] On October 20, the *Rote Fahne* was published again after an interval of two weeks, and carried an article by Brandler which made reference to the newest threat facing the Saxon proletariat. The article was entitled "Everything is at Stake," and expressed the conviction that the German workers "will not allow the Saxon proletariat to be struck down."[46]

The news of these developments took the Communists by surprise, although they were largely responsible for them. Böttcher's reckless speech at Leipzig a week earlier had started the political avalanche which was now about to descend on them. Moreover Zeigner, whom they had consciously deceived about their motives for joining his government, had unwittingly contributed to ruining their plans when he loyally defended Böttcher and refused to obey General Müller's orders to dissolve the proletarian hundreds, on the existence of which depended success or failure of the projected Communist uprising.

On October 20, as soon as the *Zentrale* received word of General Müller's proclamation, the Communist leaders met for a hasty conference. The original plan of action had been to call a national conference of factory councils, but for this there was no longer sufficient time. The conference, improvising rapidly, decided to utilize a workers' conference at Chemnitz, which had been scheduled several days earlier for October 21, to sound out the mood of the labor representatives and, if the mood was favorable, to call for a general strike which would give the signal for the uprising.[47] This decision allowed the party less than twenty-four hours of preparation.

[44] Carr, *The Interregnum*, p. 221.
[45] Wenzel, p. 224.
[46] *ibid.*; Carr, *The Interregnum*, p. 221.
[47] *Die Lehren der deutschen Ereignisse*, p. 42; Thalheimer, 1923: *Eine verpasste Revolution?*, p. 26; cf. the rather ambiguous version in Habedank, p. 82. The conference had been originally called for the purpose of deliberating on how to deal with the critical food shortage in Saxony; see Wenzel, p. 223; Remmele, *The Communist International*, 1, New Series, No. 2 (n.d.), p. 35.

The Abortive "German October"

The Chemnitz Conference opened as scheduled the following day, October 21, 1923. Its composition was fairly representative of Saxon labor. Aside from 66 KPD delegates, the conference was attended by 140 delegates of factory councils, 122 representatives of labor unions, 79 delegates of control commissions, 15 delegates of action committees, 16 unemployed, 7 representatives of the SPD and one from the practically defunct USPD.[48] The principal speakers were the Social Democratic Minister of Labor Graupe, Finance Minister Böttcher, and his fellow Communist, Minister of Economic Affairs Heckert. All three stressed the critical food shortage in the state, the equally catastrophic financial situation, and the misery of the unemployed. These reports were followed by a public discussion of the political crisis in Saxony. Repeated demands were made to resist the threatening "military dictatorship," and several speakers urged the proclamation of a general strike as a means of collective protest.[49]

Then Brandler took the floor. From the preceding discussion he may have received the impression that the suggestion he was about to make would be met with approval, for he called bluntly for the immediate proclamation of a general strike. He added that such a proclamation would serve as labor's fighting slogan against the Reichswehr, and urged that the conference put the matter to a vote at once. But Brandler's suggestion was greeted with icy silence. Whether this was due to the manner in which he had broached the question, or whether the delegates considered his proposal a case of indecent haste cannot be determined. It was evident, however, that the delegates were not prepared to make any rash decisions on the spur of the moment. After a brief moment of embarrassed silence the Saxon Minister of Labor Graupe rose and announced that if the Communists insisted on pressing the suggestion just made, he and his six fellow delegates from the SPD would at once leave the conference. Graupe's statement met with no protest. It was, in Thalheimer's words, a "third-class funeral."[50]

---

[48] Wenzel, p. 223. With a few minor exceptions, the same figures are given in Habedank, p. 86, and Thalheimer, 1923: *Eine verpasste Revolution?*, p. 26.

[49] Habedank, p. 86; *Schulthess'*, 1923, p. 200.

[50] Thalheimer, 1923: *Eine verpasste Revolution?*, p. 26; Wenzel, p. 225; Habedank, p. 86. Habedank claims that Brandler insisted on a unanimous vote, although he knew that it would be impossible to obtain. There is no corroborating evidence for this charge.

Why did the conference discuss at length the feasibility of calling a general strike, but reject out of hand Brandler's motion to proclaim one immediately? Were the non-Communist participants hypocrites? The subsequent course of the conference does not substantiate such an assumption. For as soon as Graupe had rejected the Communist motion he in turn moved that a special commission be formed, comprising an equal number of Social Democrats and Communists, to study the prospects for a general strike. Graupe's motion was adopted, and the commission formed. Its members reported back shortly and moved the creation of an action committee, likewise composed of Communists and Social Democrats, which was to contact the leading echelons (*Spitzenorganisationen*) of the political labor parties, the trade-unions, and the government of Saxony, and was to negotiate with them about the proclamation of a general strike. Only if these negotiations should fail was the action committee entitled to proclaim a general strike. The motion was passed by an overwhelming majority.[51] The outcome shows that the conference members, however much they may have been provoked by General Müller, were simply not inclined to make a weighty decision without first exploring its every aspect. Brandler's motion, as he might well have known, flew in the face of German labor's traditional insistence on proper procedure and proper channels. Moreover, the most determined resistance to Brandler's motion came from the representatives of the trade-unions and the SPD, who had no desire to let themselves be led into a possible putsch by the Communists.[52] In the end, Brandler's dutiful execution of orders, which he had only reluctantly accepted in Moscow a few weeks earlier, proved to have done more harm than good. For the special action committee apparently never reported back, and a general strike was not called in Saxony at that time.[53] Instead, Reichswehr formations began to march into the state on the day of the conference, with bands playing, flags unfurled, and rifles loaded with live ammunition.

[51] Habedank, pp. 86-87; Wenzel, p. 225.

[52] Wenzel, pp. 225-226. The reluctance of the Social Democrats, including their left wing, to risk a general strike was also due to their conviction that the Reichswehr was marching in primarily to keep the Bavarian "Fascists" in check (*ibid.*, p. 225 and *Fifth Congress of the Communist International, Abridged Report*, p. 65; also Gast, *Zeitschrift für Geschichtswissenschaft*, iv, No. 3 [1956], pp. 462-463).

[53] A general protest strike was finally called on October 30, 1923, but since it came too late and lacked support it was not very effective. See below.

The Abortive "German October"

The "third-class funeral" was over. The Communists had sounded out the collective mood of Saxony's labor representatives and had found it wanting in spirit. It was clear to Brandler and his colleagues that the party could hardly count on substantial support for their venture from German labor as a whole, if not even the Saxon proletariat was willing to take any risks.[54] That this was the consensus of the Communists present in Chemnitz became evident as soon as the general conference had adjourned. The *Zentrale* immediately summoned a meeting to discuss the situation. In addition to the members of the *Zentrale* present, the meeting was attended by several *MP* commanders and their Russian advisors. Absent were Radek and his three fellow "supervisors" who had not been in Chemnitz at all and, in fact, had not yet arrived in Germany.[55] Without waiting for Radek, the party functionaries attending the meeting agreed that no large-scale uprising could be risked under the present circum-

[54] Thalheimer, 1923: *Eine verpasste Revolution?*, p. 27; *Die Lehren der deutschen Ereignisse*, p. 6.

[55] *Die Lehren der deutschen Ereignisse*, pp. 5, 24. Radek's whereabouts were again of great concern to the German authorities. When the German press in mid-October circulated reports that Radek and six (!) companions had arrived in Berlin, Ambassador Brockdorff-Rantzau, eager as usual to avoid unnecessary friction with Russia, sent the following telegram to Berlin: "Moscow, October 16, 1923: Claims by German papers that Radek has arrived Berlin with six companions pure invention. Radek met . . . Professor Hoetzsch at Embassy two weeks ago; gave long speech at agricultural exhibition one week ago; spoke yesterday in person with Embassy Councilor Graap and Legation Councilor von Gelbsattel" ("Brockdorff-Rantzau to Foreign Office," Auswärtiges Amt, Germany, microfilm, container 1406, frame D 553265). Thus Radek could not have left Moscow before October 15, 1923. He did not arrive in Germany before October 22. On this day he may have stayed in Dresden, and may have returned to Berlin with Brandler and other KPD functionaries. This possible, though by no means conclusive, reconstruction of Radek's itinerary is based on the following accounts: *Die Lehren der deutschen Ereignisse*, pp. 5, 6, 24; Gast, *Zeitschrift für Geschichtswissenschaft*, IV, No. 3 (1956), p. 463; Herbert Dirksen, *Moskau-Tokio-London: 20 Jahre deutscher Aussenpolitik* (Stuttgart, n.d.), p. 63; Wenzel, p. 227. Cf. Fischer, p. 336, who has Radek in Chemnitz during the conference. Her account indicates, however, that she was not in Chemnitz herself but had probably remained in Berlin. Most of her descriptions of events follow nearly verbatim Thalheimer, *1923: Eine verpasste Revolution?*, although she does not identify her source. The Berlin organization was represented in Chemnitz by Hans Pfeiffer, then secretary of the Berlin district's organizational bureau. Contrary to Ruth Fischer's claim that he was liquidated during the Russian purge trials of the thirties (Fischer, p. 603, n.42), Pfeiffer lives today in East Germany; see Habedank, pp. 85, n.1, 209, and *passim*; Habedank identifies him only by his initials, but states that in 1923 he was *Organisationssekretär* of the party's Berlin district; see also *Die Gründung der Kommunistischen Partei Deutschlands, Protokoll der wissenschaftlichen Tagung des Instituts für Gesellschaftswissenschaften, der Parteihochschule "Karl Marx" und des Instituts für Marxismus-Leninismus beim ZK der SED am 22. und 23. Januar 1959 in Berlin* (Berlin, 1959), p. 181, n.1.

stances. There seemed little else to do after the original scheme, which had marked out Saxony as the starting point of the rising, had miscarried.[56] This conclusion was in accordance with the resolution taken a day earlier to await the outcome of the Chemnitz Conference before committing the party to any definite course of action.

The Chemnitz Conference, however, had a bloody sequel, an armed proletarian uprising in Hamburg. Unfortunately, many of its underlying causes are still shrouded in mystery and, pending the discovery of additional evidence, an account of its origins will have to remain tentative.[57]

[56] Wenzel, p. 226.

[57] Unless otherwise indicated, the discussion of the origins of the Hamburg uprising, given below, is based on the following accounts: Lothar Danner, *Ordnungspolizei Hamburg: Betrachtungen zu ihrer Geschichte 1918 bis 1933* (Hamburg, 1958), pp. 67-74 (the author was the commander of Hamburg's *Ordnungspolizei* in 1923); Wenzel, pp. 226-231; and Habedank, pp. 87-108. All three authors are in general agreement on the situation in Hamburg prior to the outbreak of fighting, but they differ widely on the question of how the uprising originated. Whenever there was any doubt I have adhered to the version given by Danner, the most recent and, in my opinion, also the most convincing account.

Danner's is the only version which attributes the responsibility for the decision to stage an uprising solely to the leadership of the Hamburg party organization. Every other version relies on what may be called the *"Zentrale's* roving courier" theory, which was first advanced on November 1, 1923, in *Vorwärts*. This theory held that after the failure of the Chemnitz Conference the *Zentrale* decided to start the uprising in Hamburg instead of in Saxony. A courier with the appropriate orders was sent to Hamburg where he delivered his message. But shortly after he had left Chemnitz the *Zentrale* had a change of heart and sent a second courier to countermand the original order. The second courier, for reasons which differ with each individual version, came too late, and the uprising in Hamburg began.

There are many variations of this same theme. The story most often told is that the first courier for Hamburg left the Chemnitz Conference too soon and conveyed the signal for the uprising. The courier's premature departure is frequently attributed to Ernst Thälmann's hot temper. Thälmann was allegedly so outraged over the outcome of the conference that he took it upon himself to send off the couriers to their respective districts with orders to launch the uprising at once. But all couriers could be stopped at the railway station, except for Hermann Remmele, the courier for Hamburg. A second courier was sent after Remmele to countermand his orders but was unable to make contact with the Hamburg organization. Thus the uprising began. See Zeutschel, *Im Dienst der Kommunistischen Terror-Organisation* (Berlin, 1931), p. 15; Flechtheim, *Die K.P.D. in der Weimarer Republik* (Offenbach, 1948), p. 96; Schwarz, *"Völker höret die Zentrale, KPD bankrott"* (Berlin, 1933), pp. 105-107; Valtin, *Out of the Night* (New York, 1941), p. 70. Fischer, p. 339, has both Remmele and Thälmann leave for Hamburg before they received word from Brandler that the uprising was off. Thalheimer, *1923: Eine verpasste Revolution?*, p. 27, mentions only that Remmele left too early and could not be stopped in time. So does Nollau, *Die Internationale* (Cologne, 1959), p. 74. According to Wenzel (p. 228, n.11), the story of the courier's premature departure from Chemnitz is also upheld by Brandler, who still feels bound by what he considers was then

The Abortive "German October"

The man in charge of the party's political organization in Hamburg was Hugo Urbahns, a teacher, who was secretary of the KPD District Command *Wasserkante*. After Zinoviev's telegram of October 1, 1923, when all party districts were ordered to prepare for the anticipated uprising, Urbahns complied for Hamburg by forming a committee of three on October 8. He himself retained charge of the political organization. To Hans Kippenberger was entrusted the military organization. A third, unidentified party member was to be responsible for the city's food supply in the event of armed struggle. Kippenberger's "military" superior was Albert Schreiner, *MP Oberleiter Nord-West*, who was assisted by the Russian military

---

the party's official explanation. In fact, official Communist publications of that time merely referred to the uprising but did not explain its origins. See, for instance, *Bericht über die Verhandlungen des IX. Parteitages*, p. 16; *Die Lehren der deutschen Ereignisse*, pp. 6, 43, 53; G. Zinoviev, "Lessons of German Events and United Front Tactics," *The Communist International*, 1, New Series, No. 2 (London, n.d.), p. 86; also Zinoviev's account reproduced in Eudin and Fisher, *Soviet Russia and the West 1920-1927* (Stanford, 1957), pp. 220-221.

Wenzel's account (pp. 227-228) differs somewhat from those cited above and is based on personal information given by Wollenberg in 1953 and 1954. Wollenberg claims that he heard this version in 1924 when he attended a special military training course in Moscow. His story has it that after the Chemnitz Conference was over, members of the *Zentrale* met with the party's military experts and decided to start the uprising somewhere outside of Saxony. The choice fell on Kiel where the revolution had begun in November 1918. Remmele was chosen to go to Kiel and transmit the order. (Thalheimer, *1923: Eine verpasste Revolution?*, p. 27, mentions also that Remmele had instructions to go to Kiel, not Hamburg, but then proceeds without further elaboration to discuss events in Hamburg.) On his way to Kiel, Remmele decided to pass through Hamburg first in order to check with the Communist *MP* command *Nordwest*. He was told by the men in charge that the Kiel organization was too weak to start an uprising, but that Hamburg would be suitable. Remmele agreed, and so the uprising was decided upon. In the meantime, however, the *Zentrale* had been contacted by Radek, who telephoned from either Prague or Dresden to find out what was happening in Chemnitz. When told the news, including the latest decision involving Kiel, Radek vetoed further adventures. Another courier was sent to Kiel, who delivered his message and reported by telephone that he had done so. (He apparently failed to mention that Kiel had not received orders to start an uprising in the first place.)

Habedank has still another version. According to his account, the *Zentrale* decided on October 20 to have Hamburg spearhead the uprising. On October 21, word of this decision was sent to Thälmann in Hamburg via the party's central courier service in Berlin (p. 91). The courier in question was Remmele (p. 11). Hamburg heard nothing further from the *Zentrale* until shortly before the rising was to begin, at which time Remmele reappeared in Hamburg—late on October 22—with orders to cancel the uprising. Remmele had allegedly delivered the same order to Kiel, where it was obeyed. He failed in Hamburg, however, because Thälmann refused to comply with the order (p. 112). For Habedank's rather bewildering treatment of the couriers in general, and Remmele in particular, see also pp. 11-12, 85, 202-203.

Despite Habedank's apparently serious efforts to approach his topic in a scholarly manner, the fact that he is subject to the party line of Ulbricht's East German

adviser, "General" Moishe Stern (alias Emilio Kleber, under which name he became known during the Spanish Civil War).[58] Kippenberger organized the party members in the various sections of the city into action groups, the leaders of which were given considerable leeway in training their men for the anticipated fighting. The objectives to be taken by each group were communicated to the individual leaders, who were instructed not to take action until they were ordered to do so.

On October 20, the *Zentrale* called on all German party districts to send representatives to the Chemnitz Conference. Urbahns decided to go himself and took along two workers, Inselberger and Ruhnau, who were to attend the conference officially as factory council representatives rather than as delegates of the KPD. The three men left Hamburg sometime around noon of October 21 and

---

regime may account for the author's unconvincing presentation of the origins of the Hamburg uprising. Thus he misrepresents the vital role played by the ECCI in initiating the "German October" (p. 65). He obscures the fact that the final decision on whether to start a German insurrection was deferred by the *Zentrale* until after the Chemnitz Conference was over (p. 82). He claims that Hamburg was to give the signal for a nationwide uprising on October 23 and thereby conveys the misleading impression that the original plan, which had marked out Saxony for this role, never existed (pp. 82, 85). Finally, he grossly exaggerates both Thälmann's position in the Hamburg organization and the role he played during the uprising.

Habedank's account agrees with those of Danner and Wenzel that during those crucial October days Thälmann was in Hamburg and not in Chemnitz, as most of the other versions have it. There is little doubt that he was indeed in Hamburg, but not, as Habedank claims, as head of the party's Northwest district (*Oberleitung des KPD-Oberbezirks Nordwest*, p. 202). Thälmann was a representative of the Left Opposition in the *Zentrale*, and in Hamburg just one of several prominent party functionaries. He was certainly not a leading commander, nor the guiding spirit of the uprising, a position to which East German legend has posthumously promoted him (see also Ulbricht, *Zur Geschichte der deutschen Arbeiterbewegung*, 1, pp. 139-148, which is an altogether distorted version of events).

In summary, all accounts relying on the courier version fail to explain convincingly why the *Zentrale* was unable to stop the Hamburg rising, even though thirty-six hours elapsed between the dispatch of the second courier and the start of the operation. Some versions use Thälmann as a *deus ex machina*, and most of them raise more questions than they answer. Wenzel's (actually Wollenberg's) version is a case in point. Why did the second courier sent to Kiel fail to report that Remmele had not been in that city at all? Was he such a simpleton that he delivered his message and then gave the matter no further thought? And why did Remmele fail to notify the *Zentrale* of a drastic change of plans, a decision taken on his own responsibility? We are not told. Thus Danner's hypothesis is still the most plausible, though the exact circumstances of how the Hamburg uprising originated may never be known.

[58] On Schreiner see Wollenberg, *Der Apparat* (Bonn, 1952), p. 10, and Habedank, p. 209, who gives only his initials, A. Sch. On Stern, alias Kleber, see Dallin, *Soviet Espionage* (New Haven, 1955), pp. 74, 541.

arrived in Chemnitz only after the conference was over. When Urbahns was informed that as a result of the conference the Communist plan for an uprising was canceled, he sent Inselberger back to Hamburg party headquarters with a report to this effect. The next day Urbahns proceeded first to Dresden. From there he sent Ruhnau to Hamburg with another report, the contents of which are unknown. Urbahns himself returned home via Berlin, arriving in Hamburg around midnight of October 22, and went straight to bed.

During Urbahns' absence the pace of events in Hamburg had quickened. The atmosphere in the city was tense. The dock workers went on strike on October 20, and some of the related harbor installations were likewise affected by the walkouts. The movement spread to the warehousemen and construction workers, all of whom demanded wage increases. In addition, repeated demonstrations by the unemployed led in some places to clashes with the police. On October 21 the Hamburg dock workers held a meeting, and passed a resolution to call a general strike if the federal government moved troops into Saxony. The projected *Reichsexekutive* and the resolution of the dock workers were debated the following day by a conference sponsored by the *Allgemeiner Deutscher Gewerkschaftsbund*, and attended by delegates from the SPD, KPD, and trade-unions. After some discussion a spokesman for the trade-unions proposed a resolution which urged all organizations participating in the conference to wire their respective central offices in Berlin, asking them to disregard differences dividing the workers and to issue a joint proclamation for a nationwide general demonstration strike. In the meantime, while waiting for a reply to this proposal, all workers, employees and officials were to refrain from local strikes serving the same purpose as the projected demonstration strike, and were not to leave their places of employment without prior permission from their organizations.

The resolution was immediately opposed by the two KPD representatives present, Esser and Rühl, who announced that they would consult with party headquarters and then would make known in writing the Communist position. The consultation took place during the afternoon and evening of October 22, and a statement on the party's views was drafted. It was communicated by Rühl to the city's *Gewerkschaftshaus* (trade-union headquarters) the following morning, thus after the Hamburg uprising had begun. The Communists refused to sign the resolution proposed during the joint conference of October 21. Their reply stated bluntly that as a result of the Chemnitz Conference a general strike had been proclaimed in Saxony and was already in effect. Armed clashes between workers and Reichswehr supported by Fascists, were taking place in Saxony and Thuringia, where the fighting workers had appealed for outside help. The situation in Hamburg was also becoming tenser. In view of all these developments the proposed resolution was inadequate. It was designed to deceive the Hamburg workers in order to keep them from joining the battle. The KPD demanded that the Hamburg proletariat follow the example set by Chemnitz.

Who was responsible for the misrepresentation of events in central Germany? Was it the handiwork of Urbahns' two travel companions, Inselberger and Ruhnau, or had the reports they transmitted been edited by someone at party headquarters, conceivably by Kippenberger, or perhaps Thälmann? Had Urbahns' message concerning the outcome of the Chemnitz Conference been ambiguous?[59] No conclusive answer to these questions can be given. But it can be said with reasonable certainty that both the contents and tone of the Communist response to the trade-union resolution indicate that it was drawn up *after* party headquarters had decided on staging an uprising in Hamburg the following morning. In all probability the decision was taken sometime during the course of October 22, thus in the absence of Urbahns. Throughout that day unruly crowds milled through the streets of the working-class quarters, and were addressed by Communist "minute men" who mingled with them and frequently resisted police efforts to disperse them. In many parts of the city the party conducted hastily improvised meetings, usually in rented halls, and Communist speakers promised their audiences that the KPD would soon "go into action" (*losschlagen*). This promise the men at party headquarters intended to keep. They were aware of the widespread anger which the military occupation of Saxony had evoked among the Hamburg workers. They noticed also that *Reichswehr* units, stationed in the vicinity of the city, were

[59] There is little doubt that he did not intentionally mislead his colleagues in Hamburg, for no Communist functionary with any sense of responsibility would send reports of general strike and armed clashes in Saxony, and upon his return home go straight to bed without first contacting his own party headquarters.

being transported south, presumably to Saxony. Opportunity beckoned, and men like Kippenberger and Schreiner resolved to use it. The original plan of starting a revolution in Saxony had miscarried. Could not Hamburg take the place of Saxony, acting as a signal and an example for the proletariat elsewhere in the country, perhaps even in beleaguered central Germany? Aside from Urbahns' negative report, no messages or orders had been received by the Hamburg organization. The decision thus lay with the men who were in charge of it, and they fixed the hour of the uprising for 5 A.M. the next day, October 23, 1923. And in order to justify this act in the eyes of the workers, especially of the non-Communists whose support would be so vitally needed, Communist headquarters misrepresented the facts about developments in Saxony in the party's reply to the Hamburg trade-unions.

A plan of battle was ready. It had been developed by the *Oberleitung*, the party's MP high command. The Communists were to isolate Hamburg during the night by disrupting all channels of communication, and by blocking all arterial roads and railway lines leading into the city, in order to prevent reinforcement of the police from outside. Then they were to attack police stations, army barracks, and arsenals in the working-class suburbs of the northwestern, northern, northeastern and eastern parts of the city. Once these initial objectives had been captured, the weapons thus obtained were to be distributed to the people; the Communists shock troops, which would then be reinforced by the mass of workers in the suburbs, would lead this expanding army of proletarians into the heart of Hamburg, pressing the bourgeois enemies before them toward the south and the river, and there disarm them. It was expected that once Hamburg was in the hands of the insurgents, the spirit of revolution would spread beyond the city in the course of a few days.

In accordance with this strategic blueprint, special detachments began to fell trees across some of the arterial roads at 2 A.M. on October 23. But difficulties developed even at this early stage. Some of the demolition crews failed to cut the railway lines, telephone cables, and telegraph wires, because they could not agree on whether this would really be an effective and necessary measure. Around 5 A.M. the assaults on a number of police stations began, in the suburbs of Barmbeck, Wandsbeck, Hamm, St. Georg, Schiffbeck, Eimsbüttel, Hummelsbüttel, etc. Within a few hours, seventeen out of twenty-six police stations attacked were captured by the Communists.

Despite these initial successes, the Communists were fighting a losing battle in Hamburg. The decisive factor which broke the back of the uprising by the end of the first day was that the hoped-for mass support failed to materialize. The Communists, whose small and scattered squads fought bravely against growing opposition from police, navy troops, and SPD Reichsbanner formations, remained isolated. Once again the party met the now familiar reaction of distrust, if not open hostility, from the non-Communist part of the working-class population. Not even the striking dock workers moved a finger to assist the KPD against the forces of the government. Throughout the city labor was more concerned with the negotiations for higher wages, which the trade-unions were conducting with employers, than with the handful of determined radicals who were sniping at policemen from the roofs or at armored cars from behind barricades.

When it became obvious that they could not expect support from the population, the fighting spirit of the various Communist detachments scattered throughout the northern and eastern suburbs began to decline. Communications and coordination had not been very good from the start. In some cases, party squads either ignored orders from their high command, or wilfully disobeyed them. One district after another ceased fighting, especially when the word got around that messengers from the *Zentrale* had come with orders to abandon the struggle. Only in the suburb of Barmbeck did fighting continue throughout October 24, and in some isolated areas skirmishes lasted until the 25th. After this date, Hamburg settled back to an uneasy quiet. The one and only violent manifestation of the "German October" was over.[60]

---

[60] A truly objective account of the Hamburg uprising does not yet exist. By far the best description, though written from the point of view of the police, is in Danner, pp. 74-131, including excerpts of the later court trials. Habedank's study, despite its aforementioned shortcomings, presents a detailed picture of the course of the rising. Ehrt, *Bewaffneter Aufstand* (Berlin-Leipzig, 1933), pp. 19-22, is brief and partisan but reproduces some contemporary police reports. Wenzel, pp. 226-231, and his principal source have been mentioned. Larissa Reissner, *Hamburg auf den Barrikaden: Erlebtes und Erhörtes aus dem Hamburger Aufstand 1923* (Berlin, n.d.), is an impressionistic account by Radek's mistress, who witnessed the fighting. Other eyewitness accounts by two participants are in Zeutschel, pp. 15-25, and Valtin, pp. 69-87. Neither is reliable.

The Abortive "German October"

How little the Hamburg uprising actually affected the KPD is revealed by the events which followed in the wake of the Chemnitz Conference. After the original plan for a revolution, launched from Saxony, was abandoned on the evening of October 21, the *Zentrale* settled down to await the arrival of the ECCI delegation. Radek and his companions seem to have made their appearance, presumably in Dresden, sometime on October 22. There followed a series of discussions between the ECCI delegation and members of the KPD *Zentrale* on what had taken place at Chemnitz. Radek fully approved of the party's decision not to stage an armed uprising in Saxony, but he urged the *Zentrale* to proclaim a general strike. His suggestion was met with nearly unanimous opposition. The German Communist leaders argued that if Radek did not think it wise to start a revolution, then he could not have a general strike either; as matters stood in Saxony at the moment, general strike and armed uprising were virtually interdependent. The opinion of the *Zentrale* prevailed.[61]

No attempt has been made in this study to recount in detail the various stages of the street fighting in Hamburg. Though the event was at the time vital enough to the participants on both sides, viewed in retrospect it remains an essentially accidental episode, a bloody but isolated struggle. German Communists, however, have endowed the uprising with a symbolic significance it never warranted. The Hamburg barricades became the party's Thermopylae, and Thälmann its Leonidas. See, for example, Walter Ulbricht's distorted version in *Zur Geschichte der deutschen Arbeiterbewegung*, I, pp. 139-148, a depressing example of historical myth-making, and Habedank's account, *passim*. See also Ernst Thälmann, "Die Lehren des Hamburger Aufstandes," *Zur Geschichte der Kommunistischen Partei Deutschlands*, pp. 151-157, reproduced from an article which Thälmann published in *Die Rote Fahne* on October 23, 1925. Its chief interest lies in its propagandistic approach.

Virtually no reliable figures exist on the number of participants and the casualties suffered on either side. Nor do we know how many weapons the insurgents had. The Communists, probably in an effort to emphasize the heroic nature of the rising, have given the numbers of participants as low as 300 fighters, and 1,000 "helpers" in erecting barricades (cited in Wenzel, p. 229). Thalheimer (1923: *Eine verpasste Revolution?*, p. 27) mentions only 200 fighters, whereas Valtin (p. 71) gives an estimate of 1200. Police estimates, according to Wenzel (p. 230), ran as high as 5000 insurgents, a figure which makes one suspect that it served to justify the difficulties which the force encountered in dealing with the uprising. Danner lists only scattered figures for the various engagements which he describes. The number of Communists killed was given as 24 by the *Hamburger Volkszeitung* of October 22, 1927, as reproduced in *Zur Geschichte der Kommunistischen Partei Deutschlands* (Berlin, 1955), facing p. 152. Danner, p. 99, lists police casualties as 17 dead, 69 wounded. Ehrt, *Bewaffneter Aufstand*, p. 22, estimates "at least 40" dead. There appears to be general agreement on the fact that the insurgents lacked weapons. Habedank (p. 203) says so, but gives no figures. Zeutschel (p. 23), mentions 80 rifles "and twice the number of pistols." Brandler gave Wenzel the figure of 196 rifles, although police estimates ran higher than that (Wenzel, p. 230).

[61] *Die Lehren der deutschen Ereignisse*, p. 6.

Sometime during the night of October 22 the Communist leaders left Saxony for Berlin, where they reassembled the following day and received the news of the Hamburg insurrection.[62] The *Zentrale* reconvened at once, together with Radek, to discuss what action to take in view of this new development. Two motions were made. The first came from Ruth Fischer, who suggested the proclamation of a mass strike in Berlin on October 25, in the expectation that such a strike would lead within two or three days to an armed proletarian uprising. The second motion called for the party not to engage in any action. Thereupon Radek suggested a compromise, a strike without an armed uprising. None of the motions passed, and for the next few days the Communist leaders were engaged in a series of conferences on what the party should do. The *Zentrale* appointed a committee of seven to draft a set of guiding principles for the party's policy in the immediate future. The committee reported back on October 25[63] with a resolution which, in tone and content, was a remarkable document, for it revealed that the party had learnt nothing from its recent experiences. The most pertinent sections of the resolution read as follows:

"1) The social and political opposites [in Germany] are moving daily closer toward a crisis. Every day may bring decisive struggles of the revolution and counterrevolution.

"2) The vanguard of the working class . . . presses for the resumption of the struggle; however, the working class as a whole, despite its great embitterment and misery, is not yet ready to fight.

"3) For this reason, the reserves of the proletariat must be drawn closer to the vanguard by means of resolute agitation. . . . Technical preparations must be pursued with the utmost energy. In order to achieve unity among the proletariat for the struggle ahead, [the party] must conduct negotiations with Social Democracy, centrally and locally, in order either to force the Social Democrats into battle, or to split the Social Democratic workers and their traitorous leaders.

"4) In view of these circumstances it will be necessary for the party to keep the comrades out of armed struggles, so as to gain time for the preparations. But if great spontaneous fights should break out among the working class, the party will support them with all

---

[62] *ibid.*; Gast, *Zeitschrift für Geschichtswissenschaft,* IV, No. 3 (1956), p. 463.
[63] Wenzel, p. 253 and n.4; cf. *Die Lehren der deutschen Ereignisse,* p. 8, which gives October 26 as the date.

means at its disposal. The party must also parry the blows of the counterrevolution by way of mass struggles (demonstrations, political strikes). Armed combat during these struggles is to be avoided, if possible. . . ."[64]

The resolution was adopted unanimously, and was then circulated throughout the KPD.[65] Thus the party was back where it had been before the Cuno strike three months earlier—back to those tactics of political attrition which went under the euphemism of "united front policy." The Communists had tested the revolutionary fervor of the workers in "red" Saxony, and had found it wanting. They had, inadvertently, tested it again in Hamburg, and the resulting fiasco had been nearly as complete as that of March 1921. But whether from stubbornness or from blindness, they continued to behave for the time being as if the revolution was still a real possibility.

They were soon undeceived by the actions of the central government. In the last ten days of October the Stresemann cabinet was confronted by explosive situations in central Germany and Bavaria. Of the two trouble spots Bavaria proved the more dangerous, and Berlin had to move cautiously, but without delay, in order to forestall disaster. On October 20 the Reich Defense Minister relieved General von Lossow of his command over the Reichswehr troops stationed in Bavaria, and replaced him with General Kress von Kressenstein. The Bavarian government reacted with open defiance. General Commissioner von Kahr declared at once that the decree of the federal defense minister was null and void, and appointed von Lossow *Landeskommandant* (state commander) of the Reichswehr units stationed in Bavaria. On October 22 the troops took an oath of allegiance to the Bavarian government. Stresemann faced trouble from all directions: while fruitless negotiations between Berlin and Munich continued, the Communists rose in Hamburg, and simultaneously Rhenish Separatists attempted to turn the Palatinate into an independent state.[66]

In the face of these multiple difficulties, the central government decided to move against the point of least resistance—the Zeigner government of Saxony. That state was already occupied by the Reichswehr, which on October 25 had arrested several low-ranking

[64] *Die Lehren der deutschen Ereignisse*, p. 8.
[65] *ibid.*; Wenzel, p. 233, n.4.
[66] *Schulthess'*, 1923, pp. 198-205, *passim*; Stresemann, *Vermächtnis*, 1, pp. 171-184, *passim*; Schlottner, pp. 73-79.

government officials.[67] The population was sullen and restless, but the troops were firmly in control of the situation. Aside from sporadic attempts by Communist agitators to incite the workers against the military occupation, Saxony was quiet. Nevertheless, it was in Dresden rather than in Munich that the government first asserted itself. Defense Minister Gessler was the driving force behind this move. Whether from personal pique in consequence of Zeigner's verbal attacks on the Reichswehr, or from mere tactical considerations, Gessler, during a cabinet meeting on October 27, recommended immediate intervention in Saxony. He gave as his reason the unbearable situation which the troops faced in the state. Stresemann supported Gessler, arguing that a government which contained Communist ministers was irreconcilable with the spirit of the Weimar constitution. But his real reason, which he revealed a few minutes later, was one of expediency rather than of principle. The chancellor pointed out that the government might be crushed between right-wing radicalism in Bavaria and left-wing radicalism in Saxony. If the government were to enforce the German constitution in Saxony, the position of the Reich vis-à-vis Bavaria would be strengthened, and open conflict with the latter state would be avoided. Stresemann's and Gessler's views won out, over the objections of the Social Democratic cabinet members.[68] On the same day the chancellor wrote a letter to Zeigner in which he demanded in no uncertain terms the expulsion of the Communist ministers from the Saxon cabinet.

". . . The spirit of recalcitrance and violence displayed by the Communist Party was demonstrated by the statements which the chief of your state chancellery, Herr *Ministerialdirektor* Brandler, made at Chemnitz on October 21 when he called publicly for open opposition to the Reichswehr. . . .

"In the name of the federal government I herewith demand . . . that you arrange for the resignation of the Saxon state government since in view of recent events the participation of Communist members within said government has become incompatible with constitutional conditions.

"I request that you inform me of the government's resignation by tomorrow, October 28. Should the formation of a new government

---

[67] *Verhandlungen des Sächsischen Landtages 1923*, II, p. 1834.
[68] "Reichskabinett-Protokolle," Auswärtiges Amt und Reichskanzlei, Germany, microfilm T-120, container 1749, frames 757443-757447; Stresemann, *Vermächtnis*, I, pp. 184-186.

. . . not be carried out immediately, without the participation of its Communist members . . . , the holder of executive power will designate a federal commissioner who will assume the administrative functions of the state until constitutional conditions are restored."[69]

This was the second ultimatum within a fortnight which the Saxon minister-president received, and with which he refused to comply. His Bavarian counterpart, Ritter von Kahr, was guilty of the same offense and remained unscathed, but Zeigner's disobedience led to his political demise. On October 29 President Ebert invoked Article 48 of the federal constitution, and empowered the chancellor ". . . to deprive the members of the Saxon state government and of the Saxon state and municipal administrations of their offices. . . ."[70] The presidential decree was immediately followed by the appointment of a Reichstag deputy of the People's Party, Dr. Rudolph Heinze, as *Reichskommissar* (federal commissioner) for Saxony, and the occupation of the ministerial offices in Dresden by federal troops. Zeigner "resigned" his office the following day, and on the 31st the diet elected a new minister-president, the rather moderate, left-of-center Social Democrat, Dr. Karl Fellisch. The coalition government of left-wing Social Democrats and Communists in Saxony was over.[71]

The *Reichsexekutive* against Saxony, and subsequently against Thuringia, accentuated the fact that the KPD had reached a political impasse. As soon as the federal ultimatum to Zeigner became known in Berlin, Radek instructed the Communist ministers Böttcher and Heckert not to resign without some show of resist-

---

[69] Stresemann, *Vermächtnis*, I, pp. 186-187.

[70] *Schulthess'*, 1923, p. 207.

[71] A good account of this episode is in Schlottner, pp. 79-89, 114-123. See also *Schulthess'*, 1923, pp. 207-208; Stresemann, *Vermächtnis*, I, pp. 184-191; *Verhandlungen des Sächsischen Landtages 1923*, II, pp. 1841-1849; and the recently published article by Harold J. Gordon, "Die Reichswehr und Sachsen 1923," *Wehrwissenschaftliche Rundschau*, Heft 12 (1961), pp. 677-692.

One result of Stresemann's decision to invoke the *Reichsexekutive* against Saxony was the collapse of the Great Coalition. The Social Democratic ministers in the cabinet took a dim view of the federal executive action, especially since equivalent measures were not applied against rebellious Bavaria. When Stresemann rejected Social Democratic demands for withdrawing the troops from Saxon territory and for taking a firmer stand vis-à-vis Bavaria, the Social Democratic ministers handed in their resignations on November 2, 1923. A few days later, Thuringia suffered the same fate as Saxony. Reichswehr units occupied that state on November 5 and the Communist ministers resigned from the Thuringian government on November 12, 1923 (Witzmann, pp. 99-102).

ance.[72] This was attempted. Supported by left-wing Social Democrats and some trade-unions, the Saxon Communists proclaimed a general protest strike on October 30. Although it was scheduled to last for three days, the trade-unions decided to call it off after only twenty-four hours.[73] Labor's fighting spirit in Red Saxony was broken, and only smouldering resentment over the military occupation and the forceful removal of Zeigner's working-class coalition remained. This resentment found its expression in a continued show of sympathy for the Communists by large segments of the Saxon Social Democrats, and during the months that followed the left-wing faction of the SPD made several futile attempts to form another government coalition with the KPD.[74] Interestingly enough, the opposite was true in Thuringia, where the two parties quarrelled incessantly over which was most responsible for the failure of the coalition government in that state.[75]

Meanwhile Radek tried hard, but in vain, to organize Communist protest demonstrations in Berlin. His return to Moscow was only a question of weeks, and he was not in an enviable position. As nominal supervisors of the projected uprising, he and his three colleagues from the ECCI would be held responsible for having failed to accomplish their mission. Radek tried desperately to salvage as much as possible from a situation which was actually beyond repair. He suggested that the party sponsor street demonstrations by the unemployed. They were attempted, but proved to be listless and ineffective ventures. He also demanded that the party stage protest marches which were to be protected by armed (and illegal) proletarian hundreds. Most members of the *Zentrale* declared themselves essentially in agreement with this plan, but insisted that they needed a prolonged period of preparation before they could hope to attempt such demonstrations. In contrast, Ruth Fischer flatly rejected the idea, with the argument that the masses were too disheartened by the recent events in Saxony and Hamburg to support Communist-organized protest actions.[76] For the second time within three months

[72] *Die Lehren der deutschen Ereignisse*, p. 8. By then, Brandler had apparently returned to Berlin.

[73] Wenzel, p. 238.

[74] *ibid.*, pp. 238-239. For other examples of sympathy bestowed on the Communists by left-wing Social Democrats outside of central Germany see *ibid.*, pp. 239-241.

[75] Witzmann, p. 102.

[76] *Die Lehren der deutschen Ereignisse*, pp. 9-11.

she turned down an opportunity to act in a crisis.[77] Although the arguments with which she justified her position in each case were sound, her behavior raises some doubts as to the sincerity of her often professed radicalism.

It is difficult to say how soon after Chemnitz and Hamburg the Communist leaders came to realize the full extent of the party's latest, relatively bloodless, but ultimately most decisive defeat. At the meeting of the Central Committee on November 3 the proceedings were still largely dominated by the Brandler faction, which tried to discuss the abortive uprising without lending it an air of finality. Up to that point there had been no official word from Moscow on this issue. In fact, as late as October 28, Zinoviev gave a speech in Petrograd in which he again mentioned his mythical figure of twenty million German proletarians who were still waiting to be led to the barricades.[78] As long as the Comintern had not spoken, it would have been imprudent of Brandler and Radek to admit openly the true significance of the party's October retreat, even if they had been fully aware of it, which is doubtful.[79] Thus the proceedings of the Central Committee were pervaded by an atmosphere of cautious optimism. Brandler himself delivered the principal report. He accepted full responsibility for having called off the planned insurrection, but indicated that the revolution was merely postponed, not cancelled. Most of the theses which Brandler advanced were subsequently written into the resolution which was submitted to the committee for adoption. Its text was drafted by Brandler, with the aid of Radek and Pyatakov. The main theme of the resolution was that there had been a "Fascist" victory over the "November Republic." This victory was evident from the recent events in Saxony, the repeated bans of the party press, the Bavarian situation, and related examples. The greatest share of responsibility for these developments was attributed to the Social Democrats, and to the Social Democratic leaders in particular, because they had refused to support the Communists in their struggle against the "military dictatorship." It was held that the latest betrayal of the SPD leaders required a new approach to the united front policy. From then on the party was to refrain from any dealings with the Social Democratic bureaucracy,

---

[77] The first time was on the occasion of the anti-Fascist day. See above, Ch. xi.
[78] Wenzel, p. 244.
[79] ibid., p. 245.

but was to concentrate exclusively on winning the rank and file of the SPD for the ultimate struggle against the "Fascist" dictatorship. In short, the resolution called for a united front policy "from below." As far as references to any future uprising were concerned, the resolution was ambiguous. It stated that "armed insurrection remains on the agenda," and stressed the need for "the preparation of the struggle for the proletarian dictatorship." But the radical tone of these passages was qualified by the statement that the projected struggle would have to begin by opposition to the attempted onslaughts against the eight-hour day, and by fighting unemployment, suppression of the labor press, the national state of emergency, and low wages. In other words, the qualifications embodied in the resolution indicated an implied admission that at least in the near future there would be no chance of a major revolution. The resolution was adopted at the committee meeting by a vote of 40 to 13. The majority of the party hierarchy thus endorsed the future plans of the Brandler *Zentrale,* and at the same time approved of its past policies.[80]

Had the matter been allowed to rest there, the October retreat would have remained just another episode in the history of the German Communist party, just another attempt to capture power which, though it had failed once again, would be repeated at the earliest possible opportunity. For several weeks after the meeting of the Central Committee it actually looked as if the party was returning to its old course, which consisted of probing for soft spots and at the same time continuing conspiratorial activities.[81] But the Brandler

[80] Carr, *The Interregnum,* pp. 226-227; Wenzel, pp. 241-245; *Bericht über die Verhandlungen des IX. Parteitages,* pp. 64/74-64/75 (double pagination).

[81] According to Wenzel, who has treated these developments at length (pp. 245-263), the party's *Apparat* conducted secret military preparations for a Communist uprising throughout the winter months, and terminated them only in April or May 1924. But it is exceedingly doubtful that these measures constituted genuine moves toward a revolution. To be sure, armed insurrection remained officially on the agenda of the KPD for some time to come. It is also very possible that the party's "cloak-and-dagger" units, over which the *Zentrale* had notoriously little control, continued to carry on clandestine activities beyond October 1923. But at the same time the party leaders were too deeply involved in factional struggles and too hamstrung by the restrictions imposed upon the KPD by the governmental ban of November 23, 1923 (see below) to have been either in the mood or in the position for another insurrectionist adventure. Furthermore, the departure of Radek and his colleagues for Moscow in December and the drying up of Russian funds the same month cast additional doubt on the seriousness of these clandestine activities. It is nevertheless true, and somewhat ironic, that by the end of November both government officials and the Social Democratic Party thought to have detected Communist

Zentrale was permitted neither time nor opportunity to return the KPD to the *status quo* prior to October. Both in Berlin and Moscow forces were at work which brought about a reorientation of the party, a new leadership and, involuntarily but irrevocably, a termination of the phase of revolutionary experimentation.

The month of November had few favors to bestow upon the German Communists. The abortive Hitler putsch in Munich on November 9 had a cathartic effect on all Germany: the shots at the Feldherrnhalle which killed fourteen National Socialists cleared the air and laid the basis for speedy settlement of most of the outstanding differences between Bavaria and the Reich.[82] Equally important for the nation as a whole was the issue of the new *Rentenmark* on November 16, which restored public confidence in the currency and prepared the way for the eventual economic recovery of Germany. It was only natural, however, that the transition from acute crisis to gradual stabilization, economically and politically, was accompanied by certain stresses and strains. Thus the stabilization of the mark led to a temporary dislocation of the economy because of a nationwide shortage of capital, a shift in demand from capital (or instrumental) goods to consumers' goods, and a rapid rise of unemployment which lasted until the spring of 1924.[83] On the political front,

---

plans for a revolution. Suspicions along these lines had been entertained by governmental authorities ever since September 1923, when the Russian Embassy in Berlin became implicated in what appeared to be a large-scale traffic of arms. Suspicions grew stronger when the Prussian police secured a letter which Ruth Fischer had written to Zinoviev on November 22, 1923. In it she accused Brandler and his friends of having mismanaged the projected revolution ("Foreign Office to German Embassy, Moscow, November 29, 1923," Auswärtiges Amt, Germany, microfilm, container 1406, frame D 553355). The Social Democratic Party, which also knew about this letter ("Press Department of the Foreign Office to the German Embassy, Moscow, November 28, 1923," *ibid.*, frame D 553346), announced publicly that because the KPD was preparing for a revolution on Moscow's orders, the SPD rejected henceforth any organizational or political cooperation with the already outlawed Communist Party (*Schulthess'*, 1923, p. 224). On the same day, Severing referred in the Prussian diet to Communist plans for a revolution (*ibid.*).

82 Schwend, pp. 249-251, and *passim*.

83 For details on the stabilization of the currency see Bresciani-Turroni, *The Economics of Inflation* (London, 1937), chs. ix and x; Hans Luther, *Politiker ohne Partei* (Stuttgart, 1960), pp. 109-247; Schacht, *Confessions of "The Old Wizard"* (Boston, 1956), pp. 162-178; Lüke, *Von der Stabilisierung zur Krise* (Zürich, 1959), pp. 10-36. Unemployment was relatively low until October 1923. It then rose steadily until January 1924, and gradually declined during the following months, although it did not drop to the level of before October 1923 until the end of 1924 (*Statistisches Jahrbuch für das deutsche Reich*, 1924/1925, vol. 44 (Berlin, 1925), pp. 296, 299).

full emergency powers had been temporarily granted to General von Seeckt by the Stresemann cabinet on the evening of November 8.[84] He used these powers to deal firmly with Bavaria and the Munich putsch, and on November 23, when Stresemann's chancellorship came to an end, Seeckt banned the German Communist Party, the National Socialist Party, and the *Deutsch-Völkische Freiheits-partei*.[85]

None of these events could bring comfort to the KPD. The collapse of the Hitler putsch, and the *détente* between Berlin and Munich which followed, weakened all arguments concerning the "Fascist" nature of the government. Moreover, the prevention of the attempted *coup d'état* in Bavaria had a salutary effect on the German workers.[86] So had the monetary stabilization which transformed nominal wages into real wages, and led to a sudden rise in the purchasing power of the working classes.[87] Not even the temporary increase in unemployment benefited the KPD, since a surplus of idle workers rendered strikes, and notably large-scale political strikes, illusory.[88] Finally, the enforced illegality of the party from November 23, 1923 until March 1, 1924 paralyzed all organizational activities, and for months rendered the Communists politically ineffective.

Meanwhile Radek and his ECCI delegation had made repeated attempts throughout November to prod the party's Berlin organization into showing some revolutionary spirit. But these efforts proved as futile as they had been immediately after the Chemnitz Conference. In a letter of November 20, written to the Berlin district command of the KPD, Radek complained bitterly about Ruth Fischer's failure to stage protest demonstrations in Berlin on the 9th and the 13th of that month. He called on her to make another attempt on the 22nd, urging her to mobilize as many workers as possible for a demonstration in the center of the city. The demonstration was to be accompanied by Communist disturbances in the Reichstag on the same day. Ruth Fischer answered that it was impossible to mobilize the apathetic masses within two days, but promised to try on

---

[84] Craig, *The Politics of the Prussian Army, 1640-1945* (New York and Oxford, 1956), p. 419.

[85] *Schulthess'*, 1923, p. 222.

[86] Wenzel, p. 251.

[87] Bresciani-Turroni, p. 367.

[88] Wenzel, p. 253.

the 27th. On that day, a demonstration of about three to four thousand actually took place in the Berlin Lustgarten, but it lacked spirit, and the demonstrators merely milled around the square until the police dispersed them. It was obvious that even the most radical portion of the German party could no longer be relied upon to display revolutionary *élan*.[89]

A few days later, early in December, Radek and his colleagues from the ECCI returned to the Soviet Union.[90] They departed under a cloud, for the reports that they took back with them were bound to be unpopular in Moscow. Indications of trouble ahead may have reached them prior to their departure. During November, when Radek had desperately tried over and over again to offset the undeniable letdown after the October retreat by calling for a series of spirited and face-saving demonstrations, Zinoviev, in articles and speeches, had expressed his growing, though still veiled, disapproval of the German party's recent policies and decisions. This disapproval, which was at first directed mainly against the Brandler *Zentrale*, was tied up with the inner party struggle among the Russian leadership.

This conflict had been shaping up ever since 1922, when Lenin's health began to deteriorate at an alarming pace, and it had gained momentum in 1923. On one side was the party's Secretariat, composed of the somewhat ill-matched triumvirate of Stalin, Zinoviev, and Kamenev, and on the other side Trotsky and his supporters, among them Radek. The issues on which the struggle was ostensibly fought were political and economic in nature, and were primarily restricted to party affairs and Russian domestic problems. Throughout the summer and fall of 1923, Trotsky was steadily losing ground. When Lenin died on January 21, 1924, the triumvirs were in control

[89] *ibid.*, pp. 251-252; "Foreign Office to German Embassy, Moscow, November 29, 1923," Auswärtiges Amt, Germany, mircofilm, container 1406, frame D 553355.

[90] Carr, *The Interregnum*, p. 233, gives the date as December 7, 1923; Wenzel, p. 249, says only "early in December." Although Radek had been in Germany ever since October 22, 1923, rumors of his presence there reached the German authorities only in the last week of November. From then on until he officially reappeared in Moscow—where he met Ambassador Brockdorff-Rantzau on December 13—the German government made frantic efforts to detect his whereabouts. The efforts proved unsuccessful, for although the Germans knew that he was not in Moscow, where the Russian officials claimed that he was in the Caucasus, his presence in Germany could not be established. For the rather fascinating correspondence on this matter see Auswärtiges Amt, Germany, microfilm, container 1406, frames D 553331, 553347, 553355, 553368, 553388, 553398, 553409.

of the party, and Trotsky in bitter, and daily more forlorn, opposition. The aftermath of the German October can only become comprehensible if seen against this general background.[91]

It was several weeks before Moscow fully realized that the German revolution was a failure. Zinoviev, who as chairman of the ECCI was most immediately concerned with the German events, refused to recognize for some time after the Chemnitz Conference that the October retreat was final, and not merely a temporary setback. Thus his initial reaction was approval of the tactics which the German *Zentrale* had applied in Saxony, and he blamed the Social Democrats for the failure of the Saxon experiment and the abortive Hamburg uprising. But as the weeks passed, his attitude began to change. At first he had found nothing basically wrong either with the policies which the KPD had pursued in Saxony, or with the resolution approving these policies which the party had adopted at its Central Committee meeting on November 3, but by the end of that month he severely criticized the *Zentrale* on both counts, and in December turned openly against both Brandler and Radek.

Zinoviev's volte-face was a matter not of conviction, but of expediency. As the magnitude of the German debacle was gradually revealed to the Bolshevik leaders, Zinoviev found himself in a vulnerable position. As chairman of the ECCI he formally shared the responsibility for the political actions and omissions of the KPD, a member party of the Comintern. The easiest way to escape, or at least to lessen, this responsibility was to shift it to someone else, in this case to Brandler, and subsequently to Radek as well. In reaching this decision he seems to have been prompted in part by Maslow and Fischer. The former had been in Moscow ever since September in order to submit to an investigation of his past party record. In November Zinoviev suddenly dropped his erstwhile aloofness and began to treat Maslow in a friendly fashion. During this period, Maslow wrote an article in which he strongly attacked the entry of the KPD into the Saxon government of Zeigner. Although it was not published until two months later, Zinoviev may well have known

[91] An excellent and comprehensive account of the intraparty struggle is in Carr, *The Interregnum*, pp. 257-366. A briefer version is in Schapiro, *The Communist Party of the Soviet Union* (New York, 1959), pp. 267-285. See also Deutscher, *The Prophet Unarmed: Trotsky 1921-1929* (London-New York-Toronto, 1959), ch. II and *passim*, which concentrates on Trotsky's role; and Merle Fainsod, *How Russia is Ruled* (Cambridge, Mass., 1954), pp. 138-140, for a concise, succinct description of events.

it, and at least he knew Maslow's position on the question.[92] Furthermore, Ruth Fischer wrote a letter to Zinoviev on November 22 in
which she complained bitterly about the incompetence of Brandler,
and implored Zinoviev to invite a delegation of the KPD to Moscow
for a discussion of the party's outstanding differences.[93] The letter
was intercepted by the German police, and its contents wired to the
German Embassy in Moscow, where Brockdorff-Rantzau handed
it accusingly to the Commissar for Foreign Affairs, Chicherin, on
December 2nd or 3rd.[94] There is little doubt that Chicherin showed
the letter to Zinoviev. It was probably at this point that the chairman of the ECCI sent a confidential letter to the German *Zentrale*
in which he castigated the KPD's Saxon policy.

The crucial passage in the letter, which is undated, read: "... We
here in Moscow . . . regarded the entry of Communists into the
Saxon Government only as a military-strategic maneuver. You
turned it into a political bloc with the "left" Social Democrats,
which tied your hands. We thought of your entry into the Saxon
Government as a way of winning a jumping-off ground from which
to deploy the forces of our armies. You turned participation in the
Saxon cabinet into a banal parliamentary coalition with the Social
Democrats. The result was our political defeat. . . ."[95]

By the middle of the month the German issue became intimately
fused with the Russian intraparty struggle, as Zinoviev used his
growing display of hostility against the Brandler *Zentrale* to undermine the position of his antagonist Trotsky. It was a devious approach, for Trotsky was as outspoken as Zinoviev in his condemnation of the German Communists for having bungled what he considered a perfect opportunity for a revolution. But he differed from
Zinoviev on the conclusions to be drawn. While he unhesitatingly
criticized Brandler and Radek for having blundered, he was not prepared to make either of them a scapegoat, especially since he be-

[92] On the Maslow case see Carr, *The Interregnum*, pp. 231-232, and Fischer, pp.
359-364.
[93] "Foreign Office to German Embassy, Moscow, November 29, 1923," Auswärtiges Amt, Germany, microfilm, container 1406, frame D 553355.
[94] "Brockdorff-Rantzau to Foreign Office, Berlin, December 4, 1923," *ibid.*,
frame D 553382.
[95] Quoted in Jane Degras, ed., *The Communist International 1919-1943, Documents*, II, 1923-1928 (London-New York-Toronto, 1960), p. 65. Degras dates the
letter "December?" (p. 62), as does Wenzel (pp. 264-265). Carr (*The Interregnum*, p. 231) implies that it was sent early in November.

lieved that Zinoviev himself was far from blameless.[96] Nor did Trotsky see any advantage in changing the leadership of the KPD by replacing Brandler, whom he personally liked and respected, with Fischer and Maslow, whom he distrusted. Just such a switch, however, was contemplated by Zinoviev, and it was Radek who inadvertently convinced him and his friends in the Russian party that this was not only a desirable measure, but an urgent necessity. On December 13, shortly after his return from Germany, Radek told a party meeting in Moscow that if the majority of the Russian leaders should turn against Trotsky, the majority of the German and French Communists would side with Trotsky against his opponents.[97] To the triumvirate this sounded like an open challenge. Radek was known as Trotsky's staunchest supporter in the current struggle, a fact which their differing views on the recent handling of the German situation did not alter.[98] Radek's warning seemed to be substantiated a few days later when the Central Committee, not of the French but of the Polish Communist Party, sent a letter which left no doubt about the high reputation Trotsky enjoyed in those quarters.[99] Zinoviev's faction realized the need of preventing Trotsky from acquiring more allies outside the Soviet Union. For the moment nothing could be done about the Polish party, but the abortive German October served as a convenient excuse for Russian intervention in the affairs of the KPD.

In mid-December, invitations to send representatives to Moscow by the end of the month were extended to the KPD. By that time the apparent unity (except for the Left Opposition) of the party, which had been displayed on November 3 regarding the Central Committee's resolution on the October events, had totally disappeared. The KPD *Zentrale* was split into three factions rather than the customary two, respectively representing a right wing, a center wing, and a left wing. Each faction claimed leadership over the party. The divisive issue was the interpretation of the October events. The right wing, represented by Brandler and Thalheimer, staunchly

---

[96] Trotsky, *The Third International After Lenin* (New York, 1936), pp. 94-95; Deutscher, *The Prophet Unarmed*, pp. 144-145.

[97] Thalheimer, *1923: Eine verpasste Revolution?*, p. 11. Radek made this speech two days after Trotsky's devastating letter of December 8, 1923 had been published in *Pravda*. Carr, *The Interregnum*, p. 234, has Radek refer, erroneously, to the "German and Polish" parties.

[98] Borkenau, *The Communist International* (London, 1938), p. 256.

[99] Carr, *The Interregnum*, pp. 234-235.

defended the recent "retreat," and continued to uphold the united front policy as the party's only hope of winning mass support in the future. The left wing, represented by Fischer and Thälmann (Maslow was still in Moscow), maintained that the Brandler faction had discredited the party, that the united front policy in its previous form was untenable, and that the revolution had failed because of timid and opportunist leadership. The center group, which included Remmele, Eberlein, Kleine, Stoecker, Koenen, and Pieck, was very critical of Brandler's past policies, but was not yet prepared to join forces with the radicals on the Left. Its members believed that a retreat had been necessary, but argued that it should have been "a fighting retreat" rather than a timid and passive surrender.[100]

As it turned out, the creation of a center group spelled doom to the Brandler *Zentrale*. When the party chairman departed for Moscow around the turn of the year, he could only rely on the support of Thalheimer, Pieck, and Zetkin.[101] By the time the German delegation arrived, Brandler found that Zinoviev had already taken a step toward depriving him and his remaining supporters of the party leadership: on December 27, during a session of the Politburo, Zinoviev had opened an all-out offensive against Brandler's principal mentor, Karl Radek.

The attack on Radek served a dual purpose. It was designed to strip the Brandler faction of its remaining influence in the KPD, thereby strengthening Brandler's opponents. Furthermore, by discrediting Radek, Zinoviev and his colleagues in the triumvirate could weaken the position of their opponent Trotsky.[102] Moreover,

---

[100] *ibid.*, pp. 227, 235; Degras, ed., *The Communist International, Documents,* II, pp. 64-65; Wenzel, p. 265. For a fuller picture of the respective views held by the three groups see *Die Lehren der deutschen Ereignisse, passim.* No date is given in *Bericht über die Verhandlungen des IX. Parteitages,* p. 112. Wenzel (p. 265) claims that it occurred in December, after the members of the *Zentrale* realized that Brandler had become a special target for Zinoviev's abuse.

[101] Officially at least, Pieck belonged to the center group, although his sympathies remained for the time being on Brandler's side. This is evident from Pieck's voting record in Moscow during January, 1924 (*Die Lehren der deutschen Ereignisse,* pp. 81-82, and *passim*). Clara Zetkin adopted a similar attitude, but as she was then an active member of the Presidium of the ECCI she ultimately voted with that body during the January talks.

[102] In discrediting Radek, Zinoviev also settled a score with Pyatakov, who had been a member of Radek's ECCI mission to Germany and who had invited the hostility of the triumvirate when he had signed the "Declaration of the Forty-Six." See Wenzel, p. 267; for the "Declaration," see Carr, *The Interregnum,* pp. 297-301, 367-373.

the resolution which the Politburo adopted left no doubt that the Zinoviev faction was openly bidding for the support of the Left Opposition within the German party.

"Comrade Radek directs his course entirely in support of the *Right* minority of the Central Committee [meaning the *Zentrale*] of the KPD and [tries] to disown the Left wing of the party . . . whereas the Politburo of the Central Committee of the RKP bases its policy on support of the great majority of the Central Committee of the KPD and on collaboration with the Left. . . .

"The general view of comrade Radek on the course of the further struggle in Germany arises from an incorrect assessment of the class forces in Germany: an opportunist overestimation of the differences within Fascism and an attempt to base the policy of the working class in Germany on these differences."[103]

It was as simple as that. Not only did the resolution identify Radek with the errant Brandler, it also tagged on, for good measure, an official, albeit belated, censure of Radek's Schlageter policy, which had proved a failure. The stage was now set for the final reckoning.

Despite an unprecedented, foolhardy counterattack by Radek, who informed the Russian Politburo that he was only responsible to the world congress of the Comintern for his actions in Germany —a point which Zinoviev grudgingly conceded in principle—Radek's days as the Comintern expert for Germany were numbered.[104] On January 11, 1924, the Presidium of the ECCI convened in Moscow for a joint conference with the German delegation to air the problem of the October defeat. The details of these proceedings, which lasted several days, need not detain us here.[105] Both Radek and Brandler offered a spirited defense of their views. They pointed out that the German proletariat was not yet ready for revolution, and maintained that the Communist retreat in October had been necessary and prudent. Radek also let it be known that he considered demands for a change in the leadership of the KPD unwise and uncalled-for. The two spokesmen of the Right were followed by Rem-

[103] Quoted in Carr, *The Interregnum*, p. 236. The author is probably correct in assuming that Trotsky did not attend this session of the Politburo.
[104] *ibid.*; Wenzel, p. 271. Degras, ed., *The Communist International, Documents,* II, p. 68, infers that Radek made his heretical remark prior to December 27, 1923.
[105] By far the most detailed extant source is the Comintern publication of the procedures, *Die Lehren der deutschen Ereignisse*. A good general account is in Carr, *The Interregnum*, pp. 236-240, including notes. A rather colored version of events is in Fischer, pp. 371-376.

mele, who represented the new center group. His résumé of the October events, delivered with malice toward none, was measured in tone, rational, and searching. He did not hesitate to criticize the ECCI, by implication, for its part in the defeat, especially its unrealistic assessment of the German situation, and its equally unrealistic insistence on starting an all-out revolution from Saxony. According to Remmele, the recent experience showed that the party would have to tread the road to revolution by stages, by setting for itself limited objectives, and only after having aroused the German proletariat should the party attempt to make its bid for power. As for the mistakes of the KPD, Remmele did not hesitate to enumerate them too, emphasizing especially the ineffectiveness of the Communist ministers in Zeigner's cabinet. He censured Brandler for having too often acted independently of the *Zentrale* as a whole and suggested that, if Brandler should continue to lead the KPD, he should do so in closer cooperation with his colleagues. As for the Left, Remmele praised Thälmann as a true representative of the proletariat whose help and advice were needed by the party, but left no doubt that he considered both Fischer and Maslow radical intellectuals with a lot of theories but little understanding of practical politics.[106]

Ruth Fischer, speaking for the Left Opposition, delivered one of her customarily unrestrained attacks on Radek and the Brandler faction without throwing much light on the issue in question. The only remarkable part of her speech was the courtesy which she showed to Remmele. The fact that she ignored his less than flattering remarks about herself and Maslow was probably due to her eagerness to win the support of the center group in her quarrel with the Right.[107]

The next speaker was Zinoviev, the sole representative of the Russian party except for Radek, who belonged to Trotsky's camp. Zinoviev was in a precarious position because there was still a good deal of difference between the views held by the center group and the left-wing Fischer-Maslow faction. In order to discredit Brandler, and thereby Trotsky's friend, Radek, he had to aim at a working compromise by which the potential new majority of the German party could be lined up against the Right. Taking a leaf out of Ruth

[106] *Die Lehren der deutschen Ereignisse*, pp. 38, 47.
[107] *ibid.*, pp. 48-57.

Fischer's book, Zinoviev also made a barely disguised bid for the support of the vital center group when he suggested that the present majority in the *Zentrale* should join with the Left in constituting the new KPD leadership. His censure of Brandler's policies, in particular his handling of the so-called "Saxon experiment," was nearly as unreserved as Ruth Fischer's had been, but he took the precaution of not yet identifying himself too closely with the Left Opposition, whose representative he chided good-naturedly for her tendency to exaggerate.[108]

After the reports, the matter of the German October defeat was entrusted to a commission which was given the task of drafting an official resolution. Only the left and center factions, and one representative of the Comintern (Kuusinen) were on the commission—Brandler and Radek were barred from it by an adverse vote.[109] During the commission's deliberations, Zinoviev continued to work behind the scenes for a still more unqualified condemnation of Radek. This he obtained from the Central Committee of the Russian party, which met on January 14 and 15. On January 18, when the Russian party leaders met for a conference, Zinoviev himself delivered the most blistering series of accusations that had yet been directed against his adversary. True to form, Zinoviev's charges were embedded in a party resolution, unanimously adopted but for one abstaining vote—Radek's.[110]

The commission reported the following day to the Presidium of the ECCI with its report on the draft resolution. This was a patchwork of inconclusive statements concerning the causes of the German October debacle, and bore all the marks of a Zinoviev-inspired compromise between the views of the center and the left wing. The text of these "Lessons of the German Events" incorporated criticisms raised by Remmele and Ruth Fischer as well as by Zinoviev, but ignored those of Brandler and Radek.[111] After some political maneuvering and fencing, including the submission of a minority report by Brandler, Pieck, Zetkin, and four others, protesting against the letter and spirit of the resolution draft, it was finally adopted unanimously on January 21, 1924, a few hours before Lenin died.

[108] For Zinoviev's speech see *ibid.*, pp. 58-80.
[109] *ibid.*, p. 81.
[110] Carr, *The Interregnum*, pp. 238-239.
[111] The text is in *Die Lehren der deutschen Ereignisse*, pp. 95-100.

Zinoviev had put himself on record that he considered the October retreat to have been inevitable after all.[112]

In making this gesture, Zinoviev had nothing to lose. His admission did not appear in the official resolution which, on the other hand, was now adopted without dissent. This looked good on the record and could only strengthen Zinoviev's position versus his opponents, notably Trotsky and his supporters in Russia and abroad. For although Zinoviev could not saddle Trotsky directly with responsibility for the German fiasco, he could discredit him by implication through the latter's alliance with Radek, who in turn was a staunch defender of the deviationist Brandler-Thalheimer faction. The fact that Brandler and Radek had voted for the resolution did not weaken Zinoviev's case, as their vote could easily be construed as an admission of guilt.

While Zinoviev had so far refrained from openly articulating his devious linkage, his "observer" in the German *Zentrale*, August Guralsky-Kleine, could afford to be more outspoken. Writing in the spring of 1924, he stated that "The alliance between Thalheimer-Brandler and Radek-Trotsky in the German question is no accident. It touches on a fundamental question: de-Bolshevization of the Russian Communist Party and de-Bolshevization of the European parties, or maintenance of the Bolshevik tutelage of the Russian Communist Party and Bolshevization of the European parties."[113]

Bolshevization of the European parties, including the KPD, was what the triumvirate hoped to achieve now that the recent German defeat had shown the need for such a measure. It was the third such defeat suffered by the KPD (1919, 1921, 1923), but the first for which the Bolshevik leaders, and Zinoviev as chairman of the ECCI in particular, bore a large share of responsibility. Hence their eagerness to shift the blame, a procedure which had the additional advantage of benefiting them in their vendetta against Trotsky, the only man, incidentally, who could conceivably endanger Zinoviev's leading position in the Comintern. But shifting the blame was not enough. With Lenin dead, and with the Russian intraparty struggle at its height, the triumvirs had to make sure of securing the unconditional support of non-Russian Communist parties. Such support

[112] *ibid.*, pp. 83, 90-91.
[113] *Die Internationale*, VII, No. 4 (March 31, 1924), p. 161, as quoted in Carr, *The Interregnum*, p. 241 and n.2.

could only be secured through tightening the Bolsheviks' control over the leaders of the foreign parties, who had to be relied on, in turn, to extend the same iron discipline throughout their own organizations. Since this had to be done largely through the Comintern, and since Zinoviev was chairman of its executive committee, the introduction of Bolshevik discipline required replacement of all those Communist leaders abroad who were anti-Zinoviev or pro-Trotsky, or both, by persons who would do Zinoviev's bidding. Since Zinoviev was known as a left-wing Communist, it was only logical that he would look for supporters abroad among men of his own persuasion.

The KPD was the first European party to tread the road toward Bolshevization, and the October defeat was both cause and effect of this development. For the abortive uprising, which coincided with the conflict among the Bolshevik leaders on the eve of Lenin's death, first pointed up the desirability of Bolshevization, and at the same time provided the opportunity for putting it into effect. The first step in this direction had been taken when the committee, which drafted the resolutions on the October defeat, inserted a clause making it mandatory that all party officers elected in the various district organizations have their election confirmed by the next higher echelon of the party hierarchy.[114] This eliminated for all practical purposes the remaining vestiges of democracy, and enabled the leadership to exercise a stricter control over their subordinates. Furthermore, it made it easier to suppress all oppositional trends from the outset.[115]

The stage for this process had been set in Moscow by the Comintern Presidium. Now Zinoviev could settle back and leave all further developments along these lines to the elements within the KPD which had the blessing of the Russian leaders. The first Central Committee meeting of the KPD, which convened on February 19 for the purpose of electing a new *Zentrale*, demonstrated the success of Moscow's intrigues. Pending elections at the next party congress, membership in the *Zentrale* was temporarily reduced to seven officers, five of whom belonged to the center group, two to the Left Opposition.[116] The Brandler faction was no longer represented,

---

[114] *Die Lehren der deutschen Ereignisse*, p. 116.

[115] Wenzel, p. 273.

[116] *Bericht über die Verhandlungen des IX. Parteitages*, p. 64/75 (double pagination).

and Brandler himself was permanently barred from holding office in the KPD.[117] To be sure, the Left Opposition was not yet in control of the party, but it was well on the way. By what means Ruth Fischer and her friends made their way to the top of the greasy pole is still shrouded in mystery, and numerous unsavory rumors have so far defied all attempts at substantiation.[118] What is known, however, is that the Left Opposition received a considerable amount of backing from Zinoviev, not only because the Left was anti-Brandler, but because its members were also anti-Trotsky. There was no conceivable reason for them to adopt this position, save one: calculated expediency. They knew that Trotsky was as critical of the KPD's bungling of the projected uprising as they were, but they allowed themselves to be enlisted in the camp of Trotsky's enemies because they stood to profit by it. When they voted on February 19 in favor of the Central Committee resolution which condemned Trotsky, they presumably did so less reluctantly than did Brandler, for their votes helped pay the fare to the top.[119]

Between April 7 and 10, the party held its Ninth Congress in Frankfurt am Main. Although the ban on the KPD had been official-

[117] Wenzel, p. 273. Brandler's fortunes, and those of his last remaining friend, August Thalheimer, continued to decline. At the meeting of the Central Committee on February 19, 1924, Brandler, and presumably Thalheimer also, voted in favor of a resolution which condemned the Trotsky faction within the Russian Communist Party. Yet a few weeks earlier, after his return from Moscow, Brandler had stated that he preferred the company of Radek and Trotsky to that of Zinoviev and Ruth Fischer. He and Thalheimer left Germany in April 1924, after the Ninth Party Congress, and went to Moscow. Both were wanted by the German police. In Russia they were not allowed to maintain any contact with the KPD, but they were permitted to join the Russian Communist Party as common rank-and-filers. Thalheimer earned a living by teaching, Brandler by working as an employee of a consumers' cooperative. They returned to Germany in 1928, and were expelled from the party the following year. They founded a splinter party, the *"KPD (Opposition),"* or *KPO*, which never attained any importance. It was small—with approximately 4000 members in 1933—and lacked influence. Brandler revived this "party" after the Second World War in West Germany, giving it the name *"Gruppe Arbeiterpolitik."* To my knowledge, it has never made the headlines, and probably never will. See Wenzel, p. 274, n.1.

[118] For a searching, though inconclusive analysis of the "Rise of the Left," see Wenzel, pp. 275-278.

[119] Ruth Fischer's account is curiously evasive on the attitude which the Left Opposition adopted in regard to the Trotsky crisis. The account, however, makes a great deal of the alleged betrayal of Trotsky by the Right, even though the attitude of the Brandler faction could have hardly made any difference to the outcome after the Right had been disgraced and deprived of all influence. See especially the comments on pp. 374-375. For the position of the Left see also Borkenau, *The Communist International*, p. 256.

ly rescinded on March 1, the congress did not meet in the open, but retained all the precautions of the period of illegality. Warrants of arrest against several party leaders were still pending, which made it necessary to move the place of meeting daily, and to omit mention of the speakers' names from the verbatim report of the proceedings.[120]

The composition of the congress left no doubt as to who had captured control of the KPD. There were ninety-two delegates from the Left Opposition and only thirty-four from the center group. The Brandler faction had sent no delegates at all. Once more the debates centered around the abortive October revolution, but the rhetoric—especially of the speakers of the Left, which was now in effect no longer the "Opposition"—amounted to beating a dead horse. When the new *Zentrale* was elected, only four out of fifteen party offices went to the center group. The radical wing of the party had finally arrived.[121]

The victory of the Left was a personal triumph for Ruth Fischer. Although she nominally shared power with her colleagues, her own inclination and favorable circumstances enabled her to set the tone and dominate the stage.[122] A few weeks after the Frankfurt Congress, *Die Weltbühne*, a periodical known for its sympathies with many Communist ideals, published a brief profile of Ruth Fischer. After a cursory review of her past political career, the article closed on the following note.

"Now she is the undisputed leader of the party. Radicalism has triumphed. Radicalism demands actions [*Aktionen*], demands the split of the free labor unions, demands, in order to stabilize the dictatorship of the party leadership, blind obedience from the Communist parliamentary delegates. Ruth Fischer wants to command abso-

---

[120] Flechtheim, p. 104. *Bericht über die Verhandlungen des IX. Parteitages, passim.*

[121] *Bericht über die Verhandlungen des IX. Parteitages,* pp. 341, 357, and *passim.*

[122] Since the vagaries of the Fischer-Maslow *Zentrale* lie outside the scope of this study, this episode is merely presented in a summary fashion. Zinoviev greeted the victory of the Left evidently with mixed feelings. On the one hand he welcomed it, calling it of "immense significance for the destiny of the German revolution." But he accompanied his congratulations with a warning to the new party leaders not to overplay their hand. Fischer and Maslow chose to ignore the warning, and ultimately suffered the consequences when Zinoviev was no longer politically powerful enough to shield them against Stalin when the latter decided to remove them from office. For Zinoviev's initial reaction see *Bericht über die Verhandlungen des IX. Parteitages,* pp. 65-85.

lutely, and wants to be adored ... like the Dalai Lama. But is she the spirit capable of ruling over men and objects? Or is she, since all good spirits seem to have deserted the KPD, the last glimmer of light that shines for the Communist masses in the darkness?"[123]

As it turned out, her short but turbulent reign proved disastrous for the party and her own political future.[124] What is more, it was during this "Left interlude," for such it was destined to be, that by a whimsical twist of history the revolutionary phase of German Communism came to an end. This was not apparent at the time, nor was it in any way a conscious decision taken by the new party leadership; it was primarily determined by forces beyond the control of the KPD. One important factor in this development was the economic and political stabilization of Germany which followed in the wake of the Dawes Plan. Domestic recovery, coupled with an improvement of the country's international relations, eased the tensions which had beset Germany ever since the end of the war. Furthermore, Stalin's consolidation of power in Russia marked a new era in the history of world Communism. Although the term "revolution" remained part and parcel of Communist vocabulary, in practice it became rather meaningless, after Stalin, in 1924, proclaimed a new Russian course with the slogan of "Socialism in One Country." The new course was accompanied by an emphatic return to the basis of Rapallo which, by the silent consent of both treaty partners, had weathered the October interlude. Stalin's new course also affected the position of the Comintern, which was no longer permitted to occupy an independent place in Communist strategy. Stalin converted it into a subordinate body so as to prevent it from interfering with the policies of the Politburo and the best interests of the Soviet Union. As a by-product of this measure, carried out in the midst of further intraparty struggles from which Stalin ultimately emerged the victor, Moscow also tightened its grip on the non-Russian parties.

[123] Johannes Fischart, "Neue Politikerköpfe: Ruth Fischer," *Die Weltbühne,* xx, No. 19 (May 8, 1924), p. 620.

[124] Because Maslow was arrested sometime in the spring of 1924 and remained in Moabit prison until well into 1925, and Thälmann was still largely a figurehead until his sudden "elevation" by Stalin, party policies were largely determined by Ruth Fischer. She did, however, receive assistance from Maslow who communicated with her from his cell. For a brief but excellent sketch of the Fischer-Maslow *Zentrale* see Wenzel, pp. 277-284; for a more detailed, but somewhat dated account, see Flechtheim, pp. 100-135. For Ruth Fischer's own version see pp. 387-455.

In Germany, then, the final process by which Rosa Luxemburg's party was transformed into a pawn of Stalinist Russia occurred during the "Left interlude." But after a year and a half of zealous Bolshevization, of unbridled verbal assaults on the trade-unions and the SPD, of intrigues and infighting, Fischer and Maslow were caught up in the struggle between Stalin and his two fellow-triumvirs. In the fall of 1925, Stalin removed Fischer and Maslow from the *Zentrale*, leaving the more pliable, more genuinely proletarian "Teddy" Thälmann in control of the KPD. The two ousted leaders left behind a party which they had deprived of any chance to regain the trust and sympathy of German labor. The rift in the working-class movement was beyond repair. In obediently carrying out the process of Bolshevization they had destroyed the few traces of party democracy and independence which had survived the stormy past.

CONCLUSION

AFTER THE DEBACLE of the "German October" the revolutionary phase of German Communism was over. All that remained of it for many years to come were bitter memories and vague hopes for the future. During the remaining years of the Weimar Republic the KPD increased its membership and voting strength, but never made another bid for power. Bolshevized and Stalinized, led by mediocrities who adjusted the policies of the party to the twists and turns of the official Communist course set in Moscow, the KPD eventually shared the fate of the Weimar Republic. Control of the state did not fall to the revolutionary proletariat, but to Hitler. And when after twelve years of Nazi terror and another world war the Communists did attain control over one part of Germany, they owed this achievement to the bayonets of the Russian army, not to their own revolutionary prowess.

The new East German regime, eager to claim the revolutionary tradition of the KPD, set out to rewrite and reinterpret the role which the party had played during the Weimar Republic, particularly in the early period. The result has been a legend in black and white, a tale of heroics and treason. But while it would be petty to belittle the courage and perseverance which many German Communists displayed during the early postwar years, the East German version of the party's *Kampfzeit* is on the whole incorrect.

As a revolutionary movement German Communism was most dynamic before it became formally organized into a political party, during the days of the Spartacus League. Then a small but dedicated group of radical men and women labored and made personal sacrifices for a revolution which, they hoped, would create a new society. They thought of this revolution as inspired and spearheaded by themselves, but carried out by the mass of German workers. This vision was shattered during the weeks after the collapse of the Empire, and after January 1919 ceased to be a feasible undertaking. It was a tragedy for the KPD, and, indeed, for the Weimar Republic, that the German Communists were unable to accept the finality of their defeat. Their several bids for power, which ended only with the close of 1923, were doomed to certain failure, and the party could have found little comfort in the thought that theirs was not the only abortive attempt at revolution in the history of modern Germany.

Conclusion

After German Communism had been decimated, and deprived of its most capable leader, Rosa Luxemburg, the movement began to lose the humanitarian spirit and idealism which had governed and motivated its actions in the past. Paradoxically, the decline of idealism within the KPD did not lead to the adoption of *Realpolitik*, but rather to policies that ignored the true state of existing conditions. Only the weaknesses of the formative stage survived and grew more pronounced, notably a bent for ill-fated adventures, a missing sense of proportion, and a sectarian outlook which the KPD retained even when it became a mass party. The vision of a spontaneous, popular revolution, which in Rosa Luxemburg's time had lent to the movement an air of conviction and dignity, degenerated into futile and irresponsible putschism. The free and open exchange of differing views which had marked the Spartacist phase gave way to intraparty squabbles and led to the formation of cliques, encouraged rigidity, and eventually destroyed party democracy. Hackneyed revolutionary phrases, repeated over and over with tiresome persistence, became the trademark of the KPD as the party joined in the political bickering of the Weimar Republic.

All these trends perpetuated the isolation of German Communism from the rest of the labor movement, a condition which prevailed from the day the party was founded. The majority of German workers were repelled by the extremist attitude of the KPD, looked with indifference, if not with contempt and derision, upon the party's inclination for irresponsible political ventures, and on the whole stood loyally behind the democratic republic which the Communists wanted to transform into a proletarian state.

The Communists were aware of the distrust they aroused among the trade-unions and the Social Democrats, but most of the party leaders lacked either the ability or the courage to change the situation. They preferred to deceive themselves and the rank and file by placing the blame for the party's isolation on the leaders of the trade-unions and the SPD, the *"Bonzen,"* the "traitors to the working class." They were loath to admit that their obstructionist policies, their abusive language, and their bad faith in dealing with non-Communist labor organizations condemned them to remain outcasts. In short, they failed to realize that their political methods as well as their objectives were in need of a careful and rigorous reappraisal. They chose to ignore the fact that their rigid, sectarian, and largely unimaginative approach to politics in general, and to labor politics in particular, was responsible for the refusal of most German workers to follow their lead even during a crisis as acute as that of 1923. And the few Communists who recognized and spoke out against these shortsighted policies paid for their frankness by being expelled as heretics. All that the party's tactics achieved in the long run was to do irreparable damage to the political influence of the entire German labor movement. This the Communists never intended, but their policies, especially during the party's revolutionary phase of the early twenties, made it inevitable.

This development was furthered by a steady decline in the quality of party leadership. Though all of Rosa Luxemburg's successors tried in their own way to guide the KPD toward the objective which she had set forth, none of them possessed her personal magnetism, her political astuteness, her genuine concern for, and trust in the masses. None of them won the confidence and respect of the workers outside the confines of the Communist Party which she had enjoyed. Leo Jogiches did not live long enough to affect the fate of the KPD one way or the other. Paul Levi tried hard to chart a course which embodied the principles of his dead teacher, but he was too aloof and too sceptical a man to assert himself effectively against his many critics and enemies within the party, and in the end cut his ties with a cause that was no longer his. Ernst Reuter-Friesland, after a period of trial and error, went very much the same way. Heinrich Brandler, who unlike most of his colleagues was of genuine proletarian origin, possessed courage, honesty, and loyalty; but he was too easily impressed by the counsels of his better-educated associates and thus prone to subordinate his own, often shrewd, political judgment to their arguments. Ernst Meyer, an intellectual like Levi, and probably one of the most ineffectual party leaders, was fortunate that his brief tenure as chairman of the *Zentrale* fell in a period when a revolution in Germany was temporarily off the agenda. August Thalheimer, Paul Frölich, Ruth Fischer, Hugo Eberlein and their peers also lacked the qualities which make for responsible and clear-sighted leadership. And although old Clara Zetkin occasionally displayed a spirit which lifted her temporarily above the level of mediocrity that characterized most of the party bosses, she too succumbed eventually to the paralyzing influence of centralization, bureaucratization, and Bolshevization.

Conclusion

Although all these men and women differed in outlook, personality, and ability, none of them could cope with the problem of reconciling the best interests of German Communism with the demands and "advice" of the constantly interfering Bolsheviks. It is the contention of this writer that the process of subjugating the policies of the KPD to the dictates of Moscow began, and was virtually accomplished, under Lenin and Trotsky. Stalin's completion of the process after 1923 posed very few difficulties. To be sure, the methods employed by Lenin and Trotsky were more subtle, more circumspect than were Stalin's, but they were nevertheless highly effective. The discrepancies of interests between Soviet Russia and the Comintern on the one hand, and the KPD on the other, were usually resolved in favor of the former. Moscow never permitted the German party to make to non-Communist labor organizations the concessions requisite for honest and effective cooperation. A case in point was the united front policy, which in the early 1920's purported to establish such cooperation. But Bolshevik interpretation of the nature, and especially the limits, of this policy rendered any real rapprochement between Communists and non-Communists illusory. Consequently, the KPD remained virtually isolated even on those occasions when its spokesmen professed, and possibly even believed, to be acting in behalf of the entire German proletariat. As long as the party was distrusted by the masses, its revolutionary ambitions, and with it its vision of a workers' state, were condemned to remain unfulfilled. And as long as the Communists insisted on being bound by Moscow's directives rather than on pursuing an independent policy, they could not hope to win the confidence, much less the support, of German labor. This dilemma the KPD never resolved.

And so the Party's *Kampfzeit* ultimately proved disastrous to the KPD, to German labor as a whole, and to the Weimar Republic. By the time Stalin rose to power in Russia, the KPD had lost its freedom of movement, any genuine concern for the non-Communist workers, and the vigor of its earlier idealism. All three perished in the abortive "German October" in 1923.

BIBLIOGRAPHICAL ESSAY

✎ A STUDY AS SPECIALIZED as this one does not lend itself to a conventional bibliography. Little purpose is served in crowding the pages with the titles of articles, pamphlets, or, in some cases, even monographic studies which often refer only to one specific item mentioned in the narrative. Rather than to compile a formidable list of authors and titles I have thought it more useful to append a selective bibliographical essay. This approach allows for the evaluation and criticism of the most relevant literature pertaining to the history of the German Communist Party until 1924, most of which consists of material varying widely in regard to reliability, thoroughness, and point of view.

To avoid needless duplication, an effort has been made not to repeat literature on special problems which has been previously discussed in bibliographical footnotes, particularly if such problems bear only parenthetically upon the central topic. With these considerations in mind, works on Russo-German relations, on Weimar Germany and its domestic problems, as well as the various biographies and writings of Rosa Luxemburg, to name but a few, have been omitted from the essay.

1. DOCUMENTARY SOURCES

This category includes a wide variety of material which ranges from unpublished documents available only on microfilm to newspapers and political periodicals. It does not include memoirs, biographies, collected speeches, or letters. For the sake of convenience, the section will be subdivided into "Communist" and "non-Communist" sources.

a) *Communist sources*

Basic for any study of German Communism are the published proceedings of the party congresses, *Bericht über die Verhandlungen des 1. bis 12. Parteitages der Kommunistischen Partei Deutschlands (Eine Sektion der Kommunistischen Internationale)*, herausgegeben von der Zentrale der Kommunistischen Partei Deutschlands (Berlin, 1919-1930), twelve volumes in one. Especially during the early years of the party's history, the period which has been the subject of this study, debates at the congresses were still relatively unrestricted and reveal both the nature of the problems faced by the KPD and the various viewpoints of the individual factions on party policy. In addition, each volume contains valuable data on party activities between congresses, lists of officers elected, statistical information pertaining to membership and related aspects, and a host of other useful items of information.

Equally indispensable are the proceedings of the first five congresses of the Communist International. Each of them had some influence upon the affairs of the German party. *Der I. Kongress der Kommunistischen Internationale: Protokoll der Verhandlungen in Moskau vom 2. bis zum 19. März 1919* (Hamburg, 1921), the founding congress, created the Communist International without the vote of the German delegate. *Der Zweite Kongress der Kommunistischen Internationale: Protokoll der Verhandlungen vom 19. Juli in Petrograd und vom 23. Juli bis 7. August 1920 in Moskau* (Hamburg, 1921) was mainly concerned with the adoption of the twenty-one conditions requisite for admission to the Communist International. When the next congress met in the summer of 1921, the KPD had experienced its first major leadership crisis and had suffered a grave setback as a result of the unsuccessful *März Aktion*. The record of the heated debates on both events occupies over one-half of the *Protokoll des III. Kongresses der Kommunistischen Internationale, Moskau, 22. Juni bis 12. Juli 1921* (Hamburg, 1921). The Fourth Congress, meeting shortly before the Ruhr occupation by France, was preoccupied with the united front policy. The proceedings on this issue and on the vain attempts to heal the growing rift within the KPD are in *Protokoll des Vierten Kongresses der Kommunistischen Internationale, Petrograd-Moskau vom 5. November bis 6. Dezember 1922* (Hamburg, 1923). Finally, *Fünfter Kongress der Kommunistischen Internationale. Protokoll*, 2 vols. (n.d., n.p.), deals in large part with the failure of the "German October." An earlier post-mortem, however, had been conducted in January 1924 by the ECCI and the KPD leadership. It is recorded in *Die Lehren der deutschen Ereignisse. Das Präsidium des Exekutivkomitees der Kommunistischen Internationale zur deutschen Frage, Januar 1924* (Hamburg, 1924). Because the two-volume record of the Fifth Congress was not available to me I have used the English abridgement, *Fifth Congress of the Communist International, Abridged Report of Meetings held at Moscow June 17th to July 8th, 1924* (London, n.d.). In addition to the *Protokolle*, each congress issued a separate edition of *Thesen und Resolutionen* to accompany the record of the proceedings.

While the verbatim reports of the proceedings at the Comintern congresses provide an insight into policy changes, ideological trends, and political differences within the Communist International, their special validity for this study lies in the light they shed on the relationship between the German party and the Bolshevik leaders. The *Protokolle*, however, only record the debates held during the sessions at the congresses. In order to keep abreast of Communist ideology and policy between congresses, it is necessary to supplement the *Protokolle* by examining the various Communist periodicals published during the period in question. The most widely known is *Die Kommunistische Internationale, Organ des Exekutivkomitees der Kommunistischen Internationale* (Moscow and Petrograd, 1919 *et seq.*) which appeared simultaneously in Russian, German, French, and English. The English edition, *The Communist International, Organ of the Executive Committee of the Communist International*, was published in London. Zinoviev was its editor-in-chief during the early 1920's, and there is hardly an issue which does not contain at least one contribution by him. *Die Kommunistische Internationale* served as a forum for the Communist elite. Everyone who held a leading position in the Communist hierarchy at least occasionally submitted an article on Marxist theory, on acute problems of tactics, or on local political developments. In short, the contributions dealt with anything which was held to be of interest to the worldwide revolutionary movement and thus, one would assume, to the international proletariat. But since most contributors prior to 1924-1925 tended to be intellectuals, or at least had pretensions to be such, they wrote chiefly for each other.

In September 1921 the Comintern began to publish another periodical which was primarily concerned with current news and its interpretation. It was called *Internationale-Presse Korrespondenz*, often abbreviated as *Inprekorr*, which also appeared in French and English editions. The English edition initially bore the name of *International Press Correspondence*, or *Inprecorr*, but eventually changed its name to *World News and Views*. The German edition usually had more comprehensive coverage than either its French or English counterpart. Like *Die Kommunistische Internationale*, the *Internationale Presse Korrespondenz* was published at irregular intervals, generally two to three times a month. It concentrated on international political and economic developments, especially their effects on Communism in general and Soviet Russia in particular. It also provided detailed reports on the congresses held by the various member parties of the Comintern, and discussed special problems affecting these organizations.

The KPD published its own bi-monthly periodical, *Die Internationale, Zeitschrift für Theorie und Praxis des Marxismus* (Berlin, 1919 *et seq.*), articles of which were frequently reprinted in *Die Kommunistische Internationale* or *Internationale Presse Korrespondenz*. Whereas the emphasis of *Die Internationale* was on the German scene, topics affecting the Communist movement beyond the German frontiers appeared in its columns as well.

For the day-by-day activities of the KPD *Die Rote Fahne* (November 1918–October 1923), the principal daily organ of the party, proved invaluable for this study. The paper covered party activities in the various parts of Germany, and the editorials reflected the views of the *Zentrale*, thus providing an excellent picture of the party's policies, policy changes, and factional struggles during the early twenties. *Die Rote Fahne* also contained occasional contributions from leading Russian Bolsheviks, particularly Radek and Zinoviev, and the tenor of these contributions frequently provided clues to the projected course of the party at given stages.

A useful reference work published by the KPD is the *Jahrbuch für Politik-Wirtschaft-Arbeiterbewegung* 1922-23, 1923-24, 1925-26 (Hamburg-Berlin, 1922-1926). Each volume contains articles and statistics on numerous aspects of the international labor movement, politics, and economic trends, and provides information on the various sub-organizations of the KPD such as its youth and women's branches, membership figures, and election results. Although the articles are slanted, and the data given must be used with caution, the *Jahrbuch* can be profitably consulted for research on German Communism.

When completed, the series *Dokumente und Materialien zur Geschichte der deutschen Arbeiterbewegung, Serie II: 1914-1945* (Berlin, 1958ff.), published by the Institut für Marxismus-Leninismus beim Zentralkomitee der Sozialistischen Einheitspartei Deutschlands, Berlin, should prove of value to the historian, even though the documents have been carefully selected by the East German Communists. Up to this time, the first three volumes, covering the period from 1914 through April 1919, have appeared in print. Since the archives from which most of the documents have been chosen are at present inaccessible to non-Communists, publication of the series will at least make some of this vital material available to Western scholars.

The controversy over the *März Aktion*, which divided the KPD for several months in 1921 produced a number of contemporary publications both from proponents of the *Aktion* and its critics. Heinrich Brandler, *War die März Aktion ein Bakunisten Putsch?* (Berlin-Leipzig, 1921), constitutes the party chairman's lame and unconvincing apologia. A more skillful, although ultimately specious, argument in favor of the so-called "Theory of the Revolutionary Offensive" by Thalheimer, Frölich, and others is in *Taktik und Organisation der revolutionären Offensive. Die Lehren der Märzaktion*, published by the Zentrale der Vereinigten Kommunistischen Partei Deutschlands, Sektion der Kommunistischen Internationale (Berlin-Leipzig, 1921). Despite the special pleading of *Taktik und Organisation*, the several contributions do reveal a number of relevant facts about the March uprising. The same is true of *Die Enthüllungen zu den Märzkämpfen. Enthülltes und Verschwiegenes* (Halle,

1922), published by the Kommunistische Partei Deutschlands in answer to the revelations printed by the Social Democratic newspaper *Vorwärts* in November 1921. Although *Die Enthüllungen zu den Märzkämpfen* aimed at discrediting the Social Democratic charges, the brochure's attempt to do so by disavowing the party's own agents named in the *Vorwärts* reports remained utterly ineffectual.

Two key documents pertaining to the March uprising and its origins are the pamphlets which Paul Levi published immediately after the event: *Unser Weg: Wider den Putschismus*; Zweite, mit neuem Vorwort versehene Auflage (Berlin, 1922); and *Was ist das Verbrechen? Die Märzaktion oder die Kritik daran? Rede auf der Sitzung des Zentralausschusses der V.K.P.D. am 4. Mai* 1921 (Berlin, 1921). Both publications contain Levi's unequivocal criticism of the March uprising and of the forces primarily responsible for it, i.e., the KPD *Zentrale* and the Comintern representatives in Germany. The polemical tone of the pamphlets and the strong condemnation of a policy of which he disapproved were the result of Levi's profound disillusionment with a movement to which he had dedicated years of his life. At the same time he still felt sufficiently bound by loyalty to the Communist cause and by party discipline not to reveal the names of those men and women who in his opinion had led the KPD into the wilderness of irresponsible political putschism.

Disappointingly enough, *Der Hochverratsprozess gegen Heinrich Brandler vor dem ausserordentlichen Gericht am 6. Juni* 1921 *in Berlin* (Berlin, 1921), yields little information on the March uprising. Its sole value lies in the light which it casts upon the mind and personality of the defendant.

One Communist publication which, apart from *Die Lehren der deutschen Ereignisse*, is essential for an understanding of the "German October" in 1923 is August Thalheimer, 1923: *Eine verpasste Revolution? Die deutsche Oktoberlegende und die wirkliche Geschichte von* 1923 (Berlin, 1931). These are the recollections and apologia of a bitter and disappointed man. In the pamphlet the author turns against the charges raised by the ultra-Left that circumstances in 1923 favored a revolution which then was mismanaged by the KPD *Zentrale*. Thalheimer maintains that victory by the Communists was prevented in 1923 in the first place by timely concessions on the part of the German bourgeoisie, and only in the second place by mistakes committed by the KPD *Zentrale*. He states that the reason for writing the pamphlet is his desire to discuss these mistakes so that future generations of Communists may learn from them. Although written years after the event, the pamphlet has been included in this section because its author was a member of the Brandler *Zentrale* in 1923.

b) *Non-Communist sources*

Because the Communists regarded their parliamentary activities merely as a means for political propaganda, the *Verhandlungen des Reichstags: Stenographische Berichte* (or *Anlagen*), Vols. 344-380 (Berlin, 1921-1924) were of relatively limited value for this study. However, the same cannot be said about the *Verhandlungen des Sächsischen Landtages 1922-1923*, Vol. I, Nos. 1-40, and Vol. II, Nos. 41-78 (Dresden, 1923-1924). Much of the battle between Saxony and the central government in Berlin on the one hand, between the left-wing coalition of SPD-KPD and the middle-class parties on the other, was fought out on the floor of the Saxon diet. Minister-President Erich Zeigner's position, in all its tragic facets, emerges with particular clarity from the debates.

The most valuable of the published government documents proved to be the verbatim record of the Prussian diet's investigation committee which probed into the background of the March uprising in 1921. The committee's special report is entitled *Niederschriften über die von dem Untersuchungsausschuss zur Nachprüfung der Ursachen, des Umfangs und der Wirkungen des kommunistischen Aufstandes in Mitteldeutschland im März 1921 in mündlicher Verhandlung erhobenen Beweise: Sammlung der Drucksachen des Preussischen Landtags (Anlagen zu den Sitzungsberichten)*, Drucksache Nr. 4140, 1.Wahlperiode, 1.Tagung, begonnen am 10. März 1921, VIII (Berlin, 1923). The testimonies of the various Prussian officials who were chiefly responsible for planning the police action, which then met head-on with the Communist uprising, helped to clarify the origins of the disturbances in central Germany.

With regard to unpublished documents consulted, important information was obtained from the microfilmed records of the German Foreign Ministry Archives (1867-1920) and of the German Foreign Ministry and the Reichs Chancellery covering the Weimar period, all of which are deposited at the National Archives, Washington, D.C. From the first collection, only Karl Radek's German police file was used: *Aken betreffend den Russischen Bolschewisten Karl Radek (Sobelsohn)*, Deutschland 131, adh. 3, No. 2, Vols. 1-3, December 17, 1917–February 1920. In the collection covering the Weimar period the films entitled *Russland* (Büro des Reichsministers), Serial 2860 H, Vols. 3-7. January 1, 1921–May 26, 1924, containers 1405, 1406, 1407, reveal the curiously ambivalent official German attitude toward Communism. The documents show how seriously the German ambassador to Russia and the German Foreign Office tried to improve Russo-German relations while remaining at the same time determined to suppress Communism at home. Interestingly enough, it is apparent from the documents that at least the German Ambassador to Russia, Count von Brockdorff-Rantzau, never fully believed in the feasibility of a Communist coup in Germany, and that he tended to defend the Bolshevik leaders against charges of sponsoring subversive revolutionary activities in Germany.

Equally important, especially for the attitude of the federal government toward the critical developments in 1923, are the *Stresemann Papers*, microfilm in the National Archives, Washington, D.C., particularly containers 3096 through 3099, 3104-3105, 3110-3111, 3158-3159, which supersede the earlier and selective printed version of Stresemann's *Nachlass*, entitled *Gustav Stresemann, Vermächtnis: Der Nachlass in drei Bänden*, I, *Vom Ruhrkrieg bis London*, ed. Henry Bernhard (Berlin, 1932). In addition to records of crucial cabinet meetings in September and October, 1923, the films also contain interesting correspondence between Chancellor Stresemann and prominent members of the German People's Party on the Communist threat in Saxony and Thuringia. Several of the letters indicate that Stresemann was under strong pressure from his party to proceed against the left-wing governments of these states with all the powers at his command, and it is very probable that this pressure influenced his decision to order troops into the central German region in the fall of 1923.

Besides, the "Reichskabinetts-Protokolle" (Auswärtiges Amt und Reichskanzlei), microfilm T-120, containers 1672, 1673, and 1749 have been useful in ascertaining the attitude of the German federal government toward the domestic crises in March 1921 and in October 1923.

Aside from these contemporary sources, several recently published document collections were of great assistance for research on this study: *The Communist International 1919-1943, Documents*, I, 1919-1922, II, 1923-1928, selected and edited by Jane Degras; issued under the auspices of the Royal Institute of International Affairs (London-New York-Toronto, 1956 and 1960); and Xenia Joukoff Eudin and Harold H. Fisher, in collaboration with Rosemary Brown Jones, *Soviet Russia and the West 1920-1927: A Documentary Survey* (Stanford, 1957). Miss Degras' two volumes consist of selected documents from various publications pertaining to the activities of the Third International. The documents, nearly all of them translated from the Russian, are introduced by brief annotations which acquaint the reader with the historical event to which the documents relate. A similar procedure has been adopted by the authors of *Soviet Russia and the West*, although the narrative introducing the document sections is more extensive than in Miss Degras' volumes. The two works combined give the reader an excellent picture of the trend of Bolshevik policies vis-à-vis Russia's western neighbors, and reveal clearly the differences of approach utilized by the two principal arms of Bolshevik political strategy, the Russian Foreign Office and the Comintern.

Finally, a new publication of German documents, the relevant volumes of which appeared too late to have been of use for this study, is the series *Ursachen und Folgen. Vom deutschen Zusammenbruch 1918 und 1945 bis zur staatlichen Neuordnung Deutschlands in der Gegenwart: Eine Urkunden- und Dokumentensammlung zur Zeitgeschichte,* eds. Dr. Herbert Michaelis und Dr. Ernst Schraepler unter Mitwirkung von Dr. Günter Scheel (Berlin, n.d.). The first six volumes had been published as of January 1962. When completed, this series will complement, and in part undoubtedly supersede, the earlier standard work by Johannes Hohlfeld, ed., *Deutsche Reichsgeschichte in Dokumenten. Urkunden und Aktenstücke zur inneren und äusseren Politik des deutschen Reiches,* 4 vols. (Berlin, 1934).

2. GENERAL AND SPECIAL STUDIES, INCLUDING ARTICLES

A thorough and comprehensive study of the German labor movement as a whole does not yet exist, and may, perhaps, never be written. The tendency in recent years has been to concentrate on individual parties, and even there on special phases and on specific issues. This trend emerges clearly from two recently published historiographical articles, one by William Harvey Maehl, "Recent Literature on the German Socialists, 1891-1932," *The Journal of Modern History,* xxxiii, No. 3 (September 1961), and the other by Georg Kotowski, "Zur Geschichte der Arbeiterbewegung in Mittel-und Ostdeutschland; ein Literaturbericht," *Jahrbuch für die Geschichte Mittel- und Ostdeutschlands,* viii (Tübingen, 1959). I was unable to secure a copy of the bibliographical study by Enzo Collotti, *Die Kommunistische Partei Deutschlands 1918-1933* (Milan, 1962), prior to sending the manuscript to press.

One attempt to cover the history of German labor in its entirety is the brief survey by a British writer, Evelyn Anderson, *Hammer or Anvil: The Story of the German Working-Class Movement* (London, 1945). It is a rather superficial account which, moreover, reveals the author's decidedly sceptical view concerning the political maturity of the German working class. More objective than Anderson's account, and written with much greater insight and understanding, are the chapters devoted to the subject in Carl A. Landauer, *European Socialism, A History of Ideas and Movements*, 2 vols. (Berkeley, n.d.). The chapters reflect not only the author's mature scholarly judgment, but also his many years of close association with the object of his study. For these reasons Landauer's treatment of German labor is vastly superior to the rather fleeting account given by George Douglas Howard Cole in A *History of Socialist Thought*, IV, *Communism and Social Democracy*, 2 parts (London, 1958), and even more so to what amounts to a summary of events in Adolf Sturmthal, *The Tragedy of European Labor, 1918-1939* (New York, 1943). For the period 1918-1923, Heinz Schuerer, *Die politische Arbeiterbewegung Deutschlands in der Nachkriegzeit 1918-1923* (diss. Leipzig, 1933) is a concise and succinct interpretation of the history of the German working class during this period.

Since no historical phase of the KPD can be properly understood without a knowledge of where and how the Communist movement in Germany originated, and to what socio-political circumstances it owed its existence, several special studies were found to be particularly useful for acquainting the reader with the party's antecedents and the historical climate in which it was founded. Arthur Rosenberg, *Die Entstehung der Deutschen Republik* (Berlin, 1928), still remains an incisive, convincing, and stimulating interpretation of why and how the republic was created, and of the role which German labor played in this process. Friedrich Stampfer, *Die Vierzehn Jahre der Ersten Deutschen Republik* (Karlsbad, 1936), though differing in approach and emphasis from Rosenberg's account, provides in the initial chapters a Social Democrat's view of events. Carl E. Schorske, *German Social Democracy 1905-1917: The Development of the Great Schism* (Cambridge, Mass., 1955), is a brilliant analysis of the various factors that led to the split of the SPD during the war years. By its close scrutiny of the role of trade-union influence and of the disagreements over questions of organization, political methods, and political objectives within the SPD, Schorske's study probes more deeply into this highly critical phase of Social Democratic history than does the somewhat earlier account of A. Joseph Berlau, *The German Social Democratic Party, 1914-1921* (New York, 1949). The standard work on the history of the Independent Socialists remains Eugen Prager, *Geschichte der U.S.P.D.: Entstehung und Entwicklung der Unabhängigen Sozialdemokratischen Partei Deutschlands* (Berlin, 1921), which covers events until the split of that party in Halle during the fall of 1920. Walter Tormin, *Zwischen Rätediktatur und sozialer Demokratie: Die Geschichte der Rätebewegung in der deutschen Revolution 1918/1919*, vol. 4 of *Beiträge zur Geschichte des Parlamen-*

tarismus und der politischen Parteien (Düsseldorf, 1954), is the only existing scholarly investigation of the council movement which accompanied the birth of the Weimar Republic. Dr. Tormin's discussion of the attitudes which the various revolutionary groups and factions, including the Spartacus League, adopted toward the council movement is particularly enlightening. The most recent study on the Spartacist uprising in January 1919, and its antecedents, is Eric Waldman, *The Spartacist Uprising of 1919 and the Crisis of the German Socialist Movement: A Study of the Relation of Political Theory and Party Practice* (Milwaukee, 1958). The author has set out to refute the widespread contention that the January uprising was premeditated, and instead has developed the thesis that it was "a violent outburst of the sharp hostility which then existed between the socialist factions" (p. 214). He asserts that the hostility which divided German labor during the weeks of revolutionary upheaval between November 9, 1918, and January 15, 1919, was ultimately responsible for preventing any of the various factions from attaining a dominant influence in German politics.

While all the books thus far cited touch in one way or other on the German Communists, none of them has made the study of this movement its sole concern. The first monograph dealing exclusively with the history of the German Communist Party appeared shortly after World War II: Ossip K. Flechtheim, *Die Kommunistische Partei Deutschlands in der Weimarer Republik* (Offenbach, 1948). The author states in the preface that he belongs to no political party, and that he wants neither to make revelations nor grind axes. True to his word, Flechtheim wrote a history of the KPD which is not *engagé*, and although his sympathy with the tortuous path of left-wing German labor emerges from time to time, his general approach is scholarly and objective. As a pioneering work the book is invaluable, but it has shortcomings. The account, though not devoid of critical evaluations, is by and large straight factual narration, except for an analytical chapter on the party's ideological and sociological makeup. In telling his story, however, the author has remained too close to his sources, some of which are of dubious reliability (especially Georg Schwarz, *Völker, hoeret die Zentrale, KPD bankrott* [Berlin, 1933], a polemical, distorted, and sensational book designed to appeal to anti-Communist sentiments). The author was apparently unable to secure a file of *Die Rote Fahne*, but he has made use of other Communist publications, notably the *Parteitagsberichte, Die Kommunistische Internationale*, and *Die Internationale*. In using these materials, however, he has frequently failed to evaluate them critically, so that official party opinions have become, inadvertently, the views of the author. Despite these shortcomings the book provides the first comprehensive account of the KPD from its inception until 1933. The pace is fast, and relatively little space has been given to such events as the March Uprising of 1921 and the "German October" in 1923. This is as it should be in a survey history, but unfortunately some of the author's interpretations of events suffer from the fact that the account is largely based on derivative information, much of which is either partisan or unreliable, or both.

The same year that Flechtheim published his book, Ruth Fischer's *Stalin and German Communism, A Study in the Origins of the State Party* (Cambridge, Mass., 1948) appeared on the market. The book is a historian's nightmare. Miss Fischer was deeply involved in the German Communist movement and, unlike Flechtheim, wrote her account with the passion and rancor of a disillusioned idealist. As the leader of the erstwhile Left-Wing Opposition within the KPD she approached her subject with partisan vigor. There are only villains and heroes, with Joseph Stalin heading the former, Ruth Fischer the latter. The book is essentially a lengthy polemical dispute between the author and her former comrades who turned into enemies. Apart from the bias, which can generally be discounted, the book abounds with inaccuracies and downright falsifications. Miss Fischer carefully eliminated from her account all facts which might adversely affect the picture which she tried to convey of her own role in the KPD. Furthermore, dates which the author could have easily checked are frequently inaccurate, and the reader is often at a loss as to the proper sequence of events which are described in the narrative. The footnotes rarely pertain to sources. They usually serve as an excuse for digressing on a point often only remotely pertinent to the issue under discussion. Many of these shortcomings may be explained by the fact that she wrote largely from memory, but in numerous instances the intent to mislead is too obvious to be missed. In spite of these faults the book cannot simply be dismissed as worthless. Being the personal account of one who was at the hub of events, who occupied a leading position in the KPD, and who knew personally the ins and outs of the policies, not only of the German party, but of the Russian party and the Comintern as well, it has a distinct documentary value. It does convey the flavor of the infighting, the intrigues, the personal vendettas of the Communist hierarchy, and some of the author's portraits of leading figures such as Lenin, Trotsky, Radek, et al., are vivid and convincing even when drawn, in some cases, with the intent to distort. Her book can be of use to the student of history provided it is carefully checked against other sources.

A much more substantial account of the German Communist Party and its activities through 1923 than either of the two books just men-

Bibliographical Essay

tioned is in Edward Hallett Carr, *The Bolshevik Revolution 1917-1923*, III (New York, 1953), and *The Interregnum 1923-1924* (New York, 1954), both volumes being part of the author's general work, *A History of Soviet Russia*. Although Carr's principal concern is Russia, he deals extensively with relations between the German Communists and the Russian Bolshevik leaders. In contrast to both Flechtheim and Fischer, he has made use of most of the available documentary material, including many Russian sources, and while some of his interpretations may be open to disagreement, the work sheds a great deal of light on the role of the KPD in the Comintern and on related issues. Carr's study should be read in conjunction with the older, but still useful, book by Franz Borkenau, *The Communist International* (London, 1938). The author's personal experiences in the twenties, both as a member of the KPD and of the Comintern, add astute personal observations to his account, and although some of the events related in the book require revision and reinterpretation, it is a much more reliable account than that of Ruth Fischer. Borkenau's more recent study, *Der europäische Kommunismus; seine Geschichte von 1917 bis zur Gegenwart* (Bern, 1952), adds nothing new to the story as far as the period up to 1924 is concerned. Neither does another, otherwise useful, book on the Comintern, Günther Nollau, *Die Internationale; Wurzeln und Erscheinungsformen des proletarischen Internationalismus* (Cologne, 1959). It is primarily an analysis of the organizational machinery and operational function of the Comintern, though preceded by a rather brief historical survey. Unfortunately, some of the passages pertaining to Comintern activities in Germany are not based on altogether reliable sources.

The few monographs which deal with specific aspects of either the 1921 or the 1923 uprising differ widely with regard to their usefulness. Hans Martin Meyer, *Die politischen Hintergründe des Mitteldeutschen Aufstandes von 1921* (diss. Berlin, 1935), although written at the beginning of the National Socialist regime, is a sober and balanced survey of Germany's domestic and foreign problems which, in the author's opinion, influenced the KPD in its decision to launch the March uprising. There are a number of interpretations which, upon closer examination of the evidence, require correction, especially his theory that the central German insurrection was launched in order to boost Soviet morale after the Kronstadt revolt. Although the March uprising is treated in only a dozen pages, the account as such is sound. In contrast, the East German study *Die Märzkämpfe 1921; mit Dokumentenanhang*, published by the Marx-Engels-Lenin-Stalin Institut beim ZK der SED (Berlin, 1956), is a propaganda tract dressed up as a serious historical investigation. However, the appended documents are valuable aids since most of them come from East German archives and are not readily available elsewhere. Walter Drobnig, *Der Mitteldeutsche Aufstand 1921. Seine Bekämpfung durch die Polizei* (Lübeck, 1929), describes the actual combat actions of the Prussian police in central Germany. The account is factual in its presentation, though the author's tendency to cast the police forces in a quasi-heroic role is somewhat annoying.

The most valuable study available on the "German October" of 1923 is an unpublished dissertation by Dr. Otto Wenzel, "Die Kommunist-ische Partei Deutschlands im Jahre 1923" (Freie Universität Berlin, 1955). It is a carefully conceived and thoroughly executed investigation of the party's activities during this crucial year, well documented, and on the whole convincingly presented. My book owes a great deal to Dr. Wen-zel's pioneering study, although in a number of instances my interpreta-tion differs sharply from his. The thesis advanced by the dissertation that the KPD systematically planned and prepared a revolutionary insurrection in Germany throughout the year is not borne out by the available evi-dence, unless one takes literally the revolutionary jargon which Com-munist publications and speakers employed as a matter of principle during the period under discussion. Aside from divergent interpretations, Dr. Wenzel's dissertation with its painstakingly detailed descriptions of Communist tactics in all parts of Germany is invaluable for any student of the KPD and its activities during 1923.

Heinz Habedank, *Zur Geschichte des Hamburger Aufstandes 1923* (Berlin, 1958) has been evaluated in the body of the book and needs no further comment. It should be compared with the very different account given in Lothar Danner, *Ordnungspolizei Hamburg: Betrachtungen zu ihrer Geschichte 1918 bis 1933* (Hamburg, 1958). The salient points of both studies have been considered in the footnote discussing the differ-ent interpretations of the Hamburg uprising and its origins. Helmut Gast, "Die proletarischen Hundertschaften als Organe der Einheits-front im Jahre 1923," *Zeitschrift für Geschichtswissenschaft*, IV, No. 3 (1956), pp. 439-465, elucidates the technical details pertaining to the formation and training of the red hundreds. Despite its obvious ideo-logical bias, the article is helpful for an understanding of these para-military Communist organizations. Much less enlightening is an article by another East German, Raimund Wagner, "Zur Frage der Massen-kämpfe in Sachsen vom Frühjahr bis zum Sommer 1923," *Zeitschrift für Geschichtswissenschaft*, IV, No. 1 (1956), pp. 246-264. Wagner's thesis, based largely on the interpretation given in Walter Ulbricht, *Zur Geschichte der deutschen Arbeiterbewegung; aus Reden und Auf-sätzen*, I (Berlin, 1953), is that the large-scale strike movements during the period he discusses were led and inspired by the KPD, and that their ultimate failure was due to the treasonable machinations of the Brandler *Zentrale*. The most up-to-date treatment of the Reichswehr occupation of Saxony is Harold J. Gordon, "Die Reichswehr und Sachsen 1923," *Wehrwissenschaftliche Rundschau*, No. 12 (1961), pp. 677-692. Unfortunately it appeared after the manuscript for this book was completed. For events in Thuringia the best study is Georg Witzmann, *Thüringen von 1918-1933. Erinnerungen eines Politikers* (Meisenheim am Glain, 1958). Though written from a conservative point of view, it gives a vivid picture of the short-lived left-wing coalition government of that state in 1923. The account of KPD activities in 1923, including the Hamburg uprising, which is given in the East German publication *Zur Geschichte der Kommunistischen Partei Deutschlands; eine Auswahl von Materialien und Dokumenten aus den Jahren 1914-1946*, published by the Marx-Engels-Lenin-Stalin Institut beim Zentralkomitee der SED, 2nd ed. (Berlin, 1955), has some documentary value but is otherwise useless for scholarly purposes. Interestingly enough, the March uprising of 1921 has not been included in this publication.

3. BIOGRAPHICAL AND AUTOBIOGRAPHICAL STUDIES; COLLECTED LETTERS AND SPEECHES

The pitfalls of memoirs and political biographies are well known, but nowhere are they as much in evidence as in the writings of Communists or ex-Communists. Fortunately, however, there are exceptions to the rule, and not all such materials consulted for this study have proved disappointing. By far the most useful and reliable book in this general category has been Willy Brandt and Richard Lowenthal, *Ernst Reuter: Ein Leben für die Freiheit. Eine politische Biographie* (Munich, 1957). It is indeed regrettable, from the historian's point of view, that Reuter quit the party as early as he did, for up to that point his biography provides a great deal of insight into the KPD, and especially its intraparty struggles. The authors have made use of unpublished documents and personal interviews with several of Reuter's former associates in the Communist movement. More memoirs seem to have been written by women in the revolutionary camp than by men. One of the most interesting is by Angelica Balabanoff, *My Life As a Rebel* (New York and London, 1938). Though it does not cover much beyond 1920, the book contains vivid sketches of the early Bolshevik leaders, notably of Lenin, Trotsky, Zinoviev, and Radek. Since the author was closely connected with the international revolutionary movement before the war, and for a brief period of time was secretary of the Comintern, she was well acquainted with most of the outstanding leaders of the international labor movement.

Bibliographical Essay

Equally well informed was Clara Zetkin, but she failed to write her memoirs. She did, however, leave us a small volume in which she recorded some of her conversations with Lenin, entitled *Reminiscences of Lenin* (London, 1929). The passages dealing with the March uprising of 1921, with Paul Levi, Ruth Fischer, and other members of the KPD are particularly significant. In contrast, the East German biography by Louise Dornemann, *Clara Zetkin: Ein Lebensbild* (Berlin, 1957) is a conventional Communist panegyric.

A fine description of how young people were drawn into the KPD during the party's formative years is in the autobiography of Margarete Buber-Neumann, *Von Potsdam nach Moskau; Stationen eines Irrweges* (Stuttgart, 1957). Although the emphasis of the book is on a later period, notably the 1930's, the author succeeds in conveying the initial idealism and enthusiasm which permeated German Communism during the early twenties.

Undoubtedly useful, although highly selective, are the various collections of letters and speeches by prominent German Communist leaders. All have been published in East Germany by the Institut für Marxismus-Leninismus (formerly Marx-Engels-Lenin-Stalin Institut) beim ZK der SED: *Rosa Luxemburg, Ausgewählte Reden und Schriften*, 2 vols. (Berlin, 1955); *Clara Zetkin, Ausgewählte Reden und Schriften*, 2 vols. (Berlin, 1960); *Wilhelm Pieck, Gesammelte Reden und Schriften*, 3 vols. (Berlin, 1959-1960); and *Ernst Thälmann, Reden und Aufsätze zur Geschichte der deutschen Arbeiterbewegung*, 2 vols. (Berlin, 1956). Some of these collections are not yet complete, and additional volumes will probably be published in the future.

Autobiographical accounts which must be read with extreme caution are those of the cloak-and-dagger variety. The authors, frequently ex-Communists, wrote their books primarily in order to sell; and since an exciting book sells better than a dull one, they occasionally yielded to temptation and exaggerated, or even falsified. On the other hand, not all of the experiences they relate can be discounted, either because we cannot check them and they might be true, or because we have checked them and have found them to be correct. A typical example of this genre is Jan Valtin, *Out of the Night* (New York, 1941). His description of Communist activities in Hamburg and elsewhere along Germany's northern coast in 1923 makes fascinating reading; but how reliable it is we do not know. The same is generally true for some of the other "now it can be told" accounts: Walter Zeutschel, *Im Dienst der kommunistischen Terror-Organisation (Tscheka-Arbeit in Deutschland)* (Berlin, 1931); Walter Krivitsky, *In Stalin's Secret Service; An Exposé of Russia's Secret Policies by the former Chief of the Soviet Intelligence in*

Western Europe (London, 1939); and "Ypsilon," *Pattern for World Revolution* (Chicago-New York, 1947). Somewhat less sensational, and on the whole also more trustworthy, are Boris Bajanov, *Avec Staline dans le Kremlin* (Paris, 1930), and Grigory Bessedovsky, *Revelations of a Soviet Diplomat* (London, 1931). In a slightly different category is Max Hoelz, *From White Cross to Red Flag: The Autobiography of Max Hoelz, Waiter, Soldier, Revolutionary Leader* (London-Toronto, 1930). His are the memoirs of a naïve and egocentric revolutionary idealist, inaccurate in places, but by and large believable.

Most of the memoirs and biographies of those prominent Russian Bolshevik leaders pertinent to this study shed little light on their relations with the German Communist Party during the early twenties. Neither Radek nor Zinoviev published his memoirs, nor have they found a biographer, except for two brief profiles in Oscar Blum, *Russische Köpfe* (Berlin-Leipzig-Wien-Bern, 1923). To be sure, some of Lenin's writings on particular issues, which need not be enumerated here, bear on Germany. But neither David Shub, *Lenin* (New York, 1948), nor Georg von Rauch, *Lenin, Die Grundlegung des Sowjetsystems* (Berlin-Frankfurt, 1958) adds substantially to our knowledge of Lenin's views on German developments. More informative along these lines, at least up to the Second World Congress of the Comintern in 1920, is Stanley W. Page, *Lenin and World Revolution* (New York, 1959). On Trotsky, aside from his own autobiography, Leo Trotski, *Mein Leben; Versuch einer Autobiographie* (Berlin, 1930), the most authoritative study is the still unfinished biography by Isaac Deutscher, *The Prophet Armed: Trotsky 1879-1921* (New York and London, 1954), and *The Prophet Unarmed: Trotsky 1921-1929* (London-New York-Toronto, 1959). Trotsky's memoirs do not deal at all with the KPD and its revolutionary objectives, and Deutscher's two biographical volumes touch on them only very fleetingly. More relevant to this particular subject than the aforementioned works are some of Trotsky's other writings, partly autobiographical, partly documentary, all of them written for self-justification: Leon Trotsky, *The First Five Years of the Communist International*, 2 vols. (New York, 1945, 1953), containing some of Trotsky's major speeches at various public functions; *The Third International After Lenin* (New York, 1936); and *The Stalin School of Falsification*, ed. Max Shachtman (New York, 1937).

INDEX

ADGB, *see* Allgemeiner Deutscher Gewerkschaftsbund
Abegg, Wilhelm, 110n
Adler, Friedrich, 231
Afa, *see* Allgemeiner freier Angestelltenbund
Albert, Max, *see* Eberlein
Allgemeiner Deutscher Gewerkschaftsbund, 92, 207, 230, 291n, 370, 373-74, 447; and KPD, 88, 251, 291
Allgemeiner freier Angestelltenbund, 291n
"Alliance with Soviet Russia," 140, 302, 332, 335, 336n, 340, 413
Allied Supreme Council, 59, 78
Allies, *see* Entente Powers
Alsace Lorraine, 127
Amsterdam Trade-Union International, *see* Trade-Unions, International Federation of
Anarcho-Syndicalism, *see* Syndicalists
Anglo-Russian Trade Agreement 1921, 176, 314
Antibolschewistische Bewegung, 332n
Apfelbaum, Hirsch, *see* Zinoviev
Apparat, *see* KPD, illegal activities of
Arbeitsgemeinschaft der sozialdemokratischen Reichstagsfraktion, 244
Arbeitsgemeinschaft der verfassungstreuen Mitte, 246n
Arbeitskommandos, 283, 415
Armistice 1918, 38

Baden, and Anti-Fascist Day campaign, 364
Baden riots 1923, 388, 426
Balabanov, Angelica, 50
Barth, Emil, 106
Bauer, Otto, 231
Bavaria, 124, 140, 143; and German government, 82-83, 116-17, 247n, 387, 434, 453; and "Emergency Decree for the Protection of the Republic," 247n; and homeguards, incl. Orgesch, 82-83, 117; and "Law for the Protection of the Republic," 247n; situation in 1920, 78; situation in 1923, 271, 273, 356, 378-80, 387, 389-90, 414, 434, 453; soviet republic of, 36
Bavarian People's Party, 244, 247n
Becker, Karl, 260, 262, 276n, 300
"Berlin Agreement," 242-43
Berlin, Anti-Fascist Day campaign, 364; conference of internationals at, 261;

and March Uprising, 153, 155, 165; and 1923 metal workers strike, 351-52
Berlin Left, *see* Left Opposition
Berlin Opposition, *see* Left Opposition
Bernstein, Eduard, 9
Betriebsräte, *see* factory councils
Bismarck, Otto von, 100, 304
Black Reichswehr, 355, 415, 437
Bochum riots, 323
Bolshevik leaders, Russian, 25, 32, 33, 37, 48, 58, 59, 63, 70, 77, 80, 87, 95, 96, 100, 115, 175, 183n, 207, 226, 246, 256, 262, 263, 265, 269, 288, 310, 311, 324, 334, 336, 352, 376, 377; and Berlin conference of internationals, 234; and founding of Comintern, 50; at Second Comintern congress, 65-68; at Third Comintern congress, 176-78, 181-82, 185, 189-95; and Curzon Ultimatum, 314; and "German October" preparations, 378, 391-406, 412, 415-425; and "German October" aftermath, 461-62, 469, 470; and German November Revolution, 55; and German radical groups 1918, 14n

  assess German situation summer 1923, 391-96; and KAPD, 66; summon KPD leaders in 1923, 464; and Kun mission, 120n; and "Law for the Protection of the Republic," 244; criticize March Uprising, 181-82, 223; reinterpret March Uprising, 175; and Levi Crisis, 112, 177; and Rapallo Treaty, 236; and Reuter, 208-10; and Russo-Polish war, 64; and Ruhr strikes, 323; in Russian successor crisis 1923-24, 469-70; split Socialist labor, 62, 69; and united front policy, 225, 228
Bolshevik Party, *see* Communist Party, Russia
Bombacci, Nicola, 96, 98
Bordiga, Amadeo, 68, 96, 98
Borsig, August P. E. von, 287
Bosch, Robert August, 287
Böttcher, Paul, on fascism, 337; in Saxony 1923, 385, 430-31, 435, 440-41, 455; Zentrale member, 102, 204n, 276n, 311
Bowitzki, 143, 146, 159
Brandenburg, 1923 metal workers strike, 351-52
Brandler, Heinrich, 102, 112, 114, 115,

495

Index

Communist Party, Austria, 91; Belgium, 293; Czechoslovakia, 293; France, 266, 293, 301, 464; Germany, *see* KPD; Great Britain, 293; Holland, 293; Italy, 96, 98, 185, 293; Poland, 464

    Russia, 55, 62, 120, 121n, 194, 262, 265, 311, 316n, 365, 397, 403n, 471n; All-Russian Central Executive Committee of, 236, 238, 269n, 294, 403n; congresses, *see* congresses, Russian Communist Party; and founding of Communist International, 48; and Friesland crisis, 217; intraparty struggle at Third Comintern Congress, 176; and Rapallo, 236, 238; and Russian successor crisis, 461-70; and "Workers' Opposition," 199n

Communist Trade-Union International, *see* Profintern

Communist Women's League, 175

Communist Youth International, 64n

Conference, joint KPD-ECCI, 310-12; National, of Spartacus League, 23-24; of German prime-ministers, 117

Congresses, Communist International, First (Founding), 48-51, 60, 145, 187, 193

    Second: 63, 64-70, 97, 105, 121n, 181, 187, 193, 218; and illegal party organizations, 70-71, 107, 417; and Italian Socialists, 96; and Profintern, 73

    Third: 39n, 100n, 111, 118n, 138n, 143n, 150n, 162n, 172n, 174, 197, 201, 202, 203, 204, 207n, 217, 256, 259, 262, 265, 269; effect on KPD, 198, 205; and Kun mission, 121n; Lenin on, 199; debate on Levi, 177, 180-81; and March uprising, 164, 171n, 177-92; meeting of, 176-96; organization of member parties, 226; preparations for, 175-76; Reuter on, 208; and united front, 224

    Fourth: 227, 239n, 245n, 253, 255, 268n, 269, 271, 278, 292, 308; and German situation, 265-66; and KPD, 258; meeting of, 256-65; and united front, 263, 265; and workers' governments, 264

    Fifth: 363n, 365n, 397n

Congresses, Communist Party, Germany (KPD), numbering system, 43n

    First (Founding): 33, 43; National Assembly elections issue, 23-24; and Jogiches, 24-25; and Levi, 23; and

Luxemburg, 24-25; meeting of, 23-27; and parliamentary participation, 42; and Radek, 56; and Revolutionary Shop Stewards, 25-26; and trade-union issue, 26-27n, 42

    Second (Heidelberg): 39n, 64, 66, 89, 174n; and Levi, 58; meeting of, 42-43; and Radek, 58

    Third (Karlsruhe): 39n, 44

    Fourth (Berlin): 39n, 46; and Kapp Putsch issue, 46

    Unification (First, with Left US-PD)*: 43n, 74-75, 105, 198

    Second (Jena): 43n, 197n, 209, 249; effect on KPD, 205; and Fischer, 255; and Left Opposition, 255; meeting of, 198-205; party program, 205; and united front policy, 205, 224

    Third (8th, Leipzig): 43n, 303, 305, 307, 308, 316; and Left Opposition, 267-78; meeting of, 267-78; and Radek, 270; Ruhr occupation issue, 267-68, 296; and Saxon situation, 274; and united front policy, 266-67, 269

    Ninth (Frankfurt): 471-72

Congresses, Communist Party, Russia, Ninth, 62; Tenth, 120n; Twelfth, 311, 316n; Thirteenth, 365n

Congresses, Socialist Parties, Germany, USPD, Berlin, 1919, 61; Leipzig, 1919, 61; Halle, 1920, 71, 90; Italy, Leghorn, 1921, 97-99

Congresses, others:

    National, of factory councils, 251-52; First National of German Workers' and Soldiers' Councils, 18-19, 21, 33, 55, 56; Seventh of German Communist Youth, 309; Unification of Second and Two-and-a-Half Internationals, 329-30

control commissions, proletarian, 300; and KPD, 289-90; and national congress of factory councils, 252; issue at Leipzig Congress (KPD), 274; during Ruhr strikes, 327; in Saxony, 383

Crispien, Arthur, 63, 68, 233

Cuno, Wilhelm, 265, 267, 268, 281, 282, 285, 288, 293, 294, 295, 296, 297, 304, 307, 308, 318, 355, 356, 367, 371, 375, 378, 379, 384, 385, 391, 406, 425; and government crisis, 370; and inflation, 287; KPD on, 328-29; resigns, 372; and SPD, 372

Cuno strike, 369-72, 392, 394, 406, 416n,

Index

Index

Kamenev, Lev Borisovich, 176, 461
Der Kämpfer, 433
Kantorowicz, Alfred, 89
Kapp, Wolfgang, 45
Kapp Putsch, 45-46, 60n, 63-65, 74, 78, 82, 83, 85, 101n, 111, 127, 131, 147-48, 372
Kardorff, Siegfried von, 411
Katz, Iwan, 254, 276
Kautsky, Karl, 9, 62, 63
Kippenberger, Hans, 445-46, 448-49
Klassenkampf, 146
Kleber, Emilio, *see* Stern
Kleine, August, 395; ECCI emissary to Germany, 120; and "German October," 418, 465, 469; Zentrale member, 276n, 277-78
Klöckner, Florian, 287, 340
Kolarov, Vasil P., 201-2, 301
Kollwitz, Käthe, 93, 346
Kommunistische Arbeiterpartei Deutschlands, *see* KAPD
Kommunistische Arbeitsgemeinschaft, *see* KAG
Kommunistische Partei Deutschlands, *see* KPD
Koenen, Wilhelm, 74-75n, 118n, 197, 204, 244n, 465; Zentrale member, 75n, 276n, 277
Koestler, Arthur, *Darkness at Noon*, 162
König, Arthur, 254, 276, 312
Kopisch, August, 267n
Kopp, Victor, 59, 108-9
Kornilov, Gen. Lavr, 62
Korsch, Karl, 433
Kress von Kressenstein, Friedrich Freiherr, 453
Krestinsky, Nikolai N., 317; and "German October" preparations, 395, 419
Kronstadt revolt, 120n, 121n, 176
Krupp von Bohlen and Halbach, Gustav, 295
Krupp Works, Essen incident at, 298-99
Kun, Bela, 123, 126, 140, 143, 170, 173, 176, 177n, 183, 207n; at Third Comintern Congress, 178, 189; leads Hungarian revolution, 59; and March uprising, 120-22, 125, 133, 137, 139n, 163-64, 178
Kuusinen, Otto, 468

Lange, Paul, 27
Laufenberg, Heinrich, 60, 95; and National Bolshevism, 41-43, 328

Law for the Protection of the Republic, 244-47
League of the Friends of the International Workers' Aid, 346
League of nationalist-minded Soldiers, 355
League of producing Farmers, 353
Ledebour, Georg, 4, 63
"Left Centrists," 4, 5, 7
Left Opposition, KPD, 119, 154, 201, 202, 204, 216, 253, 262, 264, 322n, 375n, 431n, 446n, 464; and Anti-Fascist Day campaign, 363, 368; in Berlin, 115, 255; and Brandler, 272-73, 309-10, 364-65, 462-63, 470-71; at central committee meetings, 198, 207, 368, 470-71; composition of, 90-91, 255; at Third Comintern Congress, 199n; at Fourth Comintern Congress, 256, 263, 265; at Leipzig (KPD) Congress, 267-78; at Jena (KPD) Congress, 203, 255; and Cuno strike aftermath, 373n

and ECCI, 310-12; and Essen conference, 307-8; and factory councils, 270; in Frankfurt/Main, 255; and "German October" preparations, 398-99, 400n, 404; and "German October" aftermath, 465-67; in Hamburg region, 255; captures party control, 471-74; Lenin on, 177n, 200, 263; and Levi, 90, 92, 94-95, 99, 102n, 114-15; and "Moscow Agreement," 312; and "Open Letter," 92; and peasantry, 353; assess prospects for German revolution, 114-15; and Radek, 270

and Rathenau campaign, 256; and Ruhr occupation, 288, 303, 305-13; in Ruhr region, 255, 308; and Russian influence on KPD, 208; and Schlageter line, 349; on Saxon situation, 387; and Stalin, 472n; strongholds of, 267n, 275-76n; and Thalheimer, 303; and trade-unions, 270; and Trotsky, 470-71; and united front, 252, 270; and workers' governments, 206, 270; and "workers' and peasants' governments," 353n, 368; and Zentrale, 95, 115, 254-78, 303, 308-13, and *passim*; and Zinoviev, 311, 466, 470-71
"Left-Wing" Communism, an Infantile Disorder, 60, 63, 227
Lemck, and March uprising, 142, 146, 148n, 159
Lenin, Vladimir Ilich, 20, 23-25, 33,

Index

39n, 54, 55, 59, 74, 173, 197, 201, 205, 208, 209, 210, 218, 335, 396, 403, 468, 469, 478; and founding of Comintern, 48-50, 15-52; at Second Comintern Congress, 65-67, 70; at Third Comintern Congress, 175-78, 181, 185-86, 188-89, 189-95; at Fourth Comintern Congress, 257, 262, 263n; and Jena (KPD) Congress, 198-200; death of, 461

on 1921 European situation, 194; on Fischer, 263; and Friesland crisis, 217; illness of, 237, 257, 265, 269-70, 288, 311, 316n, 391, 394, 461; on KAPD, 199-200; on KPD, 61, 181, 199; on Kapp Putsch, 62-63; on Kun mission, 122n; and Left Opposition, 177n, 200, 263; and *"Left-Wing" Communism*, 227; and Levi, 64-67, 177, 181, 199; and Luxemburg, 9-12, 196

reaction to March uprising, 122n, 168, 176, 181, 185, 186, 199; on Maslow, 200, 203; and NEP, 120n, 176, 257; and National Bolshevism, 42, 327; *One Step forward, two Steps back*, 10; and Radek, 60, 199; and Russian influence on KPD, 196; schism theory of, 62-63; struggle for succession of, 402ff; and twenty-one conditions, 68; and USPD, 61, 63, 66; and united front policy, 227; *What is to be done?*, 9; on world revolution, 60-61, 175, and *passim*; on Zentrale, 263; on Zetkin, 199; on Zinoviev, 51-52

Lerchenfeld-Köfering, Hugo Graf von und zu, 247n

Leuna Works and March uprising, 126, 128, 150-52, 158-59, 161-62

Levi, Paul, 12n, 44, 76, 101, 102, 105, 110, 118n, 121, 123n, 124, 142, 145, 183n, 185, 186, 188, 194, 196, 197, 201, 203, 204, 205, 211, 215, 255, 259, 305, 477; at KPD Founding Congress, 23; at Second KPD (Heidelberg) Congress, 42-43, 58; at KPD-USPD Unification Congress, 74-75; at Second Comintern Congress, 64-67, 70; criticized at Third Comintern Congress, 39n, 180-82, 192, 195; and elections to German National Assembly, 23-24; and illegal party activities, 107; and Italian Socialists, 96-98, 109; leads KPD, 27, 38-39, 75; and KPD reputation, 40-41, 89-90

leads right-wing faction, 112-14; in

KAG, 209; on Kapp Putsch, 64-65; and Kun mission, 122; and Left Opposition, 90, 92, 94-95, 99, 102n, 114-15; Lenin on, 177, 199; criticizes March uprising, 113, 119, 163, 168-73, 177; and "Open Letter," 91-92, 223, 224; purge of, 96, 99-100, 111-12, 115, 171-75, 177, 179; personality of, 39-40; and "putschism," 41; and Racosi, 99; Radek on, 98; in Reichstag, 47, 93-94

and Reuter, 95-96, 209-10, 214, 216n; on revolutionary prospects, 58; and Russian Bolsheviks, 70, 98-100, 199, 208; and Russo-German alliance, 93-95, 113-14; joins SPD, 216n; Spartacist leader, 19; and united front, 226-27; and *Vorwärts* revelations, 143n

Leviné, Eugen, 49n

Liebknecht, Karl, 7, 15, 40, 48, 74, 89, 93, 110, 115n, 294, 341, 358; assessment of, 32-33, 35; pre-1918 career of, 3-6; and founding of KPD, 23, 27, 56; murder of, 31, 33; in November Revolution (German), 19; and "Spartacus Putsch," 29-30, 34-36

Lindau, Rudolf, 276n

Linksradikale, *see* Gruppe Arbeiterpolitik

Lloyd George, David, 227

London conference, 117-18, 123

Longuet, Jean, 61, 231

Lossow, Gen. Otto Hermann von, 414, 453

Löwenhain, Walter, 64n

Lozovsky, Solomon Abramovich Dridzo, 71, 74, 208, 301, 304, 412

Ludendorff, Gen. Erich, 6, 52, 163

Lutterbeck, Dr., 323, 331, 334

Lüttwitz, Gen. Walther von, 45

Luxemburg, Rosa, 3, 37, 39, 40, 43, 52, 65, 74, 76, 89, 94n, 100, 102, 110, 111, 125, 155n, 170, 174, 193, 195, 196, 204, 341, 358, 377, 474, 476, 477; assessment of, 32-36; background of, 8; and Bernstein, 9; and founding of Comintern, 48-49; image and legacy after death, 33-36; *Junius Brochure*, 5; and founding of KPD, 22-25, 27, 33, 56; and Kautsky, 9; and Lenin, 9-12; *Mass Strike, Party and Trade-Unions*, 11; murder of, 31, 33; on elections to German National Assembly, 16-17, 21-24

in German November Revolution, 13, 15, 19; personality and ideas, 4,

Index

Index

Index

DATE DUE
